Chapter 4

Introduction to Business Telecommunications

Real World Cases
1. America Online: Success and Challenges in Online Commerce and Services, p. 131
2. Network Alchemy and Others: Virtual Private Networks and E-Commerce, p. 149

Real World Problems
1. George Margolin and Ron Ben-Israel: Cable Modems versus DSL for Web Access, p. 163
2. Sento Corporation and US West: Computer Telephony Integration, p. 163
3. Hotlinks Inc.: Building a Top Internet Service Provider, p. 164

Chapter 5

Introduction to Database Management

Real World Cases

1. EMC Corporation: The Business Value of Data Storage in the Age of E-Commerce, p. 169
2. The Chicago Stock Exchange and Enron Energy Services: Object versus Relational Databases, p. 183

Real World Problems
1. Borders Books and Music: Database Management of an E-Commerce Web Site, p. 196
2. Burlington Coat Factory Warehouse: The Business Benefits of Storage Area Networks, p. 196
3. Farmers Insurance Group: The Business Value of Data Mining and a Data Warehouse, p. 197

Chapter 6

Information Systems for Business Operations and Electronic Commerce

Real World Cases
1. Amazon.com: Success and Expansion in Electronic Commerce, p. 203
2. Buy.com: Testing a New Business Model in E-Commerce, p. 224

Real World Problems
1. Cyberian Outpost, CDNow, and AutoConnect: Improving Web Customer Retention, p. 243
2. NetBuy, Chemdex, and Others: The Business Value of Infomediaries, p. 243
3. Telefonica Servicios Avanzados de Information: Expanding Internet-Based EDI, p. 244

Introduction to Information Systems

Essentials for the Internetworked Enterprise

At **McGraw-Hill Higher Education**, we publish instructional materials targeted at the higher education market. In an effort to expand the tools of higher learning, we publish texts, lab manuals, study guides, testing materials, software, and multimedia products.

At **Irwin/McGraw-Hill** (a division of McGraw-Hill Higher Education), we realize technology will continue to create new mediums for professors and students to manage resources and communicate information with one another. We strive to provide the most flexible and complete teaching and learning tools available and offer solutions to the changing world of teaching and learning.

Irwin/McGraw-Hill is dedicated to providing the tools necessary for today's instructors and students to navigate the world of Information Technology successfully

Seminar Series - Irwin/McGraw-Hill's Technology Connection seminar series offered across the country every year, demonstrates the latest technology products and encourages collaboration among teaching professionals.

Osborne/McGraw-Hill - A division of the McGraw-Hill Companies known for its best-selling Internet titles *Harley Hahn's Internet & Web Yellow Pages* and the *Internet Complete Reference*, offers an additional resource for certification and has strategic publishing relationships with corporations such as Corel Corporation and America Online. For more information, visit Osborne at www.osborne.com.

Digital Solutions - Irwin/McGraw-Hill is committed to publishing Digital Solutions. Taking your course online doesn't have to be a solitary venture. Nor does it have to be a difficult one. We offer several solutions, which will let you enjoy all the benefits of having course material online. For more information, visit www.mhhe.com/solutions/index.mhtml.

Packaging Options - For more about our discount options, contact your local Irwin/McGraw-Hill Sales representative at 1-800-338-3987, or visit our Web site at www.mhhe.com/it.

Introduction to

Information

Systems

Essentials for the Internetworked Enterprise
Ninth Edition

James A. O'Brien
College of Business Administration
Northern Arizona University

Irwin
McGraw-Hill

Boston   Burr Ridge, IL   Dubuque, IA   Madison, WI   New York   San Francisco   St. Louis
Bangkok   Bogotá   Caracas   Lisbon   London   Madrid   Mexico City   Milan   New Delhi   Seoul
Singapore   Sydney   Taipei   Toronto

Irwin/McGraw-Hill

A Division of The **McGraw·Hill** Companies

**INTRODUCTION TO INFORMATION SYSTEMS:
ESSENTIAL FOR THE INTERNETWORKED ENTERPRISE**

This book is printed on acid-free paper.

domestic   1 2 3 4 5 6 7 8 9 0 VNH/VNH 9 0 9 8 7 6 5 4 3 2 1 0 9
international   1 2 3 4 5 6 7 8 9 0 VNH/VNH 9 0 9 8 7 6 5 4 3 2 1 0 9

ISBN 0-07-229749-2

Vice president/Editor-in-chief: *Michael W. Junior*
Publisher: *David Brake*
Senior sponsoring editor: *Rick Williamson*
Developmental editor: *Christine Wright*
Senior marketing manager: *Jodi McPherson*
Senior project manager: *Gladys True*
Production supervisor: *Lori Koetters*
Senior designer: *Michael Warrell*
Cover illustrator: *Kevin Ghiglione*
Senior photo research coordinator: *Keri Johnson*
Photo research: *Roberta Spieckerman*
Supplement coordinator: *Marc Mattson*
Compositor: *GAC Indianapolis*
Typeface: *10/12 Janson*
Printer: *Von Hoffman Press, Inc.*

Library of Congress Cataloging-in-Publication Data

O'Brien, James A.
    Introduction to information systems : essentials for the
internetworked enterprise / James A. O'Brien. -- 9th ed.
        p. cm.
    Includes bibliographical references and indexes.
    ISBN 0–07–229749–2
    1. Business--Data processing. 2. Management--Data processing.
    I. Title.
    HF5548.2.O23 2000
    658.4'038--dc21   99–31793

http://www.mhhe.com

May you love the Light within you
And in everyone you meet
And everything you experience

James A. O'Brien is an adjunct professor of Computer Information Systems in the College of Business Administration at Northern Arizona University. He completed his undergraduate studies at the University of Hawaii and Gonzaga University and earned an M.S. and Ph.D. in Business Administration from the University of Oregon. He has been coordinator of the CIS area at Northern Arizona University, professor of Finance and Management Information Systems and chairman of the Department of Management at Eastern Washington University, and a visiting professor at the University of Alberta, the University of Hawaii, and Central Washington University.

Dr. O'Brien's business experience includes working in the Marketing Management Program of the IBM Corporation, as well as serving as a financial analyst for the General Electric Company. He is a graduate of General Electric's Financial Management Program. He has also served as an information systems consultant to several banks and computer services firms.

Jim's research interests lie in developing and testing basic conceptual frameworks used in information systems development and management. He has written eight books, including several that have been published in multiple editions, as well as in Dutch, French, Japanese, or Spanish translations. He has also contributed to the field of information systems through the publication of many articles in business and academic journals, as well as through his participation in academic and industry associations in the field of information systems.

Preface

Essentials for the Internet-worked Enterprise

This new ninth edition is an introduction to information systems and information technology for today's business students, who will be tomorrow's managers, entrepreneurs, and business professionals. The goal of this text is to help business students learn how to use and manage information technology to revitalize business processes, improve managerial decision making, and gain competitive advantage. Thus, it places a major emphasis on the role of the Internet, intranets, extranets, and other information technologies in providing a technology platform for electronic commerce and collaboration within and among internetworked enterprises and global markets.

These are the essential aspects of the internetworked enterprise that this new edition brings to the study of information systems. Of course, as in all my texts, this edition:

- Loads the text with **real world cases and problems** about real people and companies in the business world.

- Organizes the text around a simple **five-level framework** that emphasizes the IS knowledge a business end user needs to know.

- Distributes and integrates IS foundation theory throughout the text instead of concentrating it in several early chapters.

- Places a major emphasis on the strategic role of information technology in gaining competitive advantage, supporting business operations and managerial decision making, and enabling electronic commerce and enterprise collaboration.

Audience

This text is designed for use in undergraduate courses in Management Information Systems, which are required in many Business Administration or Management programs as part of the common body of knowledge for all business majors. Thus, this edition treats the subject area known as Information Systems (IS), Management Information Systems (MIS), or Computer Information Systems (CIS) as a major functional area of business that is as important to management education as are the areas of accounting, finance, operations management, marketing, and human resource management.

Key Features

This new ninth edition is a major revision that retains the key features of the last edition, while significantly updating all coverage of IS technology and its business and managerial applications.

All New Real World Cases, Problems, and Application Exercises

This text provides all new up-to-date real world case studies and problems. These are not fictional stories, but actual situations faced by business firms and other organizations as reported in current business and IS periodicals. This includes two real world case studies and three real world problems in each chapter that apply specifically to that chapter's contents.

In addition, each chapter contains several application exercises, including two hands-on spreadsheet or database software assignments in Chapters 2 through 11, and Internet assignments in many chapters, especially Chapters 1, 4, 6, and 7. Also new to this edition are highlighted in-text real world examples that illustrate concepts in every chapter. The purpose of this variety of assignment options is to give instructors and students many opportunities to apply each chapter's material to real world situations.

New Chapters on Electronic Commerce and Enterprise Collaboration

This edition contains two new chapters that emphasize how the Internet, intranets, and extranets are revolutionizing the technological infrastructure and tools that enable internetworked enterprises to engage in electronic commerce and enterprise collaboration. This is demonstrated, not only in the text materials in Chapters 6 and 7, but in chapter examples and Real World Cases and Problems throughout the text. Examples include real world cases and problems like **NetFlix.com, Milacron Inc., Halco Business Products, America Online, Borders Books and Music, Amazon.com, Cyberian Outpost, CD Now and AutoConnect, Glaxo Wellcome and BC Telecom, Lockheed Martin, Dow Jones, and Charles Schwab & Co.,** to name a few.

An Information Systems Framework

This text reduces the complexity of an introductory course in information systems by using a conceptual framework that organizes the knowledge needed by business students into five major areas (see Figure 1):

- **Foundation Concepts.** Fundamental information systems concepts about the components and roles of information systems in business (Chapter 1). Other behavioral, managerial, and technical concepts are presented where appropriate in other chapters.
- **Information Technologies.** Major concepts, developments, and managerial implications involved in computer hardware, software, telecommunications, and database management technologies (Chapters 2, 3, 4, and 5). Other technologies used in computer-based information systems are discussed where appropriate in selected chapters.
- **Business Applications.** How the Internet, intranets, extranets, and other information technologies are used in modern information systems to support electronic commerce, enterprise collaboration, business operations, managerial decision making, and strategic advantage (Chapters 6, 7, 8, and 9).
- **Development Processes.** Developing information system solutions to business problems using a variety of business application development methodologies (Chapter 10).
- **Management Strategies.** The challenges of managing information systems technologies, resources, and strategies, including global IT management and security and ethical challenges (discussed in many chapters, but emphasized in Chapters 11 and 12).

The information systems framework.

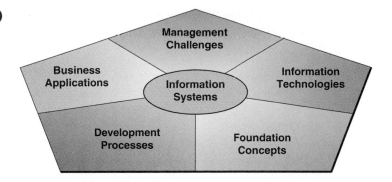

Strategic, International, and Ethical Dimensions

This text also contains substantial text material and cases reflecting the strategic, international, and ethical dimensions of information systems. This can be found not only in Chapters 9, 11, and 12, but also in all other chapters of the text. This is especially evident in many real world cases and problems, such as Boeing and Analog Devices, Mellon Bank and Bank of Montreal, Telefonica Servicios Avanzados de Information, Ford Motor Company, Barnes & Noble and Bertelsmann versus Amazon.com, Shiva Corporation, Guy Carpenter & Co. and PRT Group, SAP AG, Sara Lee and AeroGroup, Wal-Mart versus Amazon.com, EDS, Oracle, and GM-Opel, Rima Berzin and Excite Inc., and many, many others. These examples repeatedly demonstrate the strategic and ethical challenges of managing information technology for competitive advantage in global business markets and in the global information society in which we all live and work.

Modular Structure of the Text

The text is organized into four modules that reflect the five major areas of the framework for information systems knowledge mentioned earlier. See Figure 2. Also each chapter is organized into two distinct sections. This is done to avoid proliferation of chapters, as well as to provide better conceptual organization of the text and each chapter. This organization increases instructor flexibility in assigning course material since it structures the text into modular levels (i.e., modules, chapters, and sections) while reducing the number of chapters that need to be covered.

The modular organization of the text.

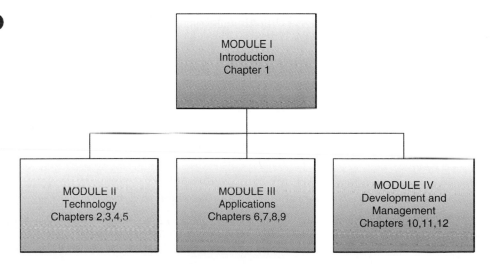

Each chapter starts with Chapter Highlights and Learning Objectives and ends with a Summary, Key Terms and Concepts, a Review Quiz tied directly to the Key Terms and Concepts, Discussion Questions, Real World Problems, Application Exercises, Review Quiz Answers, and Selected References. Real World Cases are placed at the beginning of the two sections of each chapter (with a brief analysis), to help students understand the chapter material in the context of examples from the real world of business.

Changes to This Edition

Besides providing all new Real World Cases and Problems, this edition represents a major revision of chapter contents. Highlights of the changes made to the Eighth Edition are found in the following Ninth Edition chapters:

Chapter 1: *Introduction to Information Systems in Business*

This chapter includes new and revised material in Section I on the framework of IS knowledge needed by business end users and revised coverage of key developments in the business use of information technology, including the Internet and the internetworked enterprise. The overview of the types and roles of information systems in Section II has been expanded to include enterprise collaboration systems and knowledge management systems.

Chapter 2: *Introduction to Computer Hardware*

Coverage of computer hardware has been extensively revised to emphasize the capabilities of computer systems and peripherals needed by business end users.

Chapter 3: *Introduction to Computer Software*

Updated and reorganized coverage of computer software, with new material on software suites, web browsers, electronic mail, groupware, and more.

Chapter 4: *Introduction to Business Telecommunications*

This chapter includes many new and revised topics, such as business applications and trends in telecommunications, the Internet in business, intranets, extranets, network computing, client/server, and other types of networks in Section I, and the updating of more technical topics including cellular phone systems, TCP/IP, and bandwidth and switching alternatives in Section II.

Chapter 5: *Introduction to Database Management*

Includes updated and reorganized coverage of data warehouses, hypermedia web databases, multidimensional and object-oriented data structures, and object/relational database management systems.

Chapter 6: *Information Systems for Business Operations and Electronic Commerce*

Section I of this new chapter is a major revision of material on IS support of the functional areas of business formerly in Chapter 7, and includes the impact of Internet technologies and online services. Section II introduces students to fundamental topics and business examples in electronic commerce, including EC technologies, retailing on the Web, online transaction processing, EDI, EFT, and electronic payments alternatives. Other material on transaction processing systems formerly in Chapter 7 has been eliminated.

Chapter 7: *Information Systems for Enterprise Collaboration*

Section I of this new chapter reviews topics and business examples of the intranet revolution, including intranet applications and technologies, the role of extranets, and the future of intranets and extranets. Section II covers topics, tools, and examples of team, workgroup, and enterprise collaboration, including groupware tools for electronic communications, electronic conferencing, and cooperative work management.

Chapter 8: *Information Systems for Managerial Decision Support*

This is a major revision that includes revised coverage in Section I on management information systems, online analytical processing (OLAP), and decision support and executive information systems. Section II features revised coverage of artificial intelligence and expert systems, and new material on genetic algorithms, neural networks, and other AI topics.

Chapter 9: *Information Systems for Strategic Advantage*

Section I of this chapter contains new and revised coverage of competitive strategy concepts. Section II contains revised coverage of the strategic use of IT for business, including the strategic use of the Internet, and new material on knowledge-creating companies and knowledge management systems.

Chapter 10: *Developing Business Solutions with Information Technology*

Section I features revised coverage of end user and web development issues. Section II contains revised material on managing change and implementing new information technologies in an organization.

Chapter 11: *Enterprise and Global Management of Information Technology*

Section I is a revision of managerial issues in IT including managing end user computing and Internet access. Section II contains revised material on global IT management, including cultural challenges and the Internet as a global IT platform.

Chapter 12: *Security and Ethical Challenges of Information Technology*

Section I of this chapter contains new material on IS security and controls including fire walls and encryption methods. Section II contains new material on computer crime and privacy on the Internet, as well as revised coverage of ethical and societal IT issues.

Teaching and Learning Resources

New to this edition, a **presentation manager Instructor CD-ROM** is available to adopters and offers the following resources for course presentation and management:

- An Instructor's Resource Manual, revised by Margaret Trenholm-Edmunds of Mount Allison University, contains suggestions for using the book in courses of varying lengths, detailed chapter outlines with teaching suggestions for use in lectures, and answers to all end-of-chapter questions, application exercises, and problems and case study questions. Teaching tips for incorporating the new video clips are included for many chapters.

- A printed Test Bank, containing over 3,000 true-false, multiple choice, and fill-in-the-blank questions, has been prepared by Margaret Trenholm-Edmunds of Mount Allison University.

- Computerized/Network Testing with Brownstone Diploma software is fully networkable for LAN test administration; tests also can be printed for standard paper delivery or posted to a web site for student access.

- Slide shows in Microsoft PowerPoint revised by Margaret Trenholm-Edmunds are available for each chapter to support classroom discussion of chapter concepts and real world cases.

- Data/solutions files for the database and spreadsheet application exercises in the text are included.
- Video clips are available that highlight how specific companies apply and use information technology.

The Irwin/McGraw-Hill Information Systems Video Library contains 14 10–12 minute videos on numerous companies demonstrating use of a variety of IT like intranets, multimedia, or computer-based training systems, and concepts like client/server computing and business process reengineering. This library is available free to adopters. A video lecture guide for all 14 videos is included in the Instructor's Resource Manual.

Digital Solutions

- Web site/OLC—The book's web site at http://www.mhhe.com/business/mis/obrien/obrien9e provides resources for instructors and students using the text. The Online Learning Center (OLC) builds on the book's pedagogy and features with self-assessment quizzes, additional database and spreadsheet application exercises not found in the text, technical web links, key words and glossary of terms, and other resources for students and instructors.
- Pageout/Pageout Lite—our Course Web Site Development Center. Pageout offers a syllabus page, web site address, Online Learning Center content, online quizzing, gradebook, discussion forum, and student web page creation. Pageout Lite, a scaled-down version of Pageout, offers three templates for posting your own material online and instantly converts it to HTML.

Packaging Options

The Irwin/McGraw-Hill *Advantage*, O'Leary, and Laudon Interactive computing series are collections of software application manuals and interactive computer-based training products for Microsoft Office. In addition, we offer several paperback Internet literacy books or CDs, perfect for introducing the World Wide Web, E-mail, and web page design to students. These texts and CDs are available for discounted packaging options with any Irwin/McGraw-Hill title. For more about our discount options, contact your local Irwin/McGraw-Hill sales representative or visit our web site at www.mhhe.com/it.

In addition, a software casebook—*Application Cases in MIS: Using Spreadsheet and Database Software and the Internet*, third edition, by James N. Morgan of Northern Arizona University—is available to supplement the hands-on exercises in this edition. This optional casebook contains an extensive number of hands-on cases, many of which include a suggested approach for solving each case with the Internet, spreadsheet, or database management software packages to develop solutions for realistic business problems.

Acknowledgments

The author wishes to acknowledge the assistance of the following reviewers whose constructive criticism and suggestions helped invaluably in shaping the form and content of this text.

E. Sonny Butler, *Eastern Kentucky University*
Roland G. Eichelberger, *Baylor University*
Juan Esteva, *Eastern Michigan University*

Albert L. Harris, *Appalachian State University*

Orlano K. Johnson, *University of Utah*

Naimatullah Khan, *Central Queensland University (Australia)*

Brian R. Kovar, *Kansas State University*

Stan Lewis, *University of Southern Mississippi*

Frank Merrick, *Gwynedd-Mercy College*

Alan Graham Peace, *Duquesne University*

Lora H. Robinson, *St. Cloud State University*

Mani R. Subramani, *University of Minnesota*

Rick J. Weible, *Marshall University*

My thanks also go to James N. Morgan of Northern Arizona University, who is the author of the software casebook that can be used with this text and who developed most of the hands-on Application Exercises in the text, as well as the data/solutions files on the Instructor CD-ROM. I am also grateful to Margaret Trenholm-Edmunds of Mount Allison University, the author of the Instructor's Resource Manual, Power-Point, and the Test Bank, for her revision of these valuable teaching resources.

Much credit should go to several individuals who played significant roles in this project. Thus, special thanks go to the editorial and production team at Irwin/Mc-Graw-Hill, especially Rick Williamson, senior sponsoring editor; Christine Wright, developmental editor; Jodi McPherson, senior marketing manager; Gladys True, senior project manager; and Michael Warrell, designer. Their ideas and hard work were invaluable contributions to the successful completion of the project. Thanks also to Michele Allen, Kay Pinto, and Lois Kay, whose word processing skills helped me meet my manuscript deadlines. The contributions of many authors, publishers, and firms in the computer industry that contributed case material, ideas, illustrations, and photographs used in this text are also thankfully acknowledged.

Acknowledging the Real World of Business

The unique contribution of the hundreds of business firms and other computer-using organizations that are the subject of the real world cases, problems, exercises, examples, and case studies in this text is gratefully acknowledged. The real-life situations faced by these firms and organizations provide the readers of this text with a valuable demonstration of the benefits and limitations of using the Internet and other information technologies to enable electronic commerce and enterprise collaboration in support of the business operations, managerial decision making, and strategic advantage of the internetworked business enterprise.

James A. O'Brien

Brief Contents

Module I   Introduction

1 Introduction to Information Systems in Business 2

Section I: Why Businesses Need Information Technology 4

Section II: Fundamentals of Information Systems 19

Module II   Technology

2 Introduction to Computer Hardware 47

Section I: Computer Systems: End User and Enterprise Computing 48

Section II: Computer Peripherals: Input, Output, and Storage Technologies 66

3 Introduction to Computer Software 93

Section I: Application Software: End User Applications 94

Section II: System Software: Computer System Management 109

4 Introduction to Business Telecommunications 129

Section I: Telecommunications and the Internet in Business 130

Section II: Technical Telecommunications Alternatives 148

5 Introduction to Database Management 167

Section I: Database Management: Managing Data Resources 168

Section II: Technical Foundations of Database Management 182

Module III **Applications**

6 Information Systems for Business Operations and Electronic Commerce 201

Section I: Business Information Systems 202

Section II: Fundamentals of Electronic Commerce 223

7 Information Systems for Enterprise Collaboration 249

Section I: Intranets and Extranets in Business 250

Section II: Enterprise Collaboration Systems 266

8 Information Systems for Managerial Decision Support 293

Section I: Management Information and Decision Support Systems 294

Section II: Artificial Intelligence Technologies in Business 310

9 Information Systems for Strategic Advantage 337

Section I: Fundamentals of Strategic Advantage 338

Section II: Strategic Applications and Issues in Information Technology 349

Module IV **Development and Management**

10 Developing Business Solutions with Information Technology 379

Section I: Developing Information System Solutions 380

Section II: Implementing Business Change with IT 402

11 Enterprise and Global Management of Information Technology 423

Section I: Managing Information Resources and Technologies 424

Section II: Global Information Technology Management 446

12 Security and Ethical Challenges of Information Technology 467

Section I: Security and Control Issues in Information Systems 468

Section II: Ethical and Societal Challenges of Information Technology 482

Glossary G-1

Name Index I-1

Organization Index I-7

Subject Index I-13

Contents

Module I Introduction

Chapter 1

Introduction to Information Systems in Business 2

Section I: Why Businesses Need Information Technology 4

Why Information Systems Are Important 4

The Real World of Information Systems 4

Real World Case: NetFlix.com: Challenges of a New Web Business 5

Analyzing NetFlix.com 6

What You Need to Know 6

A Framework for Business End Users 6

Information System Resources and Technologies 7

An End User Perspective 8

An Enterprise Management Perspective 8

The Fundamental Role of Information Systems 10

The Internet and Business 12

The Internetworked Enterprise 13

Globalization and Information Technology 14

Business Process Reengineering 16

Competitive Advantage with IT 16

Section II: Fundamentals of Information Systems 19

Introduction 19

Real World Case: Milacron, Inc.: Serving Small Businesses via the Web 20

Analyzing Milacron, Inc. 21

System Concepts 21

Feedback and Control 21

Other System Characteristics 23

Components of an Information System 23

Information System Resources 24

People Resources 24

Hardware Resources 26

Software Resources 26

Data Resources 26

Network Resources 27

Information System Activities 28

Input of Data Resources 28

Processing of Data into Information 28

Output of Information Products 28

Storage of Data Resources 30

Control of System Performance 30

Overview of Information Systems 30

Trends in Information Systems 30

Types of Information Systems 32

Operations Support Systems 32

Management Support Systems 33

Other Classifications of Information Systems 34

Recognizing Information Systems 36

Analyzing Milacron's Information System 36

Module II   Technology

Chapter 2

Introduction to Computer Hardware 47

Section I: Computer Systems: End User and Enterprise Computing 48

Analyzing the Mutual Group and Others 48

Real World Case: The Mutual Group and Others: Turning Mainframes into Web Servers 49

Trends in Computer Systems 50

Computer Generations 50

Microcomputer Systems 52

Multimedia Systems 55

Network Computers 55

Computer Terminals 56

Midrange Computer Systems 57

Mainframe Computer Systems 57

Supercomputer Systems 59

Technical Note: Computer System Concepts and Components 60

The Computer System Concept 60

The Central Processing Unit 62

Primary and Secondary Storage 63

Multiple Processors 63

Computer Processing Speeds 64

Section II: Computer Peripherals: Input, Output, and Storage Technologies 66

Analyzing ASD Catalogs and Ernst & Young 66

Real World Case: ASD Catalogs and Ernst & Young: The Business PC versus Consumer PC Decision 67

Introduction 68

Input Technology Trends 68

Pointing Devices 69

Pen-Based Computing 70

Voice Recognition and Response 71

Optical Scanning 72

Other Input Technologies 73

Output Technologies and Trends 74

Video Output 75

Printed Output 76

Storage Trends and Trade-Offs 76

Computer Storage Fundamentals 77

Direct and Sequential Access 79

Semiconductor Memory 79

Magnetic Disk Storage 80

Types of Magnetic Disks 80

Magnetic Tape Storage 81

Optical Disk Storage 82

Business Applications 82

Chapter 3

Introduction to Computer Software 93

Section I: Application Software: End User Applications 94

Introduction to Software 94

Analyzing Egghead.com, Aspect Telecommunications, and Others 94

Real World Case: Egghead.com, Aspect Telecommunications, and Others: Windows NT/2000 Alternatives 95

Software Trends 96

Application Software for End Users 97

Software Suites and Integrated Packages 98

Web Browsers and More 99

Electronic Mail 100

Word Processing and Desktop Publishing 101

Electronic Spreadsheets 103

Database Management 103

Presentation Graphics and Multimedia 104

Multimedia Software Technologies 105

Personal Information Managers 106

Groupware 108

Section II: System Software: Computer System Management 109

Analyzing Jay Jacobs and Burlington 109

System Software Overview 109

Real World Case: Jay Jacobs and Burlington Coat Factory: The Business Case for Linux and Open-Source Software 110
Operating Systems 111
Operating System Functions 112
Popular Operating Systems 114
Network Management Programs 115
Database Management Systems 115
Other System Management Programs 116
Programming Languages 116
Machine Languages 116
Assembler Languages 117
High-Level Languages 117
Fourth-Generation Languages 118
Object-Oriented Languages 119
HTML and Java 120
Programming Packages 121
Language Translator Programs 121
Programming Tools 122

Chapter 4

Introduction to Business Telecommunications 129

Section I: Telecommunications and the Internet in Business 130
Networking the Enterprise 130
Analyzing America Online 130
Real World Case: America Online: Success and Challenges in Online Commerce and Services 131
Business Applications of Telecommunications 132
The Business Value of Telecommunications 133
Trends in Telecommunications 134
Industry Trends 134
Technology Trends 135
Application Trends 136
The Internet Revolution 136
Internet Applications 137
Business Use of the Internet 138
Enterprise Communications and Collaboration 139
Electronic Commerce 139
Strategic Business Alliances 140

The Business Value of the Internet 140
A Telecommunications Network Model 141
Types of Telecommunications Networks 143
Wide Area Networks 143
Local Area Networks 143
Intranets and Extranets 144
Client/Server Networks 145
Network Computing 145
Interorganizational Networks 146
Section II: Technical Telecommunications Alternatives 148
Telecommunications Alternatives 148
Analyzing Network Alchemy 148
Real World Case: Network Alchemy and Others: Virtual Private Networks and E-Commerce 149
Telecommunications Media 150
Twisted-Pair Wire 150
Coaxial Cable 150
Fiber Optics 151
Terrestrial Microwave 151
Communications Satellites 151
Cellular Phone Systems 152
Wireless LANs 153
Telecommunications Processors 153
Modems 153
Multiplexers 153
Internetwork Processors 155
Telecommunications Software 155
Network Topologies 155
Network Architectures and Protocols 156
The OSI Model 158
The Internet's TCP/IP 158
Bandwidth Alternatives 158
Switching Alternatives 159

Chapter 5

Introduction to Database Management 167

Section I: Database Management: Managing Data Resources 168
Introduction 168
Analyzing EMC Corporation 168

Real World Case: EMC Corporation: The Business Value of Data Storage in the Age of E-Commerce 169

Foundation Data Concepts 170

 Character 170

 Field 170

 Record 171

 File 171

 Database 171

The Database Management Approach 172

Using Database Management Software 173

 Database Development 173

 Database Interrogation 174

 Database Maintenance 175

 Application Development 176

Types of Databases 176

 Operational Databases 176

 Data Warehouses 176

 Data Mining 177

 Distributed Databases 177

 External Databases 177

Hypermedia Databases on the Web 179

Managerial Considerations for Data Resource Management 180

 Benefits and Limitations of Database Management 181

Section II: Technical Foundations of Database Management 182

Introduction 182

 Analyzing the Chicago Stock Exchange and Enron Energy Services 182

Real World Case: The Chicago Stock Exchange and Enron Energy Services: Object versus Relational Databases 183

Database Structures 184

 Hierarchial Structure 184

 Network Structure 184

 Relational Structure 184

 Multidimensional Structure 184

 Object-Oriented Structure 186

 Evaluation of Database Structures 186

Object Technology and the Web 188

Accessing Databases 188

 Key Fields 188

 Sequential Access 189

 Direct Access 190

Database Development 190

 Data Planning and Database Design 190

Module III Applications

Chapter 6

Information Systems for Business Operations and Electronic Commerce 201

Section I: Business Information Systems 202

IS in Business 202

 Analyzing Amazon.com 202

Real World Case: Amazon.com: Success and Expansion in Electronic Commerce 203

Cross-Functional Information Systems 204

 Enterprise Resource Planning 205

Marketing Information Systems 205

 Interactive Marketing 206

 Sales Force Automation 207

 Sales and Product Management 208

 Advertising and Promotion 208

 Targeted Marketing 209

 Market Research and Forecasting 209

Manufacturing Information Systems 210

 Computer-Integrated Manufacturing 210

 Collaborative Manufacturing Networks 212

 Process Control 212

 Machine Control 212

 Robotics 212

 Computer-Aided Engineering 213

Human Resource Information Systems 214
    HRM and the Internet 214
    HRM and the Corporate Intranet 216
    Staffing and the Organization 216
    Training and Development 217
    Compensation Analysis 217
    Governmental Reporting 218
Accounting Information Systems 218
    Online Accounting Systems 218
    Order Processing 218
    Inventory Control 220
    Accounts Receivable 220
    Accounts Payable 220
    Payroll 220
    General Ledger 221
Financial Management Systems 221
    Cash Management 221
    Online Investment Management 221
    Capital Budgeting 222
    Financial Forecasting and Planning 222

Section II: Fundamentals of Electronic Commerce 223
Introduction 223
    Analyzing Buy.com 223
Real World Case: Buy.com: Testing a New Business Model in E-Commerce 224
Foundations of Electronic Commerce 225
    Electronic Commerce Technologies 225
Business-to-Consumer Commerce 226
    Retailing on the Web 226
    Amazon.com 228
Customer Value and the Internet 229
    Nortel Networks 230
Business-to-Business Commerce 231
    Supply Chain Management 232
    Wholesaling on the Web 232
    Marshall Industries 233
    Electronic Data Interchange 233
Online Transaction Processing 235
    Syntellect 235
    The Transaction Processing Cycle 235
Electronic Payments and Security 236
    Electronic Funds Transfer 237
    Secure Electronic Payments on the Internet 237

Chapter 7

Information Systems for Enterprise Collaboration 249

Section I: Intranets and Extranets in Business 250
The Intranet Revolution 250
    Analyzing Glaxo Wellcome and BC Telecom 250
Real World Case: Glaxo Wellcome and BC Telecom: The Business Value of Self-Service Intranets 251
    Intranets, Extranets, and the Internet 252
Applications of Intranets 253
    SunWeb 254
Intranet Technology Resources 256
The Business Value of Intranets 256
    Examples of Business Value 257
    Cadence OnTrack 260
The Role of Extranets 262
    Business Value of Extranets 262
    Extranet Examples 262
The Future of Intranets and Extranets 263
    US West Global Village 264

Section II: Enterprise Collaboration Systems 266
Enterprise Collaboration 266
    Analyzing Lockheed Martin 266
Real World Case: Lockheed Martin Corporation: Improving Team Collaboration via Desktop Videoconferencing 267
    Teams, Workgroups, and Collaboration 268
    Enterprise Collaboration System Components 268
Groupware for Enterprise Collaboration 270
Electronic Communication Tools 271
    Electronic Mail 271
    Internet Phone and Fax 271
    Web Publishing 271
Electronic Conferencing Tools 272
    Data and Voice Conferencing 272
    Videoconferencing 273
    Discussion Forums 275
    Chat Systems 277
    Electronic Meeting Systems 277
Collaborative Work Management Tools 279
    Calendaring and Scheduling 279
    Task and Project Management 279

Workflow Systems 280
Knowledge Management 282

Chapter 8

Information Systems for Managerial Decision Support 293

Section I: Management Information and Decision Support Systems 294

Introduction 294

Analyzing Lexis-Nexis 294

Real World Case: Lexis-Nexis Inc.: Using a Data Warehouse and Web-Based Tools for Decision Support 295

Information, Decisions, and Management 296
Decision Structure 297

Management Information Systems 297

Management Reporting Alternatives 298

Online Analytical Processing 299

OLAP at MasterCard International 301

Decision Support Systems 301

DSS Models and Software 302
Geographic Information Systems 303
DSS at PepsiCo 304

Using Decision Support Systems 304

What-If Analysis 305
Sensitivity Analysis 305
Goal-Seeking Analysis 306
Optimization Analysis 306

Executive Information Systems 307

Rationale for EIS 307
EIS at Conoco and KeyCorp 309

Section II: Artificial Intelligence Technologies in Business 310

Analyzing Dow Jones and Charles Schwab 310

Real World Case: Dow Jones and Charles Schwab & Co.: Web Applications of Intelligent Agents and Neural Nets 311

An Overview of Artificial Intelligence 312

The Domains of Artificial Intelligence 312

Neural Networks 314

Neural Nets at Infoseek 316

Fuzzy Logic Systems 316

Fuzzy Logic in Business 316

Genetic Algorithms 317

GE's Engeneous 318

Virtual Reality 318

VR Applications 318
VR at Morgan Stanley 320

Intelligent Agents 320

Wizards by Microsoft 321

Expert Systems 322

Components of an Expert System 322
Expert System Applications 322
ES for Advertising Strategy 324

Developing Expert Systems 325

Knowledge Engineering 326
ES Development at MacMillan Bloedel 327

The Value of Expert Systems 327

Benefits of Expert Systems 327
Limitations of Expert Systems 328

Chapter 9

Information Systems for Strategic Advantage 337

Section I: Fundamentals of Strategic Advantage 338

Introduction 338

Analyzing Ford Motor Company 338

Real World Case: Ford Motor Company: E-Engineering Global Business Processes 339

Competitive Strategy Concepts 340

Strategic Roles for Information Systems 341

Improving Business Processes 342
DaimlerChrysler's CATIA Pipeline 343
Promoting Business Innovation 344
Citibank and ATMs 344
Locking in Customers and Suppliers 345
Wal-Mart and Others 345
Creating Switching Costs 345
SABRE and APOLLO 345
Raising Barriers to Entry 346
Merrill Lynch 346
Leveraging a Strategic IT Platform 346
Developing a Strategic Information Base 346

The Value Chain and Strategic IS 347

Section II: Strategic Applications and Issues in Information Technology 349

Introduction 349

Analyzing Office Depot and Staples 349

Real World Case: Office Depot versus Staples: Competing with Internet Technologies 350

Reengineering Business Processes 351

The Role of Information Technology 352

CIGNA Corporation 353

Improving Business Quality 353

Total Quality Management 354

Sun Microsystems 355

Becoming an Agile Competitor 356

The Role of Information Technology 356

Ross Operating Valves 357

Creating a Virtual Company 358

Virtual Company Strategies 358

Cisco Systems 359

Building the Knowledge-Creating Company 360

Knowledge Management Systems 360

Storage Dimensions 361

Using the Internet Strategically 362

Internet Value Chains 364

McAffee Associates 364

The Challenges of Strategic IS 366

Sustaining Strategic Success 367

Module IV   Development and Management

Chapter 10

Developing Business Solutions with Information Technology 379

Section I: Developing Information System Solutions 380

Analyzing SunAmerica and A-DEC 380

Real World Case: SunAmerica Financial and A-DEC Inc.: Challenges in ERP Systems Development and Implementation 381

The Systems Approach 382

Systems Thinking 382

The Systems Development Cycle 383

Starting the Systems Development Process 384

Feasibility Studies 385

A Case Study Example: Auto Shack Stores: Solving a Business Problem 386

Systems Analysis 388

Organizational Analysis 388

Analysis of the Present System 389

Functional Requirements Analysis 389

Systems Design 390

User Interface, Data, and Process Design 390

System Specifications 392

Prototyping 393

The Prototyping Process 394

Computer-Aided Systems Engineering 395

Using CASE Tools 395

End User Development 396

Doing End User Development 397

Focus on IS Activities 398

Checklist for End User Development 399

Section II: Implementing Business Change with IT 402

Introduction 402

Analyzing Computer Associates, Microsoft, and IBM 402

Real World Case: Computer Associates, Microsoft, and IBM: Business Users Rate Software Support 403

Managing Organizational Change 404

End User Involvement 404

Change Management 404

British Petroleum Exploration 405

Implementing New Systems 405

Evaluating Hardware, Software, and Services 407

Hardware Evaluation Factors 408

Software Evaluation Factors 409

Evaluating IS Services 410

Other Implementation Activities 410

Testing 410

Documentation 412

Training 412

Conversion Methods 412

IS Maintenance 413

Chapter 11

Enterprise and Global Management of Information Technology 423

Section I: Managing Information Resources and Technologies 424

Introduction 424

Analyzing Chase Manhattan, Cigna, and PG&E 424

Real World Case: Chase Manhattan, Cigna, and PG&E: Business Managers of Information Technology 425

Managers and Information Technology 426

Poor IS Performance 427

Empire Blue Cross/Blue Shield 428

Management Involvement and Governance 428

Chemical Banking Corporation 429

Organizations and Information Technology 429

Information Resource Management 431

Strategic Management 432

The Chief Information Officer 432

Strategic Information Systems Planning 432

Information Technology Architecture 434

S. C. Johnson & Son, Inc. 435

Operational Management 435

Centralization versus Decentralization 435

Changing Trends 438

DuPont Corporation 438

Managing Systems Development 438

Managing IS Operations 439

Resource Management 440

Human Resource Management of IT 440

Careers in Information Systems 440

Technology Management 441

Network Management 442

Advanced Technology Management 443

Distributed Management 443

Managing End User Computing 444

Managing Internet Access 445

Section II: Global Information Technology Management 446

Analyzing Guy Carpenter & Co. and PRT Group 446

The International Dimension 446

Real World Case: Guy Carpenter & Co. and PRT Group: The Business Case for Global Software Development 447

Global IT Management 448

Cultural, Political, and Geoeconomic Challenges 448

Challenges in Europe and China 449

Global Business and IT Strategies 450

Global Business and IT Applications 451

Chase Manhattan Bank 452

Global IT Platforms 452

The Internet as a Global IT Platform 453

Global Data Issues 454

Global Systems Development 456

Systems Development Strategies 457

You and Global IT Management 457

Chapter 12

Security and Ethical Challenges of Information Technology 467

Section I: Security and Control Issues in Information Systems 468

Why Controls Are Needed 468

Analyzing BuyDirect and Others 468

What Controls Are Needed 468

Real World Case: BuyDirect and Others: Credit Card Fraud in E-Commerce 469

Information System Controls 471

Input Controls 471

Processing Controls 472

Output Controls 473

Storage Controls 473

Facility Controls 474

Network Security 474

Physical Protection Controls 475

Biometric Controls 476

Computer Failure Controls 477

Procedural Controls 478

Standard Procedures and Documentation 478

Authorization Requirements 478

Disaster Recovery 479

Controls for End User Computing 479

Auditing Information Systems 480

Section II: Ethical and Societal Challenges of Information Technology 482

Analyzing Warroom Research and Sun-Trust Banks 482

Real World Case: Warroom Research and Sun-Trust Banks: Defending Networks from Cyberattacks 483

The Ethical Dimension 484

Ethical Foundations 484

Business Ethics 484

Ethical and Societal Dimensions of IT 485

IT and Employment 486

IT and Individuality 488

IT and Working Conditions 489

Privacy Issues 490

Privacy on the Internet 491

Corporate E-Mail Privacy 492

Computer Matching 492

Privacy Laws 492

Computer Libel and Censorship 492

Computer Crime 493

Computer Crime Laws 494

Examples of Computer Crime 495

Health Issues 498

Ergonomics 500

Societal Solutions 500

You and Ethical Responsibility 501

Glossary G-1

Name Index I-1

Organization Index I-7

Subject Index I-13

Introduction to Information Systems

Essentials for the Internetworked Enterprise

Introduction

Why study information systems? Why do businesses need information technology? What do you need to know about the use and management of information technology in business? The introductory chapter of Module I is designed to answer these fundamental questions about information systems.

Chapter 1, "Introduction to Information Systems in Business," introduces you to the importance of information systems knowledge for business end users, some of the key issues in the business use of information technology, and the conceptual system components and basic types of information systems.

After completing this chapter, you can move on to study chapters on information technologies (Module II), business applications (Module III) and the development and management of information systems (Module IV).

Chapter

1

Introduction to Information

Systems in Business

Chapter Highlights

Section I
Why Businesses Need Information Technology

Why Information Systems Are Important
The Real World of Information Systems
Real World Case: NetFlix.com: Challenges of a New Web Business
What You Need to Know
The Fundamental Roles of Information Systems
The Internet and Business
The Internetworked Enterprise
Globalization and Information Technology
Business Process Reengineering
Competitive Advantage with IT

Section II
Fundamentals of Information Systems

Introduction
Real World Case: Milacron Inc.: Serving Small Businesses via the Web
System Concepts
Components of an Information System
Information System Resources
Information System Activities
Overview of Information Systems
Types of Information Systems
Recognizing Information Systems

Learning Objectives

After reading and studying this chapter, you should be able to:

1. Explain why knowledge of information systems is important for business end users and identify five areas of information systems knowledge they need.

2. Give examples to illustrate how information systems can help support a firm's business operations, managerial decision making, and strategic advantage.

3. Identify how businesses can use IT for strategic competitive advantage through enterprise internetworking, globalization, and business process reengineering.

4. Identify and give examples of the components and functions of the generic concept of a system introduced in this chapter.

5. Provide examples of the components of real world information systems. Illustrate that in an information system, people use hardware, software, data, and networks as resources to perform input, processing, output, storage, and control activities that transform data resources into information products.

6. Provide examples of several major types of information systems from your experiences with business organizations in the real world.

Why Businesses Need Information Technology

Why Information Systems Are Important

Information technology is reshaping the basics of business. Customer service, operations, product and marketing strategies, and distribution are heavily, or sometimes even entirely, dependent on IT. Information technology, and its expense, have become an everyday part of business life [9].

Why study information systems and information technology? That's the same as asking why anyone should study accounting, finance, operations management, marketing, human resource management, or any other major business function. Information systems and technologies have become a vital component of successful businesses and organizations. They thus constitute an essential field of study in business administration and management. That's why most business majors must take a course in information systems. Since you probably intend to be a manager, entrepreneur, or business professional, it is just as important to have a basic understanding of information systems as it is to understand any other functional area in business.

The Real World of Information Systems

Let's take a moment to bring the real world into our discussion of the importance of information systems and information technology. Read the Real World Case of Net-Flix on the next page. Then let's analyze it together. See Figure 1.1.

Figure 1.1

Chief technology and operations officer Jim Cook says NetFlix lets users check their order status at the web site using E-mail software.

Source: © Cindy Charles.

NetFlix.com: Challenges of a New Web Business

The emergence of DVDs and E-mail-based customer service technologies has unlocked a new business for online retailer NetFlix.com in Scotts Valley, California. NetFlix.com was established a little more than a year ago to target an untapped niche in the electronic-commerce market: movie rentals.

Because of the bulk and cost of delivering VHS tapes, renting tapes over the Web wasn't a popular business option, said Jim Cook, chief technology officer and director of operations at NetFlix.com. "It wasn't worth the shipping costs for a $4 rental," he said.

But the small, easy-to-ship format of a digital video disk (DVD) makes the product a better vehicle for renting movie titles online, he said. The disks cost between $20 and $30 each to buy and between $3 and $5 each to rent, plus shipping and handling charges. One disk weighs less than 1 ounce and costs about 55 cents to ship via the U.S. Postal Service.

The NetFlix.com service works like this: A customer with a PC, Web browser, and Internet access searches for and orders a movie at the www.netflix.com web site. A DVD is sent in an unmarked package along with a pread-dressed, prepaid return envelope. The customer can keep the disk for seven days from the day it arrives and then return it via U.S. mail. The company has more than 3,000 titles available for rent and offers delivery within two to three days coast to coast.

According to InfoTech research, people bought more than 1.2 million DVD players worldwide in 1998, a 140 percent increase from the previous year. InfoTech attributes the growth to Hollywood's acceptance of the medium—a large catalog of films is now available on DVD—and to falling PC hardware prices that allow more PC manufacturers to add DVD-Rom drives to their systems. Currently, only about 1 percent of households have a DVD player, but analysts expect big sales of the players this year.

Early on, NetFlix.com realized that its primary means of communication with customers would be E-mail. Since its launch, the company has been using the Enterprise Edition of Internet Message Center from Mustang Software to route hundreds of messages per day and issue automated responses.

"It's not economically viable to have a huge phone bank. So we needed a software package to serve as a dispatcher," Cook said. Besides routing and responding to E-mail, the system also provides a way to drill down and analyze questions that the company has received, he said.

For example, Cook said queries about order status are common. So NetFlix.com used that information to create a Your Account feature on the site that lets users check order status themselves. Then customer service agents can look into larger issues such as technical problems with DVDs, Cook said.

The company plans to integrate other systems within the E-mail customer database—including billing systems and personalized marketing programs, said Te Smith, NetFlix.com's marketing director.

NetFlix.com's main competition comes from video retailers such as Reel.com and Blockbuster Entertainment Group. But Cook noted that those companies are selling, not renting, DVDs over the Internet.

Dave Rochlin, vice president of marketing at Reel.com, confirmed that the retailer doesn't rent DVDs but did mention that it recently launched a DVD-only section of its online storefront. The company uses standard Web forms and E-mail routing software, Rochlin said. Reel.com briefly tried rentals over the Web but phased out the practice. "Logically, it didn't really work," a spokesperson said. "We found it hard to turn around the product to customers. And it seems like most DVD users are buying, not renting."

But NetFlix is moving aggressively to change that perception by offering free rental of the first three DVDs to new customers to encourage web site visitors to try their service. NetFlix has also established a new strategic partnership with E-commerce giant Amazon.com, which recently entered the CD and DVD market. Now visitors to either company's web site are encouraged to go to Amazon.com to buy DVD titles, and click to NetFlix for DVD rentals.

Case Study Questions

1. What are the advantages and limitations of NetFlix's present use of information technology to support its business?

2. Visit the NetFlix web site at www.netflix.com. What additional business uses of Internet and other information technologies would you recommend to NetFlix? Why?

3. What business moves should NetFlix make to improve their chances for business success? Why? How could IT help? Explain.

Source: Adapted from Roberta Fusard, "Start-Up Taps Web—To Rent DVD Films," *Computerworld*, January 4, 1999, p. 29. Copyright 1999 by Computerworld, Inc., Framingham, MA 01701. Reprinted from *Computerworld*.

Analyzing NetFlix.com

We can learn a lot about the importance of information technology and information systems from the Real World Case of NetFlix.com.

This case dramatizes just one of countless examples of how the Internet and the World Wide Web are enabling new uses of information technology to support new business ventures. For example, renting movies by mail would not be a profitable business without the development of DVD, Internet, and other information technologies. The easy-to-ship size and weight of the DVD makes mailing economically feasible. The use of Internet browser, web site, and E-mail technologies makes electronic communications and ordering quick and efficient. And the advanced capabilities of the Mustang messaging software enable NetFlix.com to extract and present information to help the company manage their operations and provide better customer service.

Thus, information technologies, including Internet-based information systems, are playing a vital and expanding role in business. Information technology can help all kinds of businesses improve the efficiency and effectiveness of their business processes, managerial decision making, and workgroup collaboration and thus strengthen their competitive positions in a rapidly changing marketplace. This is true, whether information technology is used to support product development teams, customer support processes, interactive electronic commerce transactions, or any other business activity. Internet-based information technologies and systems are fast becoming a necessary ingredient for business success in today's dynamic global environment.

What You Need to Know

As CEO of Simon & Schuster, I need to understand how information technology is changing our business, and I must ensure that our organization uses technology effectively. Consequently, I spend a lot of my time trying to understand the implications of new technologies . . .

I also expect my CIO to have a rock-solid business view of technology and my line managers to demonstrate that they understand technology and are using it [13].

Those are the words of Jonathan Newcomb, president and CEO of Simon and Schuster, the giant publishing company. So even top executives and managers must continue to learn about how to apply information systems and technologies to their unique business situations. In fact, business firms depend on all of their managers and employees to help them manage their use of information technologies. So the important question for any business end user or manager is: What do you need to know in order to help manage the hardware, software, data, and network resources of your business, so they are used for the strategic success of your company?

A Framework for Business End Users

The field of information systems encompasses many complex technologies, abstract behavioral concepts, and specialized applications in countless business and nonbusiness areas. As a manager or business end user you do not have to absorb all of this knowledge. Figure 1.2 illustrates a useful conceptual framework that organizes the knowledge in this text and outlines what end users need to know about information systems. It emphasizes that you should concentrate your efforts in five areas of knowledge:

- **Foundation Concepts.** Fundamental behavioral, technical, and managerial concepts about the components and roles of information systems. Examples include basic information system concepts derived from general systems theory

Figure 1.2

This framework outlines the major areas of information systems knowledge needed by business end users.

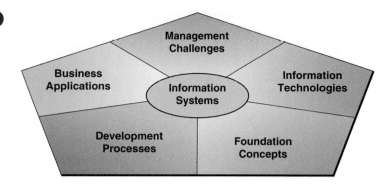

or competitive strategy concepts used to develop information systems for competitive advantage. Chapter 1 and other chapters of the text support this area of knowledge.

- **Information Technologies.** Major concepts, developments, and management issues in information technology—that is, hardware, software, networks, database management, and other information processing technologies. Chapters 2 through 5 along with other chapters of the text support this area of information systems knowledge.

- **Business Applications.** The major uses of information systems for the operations, management, and competitive advantage of an enterprise, including electronic commerce and collaboration using the Internet, intranets, and extranets, are covered in Chapters 6 to 9.

- **Development Processes.** How end users or information specialists develop information systems solutions to business problems using fundamental problem-solving and developmental methodologies. Chapter 10 helps you gain such knowledge and begin applying it to simple business problems.

- **Management Challenges.** The challenges of effectively and ethically managing the resources and business strategies involved in using information technology at the end user, enterprise, and global levels of a business. Chapters 11 and 12 specifically cover these topics, but all of the chapters in the text emphasize the managerial challenges of information technology.

Information System Resources and Technologies

An **information system** is an organized combination of people, hardware, software, communications networks, and data resources that collects, transforms, and disseminates information in an organization. See Figure 1.3. People have relied on information systems to communicate with each other using a variety of physical devices (*hardware*), information processing instructions and procedures (*software*), communications channels (*networks*), and stored data (*data resources*) since the dawn of civilization.

Today's end users rely on many types of information systems (IS). They might include simple manual (paper-and-pencil) hardware devices and informal (word-of-mouth) communications channels. However, in this text, we will concentrate on computer-based information systems that use computer hardware and software,

Information systems use people, hardware, software, data, and communications network resources to collect, transform, and disseminate information in an organization.

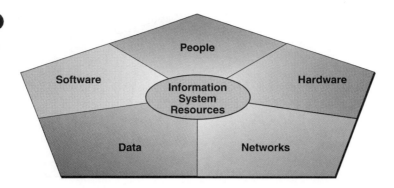

telecommunications networks, computer-based data management techniques, and other forms of **information technology** (IT) to transform data resources into a variety of information products. We will discuss this concept further in the next chapter and in the chapters of Module II on information technology.

An End User Perspective

Anyone who uses an information system or the information it produces is an **end user.** This usually applies to most people in an organization, as distinguished from the smaller number of people who are *information system specialists,* such as systems analysts or professional computer programmers. Most end users are **knowledge workers,** that is, people who spend most of their time communicating and collaborating in teams and workgroups and creating, using, and distributing information. Managerial end users are managers, entrepreneurs, or managerial-level professionals who personally use information systems. This book is written for potential managerial end users like you and other students of business administration and management.

Whatever your career will be, you can increase your opportunities for success by becoming a knowledgeable end user of information technology. Businesses and other organizations need people who can use networked computer workstations to enhance their own personal productivity and the productivity of their workgroups, process teams, departments, and organizations. For example, you should be able to use the Internet and electronic mail to communicate more effectively, spreadsheet packages to more effectively analyze decision situations, database management packages to generate better reports on organizational performance, and specialized business software to support your specific work activities.

As a prospective managerial end user and knowledge worker in a global society, you should also become aware of the **ethical responsibilities** generated by the use of information technology. For example, what uses of information technology might be considered improper, irresponsible, or harmful to other individuals or to society? What is the proper use of an organization's information resources? What does it take to be a **responsible end user** of information technology? How can you protect yourself from computer crime and other risks of information technology? These are some of the questions that outline the ethical dimensions of information systems that we will discuss and illustrate with Real World Cases in Chapter 12 and other chapters of this text. Figure 1.4 outlines some of the ethical risks that may arise in the use of information technology.

An Enterprise Management Perspective

You should also be aware of the management problems and opportunities presented by the use of information technology, and how you can effectively confront such challenges. Today's internetworked information systems play a vital role in the business success of an enterprise. For example, the Internet and Internet-like internal networks,

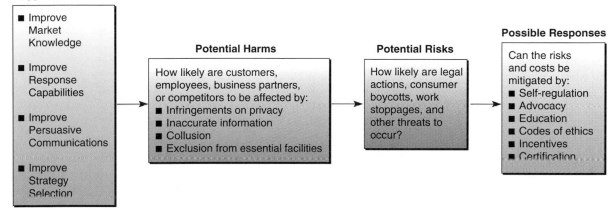

Figure 1.4 Ethical considerations of the potential harms or business risks in the business use of IT.

Applications of IT
- Improve Market Knowledge
- Improve Response Capabilities
- Improve Persuasive Communications
- Improve Strategy Selection

Potential Harms
How likely are customers, employees, business partners, or competitors to be affected by:
- Infringements on privacy
- Inaccurate information
- Collusion
- Exclusion from essential facilities

Potential Risks
How likely are legal actions, consumer boycotts, work stoppages, and other threats to occur?

Possible Responses
Can the risks and costs be mitigated by:
- Self-regulation
- Advocacy
- Education
- Codes of ethics
- Incentives
- Certification

Source: Adapted and reprinted by permission of Harvard Business School Press from Robert C. Blattberg, Rashi Glazer, and John D. C. Little, *The Marketing Information Revolution* (Boston: 1994), p. 291. Copyright © 1994 by the President and Fellows of Harvard College; all rights reserved.

or *intranets*, and external interorganizational networks, called *extranets*, can provide the information infrastructure a business needs for efficient operations, effective management, and competitive advantage. However, Figure 1.5 emphasizes that information systems must also support the business strategies, business processes, and organizational structures and culture of an enterprise.

That's because computer-based information systems, though heavily dependent on information technologies, are designed, operated, and used by people in a variety of organizational settings and business environments. Thus, the success of an information system should not be measured only by its *efficiency* in terms of minimizing costs,

Figure 1.5

Information systems and technologies must support an organization's business strategies, business processes, and organizational structures and culture to increase the business value of the enterprise in a dynamic business environment.

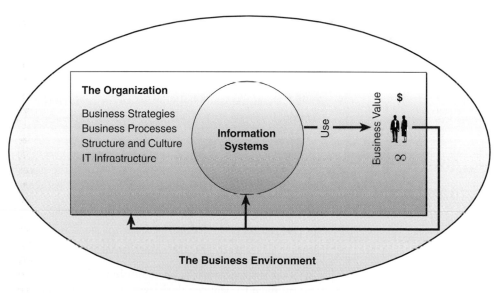

The Organization
Business Strategies
Business Processes
Structure and Culture
IT Infrastructure

Information Systems

Use → Business Value $

The Business Environment

Source: Adapted from Mark Silver, M. Lynne Markus, and Cynthia Mathis Beath, "The Information Technology Interaction Model: A Foundation for the MBA Core Course," *MIS Quarterly*, September 1995, p. 366. Reprinted with permission from the *MIS Quarterly*.

Figure 1.6

Why information technology development projects succeed or fail.

Top Five Reasons for Success:	Top Five Reasons for Failure:
● User involvement.	● Lack of user input.
● Executive management support.	● Incomplete requirements and specifications.
● Clear statement of requirements.	● Changing requirements and specifications.
● Proper planning.	● Lack of executive support.
● Realistic expectations.	● Technological incompetence.

Source: Adapted from "Few IS Projects Come in on Time, on Budget," by Rosemary Cafasso, *Computerworld*, December 12, 1994, p. 20. Copyright 1994 by Computerworld, Inc., Framingham, MA 01701. Reprinted from *Computerworld*.

time, and the use of information resources. Success should also be measured by the *effectiveness* of information technology in supporting an organization's business strategies, enabling its business processes, enhancing its organizational structures and culture, and increasing the business value of the enterprise.

However, it is important that you realize that information technology and information systems can be mismanaged and misapplied so that they create both technological and business failure. For example, Figure 1.6 outlines major reasons why information technology development projects succeed or fail in business.

So, the proper management of information systems is a major challenge for managers. In summary, the information systems function represents:

- A major functional area of business that is as important to business success as the functions of accounting, finance, operations management, marketing, and human resource management.

- An important contributor to operational efficiency, employee productivity and morale, and customer service and satisfaction.

- A major source of information and support needed to promote effective decision making by managers.

- An important ingredient in developing competitive products and services that give an organization a strategic advantage in the global marketplace.

- A major part of the resources of an enterprise and its cost of doing business, thus posing a major resource management challenge.

- A vital, dynamic, and challenging career opportunity for millions of men and women.

The Fundamental Roles of Information Systems

Figure 1.7 illustrates the fundamental reasons for the use of information technology in business. Information systems perform three vital roles in any type of organization.

- Support of its business processes and operations.
- Support of decision making by its employees and managers.
- Support of its strategies for competitive advantage.

Let's take a retail store as an example to illustrate this important point. As a consumer, you have to deal regularly with the information systems that support business operations at the many retail stores where you shop. For example, most retail stores

Figure 1.7

The three major roles of information systems. Information systems provide an organization with support for business operations, managerial decision making, and strategic advantage.

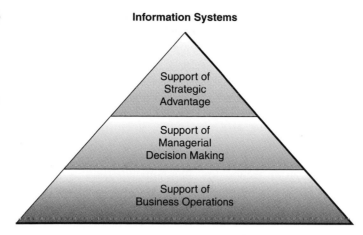

now use computer-based information systems to help them record customer purchases, keep track of inventory, pay employees, buy new merchandise, and evaluate sales trends. Store operations would grind to a halt without the support of such information systems.

Information systems also help store managers make better decisions and attempt to gain a strategic competitive advantage. For example, decisions on what lines of merchandise need to be added or discontinued, or on what kind of investment they require, are typically made after an analysis provided by computer-based information systems. This not only supports the decision making of store managers but also helps them look for ways to gain an advantage over other retailers in the competition for customers. For example, Figure 1.8 illustrates a sales analysis report produced by a management information system.

Figure 1.8

A sales analysis report produced by a management information system.

Courtesy of Lotus Development Corporation.

Gaining a strategic advantage over competitors requires innovative use of information technology. For example, store managers might make a decision to install computerized touch-screen catalog ordering systems in all of their stores, tied in with computer-based telephone ordering systems and an Internet-based computer shopping web site. This might attract new customers and lure customers away from competing stores because of the ease of ordering merchandise provided by such innovative information systems. Thus, strategic information systems can help provide products and services that give a business organization a comparative advantage over its competitors.

Now let's take a brief look at several key developments that impact the business use of information technology. These include the Internet and business, internetworking the enterprise, globalization, business process reengineering, and using information technology for competitive advantage. They are just some of the major reasons why today's businesses need information technology. We will introduce these topics here and cover them in greater detail in later chapters.

The Internet and Business

There is one major change in information technology on whose importance business executives, academicians, and technologists all agree. It is the explosive growth of the Internet and related technologies and applications, and their impact on business, society, and information technology. The Internet is changing the way businesses are operated and people work, and how information technology supports business operations and end user work activities.

The Internet has become a vital telecommunications platform for electronic communications and collaboration and electronic commerce among businesses and their employees, customers, suppliers, and business partners. Corporate web sites on the World Wide Web have become clearinghouses for the interactive exchange of information via E-mail, chat systems, discussion forums, and multimedia publishing. Business web sites also serve as electronic retail and wholesale outlets for buying and selling a wide variety of products and services.

Figure 1.9 is a sample of the Internet applications of the companies who were rated among the top 100 organizations in the United States for their use of the Internet. Notice the broad range of applications that these companies have implemented and the business benefits that have resulted. This should give you a good idea of how versatile the Internet is as an information technology platform on which to base a variety of business strategies. Now let's look in more detail at how one company is using the Internet in business.

American Airlines

Like many other companies, American Airlines offers a web site (www.aa.com) that propelled them into electronic commerce on the Internet. First, American analyzed the compelling business reasons for a business web site. Would it save money, improve customer service, shorten time to market, or transform distribution channels? Then, they decided to build a web site that their customers would find useful and that would reduce the company's customer service costs. See Figure 1.10.

American Airlines spends millions of dollars each year to staff their toll-free customer service telephone system. A large percentage of calls are not from customers wanting to book flights. Instead, many calls are from people wanting information such as how to get to the airport, how to travel with a pet, or whether they can take their skis along on a flight. American realized that many of their customers had computers at work or at home that were connected to the Internet. They assumed that

Figure 1.9

The applications of 10 top-rated business users of the Internet. Note the variety of business applications and business benefits by these companies.

Company and URL	Business Internet Applications and Benefits
A&M Records amrecords.com	Interactive site with video, audio, news, and contests. Fans get up-to-date information on clients represented by A&M. Improves name recognition and Internet presence for company.
Alaska Airlines www.alaska-air.com	Web site used for direct ticket purchases, reservations, and flight information. Customer service realized through ease and convenience of information access and improved call-wait times.
Amazon.com www.amazon.com	Online bookstore. Allows customers to search by title, author, subject, or keyword; pay by credit card; and have items shipped to them.
Federal Express www.fedex.com	Package tracking service. Customers can ship and track own packages, leading to reduced communication costs and labor costs.
First Union Corp. www.firstunion.com	Online banking service allows access to account information and transactions. Reduces telephony costs.
The Dreyfus Corp. www.dreyfus.com	Account and sales information. Customers set up new accounts, track status, and access daily rates and prices. Improves ease of transactions and security. Development cost: $127,500.
Holiday Inns www.holiday-inn.com	Customer service and marketing. Online realtime reservations. Customers can view accommodations. Development cost: $300,000.
Lands' End www.landsend.com	Interactive shopping for U.S. customers. Promotes sales and customer service by providing overstock catalog and online event information, such as quilt contest winners.
Charles Schwab Corp. www.schwab.com	Online trading, marketing, and electronic commerce. Reduces employee costs, improves customer service, and generates customer savings.
Whirlpool Corp. www.whirlpool.com	Customer service, public relations, sales, and marketing. Benefits realized through improved consumer relations and direct purchasing of small appliances. Development cost: $100,000.

Source: Adapted from "The Premier 100," The Premier 100 Supplement to *Computerworld*, February 24, 1997, pp. 56–63. Copyright 1997 by Computerworld, Inc., Framingham, MA 01701. Reprinted from *Computerworld*.

most of those customers would rather get the information they needed directly from the Web than call in and probably wait in line for answers.

So American's web site posts travel-related information such as airport layouts and logistics, aircraft seating charts, listings of in-flight movies, city ticket office locations, and flight arrival and departure times. Frequent fliers can also check the status of their accounts. Finally, American added online booking and electronic ticketing, so customers can make and pay for flight reservations on the Web [15].

The Internetworked Enterprise

Businesses are becoming **internetworked enterprises.** The Internet and Internet-like networks—inside the enterprise (intranets), between an enterprise and its trading partners (extranets), and other networks—have become the primary information technology infrastructure that supports the business operations of many organizations. This is especially evident in the areas of electronic commerce systems among businesses and their customers and suppliers, and enterprise collaboration systems among business teams and workgroups. See Figure 1.11.

Electronic commerce is the buying and selling, and marketing and servicing of products, services, and information over a variety of computer networks. An

Figure 1.10

The web site home page (www.aa.com) of American Airlines.

Courtesy of AMR Corporation.

internetworked enterprise uses the Internet, intranets, extranets, and other networks to support every step of the commercial process. This might include everything from multimedia advertising, product information, and customer support on the World Wide Web, to Internet security and payment mechanisms that ensure completion of delivery and payment processes. For example, electronic commerce could include use of multimedia web pages of product catalogs on the Internet, extranet access of inventory databases by large customers, and the use of a corporate intranet by sales reps to access customer records.

Enterprise collaboration systems involve the use of groupware tools to support communication, coordination, and collaboration among the members of networked teams and workgroups. An internetworked enterprise depends on intranets, the Internet, extranets, and other networks to implement such systems. For example, employees and external consultants may form a *virtual team* that uses a corporate intranet and the Internet for electronic mail, videoconferencing, electronic discussion groups, and multimedia web pages of work-in-progress information to collaborate on business projects. We will discuss the business impact of electronic commerce and collaboration in Chapters 6 and 7.

Globalization and Information Technology

We are living in a global economy that is increasingly dependent on the creation, management, and distribution of information resources over interconnected global networks like the Internet. Thus, many companies are in the process of **globalization;** that is, becoming internetworked global enterprises. For example, businesses are expanding into global markets for their products and services, using global production

Figure 1.11 The internetworked enterprise depends on the Internet, intranets, extranets, and other networks for enterprise collaboration among a company's business functions, and the support of electronic commerce with customers, suppliers, and other business partners.

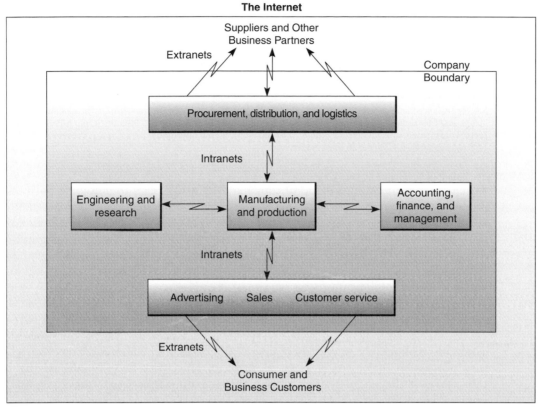

Source: Adapted from Ravi Kalakota and Andrew Whinston, *Frontiers of Electronic Commerce* (Reading, MA: Addison-Wesley, 1996), p. 219. © 1996 Addison-Wesley Publishing Company Inc. Reprinted by permission of Addison-Wesley Longman Inc.

facilities to manufacture or assemble products, raising money in global capital markets, forming alliances with global partners, and battling with global competitors for customers from all over the globe. Managing and accomplishing these strategic changes would be impossible without the Internet, intranets, and other global computing and telecommunications networks that are the central nervous system of today's global companies.

Figure 1.12 illustrates how information technology supports globalization. For example, global companies operate in a competitive environment in which internetworked computer systems make possible global markets that can instantly and cheaply process business transactions. So companies can now operate globally, sometimes by forming global business alliances with other organizations, including customers, suppliers, former competitors, consultants, and government agencies. Today's internetworked global enterprise can collectively exploit many national market niches that would be too small for any one national company to service. They can also pool skills from many countries to work on projects that need workers with a variety of skills that cannot be found in any one country [1]. We will discuss managing global IT and its impact on global business operations further in Chapter 11.

Figure 1.12

Information technology can support the globalization of business by enabling the global business operations and alliances of the internetworked global enterprise.

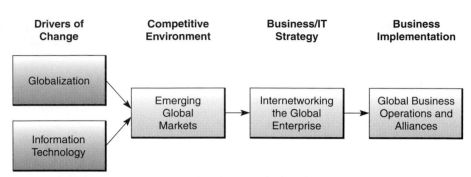

Source: Adapted and reprinted by permission of Harvard Business School Press from *Globalization, Technology, and Competition: The Fusion of Computers and Telecommunications in the 1990s* by Stephen P. Bradley, Jerry A. Hausman, and Richard L. Nolan (Boston: 1993), p. 4. Copyright © 1993 by the President and Fellows of Harvard College; all rights reserved.

Business Process Reengineering

Businesses have used information technology for many years to automate business processes and support the analysis and presentation of information for managerial decision making. However, **business process reengineering** (BPR) is an example of how information technology is being used to restructure work by transforming business processes. A business process is any set of activities designed to produce a specified output for a customer or market. The new product development process and the customer order fulfillment process are typical examples.

Reengineering guru Michael Hammer defines reengineering as "the fundamental rethinking and radical redesign of business processes to achieve dramatic improvements, such as cost, quality, service, and speed" [7]. Thus, reengineering questions all assumptions about "the way we do business." It focuses on the how and why of a business process so major changes can be made in how work is accomplished. BPR thus moves far beyond mere cost cutting or automating a process to make marginal improvements [2].

Figure 1.13 illustrates how information technology was used to help reengineer several business processes at an agricultural chemicals company. Notice that business processes at the individual, workgroup, and business unit levels can be changed by using information technologies to provide economic benefits. For example, the use of laptops for sales calls supported greater interaction between the individual salespeople and customers of an agricultural chemicals company and resulted in significantly greater sales [3]. See Figure 1.14.

Competitive Advantage with IT

Using information technology for globalization and business process reengineering frequently results in the development of information systems that help give a company a **competitive advantage** in the marketplace. These *strategic information systems* use information technology to develop products, services, processes, and capabilities that give a business a strategic advantage over the *competitive forces* it faces in its industry. These forces include not only a firm's competitors but also its customers and suppliers, potential new entrants into its industry, and companies offering substitutes for its products and services. Information technology can play a major role in implementing competitive strategies. This might include:

- **Cost strategies:** Using information technology to help you become a low-cost producer, lower your customers' or suppliers' costs, or increase the costs your competitors must pay to remain in the industry. For example, using

Figure 1.13

How information technology reengineered business processes at several levels of a business.

	IT Initiative	Process Changed	Business Benefit
Salesperson	Laptop Sales Call System	Sales Call	Increased Sales
Marketing Team	Web Site Product Database	Product Distribution	Greater Customer Satisfaction
Business Unit	Product Management System	Marketing Channel Communications	Improved Competitive Position

Source: Adapted and reprinted by permission of Harvard Business School Press from *Process Innovation: Reengineering Work through Information Technology* by Thomas H. Davenport (Boston: 1993), p. 47. Copyright © 1993 by Ernst & Young.

computer-aided manufacturing systems to lower production costs. Or creating Internet web sites for electronic commerce to lower marketing costs.

- **Differentiation strategies:** Developing ways to use information technology to differentiate your company's products or services from your competitors' so your customers perceive your products or services as having unique features or benefits. For example, providing fast and complete customer support services via an Internet web site. Or using targeted marketing systems to offer individual customers the products and services that appeal to them.

- **Innovation strategies:** Introducing unique products or services that include IT components. Or using IT to make radical changes in your business processes that cause fundamental changes in the way business is conducted in your industry.

Figure 1.14

Sales call software and laptop computers can help to reengineer the selling process.

Steve Niedorf/The Image Bank.

Figure 1.15 Examples of how companies used information technology to implement strategies for competitive advantage.

Strategy	Company	Strategic Information System	Business Benefit
Cost Leadership	Levitz Furniture	Centralized Buying	Cut Purchasing Costs
	Metropolitan Life	Medical Care Monitoring	Cut Medical Costs
	Deere & Company	Machine Tool Control	Cut Manufacturing Costs
Differentiation	Navistar	Portable Computer-Based Customer Needs Analysis	Increase in Market Share
	Setco Industries	Computer-Aided Job Estimation	Increase in Market Share
	Consolidated Freightways	Customer Online Shipment Tracking	Increase in Market Share
Innovation	Merrill Lynch	Customer Cash Management Accounts	Market Leadership
	Federal Express	Online Package Tracking and Flight Management	Market Leadership
	McKesson Corp.	Customer Order Entry and Merchandising	Market Leadership

For example, enabling customers to use Internet web sites to custom design and configure products or services for themselves. Or using corporate intranets to dramatically improve the speed and ease of collaboration of cross-functional product development teams.

Figure 1.15 provides a variety of examples of how information technology has helped businesses gain a competitive advantage using such strategies [9]. In Chapter 9, we will discuss in greater detail how businesses can gain strategic competitive advantages through the use of information technology.

Section II   Fundamentals of Information Systems

Introduction

System concepts underlie the field of information systems. That's why this section shows you how generic system concepts apply to business firms and the components and activities of information systems. Understanding system concepts will help you understand many other concepts in the technology, applications, development, and management of information systems that we will cover in this text. For example, system concepts help you understand:

- That computer networks are systems of information processing components.
- That business uses of computer networks are really interconnected business information systems.
- That developing ways to use computer networks in business includes designing the basic components of information systems.
- That managing information technology emphasizes the quality, business value, and security of an organization's information systems.

This kind of understanding will help you be a better user, developer, and manager of information systems. And that, as we have pointed out in the previous section, is important to your future success as a manager, entrepreneur, or professional in business.

Read the Real World Case on Milacron Inc. on the next page. We can learn a lot about the benefits and limitations of the use of information systems in business from this example. See Figure 1.16.

Figure 1.16

Group Vice President Alan Shaffer led the creation of Milacron's web site for their small business customers.

Source: Andy Snow.

Milacron Inc.: Serving Small Businesses via the Web

Manufacturing equipment vendor Milacron Inc. has launched an ambitious, multimillion-dollar electronic commerce site aimed at thousands of new business customers. There are about 117,000 metal-working shops with 50 or fewer employees in the United States. According to Milacron market research, about half those shops already are on the Internet.

The Milacron site, called Milpro (www.milpro.com), was designed for machine shops that previously were considered too small to merit the attention of a Milacron salesperson. Milacron customers frequently require a lot of time from the company's sales engineers for help in selecting and setting up the company's complex industrial equipment.

Now, Milacron's sales force and field-service engineers have two territories: their regular, geographic regions and new "cyberterritories." Salespeople now receive commissions for any orders secured in their cyberterritories—even if they never made actual contact with those shops.

"I'm really excited about it," said Jim VandeHel, a Milacron sales engineer who has started to call on small shops in his cyberterritory. The new web site offers customers with PCs, web browsers, and Internet access a lot of advice on how to select and use Milacron's products, as well as a multimedia catalog of more than 50,000 items.

Alan Shaffer, Milacron group vice president for industrial products, got the idea for the site two years ago after searching for a book about Russia's military bases. At two stores, he recalls, the help desk staff asked him for a specific title or author, information he didn't have.

Then he logged on to Amazon.com. "I found that book in 10 minutes with a search engine. And I said, 'Wow—we can do this with our stuff. If they could put a million books in there, we can put 50,000 inventory items into a multimedia product database,'" he said.

Milacron electronic commerce director Angela Snelling found Shaffer's enthusiasm helpful—especially when he approved her seven-figure budget for the site, even though he didn't expect a single dollar of revenue that year.

Amazon.com took six quarters to generate significant revenue, Shaffer pointed out. He said he's willing to wait for revenue to grow. But he was adamant about being first to market, cloaking the project in secrecy so competitors would not get wind of the plans.

Milacron officials are most proud of the new web site's Milpro Wizard, a knowledge-based expert system, developed in-house, that helps their customers decide which equipment, fluids, and peripherals are best for various manufacturing processes. It also offers advice for setting up machine tools. The company used software from Open Market Inc. for its catalog and transaction activities. And it hired GlobalLink New Media to help develop the site, which is hosted by the EMC Corporation's Internet Services Group hosting center in Hopkinton, Massachusetts.

Small machine shops account for only 30 percent of overall industry spending—compared with 30 percent for just the 164 largest shops—but they tend to pay higher prices because they don't receive volume discounts. "They are more than 30 percent of our profits," Shaffer said.

Case Study Questions

1. What business benefits do you foresee from Milacron's investment in its electronic commerce web site?

2. What information system resource and activities can you identify or visualize in the use of the Milpro web site by a small machine shop? Explain.

3. What should be Milacron's next step in the use of the Internet to serve their small business customers? Explain your recommendations.

Source: Adapted from Sharon Machis, "Web Site Serves the Little Guys," *Computerworld*, January 18, 1999, p. 42. Copyright 1999 by Computerworld, Inc., Framingham, MA 01701. Reprinted from *Computerworld*.

Analyzing Milacron Inc.

Milacron's web site is the hub of their electronic commerce initiatives, and a vital component in many of the types of information systems that companies are installing today. For example, the Milpro web site represents a key component of the *online transaction processing system* that Milacron uses to connect and do business with thousands of small machine shops in support of their electronic commerce activities. PCs, web browsers, and Internet access to the company web site provide customers with easy access to a wealth of information and advice from product catalog databases and *expert system* knowledge bases.

As we will see in this section, Milacron's web-based systems are just a few of many possible types of information systems, whose basic system components include:

- people, hardware, software, data, and network resources,
- which support input, processing, output, storage, and control activities,
- that produce a variety of information products for end users like Milacron's small machine shop customers.

System Concepts

What is a system? A system can be simply defined as a group of interrelated or interacting elements forming a unified whole. Many examples of systems can be found in the physical and biological sciences, in modern technology, and in human society. Thus, we can talk of the physical system of the sun and its planets, the biological system of the human body, the technological system of an oil refinery, and the socioeconomic system of a business organization. However, the following generic system concept provides a more appropriate framework for describing information systems:

A **system** is a group of interrelated components working together toward a common goal by accepting inputs and producing outputs in an organized transformation process. Such a system (sometimes called a *dynamic* system) has three basic interacting components or functions:

- **Input** involves capturing and assembling elements that enter the system to be processed. For example, raw materials, energy, data, and human effort must be secured and organized for processing.
- **Processing** involves transformation processes that convert input into output. Examples are a manufacturing process, the human breathing process, or mathematical calculations.
- **Output** involves transferring elements that have been produced by a transformation process to their ultimate destination. For example, finished products, human services, and management information must be transmitted to their human users.

Example A manufacturing system accepts raw materials as input and produces finished goods as output. An information system also is a system that accepts resources (data) as input and processes them into products (information) as output. See Figure 1.17. ●

Feedback and Control

The system concept becomes even more useful by including two additional components: feedback and control. A system with feedback and control components is sometimes called a *cybernetic* system, that is, a self-monitoring, self-regulating system.

- **Feedback** is data about the performance of a system. For example, data about sales performance is feedback to a sales manager.

Figure 1.17 This manufacturing system illustrates the generic components of many types of systems.

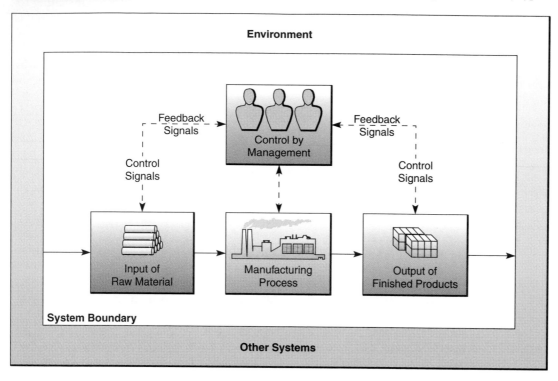

- **Control** involves monitoring and evaluating feedback to determine whether a system is moving toward the achievement of its goal. The control function then makes necessary adjustments to a system's input and processing components to ensure that it produces proper output. For example, a sales manager exercises control when he or she reassigns salespersons to new sales territories after evaluating feedback about their sales performance.

    Feedback is frequently included as part of the concept of the control function because it is such a necessary part of its operation. Figure 1.17 shows the relationship of feedback and control to the other components of a system. Note the dashed arrows indicating the flow of feedback data to the managerial control component and the resulting control signals to the other components. This emphasizes that the role of feedback and control is to ensure that other system components properly transform inputs into outputs so a system can achieve its goal.

Example

A familiar example of a self-monitoring, self-regulating system is the thermostat-controlled heating system found in many homes; it automatically monitors and regulates itself to maintain a desired temperature. Another example is the human body, which can be regarded as a cybernetic system that automatically monitors and adjusts many of its functions, such as temperature, heartbeat, and breathing. A business also has many control activities. For example, computers may monitor and control manufacturing processes, accounting procedures help control financial systems, data entry displays provide control of data entry activities, and sales quotas and sales bonuses attempt to control sales performance. ●

Other System Characteristics

Figure 1.17 points out several other system characteristics that are important to a proper understanding of information systems. Note that a system does not exist in a vacuum; rather, it exists and functions in an *environment* containing other systems. If a system is one of the components of a larger system, it is a *subsystem*, and the larger system is its environment. Also, its *system boundary* separates a system from its environment and other systems.

Several systems may share the same environment. Some of these systems may be connected to one another by means of a shared boundary, or *interface*. Figure 1.17 also illustrates the concept of an *open system;* that is, a system that interacts with other systems in its environment. In this diagram, the system exchanges inputs and outputs with its environment. Thus, we could say that it is connected to its environment by input and output interfaces. Finally, a system that has the ability to change itself or its environment in order to survive is an *adaptive system*. Now let's look at the example suggested by Figure 1.18.

Example

Organizations such as businesses and government agencies are good examples of the systems in society, which is their environment. Society contains a multitude of such systems, including individuals and their social, political, and economic institutions. Organizations themselves consist of many subsystems, such as departments, divisions, process teams, and other workgroups. Organizations are examples of open systems because they interface and interact with other systems in their environment. Finally, organizations are examples of adaptive systems, since they can modify themselves to meet the demands of a changing environment. ●

Components of an Information System

We are now ready to apply the system concepts we have learned to help us better understand how an information system works. For example, we have said that an information system is a system that accepts data resources as input and processes them into information products as output. How does an information system accomplish this? What system components and activities are involved?

Figure 1.19 illustrates an **information system model** that expresses a fundamental conceptual framework for the major components and activities of information systems. An information system depends on the resources of people (end users and IS specialists), hardware (machines and media), software (programs and procedures), data (data and knowledge bases), and networks (communications media and network support) to perform input, processing, output, storage, and control activities that convert data resources into information products.

This information system model highlights the relationships among the components and activities of information systems. It provides a framework that emphasizes four major concepts that can be applied to all types of information systems:

- People, hardware, software, data, and networks are the five basic resources of information systems.
- People resources include end users and IS specialists, hardware resources consist of machines and media, software resources include both programs and procedures, data resources can include data and knowledge bases, and network resources include communications media and networks.
- Data resources are transformed by information processing activities into a variety of information products for end users.

A business is an organizational system where economic resources (input) are transformed by various organization processes (processing) into goods and services (output). Information systems provide information (feedback) on the operations of the system to management for the direction and maintenance of the system (control), as it exchanges inputs and outputs with its environment.

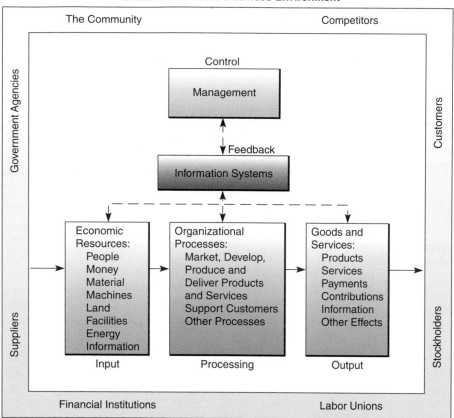

Stakeholders in the Business Environment

- Information processing consists of input, processing, output, storage, and control activities.

Information System Resources

Our basic IS model shows that an information system consists of five major resources: people, hardware, software, data, and networks. Let's briefly discuss several basic concepts and examples of the roles these resources play as the fundamental components of information systems. You should be able to recognize these five components at work in any type of information system you encounter in the real world. Figure 1.20 outlines several examples of typical information system resources and products.

People Resources

People are required for the operation of all information systems. These people resources include end users and IS specialists.

- **End users** (also called users or clients) are people who use an information system or the information it produces. They can be accountants, salespersons, engineers, clerks, customers, or managers. Most of us are information system end users.
- **IS specialists** are people who develop and operate information systems. They include systems analysts, programmers, computer operators, and other managerial, technical, and clerical IS personnel. Briefly, systems analysts design information systems based on the information requirements of end users, programmers prepare computer programs based on the specifications of systems analysts, and computer operators operate large computer systems.

Figure 1.19

The components of an information system. All information systems use people, hardware, software, data, and network resources to perform input, processing, output, storage, and control activities that transform data resources into information products.

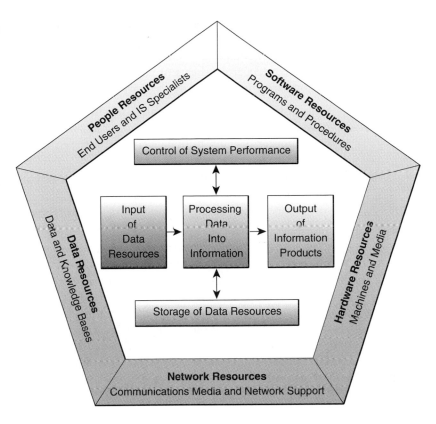

Figure 1.20

Examples of information system resources and products.

People Resources
Specialists—systems analysts, programmers, computer operators.
End Users—anyone else who uses information systems.
Hardware Resources
Machines—computers, video monitors, magnetic disk drives, printers, optical scanners.
Media—floppy disks, magnetic tape, optical disks, plastic cards, paper forms.
Software Resources
Programs—operating system programs, spreadsheet programs, word processing programs, payroll programs.
Procedures—data entry procedures, error correction procedures, paycheck distribution procedures.
Data Resources
Product descriptions, customer records, employee files, inventory databases.
Network Resources
Communications media, communications processors, network access and control software.
Information Products
Management reports and business documents using text and graphics displays, audio responses, and paper forms.

Hardware Resources

The concept of **hardware resources** includes all physical devices and materials used in information processing. Specifically, it includes not only **machines,** such as computers and other equipment, but also all data **media,** that is, tangible objects on which data are recorded, from sheets of paper to magnetic disks. Examples of hardware in computer-based information systems are:

- **Computer systems,** which consist of central processing units containing microprocessors, and a variety of interconnected peripheral devices. Examples are microcomputer systems, midrange computer systems, and large mainframe computer systems.
- **Computer peripherals,** which are devices such as a keyboard or electronic mouse for input of data and commands, a video screen or printer for output of information, and magnetic or optical disks for storage of data resources.

Software Resources

The concept of **software resources** includes all sets of information processing instructions. This generic concept of software includes not only the sets of operating instructions called **programs,** which direct and control computer hardware, but also the sets of information processing instructions needed by people, called **procedures.**

It is important to understand that even information systems that don't use computers have a software resource component. This is true even for the information systems of ancient times, or the manual and machine-supported information systems still used in the world today. They all require software resources in the form of information processing instructions and procedures in order to properly capture, process, and disseminate information to their users.

The following are examples of software resources:

- **System software,** such as an operating system program, which controls and supports the operations of a computer system.
- **Application software,** which are programs that direct processing for a particular use of computers by end users. Examples are a sales analysis program, a payroll program, and a word processing program.
- **Procedures,** which are operating instructions for the people who will use an information system. Examples are instructions for filling out a paper form or using a software package.

Data Resources

Data are more than the raw material of information systems. The concept of data resources has been broadened by managers and information systems professionals. They realize that data constitute a valuable organizational resource. Thus, you should view data as **data resources** that must be managed effectively to benefit all end users in an organization.

Data can take many forms, including traditional alphanumeric data, composed of numbers and alphabetical and other characters that describe business transactions and other events and entities. Text data, consisting of sentences and paragraphs used in written communications; image data, such as graphic shapes and figures; and audio data, the human voice and other sounds, are also important forms of data.

The data resources of information systems are typically organized into:

- Databases that hold processed and organized data.
- Knowledge bases that hold knowledge in a variety of forms such as facts, rules, and case examples about successful business practices.

For example, data about sales transactions may be accumulated and stored in a sales database for subsequent processing that yields daily, weekly, and monthly sales analysis reports for management. Knowledge bases are used by knowledge management systems and expert systems to share knowledge and give expert advice on specific subjects. We will explore these concepts further in later chapters.

Data versus Information. The word **data** is the plural of *datum*, though data commonly represents both singular and plural forms. Data are raw facts or observations, typically about physical phenomena or business transactions. For example, a spacecraft launch or the sale of an automobile would generate a lot of data describing those events. More specifically, data are objective measurements of the *attributes* (the characteristics) of *entities* (such as people, places, things, and events).

Example

Business transactions such as buying a car or an airline ticket can produce a lot of data. Just think of the hundreds of facts needed to describe the characteristics of the car you want and its financing, or the details for even the simplest airline reservation. ●

People often use the terms *data* and *information* interchangeably. However, it is better to view data as raw material resources that are processed into finished information products. Then we can define **information** as data that have been converted into a meaningful and useful context for specific end users. Thus, data are usually subjected to a value-added process (we call *data processing* or *information processing*) where (1) its form is aggregated, manipulated, and organized; (2) its content is analyzed and evaluated; and (3) it is placed in a proper context for a human user. So you should view information as processed data placed in a context that gives it value for specific end users.

Example

Names, quantities, and dollar amounts recorded on sales forms represent data about sales transactions. However, a sales manager may not regard these as information. Only after such facts are properly organized and manipulated can meaningful sales information be furnished, specifying, for example, the amount of sales by product type, sales territory, or salesperson. ●

Network Resources

Telecommunications networks like the Internet, intranets, and extranets have become essential to the successful operations of all types of organizations and their computer-based information systems. Telecommunications networks consist of computers, communications processors, and other devices interconnected by communications media and controlled by communications software. The concept of **network resources** emphasizes that communications networks are a fundamental resource component of all information systems. Network resources include:

- **Communications media.** Examples include twisted-pair wire, coaxial cable, fiber-optic cable, microwave systems, and communications satellite systems.
- **Network support.** This generic category includes all of the people, hardware, software, and data resources that directly support the operation and use of a communications network. Examples include communications processors such as

modems and internetwork processors, and communications control software such as network operating systems and Internet browser packages.

Information System Activities

Let's take a closer look now at each of the basic **information processing** (or **data processing**) activities that occur in information systems. You should be able to recognize input, processing, output, storage, and control activities taking place in any information system you are studying. Figure 1.21 lists business examples that illustrate each of these information system activities.

Input of Data Resources

Data about business transactions and other events must be captured and prepared for processing by the **input** activity. Input typically takes the form of *data entry* activities such as recording and editing. End users typically record data about transactions on some type of physical medium such as a paper form, or enter it directly into a computer system. This usually includes a variety of editing activities to ensure that they have recorded data correctly. Once entered, data may be transferred onto a machine-readable medium such as a magnetic disk until needed for processing.

For example, data about sales transactions can be recorded on source documents such as paper sales order forms. (A **source document** is the original formal record of a transaction.) Alternately, salespersons can capture sales data using computer keyboards or optical scanning devices; they are visually prompted to enter data correctly by video displays. This provides them with a more convenient and efficient **user interface,** that is, methods of end user input and output with a computer system. Methods such as optical scanning and displays of menus, prompts, and fill-in-the-blanks formats make it easier for end users to enter data correctly into an information system.

Processing of Data into Information

Data are typically subjected to **processing** activities such as calculating, comparing, sorting, classifying, and summarizing. These activities organize, analyze, and manipulate data, thus converting them into information for end users. The quality of any data stored in an information system must also be maintained by a continual process of correcting and updating activities.

For example, data received about a purchase can be (1) *added* to a running total of sales results, (2) *compared* to a standard to determine eligibility for a sales discount, (3) *sorted* in numerical order based on product identification numbers, (4) *classified* into product categories (such as food and nonfood items), (5) *summarized* to provide a sales manager with information about various product categories, and, finally, (6) used to *update* sales records.

Output of Information Products

Information in various forms is transmitted to end users and made available to them in the **output** activity. The goal of information systems is the production of appropriate **information products** for end users. Common information products include messages, reports, forms, and graphic images, which may be provided by video displays,

Figure 1.21

Business examples of the basic activities of information systems.

● **Input.** Optical scanning of bar-coded tags on merchandise.
● **Processing.** Calculating employee pay, taxes, and other payroll deductions.
● **Output.** Producing reports and displays about sales performance.
● **Storage.** Maintaining records on customers, employees, and products.
● **Control.** Generating audible signals to indicate proper entry of sales data.

audio responses, paper products, and multimedia. We routinely use the information provided by these products as we work in organizations and live in society. For example, a sales manager may view a video display to check on the performance of a salesperson, accept a computer-produced voice message by telephone, and receive a printout of monthly sales results.

What characteristics would make information products valuable and useful to you? One way to answer this important question is to examine the characteristics or attributes of **information quality.** Information that is outdated, inaccurate, or hard to understand would not be very meaningful, useful, or valuable to you or other end users. People want information of high quality, that is, information products whose characteristics, attributes, or qualities help make it valuable to them. It is useful to think of information as having the three dimensions of time, content, and form. Figure 1.22 summarizes the important attributes of information and groups them into these three dimensions.

Figure 1.22

A summary of the attributes of information quality. This outlines the attributes that should be present in high-quality information products.

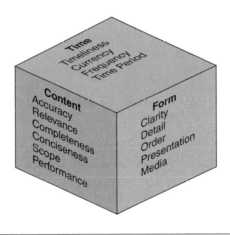

Time Dimension	
Timeliness	Information should be provided when it is needed
Currency	Information should be up-to-date when it is provided
Frequency	Information should be provided as often as needed
Time Period	Information can be provided about past, present, and future time periods

Content Dimension	
Accuracy	Information should be free from errors
Relevance	Information should be related to the information needs of a specific recipient for a specific situation
Completeness	All the information that is needed should be provided
Conciseness	Only the information that is needed should be provided
Scope	Information can have a broad or narrow scope, or an internal or external focus
Performance	Information can reveal performance by measuring activities accomplished, progress made, or resources accumulated

Form Dimension	
Clarity	Information should be provided in a form that is easy to understand
Detail	Information can be provided in detail or summary form
Order	Information can be arranged in a predetermined sequence
Presentation	Information can be presented in narrative, numeric, graphic, or other forms
Media	Information can be provided in the form of printed paper documents, video displays, or other media

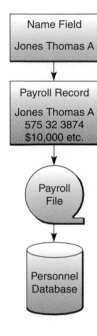

Figure 1.23

Logical data elements. This is a common method of organizing stored data in information systems.

Name Field

Jones Thomas A

- A **field** is a grouping of characters that represent a characteristic of a person, place, thing, or event. For example, an employee's *name field*.

Payroll Record

Jones Thomas A
575 32 3874
$10,000 etc.

- A **record** is a collection of interrelated fields. For example, an employee's *payroll record* might consist of a name field, a Social Security number field, a department field, and a salary field.

Payroll File

- A **file** is a collection of interrelated records. For example, a *payroll file* might consist of the payroll *records* of all employees of a firm.

Personnel Database

- A **database** is an integrated collection of interrelated records or files. For example, the *personnel database* of a business might contain payroll, personnel action, and employee skills files.

Storage of Data Resources

Storage is a basic system component of information systems. Storage is the information system activity in which data and information are retained in an organized manner for later use. For example, just as written text material is organized into words, sentences, paragraphs, and documents, stored data are commonly organized into fields, records, files, and databases. This facilitates its later use in processing or its retrieval as output when needed by users of a system. These logical data elements are shown in Figure 1.23 and will be discussed further in Chapter 5.

Control of System Performance

An important information system activity is the **control** of its performance. An information system should produce feedback about its input, processing, output, and storage activities. This feedback must be monitored and evaluated to determine if the system is meeting established performance standards. Then appropriate system activities must be adjusted so that proper information products are produced for end users.

For example, a manager may discover that subtotals of sales amounts in a sales report do not add up to total sales. This might mean that data entry or processing procedures need to be corrected. Then changes would have to be made to ensure that all sales transactions would be properly captured and processed by a sales information system.

Overview of Information Systems

There are many kinds of information systems in the real world. All of them use hardware, software, network, and people resources to transform data resources into information products. Some are simple manual information systems, where people use simple tools such as pencils and paper, or even machines such as calculators and typewriters. Others are **computer-based information systems** that rely on a variety of networked computer systems to accomplish their information processing activities.

Trends in Information Systems

The roles given to the information systems function have expanded significantly over the years. Figure 1.24 summarizes these changes.

Until the 1960s, the role of information systems was simple: transaction processing, record-keeping, accounting, and other *electronic data processing* (EDP) applications. Then another role was added, as the concept of *management information systems* (MIS) was conceived. This new role focused on providing managerial end users with

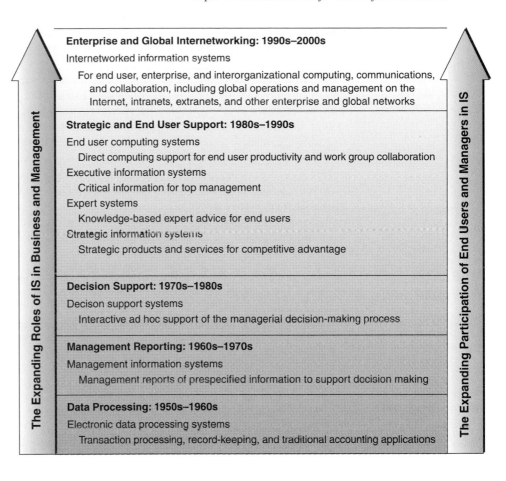

Figure 1.24

The expanding roles of information systems. Note how the roles of computer-based information systems have expanded over time. Also, note the impact of these changes on the end users and managers of an organization.

predefined management reports that would give managers the information they needed for decision-making purposes.

By the 1970s, it was evident that the prespecified information products produced by such management information systems were not adequately meeting many of the decision-making needs of management. So the concept of *decision support systems* (DSS) was born. The new role for information systems was to provide managerial end users with ad hoc and interactive support of their decision-making processes. This support would be tailored to the unique decision-making styles of managers as they confronted specific types of problems in the real world.

In the 1980s, several new roles for information systems appeared. First, the rapid development of microcomputer processing power, application software packages, and telecommunications networks gave birth to the phenomenon of *end user computing*. Now, end users can use their own computing resources to support their job requirements instead of waiting for the indirect support of corporate information services departments.

Second, it became evident that most top corporate executives did not directly use either the reports of information reporting systems or the analytical modeling capabilities of decision support systems, so the concept of *executive information systems* (EIS) was developed. These information systems attempt to give top executives an easy way to get the critical information they want, when they want it, tailored to the formats they prefer.

Third, breakthroughs occurred in the development and application of artificial intelligence (AI) techniques to business information systems. *Expert systems* (ES) and other *knowledge-based systems* forged a new role for information systems. Today, expert systems can serve as consultants to users by providing expert advice in limited subject areas.

An important new role for information systems appeared in the 1980s and continued through the 1990s. This is the concept of a strategic role for information systems, sometimes called *strategic information systems* (SIS). In this concept, information technology becomes an integral component of business processes, products, and services that help a company gain a competitive advantage in the global marketplace.

Finally, the rapid growth of the Internet, intranets, extranets, and other interconnected global networks in the 1990s has dramatically changed the capabilities of information systems in business as we move into the next century. Such **enterprise and global internetworking** is revolutionizing end user, enterprise, and interorganizational computing, communications, and collaboration that supports the business operations and management of successful global enterprises.

Types of Information Systems

Conceptually, information systems in the real world can be classified in several different ways. For example, several types of information systems can be classified conceptually as either operations or management information systems. Figure 1.25 illustrates this conceptual classification of information systems. Information systems are categorized this way to spotlight the major roles each plays in the operations and management of a business. Let's look briefly at some examples of how information systems exist in the business world.

Operations Support Systems

Information systems have always been needed to process data generated by, and used in, business operations. Such **operations support systems** produce a variety of information products for internal and external use. However, they do not emphasize producing the specific information products that can best be used by managers. Further

Figure 1.25

Operations and management classifications of information systems. Note how this conceptual overview emphasizes the main purpose of information systems that support business operations and managerial decision making.

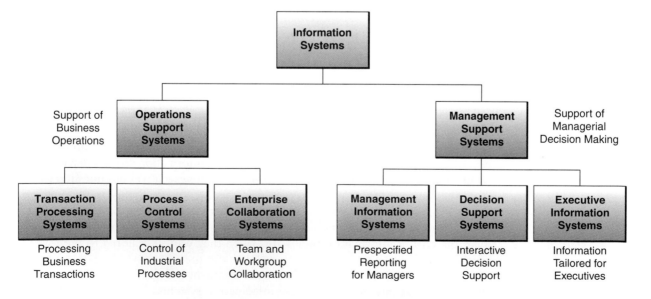

processing by management information systems is usually required. The role of a business firm's operations support systems is to efficiently process business transactions, control industrial processes, support enterprise communications and collaboration, and update corporate databases.

Transaction processing systems are an important example of operations support systems that record and process data resulting from business transactions. They process transactions in two basic ways. In *batch processing*, transactions data are accumulated over a period of time and processed periodically. In *real-time* (or online) processing, data are processed immediately after a transaction occurs. For example, point-of-sale (POS) systems at many retail stores use electronic cash register terminals to electronically capture and transmit sales data over telecommunications links to regional computer centers for immediate (real-time) or nightly (batch) processing. See Figure 1.26.

Process control systems monitor and control physical processes. For example, a petroleum refinery uses electronic sensors linked to computers to continually monitor chemical processes and make instant (real-time) adjustments that control the refinery process. **Enterprise collaboration systems** enhance team and workgroup communications and productivity. For example, knowledge workers in a project team may use electronic mail to send and receive electronic messages, and videoconferencing to hold electronic meetings to coordinate their activities.

Management Support Systems

When information systems focus on providing information and support for effective decision making by managers, they are called **management support systems.** Providing information and support for decision making by all types of managers (from top

---

Figure 1.26

QuickBooks is a popular accounting package that automates small business accounting transaction processing while providing business owners with management reports.

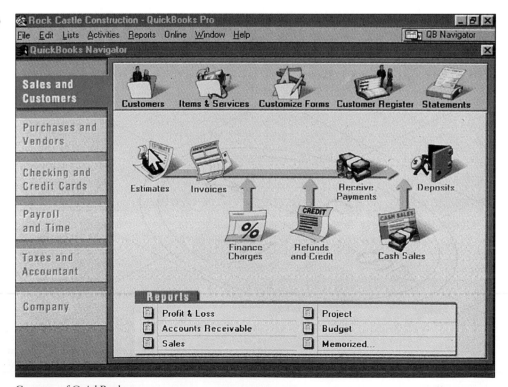

Courtesy of QuickBooks.

executives to middle managers to project supervisors) is a complex task. Conceptually, several major types of information systems support a variety of managerial end user responsibilities: (1) management information systems, (2) decision support systems, and (3) executive information systems.

Management information systems provide information in the form of reports and displays to managers. For example, sales managers may use their computer workstations to get instantaneous displays about the sales results of their products and to access weekly sales analysis reports that evaluate sales made by each salesperson. **Decision support systems** give direct computer support to managers during the decision-making process. For example, advertising managers may use an electronic spreadsheet package to do what-if analysis as they test the impact of alternative advertising budgets on the forecasted sales of new products. **Executive information systems** provide critical information in easy-to-use displays to a variety of managers. For example, top executives may use touchscreen terminals to instantly view text and graphics displays that highlight key areas of organizational and competitive performance. See Figure 1.27.

Other Classifications of Information Systems

Several other categories of information systems provide more unique or broad classifications than those we have just mentioned. That's because these information systems can support either operations or management applications. For example, **expert systems** can provide expert advice for operational chores like equipment diagnostics, or managerial decisions such as loan portfolio management. **Knowledge management systems** are knowledge-based information systems that support the creation,

Figure 1.27

Executive information systems provide information to executives in easy-to-use formats.

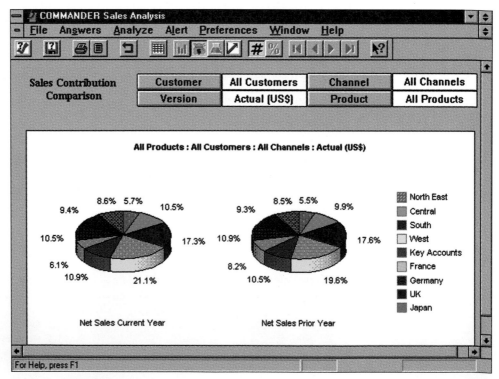

Courtesy of Comshare, Inc.

organization, and dissemination of business knowledge to employees and managers throughout a company. Information systems that focus on operational and managerial applications in support of basic business functions such as accounting or marketing are known as **business information systems.** Finally, **strategic information systems** apply information technology to a firm's products, services, or business processes to help it gain a strategic advantage over its competitors.

It is also important to realize that information systems in the real world are typically integrated combinations of several types of information systems we have just mentioned. That's because conceptual classifications of information systems are designed to emphasize the many different roles of information systems. In practice, these roles are combined into integrated or **cross-functional information systems** that provide a variety of functions. Thus, most information systems are designed to produce information and support decision making for various levels of management and business functions, as well as do record-keeping and transaction processing chores. So whenever you analyze a business information system, you will probably see that it provides information for a variety of managerial levels and business functions.

Figure 1.28 summarizes the major categories of information systems we have introduced in this section. We will explore many examples of the use of such systems in the chapters of Module III.

Figure 1.28

A summary of the major categories of information systems.

Operations support systems process data generated by business operations. Major categories are:

- **Transaction processing systems** process data resulting from business transactions, update operational databases, and produce business documents.
- **Process control systems** monitor and control industrial processes.
- **Enterprise collaboration systems** support team, workgroup, and enterprise communications and collaboration.

Management support systems provide information and support needed for effective decision making by managers. Major categories are:

- **Management information systems** provide information in the form of prespecified reports and displays to managers.
- **Decision support systems** provide interactive ad hoc support for the decision-making process of managers.
- **Executive information systems** provide critical information tailored to the information needs of executives.

Other categories of information systems can support either operations, management, or strategic applications. Major categories are:

- **Expert systems** are knowledge-based systems that provide expert advice and act as expert consultants to users.
- **Knowledge management systems** are knowledge-based systems that support the creation, organization, and dissemination of business knowledge within the enterprise.
- **Strategic information systems** provide a firm with strategic products, services, and capabilities for competitive advantage.
- **Business information systems** support the operational and managerial applications of the basic business functions of a firm.

Recognizing Information Systems

As a business end user, you should be able to recognize the fundamental components of information systems you encounter in the real world. This means that you should be able to identify:

- The people, hardware, software, data, and network resources they use.
- The types of information products they produce.
- The way they perform input, processing, output, storage, and control activities.
- How they support the business operations, managerial decision making, or competitive advantage of a business.

This kind of understanding will help you be a better user, developer, and manager of information systems. And that, as we have pointed out in this chapter, is important to your future success as a manager, entrepreneur, or professional in business.

Analyzing Milacron's Information System

Refer back to the Real World Case on Milacron Inc. on page 20. Now let's try to recognize or visualize the resources used, activities performed, and information products produced by their Milpro information system.

IS Resources. People resources include end users like Milacron's small machine shop customers and sales engineer Jim VandeHel, as well as IS specialists like E-commerce director Angela Snelling and the web site developers from GlobalLink New Media. Hardware resources would include the PC systems of Milacron's customers and the servers of their Internet service provider, EMC Corporation. Software resources mentioned in the case include the web browsers of machine shop customers, the Milpro Wizard expert system software developed by Milacron, and the E-commerce software from Open Market, Inc. Of course, the main network resource is the Internet, plus the company networks of Milacron, their customers, and their ISP. Finally, data resources mentioned include Milacron's product catalog databases and Milpro Wizard knowledge bases.

Information Products. The information products we can most easily visualize are the multitude of multimedia displays of product catalog information and product selection advice from the Milpro Wizard system that are provided to the network PCs of Milacron's customers when they access the web site.

IS Activities. Input activities that we can visualize in the Milpro system include the input of queries and data by customers about Milacron's products, as well as the continual input of new or corrected data needed to keep the site up-to-date. Processing activities are accomplished when customer PCs and web site servers execute the programs of the E-commerce and other software of this system. Output activities primarily involve the display of the many information products mentioned earlier. Storage activities take place whenever product data or other information is stored on the disk drives of customer PCs or web servers. Finally, we can visualize several control activities, including the use of security codes and passwords for entry by customers into secure parts of the Milpro site, as well as encryption of transaction details by Open Market's E-commerce software.

So you see, analyzing an information system to identify its basic components is not a difficult task. Just identify the resources that the information system uses, the information processing activities it performs, and the information products it produces. Then you will be better able to identify ways to improve these components, and thus the performance of the information system itself. That's a goal that every business end user should strive to attain.

Summary

- **Why Information Systems Are Important.** An understanding of the effective and responsible use and management of information systems and technologies is important for managers and other business knowledge workers in today's global information society. Information systems play a vital role in the efficient operations, effective management, and strategic success of businesses and other organizations that must operate in a global business environment. Thus, the field of information systems has become a major functional area of business administration.

- **Why Businesses Need Information Technology.** Information systems perform three vital roles in business firms. That is, they support an organization's business operations, managerial decision making, and strategic advantage. Information technology has also become an indispensable ingredient in several major strategies that businesses are implementing to meet the challenges of a rapidly changing business environment. These include internetworking the enterprise, globalization, business process reengineering, and using information technology for strategic competitive advantage.

- **System Concepts.** A system is a group of interrelated components working toward the attainment of a common goal by accepting inputs and producing outputs in an organized transformation process. Feedback is data about the performance of a system. Control is the component that monitors and evaluates feedback and makes any necessary adjustments to the input and processing components to ensure that proper output is produced.

- **Information System Concepts.** An information system uses the resources of people, hardware, software, data, and networks to perform input, processing, output, storage, and control activities that convert data resources into information products. Data are first collected and converted to a form that is suitable for processing (input). Then the data are manipulated and converted into information (processing), stored for future use (storage), or communicated to their ultimate user (output) according to correct processing procedures (control).

- **IS Resources and Products.** Hardware resources include machines and media used in information processing. Software resources include computerized instructions (programs) and instructions for people (procedures). People resources include information systems specialists and users. Data resources include alphanumeric, text, image, video, audio, and other forms of data. Network resources include communications media and network support. Information products produced by an information system can take a variety of forms, including paper reports, visual displays, multimedia documents, electronic messages, graphics images, and audio responses.

- **Types of Information Systems.** Major conceptual categories of information systems include operations support systems, such as transaction processing systems, process control systems, and enterprise collaboration systems, and management support systems, such as management information systems, decision support systems, and executive information systems. Other major categories are expert systems, knowledge management systems, strategic information systems, and business information systems. However, in the real world, these conceptual classifications are typically combined into cross-functional information systems that provide information and decision support for managers and also perform operational information processing activities. Refer to Figure 1.28 for a summary of the major categories of information systems.

Key Terms and Concepts

These are the key terms and concepts of this chapter. The page number of their first explanation is in parentheses.

1. Business process reengineering (16)
2. Competitive advantage (16)
3. Computer-based information system (30)
4. Control (22)
5. Data (27)
6. Data or information processing (28)
7. Data resources (26)
8. Electronic commerce (13)
9. End user (8)
10. Enterprise collaboration (14)
11. Feedback (21)
12. Globalization (14)
13. Hardware resources (26)
    a. Machines
    b. Media

14. Information (27)
    a. Products (28)
    b. Quality (29)
15. Information system (7)
16. Information system activities (28)
    a. Input
    b. Processing
    c. Output
    d. Storage
    e. Control
17. Information system model (23)
18. Information technology (8)
19. Internetworked enterprise (13)
20. Knowledge needed about information systems (6)
21. Knowledge workers (8)
22. Network resources (27)

23. People resources (24)
    a. IS specialists
    b. End users
24. Roles of information systems (10)
25. Software resources (26)
    a. Programs
    b. Procedures
26. System (21)
27. Trends in information systems (30)
28. Types of information systems (32)
    a. Cross-functional systems (35)
    b. Management support systems (33)
    c. Operations support systems (32)

Review Quiz

Match one of the previous key terms and concepts with one of the following brief examples or definitions. Look for the best fit for answers that seem to fit more than one key term or concept. Defend your choices.

1. You should know some fundamental concepts about information systems and their technology, development, applications, and management.

____ 2. People who spend most of their workday creating, using, and distributing information.

____ 3. Computer hardware and software, telecommunications, data management, and other technologies.

____ 4. Information systems support an organization's business operations, managerial decision making, and strategic competitive advantage.

____ 5. Businesses are expanding into global markets and forming alliances with global partners.

____ 6. The fundamental rethinking and redesign of business operations.

____ 7. Using information technology to gain a strategic advantage over competitors.

____ 8. A system that uses people, hardware, software, and network resources to collect, transform, and disseminate information within an organization.

____ 9. An information system that uses computers and their hardware and software.

____ 10. Anyone who uses an information system or the information it produces.

____ 11. A company can use the Internet, corporate intranets, and interorganizational extranets for electronic commerce and enterprise collaboration.

____ 12. The buying, selling, marketing, and servicing of products over the Internet and other networks.

____ 13. The use of groupware tools to support collaboration among networked teams.

____ 14. A group of interrelated components working together toward the attainment of a common goal.

____ 15. Data about a system's performance.

____ 16. Making adjustments to a system's components so that it operates properly.

____ 17. Facts or observations.

____ 18. Data that have been placed into a meaningful context for an end user.

____ 19. The act of converting data into information.

____ 20. An information system uses people, hardware, software, network, and data resources to perform input, processing, output, storage, and control activities that transform data resources into information products.

____ 21. Machines and media.

____ 22. Computers, disk drives, video monitors, and printers are examples.

____ 23. Magnetic disks, optical disks, and paper forms are examples.

____ 24. Programs and procedures.

____ 25. A set of instructions for a computer.

____ 26. A set of instructions for people.

____ 27. End users and information systems professionals.

____ 28. Using the keyboard of a computer to enter data.

____ 29. Computing loan payments.

____ 30. Printing a letter you wrote using a computer.

____ 31. Saving a copy of the letter on a magnetic disk.

____ 32. Having a sales receipt as proof of a purchase.

____ 33. Information systems can be classified into operations, management, and other categories.

____ 34. Include transaction processing, process control, and end user collaboration systems.

____ 35. Include management information, decision support, and executive information systems.

____ 36. Information systems that perform transaction processing and provide information to managers across the boundaries of functional business areas.

____ 37. Information systems have evolved from a data processing orientation to the support of strategic decision making, end user collaboration, and global internetworking.

Discussion Questions

1. How can information systems support a company's business operations and decision making by their managers, and give them a competitive advantage? Give examples to illustrate your answer.

2. Is the use of the Internet, intranets, and extranets to internetwork organizations affecting how businesses operate and how computers are used? Explain.

3. Refer to the Real World Case on NetFlix.com in the chapter. What do you think are the chances for major business success for NetFlix? Why?

4. How important is information technology to the globalization of a business? Use examples to illustrate your answer.

5. How can a manager demonstrate that he or she is a responsible end user of information systems? Give several examples.

6. Refer to the Real World Case on Milacron Inc. in the chapter. Does this case demonstrate that the Internet can be used to reach market segments that are too hard to reach by conventional means? Why or why not?

7. Can a business process be reengineered without the support of information technology? Explain.

8. Why are there so many conceptual classifications of information systems? Why are they typically integrated in the information systems found in the real world?

9. In what major ways have the roles of information systems in business expanded during the last 40 years? What is one major change you think will happen in the next 10 years?

10. Can the business use of the Internet help a company gain a competitive advantage? Give an example to illustrate your answer.

Real World Problems

1. **Boeing and Analog Devices, Inc.: Business Failure and Success with IT**

   In 1994, the Boeing Company embarked on a major business process reengineering campaign, buying off-the-shelf enterprise resource planning (ERP) software to replace hundreds of mainframe legacy systems used to manufacture commercial aircraft. For example, Boeing bought Baan's manufacturing, finance, purchasing, and distribution modules; Metaphase's product data management package; CIMLINC's Linkage for process planning; and Trilogy's SalesBUILDER for configuration management, along with other packages.

   Fast-forward to late 1998, when Boeing announced lousy financial results and major layoffs. It predicts a pathetic pretax profit margin of only 1 to 3 percent for its commercial aircraft group by the year 2000, up from 0 percent in 1998. A precipitous decline in airplane orders by Asian airlines is the culprit according to the company. But Wall Street analysts and others watching the company say production inefficiencies, poor planning, and a host of other internal failures bear part of the responsibility for the dismal margin and poor financial results, according to articles about the project in, among others, *The New York Times* and *The Wall Street Journal*. And all that ERP software Boeing purchased was supposed to avoid those production inefficiencies.

   Last year, only a few months before the roof caved in on Boeing's financial statements, a computer industry trade publication wrote a glowing report about the wonderful performance of the aircraft company's ERP implementation. But as far as the financial community is concerned, there isn't a whole lot of return on investment from five years of ERP implementation at Boeing.

   However, other ERP implementations have proved their worth through the positive results achieved. The ERP implementation at chip maker Analog Devices Inc., for instance, helped the company weather tough times in 1998, when declining prices drove down revenues and otherwise put pressure on the entire semiconductor industry. Analog has continued to show progress in reducing costs in a variety of areas, including production, staffing, and inventory.

   Bottom line: If the right combination of ERP software, business processes, and managerial expertise are working together, there should be a substantial financial return, as there was for Analog.

a. What do you think are the underlying reasons for Boeing's failure and Analog's success in the use of IT to improve their business performance?

b. What does this case reveal about the relationship between information technology, business processes, and management expertise?

Source: Adapted from Larry Marion, "Snap, Crackle, Pop, and Crash—Go the Income Statements," *Datamation*, February 1999 (www.datamation.com). © 1999 by Cahners Publishing Co.

2. Halco Business Products and Others: Small Businesses on the Web

It's everybody's dream: Take a small business and build it to national—or even international—proportions. For many Internet-wise business owners, the Web has made such growth a reality, as they are able to reach potential customers anywhere, anytime, regardless of their brick-and-mortar addresses. According to a recent study conducted by the International Data Corporation, one-third of the small businesses in the United States that use the Internet increased their revenues by at least 10 percent over the previous year. However, only a quarter of small businesses in general matched that rate of growth. Thus, a well-designed web site can help you meet your business goals, however modest or ambitious they may be. Let's look at three examples.

Halco Business Products (www.halconet.com) jumped on the Web several years ago. This Houston-area office supply and printing services company is owned by Henry Levy, who has long dreamed of taking his business national. His site now accounts for one-third of his new customers, most of whom live outside of his local area, and his overall sales increased by a whopping 50 percent.

Norman Aldinger owns Midstate Realty in Jamestown, North Dakota. Aldinger, a real estate broker for 12 years, realized that he needed a web site to compete with national franchise Realtors®. He hired a local college student, who designed the site (www.fm-net.com/midstaterealty) for $300—billed at $20 per hour, the same rate the student charges for weekly updates. Aldinger's local Internet service provider hosts his site on a server shared with other local businesses and the chamber of commerce. His total monthly fee for web access, E-mail, and 15 MB of storage space is $27. Aldinger says that since he put up his site, he's pulled in a lot more business from outside his area.

Florida resident Marcia Halpern plunked down $1,800 to set up a storefront on I-netmall to sell arthritis pain relief medicine. I-netmall, one of hundreds of Internet malls to sprout up in the last two years, promised to handle the design work, host the site, process credit card transactions, and forward her the orders.

But Halpern says I-netmall took months to get her site online and make even simple updates to it. Furthermore, the company didn't offer any compensation for lost business after its credit card processing server went down for an entire week. A company official has admitted to having had technical problems, but told us that they were being addressed. Halpern has since moved her site (www.pain-relief.net) to a local service.

a. What are some of the purposes and benefits of a web site for a small business?

b. What are several challenges faced by a small business that establishes a web site? How would you advise a small business to meet such challenges?

Source: Adapted from Victoria Hall Smith, "Got Web?" *PC World*, January 1999, pp. 161–65.

3. Mellon Bank, Bank of Montreal, and Vanguard: Targeting Customers with IT

John Doe calls Pittsburgh-based Mellon Bank and gets put on hold for several minutes. Jane Doe calls a few minutes later and immediately is patched through to a live operator.

What gives?

Simple. John's account balance is $2,500. Jane's is $25,000. And these numbers are right there on the customer service representative's screen.

So say goodbye to the first-come, first-served rule that governed the school lunch line. Thanks to information technology, a growing number of banks, airlines, and retailers are answering calls based on your profitability to their bottom line.

The most profitable customers at Bank of Montreal—identified by a new multimillion-customer knowledge database system—are assigned designated banking consultants who specialize in the banking products they use most.

Using the same system, which cost between $2 million and $5 million to develop, the Canadian bank has created hundreds of targeted marketing campaigns that have worked to boost previous customer response rates of 1 to 2 percent to as high as 20 percent, according to Dave Moxiey, vice president of data mining.

But creating classes of customers, and then treating each accordingly, has its potential pitfalls. Among them is relying too heavily on a customer's buying history rather than his potential for becoming a highly profitable customer.

Another problem with reserving extra services and special discounts for already profitable customers is that it rewards loyalty but doesn't work to increase demand, said George Cressman, an analyst at Strategic Pricing Group. In many cases, "you're giving something extra to people who would have bought your service anyway," Cressman said.

Vanguard Group, which manages more than $50 billion in mutual funds, also classifies customers, but not by profitability. Instead, Vanguard is launching a project to develop a customer relationship management (CRM) system that will let customer service workers know virtually everything about a customer, right up to his visit to Vanguard's web site the night before.

The danger, of course, is customers' fear of Big Brother. The challenge now, says Bob DiStefano,

managing director of information technology, is "differentiating between when a client would appreciate you knowing something and when that would be scary for the client. It's a hard situation to do well."

a. Do you approve of how businesses are using information technology for targeted marketing and customer service? Why or why not?

b. What ethical issues might arise in the business use of information technology revealed in this case? What would you recommend to guide businesses in such situations?

Source: Adapted from Julia King, "Customer Reps Play Favorites," *Computerworld*, February 8, 1999, pp. 1, 16. Copyright 1999 by Computerworld, Inc., Framingham, MA 01701. Reprinted from *Computerworld*.

Application Exercises

1. Using the Internet for Business Research

Search the Internet for additional information and business examples about some of the topics or companies in this chapter. For example, use search engines like Yahoo! or InfoSeek to research topics like business process reengineering, globalizing business, or using intranets and extranets. Or find and visit the web sites of companies in the Real World Cases and Problems in this chapter. Look for examples of the business use of information technology in your search.

a. Prepare a one- or two-page summary of some of your findings and the sources you used.

b. End your paper with a few sentences describing one thing you have learned from your research that might help you in your future career in business.

2. Visiting the Smart Business Supersite

The Smart Business Supersite (www.smartbiz.com) is dubbed the "how-to resource for business" site. Nearly every colorful icon on the tool bar across the top of the home page leads to useful, relevant material such as columns on electronic privacy, violence in the workplace, and internal marketing. (See Figure 1.29.)

You can also click on the browse button to call up a Windows-like menu of subjects. Then choose *Computing in Business* to get a precise index of all relevant material at the site. The Jobs/Careers section includes relevant articles and a message board. People Finder is a unique section that offers users a venue for locating speakers and consultants.

a. Prepare a one- or two-page summary describing the *Computing in Business* material you found most interesting and relevant as a business end user.

b. End your paper with a few sentences describing one thing you have learned from your research that might help you in your future career in business.

3. Jefferson State University

Students in the College of Business Administration of Jefferson State University use its microcomputer lab for a variety of assignments. For example, a student may use a word processing program stored on a microcomputer's hard disk drive and proceed to type a case study analysis. When the analysis is typed, edited, and properly formatted to an instructor's specifications, the student may save it on a floppy disk and print a copy on one of the printers in the lab network. If the student tries to save the case study analysis using a file name he or she has already used for saving another document, the program will display a warning message and wait until it receives an additional command.

Make an outline to identify the information system components in the preceding example.

a. Identify the people, hardware, software, network, and data resources and the information products of this information system.

b. Identify the input, processing, output, storage, and control activities that occurred.

4. Office Products Corporation

Office Products Corporation processes more than 10,000 customer orders a month, drawing on a combined inventory of over 1,000 office products stocked at the company's warehouse. About 60 PC workstations, many with printers, are installed at Office Products headquarters and connected in a local area

Figure 1.29   The Smart Business Supersite.

Coutesy of Smartbiz.

network to an IBM AS/400 midrange computer. Orders are received by phone or mail and entered into the system by order entry personnel at network computers, or they are entered directly by dealers who have networked their PCs to Office Products. Entry of orders is assisted by formatted screens that help operators follow data entry procedures to enter required information into the system, where it is stored on the magnetic disks of the AS/400.

As the order is entered, the AS/400 checks the availability of the parts, allocates the stock, and updates customer and part databases stored on the computer's magnetic disks. It then sends the order pick list to the warehouse printer, where it is used by warehouse personnel to fill the order. The company president has a PC workstation in her office, as do the controller, sales manager, inventory manager, and other executives. They use simple database management inquiry commands to get responses and reports concerning sales orders, customers, and inventory, and to review product demand and service trends.

Make an outline that identifies the information system components in Office Products' order processing system.

a. Identify the people, hardware, software, data, and network resources and the information products of this information system.

b. Identify the input, processing, output, storage, and control activities that occurred.

5. Western Chemical Corporation
Western Chemical has networked its computers to those of its customers and suppliers to capture data about sales orders and purchases. Such data are processed immediately, and inventory and other databases are updated. Videoconferencing and electronic mail services are also provided. Data generated by a chemical refinery process are captured by sensors and processed by a computer that also suggests answers to a complex refinery problem posed by an engineer. Managerial end users receive reports on a periodic, exception, and demand basis, and use computers to interactively assess the possible results of alternative decisions. Finally, top management can access text summaries and graphics displays that identify key elements of organizational performance and compare them to industry and competitor performance.

Western Chemical Corporation has started forming business alliances and using intranets, extranets, and the Internet to build a global telecommunications network with other chemical companies throughout the world to offer their customers worldwide products and services. Western Chemical is in the midst of making fundamental changes to their computer-based systems to increase the efficiency of their business operations and their managers' ability to react quickly to changing business conditions. Make an outline that identifies:

a. How information systems support (1) business operations, (2) management decision making, (3) strategic advantage, (4) enterprise internetworking, (5) globalization, and (6) business process reengineering at Western Chemical.

b. There are many different types of information systems at Western Chemical. Identify as many as you can in the preceding scenario. Refer to Figure 1.28 to help you. Explain the reasons for your choices.

Review Quiz Answers

1. 20	7. 2	13. 10	18. 14	23. 13b	28. 16a	33. 28
2. 21	8. 15	14. 26	19. 6	24. 25	29. 16b	34. 28c
3. 18	9. 3	15. 11	20. 17	25. 25a	30. 16c	35. 28b
4. 24	10. 9	16. 4	21. 13	26. 25b	31. 16d	36. 28a
5. 12	11. 19	17. 5	22. 13a	27. 23	32. 16e	37. 27
6. 1	12. 8					

Selected References

1. Bradley, Stephen P.; Jerry A. Hausman; and Richard L. Nolan, eds. *Globalization, Technology, and Competition: The Fusion of Computers and Telecommunications in the 1990s.* Boston: Harvard Business School Press, 1993.

2. Cash, James I., Jr.; Robert G. Eccles; Nitin Nohria; and Richard L. Nolan. *Building the Information-Age Organization: Structure, Control, and Information Technologies.* Burr Ridge, IL: Richard D. Irwin, 1994.

3. Champy, Jim. "Now Batting Cleanup: Information Technology." *Computerworld,* October 28, 1996.

4. Cronin, Mary. *Doing More Business on the Internet.* 2nd ed. New York: Van Nostrand Reinhold, 1995.

5. Davenport, Thomas H. *Process Innovation: Reengineering Work through Information Technology.* Boston: Harvard Business School Press, 1993.

6. Ewusi-Mensah, Kewku. "Critical Issues in Abandoned Information Systems Development Projects." *Communications of the ACM,* September 1997.

7. Hammer, Michael, and James Champy. *Reengineering the Corporation: A Manifesto for Business Revolution.* New York: HarperCollins, 1993.

8. Hills, Mellanie. *Intranet Business Strategies.* New York: John Wiley & Sons, 1997.

9. Keen, Peter G. W. *Shaping the Future: Business Design through Information Technology.* Cambridge: Harvard Business School Press, 1991.

10. Moschella, David. "IS Priorities as the Information Highway Begins." Special Advertising Supplement. *Computerworld,* May 22, 1995.

11. Newmann, Peter. *Computer Related Risks.* New York: ACM Press, 1995.

12. Neumann, Peter. "Systems Development Woes." *Communications of the ACM,* December 1997.

13. Neumann, Seev. *Strategic Information Systems: Competition through Information Technologies.* New York: Macmillan College Publishing Co., 1994.

14. Newcomb, Jonathan; Bob Martin; Gene Batchelder; John Rockart; Wayne Yetter; and Jerome Grossman. "The End of Delegation? Information Technology and the CIO." *Harvard Business Review,* September–October 1995.

15. Seybold, Patricia. "Don't Let PR Control Your Web Site!" *Computerworld,* April 18, 1996.

16. Silver, Mark; M. Lynn Markus; and Cynthia Mathis Beath. "The Information Technology Interaction Model: A Foundation for the MBA Core Course." *MIS Quarterly,* September 1995.

Technology

What challenges do information system technologies pose for business end users? What basic knowledge should you possess about information technology? The four chapters of this module give you an overview of the major technologies used in modern computer-based information systems and their implications for end users and managers.

Chapter 2, "Introduction to Computer Hardware," reviews trends and developments in microcomputer, midrange, and mainframe computer systems; basic computer system concepts; and the major types of technologies used in peripheral devices for computer input, output, and storage.

Chapter 3, "Introduction to Computer Software," reviews the basic features and trends in the major types of application software and system software used to support enterprise and end user computing.

Chapter 4, "Introduction to Business Telecommunications," presents a managerial overview of telecommunications networks, applications, and trends, including the Internet, intranets, extranets, client/server, and other networks, as well as technical telecommunications alternatives.

Chapter 5, "Introduction to Database Management," emphasizes management of the data resources of computer-using organizations. The chapter stresses the managerial implications of database management concepts and applications in business information systems.

Introduction to

Computer Hardware

Chapter Highlights

Section I
Computer Systems: End User and Enterprise Computing
Real World Case: The Mutual Group and Others: Turning Mainframes into Web Servers
Trends in Computer Systems
Microcomputer Systems
Midrange Computer Systems
Mainframe Computer Systems
Technical Note: Computer System
Concepts and Components

Section II
Computer Peripherals: Input, Output, and Storage Technologies
Real World Case: ASD Catalogs and Ernst & Young: The Business PC versus Consumer PC Decision
Introduction
Input Technology Trends
Pointing Devices
Pen-Based Computing
Voice Recognition and Response
Optical Scanning
Other Input Technologies
Output Technologies and Trends
Video Output
Printed Output
Storage Trends and Trade-Offs
Semiconductor Memory
Magnetic Disk Storage
Magnetic Tape Storage
Optical Disk Storage

Learning Objectives

After reading and studying this chapter, you should be able to:

1. Identify the major types, trends, and uses of microcomputer, midrange, and mainframe computer systems.

2. Outline the major technologies and uses of computer peripherals for input, output, and storage.

3. Identify and give examples of the components and functions of a computer system.

4. Identify the computer systems and peripherals you would acquire or recommend for a business of your choice, and explain the reasons for your selections.

Section I

Computer Systems: End User and Enterprise Computing

All computers are systems of input, processing, output, storage, and control components. In this section, we will discuss the trends, applications, and some basic concepts of the many types of computer systems in use today. In Section II, we will cover the changing technologies for input, output, and storage that are provided by the peripheral devices that are part of modern computer systems.

Analyzing The Mutual Group and Others

Read the Real World Case on The Mutual Group and Others on the next page. We can learn a lot about new uses of mainframe computer systems in business from this case. See Figure 2.1.

The Mutual Group, Ducks Unlimited Canada, and Diversified Investment Advisors are examples of the many companies using web-based technologies to give their employees and customers access to databases and applications on their mainframe computer systems. Web front-end software or middleware helps turn their mainframes into powerful web servers that can work with other servers at company Internet and intranet web sites.

Web middleware works with both the web browsers of users and the software of company web site servers to access mainframe data and applications via the mainframe's database management software. Though much development work may be necessary, the web/mainframe process is easier and cheaper than using traditional mainframe terminal software. Using the mainframe as a web server is also less costly and more efficient than converting mainframe applications and databases to run on networks of web servers.

Figure 2.1

Tim Wadman is a technology solutions consultant at The Mutual Group of companies. Tim leads the development of web-based applications on their mainframe.

© Peter Sibbald.

The Mutual Group and Others: Turning Mainframes into Web Servers

Webifying the mainframe may seem like a contradiction in terms—old technology in a new age. But to a growing number of companies, legacy mainframes and web software are turning out to be a hot combo.

Take The Mutual Group. Prior to installing Cyberprise Web Host and Server by Wall Data, "We actually tried to keep down the number of customers who accessed our IBM S/390 mainframe because of the headaches involved in giving all of them our software, installing it, configuring it, and supporting it," says Tim Wadman, technology solutions consultant at the Canadian insurance company. Cyberprise is web *front-end* or *middleware* software that enables users to make use of web browsers—"which everybody already has anyway," Wadman points out—to do their own mainframe querying with software they download from company Internet and intranet web servers.

More than 70 percent of corporate data in the world is still on mainframe systems, according to the Meta Group. And many companies have concluded that those legacy systems and their database management software are at least as capable as the many Unix or Windows NT servers that they typically use, when it comes to dishing out data over the Internet or an intranet. "We already know that our S/390 mainframe can share information efficiently, securely, and cost effectively to a wider universe," such as the Web, says Michael Conchatre, manager of information systems at Ducks Unlimited Canada in Oak Hammock Marsh, Manitoba. His organization uses Enterprise WebServer from Beyond Software as its web/mainframe middleware.

Another reason for slapping web front-end software onto mainframes is the huge cost savings to be gained in cost-of-ownership for web-based systems. According to a recent Gartner Group study, businesses realize 15 percent savings in software costs such as distribution and maintenance and 15 percent in technical support from replacing mainframe terminal software with web browsers.

- **Ducks Unlimited Canada,** Oak Hammock Marsh, Manitoba—Canada's largest wildlife conservation group. Eight thousand volunteer staff members in 40 offices; thousands of web-site visitors daily. Ducks Unlimited got the best of both worlds with its mainframe *webification:* "We get to keep our existing mainframe-based database management and development tools, expertise, and applications," while exploiting the Web's ability to disseminate crucial information to a highly distributed, diverse body of users, says Michael

Conchatre, manager of information systems. Hundreds of mainframe applications are now web-enabled. New ones include a web-based membership recruitment program that took six months to develop.

- **Mutual Life of Canada,** Waterloo, Ontario, lead company of The Mutual Group (group pension plans, group life and health insurance policies). Remote internal users and some external customers with direct access rights to mainframe data on Mutual Life products, customer files, and so on. 500 users, with plans to roll out to all 3,500 users in 1999, and more external customers later.

- **Diversified Investment Advisors Inc.,** Purchase, New York, a financial investment firm that specializes in corporate retirement accounts, with about 800 employees. Total potential user base is 750,000 outside customers.

To swim with the sharks in the mutual-fund market, Diversified needed a quick, inexpensive way to allow customers to access key information about their accounts on its Hitachi 9170 mainframe and perform transactions via the Web. Diversified chose WebConnect Pro from OpenConnect systems as the web middleware for their mainframe systems. It took eight months of systems development work to set up quite a sophisticated GUI-based Java web application, says Jim Stewart, telecommunications manager at Diversified. A growing number of Diversified's 750,000 customers are using the application.

Case Study Questions

1. Why would a company want to turn their mainframe into a web server? What business benefits can occur?

2. What does a company have to do to make its mainframe-based databases and applications accessible to employees and customers with web browsers?

3. When should a business use a mainframe as a web server instead of relying solely on a network of PC-based web servers?

Source: Adapted from Elisabeth Horwitt, "Webifying the Mainframe," *Computerworld*, January 25, 1999, pp. 76–79. Copyright 1999 by Computerworld, Inc., Framingham, MA 01701. Reprinted from *Computerworld*.

Trends in Computer Systems

Today's computer systems come in a variety of sizes, shapes, and computing capabilities. Rapid hardware and software developments and changing end user needs continue to drive the emergence of new models of computers, from the smallest hand-held *personal digital assistant* for end users, to the largest multiple-CPU mainframe for the enterprise.

Categories such as *mainframes, midrange computers*, and *microcomputers* are still used to help us express the relative processing power and number of end users that can be supported by different types of computers. But as Figure 2.2 illustrates, these are not precise classifications, and they do overlap each other. Thus, other names are commonly given to highlight the major uses of particular types of computers. Examples include personal computers, network servers, network computers, and technical workstations.

In addition, experts continue to predict the merging or disappearance of several computer categories. They feel, for example, that many midrange and mainframe systems have been made obsolete by the power and versatility of *client/server* networks of end user microcomputers and servers. Most recently, some industry experts have predicted that the emergence of network computers for applications on the Internet and corporate intranets will replace many personal computers, especially in large organizations and in the home computer market. Only time will tell whether such predictions will equal the expectations of industry forecasters.

Computer Generations

It is important to realize that major changes and trends in computer systems have occurred during the major stages—or **generations**—of computing, and will continue into the future. The first generation of computers developed in the early 1950s, the second generation blossomed during the late 1960s, the third generation took computing into the 1970s, and the fourth generation has been the computer technology of

---

Figure 2.2

Examples of computer system categories.

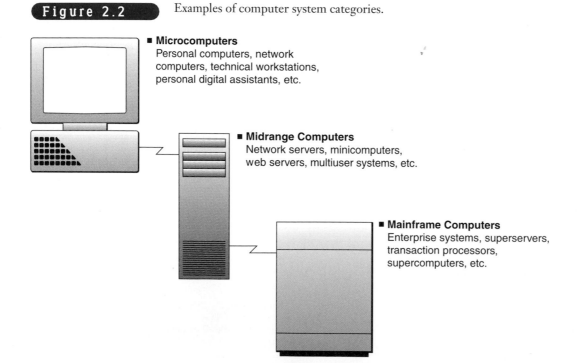

■ **Microcomputers**
Personal computers, network computers, technical workstations, personal digital assistants, etc.

■ **Midrange Computers**
Network servers, minicomputers, web servers, multiuser systems, etc.

■ **Mainframe Computers**
Enterprise systems, superservers, transaction processors, supercomputers, etc.

the 1980s and 1990s. A fifth generation of computers that accelerates the trends of the previous generations is expected to evolve as we enter the 21st century. Figure 2.3 highlights trends in the characteristics and capabilities of computers. Notice that computers continue to become smaller, faster, more reliable, less costly to purchase and maintain, and more interconnected within computer networks.

First-generation computing involved massive computers using hundreds or thousands of *vacuum tubes* for their processing and memory circuitry. These large computers generated enormous amounts of heat; their vacuum tubes had to be replaced frequently. Thus, they had large electrical power, air conditioning, and maintenance requirements. First-generation computers had main memories of only a few thousand characters and millisecond processing speeds. They used magnetic drums or tape for secondary storage and punched cards or paper tape as input and output media.

Second-generation computing used *transistors* and other solid-state, semiconductor devices that were wired to circuit boards in the computers. Transistorized circuits were much smaller and much more reliable, generated little heat, were less

Figure 2.3   Major trends in computer system capabilities.

	First Generation	Second Generation	Third Generation	Fourth Generation	Fifth Generation?
SIZE (Typical computers)	Room Size Mainframe	Closet Size Mainframe	Desk-Size Minicomputer	Desktop and Laptop Microcomputers	Networked Computers of all sizes
NETWORKING	None	Mainframe-Based Networks of Video Terminals	Mainframe and Minicomputer–Based Networks	Local Area and Client/Server Networks	The Internet, Intranets, and Extranets
CIRCUITRY	Vacuum Tubes	Transistors	Integrated Semiconductor Circuits	Large-Scale Integrated (LSI) Semiconductor Circuits	Very-Large-Scale Integrated (VLSI) Semiconductor Circuits
DENSITY (Circuits per component)	One	Hundreds	Thousands	Hundreds of Thousands	Millions
SPEED (Instructions/second)	Hundreds	Thousands	Millions	Tens of Millions	Billions
RELIABILITY (Failure of circuits)	Hours	Days	Weeks	Months	Years
MEMORY (Capacity in characters)	Thousands	Tens of Thousands	Hundreds of Thousands	Millions	Billions
COST (Per million instructions)	$10	$1.00	$.10	$.001	$.0001

expensive, and required less power than vacuum tubes. Tiny *magnetic cores* were used for the computer's memory, or internal storage. Many second-generation computers had main memory capacities of less than 100 kilobytes and microsecond processing speeds. Removable magnetic disk packs were introduced, and magnetic tape emerged as the major input, output, and secondary storage medium for large computer installations.

Third-generation computing saw the development of computers that used *integrated circuits*, in which thousands of transistors and other circuit elements are etched on tiny chips of silicon. Main memory capacities increased to several megabytes and processing speeds jumped to millions of instructions per second (MIPS) as telecommunications capabilities became common. This made it possible for *operating system* programs to come into widespread use that automated and supervised the activities of many types of peripheral devices and processing by mainframe computers of several programs at the same time, frequently involving networks of users at remote terminals. Integrated circuit technology also made possible the development and widespread use of small computers called **minicomputers** in the third computer generation.

Fourth-generation computing relies on the use of LSI (large-scale integration) and VLSI (very-large-scale integration) technologies that cram hundreds of thousands or millions of transistors and other circuit elements on each chip. This enabled the development of **microprocessors,** in which all of the circuits of a CPU are contained on a single chip with processing speeds of millions of instructions per second. Main memory capacities ranging from a few megabytes to several gigabytes can also be achieved by *memory chips* that replaced magnetic core memories. **Microcomputers,** which use microprocessor CPUs and a variety of peripheral devices and easy-to-use software packages to form small personal computer (PC) systems or *client/server* networks of linked PCs and servers, are a hallmark of the fourth generation of computing, which accelerated the **downsizing** of computing systems.

Whether we are moving into a **fifth generation** of computing is a subject of debate since the concept of generations may no longer fit the continual, rapid changes occurring in computer hardware, software, data, and networking technologies. But in any case, we can be sure that progress in computing will continue to accelerate, and that the development of Internet-based technologies and applications will be one of the major forces driving computing in the 21st century.

Microcomputer Systems

Cheaper, faster, better remains the iron law of the computer industry. The immense power of the newest microprocessors—from Intel and its competitors—means that this year's state-of-the-art personal computer is an astonishingly capable machine [5].

Microcomputers are the most important category of computer systems for end users. Though usually called a *personal computer,* or PC, a microcomputer is much more than a small computer for use by an individual. The computing power of microcomputers now exceeds that of the mainframes of previous computer generations at a fraction of their cost. Thus, they have become powerful networked *professional workstations* for end users in business.

Microcomputers come in a variety of sizes and shapes for a variety of purposes, as Figure 2.4 illustrates. For example, PCs are available as handheld, notebook, laptop, portable, desktop, and floor-standing models. Or, based on their use, they include home, personal, professional, workstation, and multiuser systems. Most microcomputers are *desktops* designed to fit on an office desk, or *notebooks* for those who want a small, portable PC for their work activities. Figure 2.5 is a checklist of some of the key

Figure 2.4

Examples of microcomputer systems.

Courtesy of International Business Machines Corporation.
Unauthorized use not permitted.
a. A notebook microcomputer.

Ed Bock/The Stock Market.
b. The microcomputer as a professional workstation.

Renee Lynn/Photo Researchers.
c. The microcomputer as a technical workstation.

features you should consider in acquiring a high-end business PC, graphics workstation, or multimedia PC. This should give you some idea of the range of features available in today's microcomputers.

Some microcomputers are powerful **workstation computers** (technical workstations) that support applications with heavy mathematical computing and graphics display demands such as computer-aided design (CAD) in engineering, or investment and portfolio analysis in the securities industry. Other microcomputers are used as **network servers.** They are usually more powerful microcomputers that coordinate telecommunications and resource sharing in small local area networks (LANs), and Internet and intranet web sites. Another important microcomputer category includes handheld microcomputer devices known as **personal digital assistants** (PDAs), designed for convenient mobile communications and computing. PDAs use touch-screens, pen-based handwriting recognition, or keyboards to help mobile workers send and receive E-mail and exchange information such as appointments, to-do lists, and sales contacts with their desktop PCs or web servers.

Figure 2.5

Business PC checklist. Some of the key features to evaluate when purchasing a high-end business PC, graphics workstation, or multimedia PC.

Dream Machine Checklist

- **The Ultimate Business Box.** If your dream machine is mainly for business, you'll want at least 64MB of RAM for those big software programs, a 56Kbps modem to pull down research and news from the Web, a 5–10GB hard drive, and a 300–400MHz processor. Don't sweat high-end graphics and audio processors, but invest in a backup Zip or SuperDisk drive.

- **The Graphics Workstation.** If you're crunching 3-D architectural renderings, you'll want 128MB of main memory, 20MB of graphics memory, a 400–450MHz microprocessor, and a replaceable 10GB hard drive for those large graphics files.

- **The Ultimate Multimedia Machine.** PC enthusiasts want it all. Top-end 400–450MHz processor, 128MB RAM, a 10GB hard drive, 56Kbps modem. For browsing multimedia on the Web, look for16-bit, full-duplex audio boards with WaveTable synthesis. If gaming is your focus, go for fast 3-D rendering boards, and even a DVD-ROM drive.

Source: Adapted from "Dream Machines," Technology Buyer's Guide, *Fortune*, Winter 1998, p. 66, and "Desktop Power," Technology Buyer's Guide, *Fortune*, Winter 1999, p. 42. © 1998 and 1999 by Time Inc. All rights reserved.

Figure 2.6

An example of a multimedia business presentation in a videoconferencing session.

Courtesy of Hewlett-Packard Company.

Multimedia Systems

While sound, video, and animation are still most important for games and educational software, multimedia technology has begun to suffuse business applications as well. The cost of videoconferencing has plummeted while its quality has improved. Film clips and animations—already a staple in PC-based presentations—are turning up in tutorials and training materials. Shared documents annotated with voice, digitized photographs, or 3-D graphics are beginning to make the rounds on the company network. The highly graphical Web, for good or ill, is as commonplace as bad coffee in today's office [7].

Multimedia PCs are designed to present you with information in a variety of media, including text and graphics displays, voice and other digitized audio, photographs, animation, and video clips. Mention multimedia, and many people think of computer video games, multimedia encyclopedias, educational videos, and multimedia home pages on the World Wide Web. However, multimedia systems are widely used in business for training employees, educating customers, making sales presentations, and adding impact to other business presentations. See Figure 2.6.

The basic hardware and software requirements of a multimedia computer system depend on whether you wish to create as well as enjoy multimedia presentations. Owners of low-cost multimedia PCs marketed for home use do not need authoring software or high-powered hardware capabilities in order to enjoy multimedia games and other entertainment and educational multimedia products. These computers come equipped with a CD-ROM drive, stereo speakers, additional memory, a high-performance processor, and other multimedia processing capabilities.

People who want to create their own multimedia productions may have to spend several thousand dollars to put together a high-performance *multimedia authoring system.* This includes a high-resolution color graphics monitor, sound and video capture boards, a high-performance microprocessor with multimedia capabilities, additional megabytes of memory, and several gigabytes of hard disk capacity. *Sound cards* and video capture boards are circuit boards that contain *digital signal processors* (DSPs) and additional megabytes of memory for digital processing of sound and video. A digital camera, digital video camcorder, optical scanner, and software such as authoring tools and programs for image editing and graphics can add several thousand dollars to the start-up costs of a multimedia authoring system.

Network Computers

Network computers (NCs) are emerging as a serious business computing platform. Though Microsoft and Intel ridiculed the NC concept at first, they have since agreed to support moves toward "thin client" as well as traditional "fat client" full-featured PCs. The Wintel duo (Windows operating system and Intel microprocessor) proposed a stripped-down, locked-up PC called the NetPC. Microsoft went one step further and proposed an even more stripped-down device than the NC or NetPC, called the *Windows terminal,* that would be dependent on network servers for software, processing power, and storage [10]. See Figure 2.7.

Network computers are thus a major new microcomputer category designed primarily for use with the Internet and corporate intranets by clerical workers, operational employees, and knowledge workers with specialized or limited computing applications. NCs are low-cost, sealed, networked microcomputers with no or minimal disk storage. Users of NCs depend primarily on Internet and intranet servers for their operating system and web browser, Java-enabled application software, and data access and storage. Examples include Sun's JavaStation, IBM's Network Station, and the NCD Explora network computers.

Network computer

- Operating system, application software, and data storage are provided by the server
- Uses a web browser and runs Java-enabled software applications called *applets*
- Managed remotely and centrally
- Generally has no hard disk drive

NetPC

- Works like a PC, with its own software
- Has a hard drive, but no floppy drive or CD-ROM
- Box is sealed so users can't change its configuration
- Operating system and applications are managed and loaded centrally

Windows terminal

- An inexpensive terminal-like device without disk storage
- Multiuser version of Windows NT as the server operating system
- Microsoft Office–like multiuser software on the server

One of the main attractions of network computers is their lower cost of purchase, upgrades, maintenance, and support compared to full-featured PCs. Other benefits to business include ease of software distribution and licensing, computing platform standardization, reduced end user support requirements, and improved manageability through centralized management and enterprisewide control of computer network resources [9, 10]. See Figure 2.8.

Special-purpose NCs that take the form of *set-top boxes* that connect to your home TV set are another category of network computer. These devices enable you to surf the World Wide Web or send and receive E-mail and watch TV programs at the same time in multiple windows. Examples include the Sony Web TV Internet Terminal and Philips Magnavox WebTV Plus Receiver, which use Microsoft's WebTV network service. Another example is the RCA Network Computer, which is based on Oracle's *information appliance* NC standards, and uses the NetChannel Internet service. The Sony and Philips models include a TV tuner, 56 Kbps modem, and 1.1 GB hard drive for downloading files. Prices for these devices start around $300, plus optional peripherals such as keyboards and printers [8].

Computer Terminals

Computer terminals are undergoing a major conversion to networked computer devices. *Dumb terminals*, which are keyboard/video monitor devices with limited processing capabilities, are being replaced by *intelligent terminals*, which are modified networked PCs, network computers, or other networked devices. Intelligent terminals can perform data entry and some information processing tasks independently. This includes the widespread use of **transaction terminals** in banks, retail stores, factories, and other work sites. Examples are automated teller machines (ATMs), factory production recorders, and retail point-of-sale (POS) terminals. These intelligent terminals use keypads, touch screens, and other input methods to capture data and interact with end users during a transaction, while relying on servers or other computers in the network for further transaction processing.

Figure 2.8   Examples of network computers.

Courtesy of Sun Microsystems, Inc.

Courtesy of NCD.

Midrange Computer Systems

Midrange computers, including microcomputers and high-end network servers, are multiuser systems that can manage networks of PCs and terminals. Though not as powerful as mainframe computers, they are less costly to buy, operate, and maintain than mainframe systems, and thus meet the computing needs of many organizations. See Figure 2.9.

Midrange computers first became popular as **minicomputers** for scientific research, instrumentation systems, engineering analysis, and industrial process monitoring and control. Minicomputers could easily handle such uses because these applications are narrow in scope and do not demand the processing versatility of mainframe systems. Thus, midrange computers serve as industrial process-control and manufacturing plant computers, and they still play a major role in computer-aided manufacturing (CAM). They can also take the form of powerful technical workstations for computer-aided design (CAD) and other computation and graphics-intensive applications. Midrange computers are also used as *front-end computers* to assist mainframe computers in telecommunications processing and network management.

> *Burgeoning data warehouses and related applications such as data mining and online analytical processing are forcing IT shops into higher and higher levels of server configurations. Similarly, Internet-based applications, such as web servers and electronic commerce, are forcing IT managers to push the envelope of processing speed and storage capacity and other [business] applications fueling the growth of high-end servers* [17].

Midrange computers have become popular as powerful **network servers** to help manage large Internet web sites, corporate intranets and extranets, and client/server networks. Electronic commerce and other business uses of the Internet are popular high-end server applications, as are integrated enterprisewide manufacturing, distribution, and financial applications. Other applications, like data warehouse management, data mining, and online analytical processing (which we discuss in Chapters 5 and 8), are contributing to the growth of high-end servers and other midrange systems [17].

Mainframe Computer Systems

Six years after dire pronouncements that the mainframe was dead, quite the opposite is true: Mainframe usage is actually on the rise. And it's not just a short-term blip. One factor that's been driving mainframe sales is cost reductions [of 35 percent or more]. Price reductions aren't the only factor fueling mainframe acquisitions. IS organizations are

Figure 2.9

The IBM Netfinity 7000 is a powerful high-end server designed for high volume electronic commerce processing at Internet web sites.

Courtesy of International Business Machines Corporation. Unauthorized use not permitted.

teaching the old dog new tricks by putting mainframes at the center stage of emerging applications such as data mining and warehousing, decision support, and a variety of Internet-based applications, most notably electronic commerce [16].

Mainframe computers are large, fast, and powerful computer systems. For example, mainframes can process hundreds of million instructions per second (MIPS). Mainframes also have large primary storage capacities. Their main memory capacity can range from hundreds of megabytes to many gigabytes of primary storage. And mainframes have slimmed down drastically in the last few years, dramatically reducing their air-conditioning needs, electrical power consumption, and floor space requirements, and thus their acquisition and operating costs. Most of these improvements are the result of a move from water-cooled mainframes to a new CMOS air-cooled technology for mainframe systems. See Figures 2.10 and 2.11.

Thus, mainframe computers continue to handle the information processing needs of major corporations and government agencies with many employees and customers or with complex computational problems. For example, major international banks, airlines, oil companies, and other large corporations process millions of sales transactions and customer inquiries each day with the help of large mainframe systems. Mainframes are still used for computation-intensive applications such as analyzing seismic data from oil field explorations or simulating flight conditions in designing aircraft. Mainframes are also widely used as *superservers* for the large client/server networks and high-volume Internet web sites of large companies. And as previously mentioned,

Figure 2.10

An air-cooled mainframe computer system, the IBM S/390.

© Dennis Brack/Black Star.

mainframes are becoming a popular business computing platform for data mining and warehousing, and electronic commerce applications. See Figure 2.12.

Supercomputer Systems

Supercomputers have now become "scalable servers" at the top end of product lines that start with desktop workstations. Market-driven companies, like Silicon Graphics, Hewlett-Packard, and IBM, have a much broader focus than just building the world's fastest computer, and the software of the desktop computer has a much greater overlap with that of the supercomputer than it used to, because both are built from the same cache-based microprocessors [12].

The term **supercomputer** describes a category of extremely powerful computer systems specifically designed for scientific, engineering, and business applications requiring extremely high speeds for massive numeric computations. The market for supercomputers includes government research agencies, large universities, and major

Figure 2.11

Comparing a traditional water-cooled mainframe with a comparable air-cooled CMOS system.

IBM	ES/3090 Model 600E (water cooled)	S/390 Ry4 (CMOS air cooled)
Processors	6-way	10-way
Processing power	390 MIPS	400 MIPS
Electrical needs	138.8 KVA	5 KVA
Floor space	974 sq. ft.	52 sq. ft.
Weight	31,590 pounds	2,057 pounds

Source: Adapted from Tim Ouellette, "Goodbye to the Glass House," *Computerworld*, May 26, 1997, pp. 1, 115. Copyright 1997 by Computerworld, Inc., Framingham, MA 01701. Reprinted from *Computerworld*.

Figure 2.12

Why companies are
using mainframes as
servers for electronic
commerce.

- Most critical business data may already be stored on the mainframe.
- Mainframe scalability can handle growing Internet traffic.
- Mainframe applications were designed to work with thin clients such as NetPCs and NCs.
- Built-in mainframe security can be combined with new cryptographic coprocessors and fire wall capabilities.
- Data are safer on the mainframe than on many servers.
- Internet tools are integrated right into the mainframe's OS/390 operating system.
- New mainframes offer huge savings in size, energy, and maintenance.

Source: Adapted from Tim Ouellette, "Mainframes Ripe for Web Serving," *Computerworld,* June 30, 1997, pp. 65, 68. Copyright 1997 by Computerworld, Inc., Framingham, MA 01701. Reprinted from *Computerworld.*

corporations. They use supercomputers for applications such as global weather forecasting, military defense systems, computational cosmology and astronomy, microprocessor research and design, large-scale data mining, and so on.

Supercomputers use *parallel processing* architectures of interconnected microprocessors (which can execute many instructions at the same time in parallel). They can perform arithmetic calculations at speeds of billions of floating-point operations per second (gigaflops). Teraflop (1 trillion floating-point operations per second) supercomputers, which use advanced massively parallel processing (MPP) designs of thousands of interconnected microprocessors, are becoming available. Purchase prices for large supercomputers are in the $5 million to $50 million range.

However, the use of symmetric multiprocessing (SMP) and distributed shared memory (DSM) designs of smaller numbers of interconnected microprocessors has spawned a breed of *minisupercomputers* with prices that start in the hundreds of thousands of dollars. For example IBM's RS/6000 SP starts at $150,000 for a one-processing-node SMP computer. However, it can be expanded to a maximum of 512 processing nodes, which drives its price into the tens of millions of dollars. Deep Blue, which beat world chess champion Garry Kasparov in May 1997, was a 32-node version of the RS/6000 SP [11]. Thus, supercomputers continue to advance the state of the art for the entire computer industry. See Figure 2.13.

Technical Note: Computer System Concepts and Components

As a business end user, you do not need a detailed technical knowledge of computers. However, you do need to understand some basic facts and concepts about computer systems. This should help you be an informed and productive user of computer system resources. Therefore, this section presents basic concepts about the components and functions of a computer system. Other topics include the central processing unit, computer memory, and variations in computer processors.

The Computer System Concept

A computer is more than a high-powered collection of electronic devices performing a variety of information processing chores. A computer is a system, an interrelated combination of components that performs the basic system functions of input, processing, output, storage, and control, thus providing end users with a powerful information processing tool. Understanding the computer as a **computer system** is vital to the effective use and management of computers. You should be able to visualize any

The supercomputer that beat world chess champion Garry Kasparov was a 32-node version of the IBM RS/6000 SP.

© Dennis Brack/Black Star.

computer this way, from a microcomputer like that shown in Figure 2.14, to a large computer system whose components are interconnected by a telecommunications network and spread throughout a building or geographic area.

Figure 2.15 illustrates that a computer is a system of hardware devices organized according to the following system functions:

- **Input.** The input devices of a computer system include keyboards, touch screens, pens, electronic mice, optical scanners, and so on. They convert data into electronic machine-readable form for direct entry or through telecommunications links into a computer system.

- **Processing.** The central processing unit (CPU) is the main processing component of a computer system. (In microcomputers, it is the main microprocessor.) In particular, the electronic circuits of the arithmetic-logic unit, one of the CPU's major components, perform the arithmetic and logic functions required in computer processing.

- **Output.** The output devices of a computer system include video display units, printers, audio response units, and so on. They convert electronic information produced by the computer system into human-intelligible form for presentation to end users.

- **Storage.** The storage function of a computer system takes place in the storage circuits of the computer's primary storage unit, or *memory*, and in secondary storage devices such as magnetic disk and tape units. These devices store data and program instructions needed for processing.

- **Control.** The control unit of the CPU is the control component of a computer system. Its circuits interpret computer program instructions and transmit directions to the other components of the computer system.

A microcomputer is a system of computing components. This microcomputer system includes (1) a keyboard and mouse for input, (2) microprocessors and other circuitry in its main system unit for processing and control, (3) a video monitor and printer for output, and (4) memory chips and a built-in floppy disk drive and hard disk unit for storage.

Courtesy of Hewlett-Packard Company.

The Central Processing Unit

The **central processing unit** is the most important hardware component of a computer system. It is also known as the CPU, the central processor or instruction processor, and the **main microprocessor** in a microcomputer. Conceptually, the circuitry of a CPU can be subdivided into two major subunits: the arithmetic-logic unit and the control unit. The CPU also includes circuitry for devices such as *registers* and *cache*

The computer system concept. A computer is a system of hardware components and functions.

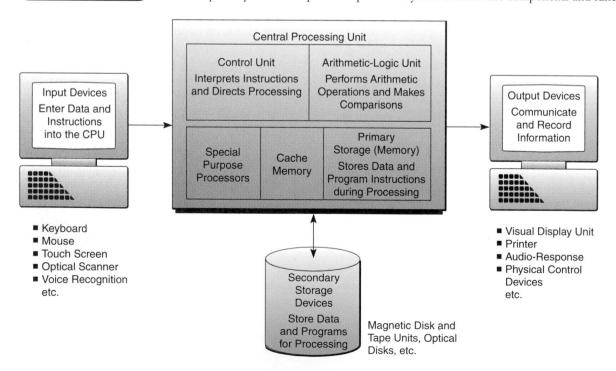

memory for high-speed, temporary storage of instruction and data elements, and various subsidiary processors such as those for arithmetic operations, input/output, and telecommunications support.

The **control unit** obtains instructions from software segments stored in the primary storage unit and interprets them. Then it transmits electronic signals to the other components of the computer system to perform required operations. The **arithmetic-logic unit** performs required arithmetic and comparison operations. A computer can make logical changes from one set of program instructions to another (e.g., overtime pay versus regular pay calculations) based on the results of comparisons made in the ALU during processing.

Primary and Secondary Storage

A computer's **primary storage unit** is commonly called **main memory,** and holds data and program instructions between processing steps and supplies them to the control unit and arithmetic-logic unit during processing. Most of a computer's memory consists of microelectronic semiconductor memory chips known as RAM (random access memory). The contents of these memory chips can be instantly changed to store new data. Other, more permanent memory chips, called ROM (read only memory), may also be used.

Secondary storage devices like magnetic disks and optical disks are used to store data and programs, and thus greatly enlarge the storage capacities of computer systems. Also, since memory circuits typically lose their contents when electric power is turned off, most secondary storage media provide a more permanent type of storage. However, the contents of hard disk drives, floppy disks, CD-ROM disks, and other secondary storage media cannot be processed without first being brought into memory. Thus, secondary storage devices play a supporting role to the primary storage of a computer system.

Multiple Processors

Many current computers, from microcomputers to large mainframes, use multiple processors for their processing functions. Instead of having one CPU with a single control unit and arithmetic-logic unit, the CPUs of these computers contain several types of processing units. Let's briefly look at the major types of such **multiprocessor** designs.

A **support processor** design relies on specialized microprocessors to help the main CPU perform a variety of functions. These microprocessors may be used for input/output, memory management, arithmetic computations, multimedia processing, and telecommunications, thus freeing the main processor to do the primary job of executing program instructions. For example, many microcomputers rely on support microprocessors such as arithmetic co-processors, video display controllers, and magnetic disk controllers to reduce the processing load on their main microprocessors. A large computer may use support microprocessors called *channels* to control the movement of data between the CPU and input/output devices. Advanced microprocessor designs integrate the functions of several support processors on a single main microprocessor. See Figure 2.16.

A **coupled processor** design uses multiple CPUs or main microprocessors to do multiprocessing, that is, executing more than one instruction at the same time. Some configurations provide a *fault-tolerant* capability in which multiple CPUs provide a built-in backup to each other should one of them fail.

A **parallel processor** design uses a group of instruction processors to execute several program instructions at the same time. Sometimes, hundreds or thousands of processors are organized in clusters or networks in *massively parallel processing* (MPP) computers. Other parallel processor designs are based on simple models of the human

The Intel Pentium II microprocessor uses 7.5 million transistors to process over 500 million instructions per second.

Courtesy of Intel.

brain called *neural networks.* All of these systems can execute many instructions at a time in parallel. This is a major departure from the traditional design of current computers, called the *Von Neuman design,* which executes instructions serially (one at a time). Though difficult to program, many experts consider parallel processor systems the key to providing advanced capabilities to future generations of computers.

RISC Processors. Many advanced technical workstations and other computers rely on a processor design called RISC (reduced instruction set computer). This contrasts with most current computers that use CISC (complex instruction set computer) processors. RISC processor designs optimize a CPU's processing speed by using a smaller *instruction set.* That is, they use a smaller number of the *basic machine instructions* that a processor is capable of executing. By keeping the instruction set simpler than CISC processors and using more complex software, a RISC processor can reduce the time needed to execute program instructions. Thus, RISC processors like Digital Equipment's Alpha chip have become popular for computers such as network servers and technical workstations. Apple's Macintosh and PowerBooks and IBM's AS/400 midrange systems use RISC microprocessors like the Power PC, codeveloped by Motorola, Apple, and IBM.

Computer Processing Speeds

How fast are computer systems? Computer operating speeds that were formerly measured in **milliseconds** (thousandths of a second) and **microseconds** (millionths of a second) are now in the **nanosecond** (billionth of a second) range, with **picosecond** (trillionth of a second) speed being attained by some computers. Such speeds seem almost incomprehensible. For example, an average person taking one step each nanosecond would circle the earth about 20 times in one second! Many microcomputers and midrange computers, and most mainframe computers, operate in the nanosecond range, and can thus process program instructions at *million instructions per second*

Figure 2.17   A comparison of the Norton Utilities multimedia performance scores for several Intel Pentium microprocessors. Notice how MMX multimedia circuitry, higher megahertz clock speeds, and level 2 (L2) external cache capacities increase multimedia processing speed so microprocessors can accomplish more multimedia operations in the same amount of time.

Processor	Pentium	Pentium–MMX™	Pentium II	Pentium II	Pentium II
Clock Speed	200MHz	200MHz	233MHz	266MHz	300MHz
Cache Memory (L2)			512KB	512KB	512KB
Overall Speed	9.8	14.1	17.5	19.8	21.7
Video	8.4	11.4	10.4	11.8	12.9
3-D Graphics	13	14.2	22.4	25.5	27.6
Imaging	5.7	28.1	41.4	46.1	50.7

(MIPS) speeds. Another measure of processing speed is *megahertz* (MHz), or millions of cycles per second. It is commonly called the *clock speed* of a microprocessor, since it is used to rate microprocessors by the speed of their timing circuits or internal clock.

However, megahertz ratings can be misleading indicators of the effective processing speed of microprocessors as measured in MIPS and other measures. That's because processing speed depends on a variety of factors besides a microprocessor's clock speed. Important examples include the size of circuitry paths, or *busses*, that interconnect microprocessor components; the capacity of instruction processing *registers*; the use of high-speed *memory caches;* and the use of specialized microprocessors such as a math co-processor to do arithmetic calculations faster. See Figure 2.17.

Section II   Computer Peripherals: Input, Output, and Storage Technologies

The right peripherals can make all the difference in your computing experience. A top-quality monitor will be easier on your eyes—and may change the way you work. A scanner can edge you closer to that ever-elusive goal—the paperless office. Backup-storage systems can offer bank-vault security against losing your work. CD-ROM drives can be essential for education and entertainment. Memory cards, 3-D graphics, and other devices will help you configure your computer to meet your needs. Some may be the digital equivalent of chrome bumpers and tailfins, but the right choice of peripherals can make a big difference [7].

Analyzing ASD Catalogs and Ernst & Young

Read the Real World Case on ASD Catalogs and Ernst & Young on the next page. We can learn a lot about the challenges of acquiring and supporting PCs and their peripherals and other components from this case. See Figure 2.18.

Jason Foster of ASD Catalogs must decide whether to replace 200 clone PCs with premium-priced business PCs or less expensive consumer PCs. Since the spread between the price of cheap consumer PCs and business PCs has widened significantly, managers like Jason are faced with a more complex business decision.

However, Al Hershey of Ernst & Young is adamant that the total cost of using a more expensive business PC with better quality standard peripherals and components

Figure 2.18

Jason Foster heads systems development at ASD Catalogs and is responsible for the acquisition and management of their PCs and workstations.

© Will Van Overbeek.

ASD Catalogs and Ernst & Young: The Business PC versus Consumer PC Decision

When Jason Foster took over systems development at ASD Catalogs a year ago, he inherited a mishmash of more than 200 clone PCs. Since then, he has hassled with inconsistent components, poor serviceability, and frequent system crashes, all of which take a serious toll on productivity.

"Order fulfillment and payment verification locked up at least once a day," says Foster, director of systems development at the Garland, Texas–based order-fulfillment company, which processes 2,000 orders daily for retail catalog and Web merchandisers. "Anytime developers doing Internet multimedia and high-end database work have to deal with the network, we're locking up three to five times a day."

Foster will be replacing the company's 230 PCs and six developer workstations soon. Should he buy business PCs for $1,700 or more, loaded with features he won't need? Or should he purchase considerably less expensive consumer PCs?

The plummeting prices of PCs are putting many information technology managers into Foster's shoes. If you multiply the price differential between a typical corporate configuration and a dirt-cheap consumer box by hundreds or thousands of end users, pretty soon you're talking about real money. But shorter product life cycles, inconsistent componentry, and difficulties in upgrades are common in such machines.

Chris Goodhue, an analyst at Gartner Group, has an unequivocal answer for Foster: "Any organization looking to improve manageability and contain total cost of ownership as their business grows should not consider the consumer PC."

Foster is still mulling his options. But he says he worries that in the long run, going with the consumer machines could land him right back where he started.

"I want consistency over time—the same processor, disk drive assemblies, BIOS, memory modules, graphics cards," says Al Hershey, a partner and buyer at Ernst & Young LLP in New York City.

Hershey oversees the purchase each month of about 2,000 IBM and Dell Computer desktops and notebooks as part of an ongoing replenishment of the organization's 65,000 computers. He says that four years ago, he haggled with Dell until it agreed to build its business line with standardized peripherals and components and with Ernst & Young's custom software installed.

"Does it cost a little more? Yes. But the cost to own the machine is actually much less because my service costs, problem resolution, help desk costs, and spare parts are all much lower," Hershey says.

Consumer PCs under $1,000 are a different story. Makers usually buy processors, hard drives, modems, sound cards, and other components and peripherals based on availability or cost, not consistency from system to system. Even larger vendors such as Dell, Compaq, Hewlett-Packard, and IBM swap components on their consumer lines too often for comfort, Hershey says.

In the case of clones, you won't even recognize the name on many of those components. Name-brand vendors also use non-Intel processors, such as those from Cyrix and Advanced Micro Devices, on their consumer lines. That's a concern for some customers. Foster says he believes the use of components from small or lesser-known vendors contributed to the frequent lockups on his consumer PCs.

Also, most business PCs ship with built-in network cards and plug-ins to leading network management software such as IBM/Tivoli, HP OpenView, or Computer Associates Unicenter. "We're not sure we want to go with a consumer PC that's not network-ready even though the direction of our systems development effort is browser-based computing which would run on a fairly limited PC," Foster says.

"Don't skimp on the hardware. Buy for your business need, not just what you can afford," Hershey says. "In the long run, if it doesn't crash and you get full production days out of the machine, you've got your money's worth."

Case Study Questions

1. Why would a company consider using consumer PCs in their business? When might such a decision be appropriate?

2. What acquisition cost/support cost trade-offs are part of business PC versus consumer PC decision making?

3. What would you advise Jason Foster of ASD Catalogs to do? Why?

Source: Adapted from Deborah Radcliff, "Bogus Bargain Boxes?" *Computerworld*, February 8, 1999, pp. 84–85. Copyright 1999 by Computerworld, Inc., Framingham, MA 01701. Reprinted from *Computerworld*.

Figure 2.19

Some advice about peripherals for a business PC.

Peripherals Checklist
● **Monitors.** Bigger is better for computer screens. Consider a 17-inch or 19-inch monitor. That gives you much more room to display spreadsheets, Web pages, lines of text, open windows, etc. The stability and clarity of a monitor's image are important, too. Look for models with a "refresh rate" of at least 75 Hz and a resolution of at least 1024×768 pixels.
● **Printers.** Your choice is between laser printers or color inkjet printers. Lasers are better suited for high-volume business use. Moderately priced color inkjets provide high-quality images and are well-suited for reproducing photographs. Per-page costs are higher than for laser printers.
● **Scanners.** You'll have to decide between a compact, sheet-fed scanner or a flatbed model. Sheet-fed scanners will save desktop space, while bulkier flat-bed models provide higher speed and resolution. Resolution is a key measure of quality; you'll want at least 300 dpi.
● **Hard Disk Drives.** Bigger is better; as with closet space, you can always use the extra capacity. So go 2 gigabytes at the minimum, 8 to 10 gigabytes at the max.
● **CD-ROM Drives.** Once considered a luxury, the CD-ROM drive is becoming a necessity for software installation and multimedia applications. Consider a high-speed variable-speed model (20X to 32X) for faster, smoother presentations.
● **Backup Systems.** Essential. Don't compute without them. Cassette tape backup is OK, but removable mag disk cartridges (like the Iomega Zip and Jazz drives) are more convenient and versatile, and faster too.

Source: Adapted from "Peripherals," Technology Buyer's Guide, *Fortune*, Winter 1997, p. 75, and Winter 1998, p. 110. Copyright © 1997 and 1998 by Time Inc. All rights reserved.

is really less over time, because their service, maintenance, and support costs are much less than consumer-grade PCs. Hershey also emphasizes that using PCs in a business work environment makes breakdowns and downtimes of PCs much more costly in lost productivity to a company, than to users of consumer PCs in a home environment. This acquisition cost versus total support cost trade-off is a major consideration in most business PC decision making today.

Introduction

A computer is just a high-powered "processing box" without peripherals. **Peripherals** is the generic name given to all input, output, and secondary storage devices that are part of a computer system. Peripherals depend on direct connections or telecommunications links to the central processing unit of a computer system. Thus, all peripherals are **online** devices; that is, they are separate from, but can be electronically connected to and controlled by, a CPU. (This is the opposite of **offline** devices that are separate from and not under the control of the CPU.) The major types of peripherals and media that can be part of a computer system are discussed in this section. See Figure 2.19.

Input Technology Trends

Figure 2.20 emphasizes that there has been a major trend toward the increased use of input technologies that provide a more **natural user interface** for computer users. You can now enter data and commands directly and easily into a computer system through pointing devices like electronic mice and touch pads, and technologies like optical scanning, handwriting recognition, and voice recognition. These developments have made it unnecessary to always record data on paper *source documents* (such as sales

Figure 2.20 Input technology trends. Note the trend toward input methods that provide a more natural user interface.

	First Generation	Second Generation	Third Generation	Fourth Generation	Fifth Generation?
INPUT MEDIA/ METHOD	Punched Cards Paper Tape	Punched Cards	Key to Tape/Disk	Keyboard Data Entry Pointing Devices Optical Scanning	Voice Recognition Touch Devices Handwriting Recognition

TREND: Toward Direct Input Devices That Are More Natural and Easy to Use .

order forms, for example) and then keyboard the data into a computer in an additional data entry step. Further improvements in voice recognition and other technologies should enable an even more natural user interface in the future.

Pointing Devices

Keyboards are still the most widely used devices for entering data and text into computer systems. However, **pointing devices** are a better alternative for issuing commands, making choices, and responding to prompts displayed on your video screen. They work with your operating system's **graphical user interface** (GUI), which presents you with icons, menus, windows, buttons, bars, and so on, for your selection. For example, pointing devices such as electronic mice and touchpads allow you to easily choose from menu selections and icon displays using point-and-click or point-and-drag methods. See Figure 2.21.

The **electronic mouse** is the most popular pointing device used to move the cursor on the screen, as well as to issue commands and make icon and menu selections. By moving the mouse on a desktop or pad, you can move the cursor onto an icon

Figure 2.21

Examples of common peripheral devices for input, output, and storage.

© Index Stock Photography Inc.
a. This PC provides a keyboard, mouse, video monitor, and CD-ROM drive.

Courtesy of Diner's Club International.
b. This laptop microcomputer features an LCD display, CD-ROM drive, and touchpad pointing device.

displayed on the screen. Pressing buttons on the mouse activates various activities represented by the icon selected.

The trackball, pointing stick, and touchpad are other pointing devices most often used in place of the mouse. A **trackball** is a stationary device related to the mouse. You turn a roller ball with only its top exposed outside its case to move the cursor on the screen. A **pointing stick** (also called a *trackpoint*) is a small buttonlike device, sometimes likened to the eraserhead of a pencil. It is usually centered one row above the space bar of a keyboard. The cursor moves in the direction of the pressure you place on the stick. The **touchpad** is a small rectangular touch-sensitive surface usually placed below the keyboard. The cursor moves in the direction your finger moves on the pad. Trackballs, pointing sticks, and touchpads are easier to use than a mouse for portable computer users and are thus built into most notebook computer keyboards.

Touch screens are devices that allow you to use a computer by touching the surface of its video display screen. Some touch screens emit a grid of infrared beams, sound waves, or a slight electric current that is broken when the screen is touched. The computer senses the point in the grid where the break occurs and responds with an appropriate action. For example, you can indicate your selection on a menu display by just touching the screen next to that menu item.

Pen-Based Computing

Handwriting-recognition systems convert script into text quickly and are friendly to shaky hands as well as those of block-printing draftsmen. The pen is more powerful than the keyboard in many vertical markets, as evidenced by the popularity of pen-based devices in the utilities, service, and medical trades [7].

Pen-based computing technologies are being used in many hand-held computers and personal digital assistants. These small PCs and PDAs contain fast processors and software that recognizes and digitizes handwriting, handprinting, and hand drawing. They have a pressure-sensitive layer like a graphics pad under their slatelike liquid crystal display (LCD) screen. So instead of writing on a paper form fastened to a clipboard or using a keyboard device, you can use a pen to make selections, send E-mail, and enter handwritten data directly into a computer. See Figure 2.22.

Figure 2.22

Using a personal digital assistant (PDA) that accepts pen-based input.

© Jose Luis Pelaez, Inc./The Stock Market.

A variety of other penlike devices are available. One example is the *digitizer pen* and *graphics tablet*. You can use the digitizer pen as a pointing device, or use it to draw or write on the pressure-sensitive surface of the graphics tablet. Your handwriting or drawing is digitized by the computer, accepted as input, displayed on its video screen, and entered into your application.

Voice Recognition and Response

It's been a staple of science fiction for decades—a space traveler speaks to a computer, and the computer automatically records every word. Thanks to [continuous] speech recognition products, speech recognition is moving from science fiction into an office-usable tool [4].

Voice recognition promises to be the easiest method for data entry, word processing, and conversational computing, since speech is the easiest, most natural means of human communication. Voice input has now become technologically and economically feasible for a variety of applications. Early voice recognition products used *discrete speech recognition*, where you had to pause between each spoken word. New *continuous speech recognition* (CSR) software recognizes continuous, conversationally paced speech. See Figure 2.23.

Voice recognition systems analyze and classify speech or vocal tract patterns and convert them into digital codes for entry into a computer system. Typically, voice recognition systems with large vocabularies require training the computer to recognize your voice in order to achieve a high degree of accuracy. Training such systems involves repeating a variety of words and phrases in a training session and using the system extensively. Trained systems regularly achieve a 95 to 99 percent word recognition rate.

Two examples of continuous speech recognition software for word processing are NaturallySpeaking by Dragon Systems and ViaVoice by IBM. Minimum requirements are a 133 MHz Pentium class microprocessor, 32 MB of RAM, an industry standard sound card, and 50 MB of available hard disk capacity. The products have 30,000-word vocabularies expandable to 60,000 words, and sell for less than $200. Training to 95 percent accuracy takes only a few hours. Longer use, faster processors, and more memory make 99 percent accuracy possible [4].

Figure 2.23

Continuous speech recognition software enables voice input for word processing, E-mail, web browsing, and other applications.

Courtesy of Andrea Electronics.

Voice recognition devices in work situations allow operators to perform data entry without using their hands to key in data or instructions and to provide faster and more accurate input. For example, manufacturers use voice recognition systems for the inspection, inventory, and quality control of a variety of products; and airlines and parcel delivery companies use them for voice-directed sorting of baggage and parcels. Voice recognition can also help you operate your computer's operating systems and software packages through voice input of data and commands. For example, such software can be voice-enabled so you can send E-mail and surf the World Wide Web via voice recognition [13].

Speaker-independent voice recognition systems, which allow a computer to understand a few words from a voice it has never heard before, are being built into products and used in a growing number of applications. Examples include *voice-messaging computers*, which use voice recognition and voice response software to verbally guide an end user through the steps of a task in many kinds of activities. Typically, they enable computers to respond to verbal and Touch-Tone input over the telephone. Examples of applications include computerized telephone call switching, telemarketing surveys, bank pay-by-phone bill-paying services, stock quotations services, university registration systems, and customer credit and account balance inquiries.

Optical Scanning

Few people understand how much scanners can improve a computer system and make your work easier. Their function is to get documents into your computer with a minimum of time and hassle, transforming just about anything on paper—a letter, a logo, or a photograph—into the digital format that your PC can make sense of. Scanners can be a big help in getting loads of paper off your desk and into your PC [7].

Optical scanning devices read text or graphics and convert them into digital input for your computer. Thus, optical scanning enables the direct entry of data from source documents into a computer system. For example, you can use a compact desktop scanner to scan pages of text and graphics into your computer for desktop publishing and web publishing applications. Or you can scan documents of all kinds into your system and organize them into folders as part of a *document management* library system for easy reference or retrieval.

There are many types of optical scanners, but they all employ photoelectric devices to scan the characters being read. Reflected light patterns of the data are converted into electronic impulses that are then accepted as input into the computer system. Compact desktop scanners have become very popular due to their low cost and ease of use with personal computer systems. However, larger, more expensive *flatbed scanners* are faster and provide higher resolution color scanning. See Figure 2.24.

The credit card billing operations of credit card companies, banks, and oil companies use a form of optical scanning called **optical character recognition** (OCR). OCR scanners read the characters and codes on credit card receipts, utility bills, insurance premiums, airline tickets, and other documents. OCR scanners are also used to automatically sort mail, score tests, and process a wide variety of forms in business and government.

Devices such as handheld optical scanning **wands** are frequently used to read OCR coding on merchandise tags and other media. Many business applications involve reading *bar coding*, a code that utilizes bars to represent characters. One common example is the Universal Product Code (UPC) bar coding that you see on packages of food items and many other products. For example, the automated checkout scanners found in supermarkets read UPC bar coding. Supermarket scanners emit laser beams that are

A compact desktop scanner.

Courtesy of Hewlett-Packard Company.

reflected off a UPC bar code. The reflected image is converted to electronic impulses that are sent to the in-store computer, where they are matched with pricing information. Pricing information is returned to the terminal, visually displayed, and printed on a receipt for the customer. See Figure 2.25.

Other Input Technologies

Magnetic stripe technology is a familiar form of data entry that helps computers read credit cards. The iron oxide coating of the magnetic stripe on the back of such cards can hold about 200 bytes of information. Customer account numbers can be recorded on the mag stripe so it can be read by bank ATMs, credit card authorization terminals, and many other types of magnetic stripe readers.

Smart cards that embed a microprocessor chip and several kilobytes of memory into debit, credit, and other cards are popular in Europe, and becoming available in the

Using an optical scanning wand to read bar coding of product data.

Douglas T. Hesney/The Stock Market.

United States. One example is Holland, where over 8 million smart debit cards have been issued by Dutch banks. Smart debit cards enable you to store a cash balance on the card and electronically transfer some of it to others to pay for small items and services. The balance on the card can be replenished in ATMs or other terminals.

The smart debit cards used in Holland feature a microprocessor and either 8 or 16 kilobytes of memory, plus the usual magnetic stripe. The smart cards are widely used to make payments in parking meters, vending machines, newsstands, pay telephones, and retail stores [6].

Digital cameras represent another fast-growing set of input technologies. Digital still cameras and digital video cameras (digital camcorders) enable you to shoot, store, and download still photos or full motion video with audio into your PC. Then you can use image-editing software to edit and enhance the digitized images and include them in newsletters, reports, multimedia presentations, and web pages [3].

The computer systems of the banking industry can magnetically read checks and deposit slips using **magnetic ink character recognition** (MICR) technology. Computers can thus sort and post checks to the proper checking accounts. Such processing is possible because the identification numbers of the bank and the customer's account are preprinted on the bottom of the checks with an iron oxide–based ink. The first bank receiving a check after it has been written must encode the amount of the check in magnetic ink on the check's lower right-hand corner. The MICR system uses 14 characters (the 10 decimal digits and 4 special symbols) of a standardized design. Equipment known as *reader-sorters* read a check by first magnetizing the magnetic ink characters and then sensing the signal induced by each character as it passes a reading head. In this way, data are electronically captured by the bank's computer system.

Output Technologies and Trends

Computers provide information to you in a variety of forms. Figure 2.26 shows you the trends in output media and methods that have developed over the generations of computing. As you can see, video displays and printed documents have been, and still are, the most common forms of output from computer systems. But other natural and attractive output technologies such as **voice response** systems and multimedia output are increasingly found along with video displays in business applications.

For example, you have probably experienced the voice and audio output generated by speech and audio microprocessors in a variety of consumer products. Voice messaging software enables PCs and servers in voice mail and messaging systems to interact with you through voice responses. And of course, multimedia output is common on the web sites of the Internet and corporate intranets.

Figure 2.26

Output technology trends. Note the trend from paper documents to more natural forms of video, audio, and multimedia output.

	First Generation	Second Generation	Third Generation	Fourth Generation	Fifth Generation?
OUTPUT MEDIA/ METHOD	Punched Cards Printed Reports and Documents	Punched Cards Printed Reports and Documents	Printed Reports and Documents Video Displays	Video Displays Audio Responses Printed Reports and Documents	Video Displays Voice Responses Hyperlinked Multimedia Documents
TREND: Toward Direct Output Methods That Communicate Naturally, Quickly, and Clearly.					

Video Output

Of all the peripherals you can purchase for your system, a [video] monitor is the one addition that can make the biggest difference. Forget about faster processors, bigger hard drives, and the like. The fact is, the monitor is the part of your system you spend the most time interacting with . . . Invest in a quality monitor, and you'll be thankful every time you turn on your computer [7].

Video displays are the most common type of computer output. Most desktop computers rely on **video monitors** that use a *cathode ray tube* (CRT) technology similar to the picture tubes used in home TV sets. Usually, the clarity of the video display depends on the type of video monitor you use and the graphics circuit board installed in your computer. These can provide a variety of graphics modes of increasing capability. A high-resolution, flicker-free monitor is especially important if you spend a lot of time viewing multimedia on CDs or the Web, or the complex graphical displays of many software packages.

The biggest use of **liquid crystal displays** (LCDs) is to provide a visual display capability for portable microcomputers and PDAs, though the use of "flat panel" LCD video monitors for desktop PC systems is growing. LCD displays need significantly less electric current and provide a thin, flat display. Advances in technology such as *active matrix* and *dual scan* capabilities have improved the color and clarity of LCD displays. See Figure 2.27.

Figure 2.27

Using a flat panel LCD video monitor for a desktop PC system.

Courtesy of Toshiba Image Bank.

Figure 2.28

An inkjet printer produces high-quality printed output.

Courtesy of Diner's Club International.

Printed Output

Printing information on paper is still the most common form of output after video displays. Thus, most personal computer systems rely on an inkjet or laser printer to produce permanent (hard copy) output in high-quality printed form. Printed output is still a common form of business communications, and is frequently required for legal documentation. Thus, computers can produce printed reports and correspondence, documents such as sales invoices, payroll checks, bank statements, and printed versions of graphic displays.

Inkjet printers, which spray ink onto a page one line at a time, have become the most popular, low-cost printers for microcomputer systems. They are quiet, produce several pages per minute of high-quality output, and can print both black-and-white and high-quality color graphics. **Laser printers** use an electrostatic process similar to a photocopying machine to produce many pages per minute of high-quality black-and-white output. More expensive color laser printers and multifunction inkjet and laser models that print, fax, scan, and copy are other popular choices for business offices. See Figure 2.28.

Storage Trends and Trade-Offs

Data and information must be stored until needed using a variety of storage methods. For example, many people and organizations still rely on paper documents stored in filing cabinets as a major form of storage media. However, you and other computer users are more likely to depend on the memory circuits and secondary storage devices of computer systems to meet your storage requirements. Figure 2.29 illustrates major trends in primary and secondary storage methods. Progress in very-large-scale integration (VLSI), which packs millions of memory circuit elements on tiny semiconductor memory chips, is responsible for continuing increases in the main-memory capacity of computers. Secondary storage capacities are also escalating into the billions and trillions of characters, due to advances in magnetic and optical media.

There are many types of storage media and devices. Figure 2.30 illustrates the speed, capacity, and cost relationships of several alternative primary and secondary storage media. Note the cost/speed/capacity trade-offs as one moves from semiconductor

Figure 2.29   Major trends in primary and secondary storage media.

	First Generation	Second Generation	Third Generation	Fourth Generation	Fifth Generation?	
PRIMARY STORAGE	Magnetic Drum	Magnetic Core	Magnetic Core	LSI Semiconductor Memory Chips	VLSI Semiconductor Memory Chips	
TREND: Toward Large Capacities Using Smaller Microelectronic Circuits.						
SECONDARY STORAGE	Magnetic Tape Magnetic Drum	Magnetic Tape Magnetic Disk	Magnetic Disk Magnetic Tape	Magnetic Disk Optical Disk Magnetic Tape	Optical Disk Magnetic Disk	
TREND: Toward Massive Capacities Using Magnetic and Optical Media.						

memories to magnetic disks, to optical disks, and to magnetic tape. High-speed storage media cost more per byte and provide lower capacities. Large-capacity storage media cost less per byte but are slower. This is why we have different kinds of storage media.

However, all storage media, especially memory chips and magnetic disks, continue to increase in speed and capacity and decrease in cost. Developments like automated high-speed cartridge assemblies have given faster access times to magnetic tape, and the speed of optical disk drives continues to increase.

Note in Figure 2.30 that semiconductor memories are used mainly for primary storage, though they are sometimes used as high-speed secondary storage devices. Magnetic disk and tape and optical disk devices, on the other hand, are used as secondary storage devices to greatly enlarge the storage capacity of computer systems. Also, since most primary storage circuits use RAM (random access memory) chips, which lose their contents when electrical power is interrupted, secondary storage devices provide a more permanent type of storage media.

Computer Storage Fundamentals

Data are processed and stored in a computer system through the presence or absence of electronic or magnetic signals in the computer's circuitry or in the media it uses. This is called a "two-state" or **binary representation** of data, since the computer and the media can exhibit only two possible states or conditions. For example, transistors and other semiconductor circuits are either in a conducting or nonconducting state.

Figure 2.30

Storage media cost, speed, and capacity trade-offs. Note how cost increases with faster access speeds, but decreases with the increased capacity of storage media.

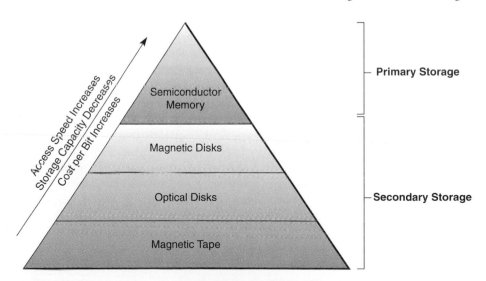

Figure 2.31

Examples of ASCII computer code.

Character	ASCII Code	Character	ASCII Code
0	00110000	I	01001001
1	00110001	J	01001010
2	00110010	K	01001011
3	00110011	L	01001100
4	00110100	M	01001101
5	00110101	N	01001110
6	00110110	O	01001111
7	00110111	P	01010000
8	00111000	Q	01010001
9	00111001	R	01010010
A	01000001	S	01010011
B	01000010	T	01010100
C	01000011	U	01010101
D	01000100	V	01010110
E	01000101	W	01010111
F	01000110	X	01011000
G	01000111	Y	01011001
H	01001000	Z	01011010

Media such as magnetic disks and tapes indicate these two states by having magnetized spots whose magnetic fields have one of two different directions, or polarities. This binary characteristic of computer circuitry and media is what makes the binary number system the basis for representing data in computers. Thus, for electronic circuits, the conducting (ON) state represents the number one, while the nonconducting (OFF) state represents the number zero. For magnetic media, the magnetic field of a magnetized spot in one direction represents a one, while magnetism in the other direction represents a zero.

The smallest element of data is called a **bit,** or binary digit, which can have a value of either zero or one. The capacity of memory chips is usually expressed in terms of bits. A **byte** is a basic grouping of bits that the computer operates as a single unit. Typically, it consists of eight bits and represents one character of data in most computer coding schemes. Thus, the capacity of a computer's memory and secondary storage devices is usually expressed in terms of bytes. Computer codes such as ASCII (American Standard Code for Information Interchange) use various arrangements of bits to form bytes that represent the numbers zero through nine, the letters of the alphabet, and many other characters. See Figure 2.31.

Storage capacities are frequently measured in **kilobytes** (KB), **megabytes** (MB), **gigabytes** (GB), or **terabytes** (TB). Although kilo means 1,000 in the metric system, the computer industry uses K to represent 1,024 (or 2^{10}) storage positions. Therefore, a capacity of 10 megabytes, for example, is really 10,485,760 storage positions, rather than 10 million positions. However, such differences are frequently disregarded in order to simplify descriptions of storage capacity. Thus, a megabyte is roughly 1 million bytes of storage, while a gigabyte is roughly 1 billion bytes and a terabyte represents about 1 trillion bytes.

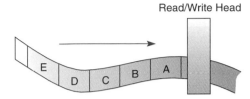

Figure 2.32 Sequential versus direct access storage. Magnetic tape is a typical sequential access medium. Magnetic disks are typical direct access storage devices.

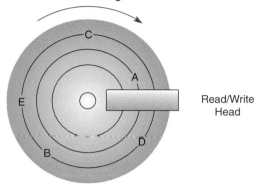

Direct and Sequential Access

Primary storage media such as semiconductor memory chips are called **direct access** or random access memories (RAM). Magnetic disk devices are frequently called direct access storage devices (DASDs). On the other hand, media such as magnetic tape cartridges are known as **sequential access** devices.

The terms *direct access* and *random access* describe the same concept. They mean that an element of data or instructions (such as a byte or word) can be directly stored and retrieved by selecting and using any of the locations on the storage media. They also mean that each storage position (1) has a unique address and (2) can be individually accessed in approximately the same length of time without having to search through other storage positions. For example, each memory cell on a microelectronic semiconductor RAM chip can be individually sensed or changed in the same length of time. Also any data record stored on a magnetic or optical disk can be accessed directly in approximately the same time period. See Figure 2.32.

Sequential access storage media such as magnetic tape do not have unique storage addresses that can be directly addressed. Instead, data must be stored and retrieved using a sequential or serial process. Data are recorded one after another in a predetermined sequence (such as in numeric order) on a storage medium. Locating an individual item of data requires searching the recorded data on the tape until the desired item is located.

Semiconductor Memory

Memory is the coalman to the CPU's locomotive: For maximum PC performance, it must keep the processor constantly stoked with instructions. Faster CPUs call for larger and faster memories, both in the cache where data and instructions are stored temporarily, and in the main memory [7].

The primary storage (main memory) of your computer consists of microelectronic **semiconductor memory** chips. Memory chips with capacities of 4 million bits (4 megabits) and 16 megabits are now common. Plug-in memory circuit boards containing 16 or 32 megabytes or more of memory chips can be added to your PC to increase its memory capacity. Specialized memory can help improve your computer's performance. Examples include external cache memory of 256 or 512 kilobytes to help your microprocessor work faster, or a video graphics accelerator card with 2 megabytes or more of RAM for faster and clearer video performance. Removable credit-card-size and smaller "flash memory" RAM cards can also provide several megabytes of erasable direct access storage for PDAs or handheld PCs.

Some of the major attractions of semiconductor memory are its small size, great speed, and shock and temperature resistance. One major disadvantage of most semi-conductor memory is its **volatility.** Uninterrupted electric power must be supplied or the contents of memory will be lost. Therefore, emergency transfer to other devices or standby electrical power (through battery packs or emergency generators) is required if data are to be saved. Another alternative is to permanently "burn in" the contents of semiconductor devices so that they cannot be erased by a loss of power.

Thus, there are two basic types of semiconductor memory: random access memory (RAM) and read only memory (ROM).

- **RAM: random access memory.** These memory chips are the most widely used primary storage medium. Each memory position can be both sensed (read) and changed (written), so it is also called read/write memory. This is a volatile memory.

- **ROM: read only memory.** Nonvolatile random access memory chips are used for permanent storage. ROM can be read but not erased or overwritten. Frequently used control instructions in the control unit and programs in primary storage (such as parts of the operating system) can be permanently burned in to the storage cells during manufacture. This is sometimes called *firmware*. Variations include PROM (programmable read only memory) and EPROM (erasable programmable read only memory) that can be permanently or temporarily programmed after manufacture.

Magnetic Disk Storage

Multi-gigabyte magnetic disk drives aren't extravagant, considering that full-motion video files, voice clips, and photo-quality images can consume colossal amounts of disk space in a blink [7].

Magnetic disks are the most common form of secondary storage for your computer system. That's because they provide fast access and high storage capacities at a reasonable cost. Magnetic disk drives contain metal disks that are coated on both sides with an iron oxide recording material. Several disks are mounted together on a vertical shaft, which typically rotates the disks at speeds of 3,600 to 7,600 revolutions per minute (rpm). Electromagnetic read/write heads are positioned by access arms between the slightly separated disks to read and write data on concentric, circular tracks. Data are recorded on tracks in the form of tiny magnetized spots to form the binary digits of common computer codes. Thousands of bytes can be recorded on each track, and there are several hundred data tracks on each disk surface, thus providing you with billions of storage positions for your software and data. See Figure 2.33.

Types of Magnetic Disks

There are several types of magnetic disk arrangements, including removable disk cartridges as well as fixed disk units. Removable disk devices are popular because they are transportable and can be used to store backup copies of your data offline for convenience and security.

- **Floppy disks,** or magnetic diskettes, consist of polyester film disks covered with an iron oxide compound. A single disk is mounted and rotates freely inside a protective flexible or hard plastic jacket, which has access openings to accommodate the read/write head of a disk drive unit. The 3 $\frac{1}{2}$-inch floppy disk, with capacities

Figure 2.33 Magnetic disk media: A hard magnetic disk drive and a 3 ½-inch floppy disk.

Courtesy of Quantum.

© Eric Kamp/Index Stock Photography, Inc.

of 1.44 megabytes, is the most widely used version, with a newer LS-120 technology offering 120 megabytes of storage.

- **Hard disk drives** combine magnetic disks, access arms, and read/write heads into a sealed module. This allows higher speeds, greater data recording densities, and closer tolerances within a sealed, more stable environment. Fixed or removable disk cartridge versions are available. Capacities of hard drives range from several hundred megabytes to gigabytes of storage.

- **RAID.** Disk arrays of interconnected microcomputer hard disk drives have replaced large-capacity mainframe disk drives to provide many gigabytes of online storage. Known as RAID (redundant arrays of independent disks), they combine from 6 to more than 100 small hard disk drives and their control microprocessors into a single unit. RAID units provide large capacities with high access speeds since data are accessed in parallel over multiple paths from many disks. RAID units also provide a *fault tolerant* capability, since their redundant design offers multiple copies of data on several disks. If one disk fails, data can be recovered from backup copies automatically stored on other disks.

Magnetic Tape Storage

Tape storage is moving beyond backup. Disk subsystems provide the fastest response time for mission-critical data. But the sheer amount of data users need to access these days as part of huge enterprise applications, such as data warehouses, requires affordable [magnetic tape] storage [14].

Magnetic tape is still being used as a secondary storage medium in business applications. The read/write heads of magnetic tape drives record data in the form of magnetized spots on the iron oxide coating of the plastic tape. Magnetic tape devices include tape reels and cartridges in mainframes and midrange systems, and small cassettes or cartridges for PCs. Magnetic tape cartridges have replaced tape reels in many applications, and can hold over 200 megabytes.

One growing business application of magnetic tape involves the use of high-speed 36-track magnetic tape cartridges in robotic automated drive assemblies that can directly access hundreds of cartridges. These devices provide lower-cost storage to supplement magnetic disks to meet massive data warehouse and other online business storage requirements. Other major applications for magnetic tape include long-term *archival* storage and backup storage for PCs and other systems [14].

Optical Disk Storage

CD-ROM technology has become a necessity. Most software companies will soon stop distributing their elephantine programs on floppies altogether. Many corporations are now rolling their own CDs to distribute product and corporate information that once filled bookshelves [7].

Optical disks are a fast-growing storage medium. The version for use with microcomputers is called **CD-ROM** (compact disk–read only memory). CD-ROM technology uses 12-centimeter (4.7-inch) compact disks (CDs) similar to those used in stereo music systems. Each disk can store more than 600 megabytes. That's the equivalent of over 400 1.44 megabyte floppy disks or more than 300,000 double-spaced pages of text. A laser records data by burning permanent microscopic pits in a spiral track on a master disk from which compact disks can be mass produced. Then CD-ROM disk drives use a laser device to read the binary codes formed by those pits.

CD-R (compact disk–recordable) is another optical disk technology. It enables computers with CD-R disk drive units to record their own data once on a CD, then be able to read the data indefinitely. The major limitation of CD-ROM and CD-R disks is that recorded data cannot be erased. However, **CD-RW** (CD-rewritable) optical disk systems have now become available that record and erase data by using a laser to heat a microscopic point on the disk's surface. In CD-RW versions using magneto-optical technology, a magnetic coil changes the spot's reflective properties from one direction to another, thus recording a binary one or zero. A laser device can then read the binary codes on the disk by sensing the direction of reflected light.

Optical disk capacities and capabilities have increased dramatically with the emergence of an optical disk technology called **DVD** (digital video disk or digital versatile disk), which can hold from 3.0 to 8.5 gigabytes of multimedia data on each side of a compact disk. The large capacities and high quality images and sound of DVD technology are expected to eventually replace CD-ROM and CD-RW technologies for data storage, and promise to accelerate the use of DVD drives for multimedia products that can be used in both computers and home entertainment systems. See Figure 2.34.

Business Applications

One of the major uses of optical disks in mainframe and midrange systems is in **image processing,** where long-term *archival storage* of historical files of document images must be maintained. Mainframe and midsize computer versions of optical disks use 12-inch plastic disks with capacities of several gigabytes, with up to 20 disks held in *jukebox* drive units. Financial institutions, among others, are using optical scanners to capture digitized document images and store them on **WORM** (write once, read many) versions of such optical disks as an alternative to microfilm media.

One of the major business uses of CD-ROM disks for personal computers is to provide a publishing medium for fast access to reference materials in a convenient, compact form. This includes catalogs, directories, manuals, periodical abstracts, part listings, and statistical databases of business and economic activity. Interactive multimedia applications in business, education, and entertainment are another major use of CD-ROM disks. The large storage capacities of CD-ROM are a natural choice for computer video games, educational videos, multimedia encyclopedias, and advertising presentations.

Thus, optical disks have become a popular storage medium for image processing and multimedia business applications, and they appear to be a promising alternative to magnetic disks and tape for very large *mass storage* capabilities for enterprise

Figure 2.34

DVD optical disk technology dramatically increases the capacity and quality of multimedia, software, and data storage.

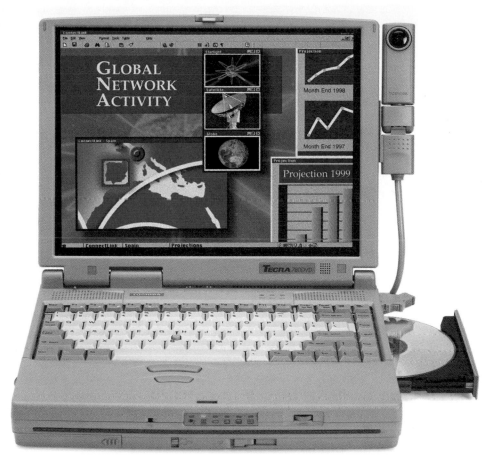

Courtesy of Toshiba Image Bank.

computing systems. However, rewritable optical technologies are still being perfected. Also, most optical disk devices are significantly slower and more expensive (per byte of storage) than magnetic disk devices. So optical disk systems are not expected to displace magnetic disk technology in the near future for most business applications.

Summary

- **Computer Systems.** Major types and trends in computer systems are summarized in Figures 2.2 and 2.3. A computer is a system of information processing components that perform input, processing, output, storage, and control functions. Its hardware components include input and output devices, a central processing unit (CPU), and primary and secondary storage devices. The major functions and hardware in a computer system are summarized in Figure 2.15.

- **Microcomputer Systems.** Microcomputers are used as personal computers, network computers, personal digital assistants, professional workstations, technical workstations, and network servers. Like most computer systems today, microcomputers are interconnected in a variety of telecommunications networks. This typically includes local area networks, client/server networks, intranets and extranets, the Internet, and other global networks. PCs are also increasingly available with built-in multimedia capabilities that enable them to provide or create video, audio, and other multimedia presentations.

- **Other Computer Systems.** Midrange computers are increasingly used as powerful network servers, and for many multiuser business data processing and scientific applications. Mainframe computers are larger and more powerful than most midsize computers. They are usually faster, have more memory capacity, and can support more input/output and secondary storage devices. They are designed to handle the information processing needs of large organizations with many customers and employees, or with complex computational problems. Supercomputers are a special category of extremely powerful mainframe computer systems designed for massive computational assignments.

- **Peripheral devices.** Refer to Figures 2.35 and 2.36 for summaries of the functions, characteristics, and capabilities of peripheral devices for input, output, and storage discussed in this chapter.

Figure 2.35

A summary of important input/output methods. Note especially the advantages and disadvantages of each method in providing hardware support of the user interface.

Peripheral Equipment	Media	Primary Functions	Comments
Video display terminals	None	Keyboard input and video output	Conventional and inexpensive, but limited display capacity and no hard copy
Printers	Paper	Printed output of paper reports and documents	Hard copy, but inconvenient and bulky; many printers are relatively slow
Pointing devices	None	Input by mouse, trackball, pointing stick, touchpad, pen, and touch screen	Input devices are easy to use and inexpensive, but may have limited applications and software
Voice input/ output devices	None	Voice input and output	Easiest I/O but is slow, has limited vocabulary, and has accuracy problems
Optical scanners	Paper documents	Direct input from written or printed documents	Direct input from paper documents, but some limitations on input format
Magnetic ink character recognition (MICR) readers	MICR paper documents	Direct input of MICR documents	Fast, high-reliability reading, but documents must be preprinted and the character set is limited

Figure 2.36

A summary of important computer storage methods. Note the advantages and disadvantages of each method.

Peripheral Equipment	Media	Primary Functions	Comments
Magnetic disk drive	Hard disk Disk cartridge	Secondary storage (direct access) and input/output	Large capacity, fast, direct access storage device (DASD), low cost/byte
Floppy disk drive	Magnetic diskette	Secondary storage (direct access) and input/output	Small, inexpensive, and convenient, but slower and smaller capacity than hard drives
Magnetic tape drive	Magnetic tape cassette and cartridge	Secondary storage (sequential access), input/output, and disk backup	Inexpensive, large capacity, with a fast transfer rate, but primarily sequential access
Optical disk drive	Optical disk: CD-ROM, WORM, CD-R, CD-RW, and DVD	Secondary storage (direct access) and archival storage	Large capacity, high-quality storage of data, text, images audio, and video. Still is primarily a read-only medium

Key Terms and Concepts

These are the key terms and concepts of this chapter. The page number of their first explanation is given in parentheses.

1. Arithmetic-logic unit (63)
2. Binary representation (77)
3. Central processing unit (62)
4. Computer system (60)
5. Computer terminal (56)
6. Control unit (63)
7. Digital cameras (74)
8. Direct access (79)
9. Downsizing (52)
10. Generations of computing (50)
11. Liquid crystal displays (75)
12. Magnetic disk storage (80)
    a. Floppy disk (80)
    b. Hard disk (81)
    c. RAID (81)
13. Magnetic ink character recognition (74)
14. Magnetic stripe (73)
15. Magnetic tape (81)
16. Mainframe computer (58)

17. Microcomputer (52)
18. Microprocessor (52)
19. Midrange computer (57)
20. Minicomputer (52)
21. Multimedia computer systems (55)
22. Multiple processors (63)
23. Network computer (55)
24. Network server (53)
25. Offline (68)
26. Online (68)
27. Optical character recognition (72)
28. Optical disk storage (82)
    a. CD ROM
    b. CD-R
    c. CD-RW
    d. DVD
    e. WORM disks
29. Optical scanning (72)

30. Pen-based computing (70)
31. Peripheral devices (68)
32. Personal digital assistant (53)
33. Pointing devices (69)
    a. Electronic mouse (69)
    b. Pointing stick (70)
    c. Touchpad (70)
    d. Trackball (70)
34. Primary storage unit (63)
35. Printers (76)
36. Secondary storage device (63)
37. Semiconductor memory (79)
    a. RAM (80)
    b. ROM (80)
38. Sequential access (79)
39. Smart cards (73)
40. Storage capacity elements (78)
    a. Bit
    b. Byte

c. Kilobyte

d. Megabyte

e. Gigabyte

f. Terabyte

41. Storage media trade-offs (76)

42. Supercomputer (59)

43. Time elements (64)

a. Millisecond

b. Microsecond

c. Nanosecond

d. Picosecond

44. Touch-sensitive screen (70)

45. Trends in computers (50)

46. Video output (75)

47. Voice recognition (71)

48. Voice response (74)

49. Volatility (80)

50. Wand (72)

51. Workstation (53)

Review Quiz

Match one of the previous key terms and concepts with one of the following brief examples or definitions. Try to find the best fit for answers that seem to fit more than one term or concept. Defend your choices.

_____ 1. Computers will become smaller, faster, more reliable, easier to use, and less costly.

_____ 2. Major stages in the development of computing.

_____ 3. A computer is a combination of components that perform input, processing, output, storage, and control functions.

_____ 4. Contains the arithmetic-logic unit and control unit.

_____ 5. Performs computations and comparisons.

_____ 6. Interprets instructions and directs processing.

_____ 7. The memory of a computer.

_____ 8. Magnetic disks and tape and optical disks perform this function.

_____ 9. Input/output and secondary storage devices for a computer system.

_____ 10. Connected to and controlled by a CPU.

_____ 11. Separate from and not controlled by a CPU.

_____ 12. Results from the presence or absence or change in direction of electric current, magnetic fields, or light rays in computer circuits and media.

_____ 13. The central processing unit of a microcomputer.

_____ 14. Can be a desktop or portable computer and a single or multiuser unit.

_____ 15. A computer category between microcomputers and mainframes.

_____ 16. A computer that can handle the information processing needs of large organizations.

_____ 17. Handheld microcomputers for communications and personal information management.

_____ 18. Low-cost networked microcomputers for use with the Internet and corporate intranets.

_____ 19. Photos or full motion video can be captured and downloaded to your PC for digital image processing.

_____ 20. A computer with several CPUs is an example.

_____ 21. A computer that manages network communications and resources.

_____ 22. The most powerful type of computer.

_____ 23. A magnetic tape technology for credit cards.

_____ 24. One billionth of a second.

_____ 25. Roughly one billion characters of storage.

_____ 26. Includes electronic mice, trackballs, pointing sticks, and touchpads.

_____ 27. You can write on the pressure-sensitive LCD screen of handheld microcomputers with a pen.

_____ 28. Moving this along your desktop moves the cursor on the screen.

_____ 29. You can communicate with a computer by touching its display.

_____ 30. Produces hard copy output such as paper documents and reports.

_____ 31. Promises to be the easiest, most natural way to communicate with computers.

_____ 32. Capturing data by processing light reflected from images.

_____ 33. Optical scanning of bar codes and other characters.

_____ 34. Bank check processing uses this technology.

35. A debit card with an embedded microprocessor and memory is an example.

_____ 36. A device with a keyboard and a video display networked to a computer is a typical example.

_____ 37. Computer voice output.

_____ 38. Combining text, graphics, voice, and video in computer input and output.

_____ 39. A handheld device that reads bar coding.

_____ 40. Storage media cost, speed, and capacity differences.

_____ 41. You cannot erase the contents of these storage circuits.

_____ 42. The memory of most computers consists of these storage circuits.

_____ 43. The property that determines whether data are lost or retained when power fails.

_____ 44. Each position of storage can be accessed in approximately the same time.

_____ 45. Each position of storage can be accessed according to a predetermined order.

_____ 46. Microelectronic storage circuits on silicon chips.

_____ 47. Uses magnetic spots on metal or plastic disks.

_____ 48. Uses magnetic spots on plastic tape.

_____ 49. Uses a laser to read microscopic points on plastic disks.

_____ 50. Vastly increases the storage capacity and image and sound quality of optical disk technology.

Discussion Questions

1. Do you agree with the statement: "The network is the computer"? Why or why not?

2. What trends are occurring in the development and use of the major types of computer systems?

3. Refer to the Real World Case on The Mutual Group in the chapter. Why are most web sites hosted on a server or a network of servers instead of a mainframe?

4. Do you think that network computers (NCs) will replace personal computers (PCs) in many applications? Explain.

5. Are networks of PCs and servers making mainframe computers obsolete? Explain.

6. Refer to the Real World Case on ASD Catalogs and Ernst & Young in the chapter. What features and ca-

pabilities would you want in a business computer for yourself? Explain the reasons for your requirements.

7. What are several trends that are occurring in the development and use of peripheral devices? Why are these trends occurring?

8. Refer to the Real World Problem on emachines Inc. in the chapter. What is the size and composition of the market for computers, like the emachines? Explain.

9. What processor, memory, magnetic disk storage, and video display capabilities would you require for a personal computer that you would use for business purposes? Explain your choices.

10. What other peripheral devices and capabilities would you want to have for your business PC? Explain your choices.

Real World Problems

1. **AmeriServe and IBM: Installing Network Computers in Business**
Dallas-based AmeriServe Inc., one of the largest food distributors in the United States, has begun a pilot project that could lead to an installation of more than 25,000 Sun JavaStation network computers at the restaurants of its customers. These include some of the country's largest food chains, such as Burger King, Taco Bell, and KFC. If the pilot project is a success, AmeriServe will move quickly to roll out JavaStations

to its customers said Dennis Rees, vice president of marketing and information technology.

AmeriServe provides food for 37,000 restaurants in the United States, Canada, and Mexico. Only 14,000 of those use PCs to order food supplies in an automated way. The rest call in orders—an average of two to three times per week—at a cost to AmeriServe of $3 to $10 per call. Rees said a web-based system would cost about 80 percent less to host.

AmeriServe has rewritten its current ordering software in Java and plans to offer the new, browser-based application to customers soon. The application will let customers place orders, view any special pricing information, track what they ordered in the past, use past orders as a suggested order menu, and confirm receipt of their orders.

The current PC-based system is costly, Rees said, not only because the hardware requires more maintenance than a network computer but also because software updates and fixes must be done locally—something that's difficult to maintain in restaurants where technical expertise isn't a given. "We can roll out incremental enhancements to the software over the network and everyone will have access overnight," Rees said.

Meanwhile, IBM continues to aggressively market network computers (NC) and has recently cut two big deals—one with food-service giant Sysco Corp., the other with insurer American General Finance Inc.—for a total of nearly 15,000 machines. The companies plan to use the devices, which start at $499, in place of terminals, and hook them into powerful IBM servers. International Data Corp. (IDC) says a total of 504,000 network computers have been sold—analysts estimate that IBM has shipped about 250,000 of those.

IBM may have almost half of the slowly emerging NC market, but it still sells a lot more PCs. For example, Dow Chemical recently announced that it will spend more than $90 million over the next three years to lease 37,500 PCs from IBM. IDC estimates IBM shipped nearly 6 million desktop PCs in 1998.

a. Why do you think the use of network computers in business has grown a lot slower than its proponents had forecasted?

b. For what type of business situations would you recommend network computers instead of PCs?

Source: Adapted from April Jacobs, "JavaStation Finally Lands Pilot Customer," *Computerworld*, December 21, 1998, pp. 55–56. Copyright 1998 by Computerworld Inc., Framingham, MA 01701. Reprinted from *Computerworld*, and Ira Sager, "IBM Stands by Its PC Alternative," *Business Week*, January 18, 1999, p. 94B. Reprinted with special permission, copyright © 1999 by The McGraw-Hill Companies, Inc.

2. Van Waters & Rogers: Taking Servers and Mainframes into the Twenty-First Century
To see where servers and mainframes may be going in the twenty-first century, take a look at how Kirkland, Washington–based Van Waters & Rogers (VW&R) manages its transactions. No client/server networks here—VW&R runs its operation with a single mainframe and 20 Windows NT servers at the Kirkland headquarters, all networked together with PCs throughout the company. Why? Because it works well and saves money.

"I'm a fervent believer in the thin client model," says Gina Martinez, director of technology planning and operations for VW&R, the largest chemical distributor in North America. It employs 2,300 people working in more than 120 offices throughout the United States and Canada. "Our IT department doesn't have the budget to send people into the field to manage server operations," she says. "I think IT managers everywhere are now finding out that the costs of distributed client/server network operations are much higher than they had anticipated."

"You can spend money on servers and on software to manage distributed networks of servers and PCs," Martinez adds, "but I'd rather spend it on network bandwidth to connect PC users to the mainframe. It costs less, and we get essentially 100 percent availability with our system."

VW&R places high demands on its mainframe. In addition to supporting roughly three-quarters of a million transactions per day, the processor serves as the central management tool for 20 Windows NT servers handling a wide range of applications, including web servers and a data warehouse.

Just a few months ago, VW&R's previous mainframe had become chronically overloaded. Now with the installation of a new mainframe from Hitachi Data Systems, usage has dropped from over 100 percent capacity to 70 percent. "This means we're ready for any new growth opportunities," says Jim Enwall, a manager of technical support.

Martinez quotes a recent survey by the Gallup Organization which measured the average downtime for PC servers at 1.6 hours per week. For IBM S/390 class mainframes clustered in a parallel sysplex configuration, availability can be as high as 99.999 percent, or less than five minutes of downtime per year. So, if your goal is $365 \times 24 \times 7$ availability, no other approach can match the mainframe, says Martinez.

a. Do you agree with Gina Martinez's positions on mainframe networks versus client/server networks? Why or why not?

b. Why does VW&R need 20 Windows NT servers as well as its mainframe?

Source: Adapted from Eva Freeman, "Mainframes in the 21st Century," *Datamation*, January 1999, at www.datamation.com. © 1999 by Cahners Publishing Co.

3. emachines Inc.: The Business Case for Cheap PCs
To judge by all the attention it has garnered, Apple Computer Inc.'s sleek, colorful iMac might seem to be the most significant high-tech hit in recent years. Not necessarily. Another computer, introduced late in 1998 with almost no fanfare, is selling almost as

quickly as the iMac and may wind up playing a bigger role in the history of computing.

It's called an emachine. It's everything the iMac isn't: bland-looking, technically unsophisticated, and cheap. Very cheap. Some models cost $499, including monitor. That's half the price of the least expensive iMac.

And that has made all the difference. emachine has become one of the best-selling computer brands and a harbinger of an era when personal computers will be as cheap and commonplace as television sets.

"We're seeing the beginning of what I'll call a structural change in what PCs cost," said Stephen Dukker, chief executive of emachines, Inc., the United States–based, Korean-owned company that makes the computer.

A dramatic cut in the cost of PCs would transform the PC from a luxury into just another home appliance, making it affordable to nearly everyone. That was Microsoft's goal when it bought WebTV, a company that makes a $300 box that pumps the Internet into a TV set. Oracle Corp. also took a swing with its Network Computer for the home. Neither product has been warmly embraced by consumers.

But prices of computer parts such as processors, hard drives, and memory chips have plunged in recent years, even as these components become much more powerful. As a result, it is now possible to make a true personal computer that is about as cheap as a WebTV unit but powerful enough to meet the needs of the average user for Internet access, E-mail, and light computing chores.

For example, emachine's cheapest systems, the etower 300 series, are just $399 plus $100 for a 14-inch color monitor. That includes a Cyrix or AMD 300 MHz processor, a 2.1 gigabyte hard drive, CD-ROM and floppy disk drives, 56K modem, and Windows 98 and Microsoft Works. There's more, as well as $499 and $599 systems with better features. Check them out at the company web site at www.e4me.com.

Customers love the low price of the emachines, but retailers like Best Buy, Costco, and Office Depot also love them because they sell so fast. PCs have almost as short a shelf life as hamburger, and dealers lose money unless they can move the merchandise quickly.

Of course, cheap is not enough. The emachines have to work, and work they do. They're far from state-of-the-art machines; but the various models contain reliable low-end processors from National

Semiconductor and Advanced Micro Devices, as well as Intel's cut-rate Celeron chips. A built-in graphics chip comes from ATI Technology, one of the industry leaders, and hard drives are supplied by Seagate Technology and Korea's Samsung Electronics.

emachines has even announced that it will try to steal some of the iMac's success with a Wintel version that will mimic the iMac's unique styling. It will have a built-in monitor, a 333-MHz Celeron processor, a 3-GB hard drive, and 32 MB of memory, as well as a built-in floppy drive, which is missing from the iMac. The computer's most compelling feature is its price: emachines plans to sell it for less than $700, slightly more than half what Apple currently charges for the cheapest iMac.

Thus, emachines hopes to define the lowest price points and minimum system combinations that lead to customer demand and satisfaction in a vast and volatile market.

"Would I buy another one? You bet!" said Ruth Sams, a senior programmer at Florida State University. Sams beefed up the memory of her emachine to 96 megabytes from the standard 32 megabytes and put in a better graphics card, but figures she still saved money on the deal. Her emachine will soon be obsolete, but so what? "For $499, I'll just keep upgrading every year," she said.

Mark Freeman, an IBM employee in Longmont, Colorado, picked an emachine when he needed a second computer at home. "No system that IBM offers can touch the price," Freeman said.

Yet these computer-savvy buyers aren't the only customers. Dukker says that 56 percent of emachine buyers have never before owned a computer, and 35 percent of them have household incomes below $30,000. In his view, the emachine is tapping a whole new market, made up of people who could never before afford a computer.

a. Will the success of PCs like emachine create a large new segment of the PC market? Why or why not?

b. Should a business buy PCs like emachine? Would you? Would you recommend such PCs to others? Explain the reasons for your answers.

Source: Adapted from Hiawatha Bray, "emachine Puts Prices at the Lowest Level Yet," *Boston Globe*, February 7, 1999, p. A10; Brian Taptich, "How the iMac Will Really Matter," *Red Herring*, January 1999, pp. 19–20; Peter Burrows, "Fast, Cheap, and Ahead of the Pack," *Business Week*, April 5, 1999, pp. 36–37; and David Batterson, "Cheap Power Tower," *Wired*, March 1999, p. 147.

Application Exercises

1. Input Alternatives
Which method of input would you recommend for the following activities? Explain your choices. Refer to Figure 2.35 to help you.

a. Entering data from printed questionnaires.

b. Entering data from telephone surveys.

c. Entering data from bank checks.

d. Entering data from merchandise tags.

e. Entering data from engineering drawings.

2. Output Alternatives
Which method of output would you recommend for the following information products? Explain your choices. Refer to Figure 2.35 to help you.

a. Visual displays for portable microcomputers.

b. Legal documents.

c. Engineering drawings.

d. Financial results for top executives.

e. Responses for telephone transactions.

3. Storage Alternatives
Indicate which secondary storage medium you would use for each of the following storage tasks. Select from the choices on the right, using Figure 2.36 to help you.

a. Primary storage.

b. Large capacity, permanent storage.

c. Large capacity, fast direct access.

d. Large capacity for multimedia.

e. Inexpensive, portable direct access.

1. Magnetic hard disk

2. Floppy disk

3. Magnetic tape

4. Semiconductor memory

5. Optical disk

4. Pricing a Personal Computer
Assume that you are in the market for a personal computer to meet your needs as a student. Get prices from at least three suppliers for a system that would meet your needs. You should specify minimum requirements for your system and also identify at least three desired upgrades. You will want to get the prices for a basic system meeting your minimum requirements and the added cost of each desired upgrade. (Many companies selling computers on the Web quote prices in this way.)

The following example describes characteristics of a basic personal computer system and some common upgrades a user might want at the time this book was written. The prices shown were obtained from the web site of a popular PC supplier (such as www.dell.com or www.gateway.com):

Basic PC unit (equipped with a 400 megahertz processor, 64 megabytes of RAM, 6.4 gigabyte hard drive, 17-inch monitor 24 speed or faster CD-ROM drive)	$1,499
Upgrade options	
450 megahertz processor	$130
128 megabytes of RAM (64 megabytes additional)	$ 79
10 gigabyte hard drive	$ 40
19-inch monitor	$199

a. Define a set of specifications for a minimum system and for upgrades that would be of interest to you. (The items in the example should be modified to reflect changes in typical PC capabilities and your personal needs.) Based on these specifications, obtain price estimates from at least three PC suppliers for the base computer and upgrades you chose. You may get price estimates from web sites, PC magazines, or local vendors. (Your instructor may require you to get your price quotes from Internet sites and turn in a printout of your price quotes.)

b. Based on price quotes you obtained, create a spreadsheet that will allow you to compare the cost of your system from each of the vendors. Your spreadsheet should show both the price of the minimum system and the price with all of the upgrades added.

c. Using a word processor, write a brief report summarizing what you found and indicating which configuration and vendor you would choose. Be sure to discuss any nonprice factors that influenced your choice (warranty and service availability differences, for instance).

5. Price and Performance Trends for Computer Hardware
The table shows a set of price and capacity figures for common components of personal computers. Typical prices for microprocessors, random access memory (RAM), and hard disk storage are shown. The performance of typical components has increased substantially over time, so the speed (for the microprocessor) or the capacity (for the storage devices) is also listed.

Although there have been improvements in these components that are not reflected in these capacity measures, it is interesting to examine trends in these measurable characteristics.

a. Create a spreadsheet based on the figures in the table, including a new column for each component showing the price per unit of capacity. (Cost per megahertz of speed for microprocessors, and cost per megabyte of storage for RAM and hard disk devices.)

b. Create a set of graphs highlighting your results and illustrating trends in price per unit of performance (speed) or capacity.

c. Using a word processor, write a short paper discussing the trends you found. How long do you expect these trends to continue? Why?

	1989	1991	1993	1995	1997	1999
Microprocessor						
Speed (megahertz)	10	25	33	100	125	350
Cost	$245	$180	$125	$275	$250	$300
RAM chip						
Megabytes per chip	1	1	4	4	16	64
Cost	$640	$55	$140	$140	$97	$125
Hard disk device						
Megabytes per disk	40	105	250	540	2,000	8,000
Cost	$435	$480	$375	$220	$250	$220

Review Quiz Answers

1. 45	9. 31	17. 32	25. 40e	33. 27	41. 37b	49. 28
2. 10	10. 26	18. 23	26. 33	34. 13	42. 37a	50. 28d
3. 4	11. 25	19. 7	27. 30	35. 39	43. 49	
4. 3	12. 2	20. 22	28. 33a	36. 5	44. 8	
5. 1	13. 18	21. 24	29. 44	37. 48	45. 38	
6. 6	14. 17	22. 42	30. 35	38. 21	46. 37	
7. 34	15. 19	23. 14	31. 47	39. 50	47. 12	
8. 36	16. 16	24. 43c	32. 29	40. 41	48. 15	

Selected References

1. *Computerworld, PC Week, PC Magazine, PC World*, and *PC Today* are just a few examples of many good magazines for current information on computer systems hardware and its use in end user and enterprise applications.

2. The World Wide Web sites of computer manufacturers such as Apple Computer, Dell Computer, IBM, Hewlett-Packard, Compaq, and Sun Microsystems are good sources of information on computer hardware developments.

3. "Desktop Power." In Technology Buyer's Guide. *Fortune*, Winter 1999.

4. Devoney, Chris. "Look, Ma, Know Hands!" *Computerworld*, September 15, 1997.

5. "Dream Machines." In Technology Buyer's Guide. *Fortune*, Winter 1998.

6. Guyon, Janet. "Smart Plastic." *Fortune*, October 13, 1997.

7. "Hardware." In Technology Buyer's Guide. *Fortune*, Winter 1999.

8. "Home Theatre." In Technology Buyer's Guide. *Fortune*, Winter 1999.

9. Jacobs, April. "Net Computers End-Run PC Migration Costs." *Computerworld*, February 17, 1997.

10. Jacobs, April, and Lisa Picatrill. "Microsoft Now Says Thin Is In." *Computerworld*, April 14, 1997.

11. Kalish, David. "IBM Boosts Strength of Supercomputer That Beat Kasparov," *PC Today*, November 1997.

12. Kennedy, Ken, and others. "A Nationwide Parallel Computing Environment." *Communications of the ACM*, November 1997.

13. Kirkpatrick, David. "Ten Tech Trends You Can Bet On." *Fortune*, November 10, 1997.

14. Ouellette, Tim. "Tape Storage Put to New Enterprise Uses." *Computerworld*, November 10, 1997.

15. "Peripherals." In Technology Buyer's Guide. *Fortune*, Winter 1998.

16. Simpson, David. "Big Iron Roars." *Datamation*, July 1997.

17. Simpson, David. "New Applications Fuel Server Sales." *Datamation*, July 1997.

18. Zander, Ed. "Endquotes." *NetReady Adviser*, Winter 1997.

Introduction to

Computer Software

Chapter Highlights

Section I
Application Software: End User Applications

Introduction to Software

Real World Case: Egghead.com, Aspect Telecommunications, and Others: Windows NT/2000 Alternatives

Application Software for End Users

Software Suites and Integrated Packages

Web Browsers and More

Electronic Mail

Word Processing and Desktop Publishing

Electronic Spreadsheets

Database Management

Presentation Graphics and Multimedia

Personal Information Managers

Groupware

Section II
System Software: Computer System Management

System Software Overview

Real World Case: Jay Jacobs and Burlington Coat Factory: The Business Case for Linux and Open-Source Software

Operating Systems

Network Management Programs

Database Management Systems

Other System Management Programs

Programming Languages

Programming Packages

Learning Objectives

After reading and studying this chapter, you should be able to:

1. Describe several major trends occurring in computer software.

2. Give examples of several major types of application and system software.

3. Explain the purpose of several popular microcomputer software packages for end user productivity and collaborative computing.

4. Outline the functions of an operating system.

5. Describe the main uses of high-level, fourth-generation, object-oriented, and web-oriented languages.

6. Explain the functions of programming language editors and translators and other programming tools.

Section I

Application Software:
End User Applications

Introduction to Software

This chapter presents an overview of the major types of software you depend on as you work with computers and access computer networks. It discusses their characteristics and purposes and gives examples of their uses. Before we begin, let's look at an example of the changing world of software in business.

Analyzing Egghead.com, Aspect Telecommunications, and Others

Read the Real World Case on Egghead.com, Aspect Telecommunications, and Others on the next page. We can learn a lot about the business impact of changes in operating systems software from this example. See Figure 3.1

The performance limitations of Microsoft's Windows NT Server 4.0 and the long delay in the release of its Windows 2000 successor have opened the door to other software alternatives for many companies. These developments have made companies more determined to avoid being dependent on any one software provider, and thus have given new life to the Unix and Novell NetWare operating systems and IBM mainframes. In addition, such developments are promoting the creation of application software versions designed to run on several different operating systems. As Kathy Cruz of Aspect Telecommunications emphasized, this enables a company to buy application software based on business needs, not on the operating system it runs on.

Figure 3.1

Kathy Cruz, chief information officer at Aspect Telecommunications, says she buys application software based on what it does for her company, not what operating system it runs on.

Source: Eric Millette.

Egghead.com, Aspect Telecommunications, and Others: Windows NT/2000 Alternatives

Back in its earthbound days, Egghead Software Inc. was a Microsoft disciple. Not only did it sell hundreds of thousands of copies a year of Microsoft Windows and Microsoft Word and Excel application software in its 150 stores, but Egghead ran its business on the software, too. On November 21, 1998, Egghead left the fold. It completed its move to a cyberspace-only business, taking on the name Egghead.com Inc.

At 4:45 A.M., in the company's offices in Vancouver, Washington, a technician switched on the new web site—one powered not by Windows software but by Sun Microsystems computers and software. "We held our breath. Fifteen minutes later, we broke out the champagne," says Egghead Chief Technologist Tom Collins.

Egghead had decided that Microsoft's Windows NT operating system was simply not up to the task of running its web site. And it couldn't afford to wait around to see if the new industrial-strength version, Windows 2000, would arrive on time.

Microsoft has promised Win2000 will ship in 1999; but buyers are becoming downright skeptical. It is, after all, the biggest commercial software project ever undertaken, with 30 million lines of code—and that figure is growing daily. Now four years under development, Win2000 is an embarrassing two years behind schedule.

Windows 2000 is missing in action at just the wrong time. Today, corporations are rushing to rejigger their businesses to take full advantage of the Internet and are clamoring for ever-more-powerful servers. But Microsoft's top-selling and widely used Windows NT 4.0 just isn't up to the biggest jobs. Even Microsoft's own 30-million-member HotMail E-mail service still runs on a version of Unix more than a year after Microsoft bought the startup. And Earthlink, an Internet service provider with 1 million subscribers, recently rejected Windows NT and chose Sun's Solaris Unix, after it estimated that it would take five times as many people to maintain Microsoft servers because things tend to go wrong with them. Other companies are turning to freeware operating systems like Linux.

In many cases, customers are concluding that Windows NT 4.0 is simply not the best operating system for their big jobs, and are unwilling to wait for Windows 2000. That's partly because corporations are consolidating their data-processing tasks on a few huge central servers rather than scattering them across hundreds of machines. Paine Webber's brokerage business just made the switch to Unix after using both Unix and NT. The goal: to cut the costs of managing their global network by 66 percent, according to Senior Vice President John Furlong.

While Microsoft would have you believe that Windows NT is an all-purpose operating system, you have to narrow down what exactly you want NT to do for you. Experienced users say NT 4.0 works well as a database, messaging, and web platform. But for large-scale network deployment or mission-critical applications requiring a stable, scalable operating system, most companies still prefer Unix on their servers, or IBM mainframes.

"It's not an all-or-nothing game at this point," says Kathy Cruz, chief information officer at Aspect Telecommunications, a computer-telephony integration firm based in San Jose, California. "We have the luxury of putting Windows NT where it works and sticking with Unix or NetWare where it doesn't. We are lucky enough to be able to buy application software based on what it does for us rather than what operating system it runs on."

Thus, corporations are deciding not to lock themselves into any one maker's software. Even at Merrill Lynch & Co., which has a policy of adopting Windows NT aggressively, software engineers have designed trading application programs so they can be switched from one operating system to another. "We have to be diligent to protect from being overly dependent on any one company," says Vice President Anthony Pizi.

Case Study Questions

1. Why are companies like Egghead and EarthLink choosing to run their business applications on Unix or other operating systems instead of Windows NT, and not waiting for Windows 2000?

2. Why is Aspect Telecommunications able to buy business application software based on what it does for the business, rather than the operating system it runs on?

3. What business strategies could Microsoft use to recapture the former business momentum of Windows NT? What should Microsoft's competitors do to capitalize on their current business opportunity?

Source: Reprinted from Steve Hamm, Marcia Stepanek, Peter Burrows, and Andy Reinhardt, "Microsoft: How Vulnerable?" *Business Week*, February 22, 1999, pp. 60–64, by special permission, copyright © 1999 by The McGraw-Hill Companies, Inc.; and Christine Burns, "A Match Made in Heaven or Integration Hell?" in "Windows NT World," IDG Special Report, *PC World*, January 1999, pp. N18–20. Reprinted with permission of *PC World* Communications Inc.

Figure 3.2

An overview of computer software. Note the major types and examples of application and system software.

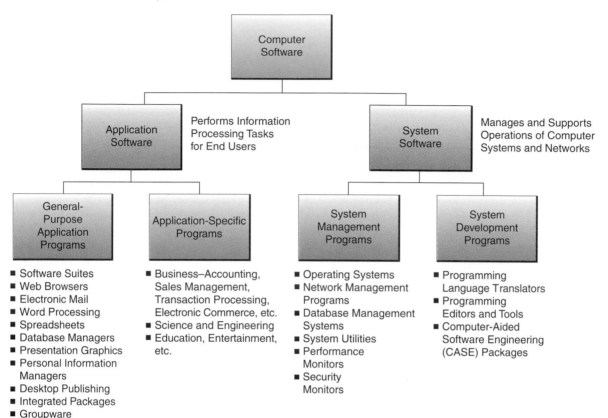

Computer Software

Application Software — Performs Information Processing Tasks for End Users

System Software — Manages and Supports Operations of Computer Systems and Networks

General-Purpose Application Programs

Application-Specific Programs

System Management Programs

System Development Programs

- Software Suites
- Web Browsers
- Electronic Mail
- Word Processing
- Spreadsheets
- Database Managers
- Presentation Graphics
- Personal Information Managers
- Desktop Publishing
- Integrated Packages
- Groupware

- Business–Accounting, Sales Management, Transaction Processing, Electronic Commerce, etc.
- Science and Engineering
- Education, Entertainment, etc.

- Operating Systems
- Network Management Programs
- Database Management Systems
- System Utilities
- Performance Monitors
- Security Monitors

- Programming Language Translators
- Programming Editors and Tools
- Computer-Aided Software Engineering (CASE) Packages

Let's begin our analysis of software by looking at an overview of the major types and functions of **application software** and **system software** available to computer users, shown in Figure 3.2. This figure summarizes the major categories of system and application software we will discuss in this chapter. Of course, this is a conceptual illustration. The types of software you will encounter depend primarily on the types of computers and networks you use, and on what specific tasks you want to accomplish.

Software Trends

Figure 3.3 emphasizes several major software trends. First, there has been a major trend away from custom-designed programs developed by the professional programmers of an organization. Instead, the trend is toward the use of off-the-shelf software packages acquired by end users from software vendors. This trend dramatically increased with the development of relatively inexpensive and easy-to-use application software packages and multipurpose *software suites* for microcomputers. The trend has accelerated recently, as software packages are designed with networking capabilities and collaboration features that optimize their usefulness for end users and workgroups on the Internet and corporate intranets and extranets.

Second, there has been a steady trend away from (1) technical, machine-specific programming languages using binary-based or symbolic codes, or (2) *procedural languages*, which use brief statements and mathematical expressions to specify the sequence of instructions a computer must perform. Instead, the trend is toward the use of a visual graphic interface for object-oriented programming, or toward nonprocedural *natural languages* for programming that are closer to human conversation. This

Figure 3.3 Trends in computer software. The trend in software is toward multipurpose, network-enabled, expert-assisted packages with natural language and graphical user interfaces.

	FIRST GENERATION	SECOND GENERATION	THIRD GENERATION	FOURTH GENERATION	FIFTH GENERATION?
Trend: Toward Easy-to-Use Multipurpose Network–Enabled Application Packages for Productivity and Collaboration					
Software Trends	User-Written Programs Machine Languages	Packaged Programs Symbolic Languages	Operating Systems High-Level Languages	Database Management Systems Fourth-Generation Languages Microcomputer Packages	Natural and Object-Oriented Languages Multipurpose Graphic-Interface Network-Enabled Expert-Assisted Packages
Trend: Toward Visual or Conversational Programming Languages and Tools					

trend accelerated with the creation of easy-to-use, nonprocedural *fourth-generation languages* (4GLs). It continues to grow as developments in object technology, graphics, and artificial intelligence produce natural language and graphical user interfaces that make both programming tools and software packages easier to use.

In addition, artificial intelligence features are built into many types of software packages. For example, software suites provide intelligent help features called *wizards* that help you perform common software functions like graphing parts of a spreadsheet or generating reports from a database. Other software packages use capabilities called *intelligent agents* to perform activities based on instructions from a user. For example, some electronic mail packages can use an intelligent agent capability to organize, send, and screen E-mail messages for you.

These major trends seem to be converging to produce a fifth generation of powerful, multipurpose, expert-assisted, and network-enabled software packages with natural language and graphical interfaces to support the productivity and collaboration of both end users and IS professionals.

Application Software for End Users

Figure 3.2 showed that application software includes a variety of programs that can be subdivided into general-purpose and application-specific categories. Thousands of **application-specific** software packages are available to support specific applications of end users in business and other fields. For example, application-specific packages in business support managerial, professional, and business uses such as transaction processing, decision support, accounting, sales management, investment analysis, and electronic commerce. Application-specific software for science and engineering plays a major role in the research and development programs of industry and the design of efficient production processes for high-quality products. Other software packages help end users with personal finance and home management, or provide a wide variety of entertainment and educational products.

General-purpose application programs are programs that perform common information processing jobs for end users. For example, word processing programs, spreadsheet programs, database management programs, and graphics programs are popular with microcomputer users for home, education, business, scientific, and many other purposes. Because they significantly increase the productivity of end users, they are sometimes known as *productivity packages*. Other examples include web browsers,

Programs	Microsoft Office	Lotus SmartSuite	Corel WordPerfect Office
Word Processor	Word	WordPro	WordPerfect
Spreadsheet	Excel	1–2–3	Quattro Pro
Presentation Graphics	PowerPoint	Freelance	Presentations
Database Manager	Access	Approach	Paradox
Personal Information Manager	Outlook	Organizer	Corel Central

electronic mail, and *groupware*, which help support communication and collaboration among workgroups and teams. We will briefly explain some of the most popular types of such packages in this section, and discuss several of them in more detail in later chapters.

Software Suites and Integrated Packages

Let's begin our discussion of popular general-purpose application software by looking at **software suites.** That's because the most widely used productivity packages come bundled together as software suites such as Microsoft Office, Lotus SmartSuite, and Corel WordPerfect Office. Examining their components gives us an overview of the important software tools that you can use to increase your productivity.

Figure 3.4 compares the basic programs that make up the top three software suites. Notice that each suite integrates software packages for word processing, spreadsheets, presentation graphics, database management, and personal information management. Microsoft, Lotus, and Corel bundle several other programs in each suite, depending on the version you select. Examples include programs for Internet access, web publishing, desktop publishing, voice recognition, financial management, electronic encyclopedias, and so on.

A software suite costs a lot less than the total cost of buying its individual packages separately. Another advantage is that all programs use a similar **graphical user interface** (GUI) of icons, tool and status bars, menus, and so on, which gives them the same look and feel, and makes them easier to learn and use. Software suites also share common tools, such as spell checkers and help wizards to increase their efficiency. Another big advantage of suites is that their programs are designed to work together seamlessly, and import each other's files easily, no matter which program you are using at the time. These capabilities make them more efficient and easier to use than using a variety of individual package versions.

Of course, putting so many programs and features together in one super-size package does have some disadvantages. Industry critics argue that many software suite features are never used by most end users. The suites take up a lot of disk space, from over 100 megabytes to over 150 megabytes, depending on which version or functions you install. So such software is sometimes derisively called *bloatware* by its critics. The cost of suites can vary from as low as $100 for a competitive upgrade to over $700 for a full version of some editions of the suites.

These drawbacks are one reason for the continued use of **integrated packages** like Microsoft Works, Lotus eSuite WorkPlace, Apple Works, and so on. Integrated packages combine some of the functions of several programs—word processing,

Figure 3.5

Using the Microsoft Works integrated package. It provides word processing, spreadsheet, file management, telecommunications, and graphics capabilities in one package.

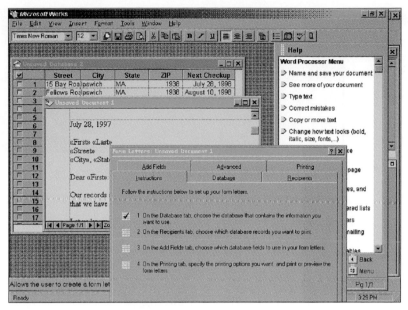

D. Moskowitz/Warm Boot.

spreadsheets, presentation graphics, database management, and so on—into one software package.

Because Works programs leave out many features and functions that are in individual packages and software suites, they cannot do as much as those packages do. However, they use a lot less disk space (less than 10 megabytes), and cost less than a hundred dollars. So integrated packages have proven that they offer enough functions and features for many computer users, while providing some of the advantages of software suites in a smaller package. See Figure 3.5.

Web Browsers and More

The most important software component for many computer users today is the once simple and limited, but now powerful and feature-rich, **web browser.** A browser like Netscape Navigator or Microsoft Explorer is the key software interface you use to point and click your way through the hyperlinked resources of the World Wide Web and the rest of the Internet, as well as corporate intranets and extranets. Once limited to surfing the Web, browsers are becoming the universal software platform on which end users launch into information searches, E-mail, multimedia file transfer, discussion groups, and many other Internet, intranet, and extranet applications. See Figure 3.6.

Industry experts are predicting that the web browser will be the model for how most people will use networked computers in the future. So now, whether you want to watch a video, make a phone call, download some software, hold a videoconference, check your E-mail, or work on a spreadsheet of your team's business plan, you can use your browser to launch and host such applications. That's why browsers are being called the *universal client,* that is, the software component installed on the workstations of all the clients (users) in client/server networks throughout an enterprise.

The web browser has also become only one component of a new suite of communications and collaboration software that Netscape and other vendors are assembling in a variety of configurations. Figure 3.7 is a summary of the software components in

Jeff Borders.

Netscape Communicator, a suite of software tools that includes the Navigator web browser, Messenger for E-mail, Conference for audio and data conferencing, Calendar for scheduling and calendaring, Netcaster for receiving web broadcasts, Composer for web page creation and publishing, and Collabra groupware for creating and managing discussion groups and their databases on intranets and extranets.

Electronic Mail

The first thing many people do at work all over the world is check their E-mail. **Electronic mail** has changed the way people work and communicate. Millions of end users now depend on E-mail software to communicate with each other by sending and receiving electronic messages via the Internet or their organizations' intranets or extranets. E-mail is stored on network servers until you are ready. Whenever you want to, you can read your E-mail by displaying it on your workstations. So, with only a few minutes of effort (and a few microseconds or minutes of transmission time), a message to one or many individuals can be composed, sent, and received. See Figure 3.8.

Figure 3.7

Components of the Netscape Communicator suite of communications and collaboration software.

Navigator	Messenger	Collabra	Conference	Calendar	Composer	Netcaster
Web browser	E-mail	Discussion forums and databases	Audio and data conferencing, chat, and Internet telephone	Group scheduling and calendaring	Web page editor	Net broadcaster via push channels

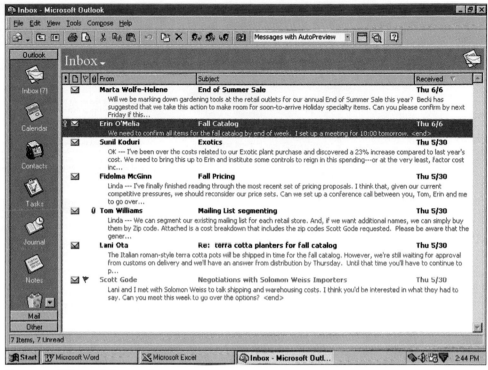

Figure 3.8

Using an E-mail package.

Courtesy of Microsoft Corporation.

As we mentioned earlier, E-mail software is now a component of top software suites and web browsers. Free E-mail packages like Microsoft HotMail and Netscape WebMail are available to Internet users from online services and Internet service providers. Full-featured E-mail software like Microsoft Exchange E-Mail or Netscape Messenger can route messages to multiple end users based on predefined mailing lists and provide password security, automatic message forwarding, and remote user access. They also allow you to store messages in folders with provisions for adding attachments to message files. E-mail packages may also enable you to edit and send graphics and multimedia as well as text, and provide bulletin board and computer conferencing capabilities. Finally, your E-mail software may automatically filter and sort incoming messages (even news items from online services) and route them to appropriate user mailboxes and folders.

Word Processing and Desktop Publishing

Software for **word processing** has transformed the process of writing. Word processing packages computerize the creation, editing, revision, and printing of *documents* (such as letters, memos, and reports) by electronically processing your *text data* (words, phrases, sentences, and paragraphs). Top word processing packages like Microsoft Word, Lotus WordPro, and Corel WordPerfect can provide a wide variety of attractively printed documents with their desktop publishing capabilities. These packages can also convert all documents to HTML format for publication as web pages on corporate intranets or the World Wide Web.

Word processing packages also provide advanced features. For example, a spelling checker capability can identify and correct spelling errors, and a thesaurus feature helps you find a better choice of words to express ideas. Or you can identify and

Figure 3.9

Using the Microsoft
Word word processing
package.

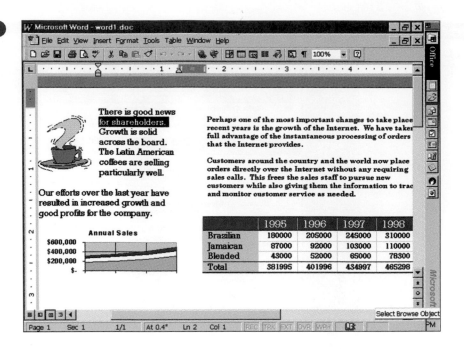

correct grammar and punctuation errors, as well as suggest possible improvements in your writing style, with grammar and style checker functions. Another text productivity tool is an idea processor or outliner function. It helps you organize and outline your thoughts before you prepare a document or develop a presentation. Besides converting documents to HTML format, you can also use the top packages to design and create web pages from scratch for an Internet or intranet web site. See Figure 3.9.

End users and organizations can use **desktop publishing** (DTP) software to produce their own printed materials that look professionally published. That is, they can design and print their own newsletters, brochures, manuals, and books with several type styles, graphics, photos, and colors on each page. Word processing packages and desktop publishing packages like Adobe PageMaker and QuarkXPress are used to do desktop publishing. Typically, text material and graphics can be generated by word processing and graphics packages and imported as text and graphics files. Optical scanners may be used to input text and graphics from printed material. You can also use files of **clip art,** which are predrawn graphic illustrations provided by the software package or available from other sources. See Figure 3.10.

The heart of desktop publishing is a page design process called *page makeup* or *page composition.* Your video screen becomes an electronic pasteup board with rulers, column guides, and other page design aids. Text material and illustrations are then merged into the page format you design. The software will automatically move excess text to another column or page and help size and place illustrations and headings. Most DTP packages provide WYSIWYG (What You See Is What You Get) displays so you can see exactly what the finished document will look like before it is printed.

Electronic Spreadsheets

Electronic spreadsheet packages like Lotus 1-2-3, Microsoft Excel, and Corel QuattroPro are used for business analysis, planning, and modeling. They help you develop

Figure 3.10

Doing desktop
publishing.

Courtesy of Adobe Systems, Inc.

an *electronic spreadsheet*, which is a worksheet of rows and columns that can be stored on your PC or a network server, or converted to HTML format and stored as a web page or *websheet* on the World Wide Web. Developing a spreadsheet involves designing its format and developing the relationships (formulas) that will be used in the worksheet. In response to your input, the computer performs necessary calculations based on the formulas you defined in the spreadsheet, and displays results immediately, whether at your workstation or web site. Most packages also help you develop graphic displays of spreadsheet results. See Figure 3.11.

For example, you could develop a spreadsheet to record and analyze past and present advertising performance for a business. You could also develop hyperlinks to a similar websheet at your marketing team's intranet web site. Now you have a decision support tool to help you answer *what-if questions* you may have about advertising. For example, "What would happen to market share if advertising expense increased by 10 percent?" To answer this question, you would simply change the advertising expense formula on the advertising performance worksheet you developed. The computer would recalculate the affected figures, producing new market share figures and graphics. You would then have a better insight on the effect of advertising decisions on market share. Then you could share this insight with a note on the websheet at your team's intranet web site.

Database Management

Microcomputer versions of **database management** programs have become so popular that they are now viewed as general-purpose application software packages like word processing and spreadsheet packages. Database management packages such as Microsoft Access, Lotus Approach, or Corel Paradox allow you to set up and manage databases on your PC, network server, or the World Wide Web. See Figure 3.12. Most database managers can perform four primary tasks, which we will discuss further in Chapter 5.

Figure 3.11

Figure 3.11

Using an electronic spreadsheet.

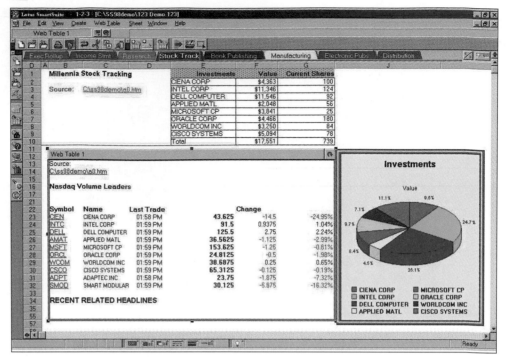

Courtesy of Lotus Development Corporation.

- **Database development.** Define and organize the content, relationships, and structure of the data needed to build a database, including any hyperlinks to data on web pages.

- **Database interrogation.** Access the data in a database to display information in a variety of formats. End users can selectively retrieve and display information and produce forms, reports, and other documents, including web pages.

- **Database maintenance.** Add, delete, update, and correct the data in a database, including hyperlinked data on web pages.

- **Application development.** Develop prototypes of web pages, queries, forms, reports, and labels for a proposed business application. Or use a built-in 4GL or application generator to program the application.

Presentation Graphics and Multimedia

Which type of display would you rather see: columns or rows of numbers, or a graphics display of the same information? **Presentation graphics** packages help you convert numeric data into graphics displays such as line charts, bar graphs, pie charts, and many other types of graphics. Most of the top packages also help you prepare **multimedia presentations** of graphics, photos, animation, and video clips, including publishing to the World Wide Web. Not only are graphics and multimedia displays easier to comprehend and communicate than numeric data but multiple-color and multiple-media displays also can more easily emphasize key points, strategic differences, and important trends in the data. Presentation graphics has proved to be much more effective than tabular presentations of numeric data for reporting and communicating in advertising media, management reports, or other business presentations.

Figure 3.12

Figure 3.12

Using a database management package. Note how Lotus Approach lets you easily obtain information from a customer order database.

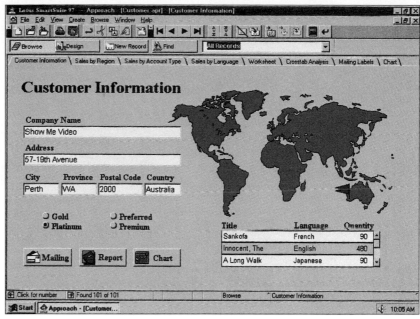

Courtesy of Lotus Development Corporation.

Presentation graphics software packages like Microsoft PowerPoint, Lotus Freelance, or Corel Presentations give you many easy-to-use capabilities that encourage the use of graphics presentations. For example, most packages help you design and manage computer-generated and -orchestrated *slide shows* containing many integrated graphics and multimedia displays. Or you can select from a variety of predesigned *templates* of business presentations, prepare and edit the outline and notes for a presentation, and manage the use of multimedia files of graphics, photos, sounds, and video clips. And of course, the top packages help you tailor your graphics and multimedia presentation for transfer in HTML format to web sites on corporate intranets or the World Wide Web. See Figure 3.13.

Multimedia Software Technologies

Hypertext and hypermedia are software technologies for multimedia presentations. By definition, **hypertext** contains only text and a limited amount of graphics. **Hypermedia** are electronic documents that contain multiple forms of media, including text, graphics, video, and so on. Key topics and other presentations in hypertext or hypermedia documents are indexed by software links so that they can be quickly searched by the reader. For example, if you click your mouse button on an underlined term on a hypermedia document, your computer may instantly bring up another display using text, graphics, and sound related to that term. Once you finish viewing that presentation, you can return to what you were reading originally, or jump to another part of the document.

Hypertext and hypermedia are developed by using software packages that rely on specialized programming languages like Java and the Hypertext Markup Language (HTML), which create hyperlinks to other parts of a document, or to other documents and multimedia files. Hypertext and hypermedia documents can thus be programmed to let a reader navigate through a multimedia database by following a chain

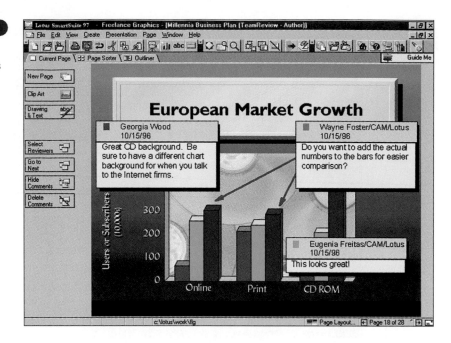

Figure 3.13

Using a presentation graphics package, Lotus Freelance. Note the collaboration on the presentation via team members' comments.

of hyperlinks through various multimedia files. The web sites on the World Wide Web of the Internet are a popular example of this technology. Thus, the use of hypertext and hypermedia software in web browsers and other programs provides an environment for online interactive multimedia presentations. See Figure 3.14.

Personal Information Managers

The **personal information manager** (PIM) is a popular software package for end user productivity and collaboration. PIMs such as Lotus Organizer and Microsoft Outlook help end users store, organize, and retrieve information about customers, clients, and prospects, or schedule and manage appointments, meetings, and tasks. The PIM package will organize data you enter and retrieve information in a variety of forms, depending on the style and structure of the PIM and the information you want. For example, information can be retrieved as an electronic calendar or list of appointments, meetings, or other things to do; the timetable for a project; or a display of key facts and financial data about customers, clients, or sales prospects. See Figure 3.15.

Personal information managers are sold as independent programs or are included in software suites, and vary widely in their style, structure, and features. For example, Lotus Organizer uses a notebook with tabs format, while Microsoft Outlook organizes data about people as a continuous A-to-Z list. Most PIMs emphasize the maintenance of *contact lists*, that is, customers, clients, or prospects. Scheduling appointments and meetings and task management are other top PIM applications. PIMs are now changing to include the ability to access the World Wide Web and provide E-mail capability. Also, some PIMs use Internet and E-mail features to support team collaboration by sharing information such as contact lists, task lists, and schedules with other networked PIM users.

Groupware

Groupware is *collaboration software*, that is, software that helps workgroups and teams work together to accomplish group assignments. Groupware is a fast-growing category of general-purpose application software that combines a variety of software

Figure 3.14

Examples of software technologies for multimedia productions and presentations available on the World Wide Web.

● **Liquid Audio www.liquidaudio.com**
Liquid Audio's Liquid Player is a program you can download for free to play web-based audio tracks. Even compressed files are reproduced with CD-quality sound. The program lets you view album art and lyrics while you listen, set up custom play lists, and purchase a copy of the music from the publisher. At Liquid's site you can also purchase premium-quality tools for encoding and posting music to the Net.

● **Macromedia Shockwave www.macromedia.com**
Macromedia makes some of the most popular software for jazzing up web pages with sound and animation. If your browser doesn't have the appropriate plug-ins, you can download them for free here. Once you've got the Shockwave and Flash players, you can experience some pretty cool and entertaining games, cartoons, and music. (Oh, and some educational stuff, too.) Check out the ShockRave web site (www.shockrave.com) for a sampling of what's out there.

● **RealNetworks www.real.com**
RealNetworks software, RealPlayer G2, provides a slick user interface and much improved transmission of compressed audio and video. G2 is free, but for $29.95 you can download a copy of RealPlayer Plus G2, which offers several advanced features: an audio equalizer, fine-tuning for video, the ability to save media clips to your hard drive, phone support, a manual and CD-ROM, and one-click searches for broadcasts on the Web.

● **Winamp www.winamp.com**
For Windows users, Winamp is a great shareware program—they ask for $10 to $20 if you keep using it—for playing back nearly every type of digital audio file you find online. Along with its virtual graphic equalizers, Winamp has a number of nifty features, such as the ability to generate 3-D images based on whatever music you're playing. You can set up a playlist of different songfiles on the Web, effectively creating an endless Internet jukebox.

Source: Adapted from "The Great Portal Race," Technology Buyers Guide, *Fortune*, Winter 1999, p. 240.
© 1999 by Time Inc. All rights reserved.

Figure 3.15

Using a personal information manager, Lotus Organizer.

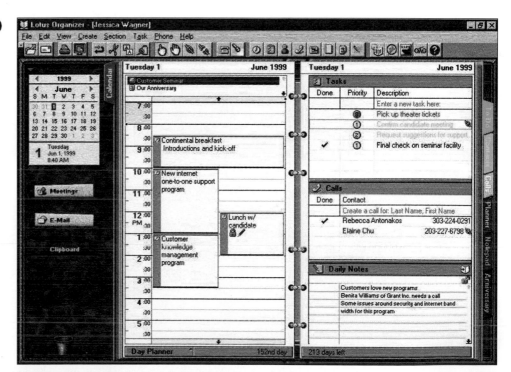

Courtesy of Lotus Development Corporation.

features and functions to facilitate collaboration. For example, groupware products like Lotus Notes, Novell GroupWise, Microsoft Exchange, and Netscape Communicator support collaboration through electronic mail, discussion groups and databases, scheduling, task management, data, audio and videoconferencing, and so on. See Figure 3.16.

Groupware products are changing in several ways to meet the demand for better tools for collaboration. Groupware is now designed to use the Internet and corporate intranets and extranets to make collaboration possible on a global scale by *virtual teams* located anywhere in the world. For example, team members might use the Internet for global E-mail, project discussion forums, and joint web page development. Or they might use corporate intranets to publish project news and progress reports, and work jointly on documents stored on web servers.

Collaborative capabilities are also being added to other software to give them groupware features. For example, in the Microsoft Office software suite, Microsoft Word keeps track of who made revisions to each document, Excel tracks all changes made to a spreadsheet, and Outlook lets you keep track of tasks you delegate to other team members.

Figure 3.16

Lotus Notes is the leading corporate groupware package. Notice how it supports team collaboration.

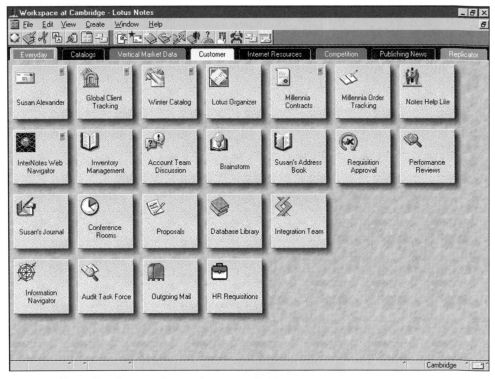

Courtesy of Lotus Development Corporation.

| Section II | # System Software: Computer System Management |

System Software Overview

Analyzing Jay Jacobs and Burlington Coat Factory

System software consists of programs that manage and support a computer system and its information processing activities. For example, operating systems and network management programs serve as a vital *software interface* between computer networks and hardware and the application programs of end users.

Read the Real World Case on Jay Jacobs and Burlington Coat Factory on the next page. We can learn a lot about the business value of new developments in system software from this example. See Figure 3.17.

Linus Torvalds created Linux by using the Internet as a development platform and enlisting the help of millions of programmers all over the world as software developers. The result is a Unix-like operating system that its users say is faster and more reliable than either Unix or Windows NT, and is available for free or at a minimal cost. These major business advantages drove Jay Jacobs and Burlington to choose Linux as the new operating system to run the servers and PCs in all of their stores. The example of Linux has encouraged the development of other successful open-source software products that are widely used in business. Thus, open-source software has become a legitimate business alternative to commercially developed software products.

| Figure 3.17 |

Chief Financial Officer Bill Lawrence supported the business decision to move to Linux at Jay Jacobs.

Source: Rex Rystedt.

Jay Jacobs and Burlington Coat Factory: The Business Case for Linux and Open-Source Software

In 1991 a very green but extraordinarily enthusiastic Linus Torvalds began to toy with an idea for a new computer operating system. Torvalds, then 21, was a Helsinki University student learning about operating systems on the fly. Through newsgroup postings on the Internet, he asked for input from his peers, made the source code available to all, and with contributions from hackers across the globe, his program began to take the shape of a free alternative to the Unix operating system. Little did he know that by 1999, his operating system, called Linux, would strike the fancy of more than a million developers and evolve into a reliable, feature-rich substitute for expensive, proprietary Unix systems, as well as begin to threaten the unquestioned dominance of Microsoft's Windows NT.

Taking what was once called *freeware* and is now more appropriately termed *open-source software* far beyond anyone's imagination, Torvalds demonstrated that even with millions of developers and extremely complex technology, peer-reviewed software development works amazingly well in the Internet world of today. Other open-source software, such as the Apache Internet/intranet server and the latest Netscape Navigator browser, owe much to Torvalds' example.

With a price of $50 for a CD-ROM version (or a free download at www.redhat.com), Linux distributors like Red Hat Software sold almost 3 million commercial copies of Linux for PCs and servers in 1998. IBM and Hewlett-Packard are working with such distributors to offer support for Linux installed on their servers and PCs. And software developers like Corel, Netscape, and Oracle are offering the WordPerfect Office suite, the Navigator browser, and other system and application software for Linux.

Users say Linux has three advantages that appeal to corporations: low cost, reliability, and fast performance. Let's take a look at two examples of why Linux is being chosen as an operating system for business applications.

Jay Jacobs

Price was the priority for Seattle-based retailer Jay Jacobs Inc., which installed Linux servers in all 120 of its stores in 1999. But CFO Bill Lawrence is also pleased by the prospect of getting fast, Unix-like performance for less than the cost of the slower Windows NT environment.

Jay Jacobs spent $1.7 million in 1999—about 2.5 percent of its revenue—to replace the ancient DOS-based systems at its headquarters and in its 120 stores. The in-store parts of the project would have cost $980,000 but by using Linux instead of another operating system, the company is saving about $80,000, or $666 per store, Lawrence said.

Burlington Coat Factory Warehouse

Burlington Coat Factory Warehouse Corp. plans to run its stores on Linux. The $1 million-plus deployment at the $1.8 billion Burlington, New Jersey, discounter is the largest Linux retail installation announced by a U.S. company. For now, Burlington will keep Windows NT for the servers and PCs of its knowledge workers at company headquarters, and continue with Unix on servers for corporate database processing.

In 1999 and 2000, Burlington is installing Linux on 1,150 computers in its 250 stores and replacing many dumb terminals and old servers. "Linux has come along so strongly, and is attractive from both a price and performance standpoint. It's free, and it runs like the wind," says CIO Mike Prince. Prince said he also expects Linux to be less costly to support and maintain than NT, which he said is less stable.

Burlington uses Red Hat Software's version of Linux. Their new PCs and servers cost $1.15 to $1.8 million, depending on the power of the machines, Prince said. The cost of Linux itself, he said, was only a few hundred dollars. Thus, Burlington saved thousands of dollars in each store by not buying a commercial operating system.

Case Study Questions

1. What are the advantages and limitations of using freeware or open-source software like Linux? Check out Linux online at www.linux.org for more information resources.

2. Why are companies like Jay Jacobs and Burlington choosing Linux instead of Unix or Windows NT to run their business operations?

3. Does the development of Linux demonstrate a major change in software development enabled by the Internet? Why or why not?

Source: Adapted from Brian Stauffer, "Freeware," *Red Herring*, February 1999, pp. 47–56; and David Orenstein, "Retailer Bets Big on Linux," *Computerworld*, February 8, 1999, p. 72; "Retailer Commits to Linux at 250 Stores," *Computerworld*, February 15, 1999, pp. 1, 97; "IBM Works to Support Linux on Its Low-End Hardware," *Computerworld*, February 22, 1999, p. 12. Copyright 1999 by Computerworld, Inc., Framingham, MA 01701. Reprinted from *Computerworld.*; and Scott Spanbauer, "Upstart Linux: Not Just for Geeks Anymore," *PC World*, March 1999, p. 64. Reprinted with the permission of *PC World* Communications Inc.

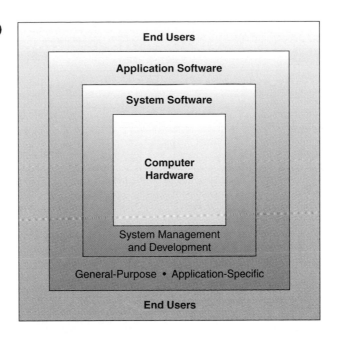

Figure 3.18

The system and application software interface between end users and computer hardware.

Figure 3.18 shows that we can group system software into two major categories:

- **System management programs.** Programs that manage the hardware, software, network, and data resources of the computer system during its execution of the various information processing jobs of users. Examples of important system management programs are operating systems, network management programs, database management systems, and system utilities.

- **System development programs.** Programs that help users develop information system programs and procedures and prepare user programs for computer processing. Major development programs are programming language translators and editors, other programming tools, and CASE (computer-aided software engineering) packages.

Operating Systems

The most important system software package for any computer is its operating system. An operating system is an integrated system of programs that manages the operations of the CPU, controls the input/output and storage resources and activities of the computer system, and provides various support services as the computer executes the application programs of users.

The primary purpose of an operating system is to maximize the productivity of a computer system by operating it in the most efficient manner. An operating system minimizes the amount of human intervention required during processing. It helps your application programs perform common operations such as accessing a network, entering data, saving and retrieving files, and printing or displaying output. If you have any hands-on experience on a computer, you know that the operating system must be loaded and activated before you can accomplish other tasks. This emphasizes the fact that operating systems are the most indispensable components of the software interface between users and the hardware of their computer systems.

Figure 3.19

The basic functions of an operating system include a user interface, resource management, task management, file management, and utilities and other functions.

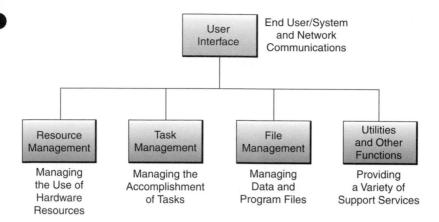

Operating System Functions

An operating system performs five basic functions in the operation of a computer system: providing a user interface, resource management, task management, file management, and utilities and support services. See Figure 3.19.

The User Interface. The **user interface** is the part of the operating system that allows you to communicate with it so you can load programs, access files, and accomplish other tasks. Three main types of user interfaces are the *command-driven, menu-driven,* and *graphical user interfaces.* The trend in user interfaces for operating systems and other software is moving away from the entry of brief end user commands, or even the selection of choices from menus of options. Instead, most software provides an easy-to-use **graphical user interface** (GUI) that uses icons, bars, buttons, boxes, and other images. GUIs rely on pointing devices like the electronic mouse or touchpad to make selections that help you get things done. See Figure 3.20.

Resource Management. An operating system uses a variety of resource management programs to manage the hardware and networking resources of a computer system, including its CPU, memory, secondary storage devices, telecommunications processors, and input/output peripherals. For example, memory management programs keep track of where data and programs are stored. They may also subdivide memory into a number of sections and swap parts of programs and data between memory and magnetic disks or other secondary storage devices. This can provide a computer system with a **virtual memory** capability that is significantly larger than the real memory capacity of its primary storage circuits. So, a computer with a virtual memory capability can process large programs and greater amounts of data than the capacity of its memory chips would normally allow.

File Management. An operating system contains file management programs that control the creation, deletion, and access of files of data and programs. File management also involves keeping track of the physical location of files on magnetic disks and other secondary storage devices. So operating systems maintain directories of information about the location and characteristics of files stored on a computer system's secondary storage devices.

Task Management. The task management programs of an operating system manage the accomplishment of the computing tasks of end users. They give each task a slice of

Figure 3.20

The graphical user interface of Microsoft's Windows 98 operating system.

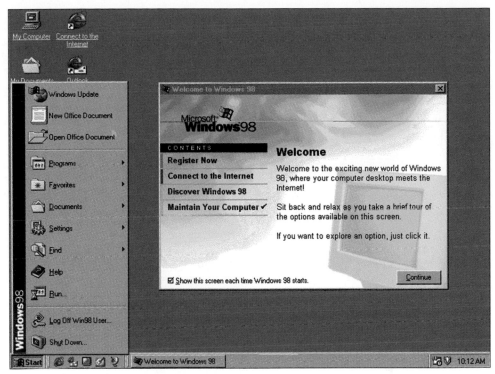

Courtesy of Microsoft Corporation.

a CPU's time and interrupt the CPU operations to substitute other tasks. Task management may involve a **multitasking** capability where several computing tasks can occur at the same time. Multitasking may take the form of *multiprogramming*, where the CPU can process the tasks of several programs at the same time, or *timesharing*, where the computing tasks of several users can be processed at the same time. The efficiency of multitasking operations depends on the processing power of a CPU and the virtual memory and multitasking capabilities of the operating system it uses.

Most microcomputer, midrange, and mainframe operating systems provide a multitasking capability. With multitasking, end users can do two or more operations (e.g., keyboarding and printing) or applications (e.g., word processing and financial analysis) concurrently, that is, at the same time. Multitasking on microcomputers has also been made possible by the development of more powerful microprocessors and their ability to directly address much larger memory capacities (up to 4 gigabytes). This allows an operating system to subdivide primary storage into several large partitions, each of which can be used by a different application program.

In effect, a single computer can act as if it were several computers, or *virtual machines*, since each application program is running independently at the same time. The number of programs that can be run concurrently depends on the amount of memory that is available and the amount of processing each job demands. That's because a microprocessor (or CPU) can become overloaded with too many jobs and provide unacceptably slow response times. However, if memory and processing capacities are adequate, multitasking allows end users to easily switch from one application to another, share data files among applications, and process some applications in a *background* mode. Typically, background tasks include large printing jobs, extensive mathematical computation, or unattended telecommunications sessions.

Figure 3.21 A comparison of popular operating systems.

Operating System	MS-DOS	Windows 98	Windows NT	OS/2 Warp 4	Macintosh System 8.5	UNIX
Developer	Microsoft	Microsoft	Microsoft	IBM	Apple	HP, Sun, IBM, etc.
Primary Market	PCs	PCs	Servers PCs	PCs Servers	Macintoshes	Workstations Servers Midrange Mainframes
Primary Micro-processors	Intel	Intel	Intel Alpha	Intel Power PC	Motorola Power PC	Many
GUI		X	X	X	X	X
Single User	X	X	X	X	X	
Multitasking		X	X	X	X	X
Virtual Memory		X	X	X	X	X
Networking		X	X	X	X	X
Multiuser			X	X		X
Network Management			X	X		X

Popular Operating Systems

For many years, MS-DOS (Microsoft Disk Operating System) was the most widely used microcomputer operating system. It is a single-user, single-tasking operating system, but was given a graphical user interface and limited multitasking capabilities by combining it with Microsoft Windows. Microsoft began replacing its DOS/Windows combination in 1995 with the **Windows 95** operating system. Windows 95 is an advanced operating system featuring a graphical user interface, true multitasking, networking, multimedia, and many other capabilities. Microsoft introduced an enhanced **Windows 98** version during 1998. See Figure 3.21.

Microsoft introduced another operating system, **Windows NT** (New Technology), in 1995. Windows NT is a powerful, multitasking, multiuser operating system that is installed on many network servers to manage client/server networks and on PCs with high-performance computing requirements. New Server and Workstation versions were introduced in 1997. Microsoft plans to merge its Windows 98 and Windows NT products into a **Windows 2000** operating system during the year 2000.

OS/2 (Operating System/2) is a microcomputer operating system from IBM. Its latest version, **OS/2 Warp 4,** was introduced in 1996 and provides a graphical user interface, voice recognition, multitasking, virtual memory, and telecommunications. A version for network servers, OS/2 Warp Server, is also available.

Originally developed by AT&T, **UNIX** now is also offered by other vendors, including Solaris by Sun Microsystems and AIX by IBM. UNIX is a multitasking, multiuser, network-managing operating system whose portability allows it to run on mainframes, midrange computers, and microcomputers. UNIX, and its *shareware* version **Linux,** is a popular choice for web and other network servers.

The Macintosh System is an operating system from Apple for Macintosh microcomputers. Now in version 8.5, the system has a popular graphical user interface as well as multitasking and virtual memory capabilities.

Figure 3.22

A display of a network management program.

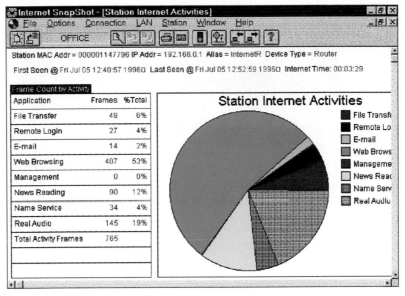

Courtesy of Tinwald Corporation.

Network Management Programs

Today's information systems rely heavily on the Internet, intranets, extranets, local area networks, and other telecommunications networks to interconnect end user workstations, network servers, and other computer systems. This requires a variety of system software for **network management,** including **network operating systems,** network performance monitors, telecommunications monitors, and so on. These programs are used by network servers and other computers in a network to manage network performance. Network management programs perform such functions as automatically checking client PCs and video terminals for input/output activity, assigning priorities to data communications requests from clients and terminals, and detecting and correcting transmission errors and other network problems. In addition, some network management programs function as *middleware* to help diverse networks communicate with each other. See Figure 3.22.

Examples of network management programs include Novell NetWare, the most widely used network operating system for complex interconnected local area networks. Microsoft's Windows NT Server and IBM's OS/2 Warp Server are two other popular network operating systems. IBM's telecommunications monitor CICS (Customer Identification and Control System) is an example of a widely used *telecommunications monitor* for mainframe-based wide area networks. IBM's NetView and Hewlett-Packard's OpenView are examples of network management programs for managing several mainframe-based or midrange-based computer networks.

Database Management Systems

In Section I, we discussed microcomputer database management programs like Microsoft Access, Lotus Approach, or Corel Paradox. In mainframe and midrange computer systems, a **database management system** (DBMS) is considered an important system software package that controls the development, use, and maintenance of the databases of computer-using organizations. A DBMS program helps organizations use their integrated collections of data records and files known as databases. It allows different user application programs to easily access the same database. For example, a DBMS makes it easy for an employee database to be accessed by payroll, employee benefits, and other human resource programs. A DBMS also simplifies the process of

Figure 3.23

The Norton System Doctor is one of the utility programs in The Norton Utilities—a top-selling set of utility programs for your PC.

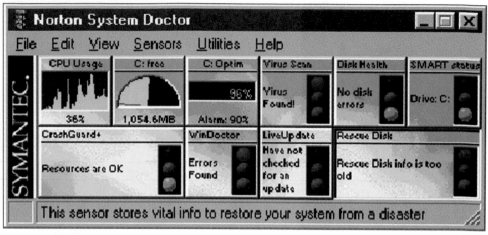

Courtesy of Symantec.

retrieving information from databases in the form of displays and reports. Instead of having to write computer programs to extract information, end users can ask simple questions in a *query language*. Thus, many DBMS packages provide *fourth-generation languages* (4GLs) and other application development features. Examples of popular mainframe and midrange packages are DB2 by IBM and Oracle 8 by Oracle Corporation. We will discuss database management software in more detail in Chapter 5.

Other System Management Programs

Several other types of system management software are marketed as separate programs or are included as part of an operating system. Utility programs, or **utilities,** are an important example. Programs like Norton Utilities perform miscellaneous house-keeping and file conversion functions. Examples include data backup, data recovery, virus protection, data compression, and file defragmentation. Most operating systems also provide many utilities that perform a variety of helpful chores for computer users. See Figure 3.23.

Other examples of system support programs include performance monitors and security monitors. **Performance monitors** are programs that monitor and adjust the performance and usage of one or more computer systems to keep them running efficiently. **Security monitors** are packages that monitor and control the use of computer systems and provide warning messages and record evidence of unauthorized use of computer resources. A recent trend is to merge both types of programs into operating systems like Microsoft's Windows NT Server, or into system management software like Computer Associates' CA-Unicenter, that can manage both mainframe systems and servers in a data center.

Programming Languages

To understand computer software, you need a basic knowledge of the role that programming languages play in the development of computer programs. A **programming language** allows a programmer to develop the sets of instructions that constitute a computer program. Many different programming languages have been developed, each with its own unique vocabulary, grammar, and uses.

Machine Languages

Machine languages (or *first-generation languages*) are the most basic level of programming languages. In the early stages of computer development, all program instructions had to be written using binary codes unique to each computer. This type of

Figure 3.24

Examples of four levels of programming languages. These programming language instructions might be used to compute the sum of two numbers as expressed by the formula X = Y + Z.

• **Machine Languages:** Use binary coded instructions 1010 11001 1011 11010 1100 11011	• **High-Level Languages:** Use brief statements or arithmetic notations BASIC: X = Y + Z COBOL: COMPUTE X = Y + Z
• **Assembler Languages:** Use symbolic coded instructions LOD Y ADD Z STR X	• **Fourth-Generation Languages:** Use natural and nonprocedural statements SUM THE FOLLOWING NUMBERS

programming involves the difficult task of writing instructions in the form of strings of binary digits (ones and zeros) or other number systems. Programmers must have a detailed knowledge of the internal operations of the specific type of CPU they are using. They must write long series of detailed instructions to accomplish even simple processing tasks. Programming in machine language requires specifying the storage locations for every instruction and item of data used. Instructions must be included for every switch and indicator used by the program. These requirements make machine language programming a difficult and error-prone task. A machine language program to add two numbers together in the CPU of a specific computer and store the result might take the form shown in Figure 3.24.

Assembler Languages

Assembler languages (or *second-generation languages*) are the next level of programming languages. They were developed to reduce the difficulties in writing machine language programs. The use of assembler languages requires language translator programs called *assemblers* that allow a computer to convert the instructions of such language into machine instructions. Assembler languages are frequently called symbolic languages because symbols are used to represent operation codes and storage locations. Convenient alphabetic abbreviations called *mnemonics* (memory aids) and other symbols represent operation codes, storage locations, and data elements. For example, the computation X = Y + Z in an assembler language might take the form shown in Figure 3.24.

Assembler languages are still widely used as a method of programming a computer in a machine-oriented language. Most computer manufacturers provide an assembler language that reflects the unique machine language instruction set of a particular line of computers. This feature is particularly desirable to *system programmers*, who program system software (as opposed to *application programmers*, who program application software), since it provides them with greater control and flexibility in designing a program for a particular computer. They can then produce more efficient software, that is, programs that require a minimum of instructions, storage, and CPU time to perform a specific processing assignment.

High-Level Languages

High-level languages (or *third-generation languages*) use instructions, which are called *statements*, that use brief statements or arithmetic expressions. Individual high-level language statements are actually *macroinstructions*; that is, each individual statement generates several machine instructions when translated into machine language by high-level language translator programs called *compilers* or *interpreters*. High-level language statements resemble the phrases or mathematical expressions required to

Figure 3.25

Highlights of several important high-level languages.

Ada: Named after Augusta Ada Byron, considered the world's first computer programmer. Developed for the U.S. Department of Defense as a standard "high-order language" to replace COBOL and FORTRAN.
BASIC: (Beginner's All-Purpose Symbolic Instruction Code). A simple procedure-oriented language designed for end user programming.
C: A mid-level structured language developed as part of the UNIX operating system. It resembles a machine-independent assembler language.
COBOL: (COmmon Business Oriented Language). An Englishlike language widely used for programming business applications.
FORTRAN: (FORmula TRANslation). A high-level language designed for scientific and engineering applications.
Pascal: Named after Blaise Pascal. Developed specifically to incorporate structured programming concepts.

express the problem or procedure being programmed. The *syntax* (vocabulary, punctuation, and grammatical rules) and the *semantics* (meanings) of such statements do not reflect the internal code of any particular computer. For example, the computation $X = Y + Z$ would be programmed in the high-level languages of BASIC and COBOL as shown in Figure 3.24.

A high-level language is easier to learn and program than an assembler language, since it has less-rigid rules, forms, and syntaxes. However, high-level language programs are usually less efficient than assembler language programs and require a greater amount of computer time for translation into machine instructions. Since most high-level languages are machine independent, programs written in a high-level language do not have to be reprogrammed when a new computer is installed, and programmers do not have to learn a different language for each type of computer. Figure 3.25 highlights some of the major high-level languages still being used in some form today.

Fourth-Generation Languages

The term **fourth-generation language** describes a variety of programming languages that are more nonprocedural and conversational than prior languages. These languages are called fourth-generation languages (4GLs) to differentiate them from machine languages (first generation), assembler languages (second generation), and high-level languages (third generation).

Most fourth-generation languages are **nonprocedural languages** that encourage users and programmers to specify the results they want, while the computer determines the sequence of instructions that will accomplish those results. Thus, fourth-generation languages have helped simplify the programming process. **Natural languages** are 4GLs that are very close to English or other human languages. Research and development activity in artificial intelligence (AI) is developing programming languages that are as easy to use as ordinary conversation in one's native tongue. For example, INTELLECT, a natural language 4GL, would use a statement like, "What are the average exam scores in MIS 200?" to program a simple average exam score task.

The ease of use of 4GLs is gained at the expense of some loss in flexibility. It is frequently difficult to override some of the prespecified formats or procedures of 4GLs. Also, the machine language code generated by a program developed by a 4GL is frequently much less efficient (in terms of processing speed and amount of storage capacity needed) than a program written in a language like COBOL. Thus, some large

Figure 3.26

An example of a bank savings account object. This object consists of data about a customer's account balance and the basic operations that can be performed on those data.

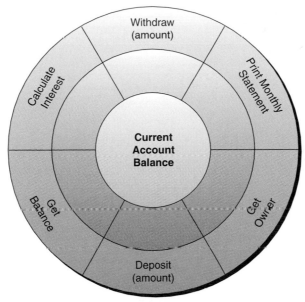

Savings Account Object

transaction processing applications programmed in a 4GL have not provided reasonable response times when faced with a large amount of realtime transaction processing and end user inquiries. However, 4GLs have shown great success in business applications that do not have a high volume of transaction processing.

Object-Oriented Languages

Object-oriented programming (OOP) languages like Visual Basic, C++, and Java have become major tools of software development. Briefly, while most other programming languages separate data elements from the procedures or actions that will be performed upon them, OOP languages tie them together into **objects.** Thus, an object consists of data and the actions that can be performed on the data. For example, an object could be a set of data about a bank customer's savings account, and the operations (such as interest calculations) that might be performed upon the data. Or an object could be data in graphic form such as a video display window, plus the display actions that might be used upon it. See Figure 3.26.

In procedural languages, a program consists of procedures to perform actions on each data element. However, in object-oriented systems, objects tell other objects to perform actions on themselves. For example, to open a window on a computer video display, a beginning menu object could send a window object a message to open and a window will appear on the screen. That's because the window object contains the program code for opening itself.

Object-oriented languages are easier to use and more efficient for programming the graphics-oriented user interfaces required by many applications. Also, once objects are programmed, they are reusable. Therefore, reusability of objects is a major benefit of object oriented programming. For example, programmers can construct a user interface for a new program by assembling standard objects such as windows, bars, boxes, buttons, and icons. Therefore, most object-oriented programming packages provide a GUI that supports a "point and click," "drag and drop" visual assembly of objects known as *visual programming*. Figure 3.27 shows a display of the Visual Basic

Figure 3.27

Using the Visual Basic object-oriented programming package.

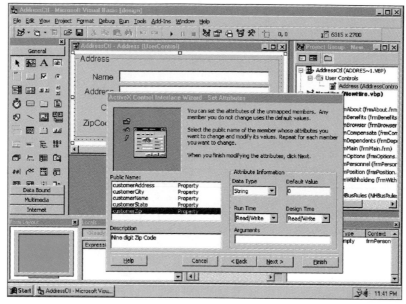

Courtesy of Microsoft Corporation.

object-oriented programming environment. Object-oriented technology is discussed further in the coverage of object-oriented databases in Chapter 5.

HTML and Java

HTML and Java are two relatively new programming languages that have become vital tools for building multimedia web pages, web sites, and web-based applications.

HTML (Hypertext Markup Language) is a page description language that creates hypertext or hypermedia documents. HTML inserts control codes within a document at points you can specify that create links (*hyperlinks*) to other parts of the document or to other documents anywhere on the World Wide Web. HTML embeds control codes in the ASCII text of a document that designate titles, headings, graphics, and multimedia components, as well as hyperlinks within the document.

As we mentioned earlier, several of the programs in the top software suites will automatically convert documents into HTML formats. These include web browsers, word processing and spreadsheet programs, database managers, and presentation graphics packages. These and other specialized *web publishing* programs like Microsoft FrontPage and Lotus FastSite, provide a range of features to help you design and create multimedia web pages without formal HTML programming.

Java is an object-oriented programming language created by Sun Microsystems that is revolutionizing the programming of applications for the World Wide Web and corporate intranets and extranets. Java is related to the C++ and Objective C programming languages, but is much simpler and secure, and is computing platform independent. Java is also specifically designed for realtime, interactive, web-based network applications. So Java applications consisting of small application programs, called **applets,** can be executed by any computer and any operating system anywhere in a network.

The ease of creating Java applets and distributing them from network servers to client PCs and network computers is a major reason for Java's popularity. Applets can be small special-purpose application programs or small modules of larger application

Using the graphical programming interface of Visual Café, a Java programming tool.

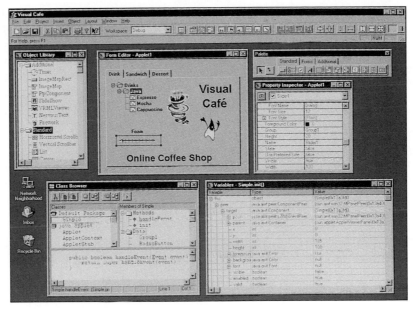

Courtesy of Symantec.

programs. Applets can reside at web sites on a network server until needed by client systems, and are easy to distribute over the Internet or intranets and extranets. Applets are platform independent too—they can run on Windows, OS/2, UNIX, and Macintosh systems without modification. Java continues to improve its speed of execution, and thus is becoming the programming language alternative to Microsoft's Active X language for many organizations intent on capitalizing on the business potential of the Internet, as well as their own intranets and extranets [5].

Programming Packages

A variety of software packages are available to help programmers develop computer programs. For example, *programming language translators* are programs that translate other programs into machine language instruction codes that computers can execute. Other software packages, such as programming language editors, are called *programming tools* because they help programmers write programs by providing a variety of program creation and editing capabilities. See Figure 3.28.

Language Translator Programs

Computer programs consist of sets of instructions written in programming languages that must be translated by a **language translator** into the computer's own machine language before they can be processed, or executed, by the CPU. Programming language translator programs (or *language processors*) are known by a variety of names. An **assembler** translates the symbolic instruction codes of programs written in an assembler language into machine language instructions, while a **compiler** translates high level language statements.

An **interpreter** is a special type of compiler that translates and executes each statement in a program one at a time, instead of first producing a complete machine language program, like compilers and assemblers do. Java is an example of an interpreted language. Thus, the program instructions in Java applets are interpreted and executed *on-the-fly* as the applet is being executed by a client PC.

Programming Tools

Most language translator programs are enhanced by a *graphical programming interface* and a variety of built-in capabilities or add-on packages. Language translators have always provided some editing and diagnostic capabilities to identify programming errors or *bugs*. However, most language translator programs now include powerful graphics-oriented *programming editors* and *debuggers*. These programs help programmers identify and minimize errors while they are programming. Such programming tools provide a computer-aided programming *environment* or *workbench*. Their goal is to decrease the drudgery of programming while increasing the efficiency and productivity of programmers. Other programming tools include diagramming packages, code generators, libraries of reusable objects and program code, and prototyping tools. Many of these same tools are part of the toolkit provided by *computer-aided software engineering* (CASE) packages.

Summary

- **Software.** Computer software consists of two major types of programs: (1) application software that directs the performance of a particular use, or application, of computers to meet the information processing needs of users, and (2) system software that controls and supports the operations of a computer system as it performs various information processing tasks. Refer to Figure 3.2 for an overview of the major types of software.

- **Application Software.** Application software includes a variety of programs that can be segregated into general-purpose and application-specific categories. General-purpose application programs perform common information processing jobs for end users. Examples are word processing, electronic spreadsheet, database management, telecommunications, and presentation graphics programs. Application-specific programs accomplish information processing tasks that support specific business functions or processes, scientific or engineering applications, and other computer applications in society.

- **System Software.** System software can be subdivided into system management programs and system development programs. System management programs manage the hardware, software, network, and data resources of a computer system during its execution of information processing jobs. Examples of system management programs are operating systems, network management programs, database management systems, system utilities, performance monitors, and security monitors. Network management programs support and manage telecommunications activities and network performance telecommunications networks. Database management systems control the development, integration, and maintenance of

databases. Utilities are programs that perform routine computing functions, such as backing up data or copying files, as part of an operating system or as a separate package. System development programs help IS specialists and end users develop computer programs and information system procedures. Major development programs are language translators, programming editors and other programming tools.

- **Operating Systems.** An operating system is an integrated system of programs that supervises the operation of the CPU, controls the input/output storage functions of the computer system, and provides various support services. An operating system performs five basic functions: (1) a user interface for system and network communications with users, (2) resource management for managing the hardware resources of a computer system, (3) file management for managing files of data and programs, (4) task management for managing the tasks a computer must accomplish, and (5) utilities and other functions that provide miscellaneous support services.

- **Programming Languages.** Programming languages are a major category of system software. They require the use of a variety of programming packages to help programmers develop computer programs, and language translator programs to convert programming language instructions into machine language instruction codes. The five major levels of programming languages are machine languages, assembler languages, high-level languages, fourth-generation languages, and object-oriented languages. Object-oriented languages like Java and special-purpose languages like HTML are being widely used for web-based business applications.

Key Terms and Concepts

These are the key terms and concepts of this chapter. The page number of their first explanation is given in parentheses.

1. Applet (120)
2. Application software (96)
3. Application-specific programs (97)
4. Assembler language (117)
5. Database management package (103)
6. Desktop publishing (102)
7. Electronic mail (100)
8. Electronic spreadsheet package (102)
9. File management (112)
10. Fourth-generation language (118)
11. General-purpose application programs (97)
12. Graphical user interface (98)
13. Groupware (106)
14. High-level language (117)
15. HTML (120)
16. Integrated package (98)
17. Java (120)
18. Language translator program (121)
19. Machine language (116)
20. Multitasking (113)
21. Natural language (118)
22. Network management programs (115)
23. Network operating systems (115)
24. Nonprocedural language (118)
25. Object-oriented language (119)
26. Operating system (111)
27. Personal information manager (106)
28. Presentation graphics package (104)
29. Programming tools (122)
30. Resource management (112)
31. Software suites (98)
32. System management programs (111)
33. System software (96)
34. Task management (112)
35. Trends in software (96)
36. User interface (112)
37. Utility programs (116)
38. Virtual memory (112)
39. Web browser (99)
40. Word processing package (101)

Review Quiz

Match one of the previous key terms and concepts with one of the brief examples or definitions that follow. Try to find the best fit for answers that seem to fit more than one term or concept. Defend your choices.

_____ 1. Programs that manage and support the operations of computers.

_____ 2. Programs that direct the performance of a specific use of computers.

_____ 3. A system of programs that manages the operations of a computer system.

_____ 4. Managing the processing of tasks in a computer system.

_____ 5. Managing the use of CPU time, primary and secondary storage, telecommunications processors, and input/output devices.

_____ 6. Managing the input/output, storage, and retrieval of files.

_____ 7. The function that provides a means of communication between end users and an operating system.

_____ 8. The use of icons, bars, buttons, and other image displays to help you get things done.

_____ 9. Provides a greater memory capability than a computer's actual memory capacity.

_____ 10. Programs that manage and support the performance of networks.

_____ 11. Software that manages telecommunications in complex local area networks.

_____ 12. Manages and supports the maintenance and retrieval of data stored in databases.

_____ 13. Translates high-level instructions into machine language instructions.

_____ 14. Performs housekeeping chores for a computer system.

15. A category of application software that performs common information processing tasks for end users.

____ 16. Software available for the specific applications of end users in business, science, and other fields.

____ 17. Helps you surf the Web.

____ 18. Use your networked computer to send and receive messages.

____ 19. Creates and displays a worksheet for analysis.

____ 20. Allows you to create and edit documents.

____ 21. You can produce your own brochures and newsletters.

____ 22. Helps you keep track of appointments and tasks.

____ 23. A program that performs several general-purpose applications.

____ 24. A combination of individual general-purpose application packages that work easily together.

____ 25. Software to support the collaboration of teams and work groups.

____ 26. Uses instructions in the form of coded strings of ones and zeros.

____ 27. Uses instructions consisting of symbols representing operation codes and storage locations.

____ 28. Uses instructions in the form of brief statements or the standard notation of mathematics.

____ 29. Might take the form of query languages and report generators.

____ 30. Languages that tie together data and the actions that will be performed upon the data.

____ 31. You don't have to tell the computer how to do something, just what result you want.

____ 32. As easy to use as one's native tongue.

____ 33. Includes programming editors, debuggers, and code generators.

____ 34. Produces hyperlinked multimedia documents for the Web.

____ 35. A popular object-oriented language for web-based applications.

____ 36. A small application program distributed from a web server.

____ 37. Toward powerful, integrated, network-enabled, expert-assisted packages with easy-to-use graphic and natural language interfaces for productivity and collaboration.

Discussion Questions

1. What major trends are occurring in software? What capabilities do you expect to see in future software packages?

2. How do the different roles of system software and application software affect you as a business end user? How do you see this changing in the future?

3. Refer to the Real World Case on Egghead.com and others in the chapter. Should the many current business users of Windows NT 4.0 switch to Windows 2000 when it becomes available? Why or why not?

4. Why is an operating system necessary? That is, why can't an end user just load an application program in a computer and start computing?

5. Should a web browser be integrated into an operating system? Why or why not?

6. Refer to the Real World Case on Jay Jacobs and Burlington Coat Factory in the chapter. What are the business benefits and limitations of using open-source software to run a company's systems?

7. Are software suites, web browsers, and groupware merging together? What are the implications for a business and its end users?

8. How are the HTML and Java programming languages affecting business applications on the Web?

9. Refer to the Real World Problem on US West and Result Communications in the chapter. What are the business implications of Citrix software, which lets FutureLink "offer up any application over any operating system to any hardware platform"?

10. Which application software packages are the most important for a business end user to know how to use? Explain the reasons for your choices.

Real World Problems

1. Recreational Equipment Inc.: Using Web Browsers for In-Store E-Commerce

As a retailer that equips explorers for the great outdoors, Recreational Equipment Inc. (REI) in Kent, Washington, has been eager to explore the Internet. In 1999, its cash registers were linked to the Web.

Selling online became a major priority in 1998, but retailers were investigating how they could use the Web in their brick-and-mortar stores as well. "Everyone assumes it's going to happen, but the question is 'How deep into the store?'" said Donald Bellomy, an analyst at Aberdeen Group.

REI, a cooperative with 1.5 million members and 51 stores nationwide, began testing new sales terminals equipped with web browsers at its Linwood, Washington, store in July of 1998. During the next nine months, the chain installed the systems in all of its stores, said Jim Smith, REI's retail operations administrator.

REI already had installed computerized kiosks that let customers order products as they browse the merchandise on the sales floor. Store clerks are able to use the new Windows NT–based registers to look up product and company information and place orders for customers via REI's web site. The three-year-old web site (www.rei.com) has been surprisingly successful. So much so, in fact, that the popular outdoors company opened an "outlet" web site (www.reioutlet.com) that features discount prices on close-out merchandise.

"The web site is becoming our major repository of product information," Smith said. The cashiers also can use REI's web site to sell items that are out of stock at a particular store but available online. Eventually, the web site will completely replace the current mainframe-based, in-store ordering system used by store buyers and managers, Smith said.

Web browsers at the point of sale are most appropriate in specialty stores, where service at the register is at least as important as speed, Bellomy said. Cashiers with access to web site product and customer data, for example, can provide more personal service and also remind customers of appropriate promotions, he said.

a. What are the benefits and limitations of using web browsers at sales terminals in retail stores?

b. Should some types of stores avoid using web browsers at sales terminals? Why or why not?

Source: Adapted from David Orenstein, "Retailers Find Uses for Web Inside Stores," *Computerworld*, January 11, 1999, p. 41. Copyright by Computerworld, Inc., Framingham, MA 01701. Reprinted from *Computerworld*.

2. US West and Result Communications: The Business Case for Software Rentals

US West Inc. pulled the plug on its in-house sales applications, crossing over to the brave new world of web-based application software rentals. Beginning in the spring of 1999, the Denver-based telecommunications company has rented Seibel Systems' sales force automation software from USInternetworking.

Under a three-year contract, USI is implementing, hosting, and managing the Seibel software, which 1,000 US West salespeople with laptop computers access over the Internet. The software is loaded on laptops, but the salespeople access the USI web server via an Internet-based secured network.

By the end of June, all 1,000 users were to be plugged in and using the new software, said Sandi Miyaki, director of channel operations at US West. "The benefit of using laptops and having Internet access is that salespeople can spend more time with customers and still access the numbers they need," Miyaki said. Prior to deploying laptops to users last year, salespeople accessed the company's sales applications from office-based PCs, which meant they had less time for sales calls.

To date, US West is the largest of a growing number of companies to rent Internet-based enterprise software applications from a growing group of so-called managed application providers.

For example, Result Communications Ltd. in Calgary, Alberta, Canada, turned to FutureLink for network operating software and services because it had neither the staff nor the expertise to build and maintain a complex network plus a wide range of graphics and business software, said Rob Skeet, director of new media.

So instead, Result pays a monthly fee of $200 per workstation for FutureLink to deliver both Macintosh graphics applications and Windows-based business applications over a single network. FutureLink's offering is based on technology from Citrix Systems that it rents out to customers of its network services. "The Citrix technology, which sits on top of the operating system software, lets us offer up any application over any operating system to any hardware platform," said FutureLink CEO Cam Chell. Calgary-based FutureLink also rents out financial applications from Great Plains Software and customer management software from Onyx Corp.

The software rental programs, which are being targeted primarily at fast-growing midmarket companies, are supposed to eliminate long, complex implementations and cut high software maintenance costs. They also make costs more predictable because users pay fixed monthly fees, which cover ongoing maintenance and software upgrades. Renting also eliminates user investment in hardware and software licenses, plus it reduces a company's need for costly and hard-to-retain in-house IT talent.

In all those cases, "the most important thing happening is that ownership of software is changing. People are starting to look at software more as a service than as property," Wainwright said.

a. Why are companies beginning to rent business application software?

b. What are the limitations of this approach?

Source: Adapted from Julia King, "US West Dials in for Web App Rentals," *Computerworld*, February 1, 1999, p. 4; "Users Buy into Software Rentals." *Computerworld*, February 16, 1999, pp. 1–16. Copyright 1999 by Computerworld, Inc., Framingham, MA 01701. Reprinted from *Computerworld*.

3. VIP Systems: Moving COBOL into the Twenty-First Century

COBOL Facts

- Amount of the world's software code in COBOL: 60 percent
- Number of COBOL applications programs: 9.5 million

Many developers think of COBOL as old, yes, but supremely effective, even for the twenty-first century. In an era of distributed and Internet computing, the 39-year-old language isn't consigned to obsolescence. Server- and workstation-based software development tools let COBOL developers design their code for client/server and Internet applications. Developing such COBOL code can be less expensive than rewrit-

ing an application in a younger language or maintaining a costly COBOL mainframe environment.

Development tools such as Net Express, Acu-COBOL-GT, and IBM's Visual-Age for COBOL let users develop applications with a point-and-click visual process in a graphical environment similar to Microsoft's Visual Basic. Net Express and Acu-COBOL also let users embed COBOL business logic in web applications.

For example, VIP Systems Inc., an insurance data processing outsourcer in Oklahoma City, is moving its COBOL applications and data from an old mainframe to Windows NT servers using Net Express 3.0, made by Micro Focus Group in Newbury, England.

"You don't want to throw 30 years of COBOL code in the trash," said Charles Ebert, a vice president at VIP. The improved code, running on VIP's NT servers connected to RAID storage, is 14 times faster than the original code on a Unisys Corporation mainframe, Ebert said.

While VIP has spent almost two years developing and testing the applications, buying a new mainframe to run their COBOL applications programs could have cost hundreds of thousands of dollars up front, thousands more to maintain, and more yet for upgrades, said David Siekman, VIP's president.

a. How and why is COBOL being improved as we enter the twenty-first century?

b. Should COBOL eventually be replaced by other languages and development environments? Why or why not?

Source: Adapted from David Orenstein, "Development Tools Keep COBOL Current," *Computerworld*, January 18, 1999, p. 14. Copyright 1999 by Computerworld, Inc., Framingham, MA 01701. Reprinted from *Computerworld*.

Application Exercises

1. ABC Department Stores

ABC Department Stores would like to acquire software to do the following tasks. Identify what software packages they need.

a. Surf the Web and their intranets and extranets.

b. Send messages to each others' computer workstations.

c. Help employees work together in teams.

d. Use a group of productivity packages that work together easily.

e. Help sales reps keep track of meetings and sales calls.

f. Type correspondence and reports.

g. Analyze rows and columns of sales figures.

h. Develop a variety of graphical presentations.

2. Evaluating Software Packages

Have you used one of the software packages mentioned in this chapter?

a. Briefly describe the advantages and disadvantages of one of the packages you have used so far.

b. How would such a package help you in a present or future job situation?

c. How would you improve the package you used?

3. Software Use at Premier Industries

Premier Industries has recently conducted a survey of the amount of time per week employees spend using various application software packages. The data from this survey follow. The values shown are the total number of workers in each department and the total hours of use of each type of package. To get the average use per worker, you would need to divide the hours shown for a package by the number of workers in the department. You have been asked to prepare a spreadsheet summarizing these data and comparing the use of the various packages across extra departments.

a. Create a spreadsheet that will emphasize the average use per worker of each type of package and make it easy to compare the usage across departments. Be sure to include an overall use category showing the combined use of all of the packages.

b. Creat a set of graphs summarizing your results.

c. A committee has been formed to schedule software training classes at your company. You have been asked to present the results of your analysis as a starting point for this committee's work. Using a word processor or presentation software, produce a brief report highlighting key results and including related spreadsheet pages and graphs needed to support your findings.

Department	Employees	Hours of Software Use			
		Word Processing	Spreadsheet	Database	Presentation
Production	50	25	80	20	0
Shipping	20	10	15	40	5
Advertising	12	60	24	6	60
Sales	25	40	15	150	10
Market research	8	30	80	60	40
Accounting	18	25	100	120	24

4. Examining Application Software Properties

Use your computer's operating system software to find the primary executable file used to run each of the application software packages on your computer; that is, the word processor, spreadsheet, database, and presentation software packages.

(Under Windows you will want to use the Windows Explorer. Search for a file with the package name followed by exe, e.g., *Excel.exe*. This will most likely be found in the Program Files subdirectory or in a subdirectory under the Program Files subdirectory. Once you have found the file you want, click on it with the right mouse button to pop up a dialog box showing its properties.)

a. For each file, find the size in kilobytes, the date the file was last changed, and the version number of the software package. Also record the total size (in kilobytes) of the directory containing these files.

b. Record this information in a spreadsheet file with appropriate headings.

c. Sort your spreadsheet in descending order based on the amount of memory used. Which applications appear to use the most storage space?

d. Now use the Find feature of your operating system (Under Explorer, Tools, Find in Windows 95, 98, and NT) to find all files created or modified in the last seven days. Count the number of files by type (e.g., DOC or PPT) and create a small spreadsheet listing this information, sorted in descending order by the count. Which types of files have you created or modified most frequently in the last week?

Review Quiz Answers

1. 33	7. 36	13. 18	18. 7	23. 16	28. 14	33. 29
2. 2	8. 12	14. 37	19. 8	24. 31	29. 10	34. 15
3. 26	9. 38	15. 11	20. 40	25. 13	30. 25	35. 17
4. 34	10. 22	16. 3	21. 6	26. 19	31. 24	36. 1
5. 30	11. 23	17. 39	22. 27	27. 4	32. 21	37. 35
6. 9	12. 5					

Selected References

1. *Business Software Review, Computerworld, PC Magazine, PC Week, Internet World, PC World,* and *Software Digest* are just a few examples of many good magazines for current information on computer software packages for end user, workgroup, and enterprise applications.

2. The World Wide Web sites of computer manufacturers and software companies like Microsoft, Sun Microsystems, Lotus, IBM, Apple Computer, and Netscape Communications are good sources of information on computer software developments.

3. Jacobsen, Ivar; Maria Ericcson; and Ageneta Jacobsen. *The Object Advantage: Business Process Reengineering with Object Technology.* New York: ACM Press, 1995.

4. The Java Language: A White Paper, from java@java.sun.com. Copyright 1996 by Sun Microsystems.

5. "Software," Technology Buyer's Guide, *Fortune,* Winter 1998 and Winter 1999.

Introduction to Business

Telecommunications

Chapter Highlights

Section I
Telecommunications and the Internet in Business
Networking the Enterprise
Real World Case: America Online: Success and Challenges in Online Commerce and Services
The Business Value of Telecommunications
Trends in Telecommunications
The Internet Revolution
Business Use of the Internet
The Business Value of the Internet
A Telecommunications Network Model
Types of Telecommunications Networks
Section II
Technical Telecommunications Alternatives
Telecommunications Alternatives
Real World Case: Network Alchemy and Others: Virtual Private Networks and E-Commerce
Telecommunications Media
Telecommunications Processors
Telecommunications Software
Network Topologies
Network Architectures and Protocols
Bandwidth Alternatives
Switching Alternatives

Learning Objectives

After reading and studying this chapter, you should be able to:

1. Identify the major types of business applications and the business value of the Internet and other telecommunications networks.

2. Identify several major developments and trends in the industries, technologies, and applications of telecommunications.

3. Identify the basic components, functions, and types of telecommunications networks.

4. Explain the functions of major types of telecommunications network hardware, software, and media.

Telecommunications and the Internet in Business

Networking the Enterprise

Businesses are becoming **internetworked enterprises.** As we said in Chapter 1, the Internet and Internet-like networks inside the enterprise (intranets), between an enterprise and its trading partners (extranets), and other types of networks have become the primary information technology infrastructure of many organizations. Such telecommunications networks enable managers, end users, teams, and workgroups to electronically exchange data and information anywhere in the world with other end users, customers, suppliers, and business partners. Companies and workgroups can thus collaborate more creatively, manage their business operations and resources more effectively, and compete successfully in today's fast-changing global economy. As a manager, entrepreneur, or business professional, you will thus be expected to make or participate in decisions regarding a great variety of telecommunications and network options. That's why you need to study the business applications, technology, and managerial implications of telecommunications.

Analyzing America Online

Read the Real World Case on America Online on the next page. We can learn a lot about the role that new business strategies and information technologies can play in electronic commerce. See Figure 4.1.

Figure 4.1

Robert W. Pittman, president (left), and Stephen M. Case, CEO, of America Online, have successfully steered AOL through the continuing challenges of electronic commerce and online services.

Source: © 1998 James Porto.

America Online: Success and Challenges in Online Commerce and Services

For Robert W. Pittman, president, and Stephen M. Case, CEO, of America Online Inc., 1998 was a year of sweet revenge. Now 1999 promises to be a year of online growth and positioning, with the year 2000 becoming a breakout year for electronic commerce and home Internet services.

As recently as two years ago, AOL was dismissed by Internet cognescenti as an idea whose time had come—and gone. All the real action was on the World Wide Web, not proprietary content services like AOL. But faster than a speeding cursor, this pair of cybermanagers has turned once-ailing AOL from a has-been to the undisputed champ of the online world.

No one who doubted AOL's staying power is skeptical anymore: In November 1998, Case, 40, harnessed the technology horsepower of Silicon Valley with his $4.2 billion purchase of Netscape Communications and a marketing agreement with Sun Microsystems. In a single stroke, AOL became a credible rival to Microsoft in the war for Internet supremacy.

Even before that deal, Pittman, 45, was building AOL into a widely recognized consumer brand, positioning it to be the Coca-Cola or McDonald's of the online world. He lured online merchants to advertise and sell their wares to AOL's over 15 million and still growing subscribers. And with the promise of a more predictable earnings stream based not just on subscription fees but also on potentially more lucrative E-commerce revenues, Case and Pittman have been able to sell AOL as the first blue-chip Internet stock. That helped AOL's shares to jump nearly 600 percent in 1998.

That's an incredible reversal from a few years ago, when AOL looked to be fading fast under a barrage of busy signals. In 1997, AOL suffered a $499 million loss. A year later, AOL hauled in $91.8 million in net income to revenues of $2.6 billion.

How did they do it? First, Case brought in Pittman as CEO to slash costs and invest in more IT capacity and capabilities to clear up AOL's horrible record for customer service and support. Second, AOL finally began making big money E-commerce deals leveraging its customer base of millions of online users. A $100 million three-year deal for exclusive rights to sell long-distance phone service to AOL members by Tel-Save broke the dam. Scores of other deals in the $20 million to $50 million range followed in books (Amazon.com *and* Barnes & Noble), online shopping (CUC International), travel (Preview Travel), flowers (1-800-flowers), music (N2K), and so on. AOL even turned to

Europe in a deal with German global media giant Bertelsmann for 10 percent of AOL and 45 percent of AOL Europe, plus a joint buyout of CompuServe Europe.

Now, new challenges await. One of the biggest online battles will see America Online facing off against Microsoft's WebTV for the Internet TV title. In one corner there's Barry Schuler, head of AOL Interactive Services, and his more than 16 million pairs of eyeballs. In the other is WebTV's scrappy Steve Perlman and his 700,000 subscribers.

Of course, waiting in the wings are cable modem Internet service providers like @Home and MediaOne that have begun to add Internet access to cable TV's list of services.

In the E-commerce game, AOL has some big advantages over other Internet portal challengers like Yahoo, Infoseek, and Excite. First, it has a key partner in newly acquired Netscape. Netscape not only has one of the biggest Internet portals in its Net Center site, but it is also a leader in E-commerce software, services, and expertise.

And as a proprietary network, AOL already has all of its 16 million members' data to leverage for revenue from online retailers. "They've already got your credit card info and billing info and E-mail address," says retail analyst Derek Brown. "They've got a head start in moving into that E-commerce transaction flow."

Case and Pittman have turned AOL around with unusually effective teamwork, despite sharply different styles. Case, an intense introvert, is the big-picture strategizer. Pittman, a talkative extrovert, is the savvy dealmaker and marketing guru. Together, they proved AOL can be cool—as well as profitable.

Case Study Questions

1. Why did the experts predict the downfall of AOL? Why did AOL succeed anyway?

2. What are some of the business challenges facing AOL? How should they confront those challenges?

3. Do you think that AOL will continue to succeed in online services and E-commerce? Why or why not?

Source: Reprinted from "Making AOL A-OK," *Business Week*, January 11, 1999, p. 65, by special permission, copyright © 1999 by the McGraw-Hill Companies, Inc.; Jeffrey Davis, "Mall Rats," *Business 2.0*, January 1999, p. 48; Marc Gaunter, "Mr. Case's Neighborhood," *Fortune*, March 30, 1998, pp. 68–80, © 1998 Time Inc. All rights reserved; and Amy Johns, "Fight!," *Wired*, March 1999, p. 53.

AOL confounded the experts who predicted that proprietary online services like AOL were out of date and unnecessary once the Internet and the World Wide Web became everyone's online destination. But CEO Steve Case and President Bob Pittman worked to solve AOL's customer service problems and thus hold on and attract even more members. Then they began to make a lot of big money deals with online retailers who wanted exclusive rights to sell to AOL's millions of members.

Now AOL and its AOL TV subsidiary face new challenges in providing home Internet services from WebTV and cable modem companies. In addition, Internet portal companies like Yahoo! and Infoseek are challenging AOL in the electronic commerce battle for the business of online merchants and customers. Only time will tell whether AOL will continue to be "the undisputed champ of the online world."

Business Applications of Telecommunications

Telecommunications is the exchange of information in any form (e.g., voice, data, text, and images) over computer-based networks. Figure 4.2 illustrates some of the many possible business applications of telecommunications. It groups telecommunications applications into the major categories of enterprise collaboration systems, electronic commerce systems, and internal business systems. Notice that these applications rely on the telecommunications capabilities of the Internet, intranets, extranets, and other types of enterprise and interorganizational networks. We will discuss some of these networks and applications in this chapter, concentrate on electronic commerce systems in Chapter 6, and intranets and enterprise collaboration systems in Chapter 7.

Enterprise collaboration applications use telecommunications networks to support communication, coordination, and collaboration among the members of business teams and workgroups. For example, employees and external consultants on a project team may use the Internet, intranets, and extranets to support electronic mail,

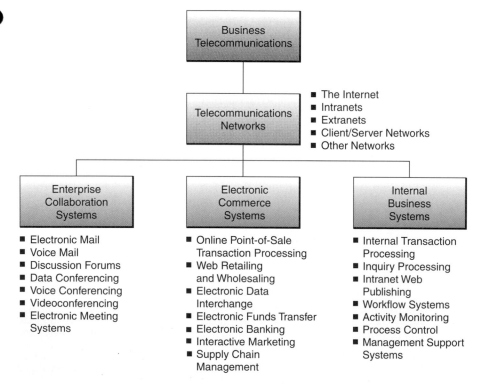

Figure 4.2

Some of the business applications of telecommunications. Note the many types of applications for enterprise collaboration, electronic commerce, and internal business operations.

videoconferencing, electronic discussion groups, and multimedia web pages to communicate and collaborate on business projects. **Electronic commerce** applications support the buying and selling of products, services, and information over the Internet and other computer networks. For example, a business could use the Internet to give customers access to multimedia product catalogs on the World Wide Web, use extranets so large customers can access the company's inventory databases, and use a corporate intranet so employees can easily look up customer records stored on intranet servers.

Internal business applications of telecommunications depend on a variety of computer networks to support a company's business operations. For example, employees may use an intranet to access benefits information on a human resource department server. Or a company may link wide area and local area networks so managers can make inquiries and generate reports from corporate databases stored on network servers and mainframe systems.

The Business Value of Telecom- munications

What *business value* is created by the business applications of telecommunications shown in Figure 4.2? That's what you need to know as a manager, entrepreneur, or business professional. A good way to answer this question is shown in Figure 4.3. Information technology, especially in telecommunications-based business applications, helps a company overcome geographic, time, cost, and structural barriers to business success. Figure 4.3 outlines examples of the business value of these four strategic capabilities of telecommunications and other information technologies. This figure emphasizes how several applications of electronic commerce can help a firm capture and provide information quickly to end users at remote geographic locations at reduced costs, as well as supporting its strategic organizational objectives.

For example, traveling salespeople and those at regional sales offices can use the Internet, extranets, and other networks to transmit customer orders from their laptop or desktop PCs, thus breaking geographic barriers. Point-of-sale terminals and an

Figure 4.3   Examples of the business value of electronic commerce applications of telecommunications.

Strategic Capabilities	EC Examples	Business Value
Overcome geographic barriers: Capture information about business transactions from remote locations	Use the Internet and extranets to transmit customer orders from traveling salespeople to a corporate data center for order processing and inventory control	Provides better customer service by reducing delay in filling orders and improves cash flow by speeding up the billing of customers
Overcome time barriers: Provide information to remote locations immediately after it is requested	Credit authorization at the point of sale using online POS networks	Credit inquiries can be made and answered in seconds
Overcome cost barriers: Reduce the cost of more traditional means of communication	Desktop videoconferencing between a company and its business partners using the Internet, intranets, and extranets	Reduce expensive business trips; allows customers, suppliers, and employees to collaborate, thus improving the quality of decisions reached
Overcome structural barriers: Support linkages for competitive advantage	Electronic data interchange (EDI) of transactions data to and from suppliers and customers using extranets or other networks	Fast, convenient service locks in customers and suppliers

Major trends in business
telecommunications.

Industry trends Toward a greater number of competitive vendors, carriers,
alliances, and network services, accelerated by deregulation
and the growth of the Internet.

Technology trends Toward the use of the Internet and other open and
interconnected local and global digital networks for voice,
data, images, and video with heavy use of high-speed fiber
optic lines and satellite channels to form a global information
superhighway system.

Application trends Toward the pervasive use of the Internet, enterprise intranets,
and interorganizational extranets to support electronic
commerce, enterprise collaboration, online business operations,
and strategic advantage in local and global markets.

online sales transaction processing network can break time barriers by supporting immediate credit authorization and sales processing. Teleconferencing can be used to cut costs by reducing the need for expensive business trips since it allows customers, suppliers, and employees to participate in meetings and collaborate on joint projects. Finally, electronic data interchange systems are used by the business to establish strategic relationships with their customers and suppliers by making the exchange of electronic business documents fast, convenient, and tailored to the needs of the business partners involved.

Trends in Telecommunications

Major trends occurring in the field of telecommunications have a significant impact on management decisions in this area. You should thus be aware of major trends in telecommunications industries, technologies, and applications that significantly increase the decision alternatives confronting the managers of business organizations. See Figure 4.4.

Industry Trends

The competitive arena for telecommunications service has changed dramatically in the United States and several other countries in recent years. The telecommunications industry has changed from a few government-regulated monopolies to a deregulated market with many fiercely competitive suppliers of telecommunications services. Numerous companies now offer businesses and consumers a choice of everything from local and global telephone services to communications satellite channels, mobile radio, cable TV, cellular phone services, and Internet access. See Figure 4.5.

The explosive growth of the Internet and the World Wide Web has spawned a host of new telecommunications products, services, and providers. Driving and responding to this growth, business firms have dramatically increased their use of the Internet and the Web for electronic commerce and collaboration. Thus, the service and vendor options available to meet a company's telecommunications needs have increased significantly, as have a business manager's decision-making alternatives.

Figure 4.5

The spectrum of telecommunications-based services available today.

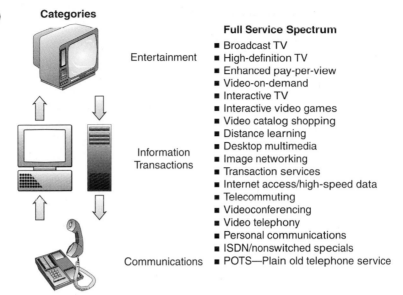

Categories

Entertainment

Information Transactions

Communications

Full Service Spectrum
- Broadcast TV
- High-definition TV
- Enhanced pay-per-view
- Video-on-demand
- Interactive TV
- Interactive video games
- Video catalog shopping
- Distance learning
- Desktop multimedia
- Image networking
- Transaction services
- Internet access/high-speed data
- Telecommuting
- Videoconferencing
- Video telephony
- Personal communications
- ISDN/nonswitched specials
- POTS—Plain old telephone service

Source: Adapted from Samir Chatterjee, "Requirements for Success in Gigabit Networking," *Communications of the ACM*, July 1997, p. 64. Copyright © 1997, Association of Computing Machinery. By permission.

Technology Trends

Open systems with unrestricted connectivity, using **Internet networking technologies** as their technology platform, are today's primary telecommunications technology drivers. Web browser suites, HTML web page editors, Internet and intranet servers and network management software, TCP/IP Internet networking products, and network security fire walls are just a few examples. These technologies are being applied in Internet, intranet, and extranet applications, especially those for electronic commerce and collaboration. This trend has reinforced previous industry and technical moves toward building client/server networks based on an open systems architecture.

Open systems are information systems that use common standards for hardware, software, applications, and networking. Open systems, like the Internet and corporate intranets and extranets, create a computing environment that is open to easy access by end users and their networked computer systems. Open systems provide greater **connectivity,** that is, the ability of networked computers and other devices to easily access and communicate with each other and share information. Any open systems architecture also provides a high degree of network **interoperability.** That is, open systems enable the many different applications of end users to be accomplished using the different varieties of computer systems, software packages, and databases provided by a variety of interconnected networks. Frequently, software known as *middleware* may be used to help diverse systems work together.

Telecommunications is also being revolutionized by the rapid change from analog to **digital network technologies.** Telecommunications has always depended on voice-oriented analog transmission systems designed to transmit the variable electrical frequencies generated by the sound waves of the human voice. However, local and global telecommunications networks are rapidly converting to digital transmission technologies that transmit information in the form of discrete pulses, as computers do. This provides (1) significantly higher transmission speeds, (2) the movement of larger amounts of information, (3) greater economy, and (4) much lower error rates than analog systems. In addition, digital technologies allow telecommunications networks to carry multiple types of communications (data, voice, video) on the same circuits.

Another major trend in telecommunications technology is a change from reliance on copper wire–based media and land-based microwave relay systems to fiber optic lines and communications satellite transmissions. Fiber optic transmission, which uses pulses of laser-generated light, offers significant advantages in terms of reduced size and installation effort, vastly greater communication capacity, much faster transmission speeds, and freedom from electrical interference. Satellite transmission offers significant advantages for organizations that need to transmit massive quantities of data, audio, and video over global networks, especially to isolated areas.

Application Trends

The changes in telecommunications industries and technologies just mentioned are causing a significant change in the business use of telecommunications. The trend toward more vendors, services, Internet technologies, and open systems, and the rapid growth of the Internet, the World Wide Web, and corporate intranets and extranets, dramatically increases the number of feasible telecommunications applications. Thus, telecommunications networks are now playing vital and pervasive roles in electronic commerce, enterprise collaboration, and internal business applications that support the operations, management, and strategic objectives of both large and small companies.

An organization's local and global computer networks can dramatically cut costs, shorten business lead times and response times, support electronic commerce, improve the collaboration of workgroups, develop online operational processes, share resources, lock in customers and suppliers, and develop new products and services. This makes telecommunications a more complex and important decision area for businesses that must increasingly find new ways to compete in both domestic and global markets.

The Internet Revolution

Suddenly it seems that the Internet is everywhere. After two decades of relative obscurity as a government and research network, the Internet burst upon the 1990s to penetrate the public consciousness, capturing headlines and attracting millions of users around the world. Every indication points to even faster growth in the future [3].

The explosive growth of the **Internet** is a revolutionary phenomenon in computing and telecommunications. The Internet has become the largest and most important network of networks today, and is evolving into the *information superhighway* of tomorrow. The Internet is constantly expanding, as more and more businesses and other organizations and their users, computers, and networks join its global web. Thousands of business, educational, and research networks now connect millions of computer systems and users in more than 200 countries to each other. The Internet has also become a key platform for a rapidly expanding list of information and entertainment services and business applications, including enterprise collaboration and electronic commerce systems.

The Internet evolved from a research and development network (ARPANET) established in 1969 by the U.S. Defense Department to enable corporate, academic, and government researchers to communicate with E-mail and share data and computing resources. The Net doesn't have a central computer system or telecommunications center. Instead, each message sent has a unique address code so any Internet server in the network can forward it to its destination. Also, the Internet does not have a headquarters or governing body. The Internet Society in Reston, Virginia, is one of several

Figure 4.6

The rapid growth of the Internet.

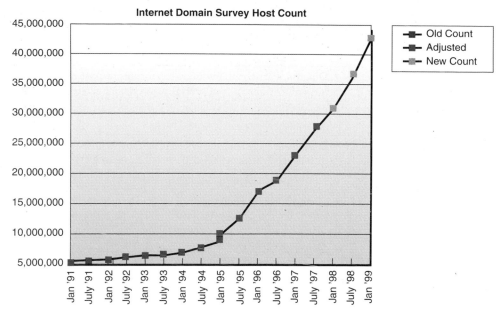

Internet Domain Survey Host Count

Legend:
- Old Count
- Adjusted
- New Count

Source: Adapted from Network Wizards (www.nw.com), March 1999.

volunteer groups of individual and corporate members who promote use of the Internet and the development of new communications standards. These common standards are the key to the free flow of messages among the widely different computers and networks in the system.

The Internet is growing rapidly. For example, the Internet grew from 30 million to over 40 million host computers from early 1998 to early 1999. Figure 4.6 gives you a good idea of the historical growth of the Internet.

Internet Applications

The most popular Internet applications are E-mail, browsing the sites on the World Wide Web, and participating in *newsgroups* and *chat rooms*. Internet E-mail messages usually arrive in seconds or a few minutes anywhere in the world, and can take the form of data, text, fax, and video files. Internet browser software like Netscape Navigator and Microsoft Explorer enables millions of users to *surf* the World Wide Web by clicking their way to the multimedia information resources stored on the hyperlinked pages of businesses, government, and other web sites. Web sites offer information and entertainment, and are the launch sites for electronic commerce transactions between businesses and their suppliers and customers. See Figure 4.7.

The Internet provides electronic discussion forums and bulletin board systems formed and managed by thousands of special-interest newsgroups. You can participate in discussions or post messages on thousands of topics for other users with the same interests to read and respond to. Other popular applications include downloading software and information files and accessing databases provided by thousands of business, government, and other organizations. You can make online searches for information at web sites in a variety of ways, using your browser and search sites such as Yahoo!, Excite, and Infoseek. Logging on to other computers on the Internet and holding realtime conversations with other Internet users in chat rooms are also popular uses of the Internet. See Figure 4.8.

Figure 4.7

Popular uses of the Internet.

• **Surf.** Point and click your way to thousands of hyperlinked web sites and resources for multimedia information, entertainment, or electronic commerce.
• **E-mail.** Exchange electronic mail with millions of Internet users.
• **Discuss.** Participate in discussion forums or post messages on bulletin board systems formed by thousands of special-interest newsgroups.
• **Chat.** Hold realtime text conversations in web site chat rooms with Internet users around the world.
• **Download.** Transfer data files, programs, reports, articles, magazines, books, pictures, sounds, and other types of files from thousands of sources to your computer system.
• **Compute.** Log on to and use thousands of Internet computer systems around the world.
• **Other Uses:** Make long-distance phone calls for free, hold desktop videoconferences, listen to radio programs, watch television, explore virtual worlds, etc.

Business Use of the Internet

As Figure 4.9 illustrates, business use of the Internet is expanding from an electronic information exchange to a broad platform for strategic business applications. Notice how applications like collaboration among business partners, providing customer and vendor support, and buying and selling products and services have become major business uses of the Internet. Other studies of leading corporations and organizations show that they are using Internet technologies primarily for marketing, sales, and customer service applications. However, these studies also show the strong growth of cross-

Figure 4.8

Some of the leading commercial online services, search sites, and Internet service providers (ISPs).

• **America Online www.aol.com** AOL is the leading commerical online service with more than 12 million members, including those added through its acquisition of CompuServe. AOL provides E-mail, news, electronic shopping, chat, and original content, as well as access to the Internet for its dial-up users.
• **AT&T WorldNet www.att.net** AT&T's dial-up Internet access is among the most reliable nationwide Internet service providers (ISPs). At the WorldNet home page, users can find links to all sorts of topics on the Net, including movies, travel, and investing. There are also connections to content providers like AOL, Snap Online, and The Mining Company.
• **Earthlink Network www.earthlink.com** Earthlink is a nationwide ISP that combines fast Internet access with content and information services. These include a shopping area that features links to well-known electronic retailers, such as American Greetings and the Disney Store, and a game room that brings together multiple online game services.
• **Metacrawler www.metacrawler.com** Instead of trying just one service, Metacrawler relays your query to a number of search sites and brings the results back quickly. There's also plenty of other information on the site from weather reports to apartment listings.
• **Yahoo! www.yahoo.com** The best-known site for online searches, Yahoo! is also an Internet "portal" that offers news, financial information, free E-mail, and other services. Its outline format is perfect for finding information in neat categories from arts and humanities to computers and business. Yahoo! also runs special sites for countries like Germany and France and for cities like Boston and Chicago.

Source: Adapted from "What's New in Web Services," in Technology Buyer's Guide, *Fortune*, Winter 1998, pp. 238–40, and "The Great Portal Race," Technology Buyer's Guide, *Fortune*, Winter 1999, pp. 238–42.

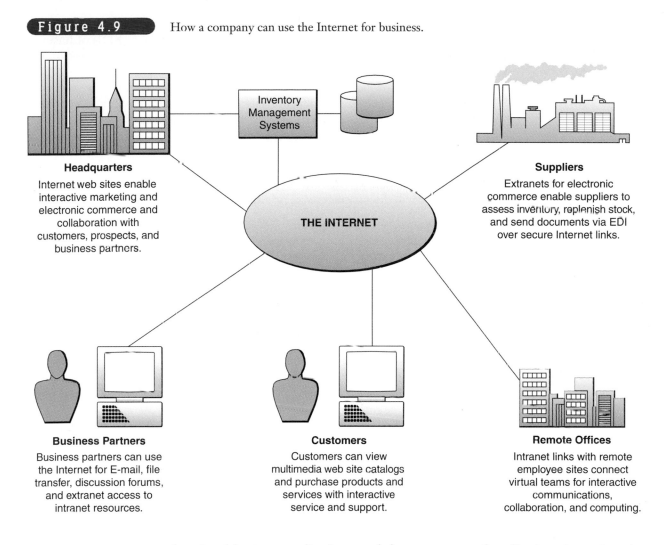

Figure 4.9   How a company can use the Internet for business.

Headquarters
Internet web sites enable interactive marketing and electronic commerce and collaboration with customers, prospects, and business partners.

Inventory Management Systems

THE INTERNET

Suppliers
Extranets for electronic commerce enable suppliers to assess inventory, replenish stock, and send documents via EDI over secure Internet links.

Business Partners
Business partners can use the Internet for E-mail, file transfer, discussion forums, and extranet access to intranet resources.

Customers
Customers can view multimedia web site catalogs and purchase products and services with interactive service and support.

Remote Offices
Intranet links with remote employee sites connect virtual teams for interactive communications, collaboration, and computing.

functional business applications, and the emergence of applications in engineering, manufacturing, human resources, and accounting [15].

Companies are using the Internet for business in a variety of ways, including enterprise communications and collaboration, electronic commerce, and strategic business alliances.

Enterprise Communications and Collaboration

The Internet, intranets, and extranets support realtime global communications and collaboration among employees, customers, suppliers, and other business partners. In teractive web sites, E-mail, bulletin board systems, discussion groups, audio- and videoconferencing, and other Internet features enable internal and external business information to be researched, solicited, disseminated, and shared. This enables members of different organizations and people at different locations to work together as members of **virtual teams** on business projects to develop, produce, market, and maintain products and services. We will discuss this development further in Chapter 7.

Electronic Commerce

The Internet, the World Wide Web, and Internet-based technologies such as intranets and extranets provide global links to a company's customers and suppliers. This enables **electronic commerce** applications—the marketing, buying, selling, and support of products and services over these networks. Such applications include interactive order processing at company web sites, electronic data interchange (EDI) of business transaction documents, and secure electronic funds transfer (EFT) payment systems, which we will discuss in Chapter 6.

Strategic Business Alliances

The Internet enables companies to form strategic alliances with customers, suppliers, consultants, subcontractors, and even competitors. Internet and extranet global links to such business partners support network organizational structures and the formation of **virtual companies.** That is, the Internet enables global alliances of business partners to be quickly formed to take advantage of market opportunities by interconnecting the unique strengths of each partner into an integrated network of business resources and capabilities. We will discuss such strategic alliances further in Chapter 9.

The Business Value of the Internet

The Internet provides a synthesis of computing and communication capabilities that adds value to every part of the business cycle [2].

What business value do companies derive from their business applications on the Internet? Figure 4.10 summarizes how 100 top-rated Internet-using organizations answered that question. Substantial cost savings can arise because applications that use the Internet and Internet-based technologies (like intranets and extranets) are typically less expensive to develop, operate, and maintain than traditional systems. For example, American Airlines saves money every time customers use their web site instead of their customer support telephone system. Another example is corporate intranet applications, which are typically a lot easier and cheaper to develop and maintain than using traditional mainframe or client/server systems.

Other primary reasons for business value include the use of the Internet and the Web for interactive marketing and customer service, as the examples in this chapter

Figure 4.10

How leading Internet-using organizations are deriving business value from their Internet applications.

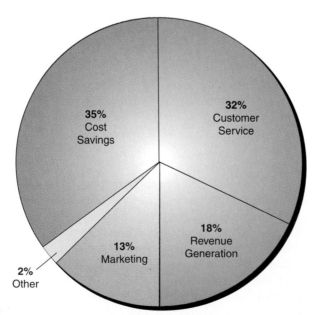

Source: Adapted from Kathleen Gow, "Risk vs. Opportunity," The Premier 100 Supplement to *Computerworld*, February 24, 1997, p. 19. Copyright 1997 by Computerworld, Inc., Framingham, MA 01701. Reprinted from *Computerworld*.

illustrate. Generating revenue from the Internet through electronic commerce applications is a growing source of business value, which we will discuss in Chapter 6. Most companies are building commercial sites on the World Wide Web to achieve four major business objectives:

- Attract new customers via web marketing and advertising.
- Improve service to existing customers via web customer service and support functions.
- Develop new web-based markets and distribution channels for existing products.
- Develop new information-based products accessible on the Web [7].

Figure 4.11 outlines examples of how 10 leading Internet-using organizations have derived cost savings or revenue benefits from their Internet applications.

A Telecommunications Network Model

Before we get any further in our discussion of telecommunications, we should understand the basic components of a **telecommunications network.** Generally, a *communications network* is any arrangement where a *sender* transmits a message to a *receiver* over a *channel* consisting of some type of *medium.* Figure 4.12 illustrates a simple con-

Figure 4.11

Examples of how top-rated companies derived cost savings or revenue from their Internet applications.

Company and URL	Internet Applications and Their Costs/Benefits
Amp, Inc. connect.amp.com	Information and electronic commerce. Allows access to current information on 75,000+ products, including application and product specs. Annual cost savings: $165,000. Development cost: $1.5M.
Arthur D. Little, Inc. www.arthurdlittle.com	Marketing of company services. Increases customer contact and global accessibility. Revenue benefits: $600,000. Development cost: $30,000.
Black & Veatch www.bv.com	Construction management system. Aids in tracking construction information across the United States. Annual cost savings: $1M.
CUC International www.cuc.com	Shoppers Advantage, online shopping service. Reduces customer service calls and telephony costs. Revenue benefits: $500,000. Development cost: $300,000.
Intellichoice, Inc. www.intellichoice.com	Automotive information and sales. Provides easy access and use of information, reduces production costs of reports. Revenue benefits: $90,000 to $100,000. Development cost: $9,000 to $10,000.
Johnson & Higgins www.jh.com	Marketing and customer services. Includes insurance policy summaries, certificate requests, manuals, and interactive service plans. Reduces costs and errors, streamlines workflow. Annual savings: $1M.
Peapod www.peapod.com	Online grocery shopping and delivery service. Saves customers time and provides information about products. Revenue benefit: $30M+. Development cost: $50,000.
MovieFone, Inc. www.movielink.com	National movie showtime guide and teleticketing service. Marketing, sales, customer service. Revenue benefit: $1M. Development cost: $1.5M.
Schnuck Markets www.schnucks.com	Marketing and electronic commerce for flowers, party goods, and movie tickets.Revenue benefit: $100,000+. Development cost: $100,000.
The Sharper Image www.sharperimage.com	Electronic commerce, marketing tool. Customer service improved in time savings, access to products, and increased sales. Annual cost savings: approximately $500,000. Revenue benefit: $1M+.

Source: Adapted from "The Premier 100," The Premier 100 Supplement to *Computerworld*, February 24, 1997, pp. 56–63. Copyright 1997 by Computerworld, Inc., Framingham, MA 01701. Reprinted from *Computerworld*.

Figure 4.12   The five basic components in a telecommunications network: (1) terminals, (2) telecommunications processors, (3) telecommunications channels, (4) computers, and (5) telecommunications software.

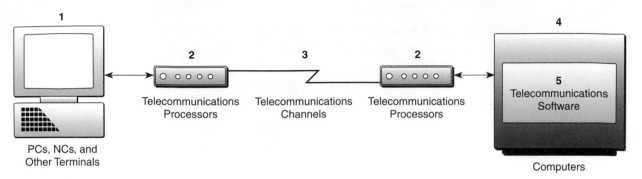

ceptual model of a telecommunications network, which shows that it consists of five basic categories of components:

- **Terminals,** such as networked personal computers, network computers, or video terminals. Of course, any input/output device that uses telecommunications networks to transmit or receive data is a terminal, including telephones and the computer terminals discussed in Chapter 2.

- **Telecommunications processors,** which support data transmission and reception between terminals and computers. These devices, such as modems, switches, and routers, perform a variety of control and support functions in a telecommunications network. For example, they convert data from digital to analog and back, code and decode data, and control the speed, accuracy, and efficiency of the communications flow between computers and terminals in a telecommunications network.

- **Telecommunications channels** over which data are transmitted and received. Telecommunications channels use combinations of **media,** such as copper wires, coaxial cables, fiber optic cables, microwave systems, and communications satellites, to interconnect the other components of a telecommunications network.

- **Computers** of all sizes and types are interconnected by telecommunications networks so that they can carry out their information processing assignments. For example, a mainframe computer may serve as a *host computer* for a large network, assisted by a midrange computer serving as a *front-end processor,* while a microcomputer may act as a *network server* for a small network of microcomputer workstations.

- **Telecommunications control software** consists of programs that control telecommunications activities and manage the functions of telecommunications networks. Examples include network management programs of all kinds, such as *telecommunications monitors* for mainframe host computers, *network operating systems* for microcomputer network servers, and *web browsers* for microcomputers.

No matter how large and complex real world telecommunications networks may appear to be, these five basic categories of network components must be at work to support an organization's telecommunications activities. This is the conceptual framework you can use to help you understand the various types of telecommunications networks in use today.

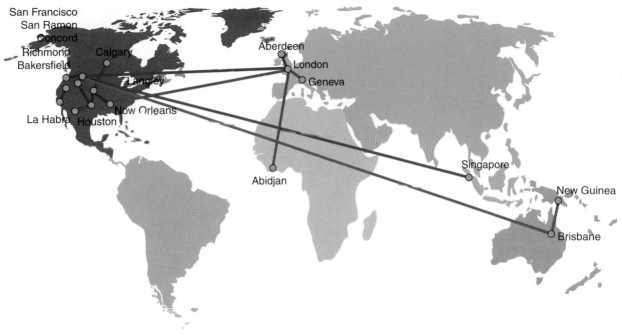

Figure 4.13   A global wide area network (WAN): the Chevron MPI (Multi-Protocol Internetwork).

Source: Courtesy of Cisco Systems, Inc.

Types of Telecommunications Networks

There are many different types of telecommunications networks. However, from an end user's point of view, there are only a few basic types, such as wide area and local area networks and interconnected networks like the Internet, intranets, and extranets, as well as client/server and interorganizational networks.

Wide Area Networks

Telecommunications networks covering a large geographic area are called **wide area networks** (WANs). Networks that cover a large city or metropolitan area (*metropolitan area networks*) can also be included in this category. Such large networks have become a necessity for carrying out the day-to-day activities of many business and government organizations and their end users. For example, WANs are used by many multinational companies to transmit and receive information among their employees, customers, suppliers, and other organizations across cities, regions, countries, and the world. Figure 4.13 illustrates an example of a global wide area network for a major multinational corporation.

Local Area Networks

Local area networks (LANs) connect computers and other information processing devices within a limited physical area, such as an office, a classroom, a building, manufacturing plant, or other work site. LANs have become commonplace in many organizations for providing telecommunications network capabilities that link end users in offices, departments, and other workgroups.

LANs use a variety of telecommunications media, such as ordinary telephone wiring, coaxial cable, or even wireless radio systems, to interconnect microcomputer workstations and computer peripherals. To communicate over the network, each PC usually has a circuit board called a *network interface card*. Most LANs use a more powerful microcomputer having a large hard disk capacity, called a *file server* or

Figure 4.14   A local area network (LAN). Note how the LAN allows users to share hardware, software, and data resources.

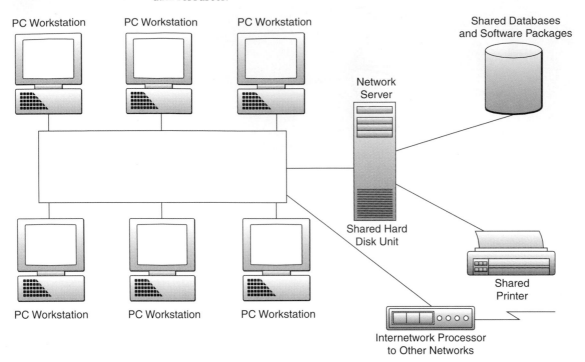

network server, that contains a **network operating system** program that controls telecommunications and the use and sharing of network resources. For example, it distributes copies of common data files and software packages to the other microcomputers in the network and controls access to shared laser printers and other network peripherals. See Figure 4.14.

Intranets and Extranets

Intranets are designed to be open, but secure, internal networks whose web browsing software provides easy point-and-click access by end users to multimedia information on internal web sites. Intranet web sites may be established on internal web servers by a company, its business units, departments, and workgroups. For example, a human resources department may establish an intranet web site so employees can easily access up-to-the-minute information on the status of their benefits accounts, as well as the latest information on company benefits options. One of the attractions of corporate intranets is that their Internet-like technology makes them more adaptable, as well as easier and cheaper to develop and use than either traditional client/server or mainframe-based legacy systems. See Figure 4.15.

Extranets are networks that link some of the intranet resources of a company with other organizations and individuals. For example, extranets enable customers, suppliers, subcontractors, consultants, and others to access selected intranet web sites and other company databases. Organizations can establish private extranets among themselves, or use the Internet as part of the network connections between them.

Many organizations use *virtual private networks* (VPNs) to establish secure intranets and extranets. A **virtual private network** is a secure network that uses the Internet as its main *backbone network*, but relies on the fire walls and other security features of its

Figure 4.15

An example of intranets and extranets.

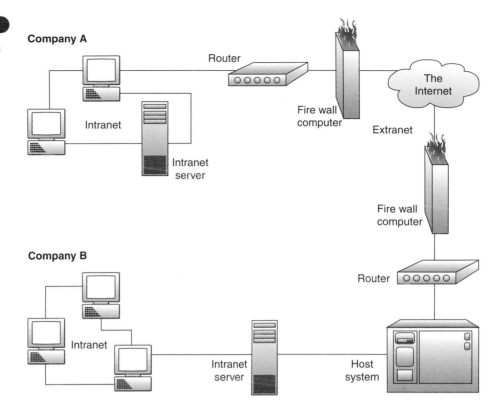

Internet and intranet connections and those of participating organizations. Thus, for example, VPNs would enable a company to use the Internet to establish secure intranets between its distant branch offices and manufacturing plants, and secure extranets between itself and its customers and suppliers [6].

Client/Server Networks

Client/server networks have become the predominate information architecture of enterprisewide computing. In a client/server network, end user PC or NC workstations are the **clients.** They are interconnected by local area networks and share application processing with network **servers,** which also manage the networks. Local area networks are also interconnected to other LANs and wide area networks of client workstations and servers. Figure 4.16 illustrates the functions of the computer systems in client/server networks.

A continuing trend is the **downsizing** of larger computer systems by replacing them with client/server networks. For example, a client/server network of several interconnected local area networks may replace a large mainframe-based network with many end user terminals. This typically involves a complex and costly effort to install new application software that replaces the software of older, traditional mainframe-based business information systems, now called **legacy systems.** Client/server networks are seen as more economical and flexible than legacy systems in meeting end user, workgroup, and business unit needs, and more adaptable in adjusting to a diverse range of computing workloads.

Network Computing

The growing reliance on the computer hardware, software, and data resources of the Internet, intranets, extranets, and other networks has emphasized that for many users, "the network is the computer." This **network computing,** or *network-centric,* concept,

The functions of the computer systems in client/server networks.

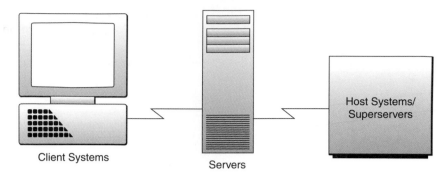

Client Systems

Servers

Host Systems/Superservers

- Types: PCs, Network Computers, Workstations, Macintoshes.
- Functions: Provide user interface, perform some/most processing on an application.

- Types: Servers, Workstations, or Midrange Systems
- Functions: Shared computation, application control, distributed databases.

- Types: Mainframes and Midrange Systems.
- Functions: Central database control, security, directory management, heavy-duty processing.

which views networks as the central computing resource of any computing environment, appears to be the architecture that will take computing into the next century.

Figure 4.17 illustrates that in network computing, **network computers** provide a browser-based user interface for processing small application programs called **applets.** Network computers are microcomputers that are designed as low-cost networked computing devices or *information appliances.* Servers provide the operating system, applets, databases, and database management software needed by the end users in the network.

Interorganizational Networks

Many business applications of telecommunications involve the use of the Internet, extranets, and other networks to form **interorganizational networks.** Such networks link a company's headquarters and other locations to the networks of its customers, suppliers, and other organizations. For example, you can think of a customer account inquiry system that provides intranet access by employees and extranet access by cus-

The functions of the computer systems in network computing.

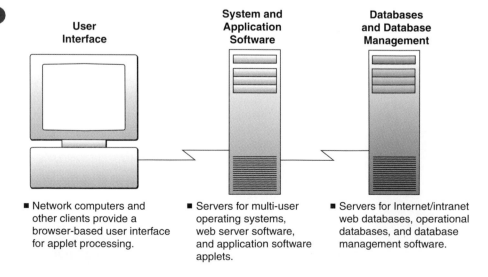

User Interface

System and Application Software

Databases and Database Management

- Network computers and other clients provide a browser-based user interface for applet processing.

- Servers for multi-user operating systems, web server software, and application software applets.

- Servers for Internet/intranet web databases, operational databases, and database management software.

tomers as an example of an interorganizational network. So is the use of electronic data interchange (EDI) systems that link the computers of a company with those of its suppliers and customers for the electronic exchange of business documents. Of course, electronic commerce applications for buying and selling products and services on the World Wide Web depend on Internet, intranet, extranet, and other interorganizational networks established among banks, businesses, customers, and suppliers.

Thus, the business use of telecommunications networks has moved beyond the boundaries of the enterprise. Now many business firms are using the Internet and other networks to extend their information systems to their customers and suppliers, both domestically and internationally. As we will see in Chapter 9, such interorganizational systems build new strategic business relationships and alliances with those stakeholders in an attempt to increase and lock in their business, while locking out competitors. Also, transaction processing costs are frequently reduced, and the quality of service to customers and suppliers improves significantly. See Figure 4.18.

Figure 4.18

The GE Trading Process Network is an example of an interorganizational network. It provides web-based marketplace services to help businesses engage in electronic commerce.

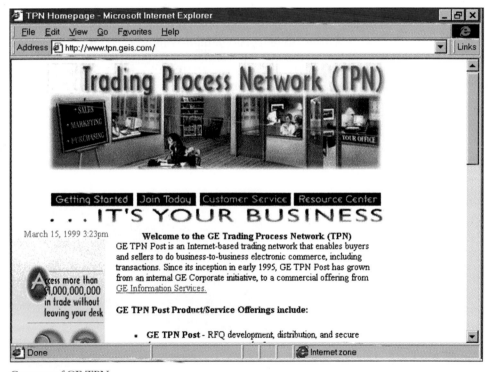

Courtesy of GE TPN.

Section II Technical Telecommunications Alternatives

Telecommunications Alternatives

Telecommunications is a highly technical, rapidly changing field of information systems technology. Most end users do not need a detailed knowledge of its technical characteristics. However, it is necessary that you understand some of the important characteristics of the basic components of telecommunications networks. This understanding will help you participate effectively in decision making regarding telecommunications alternatives.

Analyzing Network Alchemy

Read the Real World Case on Network Alchemy on the next page. We can learn a lot about the business impact of telecommunications network alternatives from this case. See Figure 4.19.

Network Alchemy believes it has the technology to take virtual private networks (VPNs) to the high level of performance and security demanded by business-to-business electronic commerce. Companies like MasterCard International and MCI WorldCom engaged in high-volume E-commerce transactions don't want to use the Internet unless VPNs can provide quality-of-service guarantees of 99.999 percent reliability for transactions processing and security. If VPNs can meet such high quality-of-service expectations, companies will be able to lower their communications costs by using the Internet for electronic commerce and other business applications.

Figure 4.20 outlines key telecommunications components and alternatives. Remember, a basic understanding and appreciation, not a detailed knowledge, are sufficient for most business end users.

Figure 4.19

Vice President Ken Adelman (left) and CEO Kenny Frerichs of Network Alchemy believe that virtual private networks are the logical technology for electronic commerce.

Source: BARTNAGEL.COM.

Network Alchemy and Others: Virtual Private Networks and E-Commerce

To some businesses, conducting commerce over the Internet is like crossing a six-lane freeway blind-folded. Sending and receiving sensitive data, conducting financial transactions, or even exchanging credit information without guaranteed delivery at prescribed transmission rates using sound security measures—a quality-of-service (QOS) guarantee—is simply too risky.

"Quality of service has been the biggest deterrent to doing big business across the Internet," says Scott Beaudoin, a network architect at MasterCard International, a company that depends on the secure and rapid electronic transmission of information.

Solving the QOS problems that have stalled the growth of business-to-business electronic commerce will help propel that market's worth from $17 billion in 1998 to $327 billion in 2002, according to Forrester Research. Beginning in 1999, guaranteed QOS has blessed the Internet in the form of *virtual private network* (VPN) technologies that offer service-level agreements guaranteeing a 99.999 percent reliability.

VPNs are really secure corporate extranets with which a company's offices, suppliers, and customers communicate via the public Internet. VPNs have always been economical—they eliminate long-distance telephone charges by allowing customers to use local ISPs for Internet access. But service providers and large corporations are still looking for a more reliable technology to send and receive sensitive financial information, like credit card and account numbers, securely from site to site.

One company, Network Alchemy, is already making this claim for its VPN hardware and software. Network Alchemy shipped the first of its secure, highly reliable VPN systems in January 1999. Its initial products are three VPN servers, bundled with client and Java-based network management software that can support small-office network traffic at 10 mbps and large network traffic of 10,000 concurrent sessions at 100 mbps, or 20,000 concurrent sessions at 200 mbps.

The company builds its products around "cryptographic clustering," a technique that groups VPN servers into a cluster, ensuring a high service quality because no single point of failure can crash the system. Network Alchemy also has a partnership agreement with PriceWaterhouseCoopers, whose security professionals will provide consulting and implementation services for Network Alchemy's VPN products.

"There's no question that E-commerce is the next step for VPNs," says Kenny Frelick, president and CEO of Network Alchemy. That's why MCI WorldCom—the global voice, data, and Internet communications services provider—has begun to play in the VPN services market, and it is considering Network Alchemy's products as a way to fulfill the data transport needs of its business customers. "The top four or five telecom providers get most of their revenue from voice, but the data segments are growing faster," says Vimal Solanki, MCI WorldCom's chief VPN architect. "That growth is absolutely being fueled by E-commerce."

MasterCard International is also evaluating Network Alchemy's offerings. "VPNs are an answer, if they can meet our QOS requirements," says Scott Beaudoin at MasterCard. QOS is critical to MasterCard's business, according to Beaudoin. "If a transaction cannot be processed, the business's preference for MasterCard as credit merchant could slide to one of our competitors," he says, "and we cannot have that."

As businesses adopt VPNs with high QOS for applications as complex as E-commerce, they will decide that the networks can support every other kind of application. In theory, say VPN proponents, a company could run all its applications over the Internet. Thus, VPNs may eventually make even local area networks unnecessary.

Suresh Joseph, a telecommunications analyst at Frost & Sullivan, points to the Automotive Network Exchange (ANX), a VPN used by the Big Three automakers and their suppliers for online procurement that may save $1.1 billion annually, "Business-to-business E-commerce will be improved by VPNs," he says. "It's simple: they cut down the cost of sales and lower the overhead of order processing and procurement."

Case Study Questions

1. What are some of the advantages and limitations of virtual private networks?

2. How could VPN technologies like Network Alchemy's solve the quality-of-service problems of business-to-business E-commerce?

3. Do you think that VPNs will make local area networks unnecessary? Why or why not?

Source: Adapted from Blaise Zerega, "The Right Stuff," *Red Herring*, February 1999, pp. 79–80; and "Quality of Service Closes the Deal," *Red Herring*, February 1999, pp. 76–77.

Figure 4.20

Key telecommunications
network components
and alternatives.

Network Component	Examples of Alternatives
Media	Twisted-pair wire, coaxial cable, fiber optics, microwave radio, communications satellites, cellular phone systems, LAN radio, infrared
Processors	Modems, multiplexers, switches, routers, hubs, gateways, front-end processors, private branch exchanges
Software	Network operating systems, telecommunications monitors, web browsers, middleware
Channels	Analog/digital, switched/nonswitched, circuit/message/packet/cell switching, bandwidth alternatives
Topology/architecture	Point-to-point, multidrop, star/ring/bus, OSI, TCP/IP

Telecommunications Media

Telecommunications channels make use of a variety of **telecommunications media.** These include twisted-pair wire, coaxial cables, and fiber optic cables, all of which physically link the devices in a network. Also included are terrestrial microwave, communications satellites, cellular phone systems, and packet and LAN radio, all of which use microwave and other radio waves. In addition, there are infrared systems, which use infrared light to transmit and receive data. See Figure 4.21.

Twisted-Pair Wire

Ordinary telephone wire, consisting of copper wire twisted into pairs **(twisted-pair wire),** is the most widely used medium for telecommunications. These lines are used in established communications networks throughout the world for both voice and data transmission. Thus, twisted-pair wiring is used extensively in home and office telephone systems and many local area networks and wide area networks.

Coaxial Cable

Coaxial cable consists of a sturdy copper or aluminum wire wrapped with spacers to insulate and protect it. The cable's cover and insulation minimize interference and distortion of the signals the cable carries. Groups of coaxial cables may be bundled together in a big cable for ease of installation. These high-quality lines can be placed underground and laid on the floors of lakes and oceans. They allow high-speed data

Figure 4.21

Telecommunications
wire and cable
alternatives.

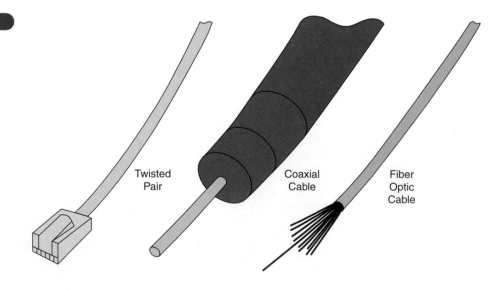

Twisted
Pair

Coaxial
Cable

Fiber
Optic
Cable

transmission and are used instead of twisted-pair wire lines in high-service metropolitan areas, for cable TV systems, and for short-distance connection of computers and peripheral devices. Coaxial cables are also used in many office buildings and other work sites for local area networks.

Fiber Optics

Fiber optics uses cables consisting of one or more hair-thin filaments of glass fiber wrapped in a protective jacket. They can conduct light pulses generated by lasers at transmission rates as high as 30 billion bits per second. This is about 60 times greater than coaxial cable and 3,000 times better than twisted-pair wire lines. Fiber optic cables provide substantial size and weight reductions as well as increased speed and greater carrying capacity. A half inch-diameter fiber optic cable can carry up to 50,000 channels, compared to about 5,500 channels for a standard coaxial cable.

Fiber optic cables are not affected by and do not generate electromagnetic radiation; therefore, multiple fibers can be placed in the same cable. Fiber optic cables have a minimal need for repeaters for signal retransmissions, unlike electrical wire media. Fiber optics also has a much lower data error rate than other media and is harder to tap than electrical wire and cable. One disadvantage of fiber optics has been the difficulty of splicing the cable to make connections, though this is also a security advantage that limits line tapping. However, improved splicing techniques have made it easier to splice fiber cables. Fiber optic cables have already been installed in many parts of the United States, and they are expected to replace other communications media in many applications in the near future.

Terrestrial Microwave

Terrestrial microwave involves earthbound microwave systems that transmit high-speed radio signals in a line-of-sight path between relay stations spaced approximately 30 miles apart. Microwave antennas are usually placed on top of buildings, towers, hills, and mountain peaks, and they are a familiar sight in many sections of the country. They are still a popular medium for both long-distance and metropolitan area networks.

Communications Satellites

Communications satellites also use microwave radio as their telecommunications medium. Many communications satellites are placed in stationary geosynchronous orbits approximately 22,000 miles above the equator. Satellites are powered by solar panels and can transmit microwave signals at a rate of several hundred million bits per second. They serve as relay stations for communications signals transmitted from earth stations. Earth stations use dish antennas to beam microwave signals to the satellites that amplify and retransmit the signals to other earth stations thousands of miles away.

While communications satellites were used initially for voice and video transmission, they are now also used for high-speed transmission of large volumes of data. Because of time delays caused by the great distances involved, they are not suitable for interactive, realtime processing. Communications satellite systems are operated by several firms, including Comsat, American Mobile Satellite, and Intellsat, an international consortium of more than 100 nations.

A variety of other satellite technologies are being implemented to improve global business communications. For example, Kmart and other companies use networks of small satellite dish antennas known as VSAT (very-small-aperture terminal) to connect their stores and distant work sties. Another example is the Iridium satellite network of hundreds of low-earth orbit (LEO) satellites orbiting at an altitude of only 485 miles above the earth. Iridium provides cellular phone, paging, and messaging services to users anywhere on the globe.

Cellular Phone Systems

Cellular phone systems use several radio communications technologies. However, all of them divide a geographic area into small areas, or *cells*, typically from one to several square miles in area. Each cell has its own low-power transmitter or radio relay antenna device to relay calls from one cell to another. Computers and other communications processors coordinate and control the transmissions of mobile phone users as they move from one area to another.

Cellular phone systems have long used analog communications technologies operating at frequencies in the 800 to 900 MHz cellular band. Newer cellular systems use digital technologies, which provide greater capacity and security, and additional services such as voice mail, paging, messaging, and caller ID. These capabilities are also available with the new PCS (Personal Communications Services) phone systems. PCS operates at 1,900 MHz frequencies using digital technologies that are related to digital cellular. However, PCS phone systems cost substantially less to operate and use than cellular systems and have lower power consumption requirements [3].

Digital cellular technologies have become an important communications medium for mobile computing and data communications. Cellular modems enable laptop computer users to use digital cellular systems for mobile computing. For example, Federal Express uses digital cellular for data communications using terminals in each of its thousands of delivery vans as part of its competitive edge. The integration of cellular and other mobile radio technologies, such as *packet radio*, and the emergence of personal telephone communications satellite systems are expected to accelerate in the next few years. These developments will provide a full range of communications and computing capabilities to mobile computer users. See Figure 4.22.

Figure 4.22

The Planet 1 personal satellite telephone is a lightweight, mobile satellite terminal that allows voice, fax, and data communication from virtually anywhere in the world.

Courtesy COMSAT Personal Communication.

Wireless LANs

Wiring an office or a building for a local area network is often a difficult and costly task. Older buildings frequently do not have conduits for coaxial cables or additional twisted-pair wire, and the conduits in newer buildings may not have enough room to pull additional wiring through. Repairing mistakes and damages to wiring is often difficult and costly, as are major relocations of LAN workstations and other components. One solution to such problems is installing a **wireless LAN,** using one of several wireless technologies. An important example is LAN radio, which may involve a high-frequency radio technology similar to digital cellular, or a low-frequency radio technology called *spread spectrum.* The other wireless LAN technology is called infrared because it uses beams of infrared light to establish network links between LAN components.

Obviously, a wireless LAN eliminates or greatly reduces the need for wires and cables, thus making a LAN easier to set up, relocate, and maintain. However, current wireless technologies have higher initial costs and other limitations. For example, an infrared LAN transmits faster than radio LANs but is limited to line-of-sight arrangements to a maximum of about 80 feet between components. High-frequency radio LANs do not need line-of-sight links, but are limited to 40 to 70 feet between components in enclosed areas. Spread spectrum LANs can penetrate masonry walls and link components from 100 to 200 feet away in enclosed areas, but are more subject to receiving or generating radio interference.

Telecommunications Processors

Telecommunications processors such as modems, multiplexers, switches, and routers perform a variety of support functions between the computers and other devices in a telecommunications network. Let's take a look at some of these processors and their functions. See Figure 4.23.

Modems

Modems are the most common type of communications processor. They convert the digital signals from a computer or transmission terminal at one end of a communications link into analog frequencies that can be transmitted over ordinary telephone lines. A modem at the other end of the communications line converts the transmitted data back into digital form at a receiving terminal. This process is known as *modulation* and *demodulation,* and the word *modem* is a combined abbreviation of those two words. Modems come in several forms, including small stand-alone units, plug-in circuit boards, and removable modem cards for laptop PCs. Most modems also support a variety of telecommunications functions, such as transmission error control, automatic dialing and answering, and a faxing capability.

Modems are used because ordinary telephone networks were primarily designed to handle continuous analog signals (electromagnetic frequencies), such as those generated by the human voice over the telephone. Since data from computers are in digital form (voltage pulses), devices are necessary to convert digital signals into appropriate analog transmission frequencies and vice versa. However, digital communications networks that use only digital signals and do not need analog/digital conversion are becoming commonplace. Since most modems also perform a variety of telecommunications support functions, devices called *digital modems* are still used in digital networks. Figure 4.24 compares several new modem and telecommunications technologies.

Multiplexers

A **multiplexer** is a communications processor that allows a single communications channel to carry simultaneous data transmissions from many terminals. Thus, a single communications line can be shared by several terminals. Typically, a multiplexer merges the transmissions of several terminals at one end of a communications channel, while a similar unit separates the individual transmissions at the receiving end.

Figure 4.23   The communications processors involved in a typical Internet connection.

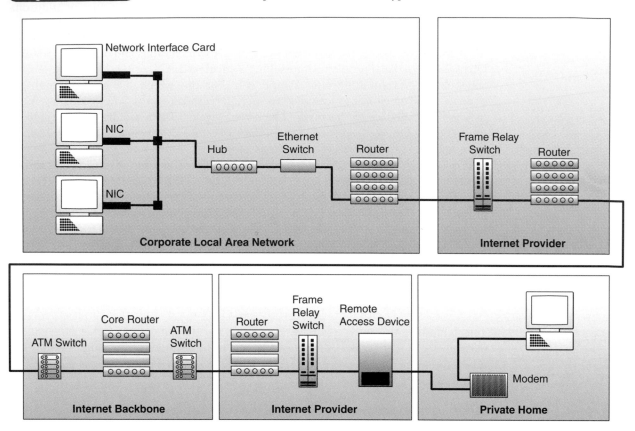

This is accomplished in two basic ways. In *frequency division multiplexing* (FDM), a multiplexer effectively divides a high-speed channel into multiple slow-speed channels. In *time division multiplexing* (TDM), the multiplexer divides the time each terminal can use the high-speed line into very short time slots, or time frames. The most advanced and popular type of multiplexer is the *statistical time division multiplexer*, most commonly referred to as a statistical multiplexer. Instead of giving all terminals equal time

Figure 4.24

Comparing new modem and telecommunications technologies.

Modem (56K bit/sec)	DSL (Digital Subscriber Line) Modem
• Receives at 56K bit/sec.	• Receives at up to 256K bit/sec.
• Sends at 28.8K bit/sec.	• Sends at 64K bit/sec.
• Slowest technology	• Users must be near switching centers
ISDN (Integrated Services Digital Network)	**Cable Modem**
• Sends and receives at 128K bit/sec.	• Receives at 1.5 to 3M bit/sec.
• Users need extra lines	• Sends at 128K bit/sec.
• Becoming obsolete	• Cable systems need to be upgraded

slots, it dynamically allocates time slots only to active terminals according to priorities assigned by a telecommunications manager.

Internetwork Processors

Telecommunications networks are interconnected by special-purpose communications processors called **internetwork processors** such as switches, routers, hubs, and gateways. A *switch* is a communications processor that makes connections between telecommunications circuits in a network so a telecommunications message can reach its intended destination. A *router* is a more intelligent communications processor that interconnects networks based on different rules or *protocols*, so a telecommunications message can be routed to its destination. A *hub* is a port switching communications processor. Advanced versions of hubs provide automatic switching among connections called *ports* for shared access to a network's resources. Workstations, servers, printers, and other network resources are connected to ports, as are switches and routers provided by the hub to other networks. Networks that use different communications architectures are interconnected by using a communications processor called a *gateway*. All these devices are essential to providing connectivity and easy access between the multiple LANs and wide area networks that are part of the intranets and client/server networks in many organizations.

Telecommunications Software

Software is a vital component of all telecommunications networks. In Chapter 3, we discussed telecommunications and network management software, which may reside in PCs, servers, mainframes, and communications processors like multiplexers and routers. For example, mainframe-based wide area networks frequently use *telecommunications monitors* or *teleprocessing* (TP) monitors. CICS (Customer Identification Control System) for IBM mainframes is a typical example. Servers in local area networks rely on Novell NetWare, IBM's OS/2 Warp Server, or Microsoft Windows NT Server.

Corporate intranets use network management software like Netscape's Enterprise Server, which is one of several programs for network management, electronic commerce, and application development in Netscape's SuiteSpot, a suite of software servers for the Internet, intranets, and extranets. Many software vendors offer telecommunications software known as *middleware*, which can help diverse networks communicate with each other. A variety of communications software packages are available for microcomputers, especially Internet web browsers like Netscape Navigator and Microsoft Explorer. See Figure 4.25.

Telecommunications software packages provide a variety of communications support services. For example, they work with a communications processor (such as a modem) to connect and disconnect communications links and establish communications parameters such as transmission speed, mode, and direction.

Network management packages such as LAN network operating systems and WAN telecommunications monitors determine transmission priorities, route (switch) messages, poll terminals in the network, and form waiting lines (queues) of transmission requests. They also detect and correct transmission errors, log statistics of network activity, and protect network resources from unauthorized access.

Network Topologies

There are several basic types of network *topologies*, or structures, in telecommunications networks. Figure 4.26 illustrates three basic topologies used in wide area and local area telecommunications networks. A *star* network ties end user computers to a central computer. A *ring* network ties local computer processors together in a ring on a more equal basis. A *bus* network is a network in which local processors share the same

Figure 4.25

A display of Netscape
Enterprise Server
intranet management
software.

bus, or communications channel. A variation of the ring network is the *mesh* network.
It uses direct communications lines to connect some or all of the computers in the ring
to each other. Another variation is the *tree* network, which joins several bus networks
together.

Client/server networks may use a combination of star, ring, and bus approaches.
Obviously, the star network is more centralized, while ring and bus networks have a
more decentralized approach. However, this is not always the case. For example, the
central computer in a star configuration may be acting only as a *switch*, or message-
switching computer, that handles the data communications between autonomous local
computers. Star, ring, and bus networks differ in their performances, reliabilities, and
costs. A pure star network is considered less reliable than a ring network, since the
other computers in the star are heavily dependent on the central host computer. If it
fails, there is no backup processing and communications capability, and the local computers are cut off from each other. Therefore, it is essential that the host computer be
highly reliable. Having some type of multiprocessor architecture to provide a fault tolerant capability is a common solution.

Ring and bus networks are most common in local area networks. Ring networks
are considered more reliable and less costly for the type of communications in such
networks. If one computer in the ring goes down, the other computers can continue to
process their own work as well as to communicate with each other.

Network Architectures and Protocols

Until quite recently, there was a lack of sufficient standards for the interfaces between
the hardware, software, and communications channels of data communications networks. For this reason, it is quite common to find a lack of compatibility between the
data communications hardware and software of different manufacturers. This situation
hampered the use of data communications, increased its costs, and reduced its efficiency and effectiveness. In response, computer manufacturers and national and inter-

Figure 4.26   The ring, star, and bus network topologies.

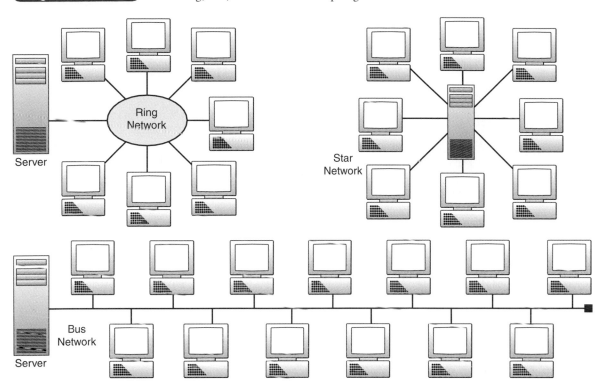

national organizations have developed standards called *protocols* and master plans called *network architectures* to support the development of advanced data communications networks.

Protocols. A **protocol** is a standard set of rules and procedures for the control of communications in a network. However, these standards may be limited to just one manufacturer's equipment, or to just one type of data communications. Part of the goal of communications network architectures is to create more standardization and compatibility among communications protocols. One example of a protocol is a standard for the physical characteristics of the cables and connectors between terminals, computers, modems, and communications lines. Other examples are the protocols that establish the communications control information needed for *handshaking*, which is the process of exchanging predetermined signals and characters to establish a telecommunications session between terminals and computers. Other protocols deal with control of data transmission reception in a network, switching techniques, internetwork connections, and so on.

Network Architectures. The goal of network architectures is to promote an open, simple, flexible, and efficient telecommunications environment. This is accomplished by the use of standard protocols, standard communications hardware and software interfaces, and the design of a standard multilevel interface between end users and computer systems.

Figure 4.27 The seven layers of the OSI communications network architecture, and the five layers of the Internet's TCP/IP protocol suite.

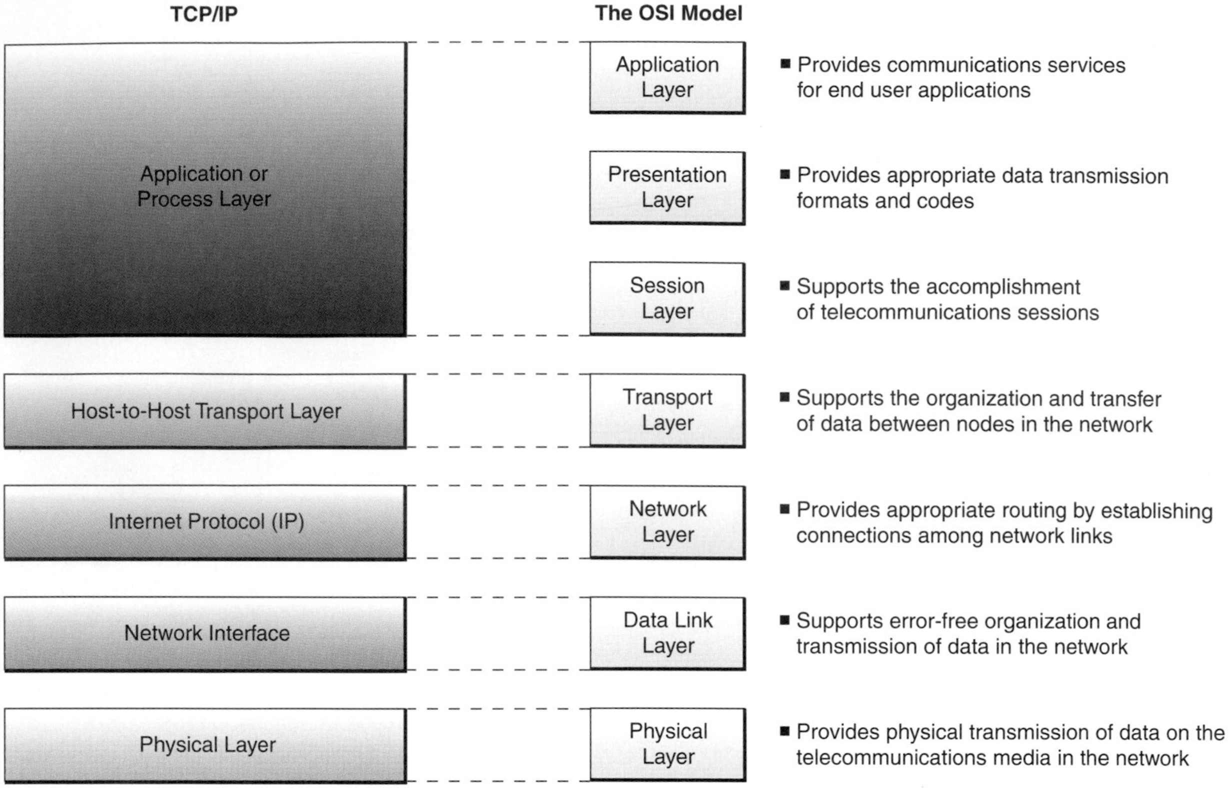

The OSI Model

The International Standards Organization (ISO) has developed a seven-layer Open Systems Interconnection (OSI) model to serve as a standard model for network architectures. Dividing data communications functions into seven distinct layers promotes the development of modular network architectures, which assists the development, operation, and maintenance of complex telecommunications networks. Figure 4.27 illustrates the functions of the seven layers of the OSI model architecture.

The Internet's TCP/IP

The Internet uses a system of telecommunications protocols that has become so widely used that it is equivalent to a network architecture. The Internet's protocol suite is called Transmission Control Protocol/Internet Protocol and is known as TCP/IP. As Figure 4.27 shows, TCP/IP consists of five layers of protocols that can be related to the seven layers of the OSI architecture. TCP/IP is used by the Internet and by all intranets and extranets. Many companies and other organizations are also converting their client/server networks to TCP/IP.

Bandwidth Alternatives

The communications speed and capacity of telecommunications networks can be classified by **bandwidth.** This is the frequency range of a telecommunications channel; it determines the channel's maximum transmission rate. The speed and capacity of data transmission rates are typically measured in bits per second (BPS). This is sometimes referred to as the *baud* rate, though baud is more correctly a measure of signal changes in a transmission line.

Figure 4.28

Examples of the telecommunications transmission speeds by type of media and network technology.

Type of Media	Maximum BPS
Twisted pair—unshielded/shielded	2M–100M
Coaxial cable—baseband/broadband	264M–550M
Satellite/terrestrial microwave	100M
Wireless LAN radio	3.3M
Infrared LAN	4M
Fiber optic cable	30G

Network Technologies	Typical/Maximum BPS
Standard Ethernet or token ring	10–16M
High-speed Ethernet	100M–1G
FDDI: fiber distributed data interface	100M
DDN: digital data network	2.4K–2M
PSN: packet switching network	2.4K–64K
Frame relay network	56K/64K–34M
ISDN: integrated services digital network	64K/128K–2M
ATM: asynchronous transfer mode	25/155M–2.4G

KBPS = thousand BPS or kilobits per second. GBPS = billion BPS or gigabits per second.
MBPS = million BPS or megabits per second.

Low-speed analog channels (*voiceband*) are typically used for transmission rates from 300 to 9,600 BPS, but can now handle up to 1 million BPS (MBPS). They are usually unshielded twisted-pair lines commonly used for voice communications, but are also used for data communications by microcomputers, video terminals, and fax machines. Medium-speed channels (*medium-band*) use shielded twisted-pair lines for transmission speeds from 9,600 BPS up to 100 MBPS.

High-speed digital channels (*broadband*) allow transmission rates at specific intervals from 256,000 BPS to several billion BPS. Typically, they use microwave, fiber optics, or satellite transmission. Examples are 1.54 million BPS for T1 communications channels developed by AT&T and up to 100 MBPS for communications satellite channels. See Figure 4.28.

Switching Alternatives

Regular telephone service relies on *circuit switching*, in which a switch opens a circuit to establish a link between a sender and receiver; it remains open until the communication session is completed. In message switching, a message is transmitted a block at a time from one switching device to another.

Packet switching involves subdividing communications messages into fixed or variable groups called packets. For example, in the X.25 protocol, packets are 128 characters long, while they are of variable length in the *frame relay* technology. Packet switching networks are frequently operated by *value-added carriers* who use computers and other communications processors to control the packet switching process and transmit the packets of various users over their networks.

Early packet switching networks were X.25 networks. The X.25 protocol is an international set of standards governing the operations of widely used, but relatively slow, packet switching networks. *Frame relay* is another popular packet switching protocol, and is used by many large companies for their wide area networks. Frame relay is considerably faster than X.25, and is better able to handle the heavy telecommunications traffic of interconnected local area networks within a company's wide area client/server network. ATM (*asynchronous transfer mode*) is an emerging high-capacity *cell switching* technology. An ATM switch breaks voice, video, and other data into fixed cells of 53 bytes (48 bytes of data and 5 bytes of control information), and routes them to their next destination in the network. ATM networks are being developed by many companies needing its fast, high-capacity multimedia capabilities for voice, video, and data communications.

Summary

- **Telecommunications Trends.** Many organizations are becoming internetworked enterprises that use the Internet, intranets, and other telecommunications networks to support business operations and collaboration within the enterprise, and with their customers, suppliers, and other business partners. Telecommunications has entered a deregulated and fiercely competitive environment with many vendors, carriers, and services. Telecommunications technology is moving toward open, internetworked digital networks for voice, data, video, and multimedia. A major trend is the pervasive use of the Internet and its technologies to build interconnected enterprise and global networks, like intranets and extranets, that form information superhighways to support enterprise collaboration, electronic commerce, and internal business applications as summarized in Figure 4.2.

- **Telecommunications Networks.** The major generic components of any telecommunications network are (1) terminals, (2) telecommunications processors, (3) communications channels, (4) computers, and (5) telecommunications software. There are several basic types of telecommunications networks, including wide area networks (WANs) and local area networks (LANs). Most WANs and LANs use client/server, network computing, and Internet technologies to form intranets, extranets, and other interorganizational networks.

- **The Internet Revolution.** The explosive growth of the Internet and the use of its enabling technologies have revolutionized computing and telecommunications. The Internet has become the key platform for a rapidly expanding list of information and entertainment services and business applications, including enterprise collaboration and electronic commerce systems. Open systems with unrestricted connectivity using Internet technologies are the primary telecommunications technology drivers in business computing. Their primary goal is to promote easy and secure access by business end users and consumers to the resources of the Internet, enterprise intranets, and interorganizational extranets.

- **Business Use of the Internet.** Businesses are broadening their use of the Internet from simple applications like E-mail and marketing themselves on the World Wide Web. Now companies are deploying a range of applications that give them strategic capabilities in enterprise communications and collaboration and electronic commerce with businesses and consumers, and forging strategic alliances with their business partners.

- **The Business Value of the Internet.** Companies are deriving business value from the Internet: strategic capabilities, which enable them to disseminate information globally, communicate interactively with customized information and services for individual customers, and foster collaboration of people and integration of business processes within the enterprise and with business partners. These capabilities allow them to generate cost savings from using Internet technologies, revenue increases from electronic commerce, and better customer service and relationships through interactive marketing.

- **Network Alternatives.** Key telecommunications network alternatives and components are summarized in Figure 4.20 for telecommunications media, processors, software, channels, and network architectures. A basic understanding of these major alternatives will help business end users participate effectively in decisions involving telecommunications issues. Telecommunications processors include modems, multiplexers, internetwork processors, and various devices to help interconnect and enhance the capacity and efficiency of telecommunications channels. Telecommunications channels use such media as twisted-pair wire, coaxial cables, fiber optic cables, terrestrial microwave, communications satellites, cellular phone systems, and wireless LAN technologies. Telecommunications software, such as network operating systems, telecommunications monitors, and web browsers, controls and supports the communications activity in a telecommunications network.

Key Terms and Concepts

These are the key terms and concepts of this chapter. The page number of their first explanation is in parentheses.

1. Bandwidth alternatives (158)
2. Business applications of telecommunications (132)
3. Business uses of the Internet (138)
4. Business value of the Internet (140)
5. Cellular phone systems (152)
6. Client/server networks (145)
7. Coaxial cable (150)
8. Communications satellites (151)
9. Downsizing (145)
10. Electronic commerce (133)
11. Enterprise collaboration (132)
12. Extranets (144)
13. Fiber optic cables (151)
14. The Internet (136)
15. Internet revolution (136)
16. Internet technologies (135)
17. Internetworked enterprise (130)
18. Internetwork processors (155)
19. Interorganizational networks (146)
20. Intranets (144)
21. Legacy systems (145)
22. Local area network (143)
23. Modem (153)
24. Multiplexer (153)
25. Network architectures (157)
    a. OSI (158)
    b. TCP/IP (158)
26. Network computing (145)
27. Network operating system (144)
28. Network server (144)
29. Network topologies (155)
30. Open systems (135)
31. Protocol (157)
32. Switching alternatives (159)
33. Telecommunications channels (142)
34. Telecommunications media (150)
35. Telecommunications network components (141)
36. Telecommunications processors (142)
37. Telecommunications software (142)
38. Trends in telecommunications (134)
39. Virtual private network (144)
40. Wide area network (143)
41. Wireless LANs (153)

Review Quiz

Match one of the key terms and concepts listed previously with one of the brief examples or definitions that follow. Try to find the best fit for answers that seem to fit more than one term or concept. Defend your choices.

_____ 1. Fundamental changes have occurred in the competitive environment, the technology, and the application of telecommunications.

_____ 2. Includes terminals, telecommunications processors, channels, computers, and control software.

_____ 3. A communications network covering a large geographic area.

_____ 4. A communications network in an office, a building, or other work site.

_____ 5. Electronic mail, videoconferencing, and electronic discussion groups can be used to manage a project.

_____ 6. Using web sites to buy and sell products and services.

_____ 7. Communications data move in these paths using various media in a network.

_____ 8. Coaxial cable, microwave, and fiber optics are examples.

_____ 9. A communications medium that uses pulses of laser light in glass fibers.

_____ 10. Supports mobile telephone and communications.

_____ 11. Includes modems, multiplexers, and internetwork processors.

_____ 12. Includes programs such as network operating systems and web browsers.

_____ 13. A common communications processor for microcomputers.

_____ 14. Helps a communications channel carry simultaneous data transmissions from many terminals.

_____ 15. Star, ring, and bus networks are examples.

_____ 16. Computers in a LAN can be interconnected by radio and infrared technologies.

_____ 17. A computer that handles resource sharing and network management in a local area network.

_____ 18. Intranets and extranets can use their network fire walls and other security features to establish secure Internet links within an enterprise or with its trading partners.

_____ 19. The software that manages a local area network.

_____ 20. An international standard, multilevel set of protocols to promote compatibility among telecommunications networks.

_____ 21. The standard suit of protocols used by the Internet, intranets, extranets, and some other networks.

_____ 22. Standard rules or procedures for control of communications in a network.

_____ 23. Information systems with common hardware, software, and network standards that provide easy access for end users and their networked computer systems.

_____ 24. Interconnected networks need communications processors such as switches, routers, hubs, and gateways.

_____ 25. A global network of millions of business, government, educational, and research networks; computer systems; databases; and end users.

_____ 26. The rapid growth in the business and consumer use of the Internet, and the use of its technologies in internetworking organizations.

_____ 27. Web sites, web browsers, HTML documents, hypermedia databases, and TCP/IP networks are examples.

_____ 28. The modern enterprise is interconnected internally and externally by the Internet, intranets, and other networks.

_____ 29. Business telecommunications supports applications in enterprise collaboration, electronic commerce, and internal business systems.

_____ 30. Networks where end user PCs are tied to network servers to share resources and application processing.

_____ 31. Network computers provide a browser-based interface for software and databases provided by servers.

_____ 32. Replacing mainframe-based systems with client/server networks.

_____ 33. Older, traditional mainframe-based business information systems.

_____ 34. Telecommunications networks come in a wide range of speed and capacity capabilities.

_____ 35. Examples are packet switching using frame relay, and cell switching using ATM technologies.

_____ 36. Telecommunications networks frequently interconnect an organization with its customers and suppliers.

_____ 37. Internet-like networks between a company and its business partners.

_____ 38. Internet-like networks within an enterprise.

_____ 39. Companies are using the Internet for more than E-mail and web site marketing.

_____ 40. Companies are cutting costs, generating revenue, improving customer service, and forming strategic business alliances via the Internet.

Discussion Questions

1. The internetworked enterprise is the best model for the business use of information technology into the next century. Do you agree or disagree? Why?

2. How is the trend toward open systems, connectivity, and interoperability related to business use of the Internet, intranets, and extranets?

3. Refer to the Real World Case on America Online in the chapter. What is the most formidable challenge facing AOL in the next five years? Explain your choice.

4. Do you think that business use of the Internet, intranets, and extranets has changed what business-

people expect from information technology in their jobs? Explain.

5. What are the business benefits and management problems of client/server networks?

6. What examples can you give that trends in telecommunications include more telecommunications providers and a greater variety of telecommunications services?

7. Why are companies expanding their use of interorganizational networks?

8. Refer to the Real World Case on Network Alchemy in the chapter. Should a company try to run all of its applications over a VPN on the Internet? Why or why not?

9. The explosive growth of the Internet and the use of its enabling technologies were the revolutionary technology phenomena of the 1990s. Do you agree or disagree? Why?

10. "The Internet is a contact sport, and if you theorize around it, you'll never win. You have to go in and you have to try. You may not be successful, but you will never get to where you want to go unless you start now." Do you agree with this statement by former chief technology officer of Sun Microsystems and now CEO of Novell, Inc., Eric Schmidt? Explain your position.

Real World Problems

1. **George Margolin and Ron Ben-Israel: Cable Modems versus DSL for Web Access**

George Margolin: Cable Modem
Thomas Edison said that genius is 1 percent inspiration and 99 percent perspiration. George Margolin, an inventor in Newport Beach, California, adds another ingredient to his own creative process: acceleration. An early cable modem user, Margolin raves, "the cable modem speeds up my patent searches, technology investigations, and trademark lookups."

But for Margolin, whose inventions include a folding computer keyboard and special-effects equipment for filmmaking, getting the service installed was like something out of the movie *The Cable Guy*. Four months elapsed between the time Comcast, his cable provider, said service would be available in his neighborhood and the day he finally got up and running—and the company had to dig an 80-foot trench in his neighbor's lawn and chop through the concrete of Margolin's garage to string a cable to his home office.

Cable modem access isn't a universal solution. Questions about service, security, and scalability keep it from being the best option for everyone. Even so, the two cable services we tested, @Home (www.home.net), via TCI, and MediaOne Express (www.mediaoneexpress.com), via MediaOne Cable, delivered an almost irresistible package: connection speeds at least 10 times faster than a 56-kbps modem for almost $40 a month—roughly twice the price of a typical dial-up account.

Ron Ben-Israel: DSL
Award-winning pastry chef Ron Ben-Israel mixes new technology with his old-fashioned business. He connects his New York bakery to the Net via a DSL line, sending photos of cakes to clients and updating his mouthwatering site at www.weddingcakes.com. "The bottom line is that DSL is fast," he says; "this gives me more time to be creative."

The same copper wire that delivers phone service can transport DSL, and some DSL versions can run over 100 times faster than dial-up. The ubiquity of phone wires makes DSL a good choice for businesses that aren't wired for cable.

DSL has various technical problems that prevent providers from deploying it everywhere the phone network goes. For one thing, it's incompatible with some phone company equipment and can reach spots only within a certain distance (usually under 18,000 feet) of switching equipment.

Unlike cable companies, most DSL providers don't bundle the network and the access. Just as with dial-up, you can get DSL service from your phone company and Internet access from an ISP. Today, only a few ISPs offer access through DSL, but more are expected to get on board. Chef Ben-Israel gets his DSL from Transwire. "I like working with a small company that knows me," he explains.

a. What are the advantages and limitations of cable modems and DSL?

b. Which one of the two Internet access methods would you prefer to have? Why?

Source: Adapted from Harry McCracken, "Bandwidth on Demand," *PC World*, March 1999, pp. 109–118. Reprinted with the permission of *PC World* Communications Inc.

2. **Sento Corporation and US West: Computer Telephony Integration**
Sento Corporation picked its phone company to set up a new $1.7 million call center at its headquarters last summer and now finds that the effort is saving 20 percent of the time its agents spend on calls. Sento CIO Keith Barr said that he's happy with the results from Denver-based US West because systems it installed have lessened by 30 seconds to two minutes the time Sento's 170 call agents spend on customer calls. Utah-based Sento is a call-center outsourcer.

"Those kinds of efficiencies are what drives the profit line," Barr said. Agents can cut the time per call without sacrificing customer assistance because the new systems can route the entire call history of a customer, including faxes and E-mail, to a Sento agent as soon as the person calls in. Agents don't have to double-check in separate PC-based files for past E-mail or get out of their seats to track down a fax, Barr said.

A suite of call center software helps provide the key function of moving data to agents. "Computer telephony integration is no simple task, especially to get the real time information synchronized," Barr said. For Sento, US West created a system that can scale to 500 agents, up from Sento's current 170. So far, call volume is 6,000 calls per day, but the center could handle 25,000, Sento officials said.

Because Sento employs computer engineers who function as help desk personnel, it's useful to have them trained in specific technologies. Routing customers to the proper agent is a key function of the new system.

The new systems can also let agents talk via the Web with customers by voice and text as well as give Sento the ability to have agents work at home or remotely. Sento is glad it chose US West, Barr said, not only for its telecommunications and network bandwidth expertise, but also for its traditional computer-integration skills.

The movement of US West and other traditional telecommunications companies into call-center integration and outsourcing is a relatively new trend but one that will continue to grow. US West installed eight call centers last year and expects to install another 20 this year, company officials said.

a. What are the business benefits of computer telephony integration?

b. What role can the World Wide Web play in computer telephony integration? What are the business benefits of this approach?

Source: Adapted from Matt Hamblin, "Revamped Call Center Brings Better Customer Service," *Computerworld*, January 18, 1999, p. 39. Copyright 1999 by Computerworld, Inc., Framingham, MA 01701. Reprinted from *Computerworld*.

3. Hotlinks Inc.: Building a Top Internet Service Provider

Company: Hotlinks Internet service provider based in Melbourne, Australia.

Business Challenge: To gain market share by offering more value than other ISPs, especially through secure Internet-based services.

Solution: Use a suite of Netscape server software to create virtual private environments that enable businesses to capture the benefits of the Internet through effective intra- and intercompany communications.

Solution Features:

1. Customers can create private newsgroups, calendars, and directories in a secure fashion through the use of digital certificates.

2. Messaging Server enhances E-mail by supporting embedded web pages and graphics.

3. Directory Services manages information that multiple applications share, such as user groups, and preferences.

Business Benefits:

1. Effective, inexpensive, Internet communications.
2. Competitive edge through ability to offer remote Internet services to customers.
3. Security of intranet and extranet resources.

An Internet service provider based in Melbourne, Australia, Hotlinks is one of the new-generation ISPs focused on providing customers with fast, sophisticated Internet access. Formed as a result of a merger between two already successful Internet companies, Hotlinks targeted a niche as a provider of superior services and support, out of reach of its competitors. "The result is a well-focused ISP dedicated to making the Internet work for everybody, with a unique focus on providing service and without the massive overhead," says Andrew Thomson, managing director.

"At the same time, you can't discount yourself into oblivion. The market has been saturated with discounting ISPs, and customers have become wary of the low levels of service and quality they are offering. The balancing act is to provide valuable services that customers will pay for." Hotlinks decided to differentiate itself by offering secure, remote access to intranet functions. In so doing, the company knew it could justify fees that would allow profitability.

Hotlinks uses the Netscape family of SuiteSpot software servers to provide private intranet facilities on the Internet. "The number of applications is enormous," says Thomson. "For example, a group of medical professionals uses secure newsgroups hosted by Collabra Server and secured by digital certificates that are authenticated by Netscape Certificate Server. This enables them to discuss complex medical issues among themselves without the rest of the world's being involved." The company also uses these Netscape servers to host secure newsgroups for its 100 technical support agents, who can privately share problems and solutions related to software installation and training.

Says Thomson: "Our ability to deliver quality performance backed by extensive customer support should place us among the top service providers in Australia within the next few years."

a. Do you agree with how Hotlinks is moving to make itself a top ISP? Why or why not?

b. What else would you recommend that Hotlinks do to be a more successful ISP?

Source: Adapted from "Hotlinks Offers Secure Access to Servers with Netscape Certificate Server," netscape.com, March 1999. Copyright 1999 Netscape Communications Corp. Used with permission. All rights reserved.

Application Exercises

1. **Evaluating Online Trading Web Sites**

It's as voyeuristic as Internet sex sites, more addictive than video games, and a lot easier to play—and you can win big money! It's online investing, one of the hottest destinations in cyberspace. Ask Ardavan Arianpour of San Diego, California, who recently turned $1,000 into $5,000 through point-and-click trading. Arianpour is his own broker, trading as often as he likes and poring over online news, quotes, and stock charts. "I just love researching and making money," says Arianpour, who has been piling up profits for retirement. That's still a long way off, though, because he is only 18.

The high school senior is one of millions of people who have hitched their computers to the stock market. Once the preserve of a few computer-literate plungers, online trading could one day account for most of the hundreds of millions in securities transactions each year.

"It's been on fire," Bill Burnham, a senior analyst at Piper Jaffray, says of online trading. "Hands down, it's the most successful area of consumer-based electronic commerce."

Some top sites:

- **Charles Schwab & Co.** (www.schwab.com). The one to beat. Leverages its huge customer base to gain the lead on the Web.
- **E*Trade** (www.etrade.com). A brash upstart whose ad push and emphasis on low prices catapulted it . . . into the top players.
- **Datek Online** (www.datek.com). Active traders paradise. Real-time quotes and trades. Refund if order not completed in a minute.

a. Surf to the online trading sites shown above. Evaluate and rank them based on ease of use, speed, cost, and quality of investment research and help provided.

b. Write up the results of your evaluations in a one- or two-page report. Which is your favorite online trading site? Why? Your least favorite? Explain.

c. Do you agree that online trading is the most successful area of consumer-based electronic commerce? Why or why not?

Source: Adapted from John Greenwald, "A Nation of Stockkeepers," *Time*, May 11, 1998, p. 48.

2. **Visiting Corporate Internet Web Sites**

Visit the Internet World Wide Web sites of Fidelity Investments in Boston, Federal Express in Memphis, and Capital One in Richmond, Virginia.

a. Use the Fidelity investment home page (www.fidelity.com) to look up information on Fidelity and its mutual funds. Then fill out the worksheet form for calculating savings needed for a college fund, and print it out on your system printer.

b. Visit the FedEx home page (www.fedex.com) to review information on FedEx and its services. You would need a user ID and a FedEx account number and package tracking number to check the status of a shipment. So just print out a screenful of information on FedEx services to document your visit.

c. Use Capital One's home page (www.capital1.com) to find out information about Capital One's banking and financial services. Then fill out and print the application form for a Visa card offered by Capital One. Don't submit the application to Capital (you can cancel the session any time) unless you are really interested in applying for their Visa card!

3. **Price and Performance Trends for Computer Hardware on the Web**

Read Application Exercise 2 back in Chapter 2. In this exercise, you are asked to update the analysis described there by adding information about microprocessors, RAM chips, and hard drives. Go onto the Internet, look up pricing information from at least three different web sites, and print out a listing of the information you found. You can look in the web sites of prominent direct retailers of personal computers and computer components (such as www.dell.com or www.gateway.com). Add your current data to the data shown in the table in Application Exercise 2 in Chapter 2, and use it to complete (or revise your results for) the three activities of that exercise.

4. **Using Electronic Communications to Compile a List of Popular Books**

This exercise requires you to assemble a list of books electronically.

a. You will first use one or more web sites for electronic retailers of books (such as amazon.com, borders.com, or BarnesandNoble.com) to obtain pricing information on at least three books of interest to you. (They can be fiction, nonfiction, technical, or any type of book you would like to list.) You are to record the set of information shown in the example for each book.

b. Next, exchange lists with at least two other students via E-mail. Your instructor may assign you a set of students to exchange lists with; if not, you may choose your own group.

c. Create a spreadsheet summarizing the lists of books that you created and you got from your fellow students. Organize your list either alphabetically by the title of the book or in ascending order based on cost.

d. E-mail your completed project to your instructor.

Student listing book	Title	Author	Price	Source
J. Morgan	The Return of Little Big Man	Berger, T.	$15.00	Amazon
J. Morgan	Learning Perl/Tk	Walsh, N., & Mui, L.	$26.36	Amazon
J. Morgan	Business at the Speed of Thought	Gates, W.	$21.00	Barnes & Noble

Review Quiz Answers

1. 38	7. 33	13. 23	19. 27	25. 14	31. 26	37. 12
2. 35	8. 34	14. 24	20. 25*a*	26. 15	32. 9	38. 20
3. 40	9. 13	15. 29	21. 25*b*	27. 16	33. 21	39. 3
4. 22	10. 5	16. 41	22. 31	28. 17	34. 1	40. 4
5. 11	11. 36	17. 28	23. 30	29. 2	35. 32	
6. 10	12. 37	18. 39	24. 18	30. 6	36. 19	

Selected References

1. Carr, Houston, and Charles Snyder. *The Management of Telecommunications.* Burr Ridge, IL: Irwin, 1997.

2. Cronin, Mary. *Doing More Business on the Internet.* 2nd ed. New York: Van Nostrand Reinhold, 1995.

3. Cronin, Mary. *Global Advantage on the Internet.* New York: Van Nostrand Reinhold, 1996.

4. Cronin, Mary. *The Internet Strategy Handbook.* Boston: Harvard Business School Press, 1996.

5. Doolittle, Sean. "Widening the Pipes." *PC Today,* December 1996.

6. Fernandez, Tony. "Beyond the Browser." *NetWorker,* March/April 1997.

7. Kalakota, Ravi, and Andrew Whinston. *Electronic Commerce: A Manager's Guide.* Reading, MA: Addison-Wesley, 1997.

8. Kalakota, Ravi, and Andrew Whinston. *Frontiers of Electronic Commerce.* Reading, MA: Addison-Wesley, 1996.

9. Keen, Peter, and Craigg Balance. *Online Profits: A Manager's Guide to Electronic Commerce.* Boston: Harvard Business School Press, 1997.

10. Kupfer, Andrew. "Four Forces That Will Shape the Internet." *Fortune,* July 6, 1998.

11. "Life on the Web." In Technology Buyer's Guide, *Fortune,* Winter 1999.

12. Martin, Chuck. *The Digital Estate: Strategies for Competing, Surviving, and Thriving in an Internetworked World.* New York: McGraw-Hill, 1997.

13. "Phones to Go." In Technology Buyer's Guide. *Fortune,* Winter 1999.

14. "The Great Portal Race." In Technology Buyer's Guide. *Fortune,* Winter 1999.

15. "The Premier 100." In The Premier 100 Supplement to *Computerworld,* February 24, 1997.

16. Wallace, Bob. "Onsite: Remote Users to Make Gains with New Network," *Computerworld,* February 2, 1998.

Chapter

5

Introduction to

Database Management

Chapter Highlights

Section I
Database Management: Managing Data Resources

Introduction

Real World Case: EMC Corporation: The Business Value of Data Storage in the Age of E-Commerce

Foundation Data Concepts

The Database Management Approach

Using Database Management Software

Types of Databases

Hypermedia Databases on the Web

Managerial Considerations for Data Resource Management

Section II
Technical Foundations of Database Management

Introduction

Real World Case: The Chicago Stock Exchange and Enron Energy Services: Object versus Relational Databases

Database Structures

Object Technology and the Web

Accessing Databases

Database Development

Learning Objectives

After reading and studying this chapter, you should be able to:

1. Outline the advantages of the database management approach.

2. Explain how database management software helps end users and supports business operations and management.

3. Explain the importance of data resource management to an organization, and how it can be implemented by database administration, data administration, and data planning activities.

4. Provide examples to illustrate each of the following concepts:

   a. Logical data elements.

   b. Fundamental database structures.

   c. Major types of databases.

   d. Database access methods.

   e. Database development.

Section I ▸ Database Management: Managing Data Resources

Introduction

Data are a vital organizational resource that need to be managed like other important business assets. Most organizations could not survive or succeed without quality data about their internal operations and external environment.

Organizations are under tremendous pressure to provide better quality decision-making information in forms easy to access and manipulate. Business users are reacting to their own mission-critical needs for better information due to rapidly changing, increasingly volatile and competitive markets, as well as ever-shortening product life cycles [13].

That's why organizations and their managers need to practice **data resource management,** a managerial activity that applies information systems technologies like *database management* and other management tools to the task of managing an organization's data resources to meet the information needs of business users. This chapter will show you the managerial implications of using database management technologies and methods to manage an organization's data assets to meet the information requirements of a business.

Analyzing EMC Corporation

Read the Real World Case on EMC Corporation on the next page. We can learn a lot from this case about the vital role that data resource management techniques play in improving the business operations and competitive decision making of companies. See Figure 5.1.

For example, Michael Ruettgers has led EMC Corporation to incredible success by correctly anticipating and meeting the insatiable need by business for huge amounts of fast, reliable data storage. EMC has captured the business of the top airlines, banks,

Figure 5.1

CEO Michael C. Ruettgers (left) has led the EMC Corporation to the forefront of data storage technology.

Source: © 1999 Seth Resnick.

EMC Corporation: The Business Value of Data Storage in the Age of E-Commerce

Michael C. Ruettgers not only saved EMC Corporation from extinction, in little more than a decade he has transformed a sputtering technology has-been into one of the hottest growth stories of the hot-growth 1990s. When Ruettgers became CEO in 1992, profits were just $30 million; they should top $1 billion in 1999. Meanwhile, he has tripled margins, to more than 20 percent, while boosting sales from $386 million in 1992 to an expected $5.3 billion this year.

EMC's computer storage equipment—big, refrigerator-size boxes full of dozens of interlinked magnetic disk drives that can store the equivalent of 100 million tax returns—hardly gets the blood rushing. But it should. Just as speedy and reliable networking opened the floodgates to cyberspace and E-commerce, ever-more-turbocharged data storage is a key building block of the Internet.

With each online mouse click, either a fresh bit of data is created or already-stored data are retrieved from all those web sites, filled with data-rich photos, stock graphs, and music videos. And the thousands of new web pages created each day need a safe, stable place to hang out. Increasingly, that place is inside one of EMC's big RAID (Redundant Array of Inexpensive Disks) boxes.

All that's on top of the heavy demand for industrial-strength storage already in use by scores of big corporations, including MCI WorldCom, Delta Air Lines, and Visa International. What's driving the growth is a crushing imperative for corporations to analyze every bit of information they can extract from their huge data warehouses for competitive advantage. That has turned the once prosaic storage industry into a key strategic player of the information age. And no one is better positioned to capitalize on it than market leader EMC. With its 35 percent market share, it boasts as customers the world's top 20 telecom outfits, 90 percent of the world's major airlines, and the 25 largest U.S. banks.

The disk drives and computer chips that go into today's large storage systems are essentially commodities. What sets EMC's technology apart is its software, which coordinates the fast movement of data in and out of its storage units, even as they perform other important tasks. Those include replicating stored data to other EMC machines for backup and ensuring that the most sought-after data are readily accessible. Developing the software has cost EMC more than $1 billion in the past nine years. But it has given the company a big lead over its rivals. And EMC plans to spend another $1 billion on software by 2001.

Now, EMC is roaring. But Ruettgers isn't standing still. For nearly the past three years, his team of engineers has been working feverishly to position the company for the vast storage needs of the new E-commerce age. Currently, E-commerce-related business accounts for only a fraction of total sales. But the company expects it to become a major driver of growth.

Already, customers like Charles Schwab & Co. and Cisco rely on EMC to store much of the data for millions of dollars of E-commerce transactions daily. EMC is also luring a new breed of customers, companies like Excite and Amazon.com, too small to fit the typical EMC customer profile in every respect except one—the massive storage requirements of their online businesses.

But even before the full punch of the E-commerce business kicks in, Ruettgers has already raised EMC's bar again. A new technology called *fiber channel* is making it possible to string together many servers with storage units that operate over a wide geographic area.

On March 1, 1998, EMC came out with the first comprehensive package allowing customers to build extensive fiber-channel *storage area networks* (SAN). The National Association of Securities Dealers will be among the first to install EMC's new network to track the billion stock trades a day in its exchange. Other EMC customers, including Citibank Group, are also making the upgrade.

Although EMC Corp. is speeding along for now, the race is on for a piece of the fast-growing data storage business. Spurred on by EMC's success, competitors from Sun Microsystems and IBM to Compaq and Dell are launching their own products in an effort to catch up. And that's why Ruettgers is stepping on the gas to stay ahead of the pack.

Case Study Questions

1. Why is E-commerce vastly increasing the need for data storage?

2. Why is there a heavy demand for data storage in many companies beyond the needs generated by E-commerce?

3. How do the data storage technologies of EMC and others help give greater business value to a company's data resources?

Source: Reprinted from Paul C. Judge, "High-Tech Star," *Business Week*, March 15, 1999, pp. 72–80, by special permission, copyright © 1999 by The McGraw-Hill Companies, Inc.

and telecommunications companies, whose already large storage requirements for their business transactions have expanded even more as they build huge data warehouses to help them use their data resources for competitive advantage.

Now the world's data storage needs are escalating dramatically to meet the vast requirements for data and multimedia storage at millions of web sites. Even this need for storage is expanding swiftly with the rapid growth of electronic commerce. EMC is poised to capture as much of this business as they can with their huge investments in new storage technologies.

Foundation Data Concepts

Before we go any further, let's review some fundamental concepts about how data are organized in information systems. As we first mentioned in Chapter 1, a hierarchy of several levels of data has been devised that differentiates between different groupings, or elements, of data. Thus, data may be logically organized into characters, fields, records, files, and databases, just as writing can be organized in letters, words, sentences, paragraphs, and documents. Examples of these logical data elements are shown in Figure 5.2.

Character

The most basic logical data element is the **character,** which consists of a single alphabetic, numeric, or other symbol. One might argue that the bit or byte is a more elementary data element, but remember that those terms refer to the physical storage elements provided by the computer hardware, discussed in Chapter 2. From a user's point of view (that is, from a *logical* as opposed to a physical or hardware view of data), a character is the most basic element of data that can be observed and manipulated.

Field

The next higher level of data is the **field,** or data item. A field consists of a grouping of characters. For example, the grouping of alphabetic characters in a person's name forms a name field, and the grouping of numbers in a sales amount forms a sales amount field. Specifically, a data field represents an **attribute** (a characteristic or

Figure 5.2 Examples of the logical data elements in information systems. Note especially the examples of how data fields, records, files, and databases are related.

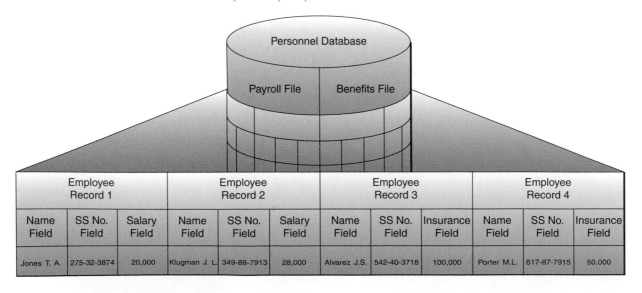

quality) of some **entity** (object, person, place, or event). For example, an employee's salary is an attribute that is a typical data field used to describe an entity who is an employee of a business.

Record

Related fields of data are grouped to form a **record.** Thus, a record represents a collection of *attributes* that describe an *entity*. An example is the payroll record for a person, which consists of data fields describing attributes such as the person's name, Social Security number, and rate of pay. *Fixed-length* records contain a fixed number of fixed-length data fields. *Variable-length* records contain a variable number of fields and field lengths.

File

A group of related records is a data **file,** or *table*. Thus, an employee file would contain the records of the employees of a firm. Files are frequently classified by the application for which they are primarily used, such as a *payroll file* or an *inventory file*, or the type of data they contain, such as a *document file* or a *graphical image file*. Files are also classified by their permanence, for example, a payroll *master file* versus a payroll weekly *transaction file*. A transaction file, therefore, would contain records of all transactions occurring during a period and might be used periodically to update the permanent records contained in a master file. A *history file* is an obsolete transaction or master file retained for backup purposes or for long-term historical storage called *archival storage*.

Database

A **database** is an integrated collection of logically related records or *objects*. As we explained in Chapter 3, an object consists of data values describing the attributes of an *entity*, plus the operations that can be performed upon the data. We will explain object-oriented databases in Section II.

A database consolidates records previously stored in separate files into a common pool of data records that provides data for many applications. The data stored in a database are independent of the application programs using them and of the type of secondary storage devices on which they are stored. For example, a personnel database consolidates data formerly segregated in separate files such as payroll files, personnel action files, and employee skills files. See Figure 5.3.

Figure 5.3

A personnel database consolidates data formerly kept in separate files.

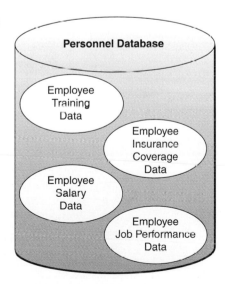

The Database Management Approach

The development of databases and database management software is the foundation of modern methods of managing organizational data. The **database management approach** consolidates data records and objects into databases that can be accessed by many different application programs. In addition, an important software package called a *database management system* (DBMS) serves as a software interface between users and databases. This helps users easily access the records in a database. Thus, database management involves the use of database management software to control how databases are created, interrogated, and maintained to provide information needed by end users and their organizations.

For example, customer records and other common types of data are needed for several different applications in banking, such as check processing, automated teller systems, bank credit cards, savings accounts, and installment loan accounting. These data can be consolidated into a common *customer database*, rather than being kept in separate files for each of those applications. See Figure 5.4.

Thus, the database management approach involves three basic activities:

- Updating and maintaining common databases to reflect new business transactions and other events requiring changes to an organization's records.

- Providing information needed for each end user's application by using application programs that share the data in common databases. This sharing of data is supported by the common software interface provided by a database management system package. Thus, end users and programmers do not have to know where or how data are physically stored.

Figure 5.4

An example of a database management approach in a banking information system. Note how the savings, checking, and installment loan programs use a database management system to share a customer database. Note also that the DBMS allows a user to make a direct, ad hoc interrogation of the database without using application programs.

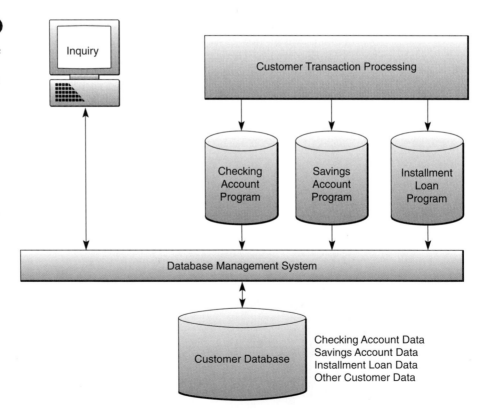

- Providing an inquiry/response and reporting capability through a DBMS package so that end users can easily interrogate databases, generate reports, and receive quick responses to their ad hoc requests for information.

Using Database Management Software

Let's take a closer look at the capabilities provided by database management software. A **database management system** (DBMS) is a set of computer programs that controls the creation, maintenance, and use of the databases of an organization and its end users. As we said in Chapter 3, database management packages are available for micro, midrange, and mainframe computer systems. The four major uses of a DBMS are illustrated in Figure 5.5. Let's take a look at each of them now.

Database Development

Database management packages like Microsoft Access or Lotus Approach allow end users to easily develop the databases they need. However, large organizations with client/server or mainframe-based systems usually place control of enterprisewide database development in the hands of **database administrators** (DBAs) and other database specialists. This improves the integrity and security of organizational databases. Database developers use the *data definition language* (DDL) in database management systems like Oracle 8 or IBM's DB2 to develop and specify the data contents, relationships, and structure of each database, and to modify these database specifications when necessary. Such information is cataloged and stored in a database of data definitions and specifications called a *data dictionary*, which is maintained by the DBA. We will discuss database development further in Section II of this chapter.

The Data Dictionary. Data dictionaries are another tool of database administration. A data dictionary is a computer-based catalog or directory containing *metadata*, that is, data about data. A data dictionary includes a software component to manage a database of data definitions, that is, metadata about the structure, data elements, and other characteristics of an organization's databases. For example, it contains the names and descriptions of all types of data records and their interrelationships, as well as information outlining requirements for end users' access use of application programs, and database maintenance and security. See Figure 5.6.

Figure 5.5   The four major uses of a DBMS package are database development, database interrogation, database maintenance, and application development.

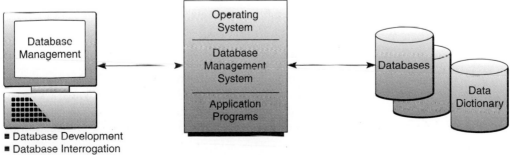

- Database Development
- Database Interrogation
- Database Maintenance
- Application Development

Using Microsoft Access to display part of the information in a data dictionary for a customer order number data element.

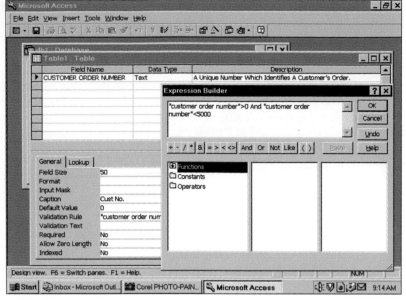

Jeff Borders.

Data dictionaries can be queried by the database administrator to report the status of any aspect of a firm's metadata. The administrator can then make changes to the definitions of selected data elements. Some *active* (versus *passive*) data dictionaries automatically enforce standard data element definitions whenever end users and application programs use a DBMS to access an organization's databases. For example, an active data dictionary would not allow a data entry program to use a nonstandard definition of a customer record, nor would it allow an employee to enter a name of a customer that exceeded the defined size of that data element.

Database Interrogation

The database interrogation capability is a major benefit of a database management system. End users can use a DBMS by asking for information from a database using a *query language* or a *report generator*. They can receive an immediate response in the form of video displays or printed reports. No difficult programming is required. The **query language** feature lets you easily obtain immediate responses to ad hoc data requests: you merely key in a few short inquiries. The **report generator** feature allows you to quickly specify a report format for information you want presented as a report. Figure 5.7 illustrates the use of a DBMS report generator.

SQL Queries. SQL, or Structured Query Language, is a query language found in many database management packages. The basic form of an SQL query is:

SELECT . . . FROM . . . WHERE . . .

After SELECT you list the data fields you want retrieved. After FROM you list the files or tables from which the data must be retrieved. After WHERE you specify conditions that limit the search to only those data records in which you are interested. Figure 5.8 compares an SQL Query to a natural language query for information on customer orders.

Graphical and Natural Queries. Many end users (and IS professionals) have difficulty correctly phrasing SQL and other database language queries. So most end user

Figure 5.7

Using the report generator of Lotus Approach to produce a customer report.

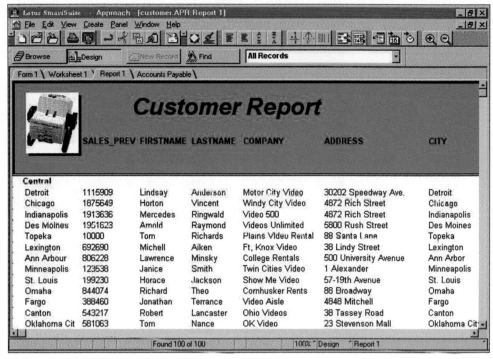

Courtesy of Lotus Development Corporation.

database management packages offer GUI (graphical user interface) point-and-click methods, which are easier to use and are translated by the software into SQL commands. See Figure 5.9. Other packages are available that use *natural language* query statements similar to conversational English (or other languages), as was illustrated in Figure 5.8.

Database Maintenance

The databases of an organization need to be updated continually to reflect new business transactions and other events. Other miscellaneous changes must also be made to ensure accuracy of the data in the databases. This **database maintenance** process is accomplished by transaction processing programs and other end user application packages, with the support of the DBMS. End users and information specialists can also employ various utilities provided by a DBMS for database maintenance.

Figure 5.8

Comparing a natural language query with an SQL query.

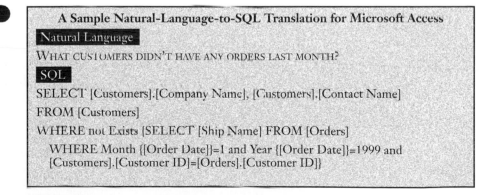

A Sample Natural-Language-to-SQL Translation for Microsoft Access

Natural Language

WHAT CUSTOMERS DIDN'T HAVE ANY ORDERS LAST MONTH?

SQL

SELECT [Customers].[Company Name], [Customers].[Contact Name]

FROM [Customers]

WHERE not Exists [SELECT [Ship Name] FROM [Orders]

WHERE Month {[Order Date]}=1 and Year {[Order Date]}=1999 and [Customers].[Customer ID]=[Orders].[Customer ID]}

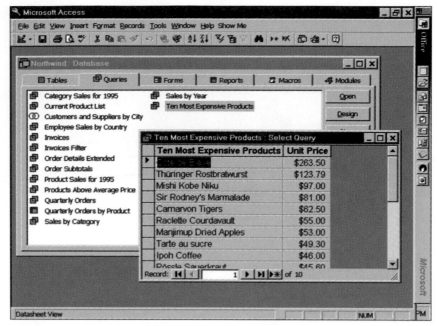

Figure 5.9

Using the Microsoft Access database management package to develop a query.

Jeff Borders.

Application Development	DBMS packages play a major role in **application development.** End users, systems analysts, and other application developers can use the internal 4GL programming language and built-in software development tools provided by many DBMS packages to develop custom application programs. For example, you can use a DBMS to easily develop the data entry screens, forms, reports, or web pages of a business application. A DBMS also makes the job of application programmers easier, since they do not have to develop detailed data-handling procedures using a conventional programming language every time they write a program. Instead, they can include *data manipulation language* (DML) statements in their programs that call on the DBMS to perform necessary data-handling activities.

Types of Databases

Continuing developments in information technology and its business applications have resulted in the evolution of several major types of databases. Figure 5.10 illustrates several major conceptual categories of databases that may be found in computer-using organizations.

Operational Databases

These databases store detailed data needed to support the operations of the entire organization. They are also called *subject area databases* (SADB), *transaction databases,* and *production databases.* Examples are a customer database, personnel database, inventory database, and other databases containing data generated by business operations.

Data Warehouses

A data warehouse stores data from current and previous years that have been extracted from the various operational databases of an organization. It is a central source of data that have been screened, edited, standardized, and integrated so they can be used by managers and other end user professionals for a variety of forms of business analysis,

Figure 5.10   Examples of the major types of databases used by organizations and end users.

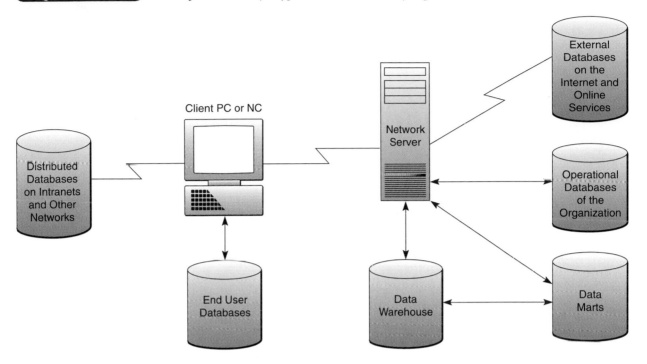

market research, and decision support. Data warehouses may be subdivided into **data marts,** which hold specific subsets of data from the warehouse. See Figure 5.11.

Data Mining

A major use of data warehouse databases is **data mining.** In data mining, the data in a data warehouse are processed to identify key factors and trends in historical patterns of business activity. This can be used to help managers make decisions about strategic changes in business operations to gain competitive advantages in the marketplace. See Figure 5.12.

Distributed Databases

Many organizations replicate and distribute copies or parts of databases to network servers at a variety of sites. These distributed databases can reside on network servers on the World Wide Web, on corporate intranets or extranets, or on other company networks. Distributed databases may be copies of operational or analytical databases, hypermedia or discussion databases, or any other type of database. Replication and distribution of databases is done to improve database performance and security. Ensuring that all of the data in an organization's distributed databases are consistently and concurrently updated is a major challenge of distributed database management.

External Databases

Access to a wealth of information from external databases is available for a fee from commercial online services, and with or without charge from many sources on the Internet, especially the World Wide Web. Web sites provide an endless variety of hyperlinked pages of multimedia documents in *hypermedia databases* for you to access. Data are available in the form of statistics on economic and demographic activity from *statistical* data banks. Or you can view or download abstracts or complete copies of

Figure 5.11

A data warehouse and its data mart subsets hold data that have been extracted from various operational databases for business analysis, market research, decision support, and data mining applications.

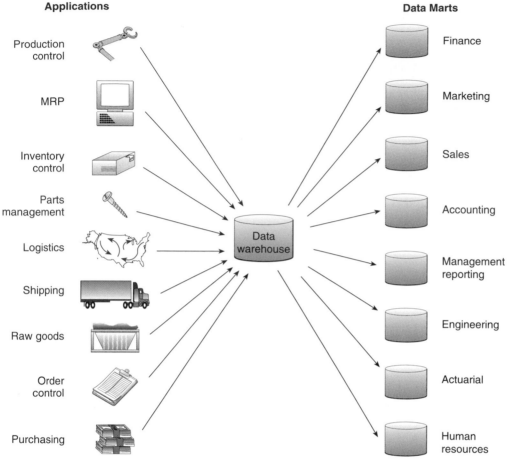

Source: Adapted from W. H. Inmon, "Does Your Datamart Vendor Care About Your Architecture?" *Datamation*, March 1997, p. 106. © 1997 by Cahners Publishing Co.

hundreds of newspapers, magazines, newsletters, research papers, and other published material and other periodicals from *bibliographic* and *full text* databases.

Data Mining at Bank of America. The Bank of America (BofA) is using data mining software to develop more accuracy in marketing and pricing financial products, such as home equity loans. BofA's data warehouse is so large—for some customers, there are 300 data points—that traditional analytic approaches are overwhelmed. For each market, BofA can offer a variety of tailored product packages by adjusting fees, interest rates, and features. The result is a staggering number of potential strategies for reaching profitable customers. Sifting through the vast number of combinations requires the ability to identify very fine opportunity segments.

Data extracted from the data warehouse were analyzed by data mining software to discover hidden patterns. For example, the software discovered that a certain set of customers were 15 times more likely to purchase a high-margin lending product.

Figure 5.12 How data mining extracts knowledge from a data warehouse.

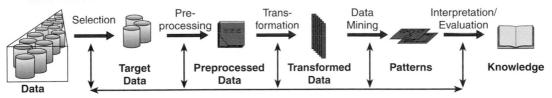

Source: Adapted from Usama Fayyad, Gregory Piatetsky-Shapiro, and Padhraic Smith, "The KDD Process for Extracting Useful Knowledge from Volumes of Data," *Communications of the ACM*, November 1996, p. 29. Copyright © 1996, Association of Computing Machinery. Used by permission.

The bank also wanted to determine the sequence of events leading to purchasing. They fed the parameters to the Discovery software from HYPERparallel and built a model for finding other customers. This model proved to be so accurate that it discovered people already in the process of applying and being approved for the lending product. Using this profile, a final list of quality prospects for solicitation was prepared. The resulting direct marketing response rates have dramatically exceeded past results [7].

Hypermedia Databases on the Web

The most compelling business driver today is the Internet. Because so much of the information flying across the Internet is [multimedia], companies need databases that can store, retrieve, and manage other data types, particularly documents, video, and sound [17].

The rapid growth of web sites on the Internet and corporate intranets and extranets has dramatically increased the use of databases of hypertext and hypermedia documents. A web site stores such information in a **hypermedia database** consisting of a home page and other hyperlinked pages of multimedia or mixed media (text, graphic and photographic images, video clips, audio segments, and so on). That is, from a database management point of view, the set of interconnected multimedia pages at a web site is a database of interrelated hypermedia pages, rather than interrelated data records [2]

Figure 5.13 shows how you might use a web browser on your client PC to connect with a web network server. This server runs web server software to access and transfer

Figure 5.13 The components of a web-based information system include web browsers, servers, and hypermedia databases.

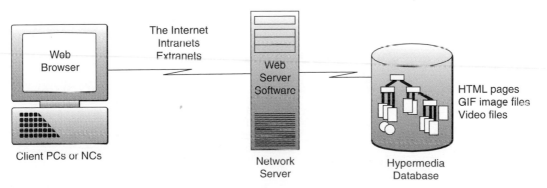

the web pages you request. The web site illustrated in Figure 5.13 uses a hypermedia database consisting of HTML (Hypertext Markup Language) pages, GIF (graphics image files) files, and video files. The web server software acts as a database management system to manage the use of the interrelated hypermedia pages of the web site.

Managerial Considerations for Data Resource Management

Managerial end users should view data as an important resource that they must learn to manage properly to ensure the success and survival of their organizations. But this is easier said than done. Database management is an important application of information systems technology to the management of a firm's data resources. However, other major data resource management efforts are needed in order to offset some of the problems that can result from the use of a database management approach. Those are (1) database administration, (2) data planning, and (3) data administration [7]. See Figure 5.14.

Database administration is an important data resource management function responsible for the proper use of database management technology. Database administration includes responsibility for developing and maintaining the organization's data dictionary, designing and monitoring the performance of databases, and enforcing standards for database use and security. Database administrators and analysts work with systems developers and end users to provide their expertise to major systems development projects.

Data planning is a corporate planning and analysis function that focuses on data resource management. It includes the responsibility for developing an overall data architecture for the firm's data resources that ties in with the firm's strategic mission and plans, and the objectives and processes of its business units. Data planning is done by organizations that have made a formal commitment to long-range planning for the strategic use and management of their data resources.

Figure 5.14

Data resource management includes database administration, data planning, and data administration activities.

Data Resource Management

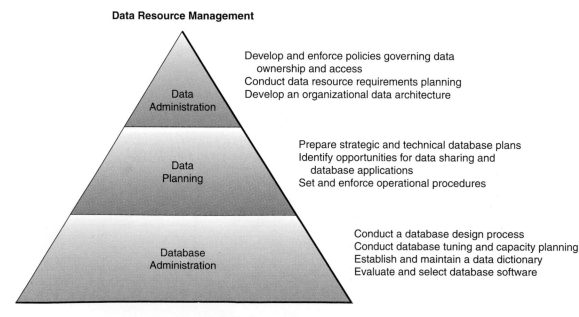

Data Administration
- Develop and enforce policies governing data ownership and access
- Conduct data resource requirements planning
- Develop an organizational data architecture

Data Planning
- Prepare strategic and technical database plans
- Identify opportunities for data sharing and database applications
- Set and enforce operational procedures

Database Administration
- Conduct a database design process
- Conduct database tuning and capacity planning
- Establish and maintain a data dictionary
- Evaluate and select database software

Data administration is another vital data resource management function. It involves administering the collection, storage, and dissemination of all types of data in such a way that data become a standardized resource available to all end users in the organization. The focus of data administration is the support of an organization's business processes and strategic business objectives. Data administration may also include responsibility for developing policies and setting standards for corporate database design, processing, and security arrangements.

Benefits and Limitations of Database Management

The database management approach provides managerial end users with several important benefits. Database management reduces the duplication of data and integrates data so that they can be accessed by multiple programs and users. Programs are not dependent on the format of the data and the type of secondary storage hardware being used. Users are provided with an inquiry/response and reporting capability that allows them to easily obtain information they need without having to write computer programs. Computer programming is simplified, because programs are not dependent on either the logical format of the data or their physical storage location. Finally, the integrity and security of the data stored in databases can be increased, since access to data and modification of the database are controlled by database management system software, a data dictionary, and a database administrator function.

The limitations of database management arise from its increased technological complexity. Developing large databases of complex data types and installing a DBMS can be difficult and expensive. More hardware capability is required, since storage requirements for the organization's data, overhead control data, and the DBMS programs are greater. Longer processing times may result from these additional data and software. Finally, if an organization relies on centralized databases, its vulnerability to errors, fraud, and failures is increased. Yet problems of inconsistency of data can arise if a distributed database approach is used. Therefore, the security and integrity of an organization's databases are major concerns of an organization's data resource management effort.

Section II Technical Foundations of Database Management

Introduction

Just imagine how difficult it would be to get any information from an information system if data were stored in an unorganized way, or if there was no systematic way to retrieve it. Therefore, in all information systems, data resources must be organized and structured in some logical manner so that they can be accessed easily, processed efficiently, retrieved quickly, and managed effectively. Thus, data structures and access methods ranging from simple to complex have been devised to efficiently organize and access data stored by information systems. In this section, we will explore these concepts, as well as more technical concepts of database management.

Analyzing the Chicago Stock Exchange and Enron Energy Services

Read the Real World Case on the Chicago Stock Exchange and Enron Energy Services on the next page. We can learn a lot about the business impact of database management technologies from this case. See Figure 5.15.

The ability of the Chicago Stock Exchange to process trades was dramatically improved when they switched from a hierarchical database to an object-oriented database management system. This change is helping them to execute trades faster and cheaper than their competitors. In addition, it has increased their flexibility and competitiveness, since the object database is easier to modify to meet changing business data requirements.

Enron Energy Services also found that they needed the help of object database technology to solve the unacceptable performance problems of their Oracle relational

Figure 5.15

John Kerin, vice president of application development, says that the Chicago Stock Exchange's move to an object database technology increased their flexibility and competitiveness.

© Marc Berlow.

The Chicago Stock Exchange and Enron Energy Services: Object versus Relational Databases

A broker sells 1,000 shares of General Electric. A receptionist checks a patient into a clinic. A mainframe printer spits out a gas bill.

At first glance, these appear to be old legacy applications that should run on traditional well-known relational database management software. But some customers are finding a new alternative—object-oriented database management systems—to run such applications faster or cheaper.

Object-oriented databases can outperform relational databases at handling complex relationships among data. But beware: It's harder to find developers and database administrators who can handle objects than it is to find specialists in more common relational products.

A relational database, which stores data in columns, rows, and tables, is usually a good choice when relationships among different types of data are fairly fixed and well-known. Relational is fine, for example, to track bumper inventory at a car factory. That's because updating the parts on hand requires fairly simple *joins* (retrieve operations), and these joins are performed across easily identifiable tables in the database.

But consider the engineer who must analyze what will happen to other parts of the car if the weight, shape, or size of that bumper is changed. A relational database might bog down as it performs complex queries across tables as it seeks out every other part that might be affected. The problem becomes acute when the business changes more quickly than a database can be redesigned to rapidly deliver necessary information.

This is where object databases can play a role. If a bumper is represented as an object rather than as an entry in a database table, associations such as parts to which the bumper is attached can be built in to the bumper object. Objects representing, say, the frame or body panels can automatically "inherit" any changes made to the bumper object, making it easier to track later.

Consider the Chicago Stock Exchange, which competes by executing trades faster and more cheaply than its rivals, according to John Kerin, vice president of application development.

Every order requires access to data such as current trading price, current quote, daily high and low prices, the status of other orders, and trading rules. Until recently, this was stored in a hierarchical, Digital VAX–based database, which was designed with pointers that sped performance by steering queries toward the proper data.

But the pointers also made it harder for the Chicago exchange to change its processes, because it essentially hard-coded business rules into the database.

To increase its flexibility and competitiveness, the exchange migrated to a Versant object-oriented database management system that can handle as many as 25 orders, 300 quotes, and 200 trades per second, a dramatic improvement over the previous system. Given that load, Kerin says, "Relational would have imposed too much overhead."

For similar reasons, Houston-based Enron Energy Services, a unit of Enron Corp., found that its Oracle relational database billing application was running out of gas.

Depending on local contracts and regulations in more than 100 markets nationwide, Enron may act as an energy wholesaler or energy retailer. Different customer types are charged different rates, pay different taxes, or get billing information in different formats.

Enron originally wrote its billing application to access an Oracle relational database that contained three dozen tables for billing alone. But performance was unacceptable. Asking the database to perform the complex queries necessary to produce the customized bills "was like assembling an automobile from scratch" tens of thousands of times per day, according to senior developer Tom Dahl.

Enron didn't replace Oracle but instead added an ObjectStore database management system from Object Design to create an object database that serves as a buffer. The daily joins are performed in Oracle, but the results are stored in an ObjectStore database, which produces the data needed to create the actual bill. Performance is faster and maintenance is easier with the new relational/object approach. Enron expects that later this year the new system will handle tens of thousands of transactions per day.

Case Study Questions

1. What is the business value of database management software to a company?

2. Why are relational database management systems used by most businesses today?

3. When are object database management systems better than relational products for a business?

database. Now Enron uses an object database management system that works with their relational database to significantly improve the performance and maintenance of their complex billing application.

Database Structures

The relationships among the many individual records stored in databases are based on one of several logical data structures, or models. Database management system packages are designed to use a specific data structure to provide end users with quick, easy access to information stored in databases. Five fundamental database structures are the hierarchical, network, relational, object-oriented, and multidimensional models. Simplified illustrations of the first three database structures are shown in Figure 5.16.

Hierarchical Structure

Early mainframe DBMS packages used the **hierarchical structure,** in which the relationships between records form a hierarchy or treelike structure. In the traditional hierarchical model, all records are dependent and arranged in multilevel structures, consisting of one *root* record and any number of subordinate levels. Thus, all of the relationships among records are *one-to-many*, since each data element is related to only one element above it. The data element or record at the highest level of the hierarchy (the department data element in this illustration) is called the root element. Any data element can be accessed by moving progressively downward from a root and along the branches of the tree until the desired record (for example, the employee data element) is located.

Network Structure

The **network structure** can represent more complex logical relationships, and is still used by some mainframe DBMS packages. It allows *many-to-many* relationships among records; that is, the network model can access a data element by following one of several paths, because any data element or record can be related to any number of other data elements. For example, in Figure 5.16, departmental records can be related to more than one employee record, and employee records can be related to more than one project record. Thus, one could locate all employee records for a particular department, or all project records related to a particular employee.

Relational Structure

The **relational model** has become the most popular of the three database structures. It is used by most microcomputer DBMS packages, as well as by many midrange and mainframe systems. In the relational model, all data elements within the database are viewed as being stored in the form of simple **tables.** Figure 5.16 illustrates the relational database model with two tables representing some of the relationships among departmental and employee records. Other tables, or **relations,** for this organization's database might represent the data element relationships among projects, divisions, product lines, and so on. Database management system packages based on the relational model can link data elements from various tables to provide information to users. For example, a DBMS package could retrieve and display an employee's name and salary from the employee table in Figure 5.16, and the name of the employee's department from the department table, by using their common department number field (Deptno) to link or join the two tables.

Multidimensional Structure

The multidimensional database structure is a variation of the relational model that uses multidimensional structures to organize data and express the relationships between data. You can visualize multidimensional structures as cubes of data and cubes within cubes of data. Each side of the cube is considered a dimension of the data.

Figure 5.16

Example of three fundamental database structures. They represent three basic ways to develop and express the relationships among the data elements in a database.

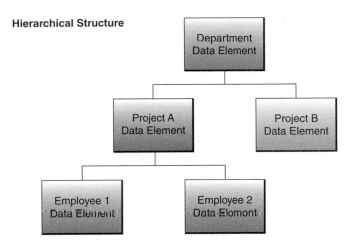

Hierarchical Structure

Network Structure

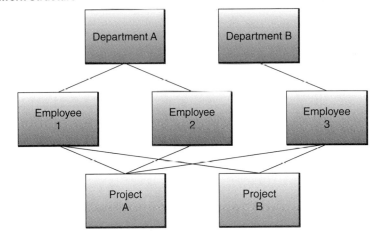

Relational Structure

Department Table

Deptno	Dname	Dloc	Dmgr
Dept A			
Dept B			
Dept C			

Employee Table

Empno	Ename	Etitle	Esalary	Deptno
Emp 1				Dept A
Emp 2				Dept A
Emp 3				Dept B
Emp 4				Dept B
Emp 5				Dept C
Emp 6				Dept B

Figure 5.17 is an example that shows that each dimension can represent a different category, such as product type, region, sales channel, and time.

Each cell within a multidimensional structure contains aggregated data related to elements along each of its dimensions. For example, a single cell may contain the total sales for a product in a region for a specific sales channel in a single month. A major benefit of multidimensional databases is that they are a compact and easy-to-understand way to visualize and manipulate data elements that have many interrelationships.

Figure 5.17 An example of the different dimensions of a multidimensional database.

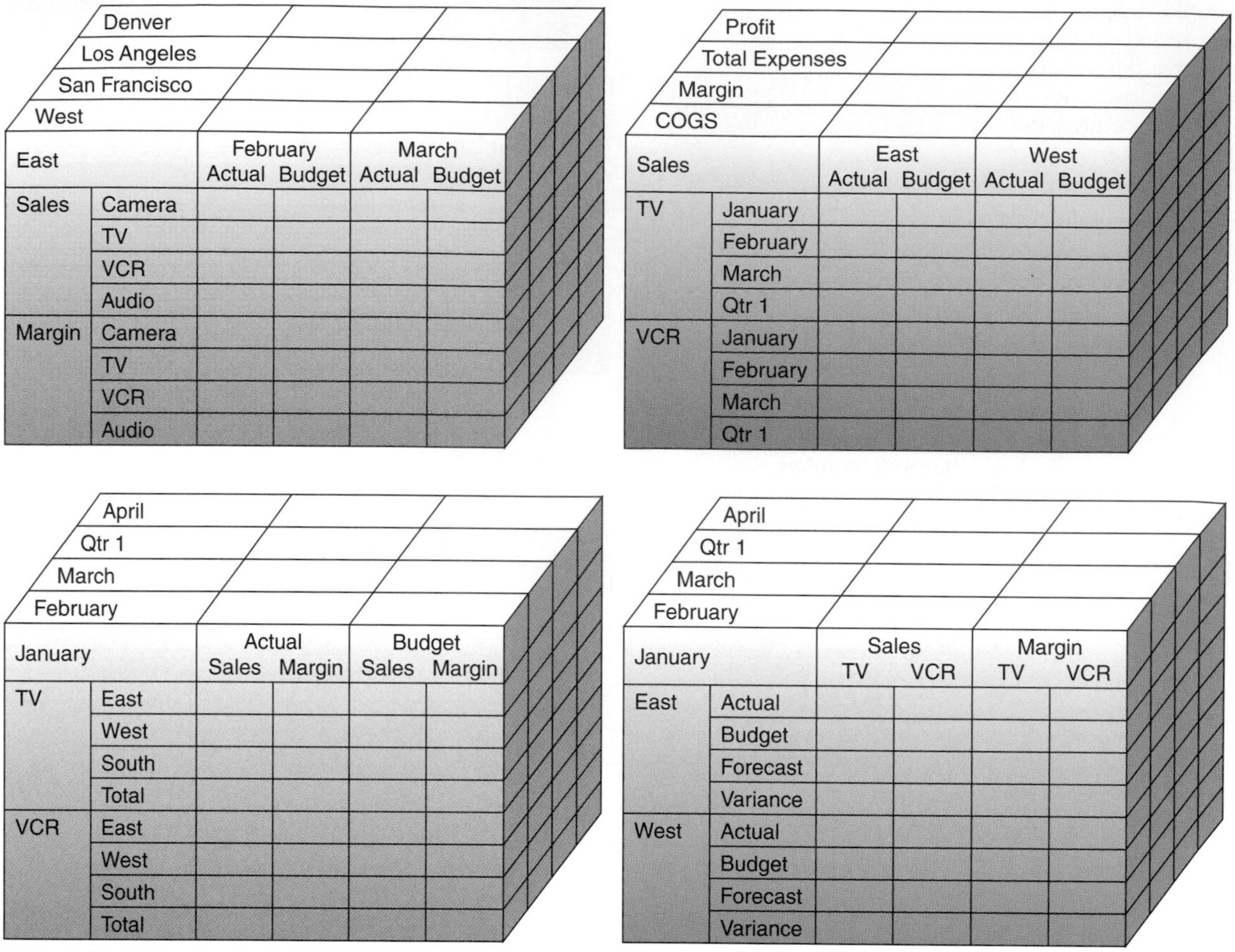

Source: Adapted from Richard Finkelstein, *Understanding the Need for On-Line Analytical Servers* (Ann Arbor, MI: Arbor Software Corporation, 1994), p. 9.

So multidimensional databases have become the most popular database structure for the analytical databases that support *online analytical processing* (OLAP) applications, in which fast answers to complex business queries are expected. We will discuss OLAP applications in Chapter 8.

Object-Oriented Structure

The **object-oriented** database model is considered to be one of the key technologies of a new generation of multimedia web-based applications. We introduced the concept of objects when we discussed object-oriented programming in Chapter 3. As Figure 5.18 illustrates, an **object** consists of data values describing the attributes of an entity, plus the operations that can be performed upon the data. This *encapsulation* capability allows the object-oriented model to better handle more complex types of data (graphics, pictures, voice, text) than other database structures.

The object-oriented model also supports *inheritance*; that is, new objects can be automatically created by replicating some or all of the characteristics of one or more *parent* objects. Thus, in Figure 5.18, the checking and savings account objects can both

The checking and savings account objects can inherit common attributes and operations from the bank account object.

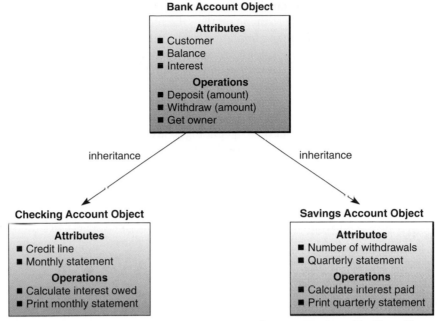

Source: Adapted from Ivar Jacobsen, Maria Ericsson, and Ageneta Jacobsen, *The Object Advantage: Business Process Reengineering with Object Technology* (New York: ACM Press, 1995), p. 65. Copyright © 1995 by Association of Computing Machinery. By permission.

inherit the common attributes and operations of the parent bank account object. Such capabilities have made *object-oriented database management systems* (OODBMS) popular in computer-aided design (CAD) and in a growing number of applications. For example, object technology allows designers to develop product designs, store them as objects in an object-oriented database, and replicate and modify them to create new product designs. In addition, multimedia web-based applications for the Internet and corporate intranets and extranets have become a major application area for object technology, as we will discuss shortly.

Evaluation of Database Structures

The hierarchical data structure was a natural model for the databases used for the structured, routine types of transaction processing that was a characteristic of many business operations. Data for these operations can easily be represented by groups of records in a hierarchical relationship. However, there are many cases where information is needed about records that do not have hierarchical relationships. For example, it is obvious that, in some organizations, employees from more than one department can work on more than one project (refer back to Figure 5.16). A network data structure could easily handle this many-to-many relationship. It is thus more flexible than the hierarchical structure in support of databases for many types of business operations. However, like the hierarchical structure, because its relationships must be specified in advance, the network model cannot easily handle ad hoc requests for information.

Relational databases, on the other hand, allow an end user to easily receive information in response to ad hoc requests. That's because not all of the relationships between the data elements in a relationally organized database need to be specified when the database is created. Database management software (such as Oracle 8, DB2, Access, and Approach) creates new tables of data relationships using parts of the data from several tables. Thus, relational databases are easier for programmers to work with and easier to maintain than the hierarchical and network models.

The major limitation of the relational model is that database management systems based on it cannot process large amounts of business transactions as quickly and efficiently as those based on the hierarchical and network models, in which all data relationships are prespecified. However, this performance gap is narrowing with the development of advanced relational DBMS software. The use of database management software based on the object-oriented and multidimensional models is growing steadily, but these technologies are still playing a supportive role to relational database software for most applications in business information systems.

Object Technology and the Web

Object-oriented database software is finding increasing use in managing the hypermedia databases and Java applets on the World Wide Web and corporate intranets and extranets. Industry proponents predict that object-oriented database management systems will become the key software component that manages the hyperlinked multimedia pages and other types of data that support corporate web sites. That's because an OODBMS can easily manage the access and storage of objects such as document and graphic images, video clips, audio segments, and other subsets of web pages.

Object technology proponents argue that an OODBMS can work with such *complex data types* and the Java applets that use them much more efficiently than relational database management systems. However, major relational DBMS vendors have countered by adding OODBMS modules to their relational software. Examples include multimedia object extensions to IBM's DB2, Informix's DataBlades for their Universal Server, and Oracle's object-based "cartridges" for their Universal Server and Oracle 8. See Figure 5.19.

Accessing Databases

Efficient access to data is important. In database maintenance, records or objects have to be continually added, deleted, or updated to reflect business transactions. Data must also be accessed rapidly so information can be produced in response to end user requests.

Key Fields

That's why all data records usually contain one or more identification fields, or *keys*, that identify the record so it can be located. For example, the Social Security number of a person is often used as a *primary* **key field** that uniquely identifies the data records of individuals in student, employee, and customer files and databases. Other methods also identify and link data records stored in several different database files. For example, hierarchical and network databases may use *pointer fields.* These are fields within a record that indicate (point to) the location of another record that is related to it in the same file, or in another file. Hierarchical and network database management systems use this method to link records so they can retrieve information from several different database files.

Relational database management packages use primary keys to link records. Each table (file) in a relational database must contain a primary key. This field (or fields) uniquely identifies each record in a file and must also be found in other related files. For example, in Figure 5.16, department number (Deptno) is the primary key in the Department table and is also a field in the Employee table. As we mentioned earlier, a relational database management package could easily provide you with information from both tables to join the tables and retrieve the information you want. See Figure 5.20.

Figure 5.19   Oracle's Universal Server is an example of a hybrid relational/object-oriented DBMS that can manage many types of data.

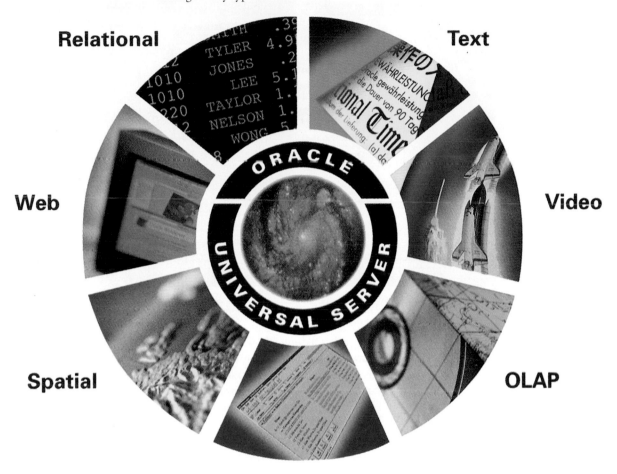

Courtesy of Oracle Corporation.

Sequential Access

One of the original and basic ways to access data is **sequential access.** This method uses a *sequential organization*, in which records are physically stored in a specified order according to a key field in each record. For example, payroll records could be placed in a payroll file in a numerical order based on employee Social Security numbers.

Figure 5.20

Joining the Employee and Department tables in a relational database enables you to selectively access data in both tables at the same time.

Department Table

Deptno	Dname	Dloc	Dmgr
Dept A			
Dept B			
Dept C			

Employee Table

Empno	Ename	Etitle	Esalary	Deptno
Emp 1				Dept A
Emp 2				Dept A
Emp 3				Dept B
Emp 4				Dept B
Emp 5				Dept C
Emp 6				Dept B

Figure 5.21

Creating a Customer
Call Tracking database
with Lotus Approach.

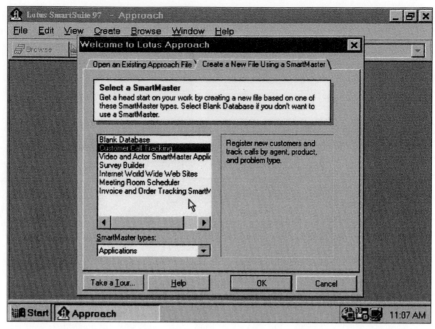

Courtesy of Lotus Development Corporation.

Sequential access is fast and efficient when dealing with large volumes of data that need to be processed periodically. However, it requires that all new transactions be sorted into the proper sequence for sequential access processing. Also, most of the database or file may have to be searched to locate, store, or modify even a small number of data records. Thus, this method is too slow to handle applications requiring immediate updating or responses.

Direct Access

When using **direct access** methods, records do not have to be arranged in any particular sequence on storage media. However, the computer must keep track of the storage location of each record using a variety of *direct organization* methods so that data can be retrieved when needed. New transactions data do not have to be sorted, and processing that requires immediate responses or updating is easily handled. There are a number of ways to directly access records in the direct organization method. Let's take a brief look at three widely used methods to accomplish such direct access processing.

One common technique of direct access is **key transformation.** This method performs an arithmetic computation on a key field of record (such as a product number or Social Security number) and uses the number that results from that calculation as an address to store and access that record. Thus, the process is called key transformation because an arithmetic operation is applied to a key field to transform it into the storage location address of a record. Another direct access method used to store and locate records involves the use of an **index** of record keys and related storage addresses. A new data record is stored at the next available location, and its key and address are placed in an index. The computer uses this index whenever it must access a record.

In the **indexed sequential access method** (ISAM), records are stored in a sequential order on a magnetic disk or other direct access storage device based on the key field of each record. In addition, each database contains an index that references

Figure 5.22

Database development
involves data planning
and database design
activities. Data models
that support business
processes are used to
develop databases that
meet the information
needs of users.

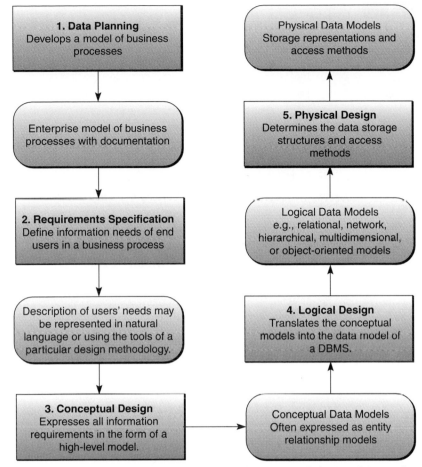

Source: Adapted from Veda Storey and Robert Goldstein, "Knowledge-Based Approaches to Database Design," *MIS Quarterly*, March 1993, p. 26. Reprinted with permission from the *MIS Quarterly*.

one or more key fields of each data record to its storage location address. Thus, an individual record can be directly located by using its key fields to search and locate its address in the database index, just as you can locate key topics in this book by looking them up in its index. As a result, if a few records must be processed quickly, the index is used to directly access the record needed. However, when large numbers of records must be processed periodically, the sequential organization provided by this method is used. For example, processing the weekly payroll for employees or producing monthly statements for customers could be done using sequential access processing of the records in the database.

Database Development

Developing small, personal databases is relatively easy using microcomputer database management packages. See Figure 5.21. However, developing a large database of complex data types can be a complex task. In many companies, developing and managing large corporate databases are the primary responsibility of the database administrator and database design analysts. They work with end users and systems analysts to model business processes and the data they require. Then they determine (1) what data

This entity relationship diagram illustrates some of the relationships among entities in a purchasing/receiving business process.

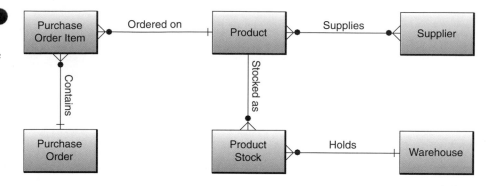

definitions should be included in the database and (2) what structure or relationships should exist among the data elements.

Data Planning and Database Design

As Figure 5.22 illustrates, database development may start with a top-down **data planning process.** Database administrators and designers work with corporate and end user management to develop an *enterprise model* that defines the basic business process of the enterprise. Then they define the information needs of end users in a business process, such as the purchasing/receiving process that all businesses have [17].

Next, end users must identify the key data elements that are needed to perform their specific business activities. This frequently involves developing *entity relationship diagrams* (ERDs) that model the relationships among the many entities involved in business processes. For example, Figure 5.23 illustrates some of the relationships in a purchasing/receiving process. End users and database designers could use ERD models to identify what supplier and product data are necessary or may be required if their company has installed enterprise resource planning (ERP) software to automate their business processes.

Such user views are a major part of a **data modeling** process where the relationships between data elements are identified. Each data model defines the logical relationships among the data elements needed to support a basic business process. For example, can a supplier provide more than one type of product to us? Can a customer have more than one type of account with us? Can an employee have several pay rates or be assigned to several project workgroups?

Answering such questions will identify data relationships that have to be represented in a data model that supports a business process. These data models then serve as logical frameworks (called *schemas* and *subschemas*) on which to base the *physical design* of databases and the development of application programs to support the business processes of the organization. A schema is an overall logical view of the relationships among the data elements in a database, while the subschema is a logical view of the data relationships needed to support specific end user application programs that will access that database.

Remember that data models represent *logical views* of the data and relationships of the database. Physical database design takes a *physical view* of the data (also called the internal view) that describes how data are to be physically stored and accessed on the storage devices of a computer system. For example, Figure 5.24 illustrates these different database views and the software interface of a bank database processing system. In this example, checking, savings, and installment lending are the business processes whose data models are part of a banking services data model that serves as a logical data framework for all bank services.

Figure 5.24 Examples of the logical and physical database views and the software interface of a banking services information system.

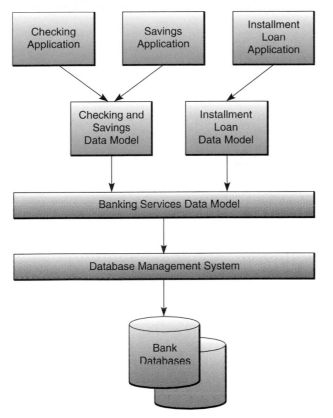

Logical User Views
Data elements and relationships (the subschemas) needed for checking, savings, or installment loan processing

Data elements and relationships (the schema) needed for the support of all bank services

Software Interface
The DBMS provides access to the bank's databases

Physical Data Views
Organization and location of data on the storage media

Summary

- **Data Resource Management.** Data resource management is a managerial activity that applies information systems technology and management tools to the task of managing an organization's data resources. It includes the database administration function that focuses on developing and maintaining standards and controls for an organization's databases. Data administration, however, focuses on the planning and control of data to support business functions and strategic organizational objectives. This includes a data planning effort that focuses on developing an overall data architecture for a firm's data resources.

- **Database Management.** The database management approach affects the storage and processing of data. The data needed by different applications are consolidated and integrated into several common databases, instead of being stored in many independent data files. Also, the database management approach emphasizes updating and maintaining common databases, having users' application programs share the data in the database, and providing a reporting and an inquiry/response capability so end users can easily receive reports and quick responses to requests for information.

- **Database Software.** Database management systems are software packages that simplify the creation, use, and maintenance of databases. They provide software tools so end users, programmers, and database administrators can create and modify databases, interrogate a database, generate reports, do application development, and perform database maintenance.

- **Types of Databases.** Several types of databases are used by computer-using organizations, including operational, distributed, data warehouse, and external databases. Hypermedia databases on the World Wide Web and corporate intranets and extranets store hyperlinked multimedia pages at a web site. Web server software can manage such databases for quick access and maintenance of the web database.

- **Database Development.** The development of databases can be easily accomplished using microcomputer database management packages for small end user applications. However, the development of large corporate databases requires a top-down data planning effort. This may involve developing enterprise and entity relationship models, subject area databases, and data models that reflect the logical data elements and relationships needed to support the operation and management of the basic business processes of the organization.

- **Data Access.** Data must be organized in some logical manner on physical storage devices so that they can be efficiently processed. For this reason, data are commonly organized into logical data elements such as characters, fields, records, files, and databases. Database structures, such as the hierarchical, network, relational, and object-oriented models, are used to organize the relationships among the data records stored in databases. Databases and files can be organized in either a sequential or direct manner and can be accessed and maintained by either sequential access or direct access processing methods.

Key Terms and Concepts

These are the key terms and concepts of this chapter. The page number of their first explanation is in parentheses.

1. Data dictionary (173)
2. Data mining (177)
3. Data modeling (192)
4. Data planning (192)
5. Data resource management (168)
6. Database administration (180)
7. Database administrator (173)
8. Database access (188)
   a. Direct (190)
   b. Sequential (189)
9. Database management approach (172)
10. Database management system (173)

11. Database structures (184)
    a. Hierarchical (184)
    b. Multidimensional (184)
    c. Network (184)
    d. Object-oriented (186)
    e. Relational (184)
12. DBMS uses (173)
    a. Application development (176)
    b. Database development (173)
    c. Database interrogation (174)
    d. Database maintenance (175)
13. Key field (188)
14. Logical data elements (170)

    a. Character (170)
    b. Field (170)
    c. Record (171)
    d. File (171)
    e. Database (171)
15. Query language (174)
16. Report generator (174)
17. Types of databases (176)
    a. Data warehouse (176)
    b. Distributed (177)
    c. External (177)
    d. Hypermedia (179)
    e. Operational (176)

Review Quiz

Match one of the key terms and concepts listed previously with one of the brief examples or definitions that follow. Try to find the best fit for answers that seem to fit more than one term or concept. Defend your choices.

_____ 1. The use of integrated collections of data records and files for data storage and processing.

_____ 2. A DBMS allows you to create, interrogate, and maintain a database, create reports, and develop application programs.

_____ 3. A specialist in charge of the databases of an organization.

_____ 4. This DBMS feature allows users to easily interrogate a database.

_____ 5. Defines and catalogs the data elements and data relationships in an organization's database.

_____ 6. Helps you specify and produce reports from a database.

_____ 7. The main software package that supports a database management approach.

_____ 8. Databases are dispersed to the Internet and corporate intranets and extranets.

_____ 9. Databases that organize and store data as objects.

_____ 10. Databases of hyperlinked multimedia documents on the Web.

_____ 11. The management of all the data resources of an organization.

_____ 12. Developing databases and maintaining standards and controls for an organization's databases.

_____ 13. Processing data in a data warehouse to discover key business factors and trends.

_____ 14. Enterprise planning that ties database development to the support of basic business processes.

_____ 15. Developing conceptual views of the relationships among data in a database.

_____ 16. A customer's name.

_____ 17. A customer's name, address, and account balance.

_____ 18. The names, addresses, and account balances of all of your customers.

_____ 19. An integrated collection of all of the data about your customers.

_____ 20. An identification field in a record.

_____ 21. A treelike structure of records in a database.

_____ 22. A tabular structure of records in a database.

_____ 23. Records are organized as cubes within cubes in a database.

_____ 24. Transactions are sorted in ascending order by Social Security number before processing.

_____ 25. Unsorted transactions can be used to immediately update a database.

_____ 26. Databases that support the major business processes of an organization.

_____ 27. A centralized and integrated database of current and historical data about an organization.

_____ 28. Databases available on the Internet or provided by commercial information services.

Discussion Questions

1. How should an internetworked business enterprise store, access, and distribute data and information about their internal operations and external environment?

2. What roles do database management, data administration, and data planning play in managing data as a business resource?

3. What are the advantages of a database management approach to organizing, accessing, and managing an organization's data resources? Give examples to illustrate your answer.

4. Refer to the Real World Case on EMC Corporation in the chapter. How would dramatic increases in the capacity of storage media affect the need for data storage in business as outlined in the case?

5. What is the role of a database management system in a business information system?

6. Databases of information about a firm's internal operations were formerly the only databases that were considered to be important to a business. What other kinds of databases are important for a business today?

7. Refer to the Real World Case on the Chicago Stock Exchange and Enron Energy Services in the chapter. As computing power continues to increase, will object database management systems replace relational database technologies?

8. What are the benefits and limitations of the relational database model for business applications today?

9. Why is the object-oriented database model gaining acceptance for developing applications and managing the hypermedia databases at business web sites?

10. How have the Internet and the World Wide Web affected the types and uses of data resources available to business end users?

Real World Problems

1. Borders Books and Music: Database Management of an E-Commerce Web Site

Borders Books and Music is writing a new chapter in the history of what has become a $2.6 billion business. Borders' new online store, located at www.borders.com, offers 10 million books, audio books, CDs, cassettes, and videos—all available to ship from stock to any home or business.

"We're the only online bookstore that couples a dominant selection with guaranteed back-end fulfillment," says Borders Senior Vice President for E-commerce and Fulfillment Rick Vanzura. "When we say a book is in stock, you can be sure it is, because of our realtime inventory checks. No other online bookseller can offer that. And it's all part of one integrated application."

Developed and deployed in less than nine months, in conjunction with IBM Interactive & New Media, Borders.com is driven by the IBM Net Commerce suite of E-business software and DB2 database management system.

The minute you enter the site, you recognize that this is no publisher's clearinghouse. More than just an online catalog, Borders.com is a place to browse, obtain recommendations, chat, and enjoy a "Borders bookstore experience." The web site's navigation model mimics a customer's typical browsing pattern—from department, to topic, to subtopic, and then to specific authors and titles.

If you want to find a particular book, CD, audio-cassette, or video, Borders.com offers the next best thing to asking a Borders sales associate: a search engine based on the DB2 Text Extender module that rapidly returns the results you want—and only the results you want—in a format most conducive to making a purchasing decision.

As simple as they may seem to the user, these searches are no trivial feat for a relational database management system. Just searching for a specific title takes three queries to three different database tables, each of which has about 20 million rows. But thanks to a unique database design and DB2 Text Extender's fast indexing scheme, the Borders search engine can return results for most searches in about four-tenths of a second.

DB2 manages a huge database that stores information on all of the items offered on the site, as well as customer registration, order, inventory, shipping, and other information required to manage the online store. Net Data Web and database connectivity software enable Net Commerce to access the database from the web server.

Borders runs its back-end systems—such as accounting, inventory, and fulfillment—on a variety of databases and hardware platforms. IBM's MQSeries middleware manages the regular updates between the DB2 database and inventory checks and realtime ordering from suppliers—something not available at any other online bookstore.

Noting that Borders' ambitious foray into the online bookselling market is beginning to bear fruit, Vanzura claims that book and music enthusiasts have been quick to embrace Borders.com. "We have hit the radar screen among the highest traffic web sites," he says. "And we have consistently been building every week on sales, orders, and profits."

a. How does the DB2 database management system support customers at the Borders.com web site?

b. What are several competitive advantages to Borders provided by their electronic commerce and database management software?

Source: Adapted from "Borders Knows No Bounds in E-Business," from www.software.ibm.com/eb/borders, March 1999. © IBM Corporation 1999. All rights reserved.

2. Burlington Coat Factory Warehouse: The Business Benefits of Storage Area Networks

Fibre channel–based storage-area networks (SAN) still may seem bleeding-edge to many mainstream business users, but Burlington Coat Factory Warehouse has had one sewn up for more than a year now. "The industry invented the buzzword—SAN—and several months later we realized we already had one in production," said Michael Prince, CIO at the discount clothier.

A SAN takes storage off isolated servers and places it on a shared, high-speed network such as fibre channel. SANs generally comprise servers, distributed storage, and networking processors like hubs and switches.

Prince says, "SANs are proving themselves as the most cost-effective way to build fast, large-scale, managed, data storage systems . . . In the low-margin, high-pressure business of discount retail, we embraced the technology."

Burlington uses three SANs, each based on multiprocessing servers from Sequent Computer Systems. The company's many databases, divided among the SANs, add up to about 4 terabytes of data. Each server houses 12 processors that connect to a disk drive pool via fibre channel switches. Each server also has a tape backup library plugged into one of the switches. Burlington Coat plans to combine the three SANs into one in about a year.

"Our current system has given us about a 3 × jump in throughput," Prince says. Furthermore, "with a faster more reliable data storage, we can take people out of the hardware-tweaking business and use them to deliver something with real business value."

For example, because of their SAN's data storage redundancy and the ability to schedule preemptive hardware maintenance, it has translated into a "more rational working environment and easier staff retention," Prince said. The three SANs' increased throughput has also enabled Burlington Coat Factory to add customer-tracking databases to the financial and inventory databases now housed on the high-speed SAN servers.

Prince plans to open a second data center at the opposite end of Burlington Coat's headquarters property. "It will only be about a half-kilometer away, so I won't be using fibre's full 10K distance capability... But we'll locate half of our disk drives and half of our servers out there so if one center goes down, we'll be protected. We couldn't do that before SAN," he said.

a. What are the advantages of storage area networks compared to previous storage systems?

b. What are the business benefits of SANs for Burlington Coat Factory warehouse?

Source: Adapted from Nancy Dillon, "Retailer Fires up SAN," *Computerworld*, March 8, 1999, p. 69. Copyright 1999 by Computerworld, Inc., Framingham, MA 01701. Reprinted from *Computerworld*.

3. Farmers Insurance Group: The Business Value of Data Mining and a Data Warehouse
Data mining tools have long been used by retailers such as Wal-Mart Stores and banks such as First Union Corp. to identify their most profitable customers. Insurance companies, though, have had other priorities, such as figuring out which markets to stay in. But now, some are using these tools to identify marketing opportunities to meet heightened competition.

Farmers Insurance Group in Los Angeles is one of them. It has developed a data mining and warehouse system for its underwriting business that's generating millions of dollars to higher revenue and lower claims.

"As competition has gotten more intense in the insurance industry, the traditional ways of segmenting risk aren't good enough at providing you competitive advantage," explained Tom Boardman, an assistant actuary at Farmers. Farmers' system should help the company's actuaries dig deeper into its customer base and understand narrower market niches and uncover hidden loss predictors, Boardman said.

Previously, Boardman and other actuaries would develop hunches about market trends—that policies for two-door convertibles are going to be more profitable than policies for two-door hardtops, for example—and put a request into the firm's information technology department "to dig up that data to prove or unprove those hunches," he said.

Farmers began to develop the customer profitability data mining system with IBM in late 1996. IBM, in turn, began to sell a customized version of the system, called Decision-Edge for Relationship Marketing/Insurance, to other insurance companies in 1998.

Boardman acknowledges that developing a data warehouse from seven databases and 35 million records was a huge undertaking. For example, because the records were spread across so many databases, locating a customer file often became a major initiative. That's why locating, cleaning up, and reformatting all of the customer data needed for the data warehouse took four months—or twice as long as Farmers expected.

But the information gained was worth the time and money spent. For example, the company was recently able to identify how insuring a certain type of high-risk sports car could be quite profitable as long as the owner had at least one other vehicle. After analyzing reams of customer policy information, Farmers discovered that it could lower its rates on the sports car's coverage and increase its market share in California and a few other states "by a couple of percentage points," said Melissa McBratney, vice president of business development for Farmers' personal lines products.

She declined to specify costs or revenue from the system, beyond saying that the revenue increases are in the millions.

a. How do data mining and a data warehouse change how a company stores and analyzes its business data?

b. How do data mining and a data warehouse provide a competitive advantage to Farmers?

Source: Adapted from Thomas Hoffman, "Finding a Rich Niche," *Computerworld*, February 8, 1999, p. 44. Copyright 1999 by Computerworld, Inc., Framingham, MA 01701. Reprinted from *Computerworld*.

Application Exercises

1. Building an Employoee Tracking Database I: Creating an Employee Table
Your organization mandates that each employee complete a specified number of hours of training each year. The number of hours depends upon the employee's existing skills and job assignment and is negotiated with his or her supervisor. Management has expressed concern that "the training requirement is

being ignored" by the more senior employees. They feel that senior employees are either negotiating for very limited training requirements or are ignoring the requirements to which they have agreed. Management would like to be able to evaluate training requirements by department and by level of seniority.

You have been asked to build a small database application to track training requirements and monitor fulfillment of those requirements. As the first step, you will need to create a database and add an employee table. Use the sample data shown in the table below as a set of test data for the employee table.

a. Create the structure for the employee table to store the required data, enter the sample data shown into your table, and print a listing of your table.

b. Write a query to show the average number of required training hours for employees who have been with the firm for more than five years. Write a query to show the average number of required training hours for employees who have been with the firm for less than five years.

c. Write a query that will display the data only for employees in the advertising department and will display them in descending order based on the number of required training hours.

d. Create a report that groups the employees by department and lists the average number of required training hours for each department and for the company as a whole.

Emp Id	Name	Department	Hire Date	Training
1234	J. Jones	Sales	18-June-92	24
2345	S. Smith	Production	12-Feb-98	40
3456	A. Adams	Sales	18-Nov-98	60
4567	B. Bates	Advertising	10-Mar-85	16
5678	D. Davis	Production	26-Jul-99	56
6789	C. Cole	Shipping	18-May-91	32
7890	E. Ellis	Sales	15-Dec-98	80
8901	F. Files	Advertising	17-Oct-90	24
9012	G. Gates	Advertising	15-Mar-99	48

2. **Building an Employee Tracking Database II: Adding a Training Table**

In order to complete the application described in the previous exercise, you need to add a table to be used in tracking each employee's attendance at training sessions. Use the list of sample values on the right to design this table and populate it with sample data. Each row of the training table is identified by the combination of the Emp. Id of the employee receiving the training and the Session Id of the training session.

a. Using the sample data shown, add an appropriate training table to the database you created in the previous exercise. Populate it with the data shown and print out a listing of these data.

b. Write a query that will join the two tables and retrieve a listing of the Session Id and hours for all of the training sessions that Employee A. Adams has completed.

c. Write a query that will join the two tables and retrieve a listing of the names of all employees who attended the session whose Id is PersMgtlA along with the number of hours attended.

Emp Id	Session Id	Hours
2345	PersMgt1A	12
3456	CompSk1A	8
3456	CompSk2A	24
3456	PersSell1A	24
4567	CompSk1A	8
5678	CompSk1A	6
5678	PersMgt1A	12
5678	ProjMgt1B	12
7890	PersMgt1A	12
7890	PersSell1A	24
8901	PersMgt1B	8
9012	PersMgt1B	12
9012	ProjMgt1B	16

d. Write a query that will join the two tables and retrieve a listing of each employee's Id number, name, and required training hours, along with the sum of the number of training hours the employee has completed.

e. Create a report based on the query described in **d** above

Review Quiz Answers

1. 9	5. 1	9. 11*d*	13. 2	17. 14*c*	21. 11*a*	25. 8*a*
2. 12	6. 16	10. 17*d*	14. 4	18. 14*d*	22. 11*e*	26. 17*e*
3. 7	7. 10	11. 5	15. 3	19. 14*e*	23. 11*b*	27. 17*a*
4. 15	8. 17*b*	12. 6	16. 14*b*	20. 13	24. 8*b*	28. 17*c*

Selected References

1. Ahrens, Judith, and Chetan Sankar. "Tailoring Database Training for End Users." *MIS Quarterly*, December 1993.

2. Atwood, Thomas. "Object Databases Come of Age," *OBJECT Magazine*, July 1996.

3. Babcock, Charles. "OLAP Leads Way to Post-Relational Era." *Computerworld*, November 21, 1997.

4. Bruegger, Dave, and Sooun Lee. "Distributed Database Systems: Accessing Data More Efficiently." *Information Systems Management*, Spring 1995.

5. Cafasso, Rosemary. "Busting Loose." *Computerworld*, April 15, 1996.

6. Chan, Hock Chuan; Kee Wei Kwock; and Keng Leng Siau. "User-Database Interface: The Effect of Abstraction Levels on Query Performance." *MIS Quarterly*, December 1993.

7. Grover, Varun, and James Teng. "How Effective Is Data Resource Management? Reassessing Strategic Objectives." *Journal of Information Systems Management*, Summer 1991.

8. Jacobsen, Ivar; Maria Ericsson; and Ageneta Jacobsen. *The Object Advantage: Business Process Reengineering with Object Technology.* New York: ACM Press, 1995.

9. Jenkings, Avery. "Warehouse Woes." *Computerworld*, February 6, 1995.

10. Kroenke, David. *Database Processing: Fundamentals, Design, Implementation.* 2nd ed. New York: Macmillan, 1996.

11. Lorents, Alden, and James Morgan. *Database Systems: Concepts, Management and Applications.* Fort Worth: The Dryden Press, 1998.

12. Pei, Daniel, and Carmine Cutone. "Object-Oriented Analysis and Design: Realism or Impressionism." *Information Systems Management*, Winter 1995.

13. "Shedding Light on Data Warehousing for More Informed Business Solutions." Special Advertising Supplement. *Computerworld*, February 13, 1995.

14. Slitz, John. "Object Technology Profiles." Special Advertising Supplement. *Computerworld*, June 13, 1997.

15. Smith, Heather A., and James D. McKeen. "Object-Oriented Technology: Getting Beyond the Hype." *The Data Base for Advances in Informatin Systems*, Spring 1996.

16. Spiegler, Israel. "Toward a Unified View of Data: Bridging Data Structure and Content." *Information Systems Management*, Spring 1995.

17. Stedman, Craig. "Databases Grab Hold of Objects, Multimedia on the Web." *Computerworld*, October 21, 1996.

18. Storey, Veda, and Robert Goldstein. "Knowledge-Based Approaches to Database Design." *MIS Quarterly*, March 1993.

19. Wilson, Linda. "Hybrid Databases Enter Warehouse." *Computerworld*, January 19, 1998.

Applications

How do the Internet, intranets, and extranets support electronic commerce and enterprise communications and collaboration? How are information systems used to support business operations, managerial decision making, and strategic advantage? The four chapters of this module show you how such business applications of information technology are accomplished in today's internetworked enterprises.

Chapter 6, "Information Systems for Business Operations and Electronic Commerce," describes how information systems support the business functions of marketing, manufacturing, human resource management, accounting, and finance. It also explores the issues, trends, and applications in electronic commerce.

Chapter 7, "Information Systems for Enterprise Collaboration," covers the use and impact of intranets within companies, and how the Internet, intranets, and extranets provide the technology platform for a variety of electronic collaboration systems in business.

Chapter 8, "Information Systems for Managerial Decision Support," shows how management information systems, decision support systems, executive information systems, expert systems, and artificial intelligence technologies have been developed and applied to business operations and decision-making situations faced by managers.

Chapter 9, "Information Systems for Strategic Advantage," introduces fundamental concepts of strategic advantage through information technology, and illustrates strategic applications of information systems that can gain competitive advantages for an organization.

Information Systems for
Business Operations
and Electronic Commerce

Chapter Highlights

Section I
Business Information Systems

IS in Business
Real World Case: Amazon.com: Success and Expansion in Electronic Commerce
Cross-Functional Information Systems
Marketing Information Systems
Manufacturing Information Systems
Human Resource Information Systems
Accounting Information Systems
Financial Management Systems

Section II
Fundamentals of Electronic Commerce

Introduction
Real World Case: Buy.com: Testing a New Business Model in E-Commerce
Foundations of Electronic Commerce
Business-to-Consumer Commerce
Customer Value and the Internet
Business-to-Business Commerce
Online Transaction Processing
Electronic Payments and Security

Learning Objectives

After reading and studying this chapter, you should be able to:

1. Give examples of how information systems support business processes within and across the business functions of accounting, finance, human resource management, marketing, and production and operations management.

2. Provide business examples that demonstrate using the Internet, intranets, or extranets to accomplish activities within each of the business functions.

3. Give examples of several ways that companies can implement business-to-consumer and business-to-business electronic commerce on the Internet.

4. Identify and give examples of several ways that electronic commerce applications provide significant business value to a company and its customers.

5. Discuss several electronic payment challenges and solutions for electronic payment security on the Internet.

Business Information Systems

IS in Business

Business managers are moving from a tradition where they could avoid, delegate, or ignore decisions about IT to one where they cannot create a marketing, product, international, organizational, or financial plan that does not involve such decisions [24].

There are as many ways to use information technology in business as there are business activities to be performed, business problems to be solved, and business opportunities to be pursued. As a business end user, you should have a basic understanding and appreciation of the major ways information systems are used to support each of the functions of business. Thus, in this section, we will discuss **business information systems,** that is, a variety of types of information systems (transaction processing, management information, decision support, etc.) that support the business functions of accounting, finance, marketing, operations management, and human resource management.

Analyzing Amazon.com

Read the Real World Case on Amazon.com on the next page. We can learn a lot about how information technology empowers the strategic moves and E-commerce success of Amazon.com from this case. See Figure 6.1.

For three years Amazon.com has concentrated on becoming the best online bookstore on the Web and one of the best web sites for customer service. They invested heavily in electronic commerce software and other information technologies to offer top-rated convenience, selection, and personalization to their customers. Now they are leveraging this investment in IT and retail E-commerce to support a strategic expansion into music, videos, software, gift items, and online auctions.

In addition, they have made investments in new E-commerce technology by acquiring companies that provide shopping agent software and online organizer services.

Figure 6.1

CEO Jeff Bezos has led Amazon.com to success as a dominant player in electronic commerce.

Amazon.com: Success and Expansion in Electronic Commerce

Amazon.com (www.amazon.com).
CEO: Jeff Bezos.
1998 Revenues: $546 million (estimated).

Net retail categories: Books, music, software, videos, gifts, online auctions.

Customer Base: Over 8 million.

Offerings: More than 3 million book, music, and other titles.

Recent Moves: Acquired Junglee and PlanetAll; launched gift-buying site; opened European book sites.

Until recently, it seemed as though the major Internet portals—with Yahoo! and America Online leading the way—held most of the keys to the future of retail commerce. As the biggest online magnets for potential shoppers, portals charge retailers dearly—in either long-term, multimillion-dollar sponsorship deals or shares of sales revenues—to stake out small plots of valuable portal real estate and drive more customer traffic to their sites.

Consumer-agent technology and price-comparison sites such as Junglee and CompareNet, on the other hand, have always held the promise of a direct consumer-retailer relationship—with shopbots (shopping software robot programs) available 24 hours a day to find any product at the best price. But it wasn't until Amazon made two major acquisitions that industry observers caught a glimpse of how the balance of retail power might shift.

Amazon's pace was blistering. In June 1998, the company added music to its offerings. In one quarter, it became the leading Net music seller, with more than $14 million in sales, much to the chagrin of stunned competitors such as CDNow and N2K. In the fall, it launched European book sites in Germany and Britain and added videos to its "media suite." Then came the acquisitions.

In August 1998, Amazon gobbled up Junglee and PlanetAll (an online address book and organizer for some 1.5 million users) for $280 million in stock. By November 1998, Amazon announced it would add software to its product line, and it opened a gift center, adding such items as Barbie dolls, watches, and PalmPilots to its array of offerings. Online auctions began a few months later.

In creating this potential powerhouse of shopping services and offerings, Amazon.com looks to be molding itself into not simply a Wal-Mart of the Web but rather a next-generation, retail commerce portal.

Imagine a customized site where—through a Junglee-like shopping service—you will not only shop easily with a trusted brand for books, videos, gifts, and more, but you will also research the features, price, and availability of millions of products from a single storefront that has Amazon's—and your—name on it. That's the promise and the challenge of Net retailing in the future.

That's what has gotten Amazon this far in its first three years of business: exhaustive focus on convenience, selection, and personalization. It lived up to its billing as Earth's Biggest Bookstore by building an inventory of more than 3 million titles. It was also among the first Net stores to facilitate credit-card purchases; greet customers by name and offer customized homepages; send purchase recommendations via E-mail; and number and explain each step in the purchasing process.

But it hasn't been all roses in Seattle, either. Amazon has been criticized for inefficient inventory management while the company continues to post multimillion-dollar losses each quarter. According to an IceGroup study of Amazon's business model in 1998, losses were running at the equivalent of $7 per transaction. (Its gross profit margins and customer-retention rates, on the other hand, continue to improve steadily, factors that keep investors happy.) The company needs to ready logistics and back-end systems to handle an expansion of product offerings. Transaction costs need to be cut to ensure the seemingly unattainable: a profitable quarter.

Amazon remains the dominant player in E-commerce, despite German media giant Bertelsmann and Amazon competitor Barnes & Noble's joint Web venture. Amazon's four-month jump to the top of the music category proved how extensible the Amazon brand is, especially as the company builds out from books, music, and videos. A profitable quarter isn't due till 2000, but if Amazon decides to begin selling ad space—which it hasn't done yet—that might change quickly.

Case Study Questions

1. Why has Amazon.com been considered a success in electronic commerce?

2. Do you think Amazon will be successful in its expansion into other products and services?

3. What advice would you give CEO Jeff Bezos to improve Amazon's chances for success in the future?

Source: Adapted from Jeffrey Davis, "Mall Rats," *Business 2.0*, January 1999, pp. 41–50.

These capabilities may enable Amazon to transform itself into a retail commerce portal for all types of products and services. Thus, if they can solve their inventory and logistics management problems, Amazon should continue to be a dominant player in electronic commerce.

Cross-Functional Information Systems

As a business end user, it is important that you have a specific understanding of how information systems affect a particular business function—marketing, for example—or a particular industry (e.g., banking) that is directly related to your career objectives. For example, someone whose career objective is a marketing position in banking should have a basic understanding of how information systems are used in banking and how they support the marketing activities of banks and other firms.

Figure 6.2 illustrates how information systems can be grouped into business function categories. Thus, information systems in this section will be analyzed according to the business function they support to give you an appreciation of the variety of business information systems that both small and large business firms may use.

Figure 6.2

Examples of business information systems. Note how they support the major functional areas of business.

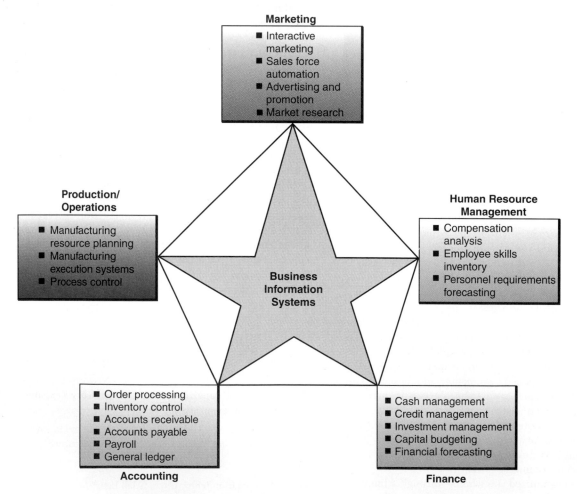

Figure 6.3
The new product development process in a manufacturing company. This business process must be supported by cross-functional information systems that cross the boundaries of several business functions.

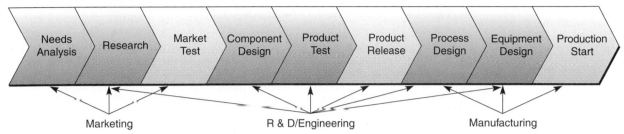

Source: Adapted and reprinted by permission of The Harvard Business School Press from *Process Innovation: Reengineering Work Through Information Technology* by Thomas H. Davenport (Boston: 1993), p. 222. Copyright © 1993 by Ernst & Young.

However, as we emphasized in Chapter 1, information systems in the real world typically are integrated combinations of functional information systems. Such systems support **business processes,** such as product development, production, distribution, order management, customer support, and so on. Many organizations are using information technology to develop **cross-functional information systems** that cross the boundaries of traditional business functions in order to reengineer and improve vital business processes. These organizations view cross-functional information systems as a strategic way to use IT to share information resources and improve the efficiency and effectiveness of business processes, thus helping a business attain its strategic objectives. See Figure 6.3.

For example, as we have seen in previous chapters, business firms are turning to Internet technologies to integrate the flow of information among their internal business functions and their customers and suppliers. Companies are using the World Wide Web and their intranets and extranets as the technology platform for their cross-functional and interorganizational information systems.

Enterprise Resource Planning

In addition, many companies have moved from functional mainframe legacy systems to cross-functional client/server network applications. This typically has involved installing **enterprise resource planning** (ERP) or *supply chain management* (SCM) software from SAP America, Baan, PeopleSoft, or Oracle Corporation. Instead of focusing on the information processing requirements of business functions, ERP software focuses on supporting the business processes involved in the operations of a business. For example, Figure 6.4 outlines how the Oracle Corporation and several business partners have developed a cross-functional suite of ERP software for the packaged goods industry. Notice all of the business processes supported by this ERP software.

Marketing Information Systems

The business function of marketing is concerned with the planning, promotion, and sale of existing products in existing markets, and the development of new products and new markets to better serve present and potential customers. Thus, marketing performs a vital function in the operation of a business enterprise. Business firms have increasingly turned to information technology to help them perform vital marketing functions in the face of the rapid changes of today's environment.

Figure 6.5 illustrates how **marketing information systems** provide information technologies that support major components of the marketing function. For example, Internet/intranet web sites and services make an *interactive marketing* process possible

Figure 6.4

A suite of cross-functional enterprise resource planning (ERP) software for the packaged goods industry developed by Oracle Corporation and its business partners.

Company	Component	Business Processes
Information Resources Inc.	Sales and marketing	Promotion analysis, product management and demand analysis, scanner data analysis
Industri-Matematic International	Order management	Finished goods inventory, picking/shipping, invoicing, sales orders, pricing and promotion
Oracle Corporation	Process manufacturing	Production management, costing, manufacturing resource planning, raw materials inventory, quality control, purchasing, finished goods inventory
Manugistics Inc.	Logistics/planning	Demand resource planning, distribution, transportation, finite scheduling
Oracle Corporation	Financials	Fixed assets, project accounting, purchasing, accounts receivable, accounts payable, general ledger

Source: Adapted from Randy Weston, "Oracle Packages Planning," *Computerworld*, February 10, 1997, p. 43. Copyright 1997 by Computerworld, Inc., Framingham, MA 01701. Reprinted from *Computerworld*.

where customers can become partners in creating, marketing, purchasing, and improving products and services. *Sales force automation* systems use mobile computing and Internet technologies to automate many information processing activities for sales support and management. Other marketing information systems assist marketing managers in product planning, pricing, and other product management decisions, advertising and sales promotion strategies, and market research and forecasting. Let's take a closer look at these computer-based applications.

Interactive Marketing

The explosive growth of Internet technologies has had a major impact on the marketing function. The term **interactive marketing** has been coined to describe a type of marketing that is based on using the Internet, intranets, and extranets to establish two-way interaction between a business and its customers or potential customers. The goal of interactive marketing is to enable a company to profitably use those networks to attract and keep customers who will become partners with the business in creating, purchasing, and improving products and services.

Figure 6.6 outlines the steps of the interactive marketing process on the Internet. Notice that the Internet has become the primary distribution channel of the new

Figure 6.5

Marketing information systems provide information technologies to support major components of the marketing function.

Figure 6.6

The interactive marketing process on the Internet.

Step 1. Segment and identify potential customers (Initial market research done by reaching relevant groups—WWW servers, listservs, newsgroups)
Step 2. Create promotional, advertising, and educational material (WWW page with multimedia effects—audio and video) (Product information and complementary products, order forms, and questionnaires)
Step 3. Put the material on customers' computer screens Push-based marketing—direct marketing using web broadcasters, newsgroups, listservs, and E-mail Pull-based marketing   indirect (static) marketing—WWW pages
Step 4. Interacting with customers Dialogue with the customer; interactive discussion among customers about various features offering endorsements, testimonials, questions/answers
Step 5. Learning from customers (repeat customers are 80 percent of the customer base) Incorporating feedback from customers in advertising, marketing strategy Identifying new markets, using experience in new product development
Step 6. Online customer service Fast, friendly solutions to customer problems

Source: Adapted from Ravi Kalakota and Andrew Whinston, *Frontiers of Electronic Commerce* (Reading, MA: Addison-Wesley, 1996), p. 499. © 1996 Addison-Wesley Publishing Company, Inc. Reprinted by permission of Addison-Wesley Longman Inc.

online marketing environment. Customers are not just passive participants who receive media advertising prior to purchase, but are actively engaged in a network-enabled proactive and interactive process.

Notice that interactive marketing views prospective customers as belonging to many distinct market segments that must be approached differently online through *targeted marketing* techniques. Interactive marketing also encourages customers to become involved in product development, delivery, and service issues. This is enabled by various Internet technologies, including chat and discussion groups, web forms and questionnaires, and E-mail correspondence. Finally, the expected outcomes of interactive marketing are a rich mixture of vital marketing data, new product ideas, volume sales, and strong customer relationships [15].

Sales Force Automation

Increasingly, computers and networks are providing the basis for **sales force automation.** In many companies, the sales force is being outfitted with notebook computers, web browsers, and sales contact management software that connect them to marketing web sites on the Internet, extranets, and their company intranets. This not only increases the personal productivity of salespeople, but dramatically speeds up the capture and analysis of sales data from the field to marketing managers at company headquarters. In return, it allows marketing and sales management to improve the delivery of information and the support they provide to their salespeople. Therefore, many companies are viewing sales force automation as a way to gain a strategic advantage in sales productivity and marketing responsiveness. See Figure 6.7.

For example, salespeople use their PCs to record sales data as they make their calls on customers and prospects during the day. Then each night sales reps in the field can connect their computers by modem and telephone links to the Internet and extranets, which can access intranet or other network servers at their company. Then they can upload information on sales orders, sales calls, and other sales statistics, as well as send

Many companies provide notebook PCs, web browsers, and sales contact management software to help their sales reps use the resources at Internet and intranet web sites to support the selling process.

Howard Grey/Tony Stone Images.

electronic mail messages and access web site sales support information. In return, the network servers may download product availability data, prospect lists of information on good sales prospects, and E-mail messages. See Figure 6.8.

Sales and Product Management

Sales managers must plan, monitor, and support the performance of the salespeople in their organizations. So in most firms, computer-based systems produce sales analysis reports that analyze sales by product, product line, customer, type of customer, salesperson, and sales territory. Such reports help marketing managers monitor the sales performance of products and salespeople and help them develop sales support programs to improve sales results.

Product managers need information to plan and control the performance of specific products, product lines, and brands. Computer-based analysis can provide price, revenue, cost, and growth information for existing products and new product development. Thus, providing information and analysis for pricing and product development decisions is a major function of a product management system.

Advertising and Promotion

Marketing managers try to maximize sales at the lowest possible costs for advertising and promotion. Marketing information systems use market research information and promotion models to help (1) select media and promotional methods, (2) allocate financial resources, and (3) control and evaluate results of various advertising and promotion campaigns. For example, the INFOSCAN system of Information

Figure 6.8

Some of the benefits of web-based sales force automation.

● Shorten the sales cycle through prequalification of prospects.
● Increase revenue through targeted marketing.
● Automate the management and qualification of web leads.
● Capture all customer information directly into a sales database.
● Enhance order management with access to data on pricing, promotions, availability, production schedules, export regulations, carriers, and transportation schedules.

Source: Adapted from Ravi Kalakota and Andrew Whinston, *Electronic Commerce: A Manager's Guide*, (Reading, MA: Addison-Wesley, 1997), p. 325. © 1997 by Addison-Wesley Publishing Company, Inc. Reprinted by permission of Addison-Wesley Longman, Inc.

Figure 6.9

The five major components of targeted marketing for electronic commerce on the World Wide Web.

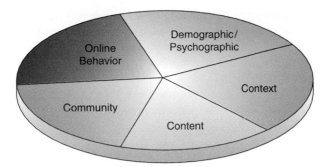

Source: Adapted from Chuck Martin, *The Digital Estate: Strategies for Competing, Surviving, and Thriving in an Internetworked World* (New York: McGraw-Hill, 1997), pp. 124-25, 206.

Resources Incorporated (IRI) tracks the sales of over 800,000 products by their universal product code (UPC) to more than 70,000 U.S. households at over 2,400 retail stores. INFOSCAN measures the effect of promotional tactics such as price discounts, coupon offers, and point-of-purchase (POP) promotions. Then INFOSCAN's computer-based marketing models produce sales forecasts and other analyses of marketing strategy [14].

Targeted Marketing

Targeted marketing has become an important tool in developing advertising and promotion strategies for a company's electronic commerce web sites. As illustrated in Figure 6.9, targeted marketing is an advertising and promotion management concept that includes five targeting components [16].

- **Community.** Companies can customize their web advertising messages and promotion methods to appeal to people in specific communities. These can be *communities of interest*, such as *virtual communities* of online sporting enthusiasts or arts and crafts hobbyists, or geographic communities formed by the web sites of a city or local newspaper.

- **Content.** Advertising such as electronic billboards or banners can be placed on various web site pages, in addition to a company's home page. These messages reach the targeted audience. An ad for a movie on the opening page of an Internet search engine is a typical example.

- **Context.** Advertising appears only in web pages that are relevant to the content of a product or service. So advertising is targeted only at people who are already looking for information about a subject matter (vacation travel, for example) that is related to a company's products (car rental services, for example).

- **Demographic/Psychographic.** Marketing efforts can be aimed only at specific types or classes of people: unmarried, twenty-something, middle income, male college graduates, for example.

- **Online behavior.** Advertising and promotion efforts can be tailored to each visit to a site by an individual. This strategy is based on "web cookie" files recorded on the visitor's disk drive from previous visits. Cookie files enable a company to track a person's online behavior at a web site so marketing efforts can be instantly developed and targeted to that individual at each visit to their web site.

Market Research and Forecasting

Market research information systems provide marketing intelligence to help managers make better marketing forecasts and develop more effective marketing strategies. Marketing information systems help market researchers collect, analyze, and maintain an enormous amount of information on a wide variety of market variables that are subject to continual change. This includes information on customers, prospects, consumers, and competitors. Market, economic, and demographic trends are also analyzed. Data can be gathered from many sources, including a company's databases, data marts and data warehouse, World Wide Web sites, and telemarketing services companies. Then, a variety of statistical software tools can help managers analyze market research data and forecast sales and other important market trends.

Manufacturing Information Systems

Manufacturing information systems support the *production/operations* function that includes all activities concerned with the planning and control of the processes producing goods or services. Thus, the production/operations function is concerned with the management of the operational processes and systems of all business firms. Information systems used for operations management and transaction processing support all firms that must plan, monitor, and control inventories, purchases, and the flow of goods and services. Therefore, firms such as transportation companies, wholesalers, retailers, financial institutions, and service companies must use production/operations information systems to plan and control their operations. In this section, we will concentrate on computer-based manufacturing applications to illustrate information systems that support the production/operations function.

Computer-Integrated Manufacturing

A variety of manufacturing information systems are used to support **computer-integrated manufacturing** (CIM). See Figure 6.10. CIM is an overall concept that stresses that the objectives of computer-based systems in manufacturing must be to:

- **Simplify** (reengineer) production processes, product designs, and factory organization as a vital foundation to automation and integration.

- **Automate** production processes and the business functions that support them with computers, machines, and robots.

Figure 6.10

Manufacturing information systems support computer-integrated manufacturing.

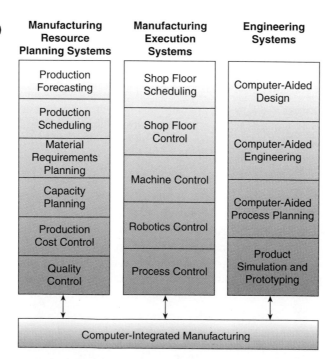

- **Integrate** all production and support processes using computers, telecommunications networks, and other information technologies.

The overall goal of CIM and such manufacturing information systems is to create flexible, agile, manufacturing processes that efficiently produce products of the highest quality. Thus, CIM supports the concepts of *flexible manufacturing systems*, *agile manufacturing*, and *total quality management*. Implementing such manufacturing concepts enables a company to quickly respond to and fulfill customer requirements with high-quality products and services.

Manufacturing information systems help companies simplify, automate, and integrate many of the activities needed to produce products of all kinds. For example, computers are used to help engineers design better products using both computer-aided engineering and computer-aided design, and better production processes with computer-aided process planning. They are also used to help plan the types of material needed in the production process, which is called *material requirements planning* (MRP), and to integrate MRP with production scheduling and shop floor operations, which is known as *manufacturing resource plannning*. See Figure 6.11.

Computer-aided manufacturing (CAM) systems are those that automate the production process. For example, this could be accomplished by monitoring and controlling the production process in a factory through *manufacturing execution systems*, or by directly controlling a physical process (process control), a machine tool (machine control), or machines with some humanlike work capabilities (robots).

Manufacturing execution systems (MES) are performance monitoring information systems for factory floor operations. They monitor, track, and control the five essential components involved in a production process: materials, equipment, personnel,

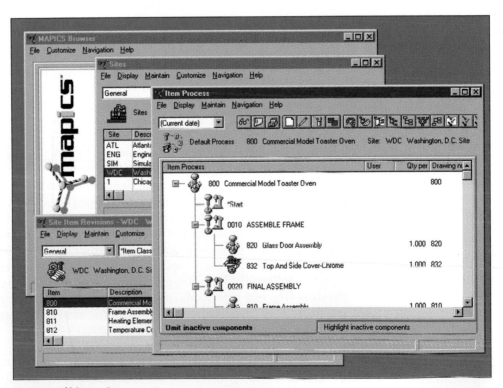

Courtesy of Mapics, Inc.

instructions and specifications, and production facilities. MES includes shop floor scheduling and control, machine control, robotics control, and process control systems. These manufacturing systems monitor, report, and adjust the status and performance of production components to help a company achieve a flexible, high-quality manufacturing process.

Collaborative Manufacturing Networks

Manufacturing processes like computer-aided engineering and design, production control, production scheduling, and procurement management typically involve a collaborative process. Increasingly, this involves using the Internet, intranets, extranets, and other networks to link the workstations of engineers and other specialists with their colleagues at other sites. These **collaborative manufacturing networks** may link employees within a company, or include representatives from a company's suppliers or customers wherever they may be located.

For example, Johnson Controls uses the Internet, intranets and other networks to link the workstations of employees at their Automotive Systems Group with their counterparts at Ford and Chrysler and other companies worldwide. The engineers and other specialists use these computer networks to collaborate on a range of assignments, including car seat design, production issues, and delivery schedules [18].

Process Control

Process control is the use of computers to control an ongoing physical process. Process control computers control physical processes in petroleum refineries, cement plants, steel mills, chemical plants, food product manufacturing plants, pulp and paper mills, electric power plants, and so on. Many process control computers are special-purpose minicomputer systems. A process control computer system requires the use of special sensing devices that measure physical phenomena such as temperature or pressure changes. These continuous physical measurements are converted to digital form by analog-to-digital converters and relayed to computers for processing.

Process control software uses mathematical models to analyze the data generated by the ongoing process and compare them to standards or forecasts of required results. Then the computer directs the control of the process by adjusting control devices such as thermostats, valves, switches, and so on. The process control system also provides messages and displays about the status of the process so a human operator can take appropriate measures to control the process. See Figure 6.12.

Machine Control

Machine control is the use of a computer to control the actions of a machine. This is also popularly called *numerical control*. The control of machine tools in factories is a typical numerical control application, though it also refers to the control of typesetting machines, weaving machines, and other industrial machinery.

Numerical control computer programs for machine tools convert geometric data from engineering drawings and machining instructions from process planning into a numerical code of commands that control the actions of a machine tool. Machine control may involve the use of special-purpose microcomputers called programmable logic controllers (PLCs). These devices operate one or more machines according to the directions of a numerical control program. Manufacturing engineers use computers to develop numerical control programs, analyze production data furnished by PLCs, and fine-tune machine tool performance.

Robotics

An important development in machine control and computer-aided manufacturing is the creation of smart machines and robots. These devices directly control their own activities with the aid of microcomputers. **Robotics** is the technology of building and

Figure 6.12

Logs at Gulf States Paper's highly automated Alabama mill get measured by Machine Vision Process Control Systems, a business application of robotics. Mindful of market conditions, a computer then calculates and displays the most profitable combination of boards to cut.

Paul Sumners.

using machines (robots) with computer intelligence and computer-controlled human-like physical capabilities (dexterity, movement, vision, etc.). Robotics has also become a major thrust of research and development efforts in the field of artificial intelligence.

Robots are used as "steel-collar workers" to increase productivity and cut costs. For example, a robot might assemble compressor valves with 12 parts at the rate of 320 units per hour, which is 10 times the rate of human workers. Robots are also particularly valuable for hazardous areas or work activities. Robots follow programs distributed by servers and loaded into separate or on-board special-purpose microcomputers. Input is received from visual and/or tactile sensors, processed by the microcomputer, and translated into movements of the robot. Typically, this involves moving its arms and hands to pick up and load items or perform some other work assignment such as painting, drilling, or welding. Robotics developments are expected to make robots more intelligent, flexible, and mobile by improving their computing, visual, tactile, and navigational capabilities [17]. Refer back to Figure 6.12.

Computer-Aided Engineering

Manufacturing engineers use **computer-aided engineering** (CAE) to simulate, analyze, and evaluate the models of product designs they have developed using **computer-aided design** (CAD) methods. Networks of powerful engineering workstations with enhanced graphics and computational capabilities and CAD software help them analyze and design products and manufacturing processes and facilities. CAD packages refine an engineer's initial drawings and provide three-dimensional computer graphics that can be rotated to display all sides of the object being designed. The engineer can zoom in for close-up views of a specific part and even make parts of the product appear to move as they would in normal operation. The design can then be converted into a finished mathematical model of the product. This is used as the basis for production specifications and machine tool programs. See Figure 6.13.

Manufacturing engineers design products according to product specifications determined in cooperation with the product design efforts of marketing research, product development, and customer management specialists. One of the final outputs of

Figure 6.13

Computer-aided design is a vital component of computer-integrated manufacturing.

Greenlar/The Image Works.

this design process is the *bill of materials* (specification of all required materials) used by the MRP application. In addition, manufacturing engineers use CAD systems to design the production processes needed to manufacture products they have developed (computer-aided process planning).

Human Resource Information Systems

The human resource management (HRM) function involves the recruitment, placement, evaluation, compensation, and development of the employees of an organization. The goal of human resource management is the effective and efficient use of the human resources of a company. Thus, **human resource information systems** are designed to support (1) planning to meet the personnel needs of the business, (2) development of employees to their full potential, and (3) control of all personnel policies and programs. Originally, businesses used computer-based information systems to (1) produce paychecks and payroll reports, (2) maintain personnel records, and (3) analyze the use of personnel in business operations. Many firms have gone beyond these traditional *personnel management* functions and have developed human resource information systems (HRIS) that also support (1) recruitment, selection, and hiring; (2) job placement; (3) performance appraisals; (4) employee benefits analysis; (5) training and development; and (6) health, safety, and security. See Figure 6.14.

HRM and the Internet

The Internet has become a major force for change in human resource management. For example, online HRM systems may involve recruiting for employees through recruitment sections of corporate web sites. Companies are also using commercial recruiting services and databases on the World Wide Web, posting messages in selected Internet newsgroups, and communicating with job applicants by Internet E-mail.

The Internet has a wealth of information and contacts for both employers and job hunters. For example, Figure 6.15 displays the home page of Top Jobs on the Net,

Figure 6.14   Human resource information systems support the strategic, tactical, and operational use of the human resources of an organization.

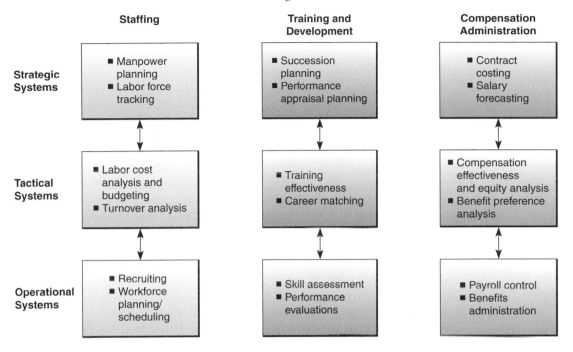

	Staffing	**Training and Development**	**Compensation Administration**
Strategic Systems	■ Manpower planning ■ Labor force tracking	■ Succession planning ■ Performance appraisal planning	■ Contract costing ■ Salary forecasting
Tactical Systems	■ Labor cost analysis and budgeting ■ Turnover analysis	■ Training effectiveness ■ Career matching	■ Compensation effectiveness and equity analysis ■ Benefit preference analysis
Operational Systems	■ Recruiting ■ Workforce planning/ scheduling	■ Skill assessment ■ Performance evaluations	■ Payroll control ■ Benefits administration

Figure 6.15

The home page of Top Jobs on the Net, a top source of international HRM information.

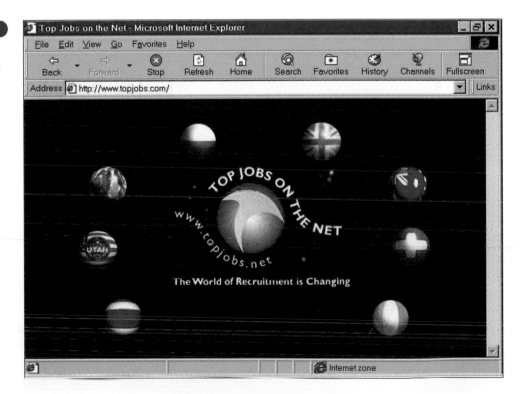

Figure 6.16

Some of the top job
hunting/recruiting sites
on the World Wide
Web.

- **America's Job Bank** (http://www.ajb.dni.us/), the largest job database site, is run by the U.S. Department of Labor. It includes listings for approximately 250,000 jobs.

- **CareerMosaic** (http://www.careermosaic.com/) has an international section that lists jobs in Asia, Australia, Canada, and Europe.

- **The Monsterboard** (http://www.monster.com/) is CareerMosaic's East Coast rival; it provides job listings, a resume database, and career counseling.

- **CareerPath.com** (http://www.careerpath.com/) lets you simultaneously search the classified job listings of 25 major U.S. newspapers by category and job title.

- **JobSmart** (http://jobsmart.org/tools/salary/sal-prof.htm) is the site to look at before you negotiate a salary for your new job. Read up on current salary statistics here.

- **DataMasters** (http://www.datamasters.com). If you're looking to relocate, find out what your salary is worth in another city here.

Source: Adapted from Kristina Klein, "Working Overtime at a Dead-End Job," James Martin, ed. *PC World*, March 1997, pp. 51–52. Reprinted with the permission of *PC World* Communications Inc.

found at www.topjobs.com. This web site is full of reports, statistics, and other useful HRM information, such as an international job report by industry, or a listing of the top recruiting markets in various countries by industry and profession. Of course, you may also want to access the job listings and resource database of commercial recruiting services on the Web. Figure 6.16 outlines the top web sites for job hunters and employers on the World Wide Web.

HRM and the Corporate Intranet

Intranet technologies allow companies to process most common HRM applications over their corporate intranets. Intranets allow the HRM department to provide around-the-clock services to their customers: the employees. They can also disseminate valuable information faster than through previous company channels. Intranets can collect information online from employees for input to their HRM files, and they can enable employees to perform HRM tasks with little intervention by the HRM department.

For example, *employee self-service* (ESS) intranet applications allow employees to view benefits, enter travel and expense reports, verify employment and salary information, access and update their personal information, and enter data that has a time constraint to it. Through this completely electronic process, employees can use their web browsers to look up individual payroll and benefits information online, right from their desktop PCs, mobile computers, or intranet kiosks located around a worksite.

Another benefit of the intranet is that it can serve as a superior training tool. Employees can easily download instructions and processes to get the information or education they need. In addition, employees using new technology can view training videos over the intranet on demand. Thus, the intranet eliminates the need to loan out and track training videos. Employees can also use their corporate intranets to produce automated paysheets, the online alternative to timecards. These electronic forms have made viewing, entering, and adjusting payroll information easy for both employees and HRM professionals [12].

Staffing the Organization

The staffing function must be supported by information systems that record and track human resources within a company to maximize their use. For example, a personnel record-keeping system keeps track of additions, deletions, and other changes to the records in a personnel database. Changes in job assignments and compensation, or hirings and terminations, are examples of information that would be used to update the personnel database. Another example is an employee skills inventory system that uses the employee skills data from a personnel database to locate employees within a company who have the skills required for specific assignments and projects.

A final example involves forecasting personnel requirements to assure a business an adequate supply of high-quality human resources. This application provides forecasts of personnel requirements in each major job category for various company departments or for new projects and other ventures being planned by management. Such long-range planning may use a computer-based simulation model to evaluate alternative plans for recruitment, reassignment, or retraining programs.

Training and Development

Information systems help human resource managers plan and monitor employee recruitment, training, and development programs by analyzing the success history of present programs. They also analyze the career development status of each employee to determine whether development methods such as training programs and periodic performance appraisals should be recommended. Computer-based multimedia training programs and appraisals of employee job performance are available to help support this area of human resource management. See Figure 6.17.

Compensation Analysis

Information systems can help analyze the range and distribution of employee compensation (wages, salaries, incentive payments, and fringe benefits) within a company and make comparisons with compensation paid by similar firms or with various economic indicators. This information is useful for planning changes in compensation, especially if negotiations with labor unions are involved. It helps keep the compensation of a company competitive and equitable, while controlling compensation costs.

Figure 6.17

An example of a performance evaluation display. Note how this employee's behavior on the job is being evaluated using intranet-based software.

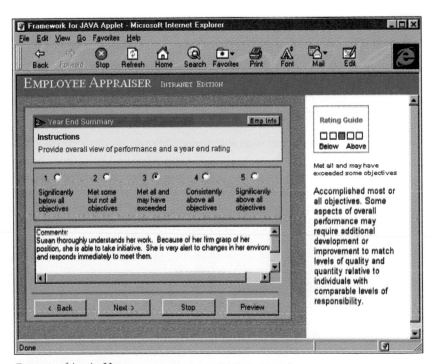

Courtesy of Austin-Hayne.

Governmental
Reporting

Nowadays, reporting to government agencies is a major responsibility of human resource management. So organizations use computer-based information systems to keep track of the statistics and produce reports required by a variety of government laws and regulations. For example, in the United States, statistics on employee recruitment and hiring must be collected for possible use in Equal Employment Opportunity Commission (EEOC) hearings; statistics for employee health, workplace hazards, accidents, and safety procedures must be reported to the Occupational Safety and Health Administration (OSHA); and statistics on the use of hazardous materials must be reported to the Environmental Protection Agency (EPA). Software packages to collect and report such statistics are available from a variety of software vendors.

Accounting Information Systems

Accounting information systems are the oldest and most widely used information systems in business. They record and report business transactions and other economic events. Accounting information systems are based on the double-entry bookkeeping concept, which is hundreds of years old, and other, more recent accounting concepts such as responsibility accounting and activity-based costing. Computer-based accounting systems record and report the flow of funds through an organization on a historical basis and produce important financial statements such as balance sheets and income statements. Such systems also produce forecasts of future conditions such as projected financial statements and financial budgets. A firm's financial performance is measured against such forecasts by other analytical accounting reports.

Operational accounting systems emphasize legal and historical record-keeping and the production of accurate financial statements. Typically, these systems include transaction processing systems such as order processing, inventory control, accounts receivable, accounts payable, payroll, and general ledger systems. Management accounting systems focus on the planning and control of business operations. They emphasize cost accounting reports, the development of financial budgets and projected financial statements, and analytical reports comparing actual to forecasted performance.

Figure 6.18 illustrates the interrelationships of several important accounting information systems commonly computerized by both large and small businesses. Many accounting software packages are available for these applications. Let's briefly review how several of these systems support the operations and management of a business firm. Figure 6.19 summarizes the purpose of six common, but important, accounting information systems.

Online Accounting
Systems

It should come as no surprise that the accounting information systems illustrated in Figures 6.18 and 6.19 are being affected by Internet and client/server technologies. Using the Internet, intranets, extranets, and other networks changes how accounting information systems monitor and track business activity. The online, interactive nature of such networks calls for new forms of transaction documents, procedures, and controls. This particularly applies to systems like order processing, inventory control, accounts receivable, and accounts payable. These systems are directly involved in the processing of transactions between a business and its customers and suppliers. So naturally, many companies are using or developing network links to these trading partners for such applications, using the Internet or other networks. We will discuss such online transaction processing systems in Section II of this chapter.

Order Processing

Order processing, or sales order processing, is an important transaction processing system that captures and processes customer orders and produces data needed for sales analysis and inventory control. In many firms, it also keeps track of the status of customer orders until goods are delivered. Computer-based sales order processing

Figure 6.18   Important accounting information systems for transaction processing and financial reporting. Note how they are related to each other in terms of input and output flows.

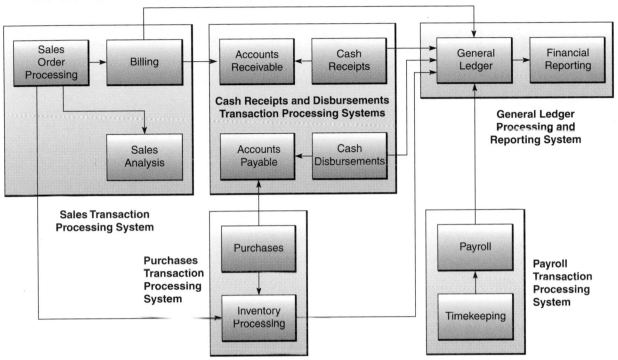

Source: Adapted from Joseph W. Wilkinson and Michael J. Cerullo, *Accounting Information Systems: Essential Concepts and Applications*, 3rd ed., p. 10. Copyright © 1997 by John Wiley & Sons, Inc. Reprinted by permission.

systems provide a fast, accurate, and efficient method of recording and screening customer orders and sales transactions. They also provide inventory control systems with information on accepted orders so they can be filled as quickly as possible. See Figure 6.20.

Figure 6.19   A summary of six widely used accounting information systems.

● **Order Processing**
Captures and processes customer orders and produces data for inventory control and accounts receivable.

● **Inventory Control**
Processes data reflecting changes in inventory and provides shipping and reorder information.

● **Accounts Receivable**
Records amounts owed by customers and produces customer invoices, monthly customer statements, and credit management reports.

● **Accounts Payable**
Records purchases from, amounts owed to, and payments to suppliers, and produces cash management reports.

● **Payroll**
Records employee work and compensation data and produces paychecks and other payroll documents and reports.

● **General Ledger**
Consolidates data from other accounting systems and produces the periodic financial statements and reports of the business.

Figure 6.20

Using the sales order processing of MYOB, a popular accounting package.

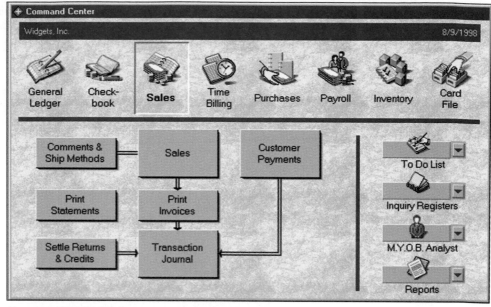

Courtesy of MYOB US, Inc.

Inventory Control

Inventory control systems process data reflecting changes to items in inventory. Once data about customer orders are received from an order processing system, a computer-based inventory control system records changes to inventory levels and prepares appropriate shipping documents. Then it may notify managers about items that need reordering and provide them with a variety of inventory status reports. Computer-based inventory control systems thus help a business provide high-quality service to customers while minimizing investment in inventory and inventory carrying costs.

Accounts Receivable

Accounts receivable systems keep records of amounts owed by customers from data generated by customer purchases and payments. They produce invoices to customers, monthly customer statements, and credit management reports. Computer-based accounts receivable systems stimulate prompt customer payments by preparing accurate and timely invoices and monthly statements to credit customers. They provide managers with reports to help them control the amount of credit extended and the collection of money owed. This activity helps to maximize profitable credit sales while minimizing losses from bad debts.

Accounts Payable

Accounts payable systems keep track of data concerning purchases from and payments to suppliers. They prepare checks in payment of outstanding invoices and produce cash management reports. Computer-based accounts payable systems help ensure prompt and accurate payment of suppliers to maintain good relationships, ensure a good credit standing, and secure any discounts offered for prompt payment. They provide tight financial control over all cash disbursements of the business. They also provide management with information needed for the analysis of payments, expenses, purchases, employee expense accounts, and cash requirements.

Payroll

Payroll systems receive and maintain data from employee time cards and other work records. They produce paychecks and other documents such as earning statements, payroll reports, and labor analysis reports. Other reports are also prepared for management and government agencies. Computer-based payroll systems help businesses make prompt and accurate payments to their employees, as well as reports to management, employees, and government agencies concerning earnings, taxes, and other deductions. They may also provide management with reports analyzing labor costs and productivity.

General Ledger

General ledger systems consolidate data received from accounts receivable, accounts payable, payroll, and other accounting information systems. At the end of each accounting period, they close the books of a business and produce the general ledger trial balance, the income statement and balance sheet of the firm, and various income and expense reports for management. Computer-based general ledger systems help businesses accomplish these accounting tasks in an accurate and timely manner. They typically provide better financial controls and management reports and involve fewer personnel and lower costs than manual accounting methods.

Financial Management Systems

Computer-based **financial management systems** support financial managers in decisions concerning (1) the financing of a business and (2) the allocation and control of financial resources within a business. Major financial management system categories include cash and investment management, capital budgeting, financial forecasting, and financial planning. See Figure 6.21.

Cash Management

Cash management systems collect information on all cash receipts and disbursements within a company on a realtime or periodic basis. Such information allows businesses to deposit or invest excess funds more quickly, and thus increase the income generated by deposited or invested funds. These systems also produce daily, weekly, or monthly forecasts of cash receipts or disbursements (cash flow forecasts) that are used to spot future cash deficits or surpluses. Mathematical models frequently can determine optimal cash collection programs and determine alternative financing or investment strategies for dealing with forecasted cash deficits or surpluses.

Online Investment Management

Many businesses invest their excess cash in short-term low-risk marketable securities (such as U.S. Treasury bills, commercial paper, or certificates of deposit) or in higher-return/higher-risk alternatives, so that investment income may be earned until the

Figure 6.21

Examples of important financial management systems.

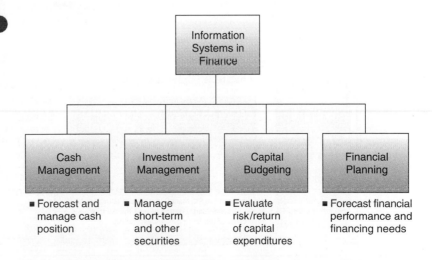

funds are required. The portfolio of such securities can be managed with the help of portfolio management software packages. Investment information and securities trading are available from hundreds of online sources on the Internet and other networks. Online investment management services help a financial manager make buying, selling, or holding decisions for each type of security so that an optimum mix of securities is developed that minimizes risk and maximizes investment income for the business. See Figure 6.22.

Capital Budgeting

The **capital budgeting** process involves evaluating the profitability and financial impact of proposed capital expenditures. Long-term expenditure proposals for plants and equipment can be analyzed using a variety of techniques. This application makes heavy use of spreadsheet models that incorporate present value analysis of expected cash flows and probability analysis of risk to determine the optimum mix of capital projects for a business.

Financial Forecasting and Planning

Financial analysts typically use electronic spreadsheets and other **financial planning** software to evaluate the present and projected financial performance of a business. They also help determine the financing needs of a business and analyze alternative methods of financing. Financial analysts use financial forecasts concerning the economic situation, business operations, types of financing available, interest rates, and stock and bond prices to develop an optimal financing plan for the business. Electronic spreadsheet packages, DSS software, and web-based groupware can be used to build and manipulate financial models. Answers to what-if and goal-seeking questions can be explored as financial analysts and managers evaluate their financing and investment alternatives.

Figure 6.22

The Motley Fool, a popular online investment site.

Fundamentals of Electronic Commerce

Introduction

What is **electronic commerce?** What is the role of the Internet in the evolution of electronic commerce (EC) for companies doing business in today's networked global markets? Defining electronic commerce as "doing business over interconnected networks using web-based technologies," as Sun Microsystems does, is a good place to start. Cathy J. Medich, executive director of CommerceNet, a consortium of major corporations that is promoting the commercial use of the Internet, has a more specific answer:

> *The Internet is redefining the model for electronic commerce to one that supports the complete seller-to-buyer relationship. This model includes promoting and communicating company and product information to a global user base, accepting orders and payment for goods and services online, delivering software and information products online, providing ongoing customer support, and engaging in online collaboration for new product development* [9].

Analyzing Buy.com

Read the Real World Case on Buy.com on the next page. We can learn a lot about the innovative business strategies and challenges and opportunities of electronic commerce from this example. See Figure 6.23.

CEO Scott Blum of Buy.com is challenging the traditional retail business model by selling products at or below cost. Blum hopes to make up the expected losses resulting from sales revenue being less than his cost of goods sold with low selling expenses and additional revenues from web site advertising, third-party marketing deals, shipping, and premium services. With a sizable venture capital investment from Softbank to cushion his startup, Blum may confound his critics and competitors and establish a legitimate new model for retail E-commerce.

Figure 6.23

CEO Scott Blum of Buy.com is selling consumer products at or below cost and hopes to make up the deficit through advertising, web site marketing deals, shipping, and services.

Real World Case

Buy.com: Testing a New Business Model in E-Commerce

Buy.com: www.buy.com
CEO: Scott Blum.
1998 revenues: $125 million.

Categories: Computers, books, games, software, videos, music.

Offerings: 1.5 million items.

Recent moves: BuyComp.com purchased more than 2,000 *buy* domain names and relaunched as Buy.com; acquired SpeedServe, the parent company of Book-Serve.com, VideoServe.com, and GameServe.com; and formed an alliance with Ingram Entertainment, SpeedServe's parent, the leading national home-entertainment distributor.

A few months ago, I suggested that in a world where Wall Street seems to value revenues and growth more than profits, the ultimate business would be to create a web site that sells dollars for 85 cents. As the argument went, you could always make up the difference through ad revenues.

This is pretty similar to what entrepreneur Scott Blum has actually done. Blum, CEO of Buy.com, is selling consumer products at or below cost, and trying to create a brand synonymous with low price—with the hope of becoming the leading E-commerce portal. He even plans to make up the deficit through advertising and services.

Buy.com's tag line, "The lowest prices on Earth," may be the most precise positioning statement ever. The company is ruthlessly committed to being the price leader—even if this means losing money on every sale. Its software searches competitors' sites to make sure Buy.com has the lowest prices on the Web. And as far as I can tell, it does.

Now Buy.com has broken Compaq's first-year sales record of $111 million, making it the fastest-growing company in U.S. history.

It's easy to be skeptical of this seemingly crazy new model. Predictably, competitors who believe in the standard notion of selling goods at a profit blast the idea. It's unproven, says Julie Wainwright, CEO of Reel.com. Others point out that retailing is about more than just pricing and that Buy.com comes up short on other important metrics, such as customer service, ease of use, and overall customer experience.

True enough. But there's a lot more to learn by considering the implications of Buy.com's success than by taking the safe route and predicting its failure.

If Buy.com succeeds, we'll have proof that it is possible to build a brand completely on price. Selection, customer service, and a good web site experience all matter, of course, but on the Web it is very simple for a consumer to experience these things on one site and close his transaction with another—the low-price leader. Buy.com thus becomes a logical final destination for any shopper.

Capital is the natural limit to a business model in which you lose money on every sale. However, the company has raised $60 million from Softbank, the Japanese conglomerate that backed Yahoo and E-Trade. Based on its employee size of about 100 people, the company should have operating expenses of $12 million. Even if it loses money on each sale and spends marginally on advertising, Buy.com should be able to run for more than a year.

Other than lack of capital, there is little restricting Buy.com's growth. Unlike traditional retailers, web-based sellers are not slowed by the friction of store growth and local marketing. Brand messages can spread like wildfire via bulletin boards and E-mail. More important, the virtual reseller—which accepts orders and passes them to someone else for fulfillment—is limited only by the capacity of its partners' inventory.

But Buy.com's critics say that it is simply buying its business, with no idea how to turn a profit. They question what value it can deliver to advertisers and wonder how loyal its customers will be.

Buy.com, however, appears quite confident that they can cover their losses and make a healthy profit with revenues from selling web site advertising, exclusive marketing deals, shipping, and premium services. Says founder and CEO Scott Blum, "It's our goal to leapfrog past Jeff Bezos and Amazon."

Case Study Questions

1. Do you think that CEO Scott Blum's E-commerce business model will eventually prove successful in generating profits? Why or why not?

2. What advice would you give to Scott Blum to improve Buy.com's chances for success?

3. What advice would you give to CEO Jeff Bezos of Amazon.com to help Amazon counter the threat posed by Buy.com?

Source: Adapted from J. William Gurley, "Buy.com May Fail, But If It Succeeds, Retailing Will Never Be the Same," *Fortune*, January 11, 1999, pp. 150–51, © 1999 Time Inc. All rights reserved; Jeffrey Davis, "Mall Rats," *Business 2.0*, January 1999, pp. 41–50; Alex Gove, "Margin of Error," *Red Herring*, February 1999, p. 140; and Brian Taptich, "Less than Zero Margins," *Red Herring*, March 1999, pp. 46–50.

Foundations of Electronic Commerce

For internetworked enterprises in the age of the Internet, intranets, and extranets, electronic commerce is more than just buying and selling products online. Instead, it encompasses the entire online process of developing, marketing, selling, delivering, servicing, and paying for products and services purchased by internetworked, global virtual communities of customers, with the support of a worldwide network of business partners. Electronic commerce systems rely on the resources of the Internet, intranets, extranets, and other computer networks to support every step of this process. For example, electronic commerce can include interactive marketing, ordering, and payment processes on the World Wide Web, extranet access of inventory databases by customers and suppliers, intranet access of customer records by sales reps and customer service, and involvement in product development via Internet newsgroups and E mail exchanges.

Companies engage in three basic categories of electronic commerce applications, which we will explore in this section: business-to-consumer, business-to-business, and internal business processes [16].

Business-to-Consumer Commerce. In this form of electronic commerce, businesses must develop attractive electronic marketplaces to entice and sell products and services to consumers. For example, companies may offer multimedia web sites that provide virtual storefronts and virtual shopping malls, interactive order processing, and secure electronic payment systems.

Business-to-Business Applications. This category of electronic commerce involves both electronic business marketplaces and direct market links between businesses. For example, many companies offer the business community a variety of marketing and product information on the World Wide Web. Others also rely on electronic data interchange (EDI) via the Internet or extranets for direct computer-to-computer exchange of business transaction documents with their business customers and suppliers.

Internal Business Processes. All business functions and many business processes are affected by electronic commerce activities. For example, many internetworked enterprises are customer-driven and market-driven. They continually monitor and evaluate online information about their customers, suppliers, and competitors from their web sites and discussion groups. This information is available via intranets to all business functions, and is used to shape a company's product development, marketing programs, customer service, and competitive strategies.

Electronic Commerce Technologies

What technologies are necessary for electronic commerce? The short answer is that most information technologies and Internet technologies that we discuss in this text are involved in electronic commerce systems. A more specific answer is illustrated in Figure 6.24.

Figure 6.24 illustrates an electronic commerce architecture proposed by Sun Microsystems and its business partners. This architecture emphasizes that:

- The Internet, intranets, and extranets are the network infrastructure or foundation of electronic commerce.
- Customers must be provided with a range of secure information, marketing, transaction processing, and payment services.
- Trading and business partners rely on the Internet and extranets to exchange information and accomplish secure transactions using electronic data interchange (EDI) and other supply chain and financial systems and databases.

Figure 6.24 The software components and functions of an integrated electronic commerce system. This architecture would enable a business to use the Internet, intranets, and extranets to accomplish electronic commerce transactions with consumers, business customers, and business partners.

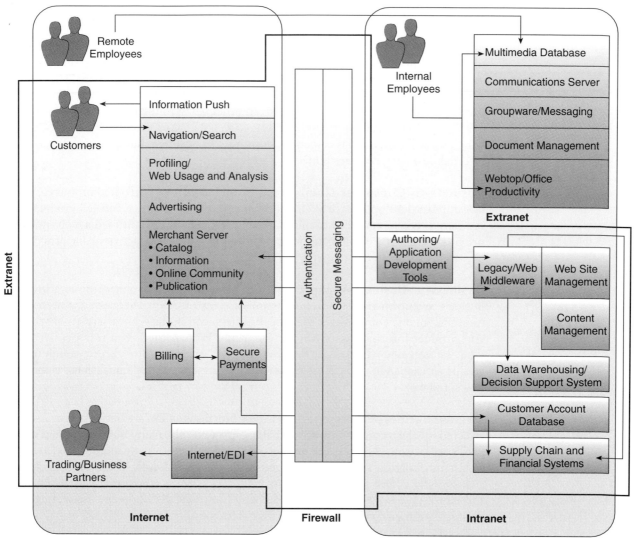

Adapted courtesy of Sun Microsystems.

- Company employees depend on a variety of Internet and intranet resources to communicate and collaborate in support of their EC work activities.
- IS professionals and end users can use a variety of software tools to develop and manage the content and operations of the web sites and other EC resources of a company.

Figure 6.25 gives examples of some of the software that enables a business to provide electronic commerce services.

Business-to-Consumer Commerce

Electronic commerce on the Internet between businesses and consumers is accelerating the impact of information technology on consumer behavior and business processes and markets.

Figure 6.25	Some of the software components developed by Netscape Communications for a company's electronic commerce systems.

Netscape EC Software	Electronic Commerce Functions
Wallet	Organizes consumers' online payment activities and provides consumers with the security of the SET electronic payment protocol for their credit/debit card transactions.
LivePayment	Allows merchants to communicate with a bank to authorize transactions and capture funds directly over the Internet.
MerchantSystem	Provides a complete retailing system for a business, including services for staging and approval; product displays based on database information, sales, and promotions; shopping cart and checkout; tax calculation; and customer support and reporting.
PublishingSystem	Provides a complete system for content publishing and account-based services, including services for membership, access control, tracking of charge events on periodic billing statements, template-based publishing, and customized content delivery.
CommunitySystem	Provides a customized system for creating online communities of interest. Integrates chat, bulletin board, and mail services with the back-end membership, billing, access-control, search, and payment services.

Source: Adapted from Echart Walther, "The Netscape One Platform Vision and Product Roadmap," White Paper, Netscape Communications Corporation, 1996, p. 13.

Technology is transforming consumer choices, which in turn transform the dynamics of the marketplace and organizations themselves. Technology embodies adaptability, programmability, flexibility, and other qualities so essential for customization. Together they have created the promise of "any thing, any way, any time" [22].

Retailing on the Web

A basic fact of Internet retailing is that all web sites are created equal as far as the "location, location, location" imperative for success in retailing is concerned. No site is any closer to its customers. This makes it vital that businesses find ways to keep customers coming back to their stores. The key to this goal is to optimize factors such as performance and service efficiency, personalization, socialization, the look and feel of the site, offering incentives to purchase, and security [23]. Let's take a look at each of these factors, which help make a retail web site a success. See Figure 6.26.

- **Performance and Service.** People don't want to be kept waiting when browsing, selecting, or paying for products in an electronic store. A site must be efficiently designed for ease of access, shopping, and buying, with sufficient server power and telecommunications capacity. Marketing, ordering, and customer service processes must also be friendly and helpful, as well as quick and easy.

- **Personalization.** Personalizing your shopping experience encourages you to make return visits. Many sites register you as a customer or have you fill out a personal interest profile. Then when you return, you are welcomed and guided just to those parts of a site that you are interested in. A lot of sites automatically record details of your visits and build similar user interest profiles.

- **Socialization.** Giving online customers with similar interests a feeling of belonging to a unique group of like-minded individuals helps build customer loyalty and value. Web-based relationship marketing and affinity marketing promote such virtual communities of customers, suppliers, company representatives, and other consumers through a variety of techniques. Examples include customer discussion forums and chat rooms, product focus groups, bulletin board systems, and cross-links to related web sites and newsgroups.

Figure 6.26

Examples of a few top-rated retail web sites.

- **Autoweb Interactive   www.autoweb.com**
  Autoweb is an online resource for buying and selling new and used cars. The site has information on every new car on the U.S. market as well as a listing of affiliated dealers to whom customers can send an electronic purchase request. Autoweb also has a database listing thousands of used cars across the country.

- **Barnes & Noble   www.barnesandnoble.com**
  The largest chain of book superstores has expanded online with sites on America Online and the Web. In addition to its one million titles—many discounted 20–30%—B&N features an online community with book-related newsgroups, daily live chat sessions with authors, and an innovative service that offers personalized book recommendations.

- **CDnow   www.cdnow.com**
  CDnow is one of the biggest music retailers on the Web. The CD superstore offers nearly every compact disk in print in the U.S. as well as 20,000 imports. Customers can listen to short song clips from many of these using RealAudio software before they buy. CDnow also offers a wide selection of movies, music videos, books, T-shirts, and DVDs.

- **Lands' End   www.landsend.com**
  The Lands' End Internet store features a selection of its product lines from the direct merchant's popular catalog. Customers can find a packable rain poncho in casualwear, a flowery tie in men's haberdashery, or a comfy quilt in the bedding department. There's also an overstock section—filled with great deals on extra stock—that gets updated weekly.

- **Virtual Emporium   www.virtualemporium.com**
  If you're unsure where to start your web shopping adventure, try the Virtual Emporium. It features links to over 200 sites in 10 different shopping zones, ranging from House & Gardens to Kids Stuff. The site also has some handy shopping tools to help you find just the right gift or even have Virtual Emporium do the shopping for you.

Source: Adapted from "What's New in Electronic Commerce," in Technology Buyer's Guide, *Fortune*, Winter 1998, pp. 266-68. © 1998 by Time Inc. All rights reserved.

- **Look and Feel.** Web sites can offer you an attractive virtual storefront. This may range from providing an exciting shopping experience with audio, motion, and striking graphics, to a more traditional look and feel, including a virtual shopping mall of related web sites. For example, Oracle software lets shoppers browse product sections, select products, drop them into a virtual shopping cart, and go to a virtual checkout stand to pay for the order.

- **Incentives.** Web stores must offer shoppers incentives to buy and return. Typically, this means coupons, discounts, special offers, and vouchers for other web services, sometimes at other cross-linked web sites. Some sites provide you with an electronic wallet where you can accumulate coupons for future use, as well as receipts and credit card information.

- **Security and Reliability.** As a customer of a web store, you must feel confident that your credit card, personal information, and details of your transactions are secure from unauthorized use. (We will discuss security issues shortly.) Having your orders filled as you requested and in the time frame promised are important measures of a web store's reliability.

Amazon.com

Lots of companies say they offer customer service on their World Wide Web sites. Few really do. In fact, we're all so starved for good customer service that we tend to notice when we're treated well. We quickly become raving fans when somebody surprises us by treating us well [39].

Figure 6.27

The home page of Amazon.com.

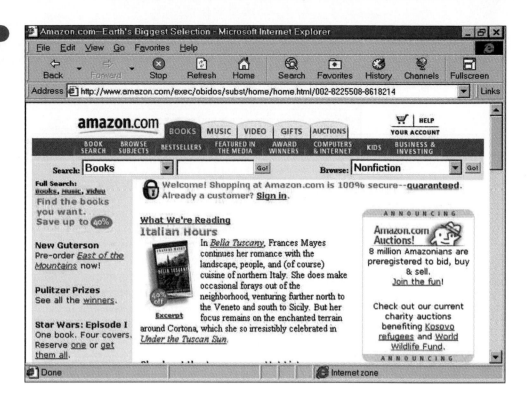

Amazon is an example of a company on the World Wide Web that consistently receives high marks for customer service. Amazon (www.amazon.com) is one of the biggest and best virtual retailers on the Web. See Figure 6.27. The site is designed to speed you through the process of browsing and ordering merchandise, while giving you reassuring, personal service at discount prices. For example, the search engine for finding the books you want is quick and accurate, and the ordering process easy and fast. Confirmation is quick, and notifications are accurate and friendly. Delivery is prompt. Orders are carefully wrapped and accompanied by handwritten notes that explain any changes in the order.

Amazon's customer service includes a personal notification system, which sends you an E-mail message when a book comes out in paperback, or when a new title in your favorite category is published. You can also read book reviews by other customers, and have books gift-wrapped and sent with a personal note. Also, at any one time, about 300,000 titles are discounted 10 to 40 percent. Buyers are E-mailed both when their order is confirmed, as well as the day their order is shipped. The company also offers customers a complete money-back guarantee. This combination of efficiency, discount prices, and personal service is why Amazon is frequently mentioned as a model of customer service for businesses on the Web [38].

Customer Value and the Internet

The driving force behind world economic growth has changed from manufacturing volume to improving customer value. As a result, the key success factor for many firms is maximizing customer value [8].

For many companies, the chief business value of the Internet lies in its ability to help them keep customers loyal, anticipate their future needs, respond to customer concerns, and improve customer service. This focus on **customer value** recognizes

Figure 6.28

Why companies are using the Internet to achieve customer value.

- Lower support costs by empowering customers to solve issues independently.
- Provide global access to critical customer service information and forums anytime.
- Improve service by focusing internal customer support resources on complex issues.
- Empower business partners with hot links to related online resolution information.
- Create proactive service and marketing programs.
- Seamless web/telephony integration for priority responsiveness.

Source: Adapted from Ravi Kalakota and Andrew Whinston, *Electronic Commerce: A Manager's Guide* (Reading, MA: Addison-Wesley, 1997), p. 331. © 1997 by Addison-Wesley Publishing Company, Inc. Reprinted by permission of Addison-Wesley Longman, Inc.

that quality, rather than price, has become the primary determinant in a customer's perception of value. From a customer's point of view, companies that consistently offer the best value are able to keep track of their customers' individual preferences; keep up with market trends; supply relevant information attractively, anytime, anywhere, in a variety of media; and provide customer services tailored to individual needs [8].

That is why so many companies have invested heavily in information technology and complex systems of interconnected computer networks. But increasingly, businesses are finding that they can reach many of their customers and prospective customers via the Internet. This fast-growing group of customers want and expect companies to communicate with them and service their needs over the Internet. And so the Internet has become a strategic and comparatively low-cost opportunity for companies large and small to offer fast, responsive, high-quality products and services tailored to individual customer preferences. Figure 6.28 lists major business objectives that companies hope to achieve by using the World Wide Web to provide customer service.

The Internet and Internet technologies can make customers the focal point of a business. The Internet, intranets, and extranets create new channels for interactive communications within a company, with customers, and with the suppliers, business partners, and others in the external environment. This enables continual interaction with customers by most business functions and encourages cross-functional collaboration with customers in product development, marketing, delivery, service, and technical support [10].

Typically, customers use the Internet to ask questions, air complaints, evaluate products, request support, and make and report their purchases. Using the Internet and corporate intranets, specialists in business functions throughout the enterprise can contribute to an effective response. This encourages the creation of cross-functional discussion groups and problem-solving teams dedicated to customer involvement, service, and support. Even the Internet and extranet links to suppliers and business partners can be used to ensure the prompt delivery of quality components and services that a company needs to meet its commitments to its customers [16]. This is how the internetworked enterprise demonstrates its focus on customer value.

Nortel Networks

Nortel Networks is a manufacturer of networking and communications equipment and software (www.nortelnetworks.com). See Figure 6.29. Nortel Networks employees interact with customers primarily through E-mail, Usenet discussion groups, telnet sessions, and file transfers of test data and software updates with customer beta test sites. Nortel Networks has integrated the Internet into the daily work of its employees across its various departments. Most Nortel Networks personnel are in regular daily contact with customers, suppliers, business partners, competitors, and

Figure 6.29

The home page of
Nortel Networks
(www.nortelnetworks.
com).

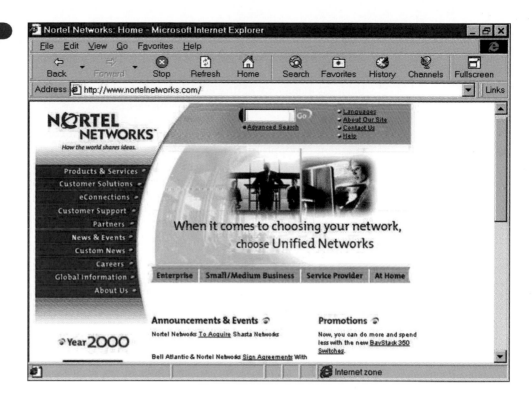

other employees. The company feels that this promotes a keener awareness of the external environment and the strategic opportunities available in the industry [8].

For example, engineers and development specialists like to evaluate newsgroup discussions to see how customers react to existing products, and what other customer needs are waiting to be met by new or improved products. Customer support specialists follow newsgroups to determine whether a performance problem is coming from Nortel Networks equipment or another part of a customer's system. They can then telnet from their computers to a customer's server to check out and solve most equipment problems quickly without having to travel to a customer's worksite.

Nortel Networks makes paying attention to customer comments on the Internet a priority for their employees. This helps build customer value and loyalty as customers notice the prompt and positive response to their questions, comments, complaints, and suggestions. Employees also find that keeping up with similar Usenet discussions on their competitors' products and service helps them do a better job of developing, marketing, and servicing their own products, especially when a customer's system contains products from multiple vendors. So for Nortel Networks, the Internet has become an essential part of business operations and the key to customer satisfaction and loyalty [8].

Business-to-Business Commerce

Because of the radical changes brought about by the Internet, centuries-old basic business processes such as buying and selling are going to change dramatically. Both buyers and sellers will be demanding more information and better information, and will demand it faster than ever. This transformation—a true paradigm shift—will forever alter the way society operates [23].

Business-to-business electronic commerce is the wholesale side of the commercial process. For example, let's suppose a company wants to build and sell a product to other businesses. Then it must buy raw materials and a variety of contracted services from other companies. The interrelationships with other businesses needed to build and sell a product make up a network of business relationships that is called the **supply chain.** Electronic commerce systems like electronic data interchange (EDI), and business management processes like supply chain management, seek to reengineer and streamline traditional supply chain processes.

Supply Chain Management

Supply chain management (SCM) is a management concept that integrates the management of supply chain processes. See Figure 6.30. The goal of SCM is to cut costs, increase profits, improve performance in relationships with customers and suppliers, and develop value-added services that give a company a competitive edge. According to the Advanced Manufacturing Council, supply chain management has three business objectives:

- Get the right product to the right place at the least cost.
- Keep inventory as low as possible and still offer superior customer service.
- Reduce cycle times. Supply chain management seeks to simplify and accelerate operations that deal with how customer orders are processed through the system and ultimately filled, as well as how raw materials are acquired and delivered for manufacturing processes [3].

Wholesaling on the Web

Wholesale electronic commerce and supply chain management rely on many different information technologies, most of which can be implemented on the Internet, the World Wide Web, and corporate intranets and extranets. These include E-mail, electronic business forms, bulletin board systems, electronic data interchange, electronic funds transfers, web sites with multimedia marketing information and product catalogs, interactive order processing systems, and so on. All of the factors for building a successful retail web site we discussed earlier also apply to wholesale web sites for business-to-business electronic commerce.

In addition, many businesses tie their Internet, intranet, and extranet electronic commerce systems to their traditional, or legacy, computer-based accounting and

Figure 6.30

The business value of each of the components of supply chain management. Note the major role of electronic commerce technologies in these management practices.

● **Supplier management.** Use electronic commerce to help reduce the number of suppliers and get them to become partners in business in a win/win relationship.
● **Inventory management.** Shorten the order-ship-bill cycle with electronic commerce processes, and keep inventory levels to a minimum.
● **Distribution management.** Use electronic data interchange to move documents related to shipping (bills of lading, purchase orders, advanced ship notices, and so on.)
● **Channel management.** Use E-mail, bulletin board systems, and newsgroups to quickly disseminate information about changing operational conditions to trading partners.
● **Payment management.** Use electronic funds transfer to link the company and systems suppliers and distributors so that payments can be sent and received electronically.
● **Financial management.** Use electronic commerce systems to enable global companies to manage their money in various foreign exchange accounts.
● **Sales force management.** Use sales force automation methods to improve the communication and flow of information among the sales, customer service, and production functions.

Source: Adapted from Ravi Kalakota and Andrew Whinston, *Frontiers of Electronic Commerce* (Reading, MA: Addison-Wesley, 1996), pp. 38–39. © 1996 by Addison-Wesley Publishing Company, Inc. Reprinted by permission of Addison-Wesley Longman, Inc.

business information systems. This ensures that all electronic commerce activities on a web site are supported by up-to-date corporate inventory and other databases, which in turn are automatically updated by web sales activities.

| Marshall Industries | Marshall Industries is a $1.2 billion electronics distributor. Their interactive marketing strategy includes a multimedia web site (www.marshall.com) and an extranet called PartnerNet that gives customers and suppliers customized entry into the company's intranets. Marshall's vision is to create a virtual distribution system where customers can learn about and buy products anytime and in any form. For example, PartnerNet creates personalized profiles of selected customers and suppliers, which give them customized views into Marshall's products, services, and inventory. See Figure 6.31.

In addition, Marshall's web site provides realtime news reports on the industry and its vendors, live audio feeds from industry trade shows, and online interactive seminars. Marshall spent $325,000 on an audio studio to host its online seminars, and hired a former radio announcer to produce live reports from industry trade shows. Their web site is so popular in the industry that Marshall is selling advertising space on their web screen to their own vendors. Marshall is confident that increased sales have more than repaid the $1 million it cost to develop the site. For example, a recent online seminar attracted 87 engineers from a dozen countries. Three or four of them also ordered software development tools during the session, which rarely happens in traditional seminars [37]. |

Electronic Data Interchange

Electronic data interchange, or EDI, involves the electronic exchange of business transaction documents over computer networks between trading partners (organizations and their customers and suppliers). Data representing a variety of business transaction documents (such as purchase orders, invoices, requests for quotations, and

Figure 6.31

The home page of Marshall Industries (www.marshall.com).

Courtesy of Marshall Industries.

shipping notices) are electronically exchanged between computers using standard document message formats. Typically, EDI software is used to convert a company's own document formats into standardized EDI formats as specified by various industry and international protocols. Thus, EDI is an example of the almost complete automation of an electronic commerce process.

Formatted transaction data are transmitted over network links directly between computers, without paper documents or human intervention. Besides direct network links between the computers of trading partners, third-party services are widely used. Value-added telecommunications carriers like GE Information Services, IBM Advantis, and Sterling Software offer a variety of EDI services. For example, they typically provide electronic mailboxes for temporary storage of EDI documents sent by a company's business partners. Many of these EDI service providers are also beginning to offer secure EDI services over the Internet [27]. Figure 6.32 illustrates a typical EDI system.

What are some of the business benefits of EDI? EDI eliminates the printing, mailing, checking, and handling by employees of numerous multiple-copy forms of business documents. Also, since standard document formats are used, the delays caused by mail or telephone communication between businesses to verify what a document means are drastically reduced. Some of the benefits of EDI that result are reductions in paper, postage, and labor costs; faster flow of transactions; reductions in errors; increases in productivity; support of just-in-time (JIT) inventory policies; and reductions in inventory levels. For example, a study by RJR Nabisco determined that the $70 cost for processing a paper purchase order using their old system dropped to less than a dollar using EDI [27]. In addition, using EDI is one of the ways a company can build strategic business links with its customers, suppliers, and other trading partners.

Figure 6.32 A typical example of electronic data interchange activities, an important form of business-to-business electronic commerce.

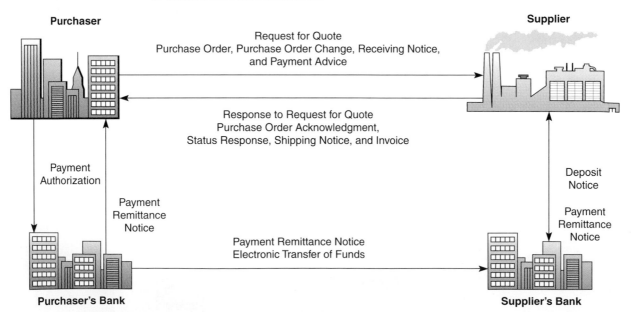

Source: Adapted from James A. Senn, "Electronic Data Interchange: Elements of Implementation," *Information Systems Management*, Winter 1992, p. 46. Reprinted from *Information Systems Management* (New York: Auerbach Publications). © 1992 by Research Institute of America. Used with permission.

Online Transaction Processing

Online transaction processing systems play a strategic role in electronic commerce. Many firms are using the Internet, extranets, and other networks that tie them electronically to their customers or suppliers for online transaction processing (OLTP). Such *realtime* systems, which capture and process transactions immediately, can help them provide superior service to customers and other trading partners. This capability adds value to their products and services, and thus gives them an important way to differentiate themselves from their competitors.

Syntellect

For example, Figure 6.33 illustrates an online transaction processing system for cable pay-per-view systems developed by Syntellect Interactive Services. Cable TV viewers can select pay-per-view events offered by their cable companies using the phone or the World Wide Web. The pay-per-view order is captured by Syntellect's interactive voice response system or web server, then transported to Syntellect database application servers. There the order is processed, customer and sales databases are updated, and the approved order is relayed back to the cable company's video server, which transmits the video of the pay-per-view event to the customer. Thus, Syntellect teams with over 700 cable companies to offer a very popular and very profitable service [21].

The Transaction Processing Cycle

Transaction processing systems, such as Syntellect's, capture and process data describing business transactions, update organizational databases, and produce a variety of information products. You should understand transaction processing as a cycle of several basic activities, as illustrated in Figure 6.34.

- **Data Entry.** The first step of the transaction processing cycle is the capture of business data. For example, transaction data may be collected by point-of-sale terminals using optical scanning of barcodes and credit card readers at a retail store or other business. Or transaction data can be captured at an electronic commerce web site on the Internet. Properly recording and editing data so they are quickly and correctly captured for processing is one of the major design challenges of information systems discussed in Chapter 10.

- **Transaction Processing.** Transaction processing systems process data in two basic ways: (1) **batch processing**, where transaction data are accumulated over a period of time and processed periodically, and (2) **realtime processing** (also called online processing), where data are processed immediately after a transaction occurs. All online transaction processing systems incorporate realtime processing capabilities. Many online systems also depend on the capabilities of *fault tolerant* computer systems that can continue to operate even if parts of the system fail. We will discuss this fault tolerant concept in Chapter 12.

- **Database Maintenance.** An organization's database must be maintained by its transaction processing systems so that they are always correct and up-to-date. Therefore, transaction processing systems update the corporate database of an organization to reflect changes resulting from day-to-day business transactions. For example, credit sales made to customers will cause customer account balances to be increased and the amount of inventory on hand to be decreased. Database maintenance ensures that these and other changes are reflected in the data records stored in the company's databases.

- **Document and Report Generation.** Transaction processing systems produce a variety of documents and reports. Examples of transaction documents include purchase orders, paychecks, sales receipts, invoices, and customer statements.

Figure 6.33 The Syntellect pay-per-view online transaction processing system.

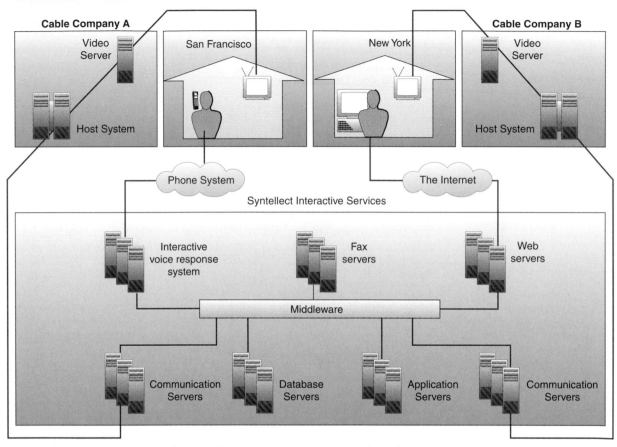

Source: Adapted from Jay Tucker, "The New Money: Transactions Pour across the Web," *Datamation*, April 1997, p. 74. © 1997 by Cahners Publishing Co.

Transaction reports might take the form of a transaction listing such as a payroll register, or edit reports that describe errors detected during processing.

- **Inquiry Processing.** Many transaction processing systems allow you to use the Internet, intranets, extranets, and web browsers or database management query languages to make inquiries and receive responses concerning the results of transaction processing activity. Typically, responses are displayed in a variety of prespecified formats or screens. For example, you might check on the status of a sales order, the balance in an account, or the amount of stock in inventory and receive immediate responses at your PC.

Electronic Payments and Security

Payment for the products and services purchased is an obvious and vital step in the electronic commerce transaction process. But the process is not simple, because of the near-anonymous electronic nature of transactions taking place between the networked computer systems of buyers and sellers, and the many security issues involved. The electronic commerce payment process is also complex because of the wide variety of debit and credit alternatives and financial institutions and intermediaries that may be part of the process. Therefore, a variety of **electronic payment systems** have evolved over time. In addition, new payment systems are being developed and tested to meet the security and technical challenges of electronic commerce over the Internet.

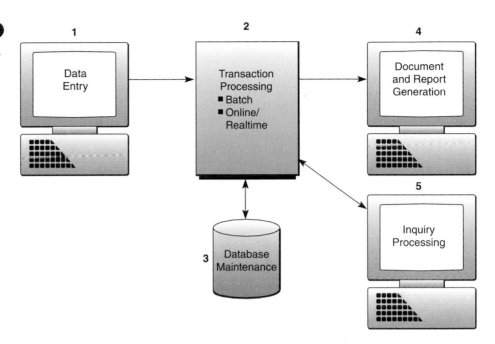

Figure 6.34

The transaction processing cycle. Note that transaction processing systems use a five-stage cycle of data entry, transaction processing, database maintenance, document and report generation, and inquiry processing activities.

Electronic Funds Transfer

Electronic funds transfer (EFT) systems are a major form of electronic payment systems in banking and retailing industries. EFT systems use a variety of information technologies to capture and process money and credit transfers between banks and businesses and their customers. For example, banking networks support teller terminals at all bank offices and automated teller machines (ATMs) at locations throughout this world. Banks may also support pay-by-phone services allowing bank customers to use their telephones as terminals to electronically pay bills. In addition, wide area networks may connect POS terminals in retail stores to bank EFT systems. This makes it possible for you to use a credit card or debit card to instantly pay for gas, groceries, or other purchases at participating retail outlets.

Secure Electronic Payments on the Internet

One of the most visible and contentious topics in Internet commerce today is the security of Internet transactions. While the technical difficulties may be soluble, a less obvious problem is how to define standards to let all consumers and merchants do business with each other while satisfying security requirements of the financial institutions involved [28].

When you make an online purchase on the Internet, your credit card information is vulnerable to interception by network sniffers, software that easily recognizes credit card number formats. Several basic security measures are being used to solve this security problem: (1) encrypt (code and scramble) the data passing between the customer and merchant, (2) encrypt the data passing between the customer and the company authorizing the credit card transaction, or (3) take sensitive information offline. (Note: Because encryption and other security issues are discussed in Chapter 12, we will not explain how they work in this section.)

For example, many companies use the Secure Socket Layer (SSL) security method developed by Netscape Communications that automatically encrypts data passing between your web browser and a merchant's server. However, sensitive information is still vulnerable to misuse once it's decrypted (decoded and unscrambled) and stored on a merchant's server. So a digital wallet approach such as the CyberCash payment system was developed. In this method, you add security software add-on modules to your web browser. That enables your browser to encrypt your credit card data in such a way that only the bank that authorizes credit card transactions for the merchant gets to see it. All the merchant is told is whether your credit transaction is approved or not [28, 29].

The Secure Electronic Transaction, or SET, standard for electronic payment security extends the CyberCash digital wallet approach. In this method, EC software encrypts a digital envelope of digital certificates specifying the payment details for each transaction. SET has been agreed to by VISA, MasterCard, IBM, Microsoft, Netscape, and most other industry players. Therefore, SET is expected to become the dominant standard for secure electronic payments on the Internet [21]. Figure 6.35 illustrates and summarizes the SET approach for electronic payment systems.

Another approach doesn't use encryption because it takes credit card and other sensitive information offline. For example, in the First Virtual payment system, you use an 800 number to set up an account, including your credit card information and E-mail address. From then on you make online purchases by giving your First Virtual ID number to the merchant. Then you must respond to an E-mail inquiry from First Virtual on whether you want to pay for the product or service with only three response options: Yes, No, or Fraud [29].

Other electronic payment systems include *micropayment* systems like DigiCash and CyberCoin. These technologies create *digital currency* or *digital cash*, sometimes called e-cash, for making payments that are too small for credit card transactions. Encryption

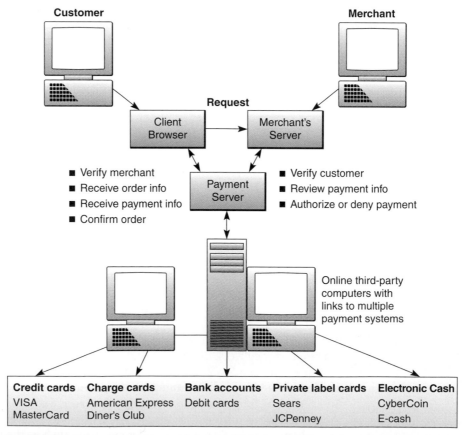

Figure 6.35

An example of secure electronic payment systems based on the SET security method.

Source: Adapted from Ravi Kalakota and Andrew Whinston, *Frontiers of Electronic Commerce* (Reading, MA: Addison-Wesley, 1996), p. 322. © 1996 Addison-Wesley Publishing Company, Inc. Reprinted by permission of Addison-Wesley Longman, Inc.

Figure 6.36

CyberCash provides electronic payment services on the World Wide Web including a digital wallet system for secure credit card transactions, and the CyberCoin digital cash system for micropayment transactions.

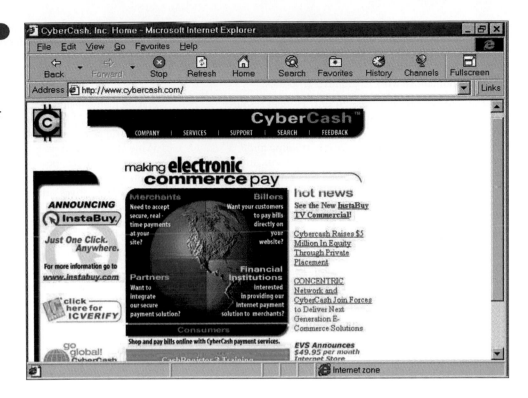

and authentication techniques are used to generate strings of data that can be handled like currency for making cash payments [29]. For example, web sites like ESPNET SportsZone, Discovery Online, and Rocket Science Games let you chat with superstars, download video segments, or play video games by using digital cash micropayment systems [31]. See Figure 6.36.

Summary

- **IS in Business.** Business information systems support the functional areas of business (marketing, production/operations, accounting, finance, and human resource management) through a wide variety of computer-based operational and management information systems.

- **Marketing.** Marketing information systems provide information for the management of the marketing function. Thus, marketing information systems assist marketing managers in market research, product development, and pricing decisions, as well as in planning advertising and sales promotion strategies and expenditures, forecasting the market potential for new and present products, and determining channels of distribution. Major types of marketing information systems include interactive marketing, sales force automation, sales management, product management,

advertising and promotion, targeted marketing, sales forecasting, and market research. Interactive marketing on the Internet and other networks is changing marketing to a more customer-driven interactive process.

- **Manufacturing.** Computer-based manufacturing information systems help a company achieve computer-integrated manufacturing (CIM), and thus simplify, automate, and integrate many of the activities needed to quickly produce high-quality products to meet changing customer demands. For example, computer-aided design (CAD) using collaborative manufacturing networks helps engineers collaborate on the design of new products and processes. Then material requirements planning (MRP) systems help plan the types of material needed in the production process. Finally, manufacturing execution systems monitor and control the manufacture of products on the factory floor through shop floor scheduling and control systems, controlling a physical process (process control), a machine tool (numerical control), or machines with some humanlike work capabilities (robotics).

● **Human Resource Management.** Human resource information systems support human resource management in organizations. They include information systems for staffing the organization, training and development, compensation administration, and governmental reporting. HRM web sites on the Internet or corporate intranets have become important tools for providing HR services to present and prospective employees.

● **Accounting and Finance.** Accounting information systems record and report business transactions and events for business firms and other organizations. Operational accounting systems emphasize legal and historical record-keeping and the production of accurate financial statements. Management accounting systems focus on the planning and control of business operations. Common operational accounting information systems include order processing, inventory control, accounts receivable, accounts payable, payroll, and general ledger systems. Information systems in finance support financial managers in decisions regarding the financing of a business and the allocation of financial resources within a business. Financial information systems include cash management, online investment management, capital budgeting, and financial forecasting and planning.

● **Electronic Commerce.** Electronic commerce encompasses the entire online process of developing, marketing, selling, delivering, servicing, and paying for products and services. The Internet's web browser and client/server architecture, and networks of hypermedia databases on the World Wide Web, serve as the technology platform for electronic commerce among internetworked communities of customers and business partners.

● **Electric Commerce Applications.** The Internet encourages innovation and entrepreneurship, thus generating many business opportunities to serve a global audience of both business and consumer customers. Successful retailing and wholesaling on the World Wide Web depend on factors such as efficient performance and service, personalization and socialization of the shopping experience, the look and feel of the web site, incentives offered, and the security and reliability of business transactions. Business-to-business applications of electronic commerce support the processes of supply chain management through a variety of Internet and web site services and network applications like electronic data interchange.

● **Online Transaction Processing.** Online transaction processing systems play a vital role in electronic commerce. Transaction processing involves the basic activities of (1) data entry, (2) transaction processing, (3) database maintenance, (4) document and report generation, and (5) inquiry processing. Many firms are using the Internet, intranets, extranets, and other networks for online transaction processing to provide superior service to their customers and suppliers.

● **Electronic Payment and Security.** The electronic payment process presents a vital and complex challenge to business and financial institutions to develop efficient, flexible, and secure payment systems for electronic commerce. A variety of payment systems have evolved for electronic funds transfers, including several major ways to provide security for transactions and payments over the Internet.

Key Terms and Concepts

These are the key terms and concepts of this chapter. The page number of their first explanation is in parentheses.

1. Accounting information systems (218)
2. Accounts payable (220)
3. Accounts receivable (220)
4. Batch processing (235)
5. Business information systems (202)
6. Collaborative manufacturing networks (212)
7. Computer-aided design (213)
8. Computer-aided engineering (213)
9. Computer-aided manufacturing (211)
10. Computer-integrated manufacturing (210)
11. Cross-functional information systems (205)
12. Customer value and the Internet (229)
13. Electronic commerce (223)
    a. Business-to-business (231)
    b. Business-to-consumer (226)
    c. Technology architecture (225)
14. Electronic data interchange (233)
15. Electronic funds transfer (237)

16. Electronic payment systems (236)
17. Financial management systems (221)
18. General ledger (221)
19. Human resource information systems (214)
20. Interactive marketing (206)
21. Inventory control (220)
22. Machine control (212)
23. Manufacturing execution systems (211)
24. Manufacturing information systems (210)
25. Marketing information systems (205)
26. Material requirements planning (211)
27. Online accounting systems (218)
28. Online HRM systems (214)
29. Online investment systems (221)
30. Online transaction processing systems (235)
31. Order processing (218)
32. Payroll (220)
33. Process control (212)
34. Realtime processing (235)
35. Retailing on the Web (226)
36. Robotics (212)
37. Sales force automation (207)
38. Security of electronic commerce (237)
39. Supply chain (232)
40. Supply chain management (232)
41. Targeted marketing (209)
42. Transaction processing cycle (235)
43. Wholesaling on the Web (232)

Review Quiz

Match one of the key terms and concepts listed previously with one of the brief examples or definitions that follow. Try to find the best fit for the answers that seem to fit more than one term or concept. Defend your choices.

_____ 1. Information systems that support marketing, production, accounting, finance, and human resource management.

_____ 2. Information systems that cross the boundaries of the functional areas of a business in order to support business processes.

_____ 3. Information systems for sales management, product management, and promotion management.

_____ 4. Collaborating interactively with customers in creating, purchasing, servicing, and improving products and services.

_____ 5. Using mobile computing networks to support salespeople in the field.

_____ 6. Information systems that support manufacturing operations and management.

_____ 7. A conceptual framework for simplifying and integrating all aspects of manufacturing automation.

_____ 8. Using computers in a variety of ways to help manufacture products.

_____ 9. Engineers and other specialists use the Internet and other networks to participate in product or process design.

_____ 10. Helps the design process using advanced graphics, networked workstations, and software.

_____ 11. Using computers to help engineers evaluate products and processes.

_____ 12. Using computers to operate a petroleum refinery.

_____ 13. Using computers to help operate machine tools.

_____ 14. Computerized devices with work capabilities that enable them to take over some production activities from human workers.

_____ 15. Translates the production schedule into a detailed plan for all materials required.

_____ 16. Information systems to support staffing, training and development, and compensation administration.

_____ 17. Using the Internet for recruitment and job hunting is an example.

_____ 18. Accomplishes legal and historical record-keeping and gathers information for the planning and control of business operations.

_____ 19. An example is using the Internet and extranets to do accounts receivable and accounts payable activities.

_____ 20. Handles sales orders from customers.

_____ 21. Keeps track of items in stock.

_____ 22. Keeps track of amounts owed by customers.

_____ 23. Keeps track of purchases from suppliers.

_____ 24. Produces employee paychecks.

_____ 25. Produces the financial statements of a firm.

_____ 26. Information systems for cash management, investment management, capital budgeting, and financial forecasting.

_____ 27. Using the Internet and other networks for investment research and trading.

_____ 28. Performance monitoring and control systems for factory floor operations.

_____ 29. Customizing advertising and promotion methods to fit their intended audience.

_____ 30. Data entry, transaction processing, database maintenance, document and report generation, and inquiry processing.

_____ 31. Collecting and periodically processing transaction data.

_____ 32. Processing transaction data immediately after they are captured.

_____ 33. Systems that immediately capture and process transaction data and update corporate databases.

_____ 34. The online process of developing, marketing, selling, delivering, servicing, and paying for products and services.

_____ 35. Selling products to consumers on the World Wide Web is an example.

_____ 36. The Internet is helping companies strengthen their relationships with customers, anticipate their future needs, respond quickly to their concerns, and improve their customer service and support.

_____ 37. Electronic data interchange between a business and its business customers and suppliers is an example.

_____ 38. The Internet and the World Wide Web depend on internetworks of web browser–equipped client/server systems and hypermedia databases.

_____ 39. The computer-to-computer exchange of business transaction documents between business partners.

_____ 40. Using information and telecommunications technologies to process money and credit transfers between businesses and financial institutions.

_____ 41. Ways to provide for efficient, flexible, and secure payments for purchases of products and services over the Internet and other networks.

_____ 42. Setting up a virtual storefront at a web site to sell products and services to networked consumers.

_____ 43. Electronic commerce transactions must be protected from fraud and theft.

_____ 44. A network of business relationships between a business that produces a product or service and the business partners that are involved in the processes that are required.

_____ 45. Integrates the management functions involved in promoting efficient and effective supply chain processes.

_____ 46. Many businesses rely on their web sites to sell products to other businesses for resale to consumers.

Discussion Questions

1. Why is there a trend toward cross-functional information systems in business?

2. What are the benefits and limitations of interactive marketing on the Internet for a business?

3. Refer to the Real World Case on Amazon.com in the chapter. Should Amazon try to become a complete retail commerce web portal? Why or why not?

4. How do you think sales force automation affects salesperson productivity, marketing management, and competitive advantage?

5. How can Internet technologies be involved in applications of computers in one of the functions of business? Choose one example and evaluate its business value.

6. How can the Internet improve customer value, relationships, and service for a business?

7. Refer to the Real World Case on Buy.com in the chapter. Who are Buy.com's competitors on the Web, other than full-price web retailers? Explain how they compete and what their prospects for success are.

8. Most businesses should engage in electronic commerce on the Internet. Do you agree or disagree with this statement? Explain your position.

9. Are you interested in owning, managing, working for, or investing in a business that is primarily engaged in electronic commerce on the Internet? Explain your position.

10. How secure are electronic payment systems on the Internet? What could be done to make electronic commerce more secure?

Real World Problems

1. Cyberian Outpost, CDNow, and AutoConnect: Improving Web Customer Retention

Online retailers are increasingly focusing on getting customers to keep coming back. Some sites are beefing up E-mail marketing and personalization; others are instituting loyalty programs to entice shoppers to make repeat buys. "You're going to see a lot more focus on retention," said Elaine Rubin, vice chairman of the industry group Shop.org.

Cyberian Outpost, for example, added a back-end system in late 1998 to improve its ability to interact with customers. Using software from Broadvision Inc. that can track user behavior and analyze patterns of activity, the online computer retailer can better target customers by geography, demographics, past purchasing habits, and other attributes. Cyberian used that type of data to design two direct E-mail promotion offers whose response rates substantially exceeded 3 percent (considered a good response rate), said Louise Cooper, vice president of worldwide marketing at the company.

CDNow Inc.—whose web site was ranked as the eighth most-visited shopping site in December 1998 by Media Metrix—launched a frequent-buyer program giving shoppers points for purchases, which they can redeem for merchandise. In the third quarter of last year, 59 percent of the site's customers were repeat buyers, according to Samantha Liss, director of brand marketing at CDNow.

In addition, the music seller has started to use Net Perceptions' GroupLens "recommendation engine" to generate suggestions about what additional music a shopper might like. Such software, also known as collaborative filtering, looks at a user's tastes and purchasing patterns and tries to match them to patterns of choices made by others. The retailer also uses personalization to let users customize the site for their tastes.

In addition to implementing marketing programs that entice customers to return, Internet retail executives said they must keep focused on such basics as customer service and strive to maintain sites that are well-designed and offer good response times and easy navigation.

"Most sites are rife with what we call 'rat holes,'" or places where users have nowhere to go except to reverse course and click back out from where they entered, said Chip Perry, CEO and president of Auto-Connect, which operates a site that offers information about used cars.

a. Which of the steps taken by the companies in this case do you think will be most successful in improving web customer retention? Why?

b. What other steps could companies take to increase the repeat business of their web customers?

Source: Adapted from Sharon Machlis, "Web Retailers Try to Keep Their Hits Up," *Computerworld*, February 8, 1999, p. 48. Copyright 1999 by Computerworld, Inc., Framingham, MA 01701. Reprinted from *Computerworld*.

2. NetBuy, Chemdex, and Others: The Business Value of Infomediaries

Business users can now buy everything, be it cows, chemicals, electronic parts, or paper, through web portals designed to help them find goods and compare suppliers' prices in specific vertical industries. Users say this emerging business-to-business purchase process will make transactions faster, simpler, and potentially more cost effective.

Take electronics components. Robert Child, director of corporate purchasing at EFTC Corp., an 1,800-employee electronics maker in Denver, said it might take two or three days and 10 or 20 calls just to locate a needed part. In some cases, there might be an 18- to 20-week lead time to get it.

By using the NetBuy portal (www.netbuy.com), which has 4,100 suppliers and $1.5 billion in inventory, Child said he can search 53 distributors in 30 seconds, find out instantly if the part is in stock, and order it.

Other third-party companies, like AgriMail.com for livestock and farm gear and biochemical supplier Chemdex Corp., are setting up vertical market electronic-commerce and information sites. Volpe Brown Whelan & Co., a San Francisco–based investment bank, predicts that the amount of purchased goods that go through such third parties will shoot from $750 million in 1999 to $211 billion by 2002. In that year, these "infomediaries" stand to make $20 billion in transaction fees and advertising.

The reason? Buyers want one-stop shopping, complete and accurate information, and trusted advice. Because they can't expect to get that from vendors with vested interests, growing numbers of third parties will set up portal sites in vertical markets, said Charles Finnie, an analyst at Volpe Brown.

"The major shift that occurs on the Web in commerce is that power shifts from sellers to buyers," Finnie said. The advantage is twofold: Buyers can access more data to help them negotiate prices and can abandon one seller for another on the Web for little or no cost.

On the www.chemdex.com site, which offers 300,000 chemical products from 130 suppliers, passwords can trigger automatic entry of information in purchase order forms such as the proper cost center, and business rules can preset spending limits and approval cycles.

Genentech Inc., a biotechnology company that helped Chemdex set up the system, uses Chemdex software that lets it enforce negotiated pricing with preferred suppliers. "What we're doing fundamentally is making a very efficient market where it's been inefficient," said David Perry, president of Chemdex.

a. Do you agree that infomediaries like NetBuy and Chemdex will become important players in business-to-business E-commerce? Why or why not?

b. Do infomediaries have a role to play in consumer-to-business E-commerce? Explain.

Source: Adapted from Sharon Machlis, "Portals Link Buyers, Sellers," *Computerworld*, January 25, 1999, pp. 1, 16. Copyright 1999 by Computerworld, Inc., Framingham, MA 01701. Reprinted from *Computerworld*.

3. **Telefónica Servicios Avanzados de Información: Expanding Internet-Based EDI**
Telefónica is Spain's largest supplier of telecommunications services, serving the Spanish-speaking and Portuguese-speaking world with affiliates in Latin America and the United States. More than 49 million customers generate over U.S. $15 billion in annual revenue for the company, making it one of Europe's leading multinational corporations. In 1998, Telefónica became one of the top five telecommunications companies in the world when it joined Worldcom/MCI's European business network as a distributor.

Telefónica Servicios Avanzados de Información (TSAI) is a subsidiary of Telefónica that handles 60 percent of Spain's electronic data interchange (EDI) traffic. TSAI's customers are trading partners—merchants, suppliers, and others involved in the supply chain from design to delivery. EDI is the data-transmission format commonly used among major trading partners, primarily to automate repetitive transactions. It automatically tracks inventory; triggers orders, invoices, and other documents related to transactions; and schedules and confirms delivery and payment. By digitally integrating the supply chain, EDI streamlines processes, saves time, and increases accuracy. Although EDI has been a boon to large businesses, it has been too costly for smaller ones.

To tap into the sizable market of smaller businesses that can't afford standard EDI services, TSAI is offering a new Internet EDI service, InfoEDI, based on Netscape ECXpert electronic commerce software. InfoEDI allows transactions to be entered and processed on the Internet, so smaller trading partners no longer have to buy and install special connections, dedicated workstations, and proprietary software. Instead, they can access the EDI network through the Internet.

InfoEDI's forms-based interface gives users the basic functionality of a remote EDI workstation; businesses can connect with InfoEDI simply by using modems and web browsers. They can then interact with the largest suppliers and retailers to send orders, issue invoices based on orders, send invoice summaries, track document status, and receive messages.

When new customers sign up for the InfoEDI service, they designate partners they trade with and specify EDI documents they can exchange. Java applets that follow EDI-specific rules provide standard document templates.

InfoEDI also provides a product database that lists all details of trading partners' products. Once a trading relationship has been established and access authorized by InfoEDI, each partner has encrypted access to details of its own products. Because those details remain accessible on the web server, users need enter only minimal information to create links to that data, which is then plugged in as needed.

To ensure that customers wanted the new service, TSAI conducted a pilot program with 70 companies. The pilot was so successful that TSAI anticipated full implementation for 2,000 trading partners by the end of 1999. An estimated 11,000 new customers could benefit from InfoEDI. As results come in and are fine-tuned, TSAI plans to expand the InfoEDI service to South American countries.

a. What are the benefits of the InfoEDI service to Telefónica and to small businesses?

b. How can Telefónica build on its InfoEDI experience to offer more services to its customers?

Source: Adapted from "Telefónica Servicios Avanzados de Información Leads Spain's Retail Industry into Global Electronic Commerce," at www.netscape.com/solutions/business/profiles, March 1999, and www.telefonica.es/foreign, March 1999.

Application Exercises

1. Business Information Systems

Which business information systems should be improved if the following complaints were brought to your attention? Identify the business function (accounting, finance, marketing, production/operations, or human resource management) and the specific information system in the functional area that is involved. (Refer to Figure 6.2.)

a. "Nobody is sure which of our sales reps is our top producer."

b. "Why was this part left out of the bill of materials?"

c. "I don't know why I didn't get a raise this year."

d. "Why were we overinvested in short-term securities?"

e. "Why are the balance sheet and income statement late this month?"

f. "Our sales reps are spending too much time on paperwork."

g. "The ROI and payback on this deal are all wrong."

h. "Which of our managers have overseas experience?"

i. "We need a workstation to design this product."

j. "Why are we being stuck with home office overhead expenses?"

2. Accounting Information Systems

Which common accounting information systems should be improved if the following complaints were brought to your attention? (Refer to Figure 6.19.)

a. "Month-end closings are always late."

b. "We are never sure how much of a certain product we have on the shelves."

c. "Many of us didn't get an earnings and deductions statement this week."

d. "We're tired of manually writing up a receipt every time a customer orders something."

e. "Our suppliers are complaining that they are not being paid on time."

f. "Our customers resent being sent notices demanding payment when they have already paid what they owe."

3. Evaluating Banking on the Web

Web banking is an idea whose time has come. Many U.S. banks let customers use the World Wide Web to access checking and savings accounts, check balances, and transfer funds. Three of those banks are West Coast heavy hitters: Wells Fargo Bank, Bank of America, and U.S. Bank. Examples of banks that offer similar services in the South are First Union Corp. and Net.B@nk. See Figure 6.37. Dozens of smaller banks and credit unions have also made the jump to the Web.

a. Surf to the web sites of the five banks shown in Figure 6.37. Evaluate them based on the same criteria used in that figure.

b. Do you agree with Frank Hayes's evaluations of these web sites? Why or why not?

c. Which of these or any other online banking web site is your favorite? Why?

4. Electronic Commerce and Payments

Figure 6.38 outlines several sources for information on electronic commerce and payments, including links to related sites.

Figure 6.37 Evaluations of the online banking web sites of five major banks.

	Net.B@nk www.netbank.com	Bank of America www.bankamerica.com	First Union www.firstunion.com	U.S. Bank www.usbank.com	Wells Fargo www.wellsfargo.com
Apply Online	Yes	Yes	Yes	Yes	Yes
Online Demonstration	Yes	Yes	Yes	No	Yes
Pay Bills	Yes	Yes	Yes	Yes	Yes
Ease of Use	Good	Good	Fair	Fair	Excellent
Speed	Good	Good	Poor	Poor	Good
Overall Grade	B	A–	B–	C+	A–

Source: Adapted and updated May 1999 from Frank Hayes, "Banks Cash in on Web," *Computerworld*, April 28, 1997, p. 60. Copyright 1997 by Computerworld, Inc., Framingham, MA 01701. Reprinted from *Computerworld*.

Figure 6.38 Examples of information sources for electronic commerce and payments on the Web.

Site	Address	Description
Center for Electronic Commerce	www.erim.org/cec/	Part of the Environmental Research Institute of Michigan (ERIM) that supports enterprise integration through EDI and electronic commerce
CommerceNet	www.commerce.net	An industry consortium addressing the needs of business for EDI and electronic commerce over the Internet
CyberCash	www.cybercash.com	Developer of secure Internet payment software and services
DigiCash	www.digicash.com	Developer of digital cash software and services
First Virtual	www.fv.com	Provider of Internet payment services
Electronic Commerce Guide	e-comm.internet.com/	Electronic commerce news, resources, and links to EC web sites

Source: Adapted from Peter Loshin, "The Electronic Marketplace," *PC Today*, July 1996, pp. 85, 88. Reprinted with permission of *PC Today* magazine: www.pc-today.com; and Leslie Goff, "Resources: Web Sites for IS Managers," *Computerworld*, June 9, 1997, p. 76. Copyright 1997 by Computerworld, Inc., Framingham, MA 01701. Reprinted from *Computerworld*.

a. Surf to these sites to find information and examples about several electronic commerce topics, such as retailing or wholesaling on the Web, electronic data interchange, or supply chain management. Choose one topic and explain how it might affect your future career in business.

b. Find information and examples of electronic payment technologies and alternatives at these sites, such as the digital wallet, digital certificates, the SET standard, and digital currency or e-cash. Which of these payment methods would you recommend to an online business? Explain the reasons for your recommendation.

5. Creating a Sales Tracking System

As sales manager for ABC Company, you are responsible for setting a quarterly sales quota for each salesperson and for monitoring each salesperson's progress in meeting the quota. To help you monitor performance more effectively, you have decided to create a database to store sales performance and quota data. You will initially create the table structure, queries, and reports you will need based on the set of sample data that follow.

a. Use database management software to create a sales tracking table appropriate for the sample data. Enter the set of data shown and get a printout listing your data.

b. Write a query that will allow you to retrieve the data for salespersons in a selected region and show their sales as a percentage of their quota.

c. Write a query that will list only those salespersons whose sales are higher than their quotas, will display the dollar amount by which they exceeded their quotas, and will list them in descending order

Employee	Region	Quarter	Quota	Sales
Davis, A.	West	1999–3	$275,000.00	$283,000.00
Jones, B.	Northeast	1999–3	350,000.00	297,231.00
Smith, L.	West	1999–3	312,500.00	362,304.50
Bates, R.	Southeast	1999–3	387,500.00	406,318.25
Vale, W.	Midwest	1999–3	295,000.00	278,320.00
Topps, P.	Northeast	1999–3	372,500.00	361,912.75
Lord, V.	Midwest	1999–3	390,000.00	417,525.00
James, M.	Southeast	1999–3	300,000.00	307,500.00
Cates, B.	West	1999–3	345,000.00	326,430.00

based on the amount by which they exceeded their quotas.

d. Create a report grouped by region lising all the items in the table and also showing the dollar amount above or below quota for each salsperson. Your report should also show summary sales performance values for each region and for all salespersons.

6. Assessing the Impact of Electronic Commerce

Your firm has an electronic commerce site that has been in operation for the past eight quarters. Your firm has three main product lines that can be selected and purchased electronically. The product lines are toys, games, and books. The table on the right shows statistics on the cumulative number of web site hits at the main HTML page for each product line. Since the numbers are cumulative, the quarterly number of hits for toys for quarter 3, for instance, is 47,623 (95,813 minus the 48,190 hits that had been received prior to the beginning of the quarter).

a. Produce a spreadsheet based on these data that can be used to analyze trends in hits across the three product groups. Your spreadsheet should record percentage changes. Also, to deal with seasonal differences in interest in your firm's products, you should have a section of the spreadsheet that compares each quarter's hits for a product category with hits in the same quarter of the prior year (quarter 5 compared to quarter 1, and so on).

b. Create appropriate graphs summarizing the trends in hits over time and across the product lines.

c. Using a word processor, write up a brief report summarizing the key results of your analysis. Based purely on the figures provided and current overall growth trends in electronic commerce, make a projection of hits over the next year for each product line.

Quarter	Toys	Games	Books
1	18,432	16,720	14,830
2	48,190	42,183	30,062
3	95,813	73,610	49,125
4	168,630	137,314	76,310
5	203,342	174,714	88,329
6	301,760	204,718	103,618
7	446,320	228,413	141,718
8	614,246	282,018	197,711

Review Quiz Answers

1. 5	8. 9	15. 26	22. 3	29. 41	36. 12	43. 38
2. 11	9. 6	16. 19	23. 2	30. 42	37. 13*a*	44. 39
3. 25	10. 7	17. 28	24. 32	31. 4	38. 13*c*	45. 40
4. 20	11. 8	18. 1	25. 18	32. 34	39. 14	46. 43
5. 37	12. 33	19. 27	26. 17	33. 30	40. 15	
6. 24	13. 22	20. 31	27. 29	34. 13	41. 16	
7. 10	14. 36	21. 21	28. 23	35. 13*b*	42. 35	

Selected References

1. Anderson, Heidi. "Surveying Via the Net." *PC Today*, April 1997.

2. Anderson, Heidi. "The Rise of the Extranet." *PC Today*, February 1997.

3. Andreessen, Marc. "The Networked Enterprise: Enterprise Vision and Product Roadmap." White Paper. Netscape Communications Corporation, 1997.

4. Asbrand, Deborah. "Squeeze Out Excess Costs with Supply Chain Solutions." *Datamation*, March 1997.

5. Blattberg, Robert C.; Rashi Glazer; and John D. C. Little, eds. *The Marketing Information Revolution.* Boston: The Harvard Business School Press, 1994.

6. Carr, Houston, and Charles Snyder. *The Management of Telecommunications.* Burr Ridge, IL: Irwin, 1997.

7. Carrol, Michael. *Cyberstrategies.* New York: Van Nostrand Reinhold, 1996.

8. Cronin, Mary. *Doing More Business on the Internet.* 2nd ed. New York: Van Nostrand Reinhold, 1995.

9. Cronin, Mary. *Global Advantage on the Internet.* New York: Van Nostrand Reinhold, 1996.

10. Cronin, Mary. *The Internet Strategy Handbook.* Boston: Harvard Business School Press, 1996.

11. Davenport, Thomas H. *Process Innovation: Reengineering Work through Information Technology.* Cambridge: The Harvard Business School Press, 1993.

12. Deck, Stewart. "The Exchanging of the Guard." *Computerworld,* October 7, 1996.

13. Eskow, Dennis. "Harvest Profits from Web Farms." *Datamation,* March 1997.

14. Gow, Kathleen. "Risk vs. Opportunity." The Premier 100 Supplement to *Computerworld,* February 24, 1997.

15. Halper, Mark. "Meet the New Middlemen." *Computerworld Commerce,* April 28, 1997.

16. Hamel, Gary, and Jeff Sandler. "The E-Corporation." *Fortune,* December 7, 1998.

17. Herringshaw, Chris. "E-Cash Gets to Work." *Internet World,* May 1997.

18. Hodges, Judy. "The Rise of the Self Service Employee." *Compterworld HR Online,* September 8, 1997.

19. Janal, Daniel. *Online Marketing Handbook.* New York: Van Nostrand Reinhold, 1995.

20. Jiang, James. "Using Scanner Data." *Information Systems Management,* Winter 1995.

21. Kalakota, Ravi, and Andrew Whinston. *Electronic Commerce: A Manager's Guide.* Reading, MA: Addison-Wesley, 1997.

22. Kalakota, Ravi, and Andrew Whinston. *Frontiers of Electronic Commerce.* Reading, MA: Addison-Wesley, 1996.

23. Kastner, Peter, and Christopher Stevens. "Electronic Commerce: A True Challenge for IT Managers." In "Enterprise Solutions: Electronic Commerce," Special Advertising Supplement to *Computerworld,* January 13, 1997.

24. Keen, Peter, and Craigg Balance. *Online Profits: A Manager's Guide to Electronic Commerce.* Boston: Harvard Business School Press, 1997.

25. LaPlante, Alice. "Think Small, Think Infinite." The Premier 100 Supplement to *Computerworld,* February 24, 1997.

26. Loeb, Larry. "The Stage Is SET." *Internet World,* August 1996.

27. Loshin, Peter. "Automating Business with EDI." *PC Today,* July 1996.

28. Loshin, Peter. "The Electronic Marketplace." *PC Today,* July 1996.

29. Loshin, Peter. "The Mechanics of Buying and Selling on the Internet." *PC Today,* February 1996.

30. Mahan, Suruchi. "Beyond HTML." The Premier 100 Supplement to *Computerworld,* February 24, 1997.

31. Martin, Chuck. *The Digital Estate: Strategies for Competing, Surviving, and Thriving in an Internetworked World.* New York: McGraw-Hill, 1997.

32. May, Thomas. "Electronic Commerce: Three Truths for IS." *Computerworld Leadership Series,* April 21, 1997.

33. O'Reilly, Tim. "Publishing Models for Internet Commerce." *Communications of the ACM,* June 1996.

34. Pussurach, Patiwat. "Money in Electronic Commerce: Digital Cash, Electronic Fund Transfer, and E-Cash." *Communications of the ACM,* June 1996.

35. Pyle, Raymond, ed. "Electronic Commerce and the Internet." *Communications of the ACM,* June 1996.

36. Renard, D. "The Truth About Electronic Cash Payments." White Paper. The Gartner Group, 1996.

37. Scheier, Robert. "Distributor Uses News to Sell Web Ads." *Computerworld,* June 10, 1996.

38. Seybold, Patricia. "Don't Let PR Control Your Web Site!" *Computerworld,* April 18, 1996.

39. Seybold, Patricia. "How to Turn Web Hits into Home Runs." *Computerworld,* September 30, 1996.

40. Tucker, Jay. "The New Money: Transactions Pour Across the Web." *Datamation,* April 1997.

41. Tucker, Michael. "EDI and the Net: A Profitable Partnering." *Datamation,* April 1997.

42. "Web Commerce." Technology Buyers Guide. *Fortune,* Winter 1999.

43. Wilkinson, Joseph W., and Michael J. Cerullo. *Accounting Information Systems: Essential Concepts and Applications.* 3rd ed. New York: John Wiley & Sons, 1997.

Information Systems for

Enterprise Collaboration

Chapter Highlights

Section I
Intranets and Extranets in Business

The Intranet Revolution

Real World Case: Glaxo Wellcome and BC Telecom: The Business Value of Self-Service Intranets

Applications of Intranets

Intranet Technology Resources

The Business Value of Intranets

The Role of Extranets

The Future of Intranets and Extranets

Section II
Enterprise Collaboration Systems

Enterprise Collaboration

Real World Case: Lockheed Martin Corporation: Improving Team Collaboration via Desktop Videoconferencing

Groupware for Enterprise Collaboration

Electronic Communication Tools

Electronic Conferencing Tools

Collaborative Work Management Tools

Learning Objectives

After reading and studying this chapter, you should be able to:

1. Give several examples of how companies are using intranets and extranets for communications and collaboration, information publishing and sharing, and business operations and management.

2. Identify several of the hardware, software, data, and network components of an intranet's information technology architecture.

3. Identify several ways that the use of intranets and extranets can provide cost savings or revenue benefits to a company

4. Identify several groupware tools for electronic communications, conferencing, and work management, and give examples of how they can enhance the collaboration of teams and workgroups in a business enterprise.

Intranets and Extranets in Business

The Intranet Revolution

How important and relevant are intranets in business? Are intranets just another technology buzzword or business fad? Let's check out some expert opinions.

- **Zona Research:** More than 80 percent of Fortune 500 companies had an intranet in place by mid-1997 [4].

- **The Gartner Group:** 75 percent of all Fortune 1,000 organizations would be using intranets by the end of 1998 [14].

- **International Data Corporation:** By the year 2000, server licenses sold for intranets [and the number of installed intranet servers] will outdistance those for Internet usage by a factor of ten to one [28].

- **Forrester Research:** By the year 2000, the intranet will be enhanced with new services that will thrust it into the limelight as the key component of corporate networks [2].

These facts and forecasts explain why so many computer industry analysts are likening the current growth in the use of intranets in business and other organizations to the tidal wave of growth in Internet usage that began in the mid-1990s.

Analyzing Glaxo Wellcome and BC Telecom

Companies like Glaxo Wellcome and BC Telecom are rapidly installing and extending intranets throughout their organizations. Like many businesses, they realize that intranets enable them to use Internet and World Wide Web technologies to support communications, collaboration, and business processes throughout the internetworked enterprise.

Read the Real World Case on Glaxo Wellcome and BC Telecom on the next page. We can learn a lot about how many companies are using intranets as a key technology platform to provide human resources services to their employees, as well as promote enterprise communications and collaboration. See Figure 7.1.

Figure 7.1

Elaine Davis, director of human resources services at Glaxo Wellcome, says that employee self-service intranets are the best way to leverage a company's investment in IT.

Source: Doug Van DeZande.

Glaxo Wellcome and BC Telecom: The Business Value of Self-Service Intranets

Glaxo Wellcome Inc., based in Research Triangle Park, North Carolina, is one of the nation's leading research-based pharmaceutical firms, and a subsidiary of London-based Glaxo Wellcome plc., with sales of $5.6 billion in 1998. Glaxo recently was voted the best company in the state to work for in a survey by a North Carolina business magazine. Glaxo Wellcome ranked highest in how it treats its employees and the services it offers them.

One of these services is an employee self-service intranet created by Glaxo's human resources services department. Self-service intranets "are really the best way to leverage a company's investment in technology," says Elaine Davis, director of human resources services at Glaxo Wellcome. Glaxo has been developing managerial and employee self-service systems using NetDynamic software since 1995.

Fortune 500 companies like Glaxo Wellcome are spending big bucks on enterprise resource planning (ERP) systems from PeopleSoft and SAP America. The problem with those investments, says Davis, is that "the only people who get to use those systems are in HR, payroll and benefits."

So Glaxo Wellcome spent a few hundred thousand dollars more to develop an integrated self-service intranet. Creating applications like a web-based compensation system for 1,500 managers "allows you to deploy that information across an organization," says Davis.

Jeff Woodrum, director of corporate payments at Glaxo Wellcome, uses the compensation system to set up employer stock option awards after annual performance reviews. "Compared to the way we used to do things in a quasi-paper environment, this system is very easy to use," Woodrum says.

Glaxo's Davis says she doesn't have any hard figures on productivity gains or cost savings. But reducing administrative costs was one of the top three goals cited by HR and IS professionals surveyed in a recent HR self-service intranet study conducted by Forrester Research. The other top two goals of such projects were increasing service levels to employees and freeing HR resources for strategic work.

HR self-service intranets initially offered mostly benefits data and information on career development. Now companies are adding functions such as health provider networks, retirement planners, and job postings. You also can register for training courses or reserve a conference room online in many HR intranets.

A good example is the corporate intranet of BC Telecom or BC TEL, part of BCT.TELUS Communications, Inc., the second largest telecommunications company in Canada, with annual revenues of almost $6 billion in 1998, and over 25,000 employees.

Among the key applications in BC TEL's corporate intranet is a feature-rich human resources web site, Virtual HR, based on Netscape Enterprise Server. With Virtual HR, employees can view information on all of the company's human resources programs. These cover health, safety, benefits, and fitness programs and schedules. Employees can also use the pension estimator to see what their pensions will be worth on retirement. Beneflex, a self-service application for viewing and changing employee benefit options, is a major service of the HR web site.

Employees can also arrange meetings through enterprisewide calendaring; make travel reservations online; and access company news, articles, and a complete company directory. Because the number of web sites and applications is growing rapidly, BC TEL's intranet site pages can be personalized to the tastes and needs of each employee.

Case Study Questions

1. What are the benefits to a company and its employees of self-service intranets for human resources applications?

2. What other types of human resources services besides those mentioned in this case would you want provided by a self-service HR intranet at a company you might work for?

3. What three business applications or services other than human resources would you want provided to employees by a company intranet? Explain the reasons for your choices.

Source: Adapted from "Employment Opportunities," at www.glaxowellcome.com, March 1999; Thomas Hoffman, "Paging People," *Computerworld Intranets*, August 24, 1998, pp. 1–7, Copyright 1998 by Computerworld, Inc., Framingham, MA 01701. Reprinted from *Computerworld*; Kathryn Brown, "Workers' Paradise," *Business North Carolina*, February 1999, pp. 23–29; "BC Telecom" at www.netscape.com/solutions/business/profiles, March 1999, Copyright 1999 Netscape Communications Corp. Used with permission. All Rights Reserved; and "Discover BC TEL," at www.bctelecom.com, March 1999.

For example, Glaxo Wellcome has a self-service human resources intranet that makes it easy for 1,500 managers to use a web browser–based system to adjust employee compensation after performance reviews. BC Telecom has a more full-service HR intranet. Employees can use their web browsers to view a full range of HR information and make adjustments to their benefits options. Self-service intranet applications like these are designed to provide more easy-to-use HR services to employees, while reducing administrative costs and freeing HR staff for more strategic applications.

Intranets, Extranets, and the Internet

Before we get any further, let's redefine the concept of an intranet, to specifically emphasize how intranets are related to the Internet and extranets. An **intranet** is a network inside an organization that uses Internet technologies (such as web browsers and servers, TCP/IP network protocols, HTML hypermedia document publishing and databases, and so on) to provide an Internet-like environment within the enterprise for information sharing, communications, collaboration, and the support of business processes. An intranet is protected by security measures such as passwords, encryption, and fire walls, and thus can be accessed by authorized users though the Internet. A company's intranet can also be accessed through the intranets of customers, suppliers, and other business partners via *extranet* links. Figure 7.2 illustrates the relationship of intranets, extranets, and the Internet of a company with several locations.

Figure 7.2

The relationship of a company's intranets to its extranets and the Internet. This company uses the Internet to interconnect its World Wide Web sites, intranets to other company locations, and extranets to business partners.

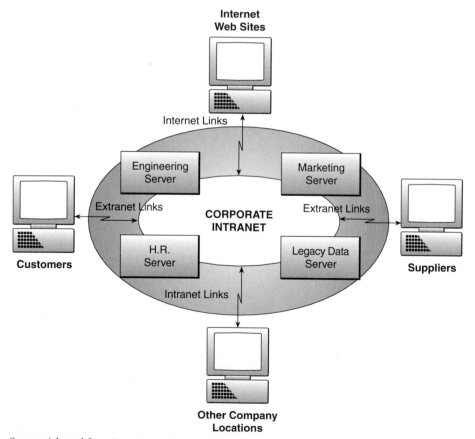

Source: Adapted from Ryan Bernard, *The Corporate Intranet* (New York: John Wiley & Sons, 1996), p.23. Copyright ©1996 by John Wiley & Sons, Inc. Reprinted by permission.

Applications of Intranets

Technology companies have the most sophisticated and widespread intranets, offering detailed data retrieval, collaboration tools, personalized customer profiles, and links to the Internet. Investing in the intranet, they feel, is as fundamental as supplying employees with a telephone [33].

Organizations of all kinds are joining technology companies in implementing a broad range of intranet uses. What are the basic business uses of intranets? One way that companies organize intranet applications is to group them conceptually into a few user services categories that reflect the basic services that intranets offer to their users. These services are provided by the intranet's browser and server software, as well as by other system and application software and groupware that are part of a company's intranet software environment [2]. Figure 7.3 illustrates how intranet applications support communications and collaboration, web publishing, business operations and management, and intranet management. Notice also how these applications can be integrated with existing IS resources and applications, and extended to customers, suppliers, and business partners.

Figure 7.3

The basic applications of intranets include communications and collaboration, business operations and management, web publishing, and intranet management.

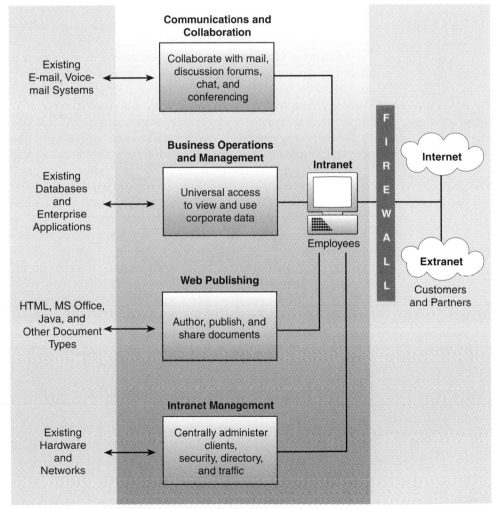

Communications and Collaboration. Intranets can significantly improve communications and collaboration within an enterprise. For example, you can use your intranet browser and your PC or NC workstation to send and receive E-mail, voicemail, paging, and faxes to communicate with others within your organization, and externally through the Internet and extranets. You can also use intranet groupware features to improve team and project collaboration with services such as discussion groups, chat rooms, and audio- and videoconferencing.

Web Publishing. The advantages of developing and publishing hyperlinked multimedia documents to hypermedia databases accessible on World Wide Web servers has moved to corporate intranets. The comparative ease, attractiveness, and lower cost of publishing and accessing multimedia business information internally via intranet web sites have been the primary reasons for the explosive growth in the use of intranets in business. For example, information products as varied as company newsletters, technical drawings, and product catalogs can be published in a variety of ways, including hypermedia web pages, E-mail, and net broadcasting, and as part of in-house business applications. Intranet software browsers, servers, and search engines can help you easily navigate and locate the business information you need.

Business Operations and Management. Intranets have moved beyond merely making hypermedia information available on web servers, or pushing it to users via net broadcasting. Intranets are also being used as the platform for developing and deploying critical business applications to support business operations and managerial decision making across the internetworked enterprise. For example, many companies are developing custom applications like order processing, inventory control, sales management, and executive information systems that can be implemented on intranets, extranets, and the Internet. Many of these applications are designed to interface with, and access, existing company databases and legacy systems. The software for such business uses (sometimes called *applets* or *crossware*) is then installed on intranet web servers. Employees within the company, or external business partners, can access and run such applications using web browsers from anywhere on the network whenever needed.

Now let's look at one company's use of an intranet in more detail to get a better idea of how intranets are used in business. The company is Sun Microsystems, whose slogan is "the network is the computer," and whose high-powered servers and Java language are helping to fuel the Internet/intranet revolution.

SunWeb

Sun Microsystems is one of the pioneers in the use of intranets in business, first implementing an intranet in 1994. Figure 7.4 shows you the main home page and a page of one of many major applications or web sites on SunWeb, the intranet of Sun Microsystems. SunWeb is huge, with over 3,000 intranet web servers available to almost 20,000 employees who support Sun workstation and server customers in over 100 countries. SunWeb has generated big cost savings versus publishing information in paper and other media. The ease and speed of sharing multimedia information on web servers have also been credited with making people and teams much more productive and creative in their jobs and projects [5].

A quick look at Sun's intranet gives us a good idea of the variety of applications and services that any business can offer its employees on an intranet [5].

• **Views.** There are three different views of the system: an organizational view (the different companies in the Sun worldwide organization), a functional view

Figure 7.4 The main home page and a page of one of many major web sites on SunWeb, the intranet of Sun Microsystems. *(Photos courtesy of Sun Microsystems.)*

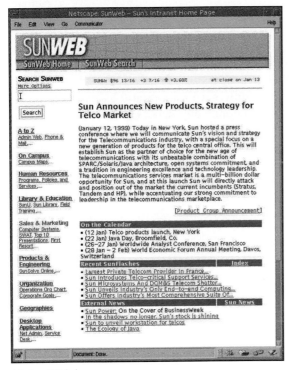

(*a*) SunWeb home page

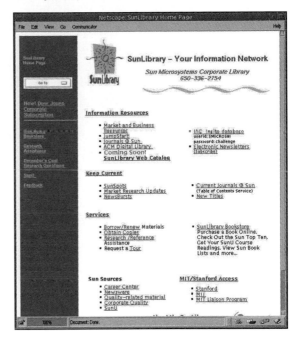

(*b*) Sun's corporate library

of the company (corporate, HR, sales, marketing, etc.), and a geographical view—all the different Sun locations throughout the world, accessible by clicking on a world map.

- **What's New.** Provides recent press releases for the company, online audio reports from Sun CEO Scott McNealy and others (called WSUN Radio), and the company's quarterly magazine *Illuminations*, which is now distributed online instead of in paper format.

- **Library & Education.** The home page for SunU, the company's name for its internal and external training course offerings. SunU also includes links to the company's libraries for access to research services and company document and electronic resources.

- **Marketing & Sales.** Contains marketing and sales databases, comparative information, marketing tools, organization information, and basic information to help sales and marketing people in the field.

- **Product Catalog.** Contains multimedia information on all the Sun products, for general reference by all employees.

- **Engineering Info.** Provides links to all the software tools that are available on each person's local file server, with a brief product profile, online documentation, and information on how to get training, how to get support, and how to get a stand-alone license.

- **Travel.** Explains how to prepare a travel expense authorization, provides current travel advisories for foreign countries, links to an international security home page, displays currency exchange rates, and includes information about transit systems in the San Francisco Bay Area where Sun headquarters is located.

- **HR & Benefits.** Information about employee benefits programs, a manager's handbook, a developer's toolkit, and corporate employment information.

- **Sun Campus.** Provides maps to all the different locations and buildings in the Bay Area, including local directories and phone numbers. This area also contains information about commuting, bus schedules, and local company-provided vans. It also shows the location of shipping and receiving areas, food services, copy centers, and conference rooms.

- **Executive Suite.** Provides external links to an "executive suite" of business references on the Internet and on the World Wide Web, including headline news, government sites, marketing information, and other popular Internet sites such as GolfWeb.

- **Construction Kit.** Contains the how-tos for building web sites on the SunWeb intranet, including policies and procedures, templates, graphics, clip art, and links to new software tools.

Intranet Technology Resources

Since intranets are Internet-like networks within organizations, they depend on all the information technologies that make the Internet possible. For example, companies using intranets must have or install TCP/IP client/server networks and related hardware and software, such as web browser and server suites, HTML web publishing software, and network management and security programs. Thus, intranets depend on the same web browser/server capabilities, TCP/IP client/server networks, and hypermedia database access available on the Internet and the World Wide Web. Figure 7.5 illustrates the components of the information technology architecture of a typical intranet.

Notice in Figure 7.5 that web browser and server software, search engines, web software tools, and network management software are key components of an open intranet. It is these software components that give intranet users the same kind of easy point-and-click navigation of hyperlinked multimedia web sites that they enjoy on the Internet. For example, Figure 7.6 outlines some of the types of intranet server software needed to power a full performance corporate intranet.

The Business Value of Intranets

The preliminary results from IDC's return on investment study of intranets found the typical ROI well over 1,000 percent—far higher than usually found with any technology investment. Adding to the benefit, with payback periods ranging from six to twelve weeks, the cost of an intranet is quickly recovered—making the risk associated with an intranet project low. The results to date clearly show that for any company, not just those already contemplating an intranet, the best strategy is to begin an intranet deployment today. The sooner an intranet becomes a core component of the corporate technology infrastructure, the sooner the company can reap the benefits [8].

Those very impressive returns, quick payback, and strong endorsement of intranets by International Data Corporation, a leading IT research group, have not gone unnoticed. Other early adopters report similar high paybacks at low cost. So the consensus

Figure 7.5

An example of the components of an intranet's information technology architecture.

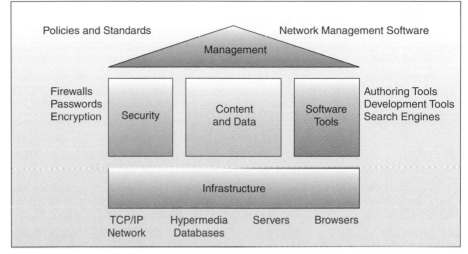

Source: Adapted from Michael Fitzgerald, "Infrastructure: Firm Foundation," *Computerworld Intranets*, October 28, 1996, p. 3. Copyright 1996 by Computerworld, Inc., Framingham, MA 01701. Reprinted from *Computerworld*.

advice of many corporate intranet users and consultants to the global business community has been that companies should get going fast on pilot intranet projects, or quickly expand any current intranet initiatives [8].

Examples of Business Value

Figure 7.7 outlines examples of how 10 leading companies in the business use of Internet and intranet technologies derived business value through cost savings or revenue benefits from their intranet applications. Many other intranet-using companies report similar cost reductions, revenue increases, or other benefits after they replaced

Figure 7.6

An example of a suite of intranet software servers that can be used to run a full-featured corporate intranet.

Netscape SuiteSpot Intranet Servers	Intranet Server Software Functions
Enterprise Server	Manages and publishes content and executes online applications to form the foundation of an intranet.
Mail Server	Provides full-featured open systems E-mail across an intranet and the Internet.
News Server	Facilitates secure groupware-style discussion groups that enable team collaboration and information sharing.
Catalog Server	Provides indexing, searching, and browsing of all content and services on an intranet.
Directory Server	Provides a universal directory service for enterprisewide management of user, access control, and server configuration information.
Certificate Server	Issues and manages public-key encryption certificates for users and servers, creating a highly secure intranet.
Proxy Server	Replicates and filters content, thus improving intranet performance, content control, and network security.

Source: Adapted from Eckart Walther, "The Netscape One Platform Vision and Product Roadmap," White Paper, Netscape Communications Corporation, 1996, p. 12. Copyright 1996 Netscape Communications Corp. Used with permission. All Rights Reserved.

Figure 7.7 Examples of how top-rated companies derived cost savings or revenue benefits from their intranet applications.

Company and URL	Business Intranet Applications and Cost Benefits
Battelle Pacific Northwest Laboratories www.pnl.gov	Provides better access to financial reports and improves productivity, speed, and control. Employees select from preformatted reports and create their own subscription lists. Annual savings: $350,000.
Bechtel Corporation www.bechtel.com	Access to engineering documents and information. Reduces paper costs and increases speed of information transfer. Development cost: $500,000.
CH2M Hill, Inc. www.ch2m.com	Global staffing tool for project teams. Able to find skilled staff and reduces time and effort to complete projects. Development cost: $30,000.
Parker Hannifin Corporation, Compumotor Division www.compumotor.com	Group intranet supports manufacturing, engineering, and marketing. Allows for easy document exchange and reduced paper costs. Annual cost savings: $130,000. Development cost: $20,000.
Gould Paper Corp. www.gouldpaper.com	Internal web site for sales and customer service. Reduces call volume and increases sales with greater salesforce involvement. Development cost: $100,000.
Hastings Entertainment www.hastings-ent.com	DataDoc Online. Reflects daily changes on video rentals, books, music, and software across 115 retail locations. Saves IS time and improves data accessibility and accuracy. Annual savings: $150,000+.
KeyCorp www.keybank.com	KeyCorp's knowledge bank distributes job postings, information on best practices and training, marketing material, and newsletters. Annual cost savings: $1.8M. Development cost: $300,000.
KPMG www.kpmg.com	Knowledge management and corporate communications system facilitates collaboration on projects. Productivity increased via information exchange and streamlining workflow. Cost: $4.5M.
Rockwell International www.rockwell.com	Each area on the manufacturing floor has its own home page updated every 60 seconds. Improves process and quality. Cost savings: $100,000. Development cost: less than $200,000
Sempra Energy www.sempra.com	Marketing, planning, and operations. Shares business information for improved decision making, efficiency, and competitiveness. Development cost: $60,000.

Source: Adapted from "The Premier 100," The Premier 100 Supplement to *Computerworld*, February 24, 1997, pp. 56-63. Copyright 1997 by Computerworld, Inc., Framingham, MA 01701. Reprinted from *Computerworld*.

traditional methods of accomplishing information publishing and other business processes with intranet-based methods. Let's look at some examples.

Publication Cost Savings. Many companies are replacing the publication of paper documents, company newsletters, and employee manuals with electronic multimedia versions published on intranet web servers. Elimination of printing, mailing, and distribution costs is a major source of cost savings. Companies are also electronically publishing telephone directories, human resource materials, company policies, job openings, and many other former paper-based communications on intranet web sites.

> *Companies that use web technology to distribute documents may experience momentous gains in productivity and incredible cost savings. Like the reengineering craze that has marked the other half of the client/server revolution, converting many paper-based systems to web systems can save both labor and overhead costs within an organization* [5].

For example, Tyson Foods saved more than $50,000 by just publishing their employee manual on their internal web instead of spending $10 per employee for a paper version for each of their 5,000 intranet users. Lockheed Martin reports saving over

$600,000 per year in paper printing and distribution costs no longer needed for over 70,000 intranet users [29, 40].

Training and Development Cost Savings. Developing information access and web publishing applications for an intranet is a lot easier than many traditional methods. Learning how to use a web browser for the company intranet is fast and easy. Many employees already know how to use a browser anyway, from surfing the World Wide Web. So training and development costs for many intranet applications are low, especially for communication, collaboration, and information sharing. For example, here's what Dave Lambe, CIO of US West Communications, said about the minimal development and training time needed for a new intranet-based customer service application they recently implemented:

> *The most exciting aspects of this application are that it was developed in less than three months and was deployed with relative ease to our 6,000 service representatives. In fact, training time was cut down to five minutes of coaching. I have never seen such a large-scale system built and deployed so quickly. That shows the power of using this technology for software applications development* [27].

In addition, putting electronic versions of training materials on intranet web sites can reduce the amount of costly classroom training in business. For example, AT&T was able to cut classroom time in half for 4,500 customer service reps because they were provided with access to intranet-based instruction [29].

Measuring Costs and Benefits. For most businesses, the benefits to be gained from intranets outweigh their limitations. See Figure 7.8. Justifying the initial cost of investing in an intranet does not seem to be a problem for many organizations. For

Figure 7.8

Some of the benefits and limitations of intranets.

Intranet Benefits	Intranet Limitations
Global, enterprisewide in scope	New evolving technology
Easy, intuitive GUI access via browsers	Lack of security features
Low-cost access	Lack of performance management
Low- or no-cost software	Minimal user support
Low-cost hardware	May require network upgrades
Runs on all platforms	Browser/server software incompatibilities between versions
Standardized file transfer	
Standardized document creation	May not scale for large enterprises with intense interactive applications
Standardized network protocol, TCP/IP	Difficult to maintain content over time
Reduces paper/printing cost	Animation, video, and audio are slow
Reduces marketing/sales costs	Unfiltered information may overwhelm users
Increases productivity via faster information access and easier collaboration	Not all employees may have personal computers

Source: Adapted from Nancy Cox, *Building and Managing a Web Services Team* (New York: Van Nostrand Reinhold, 1997), p. 13. Used by permission.

example, the Port of Los Angeles spent about $100,000 creating an intranet for 18 field offices worldwide. Payback time is estimated at three months, because one new sale attributed to the effectiveness of the intranet can justify the cost of the project. FedEx justified an intranet project by exceeding the company's minimum return on investment (ROI) criteria with projected savings from only four applications. These included cost savings from putting help desk call logs, corporate newsletters, employee benefit plan changes, and customer queries on intranet web servers [29].

Let's take a more in-depth look at one of the companies that International Data Corporation studied when they discovered the low initial costs and high return on investment possible with business intranet projects.

Cadence OnTrack	Cadence Design Systems is the leading supplier of electronic design automation (EDA) software tools and professional services for managing the design of semiconductors, computer systems, networking and telecommunications equipment, consumer electronics, and other electronics-based products. The company employs more than 3,000 people in offices worldwide to support the requirements of the world's leading electronics manufacturers. Cadence developed an intranet in 1995 for 500 managers, sales reps, and customer support staff. Called OnTrack, the intranet project provides sales support for a Cadence product line of over 1,000 products and services. Figure 7.9 summarizes the results of the IDC cost/benefit analysis of the OnTrack intranet project at Cadence [8].

The OnTrack system uses a home page with links to other pages, information sources, and other applications, to support each phase of the sales process with supporting materials and reference information. For example, at any point in the sales process, such as one called "Identify Business Issues," a sales rep can find customer presentations, sample letters, and the internal forms needed to move effectively through this step. See Figure 7.10.

With OnTrack, sales reps now use the intranet as a single tool that provides all of the information and data needed to go through the sales process, from prospecting, to closing a deal, to account management. In addition, global account teams have their own home page where they can collaborate and share information. Information on customers or competitors is now available instantly through access to an outside provider of custom news. The sales rep simply searches using a company name to get everything from financial information to recent news articles and press releases about the customer or competitor.

Maintaining the information contained in OnTrack is the responsibility of all creators of information in Cadence, from sales reps to marketing and management. To avoid the need to understand HTML, special forms allow submission of new content, or changes to any part of the information in the OnTrack system. Anyone with proper access can now add a new message to the daily alerts, modify a step in the sales process, or update a customer presentation. In addition, OnTrack generates reports highlighting frequently accessed pages and documents. For example, frequent searches are reviewed to evaluate the need for new information content or making critical information easier to access.

The high ROI achieved for the OnTrack intranet project was due to several factors. First was the relatively low cost needed to implement OnTrack. Cadence leveraged its existing computer network infrastructure and hired outside experts to create the application rather than devote internal resources. However, the most important factor was the increased profits generated by a big reduction in learning time for new sales reps. To calculate the value of this shortened learning curve, IDC

Figure 7.9

A summary of the cost/benefit results of the OnTrack intranet project at Cadence Design Systems.

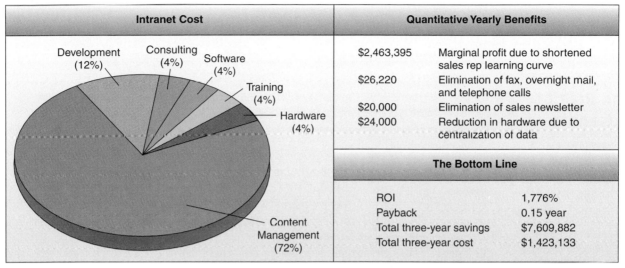

Intranet Cost	Quantitative Yearly Benefits	
Development (12%) Consulting (4%) Software (4%) Training (4%) Hardware (4%) Content Management (72%)	$2,463,395	Marginal profit due to shortened sales rep learning curve
	$26,220	Elimination of fax, overnight mail, and telephone calls
	$20,000	Elimination of sales newsletter
	$24,000	Reduction in hardware due to centralization of data

The Bottom Line	
ROI	1,776%
Payback	0.15 year
Total three-year savings	$7,609,882
Total three-year cost	$1,423,133

Source: Adapted from Ian Campbell, "The Intranet: Slashing the Cost of Doing Business," *Research Report*, International Data Corporation, 1996, pp.7–10.

Figure 7.10

The home page of the OnTrack intranet application.

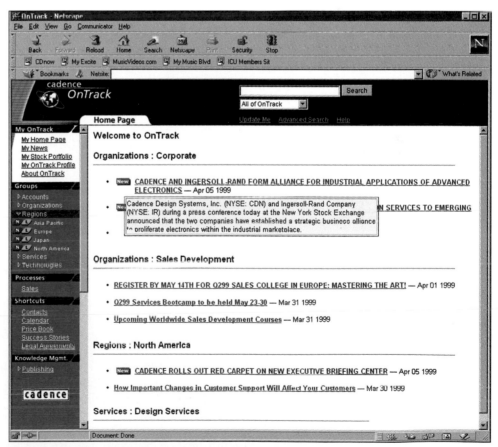

Courtesy of Cadence Design Systems, Inc./OnTrack.

estimated the additional initial profit generated by a new sales rep that was now able to meet quota in only two months, rather than the four months it took before the implementation of the OnTrack intranet application. With 40 new reps hired in the first year, and 40 planned for each of the next two years, reducing the ramp-up time by 50 percent for new sales reps has made a substantial positive impact on additional profits to Cadence [8].

The Role of Extranets

As businesses continue to use open Internet technologies [extranets] to improve communication with customers and partners, they can gain many competitive advantages along the way—in product development, cost savings, marketing, distribution, and leveraging their partnerships [4].

As we explained in Chapter 4, **extranets** are network links that use Internet technologies to interconnect the intranet of a business with the intranets of its customers, suppliers, or other business partners. Companies can establish direct private network links between themselves, or create private secure Internet links between them called *virtual private networks*. Or a company can use the unsecured Internet as the extranet link between its intranet and consumers and others, but rely on encryption of sensitive data and its own fire wall systems to provide adequate security. Thus, extranets enable customers, suppliers, consultants, subcontractors, business prospects, and others to access selected intranet web sites and other company databases. See Figure 7.11.

Business Value of Extranets

The business value of extranets is derived from several factors. First, the web browser technology of extranets makes customer and supplier access of intranet resources a lot easier and faster than previous business methods. Secondly, as you will see in three upcoming examples, extranets enable a company to offer new kinds of interactive web-enabled services to their business partners. Thus, extranets are another way that a business can build and strengthen strategic relationships with its customers and suppliers. Also, extranets can enable and improve collaboration by a business with its customers and other business partners. Extranets facilitate an online, interactive product development, marketing, and customer-focused process that can bring better-designed products to market faster [4].

Extranet Examples

Countrywide Home Loans has created an extranet called Platinum Lender Access for its lending partners and brokers. About 500 banks and mortgage brokers can access Countrywide's intranet and selected financial databases. The extranet gives them access to their account and transaction information, status of loans, and company announcements. Each lender or broker is automatically identified by the extranet and provided with customized information on premium rates, discounts, and any special business arrangements they have negotiated with Countrywide [1, 4].

Marshall Industries' extranet, called PartnerNet, was introduced in Chapter 6. The extranet provides customers and suppliers with customized 24-hour access to Marshall's intranet resources. For example, suppliers can get point-of-sale and inventory status reports about their products at any time. Customers can also check the inventory status of items they want, as well as the status of orders they previously placed. Marshall reports that the extranet has helped them to increase sales and profits, while cutting sales staff and expenses [1].

Snap-on Incorporated spent $300,000 to create an extranet link to their intranet called the Franchise Information Network. The extranet lets Snap-on's 4,000 inde-

Figure 7.11   Extranets connect the internetworked enterprise to consumers, business customers, suppliers, and other business partners.

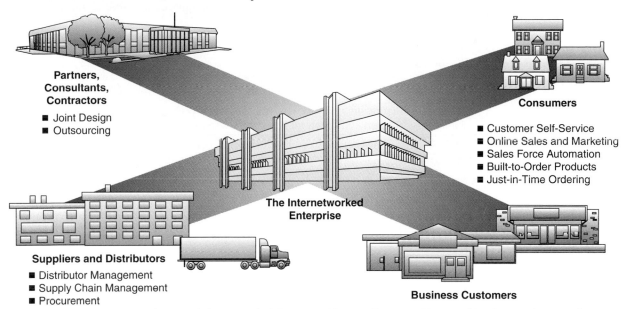

Partners, Consultants, Contractors

- Joint Design
- Outsourcing

Consumers

- Customer Self-Service
- Online Sales and Marketing
- Sales Force Automation
- Built-to-Order Products
- Just-in-Time Ordering

The Internetworked Enterprise

Suppliers and Distributors

- Distributor Management
- Supply Chain Management
- Procurement

Business Customers

Source: Adapted from Marc Andreessen, "The Networked Enterprise: Netscape Enterprise Vision and Product Roadmap," White Paper, Netscape Communications Corporation, 1997, pp. 4, 9. Copyright 1997 Netscape Communications Corp. Used with permission. All Rights Reserved.

pendent franchises for automotive tools access a secured intranet web site for customized information and interactive communications with Snap-on employees and other franchisees. Franchisers can get information on sales plus marketing updates. Tips and training programs about managing a franchise operation and discussion forums for employees and franchisees to share ideas and best practices are also provided by the extranet. Finally, the Franchise Information Network provides interactive news and information on car racing and other special events sponsored by Snap-on, as well as corporate stock prices, business strategies, and other financial information [35].

The Future of Intranets and Extranets

Mellanie Hills is the former head of the cross-functional Internet/intranet team at JCPenney Company and a leading intranet consultant and author. Hills's research and consulting with many companies shows not only their success with intranets, but that intranets and extranets will become even more pervasive in the business future. Figure 7.12 outlines what companies are expecting from intranet/extranet technologies [22].

One recurring theme for the future of intranets and extranets is the need to move beyond information publishing applications. Companies are planning more inquiry processing and transaction processing applications that tie the Internet, intranets, and extranets to mainframe and other legacy systems and databases. Though such applications are more costly and difficult to develop, many companies are forging ahead. These intranet-using companies are in the process of web-enabling operational and managerial support applications, including online transaction processing, database integration, and executive information and decision support. For example, a sales-inventory application might accept an order at a company's World Wide Web site, and

Figure 7.12

What companies are expecting from their future use of intranets and extranets.

- More and more information and applications will be put on the company intranet.
- The web browser and the intranet web will be the ubiquitous, universal user interface for timely access to business information.
- Data analysis applications and legacy systems will be front-ended by the company intranet.
- The intranet will become the primary vehicle for delivery of employee and company news, and the main source of information in our company worldwide.
- All applications, including cross-platform transaction processing, will be web-enabled or will be entered via the Internet, the intranet, or extranets.
- More processes will be added to turn information into knowledge to increase the value the intranet delivers to each employee.
- Extranets will enable a significant degree of electronic bonding with our customers and suppliers by allowing them to connect to our intranet.

Source: Adapted from Mellanie Hills, *Intranet Business Strategies*, (New York: John Wiley & Sons, 1997), p. 373. Copyright ©1997 by John Wiley & Sons, Inc. Reprinted by permission.

then trigger an intranet search engine to search an internal inventory database for the product's stock status. Then a picking list and shipping notice would be prepared at the company's warehouse intranet site. Finally, an E-mail message and invoice would be generated and sent via extranet to the customer's own company intranet workstation [4]. Now, let's look at a real world example of a web-enabled business application using an intranet.

US West Global Village

US West's Global Village intranet receives over 6.5 million hits per month, and more than 28,000 employees regularly visit the site. More than 300,000 World Wide Web pages are stored on the company's servers. "People talk about the Global Village as an integral part of running our business," says Peggy Tumey, a vice president of retail marketing.

The intranet is far more than a companywide communication tool. Every department has its own web site, and there are more than 60 applications used for everything from internal job postings to programs that cater to external business partners and customers, says Suzanne Mullison, the Global Village's webmaster. See Figure 7.13.

The real "killer application" that boosted the intranet's acceptance was Facility Check. The application give US West employees accurate estimates of when phone service will be installed—a welcome and valuable piece of information to the customers when they call.

In the last few years, with the rapid economic growth in its region and with the increased demand for second phone lines caused by the Internet, US West found that they had exhausted telephone facilities in many areas. If they promised customers the standard installation timeline, they didn't actually know whether they could deliver on that promise. Whenever they missed the promised date, they were obviously not providing the quality of service their customers expected [27].

The answer to whether telephone facilities were available was buried deep inside some very large and complex mainframe computer applications. So US West decided

Figure 7.13

The home page of US West's Global Village intranet.

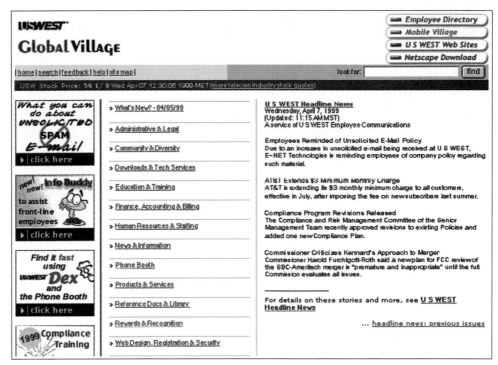

Courtesy of US West Technologies

to develop an intranet-based solution. They equipped more than 6,000 customer service reps with Netscape Navigator browsers and designed an electronic customer service form that could be accessed with the browser. Let's let Dave Lambe, VP and CIO of US West Communications, finish the story:

> *The application works like this: While on the phone with a customer, the customer service representative inputs the customer's address into the web form. Behind the scenes, a data-gathering agent accesses our mainframe engineering application. Various applications screens are captured, parsed, and interpreted into HTML. The telephone facility information is then delivered in plain language via Netscape Navigator to the customer service representative's desktop. This enables them to make a realistic service commitment to the US West customer. The result is that missed commitments and customer complaints have been reduced* [27].

US West Communications is planning to greatly expand its Global Village intranet. Besides mainframe database access, the intranet is used for publishing internal newsletters, news bulletins, and corporate documents such as policies, standards, and best practices. Employees also use the intranet for work time reporting and internal job searches. But CIO Dave Lambe says:

> *We have really just scratched the surface for its uses. With more than 20,000 employees accessing it, our intranet infrastructure is in place. I now expect that the Global Village's uses will multiply geometrically. It has truly become one of the most important tools in our entire computing portfolio* [27].

Enterprise Collaboration Systems

Enterprise Collaboration

The Internet phenomenon has permanently changed the computing mentality of business-people. Today's users expect any computing experience to include on-demand Internet access and tools for collaborating with other people [35]

Most of us have to interact with others to get things done. And as you already know, information technology is changing the way we work together. Enterprise collaboration systems provide tools to help us collaborate—to communicate ideas, share resources, and coordinate our cooperative work efforts as members of the many formal and informal process and project teams and workgroups that make up many of today's organizations.

The goal of enterprise collaboration systems is to enable us to work together more easily and effectively by helping us to:

- **Communicate:** Sharing information with each other.

- **Coordinate:** Coordinating our individual work efforts and use of resources with each other.

- **Collaborate:** Working together cooperatively on joint projects and assignments.

Analyzing Lockheed Martin

Read the Real World Case on Lockheed Martin on the next page. We can learn a lot about the business value and challenges of enterprise collaboration systems from this example. See Figure 7.14.

Figure 7.14

Engineering specialist Wynn Joness of Lockheed Martin uses desktop videoconferencing to collaborate with colleagues in Texas, California, Georgia, and Great Britain.

Source: Danny Turner.

Lockheed Martin Corporation: Improving Team Collaboration via Desktop Videoconferencing

Don't buy a videoconferencing system to save money in the travel budget. Users say the savings are small. But if you want to improve face-to-face communications and keep employees happy, the investment pays off big time.

More companies use videoconferencing now that it's more affordable and backed by standards. Benefits include convenient work access on the desktop, ease of training, improving and involving more people in collaboration, and enhancing employees' quality of life by letting them stay at home more often.

For example, Lockheed Martin Tactical Aircraft Systems in Fort Worth, Texas, wants everyone involved in the production of its new Joint Strike Fighter working as if they were side by side. Actually, its testing methodology requires it.

Lockheed uses the Fagen inspection methodology, which involves a team of four people conducting formalized walk-throughs designed to detect defects in software and its documentation as early as possible. But because the Fagen system calls for the players to be face-to-face so that facial expressions and body language can be recorded, Lockheed had to create a virtual enterprise for its geographically dispersed team members.

"Nonverbal communication is critical to this inspection process," says Wynn Joness, engineering specialist. "Things like raising an eyebrow when you don't understand something—that gets lost in conference calls."

Lockheed chose the MMCX desktop videoconferencing server from Lucent Technologies for many reasons: foremost for its application sharing, which is handled through Microsoft NetMeeting. With it, team members can work together in shared applications, passing documents back and forth while talking in two-way conversations. The system connects Lockheed's Fort Worth campus with its divisions in Marietta, Georgia; Palmdale, California; and in British Aerospace in the United Kingdom.

Image size and quality were also priorities because it was important for workers to clearly see facial expressions. But Lockheed needed to decide how far back from broadcast quality would be acceptable because the 30 frame/sec.

needed for real-time video wasn't possible on its private network. "We found that a frame rate about half that of real time was acceptable for us," Joness says. But Lockheed is upgrading its global network to improve its speed and capacity. Although 15 frame/sec. is workable, Lockheed wants it to be better.

Aside from the Fagen inspection teams, Lockheed Martin's engineers will likely benefit the most because they are seldom selected to travel to off-site meetings. According to Joness, "Not only are we now involving more engineers who should've been in these production design and management meetings all along, but the system is helping us to reduce the risks normally associated with multisite development projects." For instance, the later a defect is found in the development cycle, the more costly it is to fix. "Because we can now have impromptu live meetings, we expect to find more defects sooner than if we were working through conference calls," Joness says.

Attending meetings from your desktop is also just convenient. "When you meet in a conference room, you try to take everything you need with you. But your desktop is your power base; there is nothing to forget since everything is right there," Joness says.

Case Study Questions

1. How does desktop videoconferencing enhance team collaboration at Lockheed Martin or any company?

2. What are the limitations or disadvantages of desktop videoconferencing for enterprise collaboration?

3. When would you recommend desktop videoconferencing for team collaboration to supplement E-mail, chat, or discussion groups, and data and voice conferencing?

Source: Adapted from Kevin Burden, "Coming into Focus," *Computerworld*, January 11, 1999, pp. 91–94. Copyright 1999 by Computerworld, Inc., Framingham, MA 01701. Reprinted from *Computerworld*.

Desktop videoconferencing enables Lockheed Martin to use virtual teams of geographically dispersed specialists to implement a software inspection methodology that requires a formal walk-through process by teams of four people. In addition, more engineers are being involved in production design and management meetings, and errors are being found earlier in the production process. One of the key capabilities of desktop videoconferencing is the ability of team members to see each other's nonverbal communications, thus improving the team collaboration process.

Teams, Workgroups, and Collaboration

There are many types of teams and workgroups, each with its own work styles, agendas, and computing needs. A **workgroup** can be defined as two or more people working together on the same task or assignment. A **team** can be defined as a *collaborative workgroup*, whose members are committed to **collaboration,** that is, working with each other in a cooperative way that transcends the coordination of individual work activities found in a typical workgroup. So collaboration is the key to what makes a group of people a team, and what makes a team successful.

> *Collaboration is about working together to produce a product that's much greater than the sum of its parts. Collaborators develop a shared understanding that's much deeper than they could have developed working on their own or contributing pieces to the product. The power is so great that unless you've experienced it, it's really hard to understand. The process taps into the collective wisdom, knowledge, and even subconscious minds of the collaborators. This powerful phenomenon is becoming a requirement to effectively compete in today's marketplace* [21].

Teams and workgroups can be as formal and structured as a traditional business office or department. Or they can be less formal and structured like the members of *process teams* in a manufacturing environment. Or they can be as informal, unstructured, and temporary as an ad hoc task force or a *project team* whose members work for different organizations in different parts of the world.

Thus, the members of a team or workgroup don't have to work in the same physical location. They can be members of a **virtual team,** that is, one whose members are united by the tasks on which they are collaborating, not by geography or membership in a larger organization. In sociology and cultural anthropology, these workgroups are called *social fields*—semiautonomous and self-regulating associations of people with their own work agendas, rules, relationships, and norms of behavior. Enterprise collaboration systems make *electronic social fields* possible. Computers, groupware, and telecommunications networks allow end users to work together in virtual teams without regard to time constraints, physical location, or organizational boundaries [36]. See Figure 7.15.

Enterprise Collaboration System Components

Figure 7.16 emphasizes that an **enterprise collaboration system** is an *information system.* Therefore, it uses hardware, software, data, and network resources to support communication, coordination, and collaboration among the members of business teams and workgroups. For example, engineers, business specialists, and external consultants may form a virtual team for a project. The team may rely on intranets and extranets to collaborate via E-mail, videoconferencing, discussion forums, and a multimedia database of work-in-progress information at a project web site. The enterprise collaboration system may use PC workstations networked to a variety of servers on which project, corporate, and other databases are stored. In addition, network servers may provide a variety of software resources, such as web browsers, groupware, and application packages, to assist the team's collaboration until the project is completed.

Figure 7.15

A virtual team can include members from other teams, departments, organizations, and locations interconnected by information technology.

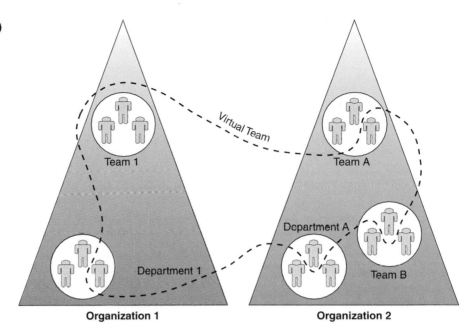

- Temporary, fluid, collaborating to achieve an objective
- Connected by shared interests and complementary expertise
- Communication and collaboration supported by information technology

Source: Adapted and reprinted from Don Mankin, Susan Cohen, and Tora Bikson, *Teams and Technology: Fulfilling the Promise of the New Organization* (Boston: Harvard Business School Press, 1996), p. 33, by permission of Harvard Business School Press. Copyright ©1996 by The President and Fellows of Harvard College; all rights reserved.

Figure 7.16

The components of an enterprise collaboration system.

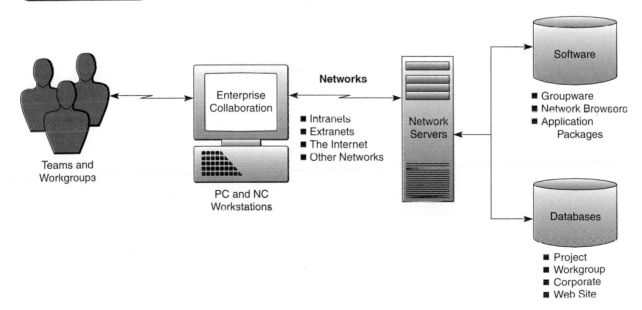

Groupware for Enterprise Collaboration

Groupware is one of the most poorly defined terms in computing. Its most general definition—software that enables multiple users to share information with one another and work together on multiple projects—can include products of many disparate types, from contact management and E-mail to document-sharing programs [19].

In Chapter 3, we defined **groupware** as *collaboration software*, that is, software that helps teams and workgroups work together in a variety of ways, to accomplish joint projects and group assignments. For example, we mentioned that groupware products like Lotus Notes, Novell GroupWise, Microsoft Exchange, and Netscape Communicator support collaboration through E-mail, data and audioconferencing, discussion forums, scheduling and calendaring, and so on. You should also be aware that groupware is changing as developers attempt to tailor it for use over the Internet or corporate intranets and extranets. In addition, as we mentioned in Chapter 3, application software suites like Microsoft Office, Lotus SmartSuite, and Corel WordPerfect Office are adding Internet/intranet access, joint document creation, and other collaborative capabilities that provide users with some groupware features.

Groupware is designed to make communication and coordination of workgroup activities and cooperation among end users significantly easier, no matter where the members of a team are located. So though groupware packages provide a variety of software tools that can accomplish many important jobs, the team and workgroup cooperation and coordination they make possible are their key feature. Groupware helps the members of a team collaborate on group projects, at the same or different times, and at the same place, or at different locations.

Many industry analysts believe that the capabilities and potential of the Internet, as well as intranets and extranets, are driving the demand for enterprise collaboration tools in business. On the other hand, it is Internet technologies like web browsers and servers, hypermedia documents and databases, and intranets and extranets that are providing the hardware, software, data, and network platforms for many of the groupware tools for enterprise collaboration that business users want. Figure 7.17 provides an overview of some of the groupware tools we will discuss in this section. Notice that groupware provides software tools for electronic communications, electronic conferencing, and collaborative work management.

Figure 7.17

Groupware for electronic communications, conferencing, and collaborative work provides software tools for enterprise collaboration.

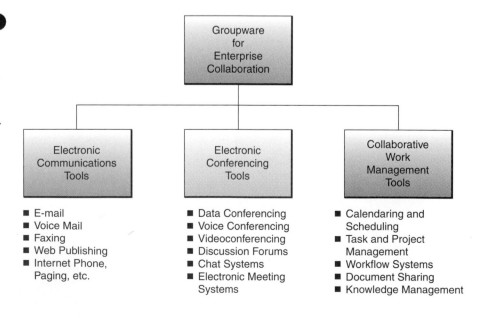

Electronic Communication Tools

Electronic communication tools include electronic mail, voice mail, faxing, web publishing, bulletin board systems, paging, and Internet phone systems. These tools enable you to electronically send messages, documents, and files in data, text, voice, or multimedia over computer networks. This helps you share everything from voice and text messages to copies of project documents and data files with your team members, wherever they may be. The ease and efficiency of such communications are major contributors to the collaboration process.

Electronic Mail

Pulled headlong by a powerful team of new standards and protocols, Internet E-mail is surging ahead of LAN-based E-mail and postal mail—even the telephone—as our primary medium of long-distance communication. Whether or not this is true in your organization, it's pretty clear that as an active Internet user you'll be spending an increasing portion of your life over the coming months and years dealing with E-mail. [25]

We introduced electronic mail software in Chapter 3 and emphasized how vital E-mail has become as a fast and convenient way to communicate and build strategic relationships with each other in business. E-mail has also been transferred into an important medium for transporting electronic copies of documents, data files, and multimedia content. This includes net broadcasters automatically *pushing* information from Internet and intranet sources into your E-mail in-box.

Your choice of Internet E-mail software will have a growing impact on your working and other communications. Ideally, your mail client should be an active ally that will do a lot more than shuffle messages from one place to another. It should help you organize your burgeoning store of messages, filter out unwanted junk mail, transfer files, put an elegant face on your correspondence, and keep your private messages private [25].

The downside of the E-mail phenomenon is the *information overload* caused by too many messages from too many sources. Especially controversial is the torrent of unsolicited *junk E-mail* (called *spamming*) that is flooding many users' Internet E-mail boxes [32]. Many solutions for this problem are being tried, including legal action and organizational restrictions on E-mail use. But experts agree that using E-mail software with good E-mail management capabilities should be every user's first line of defense.

Internet Phone and Fax

The Internet isn't just for sending E-mail and surfing the Web anymore. It's turning into a low-cost and nearly universal communications medium, helping to send faxes, retrieve voicemail, and carry two-way conversations [11].

You can now use the Internet for telephone, voice mail, faxing, and paging services. All you need is a suitably equipped PC and software such as Internet Phone by Vocal-Tech, or Netscape Conference or Microsoft NetMeeting (which are part of Netscape Communicator and Microsoft Internet Explorer).

Depending on your PC's configuration (and that of the person you're calling) and the speed of your Internet connection, the sound quality of your phone call can vary from poor to very good. Internet voice mail and faxing work better, as does paging. In fact, many companies now offer unified Internet messaging services that will collect all your voice, fax, and E-mail in one web site box (or *virtual office*) you can access with your browser. For an additional fee, you can be paged when new messages arrive [11]. See Figure 7.18.

Web Publishing

Web publishing can be viewed as an important electronic communications tool for enterprise collaboration. In Chapter 3, we mentioned how application software suites like Microsoft Office, browser suites like Netscape Communicator, and other web

Figure 7.18

Using the JFax In-Box
service to collect
Internet voice mail,
E-mail, and faxes in a
web site messaging box.

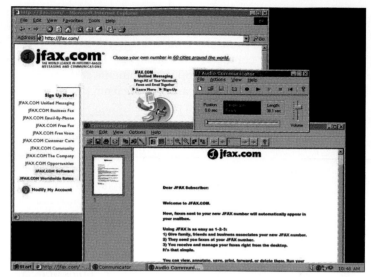

Courtesy of JFax.

publishing and web site development programs now enable you to publish hyperlinked documents in HTML directly to Internet or intranet web sites. As Figure 7.19 illustrates, a team member can publish a project report or other hyperlinked document directly to an intranet/extranet web server for viewing and comments by other members of a project team. Other project messages and news can be broadcast (pushed) to team members' video screens or E-mail boxes. Thus, intranet web publishing has become a much more efficient and effective way of communicating among teams and workgroups than previous paper or electronic methods.

Electronic Conferencing Tools

Electronic conferencing tools help people communicate and collaborate while working together. A variety of conferencing methods enable the members of teams and workgroups at different locations to exchange ideas interactively at the same time, or at different times at their convenience. Electronic conferencing options also include *electronic meeting systems*, where team members can meet at the same time and place in a *decision room* setting. Let's take a brief look at these collaboration tools, which include data and voice conferencing, videoconferencing, chat systems, discussion forums, and electronic meeting systems.

Data and Voice Conferencing

Data and voice conferencing are frequently mentioned together because they are frequently used together in work situations. **Voice conferencing** formerly relied on speaker-phone systems, but now can be accomplished with browser modules like Netscape Conference or Microsoft NetMeeting, and other Internet telephone software and groupware. These packages support telephone conversations over the Internet or intranets between your PC and other voice-enabled networked PCs.

Data conferencing is also popularly called **whiteboarding.** In this method, a groupware package connects two or more PCs over the Internet or intranets so a team can share, mark up, and revise a *whiteboard* of drawings, documents, and other material displayed on their screens. For example, groupware like Netscape Conference or Microsoft NetMeeting lets you have a voice and data conference with other networked

Figure 7.19

The traditional versus the intranet/extranet way of web publishing to share team and work-group information.

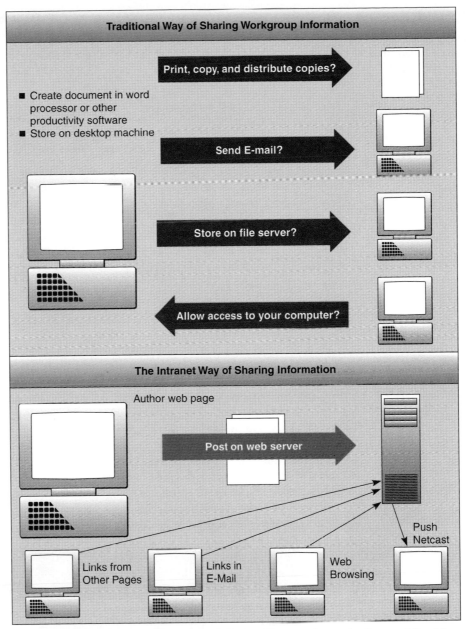

Source: Adapted from Jerry Bowles, "The Web Within: The Next Generation Intranet," Special Advertising Supplement, *Fortune*, April 14, 1997, p. 4. © 1997 Time Inc. All rights reserved.

team members. You can all view the same document or graphic image on your PCs; mark it up in realtime with painting, drawing, and highlighting tools; and save the annotated document file in your project database. See Figure 7.20.

Videoconferencing

Videoconferencing is an enterprise collaboration tool that enables realtime video/audio conferences among (1) networked PCs, known as **desktop videoconferencing**, or (2) networked conference rooms or auditoriums in different locations, called *teleconferencing*. In either case, team and enterprise collaboration can be enhanced with a

Figure 7.20

Data conferencing supports team collaboration using a shared whiteboard of project information.

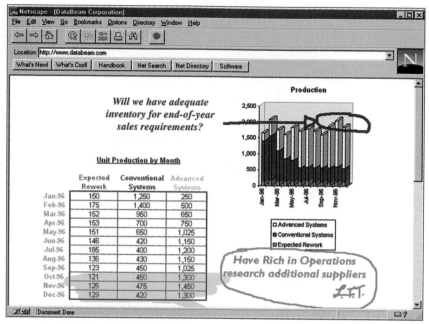

Courtesy of DataBeam Corporation.

full range of interactive video, audio, document, and whiteboard communications among the online participants. Desktop videoconferencing can now take place over the Internet, intranets, extranets, as well as public telephone and other networks. Desktop videoconferencing software such as White Pine's CU-SeeMe and Intel's ProShare are market leaders. See Figure 7.21.

Teleconferencing is an important form of enterprise collaboration. Sessions are held in realtime, with major participants being televised while participants at remote sites may only take part with voice input of questions and responses. See Figure 7.22. Teleconferencing can also consist of using closed-circuit television to reach multiple small groups, instead of using television broadcasting to reach large groups at multiple sites. Several major communications carriers offer teleconferencing services for such

Figure 7.21

Using a laptop computer for desktop video-conferencing.

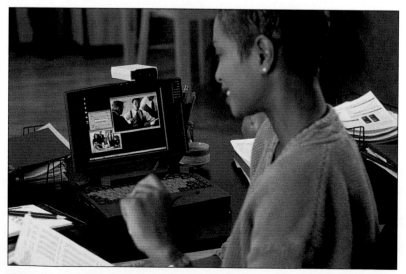

© Jon Feingersh/The Stock Market.

Figure 7.22   Teleconferencing in action.

Courtesy of Kinko's.

events as sales meetings, new product announcements, and employee education and training. However, some organizations have found that teleconferencing may not be as effective as face-to-face meetings, especially when important participants are not trained in how to communicate using their systems. Also, the cost of providing teleconferencing services and facilities can be substantial and make teleconferencing not as cost effective as expected.

Desktop videoconferencing has a few limitations as well. Complaints include jerky motions of video images and the lack of nonverbal communications from "talking heads" displays of videoconference participants. These complaints are being addressed by improvements in the software compression of video images, and the use of higher-speed modems and communications lines like ISDN or ADSL. Using more of the display screen to show more complete images of the conferencing participants is another recommended solution [42].

However, desktop videoconferencing over the Internet, intranets, and extranets is proving to be an efficient, economical, and effective way of supporting communications and collaboration among physically displaced teams and workgroups. Reducing travel time and money to attend meetings results in increased team productivity as well as cost and time savings. For example, a product development team of engineers and marketing executives from several company locations will typically use desktop videoconferencing for weekly project status meetings, as well as ad hoc meetings of team subgroups to review detailed product drawings and proposed specifications.

Discussion Forums

This category of collaboration tools includes Internet and intranet newsgroups, discussion groups, and discussion databases. Discussion forums are an extension of the earlier concept of online *bulletin board systems* (BBS), which allowed users to post

Figure 7.23

Using Netscape Instant
Teamroom discussion
forum groupware
for project team
collaboration.

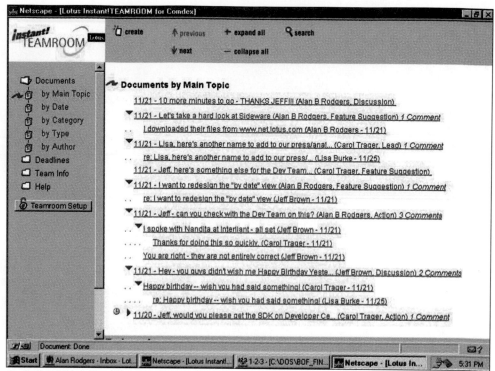

Courtesy of Lotus Development Corporation.

messages and download data and program files from the online services, businesses,
and individual BBS operators. Discussion forums are also an outgrowth of the widespread use of *newsgroups* to provide a forum for online text discussions by members of
special interest user groups on the Internet and the major online services. As we mentioned in Chapter 6, discussion forums and newsgroups can be used by companies to
create or encourage *communities of interest* or *virtual communities.* Customers, suppliers,
prospects, company representatives, and others can develop a rapport that strengthens
their relationship and loyalty to a company and its products.

Figure 7.23 shows the use of discussion forum groupware, which encourages
and manages discussion by members of a project team. Team members can ask for and
make comments, post messages, brainstorm, review documents, and even vote and
make decisions online. Discussion forums are a good tool for collaboration when you
don't really need to get a team together for meeting, but still want to encourage and
share the contribution of everyone on the project team.

Discussion forum groupware like Lotus Notes, Netscape Collabra, and several
others significantly improves the collaboration capabilities of discussion forums by
providing for *threaded discussions, virtual discussion groups, discussion tracking*, and *discussion databases.* What this means is that the groupware can keep track of the discussion
contributions of each participant, organize them by a variety of key word discussion
topics, and store them in a discussion database. This creates *threads* of discussion contributions on each topic over a period of time that can be tracked and retrieved from
the discussion database for analysis.

For example, a company could use discussion forum groupware to monitor a customer service discussion group they created on the Internet. A sales rep could select
only the discussion contributions of the employees of a particular business customer to
evaluate their feedback. Or a customer service analyst could create a *virtual discussion*

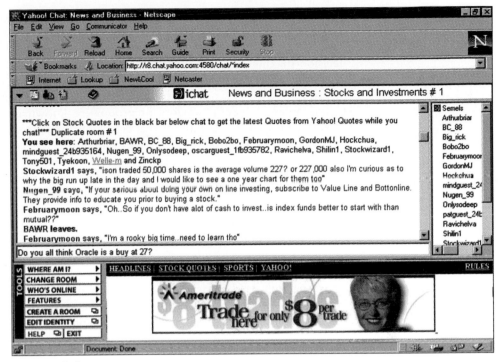

Courtesy of ichat

group. The groupware could track any discussion contributions about the company and its products across several Internet, intranet, extranet, and online service discussion groups. Thus, the discussion forum groupware would create a virtual discussion group by weaving together the threads of contributions on the same topic by people who had really been participants in other online discussion groups [2].

Chat Systems

Chat capabilities are built into many groupware products, including Microsoft Net-Meeting and Netscape Conference. Chat software by ichat Inc. is licensed to companies like Yahoo!, Merrill Lynch, and TimeWarner, and bundled into Lotus Notes. These tools are a groupware version of the Internet's Internet Relay Chat (IRC) and the *chat rooms* of America Online and the other online services. Chat enables two or more people to carry on online realtime text conversations. With chat, you can converse and share ideas interactively by typing in your comments and seeing the responses on your display screen. See Figure 7.24.

Chat is an important tool for enterprise collaboration on corporate intranets, especially where voice and videoconferencing have not been implemented. One advantage of chat is that it records and stores the dialogues of all participants, so that other team members can review them later. Chat rooms are also being added to Internet and intranet web sites as another way to encourage participation and collaboration by customers or employees. For example, companies like K-Swiss, Kendall-Jackson Wines, and Nations Bank have created regularly scheduled and moderated chat rooms at their Internet web sites. Even Microsoft Corporation has scheduled moderated chat rooms on their corporate intranet to replace events like executive question-and-answer sessions at employee meetings [10, 38].

Electronic Meeting Systems

Organizations frequently schedule meetings as decision-making situations that require interaction among groups of people. The success of group decision making during meetings depends on such factors as (1) the characteristics of the group itself, (2) the characteristics of the task on which the group is working, (3) the organizational context in which the group decision-making process takes place, (4) the use of information technology such as electronic meeting systems, and (5) the communication and decision-making processes the group utilizes [33].

Information technology can provide a variety of tools to increase the effectiveness of group decision making. Known generically as *group support systems* (GSS), these technologies include a category of groupware known as *electronic meeting systems* (EMS). Research studies indicate that electronic meeting systems produce several important benefits. For example, computer support makes group communications easier, protects the anonymity of participants, and provides a public recording of group communications (*group memory*). This significantly improves the efficiency, creativity, and quality of communication, collaboration, and group decision making in business meetings.

Electronic meeting systems packages are available that facilitate the group decision-making activities that take place in a computer-based *decision room* setting. Other types of *group decision support systems* (GDSS) may be designed to support a specific application or task, such as a groupware package for labor/management negotiations or a package that merely supports anonymous voting during a meeting. Figure 7.25 illustrates the activities supported by the software tools in the GroupSystems EMS software package. Figure 7.26 shows a typical EMS decision room in action.

Figure 7.25

An example of the use of the groupware tools in the GroupSystems package for conducting electronic meetings. Note the various group activities supported by this EMS package.

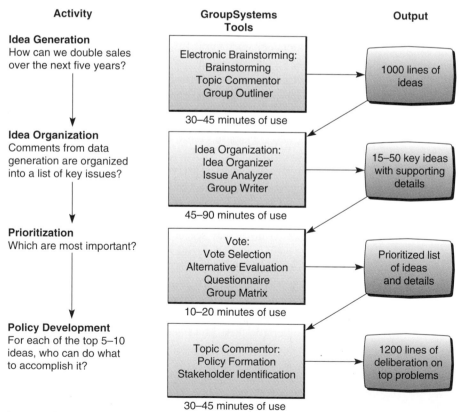

Source: Adapted from H. Chen, P. Hsu, R. Orwig, L. Hoopes, and J. F. Nunamaker, "Automated Classification from Electronic Meetings," *Communications of the ACM*, October 1994, p. 57. Copyright 1994, Association for Computing Machinery, Inc. By permission.

Figure 7.26

Using an electronic meeting system in a decision room setting.

Courtesy of Ventana Corporation.

Collaborative Work Management Tools

Collaborative work management tools help people accomplish or manage group work activities. This category of groupware includes calendaring and scheduling tools, task and project management, workflow systems, and knowledge repositories. Other tools for joint work, such as joint document creation, editing, and revision, are found in the software suites we discussed in Chapter 3. The tools in this category are so diverse that we need to explain them individually in order to understand how they support enterprise collaboration.

Calendaring and Scheduling

Calendaring and scheduling tools are a groupware extension of many of the capabilities provided by *time management* software such as *desktop accessory* packages, personal information managers, and mainframe *office automation systems*. These packages enable you to use electronic versions of a variety of office tools such as a calendar, appointment book, contact list, and task to-do list.

Groupware calendaring and scheduling tools are included in packages like Novell GroupWise, Netscape Communicator, and Microsoft Exchange. They can automatically check the electronic calendar of team members for open time slots, propose alternative meeting times, schedule team meetings or appointments, and notify and remind participants by E-mail. Some intranet packages even let you schedule meeting rooms and presentation equipment. Most calendaring and scheduling groupware can also send meeting notices containing a detailed agenda along with individual to-do lists to help each participant prepare for a meeting [22]. See Figure 7.27.

Task and Project Management

Project management and personal information packages can be used to do task and project management on your PC. Examples are Microsoft Project and Outlook, Lotus Organizer, and CA-Super Project. However, groupware packages like Lotus Notes and Netscape Communicator are adding this capability to their repertoire, while Microsoft is integrating Outlook's task management feature into its Exchange groupware product.

Project management groupware helps project teams work together, and helps team members keep track of the many tasks and timelines involved. These tools produce

Figure 7.27

Lotus Organizer can maintain electronic calendars for individuals and projects at Internet or intranet web sites.

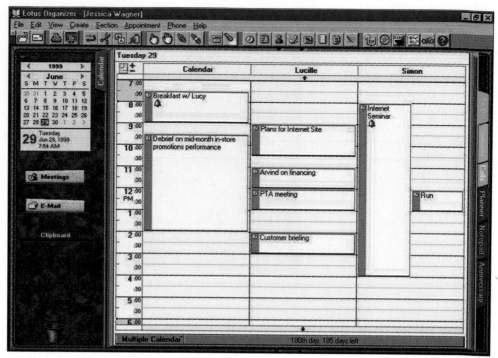

Courtesy of Lotus Development Corporation.

project schedules, program reports, and automatic reminders of due dates for project tasks. Task and project management groupware also produces charts to help plan and track projects. One is the Gantt chart that specifies the times allowed for the various activities required in a business project. Other charts use network methodologies such as CPM (critical path method) and the PERT system (Program Evaluation and Review Technique), which develop a network diagram of required activities. These techniques view a project as a series or network of distinct tasks and milestones, and specify the amount of time budgeted for the completion of each task. Figure 7.28 is an example of a Gantt chart prepared by a project management groupware package.

Workflow Systems

Workflow systems are related to task and project management, as well as a type of electronic document processing called *document image management*. However, work-flow systems involve helping knowledge workers collaborate to accomplish and manage structured work tasks within a knowledge-based business process. Workflow systems are typically based on rules that govern the flow of tasks and task information contained in business forms and other documents.

For example, you could fill out an electronic application form for a bank loan at a bank's web site and download it to a bank loan officer's networked PC. Then the ap-plication could be completed by the loan officer during an interview with you and routed to other loan specialists' networked PCs for a credit check and the preparation of additional electronic forms and documents. Finally, your loan application could be electronically rerouted to the loan officer's workstation where the loan decision would be made.

Workflow systems tools are found in groupware like Novell GroupWise, Lotus Notes, and Microsoft Exchange. Some groupware workflow products, like Livelink Intranet by Open Text, have been created to work on corporate intranets. Workflow software includes forms designers to help you create electronic forms and workflow

Figure 7.28

A Gantt chart for a business project produced by Microsoft Project.

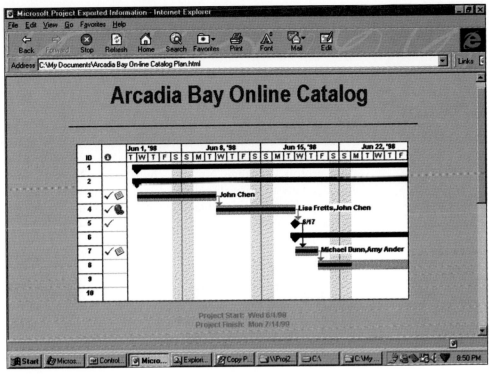

Courtesy of Microsoft Corporation.

engines to process rules for completing and routing the forms. Workflow systems may access document image management databases or send E-mail to route documents to their next destination in the business process [6, 21]. See Figure 7.29.

Figure 7.29

Using Novell Group-Wise to manage a business workflow.

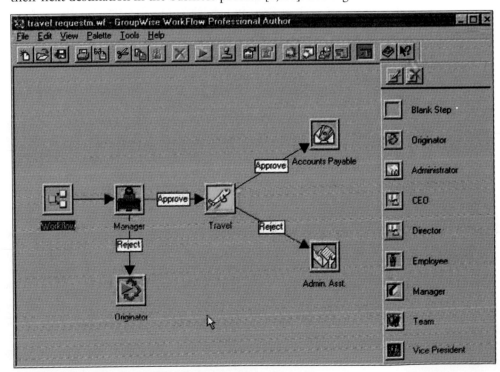

Courtesy of Novell.

Knowledge Management

What is knowledge and how do you capture and share it? We've found over the years that we can take data and put it in reports, but to make it truly useful, someone must interpret the data and do something with it. In the past few years, we've added tools to turn data into information by identifying trends. With knowledge, we move forward another step. We capture more than just the numbers and their potential impact. We capture the organization's expertise to share with everyone . . . Collecting and maintaining that knowledge is one of the many roles of groupware [21].

Knowledge management is a tool of enterprise collaboration that groupware packages use to organize, manage, and share the diverse forms of business information created by individuals and teams in an organization. Groupware such as Lotus Notes, Microsoft Exchange, Novell GroupWise, and many others store this information in document libraries, discussion databases, knowledge repositories, and web site hypermedia databases. These forms of stored information help create a *knowledge base* or *organizational memory* of strategic business information to be shared within the organization. Knowledge bases are part of the *knowledge management systems* being developed and used by many companies. We will cover knowledge management systems in Chapter 9.

For example, Compaq Computer Corporation's AltaVista Forum groupware package creates a *knowledge repository* at an intranet web site to share documents and organize a team's project knowledge. Team members can store information they want to share (such as memos, reports, spreadsheets, and multimedia presentations) in shared folders. Forum can manage multiple versions of project files for different team members and time periods. Team members can also use a search tool to find project information and receive automatic notification whenever new documents are added to the knowledge repository [21].

Another example is provided by the Livelink Intranet groupware package. With Livelink you can create a *document management library* at an intranet web site. Livelink lets you check in and check out project documents of all kinds and use a browser and search engine to find project information you need. This groupware also has a *version control* capability to manage multiple versions of project documents prepared or revised over time by team members [21]. See Figure 7.30.

Figure 7.30

Livelink by Open Text enables you to search a document management library at an intranet web site for project information.

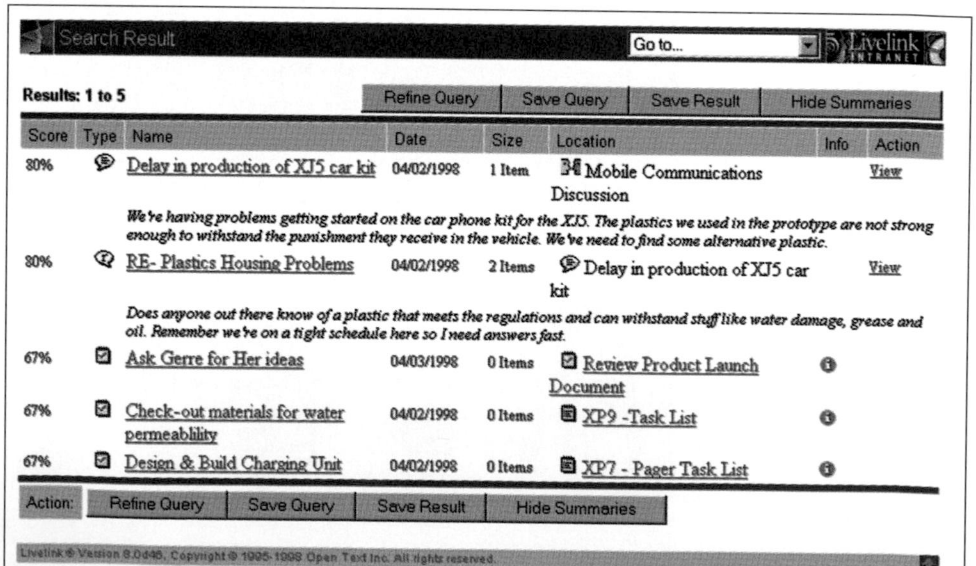

Courtesy of Open Text Corporation.

Figure 7.31 closes this section with a summary of the major categories of groupware tools that many businesses are using for enterprise collaboration. Remember that this summary is not intended to be a list of technical definitions. Instead, it briefly expresses how these tools can contribute to collaboration between teams and workgroups within the internetworked enterprise.

Figure 7.31 A summary of the major categories of groupware tools for enterprise collaboration.

Electronic Communication Tools help you to communicate and collaborate with others by electronically sending messages, documents, and files in data, text, voice, or multimedia over the Internet, intranets, extranets, and other computer networks.

- **Electronic Mail.** Widely used to send and receive text messages between networked PCs over telecommunications networks. E-mail can also include data files, software, and multimedia messages and documents as attachments.
- **Voice Mail.** Unanswered telephone messages are digitized, stored, and played back to you by a voice messaging computer.
- **Faxing.** Transmitting and receiving images of documents over telephone or computer networks using PCs or fax machines.
- **Web Publishing.** Creating, converting, and storing hyperlinked documents and other material on Internet or intranet web servers so they can easily be shared via web browsers or netcasting with teams, workgroups, or the enterprise.

Electronic Conferencing Tools help networked computer users share information and collaborate while working together on joint assignments, no matter where they are located.

- **Data Conferencing.** Users at networked PCs can view, mark up, revise, and save changes to a shared whiteboard of drawings, documents, and other material.
- **Voice Conferencing.** Telephone conversations shared among several participants via speaker phones or networked PCs with *Internet telephone* software.
- **Videoconferencing.** Realtime video- and audioconferencing (1) among users at networked PCs (desktop videoconferencing) or (2) among participants in conference rooms or auditoriums in different locations (teleconferencing). Videoconferencing can also include whiteboarding and document sharing.
- **Discussion Forums.** Provide a computer network discussion platform to encourage and manage online text discussions over a period of time among members of special interest groups or project teams.
- **Chat Systems.** Enable two or more users at networked PCs to carry on online, realtime text conversations.
- **Electronic Meeting Systems.** Using a meeting room with networked PCs, a large-screen projector, and EMS software to facilitate communication, collaboration, and group decision making in business meetings.

Collaborative Work Management Tools help people accomplish or manage joint work activities.

- **Calendaring and Scheduling.** Using electronic calendars and other groupware features to automatically schedule, notify, and remind the computer networked members of teams and workgroups of meetings, appointments, and other events.
- **Task and Project Management.** Managing team and workgroup projects by scheduling, tracking, and charting the completion status of tasks within a project.
- **Workflow Systems.** Help networked knowledge workers collaborate to accomplish and manage the flow of structured work tasks and electronic document processing within a business process.
- **Knowledge Management.** Organizing and sharing the diverse forms of business information created within an organization. Includes managing project and enterprise document libraries, discussion databases, hypermedia web site databases, and other types of knowledge bases.

Summary

- **Applications of Intranets.** Businesses are rapidly installing and extending intranets throughout their organizations (1) to improve communications and collaboration among individuals and teams within the enterprise; (2) to publish and share valuable business information easily, inexpensively, and effectively via intranet web sites and other intranet services; and (3) to develop and deploy critical applications to support business operations and management decision making.

- **Intranet Technology Resources.** Intranets depend on all of the information technologies that make the Internet possible. Thus, companies must have or install web browsers and servers, TCP/IP client/server networks, hypermedia database management systems, HTML web publishing software, and network management and security programs as part of the technology platform for their corporate intranets.

- **The Business Value of Intranets.** The early intranet applications of companies have demonstrated impressive returns, quick payback, and other strategic benefits. Major cost savings come from replacing company publications and documents on paper with electronic multimedia versions published to web servers. Intranet-based employee training and customer service programs are also proving much more cost-effective than traditional methods.

- **The Role of Extranets.** The primary role of extranets is to link the intranet resources of a company to the intranets of its customers, suppliers, and other business partners. Extranets can also provide access to operational company databases and legacy systems to business partners, as well as limited access to intranet resources by consumers and others over the Internet. Thus, extranets provide significant business value by facilitating and strengthening the business relationships of a company with customers and suppliers, improving collaboration with its business partners, and enabling the development of new kinds of web-based service for its customers, suppliers, and others.

- **Enterprise Collaboration Systems.** The goal of enterprise collaboration systems is to help us work together more efficiently and effectively as members of the many process and project teams and workgroups that make up many organizations today. Collaboration technologies help us to share information with each other (communication), coordinate our work efforts and resources with each other (coordination), and work together cooperatively on joint assignments (collaboration).

- **Groupware Tools for Enterprise Collaboration.** Groupware is collaborative software that helps teams and workgroups work together in a variety of ways. Groupware provides many software tools for electronic communications, electronic conferencing, and collaborative work management. Refer to Figure 7.31 for a summary of the groupware tools we covered in this chapter.

Key Terms and Concepts

These are the key terms and concepts of this chapter. The page number of their first explanation is in parentheses.

1. Applications of extranets (262)
2. Applications of intranets (253)
3. Business value of extranets (262)
4. Business value of intranets (256)
5. Calendaring and scheduling (279)
6. Chat systems (277)
7. Collaboration (268)
8. Collaborative work management tools (279)
9. Data conferencing (272)
10. Desktop videoconferencing (273)
11. Discussion forums (275)
12. Electronic communication tools (271)
13. Electronic conferencing tools (272)
14. Electronic mail (271)
15. Electronic meeting systems (277)
16. Enterprise collaboration (266)
17. Extranets (262)
18. Faxing (271)
19. Groupware (270)
20. Intranets (252)
21. Intranet technology resources (256)
22. Knowledge management (282)
23. Task and project management (279)
24. Team (268)
25. Teleconferencing (274)
26. Videoconferencing (273)
27. Virtual teams (268)
28. Voice conferencing (272)
29. Voice mail (271)
30. Web publishing (271)
31. Whiteboarding (272)
32. Workflow system (280)
33. Workgroup (268)

Review Quiz

Match one of the key terms and concepts listed previously with one of the brief examples or definitions that follow. Try to find the best fit for answers that seem to fit more than one term or concept. Defend your choices.

_____ 1. An Internet-like network within a company.

_____ 2. Networks that link some of the Internet resources of a company to the intranets of their customers or suppliers.

_____ 3. Intranets use web browsers and servers, TCP/IP client/server networks, hypermedia databases at networked web sites, and so on.

_____ 4. Intranets are being used to improve communications and collaboration, publish and share information, and develop applications to support business operations and managerial decision making.

_____ 5. Extranets provide access to a company's operational databases and legacy systems by its customers and suppliers.

_____ 6. Extranets can facilitate and strengthen the collaboration and relationships between a company and its business partners.

_____ 7. Intranets have demonstrated impressive returns, quick payback, and other strategic benefits.

_____ 8. Enables you to automatically check the electronic calendars of team members to schedule a meeting.

_____ 9. Two or more users at networked PCs can carry on online, interactive text conversations.

_____ 10. Working together cooperatively on joint assignments.

_____ 11. Includes calendaring and scheduling, tasks and project management, and workflow systems.

_____ 12. Users at networked PCs can view, mark up, revise, and save changes to a shared whiteboard of drawings and documents.

_____ 13. Same as data conferencing.

_____ 14. Enables realtime audio and video conferences.

_____ 15. Videoconferencing among networked PC users.

_____ 16. Videoconferencing among participants in conference rooms or auditoriums.

_____ 17. Encourages online text discussions over a period of time among members of teams or special-interest groups.

_____ 18. Includes E-mail, voice mail, faxing, and web publishing.

_____ 19. Includes data conferencing, videoconferencing, voice conferencing, and discussion forums.

_____ 20. Widely used to send electronic text messages between networked PCs.

_____ 21. Helps to facilitate communication, collaboration, and group decision making in business meetings.

_____ 22. Information systems that use hardware, software, data, and network resources to help us work together more efficiently and effectively.

_____ 23. Transmitting or receiving images of documents.

_____ 24. Collaboration software for teams, workgroups, and the enterprise.

_____ 25. Organizing and sharing business information created within or imported into an organization.

_____ 26. Helps you schedule, track, and chart the status of tasks within a project.

_____ 27. A collaborative workgroup.

_____ 28. Telephone conversations shared among several participants.

_____ 29. Telephone messages to you are digitized, stored, and played back at your convenience.

_____ 30. Enterprise collaboration systems enable people from various business functions, locations, or companies to work together on a project.

_____ 31. Two or more people working together on the same task or assignment.

_____ 32. Creating, converting, and storing hyperlinked documents on web servers.

_____ 33. Helps knowledge workers accomplish and manage the flow of structured work tasks and electronic documents in a business process.

Discussion Questions

1. What is the business value driving so many companies to rapidly install and extend intranets throughout their organizations?

2. Do you agree with technology companies that investing in an intranet "is as fundamental as supplying employees with a telephone"? Why or why not?

3. Refer to the Real World Case on Glaxo Wellcome and BC Telecom in the chapter. Why do intranets make it easier to develop applications like those in the case?

4. What might be some of the limitations of using intranets in business today?

5. What strategic competitive benefits do you see in a company's use of extranets?

6. Refer to the Real World case on Lockheed Martin in the chapter. Will desktop videoconferencing eventually become the only form of electronic conferencing in business? Why or why not?

7. Do you agree that "today's users expect any computing experience to include on-demand Internet access and tools for collaborating with other people"? Why or why not?

8. Which of the 14 groupware tools summarized in Figure 7.31 do you feel are essential for any business to have today? Which of them do you feel are optional, depending on the type of business or other factor? Explain.

9. Refer to the Real World Problem on Xilinx in the chapter. What is the business value of extranets for enterprise collaboration?

10. Do you use E-mail or Internet chat, or take part in any newsgroups or discussion forums? How well do any of those tools help your communication and collaboration with others? Explain.

Real World Problems

1. The Boeing Company: Managing the Intranet Explosion

Send a sniffer out on the network of a large corporation and you may discover dozens, maybe hundreds, even thousands of baby "intranettes" in various nooks and crannies of the organization.

The Boeing Co. in Seattle, for example, discovered more than 1 million pages hosted by at least 2,300 major intranet sites on more than 1,000 web servers. And there could be even more intranet sites, company officials acknowledged. Intranets have sprouted like weeds in many corporations, which isn't surprising because they're reasonably cheap and easy to set up. But some of those far-flung intranets grow up unsupported by the information technology department and hidden from management's view.

Companies face a balancing act in trying to rein in the intranets while leaving employees enough freedom to meet their business needs. Too much control can dampen the entrepreneurial spirit that made the intranets grow and thrive in the first place, IT managers said. Left unchecked, however, unsupported intranets can give company officials a headache.

Boeing, for instance, was happy that an industrious employee had built a corporate "Boeing Look Up Everything Site," or BLUES. Colleagues had grown to depend on it. But when the employee left Boeing for another job, the company had to find a new owner to tend the orphaned site.

Inappropriate content for a business-oriented intranet—whether a personal page, offensive information, or sensitive company data—is another persistent concern among companies with loosely controlled intranets.

"You wind up with some aberrations, and the fear is that the aberrations are going to be the majority, and that scares you to death," said Graeber Jordan, web program manager at Boeing.

But Jordan has found that the vast majority of employees stick to the Boeing guidelines that govern proprietary information in any format. Not wanting to send a "chill factor" through the employee ranks, Boeing prefers to deal with wayward sites quietly, Jordan said. "We try not to condemn the 99.9 percent," he said, "for the weirdness of one or two."

So companies like Boeing are taking the carrot-and-stick approach. Intranet web site developers gain exposure and the benefits of the company's intranet search engine if they choose to register their sites through the Boeing technical library. The company, in turn, can more easily support their sites, verify their authenticity, and check for broken links between intranet web sites.

a. Why has there been such an explosion of intranet web sites at many companies?

b. What steps should companies take to manage the development of intranet Web sites?

Source: Adapted from Carol Sliwa, "Maverick Intranets a Challenge for IT," *Computerworld*, March 15, 1999, pp. 1, 20. Copyright 1999 by Computerworld, Inc., Framingham, MA 01701. Reprinted from *Computerworld*.

2. US West and Charles Schwab & Co.: The Business Case for Intranet Portals

At Denver-based US West Inc., intranet web sites deemed critical to the business must conform to company standards to be included on its Global Village home page, which serves as a "portal" to their huge corporate intranet. That means using a designated set of servers, conforming to design requirements, and carrying the site creator's contact information.

For capacity planning purposes, US West audits its 600 intranet web sites to monitor network activity and track growth rates. "It's our obligation in the IT shop that we keep the central tool of the business up and functioning properly," CIO David Lambe noted.

The company's next project is figuring out what corporate data are on the sites, so it can decide if it wants to label sensitive content "US West confidential" or place it inside password-protected sites.

Charles Schwab, which has close to 100 web servers dishing out intranet content, plans to take an extra step: Get as many sites as possible to use a new, structured content-management system. "More and more intranet sites will migrate as people see the benefit of this portal approach," said Tom Voltz, managing director of the San Francisco brokerage's intranet services.

Schwab also is migrating to a web farm of servers and related services. Users who choose to host their intranet sites through the web farm will get a more reliable site because the IT department will worry about load balancing and redundant hardware. IT staffers, meanwhile, will be able to enforce technology standards.

Consultants and analysts agreed that portals or some level of central IT department control are needed to ensure the intranet stays up and running, security policies are maintained, and content is managed.

For companies just getting started with intranets, that could mean adding a front-end search engine, requiring page design templates, or building a centralized intranet portal that provides structure and navigational aids. Companies that already have portals can add a more sophisticated search tool or content-management system or try to bring more grassroots sites into the fold.

Eric Brown, an analyst at Forrester Research, said having a portal "is the new bar that defines what an intranet is." "It's not sufficient to just have a bunch of internal web sites and browsers," he said. "It's not an intranet until companies have some unifying force that pulls all of these things together into something that's usable."

a. What are the benefits and limitations of a portal approach to managing a company's intranet web sites?

b. What other steps do you recommend to enhance the benefits of an intranet to a company's employees?

Source: Adapted from Carol Sliwa, "Maverick Intranets a Challenge for IT," *Computerworld*, March 15, 1999, pp. 1, 20. Copyright 1999 by Computerworld, Inc., Framingham, MA 01701. Reprinted from *Computerworld*.

3. Xilinx, Inc.: Using Intranets and Extranets for Enterprise Collaboration

Xilinx is the world's leading supplier of programmable logic microprocessors and related development software.

Intranet

Xilinx's corporate intranet, Xilinx Crossroads, was developed by a team led by Sandy Sully, vice president and chief information officer. The intranet supports Xilinx work groups with groupware and workflow solutions and allows the company's global workforce to collaborate and share information easily through E-mail and discussion groups.

Employees use the Xilinx intranet to find competitive marketing information, sales materials, legal documents, product-specific information, and project information from the company's various departments and groups. Xilinx also built a seamless interface between its corporate intranet and the Internet to avoid replicating information that is already available. Xilinx Crossroads simply points to information that exists in another Internet location.

In the last few months, the intranet's capabilities have expanded to include workflow applications. For example, executive approvals for products are conducted through the intranet. Product specifications are posted to the intranet and the workflow/approval process is controlled by a workflow software application.

Extranet

Getting information, much of it confidential, out to sales partners often proved challenging before Xilinx developed its extranet. Xilinx needs to distribute materials such as updated product-status information, sales presentations, technical newsletters, competitive information, order lead time information, and selling tips in a timely manner while ensuring the utmost security.

Sales partners can now get a wealth of information from the Xilinx extranet, including sales tools on demand. "Our sales consultants can get in-depth customer information, such as the number of problems reported to technical support, or even request a quote for special types of products," says Sully. Xilinx protects its confidential information by authenticating users with Netscape security software.

Xilinx also uses its extranet to better collaborate with its manufacturing partners. The complex, graphically rich manufacturing specifications for Xilinx's products change frequently. Says Sully, "Our extranet provides the ideal way to give our manufacturing partners real-time information access. We have partners in Japan, Taiwan, and Korea and the worldwide acceptance of web browser technology is what allows us to share web site information seamlessly."

a. Choose an intranet application at Xilinx. What is its business value to the company?

b. Choose an extranet application at Xilinx. What is its business value to Xilinx and its business partners?

Source: Adapted from "Xilinx Succeeds at Being a Virtual Enterprise," from www.netscape.com/solutions/business/profiles, March 1999. Copyright 1999 Netscape Communications Corp. Used with permission. All Rights Reserved.

Application Exercises

1. Microsoft Newsgroups: Collaboration for Technical Support

Microsoft has found a way to provide technical support to its customers through an assortment of free semi-public Usenet newsgroups available only on Microsoft's own server (msnews.microsoft.com). Anyone on the Internet can ask technical questions about a multitude of Microsoft products and programming languages.

There are over 200 newsgroups that cover Microsoft's Internet-related products, including Office, Front Page, ActiveX, and Internet Explorer. The newsgroups are monitored by Microsoft employees for accuracy, although the bulk of the tech-support questions are answered by MVPs (most valuable professionals)—volunteers who have proven their value as support personnel on other online services.

a. Do you have a question or need help with a Microsoft software product? Check out the Microsoft newsgroups for help, or just to view the newsgroup postings if you do not want to participate.

b. Evaluate the Microsoft newsgroups as a business user. Do they provide a helpful service to Microsoft's customers? Do they provide business benefits to Microsoft? Do you have any suggestions for improvement for Microsoft? Explain your position.

2. ichat Inc.: Internet Chat in Business

The man perhaps most responsible for the current vogue of electronic communities is a soft-spoken bespectacled veteran of the Internet era. Meet Andrew Busey, 26. "I remember back when Mosaic took off. Suddenly 20 different companies announced they were building browsers," he reminisces. "There's an interesting déjà vu going on now with ichat."

ichat Inc., Busey's creation, is the leading provider of software that enables web surfers to converse by typing messages that can be instantly read on computer screens around the globe. While chat is infamous as a way for the sex-starved to play out fantasies, it has also become a key part of doing business on the Web. Sites that add chat to their offerings have found that traffic rises and visitors stick around longer.

That's important to corporate advertisers looking to make an impression on the Web. Even more valuable is chat's ability to give users a sense of community. A bicycling web site that offers nothing but products and articles about tours is little more than a catalogue; add chat, and it becomes a meeting place, the digital equivalent of the neighborhood bike shop. That's a site worth sponsoring.

Anyone with a web browser can download ichat's software free from the company web site at www.ichat.com. According to ichat, three million people have done so. ichat makes its money when other sites buy the server software to host and organize chats. Customers include Yahoo!, Time Warner, Universal Studios, and the Sporting News.

Unfortunately for Busey, ichat's success has not gone unnoticed. The competitors that keep him up at night are America Online and Microsoft. AOL provides free software that allows its millions of subscribers to chat with anyone on the Net who downloads the same program. Microsoft has integrated chat capability in its server software for corporate intranets.

To stave off these rivals, Busey is pushing ichat into the financial marketplace, selling to brokerages like Merrill Lynch, which will use the products to communicate with customers and alert them to news affecting their portfolios. He has also engineered a deal with IBM in which Big Blue's Lotus division will bundle ichat's software with its Internet-ready version of Notes. When you're up against Microsoft, it helps to have allies like that.

a. What is the value of Internet chat systems at business web sites?

b. Why has ichat been successful? What challenges do they face? How are they trying to meet these challenges?

c. Download chat software from ichat's web site, unless you already have a chat program in your browser or on your system.

d. Surf to several business web sites that have chat rooms, such as companies like K-Swiss, Kendall-Jackson Wines, and Nations Bank that were mentioned in the chapter. Compare the chat room experience to newsgroup discussion forums. Which do you prefer? Which has more business value and potential for a company? Explain your reasoning.

Source: Adapted from Rick Tetzeli, "Cool Companies," *Fortune*, July 7, 1997, p. 94 © 1997 by Time Inc. All rights reserved.

3. Premier Products Global Web Site Management

Premier Products is an international company with a number of sales offices throughout the world. To provide World Wide Web access to all of Premier's customers in their native languages, Premier Products has decided to offer local web sites based at its various sales offices and managed by local web masters.

You have been asked to maintain a file to track the development and operation of these sites.

City	Country	Web Master	Last Update	Size of Site
Berlin	Germany			0.00
Boston	United States	Jones, J.	15-Jul-99	48.50
Brussels	Belgium	Law, P.		0.00
Cairo	Egypt	Palmer, R.	25-Jun-99	15.00
Denver	United States	Davis, R.	18-Aug-99	52.50
Honolulu	United States			0.00
Mexico City	Mexico	Gomez, J.	14-Aug-99	65.50
Paris	France	Levin, J.	12-Aug-98	17.00
San Francisco	United States	Tower, P.	02-Sep-98	15.50
São Paulo	Brazil	Wentz, J.		0.00
Tokyo	Japan	Chen, A.	15-Mar-99	72.50
Toronto	Canada	Walls, M.	18-Sep-98	45.00

Management wants to know who is responsible for each site (the web master), when each site was last updated, and the size of each site as measured by the size of the site's file in megabytes.

The sites are in various stages of completion and some sites do not yet have a web master assigned. The sample data show the type of information that is needed and should be used in developing your database.

a. Create a database table to store the set of sample data.

b. Print a report showing all available data for each city that has a completed web site. Sort the data in your report in descending order based on the date the web site was last updated.

c. Run a query and print out a listing of all sites that have a web master but do not have a web site that has been updated since the end of 1998.

4. Firm and Industry Financial Analysis

Most large firms now have financial information for investors (annual reports, financial statements, etc.) available on the World Wide Web. Select an industry of interest to you and a prominent firm in that industry that you would like to investigate. (If parts c and d of this exercise have been assigned, your instructor will have assigned you to a team and the team will get together to select the industry to be investigated and to assign a firm for each member to investigate.)

Go to the web site of the firm you are investigating and obtain information about financial operations including at least net sales (or net revenue) and net after-tax income for the three most recent years available. Also, read the company's annual report and search the Web for current information affecting your firm and its industry.

a. Create a simple spreadsheet with a chart highlighting trends in your firm's net revenue and net income. Include a projection for income for the next year.

b. Using a word processor, write a brief report describing the income statistics of your spreadsheet, discussing current trends affecting your firm, and justifying your projection of income for the upcoming year.

c. Exchange your spreadsheet and paper with the other members of your group via E-mail. Review the income data and analysis of the other firms provided by the other members of your group. If appropriate, revise your income projections and/or your description based on what you have learned from the other members of your group.

d. Work together to produce a group report that will contain a group-written industry overview, followed by the reports on individual firms. Use E-mail and any collaborative document creation software available to you in preparing the group report.

Review Quiz Answers

1. 20	6. 3	11. 8	16. 25	21. 15	26. 23	31. 33
2. 17	7. 4	12. 9	17. 11	22. 16	27. 24	32. 30
3. 21	8. 5	13. 31	18. 12	23. 18	28. 28	33. 32
4. 2	9. 6	14. 26	19. 13	24. 19	29. 29	
5. 1	10. 7	15. 10	20. 14	25. 22	30. 27	

Selected References

1. Anderson, Heidi. "The Rise of the Extranet." *PC Today*, February 1997

2. Andreessen, Marc. "The Networked Enterprise: Netscape Enterprise Vision and Product Roadmap." White Paper, Netscape Communications Corporation, 1997.

3. Baer, Tony. "Webcasting: Now Showing on the Company Channel." *Computerworld Intranets*, March 24, 1997.

4. Barksdale, Jim. "The Next Step: Extranets." *Netscape Columns: The Main Thing*, December 3, 1996.

5. Bernard, Ryan. *The Corporate Intranet.* New York: Wiley, 1996.

6. Bly, Bob. "Workflow: The Key to Increasing Business Productivity." Special Advertising Section, *Fortune*, March 17, 1997.

7. Bowles, Jerry. "The Web Within: The Next Generation Intranet." Special Advertising Supplement, *Fortune*, April 14, 1997.

8. Campbell, Ian. "The Intranet: Slashing the Cost of Doing Business." Research Report, International Data Corporation, 1996.

9. Chen, H.; P. Hsu; R. Orwig; L. Hoopes; and J. F. Nunamaker. "Automated Classification for Electronic Meetings." *Communications of the ACM*, October 1994.

10. Cole-Gomolski, Barb. "Chat Rooms Move into Board Rooms." *Computerworld*, November 3, 1997.

11. "Conversation Piece." In Technology Buyers Guide. *Fortune*, Winter 1998.

12. "Cooperative Computing." In Technology Buyers Guide. *Fortune*, Winter 1997.

13. Cox, Nancy. *Building and Managing a Web Services Team.* New York: Van Nostrand Reinhold, 1997.

14. Doolittle, Sean. "Intranets: The Next Level." *PC Today*, June 1997.

15. Fernandez, Tony. "Beyond the Browser." *NetWorker*, March/April 1997.

16. Fitzgerald, Michael. "Infrastructure: Firm Foundations." *Computerworld Intranets*, October 28, 1996.

17. Gagne, Cathleen. "Grapplin' with Groupware." *Computerworld*, September 30, 1996.

18. Gold, Elliot, and Stephen Shaw. "Enterprisewide Conferencing: The Era of Networked Teams." Special Advertising Supplement, *Fortune*, April 1997.

19. Gow, Kathleen. "Risk vs. Opportunity." The Premier 100 Supplement to *Computerworld*, February 24, 1997.

20. Haskin, David. "Suite Decisions." *Internet World*, December 1997.

21. Hills, Mellanie. *Intranet as Groupware.* New York: Wiley, 1997.

22. Hills, Mellanie. *Intranet Business Strategies.* New York: Wiley, 1997.

23. Holtz, Shel. *PC Week: The Intranet Advantage.* Emeryville, CA:Ziff-Davis Press, 1996.

24. Kalakota, Ravi, and Andrew Whinston. *Electronic Commerce: A Managers Guide.* Reading, MA: Addison-Wesley, 1997.

25. King, Nelson. "E-Mail Reinvents Itself." *Internet World*, November 1997.

26. LaPlante, Alice. "Think Small, Think Infinite." The Premier 100 Supplements to *Computerworld*, February 24, 1997.

27. Laube, Dave. "Global Village Helps US West Improve Customer Service." *Netscape Columns: Intranet Executive*, November 1, 1996.

28. Levitt, Lee. "Intranets: Internet Technologies Deployed behind the Fire Wall for Corporate Productivity." Research Paper, Process Software Corporation, 1996.

29. Maglitta, Joseph. "Net Gain, Net Pain." *Computerworld Intranets*, June 24, 1996.

30. Mankin, Don; Susan Cohen; and Tora Bikson. *Teams and Technology: Fulfilling the Promise of the New Organization*. Boston: Harvard Business School Press, 1996.

31. Nash, Kim. "Integrating Legacy Databases: Old Iron, New Links." *Computerworld Intranets*, September 23, 1996.

32. Neumann, Peter, and Lauren Weinstein. "Spam, Spam, Spam!" *Communications of the ACM*, June 1997.

33. O'Brien, Atiye. "Friday Intranet Focus." *Upside.com: Hot Private Companies*, Upside Publishing Company, 1996.

34. Panatera, Lawrence. "Intranet Strategies." *SIM Network*, April 1996.

35. Papows, Jeff. "Endquotes." *NetReady Adviser*, Winter 1997.

36. Perin, Constance. "Electronic Social Fields in Bureaucracies." *Communications of the ACM*, December 1991.

37. Phillips, Ronald. "The Entergy NET." *Netscape Columns: Intranet Executive*, November 1, 1996.

38. Reichard, Kevin. "Hosting Your Own Chat." *Internet World*, October 1997.

39. Scheier, Robert. "Distributor Uses News to Sell Web Ads." *Computerworld*, June 10, 1996.

40. Scheier, Robert. "Role Models: IS Must Lead Not Impede." *Computerworld Intranets*, August 26, 1996.

41. Strom, David. "Videoconferencing in Focus." *Internet World*, September 1997.

42. "Talking Pictures." In Technology Buyer's Guide. *Fortune*, Winter 1997.

43. "3M Takes Intranet Global with Netscape SuiteSpot." *Netscape Intranet Solutions*, 1996.

44. Truong, Lam H. "Planet LSI Fosters Global Communication and Collaboration." *Netscape Columns: Intranet Executive*, December 3, 1996.

45. Waltner, Charles. "Intranets: Building Better Links." *Communications Week*, November 11, 1996.

Chapter

8

Information Systems

for Managerial

Decision Support

Chapter Highlights

Section I
Management Information and Decision Support Systems
Introduction
Real World Case: Lexis-Nexis Inc.: Using a Data Warehouse and Web-Based Tools for Decision Support
Management Information Systems
Online Analytical Processing
Decision Support Systems
Using Decision Support Systems
Executive Information Systems

Section II
Artificial Intelligence Technologies in Business
Real World Case: Dow Jones and Charles Schwab & Co.: Web Applications of Intelligent Agents and Neural Nets
An Overview of Artificial Intelligence
Neural Networks
Fuzzy Logic Systems
Genetic Algorithms
Virtual Reality
Intelligent Agents
Expert Systems
Developing Expert Systems
The Value of Expert Systems

Learning Objectives

After reading and studying this chapter, you should be able to:

1. Identify the role and reporting alternatives of management information systems.

2. Describe how online analytical processing can meet key information needs of managers.

3. Explain the decision support system concept and how it differs from traditional management information systems.

4. Explain how executive information systems can support the information needs of executives and managers.

5. Identify how neural networks, fuzzy logic, genetic algorithms, virtual reality, and intelligent agents can be used in business.

6. Give examples of several ways expert systems can be used in business decision-making situations.

Management Information and Decision Support Systems

Introduction

Previous chapters of this text have emphasized that information systems can support the diverse information and decision-making needs of managers. In this section, we will explore in more detail how this is accomplished by management information, decision support, and executive information systems. We will concentrate our attention on how information technology has significantly strengthened the role information systems play in supporting the decision-making activities of managerial end users.

Analyzing Lexis-Nexis

Read the Real World Case on Lexis-Nexis on the next page. We can learn a lot from this case about how data warehouse and intranet technologies are changing the face of traditional information systems for managerial information and decision support. See Figure 8.1.

When Lexis-Nexis began offering information products over the Web, it began to change the firm's customer mix and the selling effort required. So the company needed a new decision support technology strategy.

Lexis-Nexis built a customer-based data warehouse and then bought web-based software that could access and analyze warehouse data for decision support. Now the company's analysts and salespeople can use web browsers and the corporate intranet to analyze the information services used by their customers. This new DSS approach

Figure 8.1

Pam Dunsky, vice president of information systems at Lexis-Nexis, led the development of a web-based decision support system.

Source: Ted Rice.

Lexis-Nexis Inc.: Using a Data Warehouse and Web-Based Tools for Decision Support

Whenever Bill Gates talks about Microsoft's own intranet, which spans 2,000 servers and connects 26,000 employees, he talks about wanting bad news to travel fast. Company executives need to know what's going on so they can make changes on the fly. Good news shouldn't require much behavioral change; bad news might.

In simpler days, company executives might find out what's going on by checking ledgers, walking through a warehouse, or talking to the guys in engineering. Today, the information we need is buried somewhere in the great googolplex of data spawned by our modern computer systems. It's in millions of cells in the thousands of rows and tables in hundreds of relational databases.

A common approach to digging out the relevant data is to build a data warehouse that taps into and consolidates the data from operational and transaction systems and their databases. Then a company might overlay analytical decision support applications on top of that, or build data marts that could sit on top of the data warehouse to make it easier to pull up application-specific information for users. Either way, it's still a chore.

Lexis-Nexis was determined not to fall into the swamp that such a data warehouse project can become. The Dayton, Ohio–based provider of legal and news documents wanted to know more about its 1.7 million subscribers. But the company's information technology staff knew what a quagmire a large warehouse could turn into. So the company started the project with simple goals that included a small data warehouse and web-based access for users, and had the first working pieces in place in three months.

"We are taking our present analytical reporting system and rebuilding it as a customer-centric warehouse with web browser–based reporting tools for analyzing customer information so that we can better understand and predict customers' needs," said Pam Dunsky, vice president of information systems at Lexis-Nexis. "This combination gives us a very scalable reporting platform, with a better distinction between our operational and analytical data and applications. And this technology gives us a good place to start," Dunsky said.

"Our new subscribers will grow geometrically with web-based access to our information services," explained Keith Hawk, vice president of sales for the Nexis division of Lexis-Nexis. "And therefore our business model is changing from selling primarily to organizations to selling to individual users."

To track those new customers, Lexis-Nexis replaced its old decision support system—a thicket of legacy systems and an IBM DB2 database—with new DSS tools and an NCR Teradata database management system. The new customer data warehouse lets 475 salespeople and in-house analysts use the corporate intranet and web browsers to look up daily detailed customer usage data.

The type of data that company's salespeople sort through and analyze includes subscriber usage patterns—what they look up, what sources they use most often, when they're connecting—along with customer contract details.

To get to that data, Lexis-Nexis uses decision support software from MicroStrategy Inc. Field sales representatives who need ad hoc reporting capabilities use Micro-Strategy DSS WebPE, a web-based reporting tool. Power users, such as market research analysts, use DSS Agent, an analytical modeling tool with web access, to closely analyze and model business processes. Either way, the new approach provides a big improvement in decision support over the previous analytical reporting system.

Case Study Questions

1. What is the role of a data warehouse in decision support systems? Use Lexis-Nexis as an example.

2. What are the advantages of using a corporate intranet and web browser access in a decision support system?

3. What is the business value of the Lexis-Nexis DSS?

Source: Adapted from John Gantz, "The New World of Enterprise Reporting Is Here," *Computerworld*, February 1, 1999, p. 34; and Stewart Deck, "Data Warehouse Project Starts Simply," *Computerworld*, February 15, 1999, p. 63. Copyright 1999 by Computerworld, Inc., Framingham, MA 01701. Reprinted from *Computerworld*.

should help to improve sales efforts, as well as help management design new sales strategies and information products to offer to a new generation of customers.

Information, Decisions, and Management

Figure 8.2 emphasizes that the type of information required by decision makers is directly related to the **level of management decision making** and the amount of structure in the decision situations they face. You should realize that the framework of the classic *managerial pyramid* shown in Figure 8.2 applies even in today's *downsized* organizations and *flattened* or nonhierarchical organizational structures. Levels of management decision making still exist, but their size, shape, and participants continue to change as today's fluid organizational structures evolve. Thus, the levels of managerial decision making that must be supported by information technology in a successful organization are:

- **Strategic Management.** Typically, a board of directors and an executive committee of the CEO and top executives develop overall organizational goals, strategies, policies, and objectives as part of a strategic planning process. They also monitor the strategic performance of the organization and its overall direction in the political, economic, and competitive business environment.

- **Tactical Management.** Increasingly self-directed teams as well as business unit managers develop short- and medium-range plans, schedules, and budgets and specify the policies, procedures, and business objectives for their subunits of the organization. They also allocate resources and monitor the performance of their organizational subunits, including departments, divisions, process teams, project teams, and other workgroups.

- **Operational Management.** The members of self-directed teams or operating managers develop short-range plans such as weekly production schedules. They direct the use of resources and the performance of tasks according to procedures and within budgets and schedules they establish for the teams and other workgroups of the organization.

Figure 8.2

Information requirements of decision makers. The type of information required by directors, executives, managers, and members of self-directed teams is directly related to the level of management decision making involved and the structure of decision situations they face.

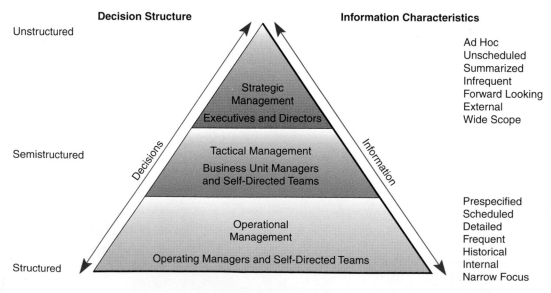

Figure 8.3   Examples of decisions by the type of decision structure and by level of management.

Decision Structure	Operational Management	Tactical Management	Strategic Management
Unstructured		Business process reengineering	New business planning
	Cash management	Work group performance analysis	Company reorganization
Semistructured	Credit management	Employee performance appraisal	Product planning
	Production scheduling	Capital budgeting	Mergers and acquisitions
	Daily work assignment	Program budgeting	Site location
Structured	Inventory control	Program control	

Decision Structure

Decisions made at the operational management level tend to be more *structured*, those at the tactical level more *semistructured*, and those at the strategic management level more *unstructured*. Structured decisions involve situations where the procedures to follow when a decision is needed can by specified in advance. The inventory reorder decisions faced by most businesses are a typical example. Unstructured decisions involve decision situations where it is not possible to specify in advance most of the decision procedures to follow. At most, many decision situations are semistructured. That is, some decision procedures can be prespecified, but not enough to lead to a definite recommended decision. For example, decisions involved in starting a new line of products or making major changes to employee benefits would probably range from unstructured to semistructured. Figure 8.3 provides a variety of examples of business decisions by type of decision structure and level of management.

Therefore, information systems must be designed to produce a variety of information products to meet the changing needs of decision makers throughout an organization. For example, decision makers at the strategic management level require more summarized, ad hoc, unscheduled reports, forecasts, and external intelligence to support their more unstructured planning and policy-making responsibilities. Decision makers at the operational management level, on the other hand, may require more prespecified internal reports emphasizing detailed current and historical data comparisons that support their more structured responsibilities in day-to-day operations.

Providing information and support for all levels of management decision making is thus no easy task. Conceptually, several major types of information systems are needed: (1) management information systems, (2) decision support systems, and (3) executive information systems. Developing such **management support systems** has been one of the primary thrusts of the business use of information technology.

Management Information Systems

Management information systems were the original type of management support systems, and are still a major category of information system. An MIS produces information products that support many of the day-to-day decision-making needs of management. Reports, displays, and responses produced by such systems provide information that managers have specified in advance as adequately meeting their information needs. Such predefined information products satisfy the information needs of decision makers at the operational and tactical levels of the organization who are faced with more structured types of decision situations. For example, sales managers rely heavily on sales analysis reports to evaluate differences in performance among salespeople who sell the same types of products to the same types of customers. They have a pretty good idea of the kinds of information about sales results they need to manage sales performance effectively.

Managers and other decision makers use an MIS to request information at their networked workstations that supports their decision-making activities. This information takes the form of periodic, exception, and demand reports and immediate responses to inquiries. Web browsers, application programs, and database management software provide access to information in the intranet and other operational databases of the organization. Remember, operational databases are maintained by transaction processing systems. Data about the business environment are obtained from Internet or extranet databases when necessary.

Management Reporting Alternatives

Management information systems provide a variety of information products to managers. Four major reporting alternatives are provided by such systems. Figure 8.4 is an example of a push reporting alternative.

- **Periodic Scheduled Reports.** This traditional form of providing information to managers uses a prespecified format designed to provide managers with information on a regular basis. Typical examples of such periodic scheduled reports are daily or weekly sales analysis reports and monthly financial statements.

- **Exception Reports.** In some cases, reports are produced only when exceptional conditions occur. In other cases, reports are produced periodically but contain information only about these exceptional conditions. For example, a credit manager can be provided with a report that contains only information on customers who exceed their credit limits. Exception reporting reduces *information overload*, instead of overwhelming decision makers with periodic detailed reports of business activity.

- **Demand Reports and Responses.** Information is available whenever a manager demands it. For example, web browsers and DBMS query languages and report

Figure 8.4

Web-based software can push selected information to business managers and specialists on corporate intranets.

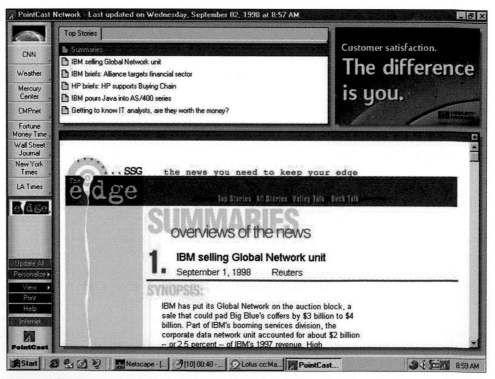

Courtesy of PointCast Incorporated.

Figure 8.5 An example of the push components in a marketing intelligence information system.

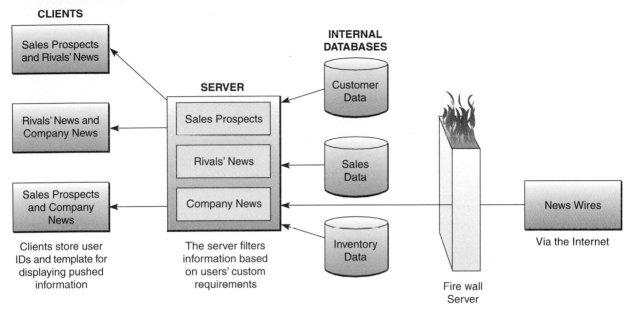

Source: Adapted from Robert Scheier, "Will 'Push' Pan Out?" *Computerworld*, February 17, 1997, p. 68. Copyright 1997 by Computerworld, Inc., Framingham, MA 01701. Reprinted from *Computerworld*.

generators enable managers at PC workstations to get immediate responses or find and obtain customized reports as a result of their requests for the information they need. Thus, managers do not have to wait for periodic reports to arrive as scheduled.

- **Push Reporting.** Information is *pushed* to a manager's networked workstation. As we discussed in Chapter 7, many companies are using webcasting software to selectively broadcast reports and other information to the networked PCs of managers and specialists over their corporate intranets. See Figure 8.5.

Online Analytical Processing

At a recent stockholder meeting, the CEO of PepsiCo, D. Wayne Calloway, said: "Ten years ago I could have told you how Doritos were selling west of the Mississippi. Today, not only can I tell you how well Doritos sell west of the Mississippi, I can also tell you how well they are selling in California, in Orange County, in the town of Irvine, in the local Von's supermarket, in the special promotion, at the end of Aisle 4, on Thursdays" [37].

The competitive and dynamic nature of today's global business environment is driving demands by business managers and analysts for information systems that can provide fast answers to complex business queries. The IS industry has responded to these demands with developments like the analytical databases, data marts, data warehouses, data mining techniques, and multidimensional database structures introduced in Chapter 5, and with specialized servers and software products that support **online analytical processing** (OLAP). Online analytical processing is a capability of management, decision support, and executive information systems that enables managers and analysts to interactively examine and manipulate large amounts of detailed and consolidated data from many perspectives. OLAP involves analyzing complex relationships among thousands or even millions of data items stored in multidimensional databases to discover patterns, trends, and exception

Figure 8.6 Online analytical processing may involve the use of specialized servers and multidimensional databases. OLAP provides fast answers to complex queries posed by managers and analysts using management, decision support, and executive information systems.

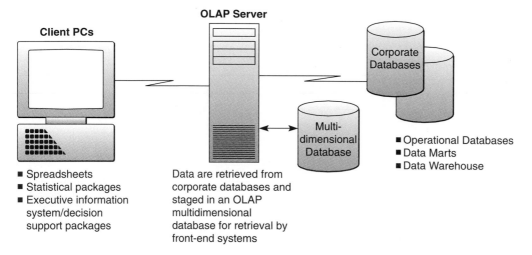

OLAP Server

Client PCs

Corporate
Databases

Multi-
dimensional
Database

- Operational Databases
- Data Marts
- Data Warehouse

- Spreadsheets
- Statistical packages
- Executive information
  system/decision
  support packages

Data are retrieved from
corporate databases and
staged in an OLAP
multidimensional
database for retrieval by
front-end systems

conditions. An OLAP session takes place online in realtime, with rapid responses to a manager's or analyst's queries, so that their analytical or decision-making process is undisturbed [17]. See Figure 8.6.

Online analytical processing involves several basic analytical operations, including consolidation, "drill-down," and "slicing and dicing" [14]. See Figure 8.7.

- **Consolidation.** Consolidation involves the aggregation of data. This can involve simple roll-ups or complex groupings involving interrelated data. For example, sales offices can be rolled up to districts and districts rolled up to regions.

- **Drill-Down.** OLAP can go in the reverse direction and automatically display detail data that comprise consolidated data. This is called drill-down. For example, the sales by individual products or sales reps that make up a region's sales totals could be easily accessed.

- **Slicing and Dicing.** Slicing and dicing refers to the ability to look at the database from different viewpoints. One slice of the sales database might show all sales of product type within regions. Another slice might show all sales by sales channel within each product type. Slicing and dicing is often performed along a time axis in order to analyze trends and find patterns.

Example

A marketing manager or analyst might use online analytical processing to access a multidimensional database consisting of sales data that have been aggregated by region, product type, and sales channel. In a typical OLAP query, a manager might access a multigigabyte/multiyear sales database in order to find all product sales in each region for each product type. After reviewing the results, the manager might refine his or her query to find the sales volume for each marketing channel within each sales region and product classification. Finally, the marketing manager might perform quarter-to-quarter or year-to-year comparisons of each marketing channel. ●

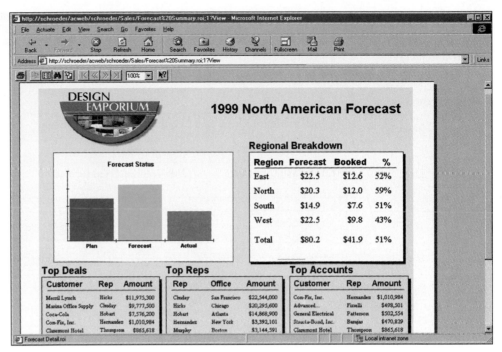

Figure 8.7

An example of a display produced by an online analytical processing package.

Courtesy of Actuate.

OLAP at MasterCard International

MasterCard International developed OLAP software called Market Advisor, which enables members to query a data warehouse and drill down into information to analyze transactions and trends online. Market Advisor also provides a 13-month historical database, extended report graphing, and triggered marketing alerts based on above- or below-average merchant or cardholder activity.

In a typical application marketing analysts can examine a trend in spending at aggregate levels for a particular merchant category, such as hardware store, restaurant, car rental agency, or gas station. By using Market Advisor, analysts can determine which states or provinces accounted for the volume and identify which merchants accounted for the greatest volume. An analyst can even drill into the data to find which cardholder accounts were used at a particular store over a period of time. The analyst can then find common spending patterns among certain categories of cardholders, and tailor marketing promotions appropriately [18].

Decision Support Systems

Decision support systems are a major category of management support systems. They are computer-based information systems that provide interactive information support to managers during the decision-making process. Decision support systems use (1) analytical models, (2) specialized databases, (3) a decision maker's own insights and judgments, and (4) an interactive, computer-based modeling process to support the making of semistructured and unstructured decisions by individual managers. See Figure 8.8.

Example

An example might help at this point. Sales managers typically rely on management information systems to produce sales analysis reports. These reports contain sales performance figures by product line, salesperson, sales region, and so on. A decision

Figure 8.8

Comparing decision support systems and management information systems. Note the major differences in the information and decision support they provide.

	Management Information Systems	Decision Support Systems
● Decision support provided	Provide information about the performance of the organization	Provide information and decision support techniques to analyze specific problems or opportunities
● Information form and frequency	Periodic, exception, demand, and push reports and responses	Interactive inquiries and responses
● Information format	Prespecified, fixed format	Ad hoc, flexible, and adaptable format
● Information processing methodology	Information produced by extraction and manipulation of business data	Information produced by analytical modeling of business data

support system, on the other hand, would also interactively show a sales manager the effects on sales performance of changes in a variety of factors (such as promotion expense and salesperson compensation). The DSS could then use several criteria (such as expected gross margin and market share) to evaluate and rank several alternative combinations of sales performance factors. ●

Therefore, DSS are designed to be ad hoc, quick-response systems that are initiated and controlled by managerial end users. Decision support systems are thus able to directly support the specific types of decisions and the personal decision-making styles and needs of individual managers.

DSS Models and Software

Unlike management information systems, decision support systems rely on **model bases** as well as databases as vital system resources. A DSS model base is a software component that consists of models used in computational and analytical routines that mathematically express relationships among variables. For example, a spreadsheet program might contain models that express simple accounting relationships among variables, such as Revenue − Expenses = Profit. Or a DSS model base could include models and analytical techniques used to express much more complex relationships. For example, it might contain linear programming models, multiple regression forecasting models, and capital budgeting present value models. Such models may be stored in the form of spreadsheet models or templates, or statistical and mathematical programs and program modules. See Figure 8.9.

DSS software packages can combine model components to create integrated models that support specific types of decisions. DSS software typically contains built-in analytical modeling routines and also enables you to build your own models. Many DSS packages are now available in microcomputer and web-enabled versions (e.g., PC/FOCUS, IFPS Personal, and Decision-Web). Of course, electronic spreadsheet packages also provide some of the model building (spreadsheet models) and analytical modeling (what-if and goal-seeking analysis) offered by more powerful DSS software. See Figure 8.10.

Figure 8.9

Components of a marketing decision support system. Note the hardware, software, model, data, and network resources involved.

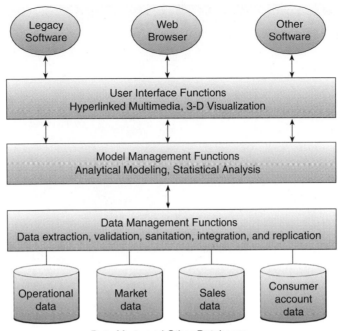

Source: Adapted from Ravi Kalakota and Andrew Whinston, *Electronic Commerce: A Manager's Guide* (Reading, MA: Addison-Wesley, 1997), p. 343. © 1997 by Addison-Wesley Publishing Company, Inc. Reprinted by permission of Addison-Wesley Longman, Inc.

Geographic Information Systems

Geographic information systems (GIS) are a special category of DSS that integrate computer graphics and geographic databases with other DSS features. A geographic information system is a DSS that constructs and displays maps and other graphics displays that support decisions affecting the geographic distribution of people and other resources. Many companies are using GIS technology to choose new retail store locations, optimize distribution routes, or analyze the demographics of their target audiences. For example, companies like Levi Strauss, Arby's, Consolidated Rail, and Federal Express use GIS packages to integrate maps, graphics, and other geographic data with business data from spreadsheets and statistical packages. GIS software for microcomputers such as MapInfo and Atlas GIS is used for most business GIS

Figure 8.10

Examples of special-purpose DSS packages.

● **Retail:** Information Advantage and Unisys offer the Category Management Solution Suite, an OLAP decision support system and industry-specific data model.
● **Insurance:** Platinum Technology offers RiskAdvisor, a data warehouse and decision support system whose data model stores information in insurance-industry specific tables designed for optimal query performance.
● **Telecom:** NCR and SABRE Decision Technologies have joined forces to create the NCR Customer Retention program for the communications industry including data marts for telephone companies to use for decision support in managing customer loyalty, quality of service, network management, fraud, and marketing.

Source: Adapted from Charles B. Darling, "Ease Implementation Woes with Packaged Data Marts," *Datamation*, March 1997, p. 103. © 1997 by Cahners Publishing Co.

Figure 8.11

Using a geographic
information system
package to analyze the
risk of earthquakes on
insurance decisions
in California.

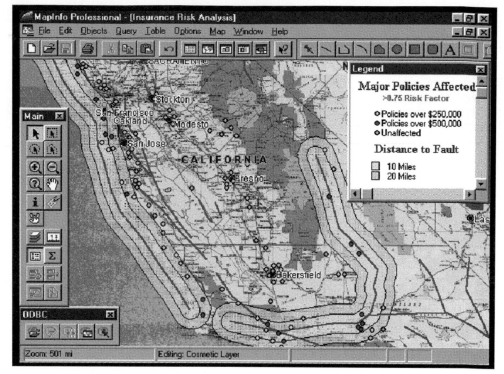

Courtesy of MapInfo, Inc.

applications. The use of the GIS for decision support has also expanded with the
mapping capabilities that have been integrated into electronic packages [26]. See Figure 8.11.

DSS at PepsiCo	PepsiCo and Sedgwick James Inc., the world's second largest insurance broker, developed a risk management DSS to help minimize PepsiCo's losses from accidents, theft, and other causes. Every week, Sedgwick loads the latest casualty claims data from the nation's leading insurance carriers into a DSS database resident on IBM RS/6000 servers in the PepsiCo intranet. The database is then accessed by managers and analysts using desktop PCs and remote laptops equipped with the INFORM risk management system. Both the RS/6000 servers and local PCs use Information Builders' middleware to provide PepsiCo managers and business analysts with transparent data access from a variety of hardware/software configurations.
	The INFORM risk management system combines the analytical power of FOCUS decision support modeling with the graphical analysis capabilities of FOCUS/EIS for Windows. As a result, PepsiCo managers at all levels can pinpoint critical trends, drill down for detailed backup information, identify potential problems, and plan ways to minimize risks and maximize profits [30].

Using Decision Support Systems

Using a decision support system involves an interactive **analytical modeling** process.
For example, using a DSS software package for decision support may result in a series
of displays in response to alternative what-if changes entered by a manager. This differs from the demand responses of information reporting systems, since managers are

Figure 8.12

Activities and examples of the major types of analytical modeling.

Type of Analytical Modeling	Activities and Examples
What-if analysis	Observing how changes to selected variables affect other variables. *Example:* What if we cut advertising by 10 percent? What would happen to sales?
Sensitivity analysis	Observing how repeated changes to a single variable affect other variables. *Example:* Let's cut advertising by $100 repeatedly so we can see its relationship to sales.
Goal-seeking analysis	Making repeated changes to selected variables until a chosen variable reaches a target value. *Example:* Let's try increases in advertising until sales reach $1 million.
Optimization analysis	Finding an optimum value for selected variables, given certain constraints. *Example:* What's the best amount of advertising to have, given our budget and choice of media?

not demanding prespecified information. Rather, they are exploring possible alternatives. Thus, they do not have to specify their information needs in advance. Instead, they use the DSS to find the information they need to help them make a decision. That is the essence of the decision support system concept.

Using a decision support system involves four basic types of analytical modeling activities: (1) what-if analysis, (2) sensitivity analysis, (3) goal-seeking analysis, and (4) optimization analysis. Let's briefly look at each type of analytical modeling that can be used for decision support. See Figure 8.12.

What-If Analysis

In **what-if analysis,** an end user makes changes to variables, or relationships among variables, and observes the resulting changes in the values of other variables. For example, if you were using a spreadsheet, you might change a revenue amount (a variable) or a tax rate formula (a relationship among variables) in a simple financial spreadsheet model. Then you could command the spreadsheet program to instantly recalculate all affected variables in the spreadsheet. A managerial user would be very interested in observing and evaluating any changes that occurred to the values in the spreadsheet, especially to a variable such as net profit after taxes. To many managers, net profit after taxes is an example of *the bottom line*, that is, a key factor in making many types of decisions. This type of analysis would be repeated until the manager was satisfied with what the results revealed about the effects of various possible decisions. Figure 8.13 is an example of what-if analysis.

Sensitivity Analysis

Sensitivity analysis is a special case of what-if analysis. Typically, the value of only one variable is changed repeatedly, and the resulting changes on other variables are observed. So sensitivity analysis is really a case of what-if analysis involving repeated changes to only one variable at a time. Some DSS packages automatically make repeated small changes to a variable when asked to perform sensitivity analysis. Typically, sensitivity analysis is used when decision makers are uncertain about the assumptions made in estimating the value of certain key variables. In our previous spreadsheet example, the value of revenue could be changed repeatedly in small increments, and

Figure 8.13

What-if analysis involves the development of alternative scenarios based on changing assumptions as part of the decision-making process.

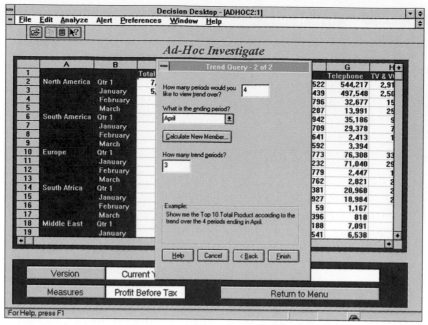

Courtesy of Lotus Development Corporation.

the effects on other spreadsheet variables observed and evaluated. This would help a manager understand the impact of various revenue levels on other factors involved in decisions being considered.

Goal-Seeking Analysis

Goal-seeking analysis reverses the direction of the analysis done in what-if and sensitivity analysis. Instead of observing how changes in a variable affect other variables, goal-seeking analysis (also called *how can* analysis) sets a target value (a goal) for a variable and then repeatedly changes other variables until the target value is achieved. For example, you could specify a target value (goal) of $2 million for net profit after taxes for a business venture. Then you could repeatedly change the value of revenue or expenses in a spreadsheet model until a result of $2 million is achieved. Thus, you would discover what amount of revenue or level of expenses the business venture needs to achieve in order to reach the goal of $2 million in after-tax profits. Therefore, this form of analytical modeling would help answer the question, "How can we achieve $2 million in net profit after taxes?" instead of the question, "What happens if we change revenue or expenses?" Thus, goal-seeking analysis is another important method of decision support.

Optimization Analysis

Optimization analysis is a more complex extension of goal-seeking analysis. Instead of setting a specific target value for a variable, the goal is to find the optimum value for one or more target variables, given certain constraints. Then one or more other variables are changed repeatedly, subject to the specified constraints, until the best values for the target variables are discovered. For example, you could try to determine the highest possible level of profits that could be achieved by varying the values for selected revenue sources and expense categories. Changes to such variables could be subject to constraints such as the limited capacity of a production process or limits to available financing. Optimization, typically, is accomplished by special-purpose software packages for optimization techniques such as linear programming, or by advanced DSS generators.

Executive Information Systems

Executive information systems (EIS) are information systems that combine many of the features of management information systems and decision support systems. However, when they were first developed, their focus was on meeting the strategic information needs of top management. Thus, the first goal of executive information systems was to provide top executives with immediate and easy access to information about a firm's *critical success factors* (CSFs), that is, key factors that are critical to accomplishing an organization's strategic objectives. For example, the executives of a department store chain would probably consider factors such as its sales promotion efforts and its product line mix to be critical to its survival and success.

In an EIS, information is presented in forms tailored to the preferences of the executives using the system. For example, most executive information systems stress the use of a graphical user interface and graphics displays that can be customized to the information preferences of executives using the EIS. Other information presentation methods used by an EIS include exception reporting and trend analysis. The ability to *drill down*, which allows executives to quickly retrieve displays of related information at lower levels of detail, is another important capability. And of course, the growth of Internet and intranet technologies has added web browsing to the list of EIS capabilities.

Figure 8.14 shows actual displays provided by the Commander executive information system. Notice how simple and brief these displays are. Also note how they provide executives with the ability to drill down quickly to lower levels of detail in areas of particular interest to them. Besides the drill-down capability, the Commander EIS also stresses trend analysis and exception reporting. Thus, an executive can quickly discover the direction key factors are heading and the extent to which critical factors are deviating from expected results [36].

Rationale for EIS

Studies have shown that top executives get the information they need from many sources. These include letters, memos, periodicals, and reports produced manually or by computer systems. Other major sources of executive information are meetings, telephone calls, and social activities. Thus, much of a top executive's information comes from noncomputer sources. Computer-generated information has not played a major role in meeting many top executives' information needs [36].

Therefore, computer-based executive information systems were developed to meet the information needs of top management that were not being met by other forms of MIS. IS specialists have capitalized on advances in computer technology to develop attractive, easy-to-use ways to provide executives with the information they need. Executive information systems are still faced with resistance by some executives, are plagued by high costs, and have had many publicized failures. However, their use is growing rapidly. EIS have spread into the ranks of middle management as more executives come to recognize their feasibility and benefits, and as less-expensive systems for client/server networks and corporate intranets have become available.

For example, according to one study, 25 percent of the world's corporate executives are likely to be using an EIS. One popular EIS software package reports that only 3 percent of its users are top executives. Another example is the EIS of Conoco, one of the world's largest oil companies. Conoco's EIS is used by most senior managers, and by over 4,000 employees located at corporate headquarters in Houston and throughout the world [4, 33, 36].

Figure 8.14

Displays provided by the Commander executive information system. Note the simplicity and clarity in which key information is provided, and the ability to drill down to lower levels of detail.

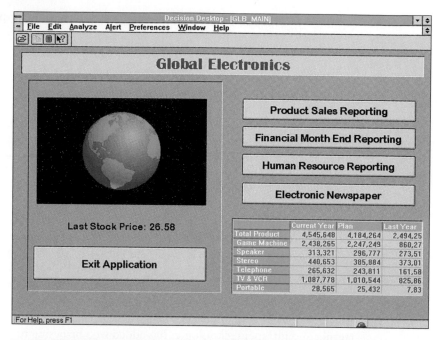

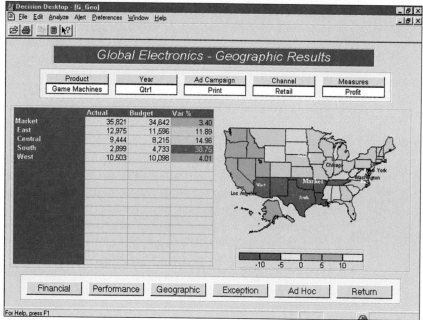

Courtesy of Comshare, Inc.

Thus, executive information systems are becoming so widely used by managers, analysts, and other knowledge workers that they are sometimes humorously called "everyone's information systems." More popular alternative names are executive support systems (ESS) and enterprise information systems (EIS). These names also reflect the fact that more features, such as web browsing, electronic mail, groupware tools, and DSS and expert system capabilities, are being added to many systems to make them more useful to managers.

EIS at Conoco and KeyCorp

As we mentioned earlier, Conoco, Inc., has a widely used EIS. Conoco's EIS is a large system with 75 different applications and hundreds of screen displays. Senior executives and over 4,000 managers and analysts worldwide use EIS applications ranging from analyzing internal operations and financial results to viewing external events that affect the petroleum industry. Conoco's EIS is popular with its users and has resulted in improved employee productivity and decision making, and significant cost savings compared to alternative methods of generating information for managers and analysts [4].

KeyCorp is a large banking and financial services holding company. It developed Keynet, a corporate intranet that transformed their mainframe-based EIS into what they call "everyone's information system." Now more than 1,000 managers and analysts have access to 40 major business information areas within Keynet, ranging from sales and financial statistics to human resource management. And savings on printing and distribution costs have easily covered the $300,000 development cost of the project [19].

Section II   Artificial Intelligence Technologies in Business

Artificial intelligence is making its way back to the mainstream of corporate technology. Designed to leverage the capabilities of humans rather than replace them, today's AI technology enables an extraordinary array of applications that forge new connections among people, computers, knowledge, and the physical world. AI-enabled applications are at work in information distribution and retrieval, database mining, product design, manufacturing, inspection, training, user support, surgical planning, resource scheduling, and complex resource management.

Indeed, for anyone who schedules, plans, allocates resources, designs new products, uses the Internet, develops software, is responsible for product quality, is an investment professional, heads up IT, uses IT, or operates in any of a score of other capacities and arenas, new AI technologies already may be in place and providing competitive advantage [38].

Analyzing Dow Jones and Charles Schwab

Read the Real World Case on Dow Jones and Charles Schwab on the next page. We can learn a lot about the business value and challenges of using artificial intelligence technologies from this example. See Figure 8.15.

Dow Jones uses intelligent agent and other AI and information technologies to provide valuable information services to the hundreds of thousands of paying customers at their Dow Jones Interactive site. Topping the list is their Custom Clips service that uses artificial intelligence software to automatically sort through thousands of news stories and articles each day to selectively send to almost 600,000 customers via web pages or E-mail.

Figure 8.15

Tim Andrews, vice president of Enterprise Products at Dow Jones & Co., helped develop their Dow Jones Interactive service using intelligent agent and other AI technologies.

Courtesy of Dow Jones.

Dow Jones and Charles Schwab & Co.: Web Applications of Intelligent Agents and Neural Nets

Intelligent agents (also called software robots or "bots") and neural network software can help automate the process of searching through and evaluating reams of information on the Web. For example, web sites such as Amazon.com's Shop the Web, Excite's Jango.com, and MySimon's MySimon.com use agent technology to help users compare prices for fragrances, book titles, or other items on multiple sites.

Other types of agents can answer E-mail, conduct intelligent searches, or help users find news reports and useful sites based on stated preferences. For example, dozens of sites can show you the news, but Dow Jones & Co.'s Dow Jones Interactive (www.djinteractive.com) is different. Nearly 600,000 customers pay to search through stories from its 6,000 licensed and internal publications. That's a huge amount of data to filter and the company has applied intelligent agent and other artificial intelligence (AI) technologies to manage the task.

One of the site's most important features is Custom Clips, which allows users to create folders based on predefined topics—such as agribusiness or IBM—or to build their own using custom key words. When the site IS agent retrieves relevant articles, it can post them to a database-generated web page or send the stories to the user's E-mail address.

At the service's core lives software developed by Verity Inc. (www.verity.com) and Dow Jones, says Tim Andrews, vice president and editor for enterprise products at Dow Jones. Every word of the 40,000 stories sent to the service each day goes through the software, where it can be compared to the various searches users have requested.

The Verity software isn't the only piece of the puzzle. The product is surrounded by relational databases that store the indexed hits and the full text of every story. And there's an E-mail server that sends the requested data to the customers. Integrating all the products wasn't easy, Andrews says.

Verity's other agent and AI products include Agent Server, which monitors, filters, and publishes information for Internet and intranet web sites, and Information Server, which searches for, organizes, and publishes information on corporate intranets.

Automatic answering of E-mail is another popular application for agents and neural network software.

Companies on the Web now get lots of E-mail. Lots of complaints, questions, and kudos from customers. Electronic mail is fast and direct, and an increasing number of companies encourage its use in an effort to stay close to customers without spending a fortune on toll-free tele-

phone lines. And customers like E-mail because there's no per-minute charge and no holding for a customer service rep. As a consequence, however, companies are bombarded with hundreds of messages per day, each from a valued customer who expects a rapid response.

Enter Brightware and Aptex, two of the leading companies offering software that helps automate the process of answering E-mail as part of larger customer service applications. For example, Brightware searches for keywords in E-mails and answers them automatically or routes them to the proper person within a company. Aptex's Select Response uses "technology based on neural networks," says Gaylin Allbaugh, product manager for the company, "to automatically answer and route E-mail to the appropriate party with attached information related to any other E-mails that might have come in on the topic."

Both companies already include on their client lists some heavy hitters such as Charles Schwab, Pacific Bell Internet Services, and Chase Manhattan. Mary Kelley, vice president of database and relationship marketing at Schwab, says, "Given our business—we have over 900,000 online accounts, with about $87 billion under management—we have to deal with E-mail volume of 8,000–10,000 messages a week. Aptex Select Response lets us reduce head count significantly, and its categorization method for automatic E-mail response is more consistent than what people can do."

Case Study Questions

1. How effective are intelligent agents in electronic commerce? Check out the shopping agent web sites mentioned in the case to help you answer.

2. How would neural network technology help to automatically answer E-mail for companies like Charles Schwab? Visit the www.aptex.com/ site to help you answer.

3. Surf to the Dow Jones Interactive site. How else could AI technologies help them improve their site and its services?

Source: Adapted from Sharon Machris, "Agent Technology," *Computerworld*, March 22, 1999, p. 69; Christopher Lundquist, "Personalization in E-Commerce," *Computerworld*, March 22, 1999, pp. 74–77, Copyright 1999 by Computerworld, Inc., Framingham, MA 01701. Reprinted from *Computerworld*; Richard Schaffer, "Handling Customer Service on the Web," *Fortune*, March 1999, pp. 204–205, © 1999 by Time Inc. All rights reserved; Eric Hellweg, "No, Really. Urgent!" *Business 2.0*, January 1999, p. 109; and "What They Say," at www.aptex.com/, March 1999.

Charles Schwab & Co., on the other hand, relies on Aptex Select Response software, which uses neural network technology to screen and respond to E-mail. Schwab's application uses Select Response to automatically answer and route thousands of E-mails a week to the appropriate specialists in the organization.

An Overview of Artificial Intelligence

But what is artificial intelligence? **Artificial intelligence** (AI) is a field of science and technology based on disciplines such as computer science, biology, psychology, linguistics, mathematics, and engineering. The goal of AI is to develop computers that can think, as well as see, hear, walk, talk, and feel. A major thrust of artificial intelligence is the development of computer functions normally associated with human intelligence, such as reasoning, learning, and problem solving, as summarized in Figure 8.16. That's why the term *artificial intelligence* was coined by John McCarthy at MIT in 1956. Besides McCarthy, AI pioneers included Herbert Simon and Allen Newell at Carnegie-Mellon, Norbert Wiener and Marvin Minsky at MIT, Warren McCulloch and Walter Pitts at Illinois, Frank Rosenblatt at Cornell, Alan Turing at Manchester, Edward Feigenbaum at Stanford, Roger Shank at Yale, and many others [27].

Debate has raged around artificial intelligence since serious work in the field began in the 1950s. Not only technological, but moral and philosophical questions abound about the possibility of intelligent, thinking machines. For example, British AI pioneer Alan Turing in 1950 proposed a test for determining if machines could think. According to the Turing test, a computer could demonstrate intelligence if a human interviewer, conversing with an unseen human and an unseen computer, could not tell which was which [27].

Though much work has been done in many of the subgroups that fall under the AI umbrella, critics believe that no computer can truly pass the Turing test. They claim that developing intelligence to impart true humanlike capabilities to computers is simply not possible. But progress continues, and only time will tell if the ambitious goals of artificial intelligence will be achieved and equal the popular images found in science fiction.

The Domains of Artificial Intelligence

Figure 8.17 illustrates the major domains of AI research and development. Note that AI applications can be grouped under the three major areas of cognitive science, robotics, and natural interfaces, though these classifications do overlap each other, and other classifications can be used. Also note that expert systems are just one of many important AI applications. Let's briefly review each of these major areas of AI and

Attributes of intelligent behavior. AI is attempting to duplicate these capabilities in computer-based systems.

- Think and reason.
- Use reason to solve problems.
- Learn or understand from experience.
- Acquire and apply knowledge.
- Exhibit creativity and imagination.
- Deal with complex or perplexing situations.
- Respond quickly and successfully to new situations.
- Recognize the relative importance of elements in a situation.
- Handle ambiguous, incomplete, or erroneous information.

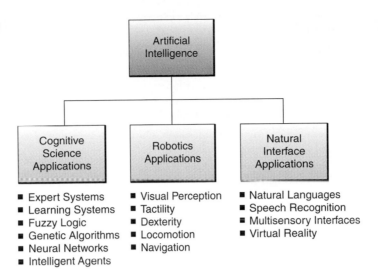

The major application areas of artificial intelligence. Note that the many applications of AI can be grouped into the three major areas of cognitive science, robotics, and natural interfaces.

some of their current technologies. Figure 8.18 outlines some of the latest developments in commercial applications of artificial intelligence.

Cognitive Science. This area of artificial intelligence is based on research in biology, neurology, psychology, mathematics, and many allied disciplines. It focuses on researching how the human brain works and how humans think and learn. The results of such research in *human information processing* are the basis for the development of a variety of computer-based applications in artificial intelligence.

Applications in the cognitive science area of AI include the development of *expert systems* and other *knowledge-based systems* that add a knowledge base and some reasoning capability to information systems. Also included are *adaptive learning systems* that can modify their behaviors based on information they acquire as they operate. Chess-playing systems are primitive examples of such applications, though many more applications are being implemented. *Fuzzy logic* systems can process data that are incomplete or ambiguous, that is, *fuzzy data*. Thus, they can solve unstructured problems with incomplete knowledge by developing approximate inferences and answers, as humans do. *Neural network* software can learn by processing sample problems and their solutions. As neural nets start to recognize patterns, they can begin to program themselves to solve such problems on their own. *Genetic algorithm* software uses Darwinian (survival of the fittest), randomizing, and other mathematical functions to simulate evolutionary processes that can generate increasingly better solutions to problems. And *intelligent agents* use expert system and other AI technologies to serve as software surrogates for a variety of end user applications.

Robotics. AI, engineering, and physiology are the basic disciplines of robotics. This technology produces robot machines with computer intelligence and computer-controlled, humanlike physical capabilities. This area thus includes applications designed to give robots the powers of sight, or visual perception; touch, or tactile capabilities; dexterity, or skill in handling and manipulation; locomotion, or the physical ability to move over any terrain; and navigation, or the intelligence to properly find one's way to a destination [27]. The use of robotics in computer-aided manufacturing was discussed in Chapter 6.

Figure 8.18

Examples of some of the latest commercial applications of AI.

Decision Support

- Intelligent work environment that will help you capture the *why* as well as the *what* of engineered design and decision making

- Intelligent human–computer interface (HCI) systems that can understand spoken language and gestures, and facilitate problem solving by supporting organizationwide collaborations to solve particular problems

- Situation assessment and resource allocation software for uses that range from airlines and airports to logistics centers

Information Retrieval

- AI-based intra- and Internet systems that distill tidal waves of information into simple presentations

- Natural language technology to retrieve any sort of online information, from text to pictures, videos, maps, and audio clips, in response to English questions

- Database mining for marketing trend analysis, financial forecasting, maintenance cost reduction, and more

Virtual Reality

- X-ray-like vision enabled by enhanced-reality visualization that allows brain surgeons to "see through" intervening tissue to operate, monitor, and evaluate disease progression

- Automated animation and haptic interfaces that allow users to interact with virtual objects via touch (i.e., medical students to "feel" what it's like to suture severed aortas)

Robotics

- Machine vision inspections systems for gauging, guiding, identifying, and inspecting products and providing competitive advantage in manufacturing

- Cutting-edge robotics systems from micro robots and hands and legs to cognitive robotic and trainable modular vision systems

Source: Adapted from Patrick Winston, "Rethinking Artificial Intelligence," Program Announcement: Massachusetts Institute of Technology, September 1997, p. 3.

Natural Interfaces. The development of natural interfaces is considered a major area of AI applications and is essential to the natural use of computers by humans. For example, the development of *natural languages* and speech recognition are major thrusts of this area of AI. Being able to talk to computers and robots in conversational human languages and have them "understand" us as easily as we understand each other is a goal of AI research. This involves research and development in linguistics, psychology, computer science, and other disciplines. This area of AI drives developments in the voice recognition and response technology discussed in Chapter 2 and the natural programming languages discussed in Chapter 3. Other natural interface research applications include the development of multisensory devices that use a variety of body movements to operate computers. This is related to the emerging application area of *virtual reality*. Virtual reality involves using multisensory human–computer interfaces that enable human users to experience computer-simulated objects, spaces, activities, and "worlds" as if they actually exist.

Neural Networks

Neural networks are computing systems modeled after the brain's meshlike network of interconnected processing elements, called *neurons*. Of course, neural networks are a lot simpler in architecture (the human brain is estimated to have over 100 billion neuron brain cells!). However, like the brain, the interconnected processors in a neural network operate in parallel and interact dynamically with each other. This enables the network to "learn" from data it processes. That is, it learns to recognize patterns and relationships in the data it processes. The more data examples it receives as input, the better it can learn to duplicate the results of the examples it processes. Thus, the neural network will change the strengths of the interconnections between the processing elements in response to changing patterns in the data it receives and the results that occur [7, 27].

For example, a neural network can be trained to learn which credit characteristics result in good or bad loans. Developers of a credit evaluation neural network could provide it with data from many examples of credit applications and loan results to process, and opportunities to adjust the signal strengths between its neurons. The neural network would continue to be trained until it demonstrated a high degree of accuracy in correctly duplicating the results of recent cases. At that point it would be trained enough to begin making credit evaluations of its own.

Neural networks can be implemented on microcomputers and other traditional computer systems by using software packages that simulate the activity of a neural network. Specialized neural network coprocessor circuit boards for PCs are also available that provide significantly greater processing power. In addition, special-purpose neural net microprocessor chips are being used in specific application areas such as military weapons systems, image processing, and voice recognition. However, most business applications depend primarily on neural net software packages to accomplish applications ranging from credit risk assessment to check signature verification, investment forecasting, data mining, and manufacturing quality control [7, 37]. See Figure 8.19.

Figure 8.19

A display of a data mining software package that uses neural network technology.

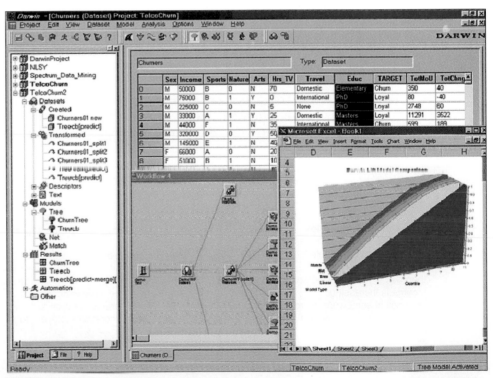

Courtesy of Thinking Machines.

Neural Nets at Infoseek	Infoseek has developed a targeted marketing service that more closely targets advertising on its Internet search engine to users' interests by keeping track of every search that a user makes. The service uses neural network technology from Aptex Software to observe all the searches users run every time they visit the InfoSeek search engine. The neural net software then calculates a numeric value, or "vector," that describes users' interests. InfoSeek uses that information to match users to the online ads it sells to advertisers on its Web search pages.
	Other commercial World Wide Web sites use this technology to build up the usefulness of their web sites or encourage repeat business. Many electronic commerce web sites use customizing software to track user behavior and predict what a user will be interested in seeing in the future. For example, Aptex has a version of its neural net software designed for sites that sell products and services online. Select-Cast for Commerce Servers analyzes customer buying patterns, and predicts products and services the customer will be likely to buy, based on past behavior [34].

Fuzzy Logic Systems

In spite of the funny name, **fuzzy logic** systems represent a small, but serious and growing, application of AI in business. Fuzzy logic is a method of reasoning that resembles human reasoning since it allows for approximate values and inferences (fuzzy logic) and incomplete or ambiguous data (fuzzy data) instead of relying only on *crisp data*, such as binary (yes/no) choices. For example, Figure 8.20 illustrates a partial set of rules (fuzzy rules) and a fuzzy SQL query for analyzing and extracting credit risk information on businesses that are being evaluated for selection as investments.

Notice how fuzzy logic uses terminology that is deliberately imprecise, such as *very high, increasing, somewhat decreased, reasonable,* and *very low.* This enables fuzzy systems to process incomplete data and quickly provide approximate, but acceptable, solutions to problems that are difficult for other methods to solve. Fuzzy logic queries of a database, such as the SQL query shown in Figure 8.20, promise to improve the extraction of data from business databases. Queries can be stated more naturally in words that are closer to the way business specialists think about the topic for which they want information [11, 23].

Fuzzy Logic in Business

Examples of applications of fuzzy logic are numerous in Japan, but rare in the United States. The United States has tended to prefer using AI solutions like expert systems or neural networks. But Japan has implemented many fuzzy logic applications,

---

Figure 8.20 An example of fuzzy logic and a fuzzy logic SQL query in a credit risk analysis application.

Fuzzy Logic Rules

Risk should be acceptable
If debt-equity is very high
  then risk is positively increased
If income is increasing
  then risk is somewhat decreased
If cash reserves are low to very low
  then risk is very increased
If PE ratio is good
  then risk is generally decreased

Fuzzy Logic SQL Query

Select companies
  from financials
    where revenues are very large
    and pe_ratio is acceptable
    and profits are high to very high
    and (income/employee_tot) is reasonable

especially the use of special-purpose fuzzy logic microprocessor chips, called fuzzy process controllers. Thus, the Japanese ride on subway trains, use elevators, and drive cars that are guided or supported by fuzzy process controllers made by Hitachi and Toshiba. They can even trade shares on the Tokyo Stock Exchange using a stock-trading program based on fuzzy logic rules. Many new models of Japanese-made products also feature fuzzy logic microprocessors. The list is growing, but includes auto-focus cameras, auto-stabilizing camcorders, energy-efficient air conditioners, self-adjusting washing machines, and automatic transmissions [31].

Genetic Algorithms

The use of **genetic algorithms** is a growing application of artificial intelligence. Genetic algorithm software uses Darwinian (survival of the fittest), randomizing, and other mathematical functions to simulate an evolutionary process that can yield increasingly better solutions to a problem. Genetic algorithms were first used to simulate millions of years in biological, geological, and ecosystem evolution in just a few minutes on a computer. Now genetic algorithm software is being used to model a variety of scientific, technical, and business processes [3, 20].

Genetic algorithms are especially useful for situations in which thousands of solutions are possible and must be evaluated to produce an optimal solution. Genetic algorithm software uses sets of mathematical process rules *(algorithms)* that specify how combinations of process components or steps are to be formed. This may involve trying random process combinations *(mutation)*, combining parts of several good processes *(crossover)*, and selecting good sets of processes and discarding poor ones *(selection)* in order to generate increasingly better solutions. Figure 8.21 illustrates a business use of genetic algorithm software.

Figure 8.21

Using genetic algorithm software for business problem solving.

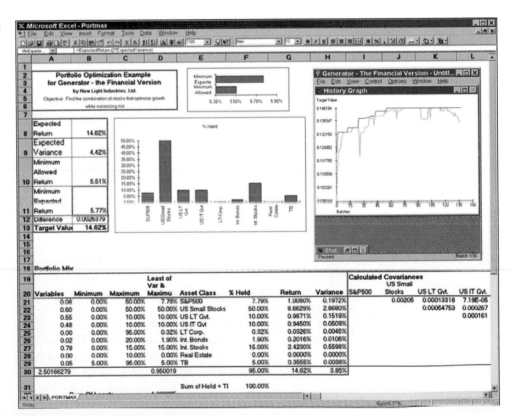

Courtesy of New Light Industries.

GE's Engeneous	General Electric's design of a more efficient jet engine for the Boeing 777 is a classic example of a genetic algorithm application in business. A major engineering challenge was to develop more efficient fan blades for the engine. GE's engineers estimated that it would take billions of years, even with a supercomputer, to mathematically evaluate the astronomical number of performance and cost factors and combinations involved. Instead, GE used a hybrid genetic algorithm/expert system, called Engeneous, that produced an optimal solution in less than a week [3].

Virtual Reality

Virtual reality (VR) is computer-simulated reality. Virtual reality is a fast-growing area of artificial intelligence that had its origins in efforts to build more natural, realistic, multisensory human–computer interfaces. So virtual reality relies on multisensory input/output devices such as a tracking headset with video goggles and stereo earphones, a *data glove* or jumpsuit with fiber-optic sensors that track your body movements, and a *walker* that monitors the movement of your feet. Then you can experience computer-simulated "virtual worlds" three-dimensionally through sight, sound, and touch. Thus, virtual reality is also called *telepresence*. For example, you can enter a computer-generated virtual world, look around and observe its contents, pick up and move objects, and move around in it at will. Thus, virtual reality allows you to interact with computer-simulated objects, entities, and environments as if they actually exist [2, 32]. See Figure 8.22.

VR Applications

Current applications of virtual reality are wide ranging and include computer-aided design (CAD), medical diagnostics and treatment, scientific experimentation in many physical and biological sciences, flight simulation for training pilots and astronauts, product demonstrations, employee training, and entertainment, especially 3-D video arcade games. CAD is the most widely used industrial VR application. It enables architects and other designers to design and test electronic 3-D models of products and structures by entering the models themselves and examining, touching, and manipulating sections and parts from all angles. This scientific-visualization capability is also used by pharmaceutical and biotechnology firms to develop and observe the behavior of computerized models of new drugs and materials, and by medical researchers to develop ways for physicians to enter and examine a virtual model of a patient's body.

VR designers are creating everything from virtual weather patterns and virtual wind tunnels to virtual cities and virtual securities markets. For example, by converting stock market and other financial data into three-dimensional graphic form, securities analysts can us VR systems to more rapidly observe and identify trends and exceptions in financial performance. Also promising are applications in information technology itself. This includes the development of 3-D models of telecommunications networks and databases. These virtual graphical representations of networks and databases make it easier for IS specialists to visualize the structure and relationships of an organization's telecommunications networks and corporate databases, thus improving their design and maintenance.

VR becomes *telepresence* when users that can be anywhere in the world use VR systems to work alone or together at a remote site. Typically, this involves using a VR system to enhance the sight and touch of a human who is remotely manipulating equipment to accomplish a task. Examples range from virtual surgery, where surgeon and patient may be on either side of the globe, to the remote use of equipment in hazardous environments such as chemical plants or nuclear reactors.

Figure 8.22

Using virtual reality for
computer-aided
automobile design
and testing.

Courtesy of Ford.

VR Limitations. The use of virtual reality seems limited only by the performance and cost of its technology. For example, some VR users develop *cybersickness*, such as eyestrain and motion sickness, from performance problems in the realism of VR systems. The cost of a virtual reality system is another limitation. A VR system consisting of a headset with goggles and headphones, a fiber-optic data glove, motion-sensing devices, and a powerful engineering workstation with top-quality 3-D modeling software can exceed $50,000. If you want less-cumbersome devices, more realistic displays, and a more natural sense of motion in your VR world, costs can escalate into several hundred thousand dollars. CAVEs (*cave automatic virtual environments*), virtual reality rooms that immerse you in a virtual reality experience, cost several million dollars to set up [10, 32].

Organizations such as NASA, the U.S. Department of Defense, IBM, Lockheed, Matsushita Electric, Caterpillar, and several universities are investing millions of dollars in virtual reality R&D projects involving the use of supercomputers, complex modeling software, and custom-made sensing devices. However, the cost of highly realistic multisensory VR systems is dropping each year. In the meantime some VR developers are using the VRML (*virtual reality modeling language*) to develop 3-D hypermedia graphics and animation products that provide a primitive VR experience for PC users on the World Wide Web and corporate intranets. Further advances in these and other VR technologies are expected to make virtual reality useful for a wide array of business and end user applications [2, 5, 32].

VR at Morgan Stanley

The Market Risks Department of Morgan Stanley & Co. uses Discovery virtual reality software by Visible Decisions to model risks of financial investments in varying market conditions. Discovery displays three-dimensional results using powerful Silicon Graphics workstations.

Morgan Stanley also uses VRML (virtual reality modeling language) as a way to display the results of risk analyses in three dimensions on PCs in their corporate intranet. (VRML allows developers to create hyperlinks between 3-D objects in files and databases on the World Wide Web and corporate intranets.) 3-D results are displayed on ordinary PCs in a virtual reality experience over an intranet connection to a Sun Microsystems SPARCstation server running a Sun VRML browser. Seeing data in three dimensions and experiencing relationships among data in a virtual reality process make it easier for analysts to make intuitive connections than it would be with a 2-D chart or table of numbers [35].

Intelligent Agents

Intelligent agents are growing in popularity as a way to use artificial intelligence routines in software to help users accomplish many kinds of tasks. An intelligent agent is a *software surrogate* for an end user or a process that fulfills a stated need or activity. An intelligent agent uses its built-in and learned knowledge base about a person or process to make decisions and accomplish tasks in a way that fulfills the intentions of a user. Sometimes an intelligent agent is given a graphic representation or persona, such as Einstein for a science advisor, Sherlock Holmes for an information search agent, and so on. Thus, intelligent agents (also called intelligent assistants and Wizards) are special-purpose knowledge-based information systems that accomplish specific tasks for users. Figure 8.23 summarizes major types of intelligent agents [22, 25].

Figure 8.23

Types of intelligent agents.

User Interface Agents

- **Interface Tutors.** Observe user computer operations, correct user mistakes, and provide hints and advice on efficient software use.

- **Presentation Agents.** Showing information in a variety of reporting and presentation forms and media based on user preferences.

- **Network Navigation Agents.** Discover paths to information and provide ways to view information that are preferred by a user.

- **Role-Playing Agents.** Play what-if games and other roles to help users understand information and make better decisions.

Information Management Agents

- **Search Agents.** Help users find files and databases, search for desired information, and suggest and find new types of information products, media, and resources.

- **Information Brokers.** Provide commercial services to discover and develop information resources that fit the business or personal needs of a user.

- **Information Filters.** Receive, find, filter, discard, save, forward, and notify users about products received or desired, including E-mail, voice mail, and all other information media.

Intelligent agents like those in Ask Jeeves help you find information in a variety of categories from many online sources.

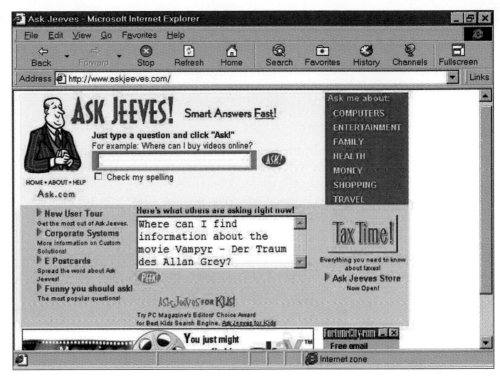

As we mentioned in Chapter 3, intelligent agents are evidence of a trend toward expert-assisted software packages. One of the most well-known uses of intelligent agents is the wizards found in Microsoft Office and other software suites. These wizards are built-in capabilities that can analyze how an end user is using a software package and offer suggestions on how to complete various tasks. Thus, wizards might help you change document margins, format spreadsheet cells, query a database, or construct a graph. Wizards and other software agents are also designed to adjust to your way of using a software package so that they can anticipate when you will need their assistance. See Figure 8.24.

The use of intelligent agents is expected to grow rapidly as a way to simplify software use, search the Internet and corporate intranets, and automate information screening and retrieval for users. Intelligent agents are becoming necessary as software packages become more sophisticated and powerful, as networks like the Internet and the World Wide Web become more vast and complex, and as information sources and media proliferate exponentially. In fact, some commentators forecast that much of the future of computing will consist of intelligent agents performing their work for users. So instead of using agents to help us accomplish computing tasks, we will be managing the performance of intelligent agents as they perform computing tasks for us [25].

Wizards by Microsoft

Microsoft has developed a series of Troubleshooting Wizards available on its World Wide Web site (www.microsoft.com/support/tshoot/). The Troubleshooting Wizards are similar to the intelligent agents in Windows 95 that solve simple interoperability problems. But Troubleshooting Wizards are based on a new inference engine that chooses the most likely reasons for user problems. After installation, users who click on the Help option are directed to the wizards, which pose questions aimed at identifying the problem and the fix. The wizards are intelligent software agents designed to help users fix minor problems with Microsoft software without calling Microsoft technical support. Such calls can cost users $150 or more and strain Microsoft's support organization. Large organizations can use the wizards to quickly solve routine glitches and common network configuration or interoperability problems in products like Windows NT Server [14].

Expert Systems

One of the most practical and widely implemented applications of artificial intelligence in business is the development of expert systems and other knowledge-based information systems. A *knowledge-based information system* (KBIS) adds a knowledge base to the major components found in other types of computer-based information systems. An **expert system** (ES) is a knowledge-based information system that uses its knowledge about a specific, complex application area to act as an expert consultant to end users. Expert systems provide answers to questions in a very specific problem area by making humanlike inferences about knowledge contained in a specialized knowledge base. They must also be able to explain their reasoning process and conclusions to a user. So expert systems can provide decision support to end users in the form of advice from an expert consultant in a specific problem area [15, 27].

Components of an Expert System

The components of an expert system include a knowledge base and software modules that perform inferences on the knowledge and communicate answers to a user's questions. Figure 8.25 illustrates the interrelated components of an expert system. Note the following components:

- **Knowledge Base.** The knowledge base of an expert system contains (1) facts about a specific subject area (for example, *John is an analyst*) and (2) heuristics (rules of thumb) that express the reasoning procedures of an expert on the subject (for example: IF John is an analyst, THEN he needs a workstation). There are many ways that such knowledge is represented in expert systems. Examples are *rule-based*, *frame-based*, *object-based*, and *case-based* methods of knowledge representation. See Figure 8.26.

- **Software Resources.** An expert system software package contains an inference engine and other programs for refining knowledge and communicating with users. The **inference engine** program processes the knowledge (such as rules and facts) related to a specific problem. It then makes associations and inferences resulting in recommended courses of action for a user. User interface programs for communicating with end users are also needed, including an explanation program to explain the reasoning process to a user if requested. Knowledge acquisition programs are not part of an expert system but are software tools for knowledge base development, as are *expert system shells*, which are used for developing expert systems.

Expert System Applications

Using an expert system involves an interactive computer-based session in which the solution to a problem is explored, with the expert system acting as a consultant to an end user. The expert system asks questions of the user, searches its knowledge base for facts and rules or other knowledge, explains its reasoning process when asked, and gives expert advice to the user in the subject area being explored. For example, Figure 8.27 illustrates one of the displays of an expert system.

Expert systems are being used for many different types of applications, and the variety of applications is expected to continue to increase. However, you should realize

Figure 8.25

Components of an expert system. The software modules perform inferences on a knowledge base built by an expert and/or knowledge engineer. This provides expert answers to an end user's questions in an interactive process.

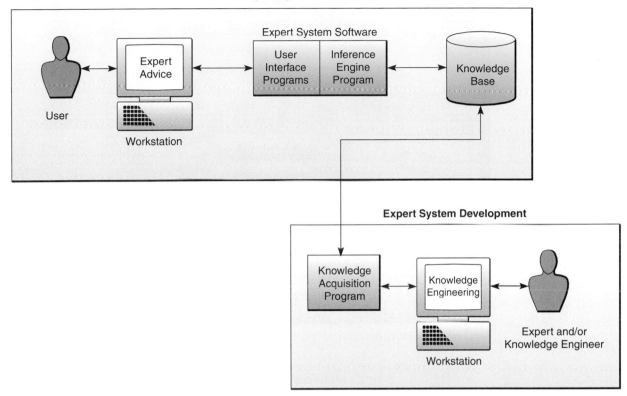

that expert systems typically accomplish one or more generic uses. Figure 8.28 outlines six generic categories of expert system activities, with specific examples of actual expert system applications. As you can see, expert systems are being used in many different fields, including medicine, engineering, the physical sciences, and business. Expert systems now help diagnose illnesses, search for minerals, analyze compounds, recommend repairs, and do financial planning. So from a strategic business standpoint, expert systems can and are being used to improve every step of the product cycle of a business, from finding customers to shipping products to them.

Figure 8.26

A summary of four ways that knowledge can be represented in an expert system's knowledge base.

- **Case-Based Reasoning.** Representing knowledge in an expert system's knowledge base in the form of cases, that is, examples of past performance, occurrences, and experiences.

- **Frame-Based Knowledge.** Knowledge represented in the form of a hierarchy or network of *frames*. A frame is a collection of knowledge about an entity consisting of a complex package of data values describing its attributes.

- **Object-Based Knowledge.** Knowledge represented as a network of objects. An object is a data element that includes both data and the methods or processes that act on those data.

- **Rule-Based Knowledge.** Knowledge represented in the form of rules and statements of fact. Rules are statements that typically take the form of a premise and a conclusion such as: If (condition), Then (conclusion).

Figure 8.27

One of the displays of a chemical process monitoring expert system. Note one of the acidity monitoring rules in its knowledge base.

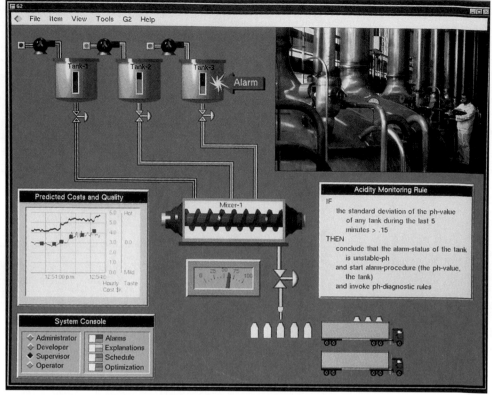

Courtesy of Gensym Corporation.

ES for Advertising Strategy

ADCAD (ADvertising Communications Approach Designer) is an expert system that assists advertising agencies in setting marketing and communications objectives, selecting creative strategies, and identifying effective communications approaches. In particular, it is designed to help advertisers of consumer products with the development of advertising objectives and ad copy strategy, and the selection of communications techniques. ADCAD's knowledge base consists of rules derived from various sources, including consultations with the creative staff of the Young & Rubicam advertising agency. Figure 8.29 gives examples of two of the hundreds of rules in ADCAD's knowledge base [6].

ADCAD uses a question-and-answer format, asking the user a series of questions about the advertising problem. It then searches through its knowledge base, matching user answers against its rules to draw inferences. Then ADCAD presents its recommendations, along with a rationale for each recommendation if asked. For example, Figure 8.29 shows how ADCAD responded when asked to explain its recommendation to use a celebrity to present an ad on television for a shampoo product.

ADCAD has been popular with advertising and brand managers since it provides them with a rationale for their current advertising, as well as ideas for new communications approaches. Another benefit of ADCAD is its support of what-if analysis of advertising options. ADCAD allows users to easily change their responses to questions and investigate the impact of alternative product or market assumptions. This feature has also made ADCAD a valuable training tool for students and novice advertising managers [6].

Figure 8.28

Major application categories and examples of typical expert systems. Note the variety of applications that can be supported by such systems.

Decision management—Systems that appraise situations or consider alternatives and make recommendations based on criteria supplied during the discovery process:
Loan portfolio analysis
Employee performance evaluation
Insurance underwriting
Demographic forecasts

Diagnostic/troubleshooting—Systems that infer underlying causes from reported symptoms and history:
Equipment calibration
Help desk operations
Software debugging
Medical diagnosis

Maintenance/scheduling—Systems that prioritize and schedule limited or time-critical resources:
Maintenance scheduling
Production scheduling
Education scheduling
Project management

Design/configuration—Systems that help configure equipment components, given existing constraints:
Computer option installation
Manufacturability studies
Communications networks
Optimum assembly plan

Selection/classification—Systems that help users choose products or processes, often from among large or complex sets of alternatives:
Material selection
Delinquent account identification
Information classification
Suspect identification

Process monitoring/control—Systems that monitor and control procedures or processes:
Machine control (including robotics)
Inventory control
Production monitoring
Chemical testing

Developing Expert Systems

The easiest way to develop an expert system is to use an **expert system shell** as a developmental tool. An expert system shell is a software package consisting of an expert system without its kernel, that is, its knowledge base. This leaves a *shell* of software (the inference engine and user interface programs) with generic inferencing and user interface capabilities. Other development tools (such as rule editors and user interface generators) are added in making the shell a powerful expert system development tool.

Expert system shells are now available as relatively low-cost software packages that help users develop their own expert systems on microcomputers. They allow trained users to develop the knowledge base for a specific expert system application. For example, one shell uses a spreadsheet format to help end users develop IF-THEN rules, automatically generating rules based on examples furnished by a user. Once a knowledge base is constructed, it is used with the shell's inference engine and user interface modules as a complete expert system on a specific subject area. Expert system shells have accelerated the development and use of expert systems. See Figure 8.30.

Figure 8.29

Examples of the rules
and explanations of the
ADCAD expert system
for developing advertis-
ing strategies.

Examples of ADCAD's rules

- **IF** ad objective = convey brand image or reinforce brand image
  AND brand purchase motivation = sensory stimulation
  AND message processing motivation = high
  THEN emotional tone = elation.

- **IF** ad objective = change brand beliefs
  AND message processing motivation = low
  AND purchase anxiety = low
  AND brand use avoids fearful consequences = yes
  THEN emotional tone = high fear.

Example of an ADCAD explanation of its recommendation to use a celebrity

- Just a moment please . . .
  The advertising objective is to communicate or reinforce your brand's image, mood, or
  an associated lifestyle to consumers who are not highly motivated to process your ad
  message. A celebrity presenter can attract the consumer's attention, enhance your brand's
  image, and become a memorable cue for brand evaluation.

Knowledge Engineering

A **knowledge engineer** is a professional who works with experts to capture the knowledge (facts and rules of thumb) they possess. The knowledge engineer then builds the
knowledge base (and the rest of the expert system if necessary), using an iterative, prototyping process until the expert system is acceptable. Thus, knowledge engineers perform a role similar to that of systems analysts in conventional information systems
development.

Once the decision is made to develop an expert system, a team of one or more domain experts and a knowledge engineer may be formed. Or experts skilled in the use

Figure 8.30

Using an expert system
shell to develop an ex-
pert system.

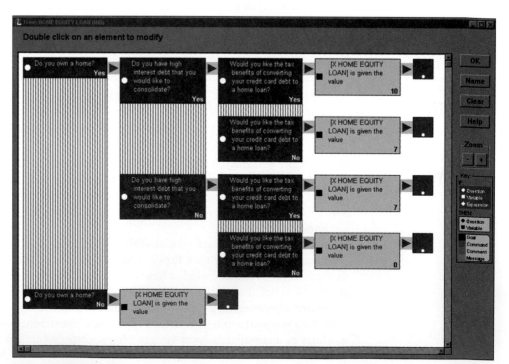

Courtesy of MultiLogic, Inc.

of expert system shells could develop their own expert systems. If a shell is used, facts and rules of thumb about a specific domain can be defined and entered into a knowledge base with the help of a rule editor or other knowledge acquisition tool. A limited working prototype of the knowledge base is then constructed, tested, and evaluated using the inference engine and user interface programs of the shell. The knowledge engineer and domain experts can modify the knowledge base, then retest the system and evaluate the results. This process is repeated until the knowledge base and the shell result in an acceptable expert system.

ES Development at MacMillan Bloedel

MacMillan Bloedel Corp. is a forest products conglomerate in British Columbia, Canada, that produces particle board used in building items such as bookshelves, furniture, and kitchen cupboards. Due to high staff turnover and a reorganization of divisional personnel at the particle board plant, only two senior employees had the comprehensive, operational know-how and training needed to operate the facility. After they retired, MacMillan had to call back a former manager, named Herb, as a very expensive consultant to keep the mill running. So MacMillan decided to develop an expert system to capture his knowledge of plant operations. The expert system that resulted documents the procedures needed to efficiently run the facility, and is also used for training and upgrading employees.

Knowledge engineers used the ACQUIRE expert system shell from Acquired Intelligence to develop the system. The ACQUIRE knowledge-based acquisition system was used to pick Herb's brain for his knowledge of how to start up, clean up, and set up the particle board coating line. The line consisted of machines whose operations parameters changed according to the coating to be applied. Herb was able to provide expert information, in the form of facts and rules, that was captured in the expert system's knowledge base. The resulting expert system consistently provides quality maintenance and operations advice to the mill operators [15].

The Value of Expert Systems

Obviously, expert systems are not the answer to every problem facing an organization. People using other types of information systems do quite well in many problem situations. So what types of problems are most suitable to expert system solutions? One way to answer this is to look at examples of the applications of current expert systems, including the generic tasks they can accomplish, as were summarized in Figure 8.28. Another way is to identify criteria that make a problem situation suitable for an expert system. Figure 8.31 outlines some important criteria.

Figure 8.31 should emphasize that many real-world situations do not fit the suitability criteria for expert system solutions. Hundreds of rules may be required to capture the assumptions, facts, and reasoning that are involved in even simple problem situations. For example, a task that might take an expert a few minutes to accomplish might require an expert system with hundreds of rules and take several months to develop. A task that may take a human expert several hours to do may require an expert system with thousands of rules and take several years to build [1, 9].

Benefits of Expert Systems

An expert system captures the expertise of an expert or group of experts in a computer-based information system. Thus, it can outperform a single human expert in many problem situations. That's because an expert system is faster and more consistent, can have the knowledge of several experts, and does not get tired or distracted by overwork or stress.

Figure 8.31

Criteria for applications
that are suitable for
expert systems
development.

Suitability Criteria for Expert Systems

Domain: The domain, or subject area, of the problem is relatively small and limited to a well-defined problem area.

Expertise: Solutions to the problem require the efforts of an expert. That is, a body of knowledge, techniques, and intuition is needed that only a few people possess.

Complexity: Solution of the problem is a complex task that requires logical inference processing, which would not be handled as well by conventional information processing.

Structure: The solution process must be able to cope with ill-structured, uncertain, missing, and conflicting data, and a problem situation that changes with the passage of time.

Availability: An expert exists who is articulate and cooperative, and who has the support of the management and end users involved in the development of the proposed system.

Expert systems also help preserve and reproduce the knowledge of experts. They allow a company to preserve the expertise of an expert before she leaves the organization. This expertise can then be shared by reproducing the software and knowledge base of the expert system. This allows novices to be trained and supported by copies of an expert system distributed throughout an organization. Finally, expert systems can have the same competitive advantages as other types of information technology. That is, the effective use of expert systems can allow a firm to significantly improve the efficiency of its business processes, or produce new knowledge-based products and services.

Limitations of Expert Systems

The major limitations of expert systems arise from their limited focus, inability to learn, maintenance problems, and developmental cost. Expert systems excel only in solving specific types of problems in a limited domain of knowledge. They fail miserably in solving problems requiring a broad knowledge base and subjective problem solving. They do well with specific types of operational or analytical tasks, but falter at subjective managerial decision making. For example, an expert system might help a financial consultant develop alternative investment recommendations for a client. But it could not adequately evaluate the nuances of current political, economic, and societal developments, or the personal dynamics of a session with a client. These important factors would still have to be handled by the human consultant before a final investment decision could be reached.

Expert systems may also be difficult and costly to develop and maintain properly. The costs of knowledge engineers, lost expert time, and hardware and software resources may be too high to offset the benefits expected from some applications. Also, expert systems can't maintain themselves. That is, they can't learn from experience but must be taught new knowledge and modified as new expertise is needed to match developments in their subject areas. However, some of these limitations can be overcome by the use of expert system developmental tools that make the job of development and maintenance easier.

Summary

- **Information, Decisions, and Management.** Information systems can support a variety of management decision-making levels and decisions. These include the three levels of management activity (strategic, tactical, and operational decision making) and three types of decision structures (structured, semistructured, and unstructured). Information systems provide a wide range of information products to support these types of decisions at all levels of the organization.

- **Management Information Systems.** Management information systems provide prespecified reports and responses to managers on a periodic, exception, demand, or push reporting basis, to meet their need for information to support decision making.

- **Online Analytical Processing.** Online analytical processing interactively analyzes complex relationships among large amounts of data stored in multidimensional databases. Managers and analysts can discover patterns, trends, and exception conditions in an online, realtime process that supports their business analysis and decision making.

- **Decision Support Systems.** Decision support systems are interactive, computer-based information systems that use DSS software and a model base and database to provide information tailored to support semistructured and unstructured decisions faced by individual managers. They are designed to use a decision maker's own insights and judgments in an ad hoc, interactive, analytical modeling process leading to a specific decision.

- **Analytical Modeling.** Using a decision support system is an interactive, analytical modeling process, consisting of what-if analysis, sensitivity analysis, goal-seeking analysis, and optimization analysis activities. Decision support system applications may be institutional or ad hoc but are typically developed to support the types of decisions faced by specific industries, functional areas, and decision makers.

- **Executive Information Systems.** Executive information systems are information systems designed to support the strategic information needs of top management. However, their use is spreading to lower levels of management. EIS are easy to use and enable executives to retrieve information tailored to their needs and preferences. Thus, EIS can provide information about a company's critical success factors to executives to support their planning and control responsibilities.

- **Artificial Intelligence.** The major application domains of artificial intelligence (AI) include a variety of applications in cognitive science, robotics, and natural interfaces. The goal of AI is the development of computer functions normally associated with human physical and mental capabilities, such as robots that see, hear, talk, feel, and move, and software capable of reasoning, learning, and problem solving. Thus, AI is being applied to many applications in business operations and managerial decision making, as well as in many other fields.

- **AI Technologies.** The many application areas of AI are summarized in Figure 8.17, including neural networks, fuzzy logic, genetic algorithms, virtual reality, and intelligent agents. Neural nets are hardware or software systems based on simple models of the brain's neuron structure that can learn to recognize patterns in data. Fuzzy logic systems use rules of approximate reasoning to solve problems where data are incomplete or ambiguous. Genetic algorithms use selection, randomizing, and other mathematical functions to simulate an evolutionary process that can yield increasingly better solutions to problems. Virtual reality systems are multisensory systems that enable human users to experience computer-simulated environments as if they actually existed. Intelligent agents are knowledge-based software surrogates for a user or process in the accomplishment of selected tasks.

- **Expert Systems.** Expert systems are knowledge-based information systems that use software and a knowledge base about a specific, complex application area to act as expert consultants to users in many business and technical applications. Software includes an inference engine program that makes inferences based on the facts and rules stored in the knowledge base. A knowledge base consists of facts about a specific subject area and heuristics (rules of thumb) that express the reasoning procedures of an expert. The benefits of expert systems (such as preservation and replication of expertise) must be balanced with their limited applicability in many problem situations.

Key Terms and Concepts

These are the key terms and concepts of this chapter. The page number of their first explanation is in parentheses.

1. Analytical modeling (304)
   a. Goal-seeking analysis (306)
   b. Optimization analysis (306)
   c. Sensitivity analysis (305)
   d. What-if analysis (305)
2. Artificial intelligence (312)
   a. Application areas (312)
   b. Objectives (312)
3. Decision structure (297)
4. Decision support versus management reporting (302)
5. Decision support system (301)
6. DSS software (302)
7. Executive information system (307)

8. Expert system (322)
   a. Applications (322)
   b. Benefits and limitations (327)
   c. Components (322)
   d. System development (325)
9. Expert system shell (325)
10. Fuzzy logic (316)
11. Genetic algorithms (317)
12. Geographic information system (303)
13. Inference engine (322)
14. Intelligent agent (320)
15. Knowledge base (322)
16. Knowledge engineer (326)

17. Level of management decision making (296)
18. Management information system (297)
19. Management support system (297)
20. Model base (302)
21. Neural network (314)
22. Online analytical processing (299)
23. Reporting alternatives (298)
24. Robotics (313)
25. Virtual reality (318)

Review Quiz

Match one of the key terms and concepts listed previously with one of the brief examples or definitions that follow. Try to find the best fit for answers that seem to fit more than one term or concept. Defend your choices.

_____ 1. A CEO and a production team may have different needs for decision making.

_____ 2. Decision-making procedures cannot be specified in advance for some complex decision situations.

_____ 3. An information system category that includes management information systems, decision support systems, and executive information systems.

_____ 4. Systems that produce predefined reports for management.

_____ 5. Managers can receive reports periodically, on an exception basis, or on demand.

_____ 6. Provide an interactive modeling capability tailored to the specific information needs of managers.

_____ 7. Interactive responses to ad hoc inquiries versus prespecified information.

_____ 8. A collection of mathematical models and analytical techniques.

_____ 9. Analyzing the effect of changing variables and relationships and manipulating a mathematical model.

_____ 10. Changing revenues and tax rates to see the effect on net profit after taxes.

_____ 11. Changing revenues in many small increments to see revenue's effect on net profit after taxes.

_____ 12. Changing revenues and expenses to find how you could achieve a specified amount of net profit after taxes.

_____ 13. Changing revenues and expenses subject to certain constraints in order to achieve the highest profit after taxes.

_____ 14. Information systems for the strategic information needs of top and middle managers.

_____ 15. Realtime analysis of complex business data.

16. Information technology that focuses on the development of computer functions normally associated with human physical and mental capabilities.

____ 17. Applications in cognitive science, robotics, and natural interfaces.

____ 18. Development of computer-based machines that possess capabilities such as sight, hearing, dexterity, and movement.

____ 19. Computers can provide you with computer-simulated experiences.

____ 20. An information system that integrates computer graphics, geographic databases, and DSS capabilities.

____ 21. A knowledge-based information system that acts as an expert consultant to users in a specific application area.

____ 22. Applications such as diagnosis, design, prediction, interpretation, and repair.

____ 23. These systems can preserve and reproduce the knowledge of experts but have a limited application focus.

____ 24. A collection of facts and reasoning procedures in a specific subject area.

____ 25. A software package that manipulates a knowledge base and makes associations and inferences leading to a recommended course of action.

____ 26. A software package consisting of an inference engine and user interface programs used as an expert system development tool.

____ 27. One can either buy a completely developed expert system package, develop one with an expert system shell, or develop one from scratch by custom programming.

____ 28. An analyst who interviews experts to develop a knowledge base about a specific application area.

____ 29. AI systems that use neuron structures to recognize patterns in data.

____ 30. AI systems that use approximate reasoning to process ambiguous data.

____ 31. Knowledge-based software surrogates that do things for you.

____ 32. Software that uses mathematical functions to simulate an evolutionary process.

Discussion Questions

1. Has the growth of self-directed teams to manage work in organizations changed the need for strategic, tactical, and operational decision making in business?

2. What is the difference between the ability of a manager to retrieve information instantly on demand using an MIS and the capabilities provided by a DSS?

3. Refer to the Real World Case on Lexis-Nexis in the chapter. Why does Bill Gates want bad news to travel fast on the Microsoft intranet? Do you agree? Why or why not?

4. In what ways does using an electronic spreadsheet package provide you with the capabilities of a decision support system?

5. Why is the use of executive information systems expanding into the ranks of middle management and throughout an organization?

6. Refer to the Real World Case on Dow Jones and Charles Schwab in the chapter. How could AI technologies help provide customer service on the Web? Talk to the Shallow Red (not Deep Blue) software robot at www.neuromedia.com to help you answer this question.

7. Can computers think? Will they ever be able to? Explain why or why not.

8. What are some of the most important applications of AI in business? Defend your choices.

9. Refer to the Real World Problem on Dayton Hudson in the chapter. What benefits does online analytical processing provide to support business decision making?

10. What are some of the limitations or dangers you see in the use of AI technologies such as expert systems, virtual reality, and intelligent agents? What could be done to minimize such effects?

Real World Problems

1. Key Corp. and Peoples Bank: Using Decision Support Systems in Banking

Quick payback and support for some surprising, counterintuitive decisions have been among the benefits early users found with IBM's DecisionEdge for Relationship Marketing decision support software. "We had a full return on our investment 14 months after installing the data warehouse component," said Jo Ann Boylan, an executive vice president in the Key Technology Service division at Key Corp., the nation's 13th largest retail bank with 7 million customers.

She added that the data warehousing and analysis system helped raise the bank's direct-mail response rate from 1 to as high as 10 percent. It also helped identify unprofitable product lines.

The DecisionEdge decision support package includes application suites, analytical tools, a data warehouse, industry-specific data models, and consulting services. Pricing begins at around $150,000.

Peoples Bank & Trust Co. in Indianapolis used the DecisionEdge for relationship marketing to delve into some highly profitable bank offerings that turned out to be prohibitively expensive, said Bob Connors, a senior vice president of information services. The DSS pointed out how much it actually costs to bring in each highly profitable home equity loan customer.

"Because those loans can be so profitable, it seems like a no-brainer that you'd want to market them," Connors explained. "But we found that the costs to bring them in were far too high, so we've cut way back on that spending. We still offer the loans, but we don't spend so much on advertising or direct mail any more."

Peoples Bank's data warehouse is much smaller than Key's—which has over 65 million records—but it is similarly used to better understand its 50,000 customers. "We recently used the DSS to help identify maturing certificates of deposit and offer different types of accounts to those customers to retain those deposits. We achieved 135 percent of our goal," Connors noted.

a. What is the business value of the DecisionEdge system to Key Corp. and Peoples Bank?

b. Why might a DSS provide support for "surprising, counterintuitive decisions"?

Source: Adapted from Stewart Deck, "Early Users Give Nod to Analysis Package," *Computerworld*, February 22, 1999, p. 14. Copyright 1999 by Computerworld, Inc., Framingham, MA 01701. Reprinted from *Computerworld*.

2. NDC Health Information Services: Web-Based Decision Analysis and Reporting

The world's largest web-based data warehouse sits quietly in a Phoenix, Arizona, office building, compiling data from more than 35,000 pharmacies and quickly making them available to people around the country via the Web. It contains 24 months of data representing more than 70 percent of the prescriptions written in the United States. Each month, the warehouse is fed data on 130 to 150 million new prescriptions. The warehouse and its decision-support front end—together called Intellect Q&A—are maintained by NDC Health Information Services. NDC provides prescription, pharmacy, and managed-care database and information solutions to pharmaceutical and healthcare companies across the United States.

Until Intellect Q&A went into production in February 1998, most organizations received critical sales data 45 to 60 days after month's end. After the data was in-house, all reporting requests had to go through the IS department, where they typically took at least a week to process.

The new system, based on DSS tools from MicroStrategy's DSS suite, allows anyone at any member organization to pose a business question, access the data, and produce a customized report in seconds or minutes, depending on its complexity. Best of all, this can be done any time after a transaction takes place from any Internet connection using the NDC extranet. Thus, NDC customers now have a much better sense of the market conditions they're facing.

To access information, subscribers simply log into the Web and enter the Intellect Q&A web site address. They can use a variety of browsers, running on all major operating systems. After providing a login and password, users are presented with a set of folders containing more than 70 analytical reports. Clicking on a report issues a query request to NDC's data warehouse, and a report is returned to the user's desktop. Users can then drill down to another level of detail, request more information or export the data to a spreadsheet for further mathematical manipulation. Users can also perform critical analytical functions such as ranking, trend analysis, market share, and exception reporting.

Intellect Q&A has helped make pharmaceutical market data available to a broader audience than NDC's traditional customers, from advertising agencies to biotech firms and Wall Street analysts. These new customers can access and analyze critical healthcare data at a fraction of the time and cost previously required. As a result, NDC expects to add $50 million to its revenue stream from these new markets over the next three years.

a. What are the business benefits of the web-based DSS at NDC Health Information Services?

b. How does an extranet help companies like NDC provide decision support services?

Source: Adapted from "MicroStrategy Inc: Web-Based Warehousing at NDC," *Intelligent Enterprise*, Advertising Section, January 5, 1999, p. R8.

3. Dayton Hudson Corporation: Using Decision Support Systems in Retailing

To succeed in retail merchandising, you must have a timely, accurate understanding of what your customers want. But you also must be able to respond quickly to market shifts and product trends. Leading mass-market retailers are discovering that data warehouses combined with powerful decision analysis tools can help them gain insights into their customer base, manage inventories more tightly, and keep the right products in front of the right people at the right place and time.

Leading the pack is Dayton Hudson Corporation, the fourth largest general merchandise retailer in the United States, with over 230,000 employees and almost 1,200 stores in 39 states. With such geographically distributed operations, Dayton Hudson executives realized the critical need for a common data and decision support platform that would span all divisions. To this end, the company embarked on a project to standardize its decision support systems across three key operating units: Target Stores, Mervyn's, and the Dayton Hudson Department Store Division, which includes the Marshall Field's, Dayton's, and Hudson stores.

The first system was developed for Target Stores. Driven by competition, the Target system focuses on the high end of the discount retail market, with the ability to respond to micro-market conditions more quickly and effectively than competitors. To accomplish this, they needed to be able to analyze massive volumes of information interactively.

The decision support system is composed of several applications known collectively as the Decision Maker's Workbench, which use Decision Suite and WebOLAP software from Information Advantage.

The DSS and Dayton Hudson's corporate intranet support more than 1,700 active users creating more than 60,000 ad-hoc OLAP reports each month. During the Christmas season, more than 20,000 analytic OLAP reports are produced each day.

By integrating the Web with its corporate data warehouse, Target has also enabled its vendors to access its data warehouse to monitor the sales and performance of their own products via secure extranet links across the Internet.

With the Target system complete, Dayton Hudson has standardized it as a model for the entire company. Already the standardized warehouse has enabled Dayton Hudson to obtain more accurate data on how items are performing across divisions, across the company. This has improved vendor negotiations considerably by enabling the different divisions to consolidate orders and receive a better price. The standardized DSS applications also allow for cross-referencing of fashion trends across divisions, and they have helped validate merchandising hunches through the analysis of cross-company data.

Standardizing on a common system of this magnitude across multiple divisions is something few corporations have dared attempt. However, as Mike Peterson, vice president of marketing at Target Stores, puts it, "People who are making million-dollar decisions on a regular basis deserve the best decision support systems we can give them."

a. What is the business value of decision support systems for retailers like the stores of Dayton Hudson?

b. What benefits result from the use of intranets and extranets in retail decision support systems like Dayton Hudson's?

Source: Adapted from "Dayton Hudson Knows What's in Store for Their Customers," *Intelligent Enterprise*, Advertising Section, January 5, 1999, p. R2; and David Orenstein, "Application Keeps Merchandise Moving," *Computerworld*, February 22, 1999, p. 42. Copyright 1999 by Computerworld, Inc., Framingham, MA 01701. Reprinted from *Computerworld*.

Application Exercises

1. The ADCAD System

Evaluate the ADCAD expert system on page 324 in the chapter. Write up your evaluation based on the following points.

a. The components of an expert system that you recognize. (See Figure 8.25.)

b. How well it fits the suitability criteria and application categories for expert systems. (See Figures 8.28 and 8.31.)

c. The benefits and limitations of this expert system.

2. ES at MacMillan Bloedel

Evaluate the ACQUIRE expert system of MacMillan Bloedel on page 327 in the chapter. Write up your evaluation based on the following points:

a. The components of an expert system that you recognize. (See Figure 8.25.)

b. How well it fits the suitability criteria and application categories for expert systems. (See Figures 8.28 and 8.31.)

c. The benefits and limitations of this expert system.

3. **Springville School District**

The Springville School District has seven elementary schools. The following table shows the current enrollment in each elementary school and the number of teachers currently assigned to each school. The district has established a goal of ensuring that there is at least one teacher for every 20 students in each elementary school. (You can divide the number of students by the number of teachers to determine this ratio for each school.) Is it possible to achieve this goal without increasing the number of teachers in the district?

a. Build a spreadsheet to perform the ratio analysis described above and print it out.

b. One suggested method for achieving the district's goal is to pay transportation expenses for parents who are willing to transfer their children from overcrowded schools to schools that are less crowded. Use goal-seeking analysis on your spreadsheet to determine the number of students who would have to move so that all of the schools are below the 20 to 1 ratio.

c. A second alternative is to transfer teachers from less-crowded schools to schools that are overcrowded. Use goal-seeking analysis on your spreadsheet to determine the number of teachers who would have to transfer to each overcrowded school so that all schools are below the 20 to 1 ratio.

School	Students	Teachers
Cleveland	741	43
Parkside	884	38
Powers	643	37
Lakeview	906	39
Sunnyslope	704	40
Praireview	715	41
Mountainview	793	40

4. **Software Licensing at Ace Enterprises**

You have been asked to evaluate your department's need for several types of common business applications software and to examine the cost of the needed software. A survey of your department indicates the following needs:

Word processing software	70 employees
Spreadsheet software	35 employees
Database management software	12 employees

This software can be purchased through individual licenses or through a site license with an upper limit on the amount of users. For example, a 20-user license would allow you to have any number of users up to 20 using the software. In addition, each piece of software is available separately or you can purchase an integrated package containing all three. You have obtained the following set of price quotes. The vendor has indicated that some of the prices may be subject to change, but the structure of the rates will not change.

	Individual	40-User License	100-User License
Word processing software	$100	$2,000	$4,000
Spreadsheet software	100	2,000	4,000
Database management software	150	3,000	6,000
Integrated package	250	4,500	9,000

Preliminary evaluation suggests that three alternatives should be considered:

1. Buying a 40-unit site license to the integrated package and buying additional individual licenses needed for the word processing software.

2. Buying a 100-unit site license for word processing, a 40-unit site license for the spreadsheet, and 15 individual licenses for database management software.

3. Buying a 100-unit site license for the integrated package.

a. Use a spreadsheet to analyze the three alternatives described. First, create a pricing area with appropriate headings to record the price list information. Then add an area for the calculations for each of the alternatives. This area should show the number of licenses needed and number of licenses provided for each type of software under each license. It should also contain a column for calculations of the cost for each component (if needed) and a summary row showing the total cost for each alternative. Your calculations should reference the pricing area so that changes in that area will automatically change the cost estimates.

b. Write a brief report summarizing your findings and including a recommendation.

c. Suppose the vendor offered to lower the price of all 100-user licenses by 20 percent. Print out a listing showing how this would affect the cost of each alternative. Would this cause your recommendation to change?

Review Quiz Answers

1. 17	6. 5	11. 1c	16. 2	21. 8	26. 9	31. 14
2. 3	7. 4	12. 1a	17. 2a	22. 8a	27. 8d	32. 11
3. 19	8. 20	13. 1b	18. 24	23. 8b	28. 16	
4. 18	9. 1	14. 7	19. 25	24. 15	29. 21	
5. 23	10. 1d	15. 22	20. 12	25. 13	30. 10	

Selected References

1. Allen, Bradley. "Case-Based Reasoning: Business Applications." *Communications of the ACM*, March 1994.

2. Ashline, Peter, and Vincent Lai. "Virtual Reality: An Emerging User-Interface Technology." *Information Systems Management*, Winter 1995.

3. Begley, Sharon. "Software Au Naturel." *Newsweek*, May 8, 1995.

4. Belcher, Lloyd, and Hugh Watson. "Assessing the Value of Conoco's EIS." *MIS Quarterly*, September 1993.

5. Blackburn, David; Rik Henderson; and Gary Welz. "VRML Evolution: State of the Art Advances." *Internet World*, December 1996.

6. Blattberg, Robert C.; Rashi Glazer; and John D. C. Little. *The Marketing Information Revolution*. Boston: The Harvard Business School Press, 1994.

7. Botchner, Ed. "Data Mining: Plumbing the Depths of Corporate Databases." *Computerworld*, Special Advertising Supplement, April 21, 1997.

8. Burden, Kevin. "The CW Guide to Business Intelligence Software." *Computerworld*, December 19, 1994.

9. Buta, Paul. "Mining for Financial Knowledge with CBR." *AI Expert*, February 1994.

10. Bylinsky, Gene. "To Create Products, Go into a CAVE." *Fortune*, February 5, 1996.

11. Cox, Earl. "Relational Database Queries Using Fuzzy Logic." *AI Expert*, January 1995.

12. Cronin, Mary. "Using the Web to Push Key Data to Decision Makers." *Fortune*, September 29, 1997.

13. Darling, Charles. "Ease Implementation Woes with Packaged Datamarts." *Datamation*, March 1997.

14. DiDio, Laura. "Microsoft's Cost Cutting Helps Users." *Computerworld*, April 21, 1997.

15. Egan, Richard. "The Expert Within." *PC Today*, January 1995.

16. Finkelstein, Richard. *Understanding the Need for Online Analytical Servers*. Ann Arbor, MI: Comshare, 1994.

17. Finkelstein, Richard. "When OLAP Does Not Relate." *Computerworld*, December 12, 1994.

18. Freeman, Eva. "Birth of a Terabyte Data Warehouse." *Datamation*, April 1997.

19. Freeman, Eva. "Desktop Reporting Tools." *Datamation*, June 1997.

20. Goldberg, David. "Genetic and Evolutionary Algorithms Come of Age." *Communications of the ACM*, March 1994.

21. Gorry, G. Anthony, and Michael Scott Morton. "A Framework for Management Information Systems." *Sloan Management Review*, Fall 1971; republished Spring 1989.

22. Higgins, Kelly. "Your Agent Is Calling." *Communications Week*, August 5, 1996.

23. Jablonowski, Mark. "Fuzzy Risk Analysis: Using AI Systems." *AI Expert*, December 1994.

24. Kalakota, Ravi, and Andrew Whinston. *Electronic Commerce: A Manager's Guide*. Reading, MA: Addison-Wesley, 1997.

25. King, James. "Intelligent Agents: Bringing Good Things to Life." *AI Expert*, February 1995.

26. King, Julia. "Sharing GIS Talent with the World." *Computerworld*, October 6, 1997.

27. Kurzweil, Raymond. *The Age of Intelligent Machines*. Cambridge, MA: The MIT Press, 1992.

28. LaPlante, Alice. "Start Small, Think Infinite." *Computerworld Premier 100*, February 24, 1997.

29. Lasker, Harry, and David Norton. "The New CEO/CIO Partnership." *Computerworld Leadership Series*, January 22, 1996.

30. Mailoux, Jacquiline. "New Menu at PepsiCo." *Computerworld*, May 6, 1996.

31. McNeill, F. Martin, and Ellen Thro. *Fuzzy Logic: A Practical Approach*. Boston: AP Professional, 1994.

32. Pimentel, Ken, and Kevin Teixeira. *Virtual Reality Through the New Looking Glass*. 2nd ed. New York: Intel/McGraw-Hill, 1995.

33. Vandenbosch, Betty, and Sid Huff. "Searching and Scanning: How Executives Obtain Information from Executive Information Systems." *MIS Quarterly*, March 1997.

34. Wagner, Mitch. "Engine Links Ads to Searches." *Computerworld*, June 2, 1997.

35. Wagner, Mitch. "Reality Check." *Computerworld*, February 26, 1997.

36. Watson, Hugh, and John Satzinger. "Guidelines for Designing EIS Interfaces." *Information Systems Management*, Fall 1994.

37. Watterson, Karen. "Parallel Tracks." *Datamation*, May 1997.

38. Winston, Patrick. "Rethinking Artificial Intelligence." Program Announcement, Massachusetts Institute of Technology, September 1997.

Information Systems for

Strategic Advantage

Chapter Highlights

Section I
Fundamentals of Strategic Advantage

Introduction
Real World Case: Ford Motor Company: E-Engineering Global Business Processes
Competitive Strategy Concepts
Strategic Roles for Information Systems
The Value Chain and Strategic IS

Section II
Strategic Applications and Issues in Information Technology

Introduction
Real World Case: Office Depot versus Staples: Competing with Internet Technologies
Reengineering Business Processes
Improving Business Quality
Becoming an Agile Competitor
Creating a Virtual Company
Building the Knowledge-Creating Company
Using the Internet Strategically
The Challenges of Strategic IS
Sustaining Strategic Success

Learning Objectives

After reading and studying this chapter, you should be able to:

1. Identify several basic competitive strategies and explain how they can be used to confront the competitive forces faced by a business.

2. Identify several strategic roles of information systems and give examples of how information technology can implement these roles and give competitive advantages to a business.

3. Give examples of how business process reengineering involves the strategic use of information technology.

4. Identify how total quality management differs from business process reengineering in its use of information technology.

5. Identify how information technology can be used to help a company be an agile competitor, or to form a virtual company to meet strategic business opportunities.

6. Explain how knowledge management systems can help a business build a knowledge-creating company.

7. Identify several strategic uses of Internet technologies in business and give examples of each.

Fundamentals of Strategic Advantage

Introduction

IT has become a strategic necessity. Believe it, act on it, or become a footnote in history [7].

So says James Champy, one of the founders of the business reengineering revolution of the 1990s. Thus, it is important that you view information systems as more than a set of technologies that support workgroup and enterprise collaboration, efficient business operations, or effective managerial decision making. Information technology can change the way businesses compete. So you should also view information systems strategically, that is, as vital competitive networks, as a means of organizational renewal, and as a necessary investment in technologies that help an enterprise achieve its strategic objectives.

Analyzing Ford Motor Company

Read the Real World Case on the Ford Motor Company on the next page. We can learn a lot about the strategic use of information technology for competitive advantage from this case. See Figure 9.1.

Ford is using Web technologies to reengineer its internal business processes as well as those between the company and its dealers, suppliers, and customers. Ford's site on the Web encourages customers to shop and passes their feedback to local dealers and their own marketing and design specialists. Ford's global intranet connects thousands of designers in the United States and Europe so they can collaborate on design

Figure 9.1

Bernard Mathaisel is Ford's chief information officer and leader of Ford's new web-based reengineering strategy.

Source: Michael L. Abramson.

Ford Motor Company: E-Engineering Global Business Processes

Reengineering. It was all the rage in the mid-90s. But the vast speedy Internet is ushering in an even bigger wave of business transformation. Call it E-engineering. Companies realize it's not enough to put up simple web sites for customers, employees, and partners. To take full advantage of the Net, they've got to reinvent the way they do business—changing how they distribute goods, collaborate inside the company, and deal with suppliers.

Ford Motor Company is taking on the E-engineering challenge holistically. One executive, Bernard Mathaisel, is both chief information officer and leader of its reengineering efforts. His plan is to fundamentally retool the way Ford operates with the help of the Web, cementing lifelong relationships with customers and slashing costs. "We're bringing new practices into every aspect of the company," says Mathaisel.

Already, E-business has begun to spread through the organization from front to back. Rather than relying on dealers to handle all customer contacts, Ford has put up a site on the Web that web shoppers can use to pick and price cars—and refers them to dealers. Ford then routes the customer feedback from the web site to its marketers and designers to help them plan new products.

In the design process, Ford's global intranet brings 4,500 engineers from labs in the United States, Germany, and England together in cyberspace to collaborate on projects. The idea is to break down the barriers between regional operations so basic auto components are designed once and used everywhere. When design plans conflict, the software automatically sends out E-mail alerts. Next, Ford's going to roll out an extranet-based system for ordering parts from suppliers. When all of these pieces are in place, the company hopes to transform the way it produces cars by building them quickly to order, rather than to forecasts.

For example, Ford has teamed with Structural Dynamics Research Corporation to link several hundred suppliers around the globe to the automaker's computer-aided design and manufacturing and computer-aided engineering system so they can participate in what has become an interactive vehicle design process.

Here's how the Ford process works: Ford is giving suppliers equipped with the same CAD software extranet access to its design database so they can collaborate via file transfer with Ford technicians on model designs. A seat supplier sends a design for a seat assembly from his Unix workstation over a secure extranet link from Japan to Ford's product data management system, which places it in the design database and notifies all parties via e-mail that information has arrived. A Ford engineer reviews the design to see if it will fit cleanly in the vehicle's interior. If it won't, a file with data on the assembly's surroundings is sent to the supplier so changes can be made.

"By outsourcing to suppliers, we get expertise in designing particular components that we no longer need to design here," said Dan Snedecor, global supplier systems manager at Ford in Dearborn, Michigan. "We're not training or creating expertise; we're taking advantage of it where it already exists and can be done for us at a lower cost."

"What we hope to gain is consistency in quality of designs," Snedecor said. The automaker also expects to reduce its head count as a result of the project. "We can reduce the workforce by relying on the supplier community to do our design, manufacturing and assembly," he said.

Snedecor declined to discuss Ford's investment in the project and said it's too early to estimate any cost savings. Ford suppliers in North America, Europe, South America, Australia, Japan, and Taiwan are participating in the program.

Case Study Questions

1. How is Ford using web technologies to reengineer its business processes? Visit www.ford.com to learn more about what Ford is doing.

2. Does Ford's E-engineering efforts give them potential for competitive advantage? Why or why not?

3. How else might Ford use web technologies to reengineer its business processes for competitive advantage? Use an example to illustrate your proposal.

Source: Reprinted from Steve Hamm and Marcia Stepanek, "From Reengineering to E-Engineering," *Business Week e.biz*, March 22, 1999, pp. EB 14–18, by special permission, copyright © 1999 by The McGraw-Hill Companies, Inc.; and Bob Wallace, "Ford Suppliers Get Call to Design," *Computerworld*, March 8, 1999, pp. 1, 97. Copyright 1999 by Computerworld, Inc., Framingham, MA 01701. Reprinted from *Computerworld*.

projects. Also, extranet links enable suppliers from all over the world to collaborate on the design, manufacture, and assembly of automotive components. All of these E-engineering initiatives are designed to slash costs, reduce time to market, and lower inventory and workforce levels, while improving the sales, quality, and consistency of Ford's products.

Competitive Strategy Concepts

The strategic role of information systems involves using information technology to develop products, services, and capabilities that give a company strategic advantages over the competitive forces it faces in the global marketplace. This creates **strategic information systems,** information systems that support or shape the competitive position and strategies of an enterprise. So a strategic information system can be any kind of information system (TPS, MIS, DSS, etc.) that helps an organization gain a competitive advantage, reduce a competitive disadvantage, or meet other strategic enterprise objectives [27]. Let's look at several basic concepts that define the role of such strategic information systems.

How should a managerial end user think about competitive strategies? How can competitive strategies be applied to the use of information systems by an organization? Figure 9.2 illustrates an important conceptual framework for understanding and applying competitive strategies. A firm can survive and succeed in the long run if it successfully develops strategies to confront five **competitive forces** that shape the structure of competition in its industry. These are: (1) rivalry of competitors within its industry, (2) threat of new entrants, (3) threat of substitutes, (4) the bargaining power of customers, and (5) the bargaining power of suppliers [30].

Figure 9.2

Businesses can develop competitive strategies to counter the actions of the competitive forces they confront in the marketplace.

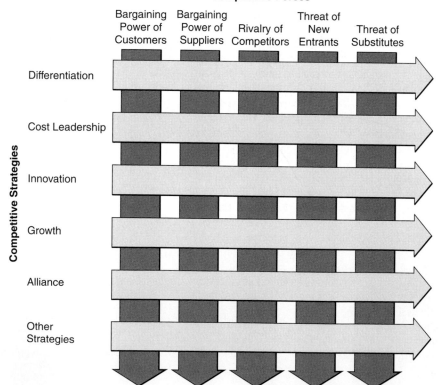

A variety of competitive strategies can be developed to help a firm confront these competitive forces. For example, businesses may try to counter the bargaining power of their customers and suppliers by developing unique business relationships with them. This effectively locks in customers or suppliers by creating "switching costs" that make it expensive or inconvenient for them to switch to another firm. Thus, competitors are also locked out by such strategies. Companies may use other strategies to protect themselves from the threat of new businesses entering their industry, or the development of substitutes for their products or services. For example, businesses may try to develop legal, financial, or technological requirements that create barriers to entry to discourage firms from entering an industry, or make substitution unattractive or uneconomical.

Figure 9.2 also emphasizes that businesses can counter the threats of competitive forces that they face by implementing five basic **competitive strategies** [27].

- **Cost Leadership Strategy.** Becoming a low-cost producer of products and services in the industry. Also, a firm can find ways to help its suppliers or customers reduce their costs or to increase the costs of their competitors.

- **Differentiation Strategy.** Developing ways to differentiate a firm's products and services from its competitors' or reduce the differentiation advantages of competitors. This may allow a firm to focus its products or services to give it an advantage in particular segments or niches of a market.

- **Innovation Strategy.** Finding new ways of doing business. This may involve the development of unique products and services, or entry into unique markets or market niches. It may also involve making radical changes to the business processes for producing or distributing products and services that are so different from the way a business has been conducted that they alter the fundamental structure of an industry.

- **Growth Strategies.** Significantly expanding a company's capacity to produce goods and services, expanding into global markets, diversifying into new products and services, or integrating into related products and services.

- **Alliance Strategies.** Establishing new business linkages and alliances with customers, suppliers, competitors, consultants, and other companies. These linkages may include mergers, acquisitions, joint ventures, forming of "virtual companies," or other marketing, manufacturing, or distribution agreements between a business and its trading partners.

Strategic Roles for Information Systems

How can the preceding competitive strategy concepts be applied to the **strategic role of information systems** in an organization? Put another way, how can managers use investments in information technology to directly support a firm's competitive strategies? These questions can be answered in terms of the key strategic roles that information systems can perform in a firm. Figure 9.3 summarizes how information technology can be used to implement a variety of competitive strategies. These include not only the five basic competitive strategies, but also other ways that companies can use information systems strategically to gain competitive edge. Figure 9.4 provides examples of how many corporations have used strategic information systems to implement each of the five basic strategies for competitive advantage. In the rest of this chapter, we will discuss and provide other examples of such strategic uses of information technology.

Figure 9.3

A summary of how information technology can be used to implement competitive strategies.

Lower Costs
- Use IT to substantially reduce the cost of business processes.
- Use IT to lower the costs of customers or suppliers.

Differentiate
- Develop new IT features to differentiate products and services.
- Use IT features to reduce the differentiation advantages of competitors.
- Use IT features to focus products and services at selected market niches.

Innovate
- Create new products and services that include IT components.
- Make radical changes to business processes with IT.
- Develop unique new markets or market niches with the help of IT.

Promote Growth
- Use IT to manage regional and global business expansion.
- Use IT to diversify and integrate into other products and services.

Develop Alliances
- Use IT to create virtual organizations of business partners.
- Develop interorganizational information systems linked by the Internet, extranets, or other networks that support strategic business relationships with customers, suppliers, subcontractors, and others.

Improve Quality and Efficiency
- Use IT to dramatically improve the quality of products and services.
- Use IT to make continuous improvements to the efficiency of business processes.
- Use IT to substantially shorten the time needed to develop, produce, and deliver products and services.

Build an IT Platform
- Leverage investment in IS people, hardware, software, and networks from operational uses into strategic applications.
- Build a strategic information base of internal and external data collected and analyzed by using IT.

Other Strategies
- Use interorganizational information systems to create switching costs that lock in customers and suppliers.
- Use investment in IT to build barriers to entry against industry outsiders.
- Use IT components to make substitution of competing products unattractive.
- Use IT to help create, share, and manage business knowledge.

Improving Business Processes

One of the strategic business values of information technology is its role in making major improvements in a company's business processes. Investments in information technology can help make a firm's operational processes substantially more efficient, and its managerial processes much more effective. Making such improvements to its business processes could enable a company to cut costs, improve quality and customer service, and develop innovative products for new markets. For example, manufacturing processes for everything from automobiles to watches have been automated and significantly improved by computer-aided design, engineering, production, and manufacturing resource management technologies. In the automobile industry, the process for the production, distribution, and sales of cars and parts and the sharing of vital

Figure 9.4   Examples of how companies used information technology to implement five competitive strategies for strategic advantage.

Strategy	Company	Strategic Information System	Business Benefit
Cost Leadership	Levitz Furniture	Centralized buying	Cut purchasing costs
	Metropolitan Life	Medical care monitoring	Cut medical costs
	Deere & Company	Machine tool control	Cut manufacturing costs
Differentiation	Navistar	Portable computer-based customer needs analysis	Increase in market share
	Setco Industries	Computer-aided job estimation	Increase in market share
	Consolidated Freightways	Customer online shipment tracking	Increase in market share
Innovation	Merrill Lynch	Customer cash management accounts	Market leadership
	Federal Express	Online package tracking and flight management	Market leadership
	McKesson Corp.	Customer order entry and merchandising	Market leadership
Growth	Citicorp	Global telecommunications network	Increase in global market
	Wal-Mart	Merchandise ordering by satellite network	Market leadership
	Toys 'Я' Us Inc.	POS inventory tracking	Market leadership
Alliance	Wal-Mart/Procter & Gamble	Automatic inventory replenishment by supplier	Reduced inventory cost/increased sales
	Levi Strauss/Designs Inc.	Electronic data interchange	Just-in-time merchandise replenishment
	Airborne Express/ Rentrak Corp.	Online inventory management/ shipment tracking	Increase in market share

business data by managers and others has been substantially improved by using the Internet, extranets, and other networks that electronically connect an automobile manufacturer's production and distribution facilities with car dealers and suppliers. Figure 9.5 outlines many of the ways that information technology can improve business processes.

Daimler Chrysler's CATIA Pipeline

DaimlerChrysler has reorganized its vehicle development process into multidisciplinary platform teams interconnected by the CATIA Pipeline, a telecommunications network that connects nearly every part of the company's "extended enterprise" to every other, including external suppliers and contractors. The software engine that moves data through the network and manages its database is CATIA (Computer-Aided Three-Dimensional Interactive Application), an integrated computer-aided design, development, engineering, and manufacturing execution system from Dassault Systems of France. Product information flows instantaneously from all directions and in all directions, linking managers, designers, engineers, marketers, service technicians, suppliers, and manufacturing.

The 1998 Dodge Intrepid and Chrysler Concorde were the first products developed with the CATIA Pipeline. The cars and almost all of their components were electronically designed, tested, and stored in the CATIA database before any physical models or prototypes were made. Designers and engineers are able to design and

Figure 9.5

How information technology can improve business processes.

IT Capability	How IT Improves Business Processes
Transactional	Transform unstructured processes into routine transactions
Geographical	Transform information quickly and easily across large distances, making processes independent of geography
Automational	Reduce or replace human labor in a process
Analytical	Bring complex analytical methods to bear on a process
Informational	Bring large amounts of detailed information into a process
Sequential	Enable changes in the sequence of tasks, often allowing multiple tasks to be worked on simultaneously
Knowledge	Allow the capture and dissemination of knowledge and expertise to improve a process
Tracking	Allow the detailed tracking of the status, inputs, and outputs of a process
Disintermediation	Connect two parties within a process that would otherwise communicate through an intermediary.

Source: Adapted and reprinted by permission of The Harvard Business School Press from *Process Innovation: Reengineering Work through Information Technology* by Thomas M. Davenport (Boston: 1993), p. 51, Copyright © 1993 by Ernst & Young.

test every part thousands of times, simulate crashes, test air conditioners, plan production processes, and practice servicing procedures—all electronically. More importantly, CATIA determines how any design change affects any others and instantly notifies everyone affected. CATIA has thus made significant improvements to DaimlerChrysler's business process. The payoff has been dramatic reductions in costs, and major improvements in production efficiency and in product quality and performance [2].

Promoting Business Innovation

Investments in information systems technology can result in the development of unique products and services or processes. This can create new business opportunities and enable a firm to expand into new markets or into new segments of existing markets. We discussed such innovative use of the Internet for electronic commerce in Chapter 6. The use of automated teller machines (ATMs) in banking is another classic example of an innovative investment in information systems technology.

Citibank and ATMs

By being first to install ATMs, Citibank and several other large banks were able to gain a strategic advantage over their competitors that lasted for several years [22, 24]. ATMs lured customers away from other financial institutions by cutting the cost of delivering bank services and increasing the convenience of such services. The more costly and less convenient alternative would have been to establish new bank branch offices. ATMs are also an example of product differentiation, since bank services are now provided in a new way. ATMs raised the cost of competition, which forced some smaller banks that could not afford the investment in new technology to merge with larger banks. ATMs represented an attractive and convenient new banking service produced and distributed to customers by making innovative changes in the delivery of bank services. Thus, information systems technology was used to develop a strategic new distribution process for bank services.

Locking In Customers and Suppliers

Investments in information technology can also allow a business to **lock in customers and suppliers** (and lock out competitors) by building valuable new relationships with them. This can deter both customers and suppliers from abandoning a firm for its competitors or intimidating a firm into accepting less-profitable relationships. Early attempts to use information systems technology in these relationships focused on significantly improving the quality of service to customers and suppliers in a firm's distribution, marketing, sales, and service activities. Then businesses moved to more innovative uses of information technology.

Wal-Mart and Others

For example, Wal-Mart built an elaborate satellite network linking all of its stores. The network was designed to provide managers, buyers, and sales associates with up-to-date sales, shipping, inventory, and account status information to improve product buying, inventories, and store management. Then the firm began to use the operational efficiency of such information systems to offer better-quality products and services and thereby differentiate itself from their competitors.

Companies like Wal-Mart began to extend their networks to their customers and suppliers in order to build innovative relationships that would lock in their business. This creates **interorganizational information systems** in which the Internet, extranets, and other networks electronically link the computers of businesses with their customers and suppliers, resulting in new business alliances and partnerships. Electronic data interchange (EDI) links between businesses and their suppliers, such as those we mentioned in Chapter 6, are a prime example of such strategic linkages. An even stronger link is formed by automatic inventory replenishment systems such as those between Wal-Mart and Procter & Gamble. In that system, Procter & Gamble automatically replenishes Wal-Mart's stock of Procter & Gamble products. [8, 24].

Creating Switching Costs

A major emphasis in strategic information systems has been to find ways to build **switching costs** into the relationships between a firm and its customers or suppliers. That is, investments in information systems technology have attempted to make customers or suppliers dependent on the continued used of innovative, mutually beneficial interorganizational information systems. Then, they become reluctant to pay the costs in time, money, effort, and inconvenience that it would take to change to a company's competitors.

SABRE and APOLLO

A classic example is the computerized airline reservation systems, such as the SABRE system of AMR Corporation (American Airlines) and the APOLLO system of COVIA (United Airlines), used by most travel agents. Once a travel agency has invested a substantial sum in installing such an interorganizational system, and travel agents have been trained in its use, the agency is reluctant to switch to another reservation system.

Thus, what seemed to be just a more convenient and efficient way of processing airline reservations became a strategic weapon that gave these providers a major competitive advantage. Not only does an airline reservation system raise competitive barriers and increase switching costs, it also continues to give their providers an advantage in gaining reservations for themselves, even with the enforcement of new legal guidelines to protect competition. Such systems also provide these companies with a major new line of information products. Thus, computer-based reservation services are a major source of revenue for their providers, which charge a variety of fees to travel agencies and airlines who use their systems. Both companies have now extended these systems to the Internet. It will be interesting to see how well their services compete with other airlines and online travel services on the World Wide Web. The low cost and easy access of Internet-based services tend to significantly reduce switching costs [14].

Raising Barriers to Entry

By making investment in information technology to improve its operations or promote innovation, a firm could also erect barriers to entry that would discourage or delay other companies from entering a market. Typically, this happens by increasing the amount of investment or the complexity of the technology required to compete in an industry or a market segment. Such actions would tend to discourage firms already in the industry and deter external firms from entering the industry.

Merrill Lynch

Merrill Lynch's cash management account is a classic example. By making large investments in information technology, along with a groundbreaking alliance with BancOne, they became the first securities brokers to offer a credit line, checking account, Visa credit card, and automatic investment in a money market fund, all in one account. This gave them major competitive advantage for several years before their rivals could develop the IT capability to offer similar services on their own [27]. Thus, large investments in computer-based information systems can make the stakes too high for some present or prospective players in an industry.

Leveraging a Strategic IT Platform

Investing in information technology enables a firm to build a **strategic IT platform** that allows it to take advantage of strategic opportunities. In many cases, this results when a company invests in advanced computer-based information systems to improve the efficiency of its own business processes. For example, they may develop client/server networks of PC and NC clients and network servers; develop intranets, extranets, and Internet services; hire more IS specialists; and do extensive multimedia training of end users. Then, armed with this technology platform, the firm can **leverage investment in information technology** by developing new products and services that would not be possible without strong IT capability.

An important current example is the development of corporate intranets and extranets by many companies, which enables them to leverage their previous investments in Internet browsers, servers, and client/server networks. Another classic example was the development by banks of remote banking services using automated teller machines. This innovative business use of IT was based in part on leveraging their expertise in teller terminal networks, which already interconnected their branches.

Developing a Strategic Information Base

Information systems also allow a firm to develop a **strategic information base** that can provide information to support the firm's competitive strategies. Information in a firm's corporate databases has always been a valuable asset in promoting efficient operations and effective management of a firm. However, information about a firm's operations, customers, suppliers, and competitors, as well as other economic and demographic data, stored in data warehouses, data marts, and other corporate databases, is now viewed as a strategic resource. That is, it is used to support strategic planning, marketing, and other strategic initiatives. In much the same way, information about *best business practices* and other business knowledge stored in intranet web site databases is a **strategic knowledge base.** We will discuss knowledge management in Section II.

For example, many businesses are now using data mining and online analytical processing to help design targeted marketing campaigns to selectively sell customers new products and services. This is especially true of firms that include several subsidiaries offering a variety of products and services. For example, once you become a customer of a subsidiary of American Express, you quickly become a target for marketing campaigns by their many other subsidiaries, based on information provided by the American Express strategic information resource base. This is one way a firm can leverage its investment in electronic commerce, transaction processing, and customer management systems—by linking its databases to its strategic planning and marketing systems. This strategy helps a firm create better marketing campaigns for new products and services, build better barriers to entry for competitors, and find better ways to lock in customers and suppliers.

The Value Chain and Strategic IS

Let's look at one final important concept that can help a manager identify opportunities for strategic information systems. The value chain concept was developed by Michael Porter [30] and is illustrated in Figure 9.6. It views a firm as a series, or chain, of basic activities that add value to its products and services, and thus add a margin of value to the firm. In the value chain conceptual framework, some business activities are primary processes; others are support processes. This framework can highlight where competitive strategies can best be applied in a business. That is, managerial end users should try to develop a variety of strategic information systems for those basic processes that add the most value to a company's products or services, and thus to the overall business value of the company. Figure 9.6 provides examples of how and where

Figure 9.6

The value chain of a firm. Note the examples of the variety of strategic information systems that can be applied to a firm's basic business processes for competitive advantage.

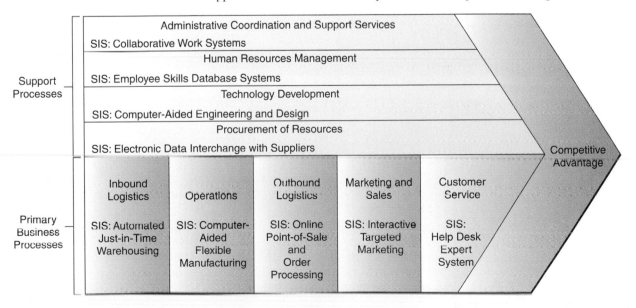

information systems technology can be applied to basic business processes using the value chain framework.

For example, Figure 9.6 emphasizes that collaborative work systems can increase the communications and collaboration needed to dramatically improve administrative coordination and support services. Employee skills database systems can help the human resources management function quickly locate and assign employees to important positions and projects. Computer-aided engineering and design systems can automate the design of products and processes as part of technology development. Finally, extranets and electronic data interchange (EDI) systems can help improve procurement of resources by providing online telecommunications links to a firm's suppliers.

Other examples of strategic applications of information systems technology to primary business processes are identified in Figure 9.6. These include automated just-in-time warehousing systems to support inbound logistic processes involving storage of inventory, computer-aided flexible manufacturing (CAM) systems for manufacturing operations, and online point-of-sale and order processing systems to improve outbound logistics processes that process customer orders. Information systems can also support marketing and sales processes by developing an interactive targeted marketing capability on the Internet and its World Wide Web. Finally, customer service can be dramatically improved by offering expert system help desk services to customers.

Thus, the value chain concept can help managers decide where and how to apply the strategic capabilities of information technology. It shows how various types of strategic information systems can be applied to the specific business processes that help a firm gain competitive advantages in the marketplace.

Section II **Strategic Applications and Issues in Information Technology**

Introduction

How do most companies use information technology? There are many ways that organizations may view and use information technology. Companies may use information systems strategically, or may use them in defensive or controlled ways. For example, if a company emphasized strategic business uses of information technology, its management would view IT as a major competitive differentiator. It would then devote significant amounts of technology to support decision making and to improve business processes. More and more businesses are beginning to use information systems strategically for competitive advantage. In this section, we will provide many examples of such strategic business applications of information technology.

Analyzing Office Depot and Staples

Read the Real World Case on Office Depot and Staples on the next page. We can learn a lot about the strategic applications of electronic commerce from this example. See Figures 9.7 and 9.8.

Office Depot and Staples are using business-to-business and business-to-consumer E-commerce strategies to compete against each other in the office supplies market. They hope to capture the business of companies by using extranet-based E-commerce processes to help them lower the costs and increase the efficiency of their purchasing process for office supplies. And they want to capture the business of consumers and small businesses by making the Web shopping experience so easy and attractive that customers will do all of their shopping for office supplies at the company web sites. To make this happen, both companies are investing millions of dollars in their E-commerce systems.

Figure 9.7

Jeff Levitan (left), head of Staples.com, and Bill Seltzer, CIO of Office Depot, see E-commerce as a strategic area for growth in their low-margin business.

Source: Stella Johnson.

Source: Mike Price.

Office Depot versus Staples: Competing with Internet Technologies

Rounding the corner and into the middle stretch, here comes Office Depot, the leading vendor of office supplies. Pulling up on Office Depot's flank: Staples, the feisty No. 2 player that tried to acquire the bigger rival two years ago.

Talk about a horse race! In every quarter during the past 18 months, Office Depot, in Delray Beach, Florida, has led its Westboro, Massachusetts–based competitor in sales. Yet when it comes to profits, it's continually exchanging the lead with Staples. Perhaps that's why Wall Street analysts tend to recommend smaller Staples over its erstwhile sweetheart. Staples—with a 14.6 percent return on equity versus Office Depot's 8.4 percent—just seems to be run better in their eyes.

But now a new competitive front has opened up that's particularly well-suited to the office-supply business, with its constant aim to trim shipping costs and distribute low-margin, commodity products. The front is the Internet.

During the past year, both companies have gone live with private, business-to-business Internet sites for their large corporate customers: Office Depot's QuickOrder and Staples Network Advantage Plus (SNAP). Both also now offer public Internet sites www.officedepot.com and www.staples.com for their small office/home office customers. And though neither Jeff Levitan, head of Staples.com, or Bill Seltzer, Office Depot's executive vice president and CIO, will reveal what they have spent so far, analysts estimate that each company has invested nearly $10 million in efforts to encourage customers to place orders online.

With QuickOrder and SNAP, customers link in from their own intranets, traverse the Internet's public lines and, using their passwords, sign onto private Internet web sites.

"Each company sends us purchasing rules for each user, so we know if a company restricts the purchase of certain products and what the user does or doesn't have the authority to buy," says Monica Luechtefeld, Office Depot's vice president of marketing, who's in charge of QuickOrder. "If a purchase exceeds the cost that's been authorized for a particular user, the system E-mails the appropriate managers for approval, plus sends notice of the purchase to the company's purchasing department."

QuickOrder has features that SNAP still lacks, however. For example, when any user at a large company signs on to QuickOrder, that password triggers a host of activities—telling Office Depot where the user is located and checking the nearest of its 21 warehouses for the ordered stock. As users check for items, they immediately know inventory levels, the ship date, and a history of what they've ordered. They also can track the order at their desks.

Today, Office Depot's E-commerce extranet handles 40,000 users in 5,800 companies. Every week it adds 200 companies representing 700 to 1,000 new users. Staples won't reveal its numbers, saying only that it expects to see a 25 percent increase in business in the coming year. Neither will say what percentage of total revenue stems from their electronic business-to-business web sites.

Another big battleground for both companies is their competing public web sites, which are intended for small office/home office customers and consumers, and which try to spur impulse buys. It's here at their public sites that the two companies are waging an equally public war. Office Depot launched Officedepot.com in January 1998, 11 months ahead of the Staples.com debut. Their shared aim is to make the shopping experience so easy and delightful that their smaller customers won't bother looking elsewhere on the Internet to save a few pennies.

Such systems aren't cheap and they require the endorsement of top executives. Each company has that backing. Staples' executives have demonstrated the value they place on the Internet. In December 1998, only one month after launching its public web site, the company announced it would make Staples.com a separate business unit responsible for its own success, and allocated an additional $10 million to $12 million for Staples.com on top of the $10 million it already had earmarked for the year.

At Office Depot, the first topic at the weekly top executive committee meeting centers on technology projects and their business impact. "I know of no other company where IT gets that kind of attention," says Seltzer, who's a member of the executive steering team. "We are viewed as that strategic."

Case Study Questions

1. What are the strategic benefits to Office Depot and Staples of their business-to-business E-commerce systems?

2. Visit the Office Depot and Staples web sites. Which company is doing a better job of implementing a business-to-business E-commerce strategy? Explain.

3. Should Office Depot make their E-commerce web site a separate business unit? Why or why not?

Figure 9.8   How a business may view and employ information technology.

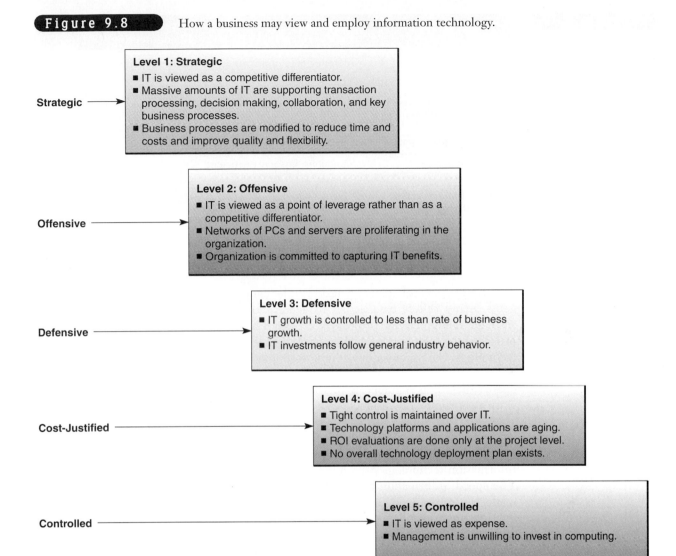

Source: Adapted from Richard Murray, "The Quest for World Class IT Capability," *Information Systems Management* (New York: Auerbach Publications), Summer 1991, p. 13. © 1991 Research Institute of America. Used with permission.

Reengineering Business Processes

One of the most important competitive strategies today is **business process reengineering** (BPR), most often simply called reengineering. In Chapter 1, we stressed that reengineering is more than automating business processes to make modest improvements in the efficiency of business operations. We defined reengineering as a fundamental rethinking and radical redesign of business processes to achieve dramatic improvements in cost, quality, speed, and service [19]. So BPR combines a strategy of promoting business innovation with a strategy of making major improvements to business processes so that a company can become a much stronger and more successful competitor in the marketplace. See Figure 9.9

However, Figure 9.9 points out that while the potential payback of reengineering is high, so is its risk of failure and level of disruption to the organizational environment. Making radical changes to business processes to dramatically improve efficiency

How business process reengineering differs from business improvement.

	Business Improvement	Business Reengineering
Definition	Incrementally improving existing processes	Radically redesigning business processes
Target	Any process	Strategic business processes
Primary Enablers	IT and work simplification	IT and organizational redesign
Potential Payback	10%–50% improvements	10-fold improvements
What Changes?	Same jobs, just more efficient	Big job cuts; new jobs; major job redesign
Risk of Failure and Level of Disruption	Low	High

Source: Adapted from Colleen Frye, "Imaging Proves Catalyst for Reengineering," *Client/Server Computing*, November 1994, p. 54.

and effectiveness is not an easy task. While many companies have reported impressive gains, many others have failed to achieve the major improvements they sought through reengineering projects [12, 21]. That's why organizational redesign approaches are an important enabler of reengineering, along with the use of information technology. For example, one common approach is the use of self-directed cross-functional or multidisciplinary *process teams*. Employees from several departments or specialties including engineering, marketing, customer service, and manufacturing may work as a team on the product development process. Another example is the use of *case managers*, who handle almost all tasks in a business process, instead of splitting tasks among many different specialists.

The Role of Information Technology

Information technology plays a major role in reengineering most business processes. The speed, information processing capabilities, and connectivity of computer networks can substantially increase the efficiency of business processes, as well as communications and collaboration among the people responsible for their operation and management. For example, the order management process illustrated in Figure 9.10 is vital to the success of most companies. Many of them are reengineering this process with the help of the information technologies listed in Figure 9.11 [11].

The order management process consists of several business processes and crosses the boundaries of traditional business functions.

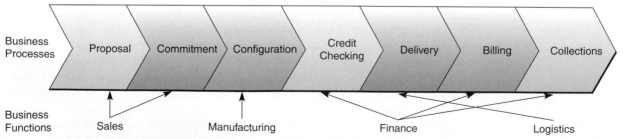

Sources: Adapted and reprinted by permission of The Harvard Business School Press from *Process Innovation: Reengineering Work through Information Technology* by Thomas H. Davenport (Boston: 1993), p. 248. Copyright © 1993 by Ernst & Young.

Figure 9.11

Examples of information technologies that support reengineering the sales and order management processes.

- Prospect tracking and management systems using corporate intranets.
- Portable sales force automation systems using the Internet and extranets.
- Portable networking for field and customer site communications.
- Customer site workstations for order entry and status checking.
- Expert systems that match products and services to customer needs.
- Electronic data interchange and electronic funds transfer between firms.
- Expert systems for configuration, shipping, and pricing.
- Predictive modeling for continuous product replenishment.
- Composite systems that bring cross-functional information to employee workstations.
- Customer, product, and production databases.

CIGNA Corporation

CIGNA Corporation is a leading worldwide insurance and financial services company and employs 50,000 people in almost 70 countries. Between 1989 and 1993, CIGNA completed more than 20 reengineering projects, saving over $100 million. At CIGNA,

reengineering was refocused from excellence in operational business processes to enabling new business growth. Along the way, reengineering has begun to become part of the way that CIGNA employees and managers think. To CIGNA, business reengineering means "break-through innovation focused on customer needs." It is a vehicle to realign strategy, operations, and systems to deliver significantly increased financial results [5].

Thus, reengineering at CIGNA is a strategic business initiative. Figure 9.12 summarizes the accomplishments of reengineering programs at four major business units at CIGNA. Major changes in business information systems and the use of information technology were involved in all of the projects. For example, CIGNA reengineered the corporate medical presale process by making major revisions to work activities and manual and computer-based procedures. The company reduced the time to deliver a quote to a customer for corporate medical insurance from 17 days to 3. Fourteen manual hand-offs of work from one person to another were reduced to three all-electronic transfers. See Figure 9.13.

Improving Business Quality

No single approach to organizational change, including reengineering, is appropriate for all circumstances. Many companies have a portfolio of approaches to operational change including reengineering, continuous [quality] improvement, incremental approaches, and restructuring techniques. Some combine multiple approaches in one initiative—for example, using reengineering for a long-run solution and short-term process improvements in the current process to deliver quick benefits [12].

Thus, information technology can be used strategically to improve business performance in many ways other than in supporting reengineering initiatives. One important strategic thrust is continuous quality improvement, popularly called **total quality management** (TQM). Previous to TQM, quality was defined as meeting established standards or specifications for a product or service. Statistical *quality control* programs were used to measure and correct any deviations from standards [11].

Figure 9.12

Some of the accomplishments of reengineering projects at CIGNA.

Business Unit	Accomplishments
CIGNA Re	• Staff reduced by 50%. • Operating expenses reduced by 42%. • 1,200% transaction time improvement. • Team-based organization. • Systems reduced from 17 mainframe-based systems to five PC-based systems.
CIGNA International Life and Employee Benefits–UK	• 30% improvement in cost. • 75% improvement in quality. • 100% improvement in cycle time. • 50% improvement in customer satisfaction.
Global Risk Management	• New products offered to customers. • 25% staff reduction. • $25 million reduction in operating expenses. • Client/server-based system that prices products considering local conditions and local losses.
Property and Casualty	• Three organizational layers were flattened. • Team-based organization. • 32% reduction in systems staff. • 63% reduction in reported systems problems. • 100% accuracy on systems fixes. • 43% reduction in systems requests.

Source: Adapted form J. Raymond Caron, Sirkka Jarvenpaa, and Donna Stoddard, "Business Reengineering at CIGNA Corporation: Experiences and Lessons from the First Five Years," *MIS Quarterly*, September 1994, p. 240. Reprinted with permission from the *MIS Quarterly*.

Total Quality Management

Total quality management is a much more strategic approach to business improvement. Quality is emphasized from the customer's viewpoint, rather than the producer's. Thus, quality is defined as meeting or exceeding the requirements and expectations of customers for a product or service. This may involve many features and

Figure 9.13

The results of reengineering the process to deliver an insurance quote to a corporate customer at CIGNA International–United Kingdom.

Corporate Medical Presale Process	
Before Reengineering	**After Reengineering**
• Seventeen-day cycle time.	• Three-day cycle time.
• Fourteen hand-offs—manual.	• Three hand-offs—all electronic.
• Seven authorization steps.	• Zero authorization steps.
• Six hours of total work.	• Three hours of total work.
• Four hours of value-added work.	• Three hours of value-added work.
• Two hours of rework.	• Zero hours of rework.

Source: Adapted form J. Raymond Caron, Sirkka Jarvenpaa, and Donna Stoddard, "Business Reengineering at CIGNA Corporation: Experiences and Lessons from the First Five Years," *MIS Quarterly*, September 1994, p. 240. Reprinted with permission from the *MIS Quarterly*.

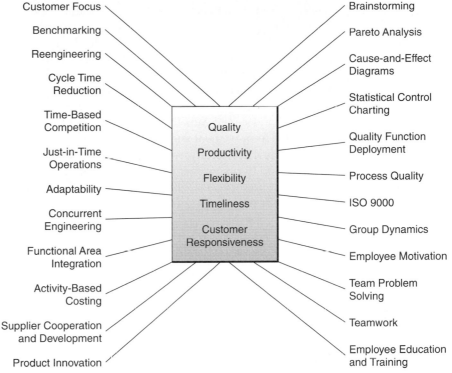

Source: Adapted and reproduced from C. Carl Pegels, *Total Quality Management: A Survey of Its Important Aspects*, 1995, p. 6, with the permission of boyd & fraser publishing company. Copyright 1995 by boyd & fraser publishing company. All rights reserved.

attributes, such as performance, reliability, durability, responsiveness, aesthetics, and reputation, to name a few [13, 26].

Total quality management is also a much broader management approach than quality control. As Figure 9.14 illustrates, TQM may use a variety of tools and methods to seek continuous improvement of quality, productivity, flexibility, timeliness, and customer responsiveness. According to quality guru Richard Schonberger, companies that use TQM are committed to:

1. Even better, more appealing, less-variable quality of the product or service.

2. Even quicker, less-variable response—from design and development through supplier and sales channels, offices, and plants all the way to the final user.

3. Even greater flexibility in adjusting to customers' shifting volume and mix requirement.

4. Even lower cost through quality improvement, rework reduction, and non-value-adding waste elimination [26].

| **Sun Microsystems** | Sun Microsystems describes its total quality management process as "embedding quality in Sun's DNA." The emphasis at Sun is on alignment—tying together key quality initiatives with Sun's core business drivers and using Sun's technology to drive and manage quality. Sun is one of the world's more "wired" companies with all employees connected through SunWeb—its corporate intranet. The combination of electronic networking and culture enables Sun to gather and distribute timely |

feedback from quality indicators like the Customer Quality Index (CQI), which measures "train wrecks," such as late delivery, discrepant orders, hardware calls, software calls, problem escalations, and "DOA" (dead on arrival) products. Another widely shared metric is the Employee Quality Index (EQI), an online, Java-based survey of 3,500 randomly selected employees every month designed to gauge employee satisfaction and reduce "performance inhibitors."

Other elements of Sun's quality process are a sophisticated Customer Loyalty Index (CLI) and survey; Sun Teams, a grassroots employee-involvement effort focusing on process improvement and teamwork; and RAS4net, a Sun-wide initiative to meet the reliability, availability, and serviceability (RAS) requirements of enterprise computing. In addition, most employees' compensation is based on quality and customer satisfaction performance. Sun says that its TQM program is producing both real reductions in customer dissatisfiers and increases in customer satisfaction [3].

Becoming an Agile Competitor

We are changing from a competitive environment in which mass-market products and services were standardized, long-lived, information-poor, and exchanged in one-time transactions, to an environment in which companies compete globally with niche market products and services that are individualized, short-lived, information-rich, and exchanged on an ongoing basis with customers [18].

Agility in competitive performance is the ability of a business to prosper in rapidly changing, continually fragmenting global markets for high-quality, high-performance, customer-configured products and services. An agile company can make a profit in markets with broad product ranges and short model lifetimes, can process orders in arbitrary lot sizes, and can offer individualized products while maintaining high volumes of production. Agile companies depend heavily on information technology to support and manage business processes, while providing the information processing capability to treat masses of customers as individuals.

Figure 9.15 illustrates that to be an agile competitor, a business must implement four basic strategies of agile competition. First, customers of an agile company feel enriched by products or services that they perceive as solutions to their individual problems. Thus, products can be priced based on their value as solutions, not on their cost to produce. Second, an agile company cooperates internally and with other companies, even competitors. This allows a business to bring products to market as rapidly and cost-effectively as possible, no matter where resources are located and who owns them. Third, an agile company organizes so that it thrives on change and uncertainty. It uses flexible, multiple organizational structures keyed to the requirements of different and constantly changing customer opportunities. Finally, an agile company leverages the impact of its people and the information and knowledge that they possess. By nurturing an entrepreneurial spirit, an agile company provides powerful incentives for employee responsibility, adaptability, and innovation [19].

The Role of Information Technology

The bottleneck to higher levels of performance in an agile company is not equipment but information flow, internally and among cooperating companies. Information is already an increasingly important and increasingly valuable component of consumer and commercial products. Packaging information, providing access to information, and information "tools"—for example, design software and database search software—will become increasingly valuable products in their own right, as well as increasingly valuable elements of hardware products, such as automobiles [18].

Figure 9.15

The four fundamental strategies of agile competition.

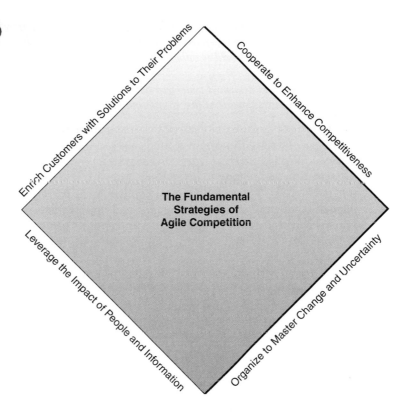

Enrich Customers with Solutions to Their Problems

Cooperate to Enhance Competitiveness

The Fundamental Strategies of Agile Competition

Leverage the Impact of People and Information

Organize to Master Change and Uncertainty

So information technology is a strategic requirement for agile product development and delivery. Information systems provide the information that people need to support agile operations, as well as the information built into products and services.

| Ross Operating Valves | Ross Operating Valves manufactures hydraulic valves in Madison Heights, Michigan; in Lavonia, Georgia; in Frankfurt, Germany; and in Tokyo, Japan. Ross uses a manufacturing system called Ross/Flex at the Lavonia plant. Ross/Flex consists of proprietary computer-aided design (CAD) software and a database of digitized valve designs. Ross/Flex enables valves to be custom-designed jointly by customers and by Ross "integrators"—engineers and skilled machinists. Designs are downloaded to computer-controlled machine tools. Prototypes are completed in one day at a typical cost of $3,000, one-tenth of the previous cost and time.

After the prototype is tested, customers can request changes to produce improved prototypes. When they are satisfied, customers can then approve production of the valves. Since introducing Ross/Flex as a free service, business has increased dramatically and Ross has enjoyed extraordinary market success. After several years, Ross began offering customers the option of remotely accessing its design software and database for a fee. Customers can then design their own valves and download them to Ross computer-controlled machinery for production [1, 18].

Ross/Flex demonstrates the strategic use of information technology to support agile competition. Ross (1) enriches customers with custom-designed solutions, (2) cooperates with them to enhance their own competitiveness, (3) organizes innovatively with teams of integrators who can easily handle changing customer needs, and (4) leverages their people and information resources to produce innovative and profitable business opportunities in a dynamic global market. |

Creating a Virtual Company

These days, thousands of companies, large and small, are setting up virtual corporations that enable executives, engineers, scientists, writers, researchers, and other professionals from around the world to collaborate on new products and services without ever meeting face to face. Once the exclusive domain of Fortune 500 companies with banks of powerful computers and dedicated wide area networks, remote networking is now available to any company with a phone, a fax, and E-mail access to the Internet or an online service [32].

In today's dynamic global business environment, forming a **virtual company** can be one of the most important strategic uses of information technology. A virtual company (also called a *virtual corporation* or *virtual organization*) is an organization that uses information technology to link people, assets, and ideas. Figure 9.16 outlines six basic characteristics of successful virtual companies. It emphasizes that to be successful, a virtual company must be an adaptable and opportunity-exploring organization, providing world-class excellence in its competencies and technologies, which transparently create integrated customer solutions in business relationships based on mutual trust [15].

Figure 9.17 illustrates that virtual companies typically use an organizational structure called a **network structure.** And since most virtual companies are interlinked by the Internet, intranets, and extranets, their structure may also be called a **hyperarchy,** modeled after the hyperlinked structure of the World Wide Web [14]. Notice that this company has organized internally into clusters of process and cross-functional teams linked by intranets. It has also developed alliances and extranet links that form **interorganizational information systems** with suppliers, customers, subcontractors, and competitors. Thus, the network and hyperarchy structures create flexible and adaptable virtual companies keyed to exploit fast-changing business opportunities [6].

Virtual Company Strategies

Why are people forming virtual companies? Several major reasons stand out and are summarized in Figure 9.18. People and corporations are forming virtual companies as the best way to implement key business strategies that promise to ensure success in today's turbulent business climate.

For example, in order to exploit a diverse and fast-changing market opportunity, a business may not have the time or resources to develop the manufacturing and distribution infrastructure, people competencies, and information technologies needed. Only by quickly forming a virtual company of all-star partners can it assemble the components it needs to provide a world-class solution for customers and capture the

Figure 9.16

Six basic characteristics of successful virtual companies.

- **Adaptability.** Able to adapt to a diverse, fast-changing business environment.
- **Opportunism.** Created, operated, and dissolved to exploit business opportunities when they appear.
- **Excellence.** Possess all-star, world-class excellence in the core competencies that are needed.
- **Technology.** Provide world-class information technology and other required technologies in all customer solutions.
- **Borderless.** Easily and transparently synthesize the competencies and resources of business partners into integrated customer solutions.
- **Trust-Based.** Members are trustworthy and display mutual trust in their business relationships.

Figure 9.17

Network and hyperarchy structures facilitate the creation of virtual companies.

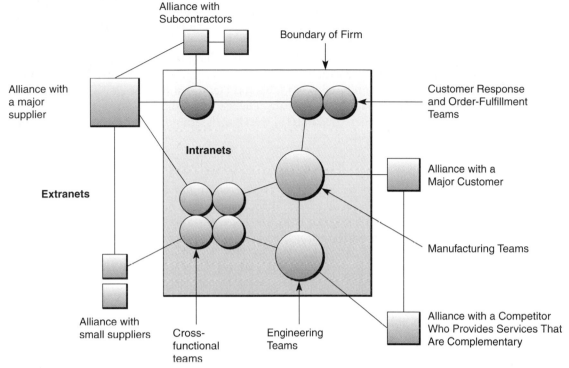

Source: Adapted from James I. Cash Jr., Robert G. Eccles, Nitin Nohria, and Richard L. Nolan, *Building the Information-Age Organization: Structure, Control, and Information Technologies* (Burr Ridge, IL: Richard D. Irwin, 1994), p. 34.

market opportunity. Of course, computer systems, the Internet, intranets, extranets, and a variety of other information technologies will be vital components in creating a successful solution.

Cisco Systems

Cisco Systems is the world's largest manufacturer of telecommunications products. Jabil Circuit is the fourth largest company in the electronics contract manufacturing industry, with annual sales approaching $1 billion. Cisco has a *virtual manufacturing company* arrangement with Jabil and Hamilton Corporation, a major electronics parts supplier. Let's look at an example of how these three companies are involved in a typical business transaction.

Figure 9.18

Business strategies of virtual companies.

- Share infrastructure and risk.
- Link complementary core competencies.
- Reduce concept-to-cash time through sharing.
- Increase facilities and market coverage.
- Gain access to new markets and share market or customer loyalty.
- Migrate from selling products to selling solutions.

An order placed for a Cisco 1600 series router (an internetwork processor used to connect small offices to networks) arrives simultaneously at Cisco in San Jose, California, and Jabil in St. Petersburg, Florida. Jabil immediately starts to build the router by drawing parts from three on-site inventories: Jabil's, one belonging to Cisco, and one owned and controlled by Hamilton. When completed, the router is tested and checked against the order in St. Petersburg by computers in San Jose, then shipped directly to the customer by Jabil. That triggers a Cisco invoice to the customer and electronic billings from Jabil and Hamilton to Cisco in San Jose. Thus, Cisco's virtual manufacturing company alliance with Jabil and Hamilton gives them an agile, build-to-order capability in the fiercely competitive telecommunications equipment industry [34].

Building the Knowledge-Creating Company

In an economy where the only certainty is uncertainty, the one sure source of lasting competitive advantage is knowledge. When markets shift, technologies proliferate, competitors multiply, and products become obsolete almost overnight, successful companies are those that consistently create new knowledge, disseminate it widely throughout the organization, and quickly embody it in new technologies and products. These activities define the "knowledge-creating" company, whose sole business is continuous innovation [28].

To many companies today, lasting competitive advantage can only be theirs if they become **knowledge-creating companies** or *learning organizations.* That means consistently creating new business knowledge, disseminating it widely throughout the company, and quickly building the new knowledge into their products and services.

Knowledge-creating companies exploit two kinds of knowledge. One is *explicit knowledge*—data, documents, things written down or stored on computers. The other kind is tacit knowledge—the "how-tos" of knowledge, which reside in workers. Successful **knowledge management** creates techniques, technologies, and rewards for getting employees to share what they know and to make better use of accumulated workplace knowledge. In that way, employees of a company are leveraging knowledge as they do their jobs [28].

Knowledge Management Systems

New knowledge always begins with the individual. A brilliant researcher has an insight that leads to a new patent. A middle manager's intuitive sense of market trends becomes the catalyst for an important new product concept. A shop-floor worker draws on years of experience to come up with new process innovation. In each case, an individual's personal knowledge is transformed into organizational knowledge valuable to the company as a whole.

Making personal knowledge available to others is the central activity of the knowledge-creating company. It takes place continuously and at all levels of the organization [28].

Knowledge management has thus become one of the major strategic uses of information technology. Many companies are building **knowledge management systems** (KMS) to manage organizational learning and business know-how. The goal of knowledge management systems is to help knowledge workers create, organize, and make available important business knowledge, wherever and whenever it's needed in an organization. This includes processes, procedures, patents, reference works, formulas, "best practices," forecasts, and fixes. Internet and intranet web sites, groupware, data mining, knowledge bases, discussion forums, and videoconferencing are some of the key information technologies for gathering, storing, and distributing this knowledge.

Figure 9.19   Comparing the adaptive learning systems of knowledge management to traditional knowledge-based expert systems.

	Traditional Expert Systems	Adaptive Learning Systems
Knowledge Capture	Time spent building workable rules and cases is prohibitive.	On-the-fly knowledge capture such that knowledge base learns quickly and easily.
Knowledge Retrieval	Unsuited to solution-in-progress. Requires large number of cases to provide problem-solving accuracy.	Accommodates changing solutions and solutions that have fuzzy and incomplete knowledge.
Knowledge Base Maintenance	Very high effort to maintain changing rules with large numbers of cases.	Self-organizing adaptive knowledge structure.
Skill of Knowledge Engineer	Requires skilled knowledge engineers to translate knowledge to rules and develop expert system.	Problem/solution/symptom structure is intuitive and requires no special skill.

Source: Adapted from Omar El Sawy and Gene Bowles, "Redesigning the Customer Support Process for the Electronic Economy: Insights from Storage Dimensions," *MIS Quarterly*, December 1997, p. 479. Reprinted with permission from the *MIS Quarterly*.

Therefore, knowledge management systems are information systems that facilitate organizational learning and knowledge creation. They use a variety of information technologies to collect and edit information, assess its value, disseminate it within the organization, and apply it as knowledge to the processes of a business. KMS are sometimes called *adaptive learning systems*. That's because they create cycles of organizational learning called *learning loops*, where the creation, dissemination, and application of knowledge produces an adaptive learning process within a company [13, 20]. See Figure 9.19.

Knowledge management systems can thus provide rapid feedback to knowledge workers, encourage behavior changes by employees, and significantly improve business performance. As the organizational learning process continues and its knowledge base expands, the knowledge-creating company integrates its knowledge into its business processes, products, and services. This makes it a highly innovative and agile provider of high-quality products and customer services, and a formidable competitor in the marketplace [32]. Now let's look at an example from the real world.

Storage Dimensions

Storage Dimensions is a manufacturer and developer of high-availability RAID disk storage systems, high-capacity tape backup systems, and network storage management software. It markets and supports customers in Fortune 1000 companies in North America, Europe, and the Pacific Rim. Figure 9.20 illustrates the adaptive learning loop of Storage Dimensions' knowledge management system. This KMS is a key component of their TechConnect customer support management system, which has dramatically improved Storage Dimensions' customer service and support.

TechConnect relies on unique problem resolution software, use of the Internet and intranets, and an online web site knowledge base of hyperlinked solution documents. Customer problems are quickly analyzed and resolved by product managers, development engineers, technical support specialists, or the customers themselves. Solutions are incorporated into the TechConnect knowledge base as solutions documents. The new knowledge is automatically linked with related symptoms and

Figure 9.20

The adaptive learning loop of the knowledge management system used by Storage Dimensions' TechConnect customer support management system.

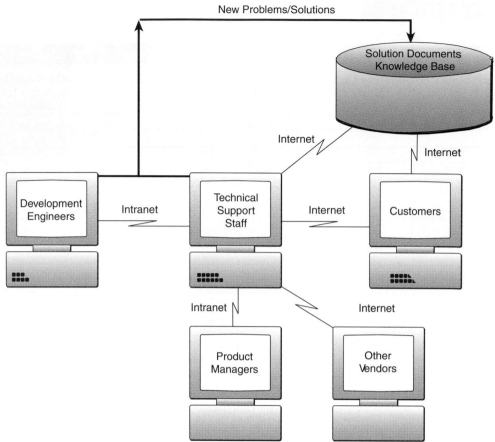

Source: Adapted from Omar El Sawy and Gene Bowles, "Redesigning the Customer Support Process for the Electronic Economy: Insights from Storage Dimensions," *MIS Quarterly*, December 1997, p. 467. Reprinted with permission from the *MIS Quarterly*.

solutions to update the knowledge base. TechConnect's software also automatically prioritizes solutions based on their usefulness or frequency of use in resolving specific kinds of problems. Thus, TechConnect learns, and new business knowledge is created each time it is used [13].

Using the Internet Strategically

Companies need a strategic framework that can bridge the gap between simply connecting to the Internet and harnessing its power for competitive advantage. The most valuable Internet applications allow companies to transcend communication barriers and establish connections that will enhance productivity, stimulate innovative development, and improve customer relations [10].

The Internet can be used strategically for competitive advantage, as this and many previous chapters have demonstrated. However, in order to optimize this strategic impact, a company must continually assess the strategic position of its Internet-based applications. Figure 9.21 is a strategic positioning matrix that can help a company identify where to concentrate its use of the Internet to gain competitive advantage. Let's take a look at the strategies that each quadrant of this matrix represents [10].

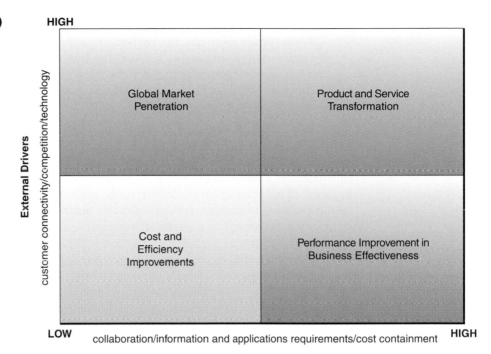

Figure 9.21

A strategic positioning matrix helps a company optimize the strategic impact of its Internet-based applications.

Internal Drivers

Source: Adapted and reprinted by permission of The Harvard Business School Press from Mary Cronin, *The Internet Strategy Handbook* (Boston: 1996), p. 20. Copyright © 1996 by the President and Fellows of Harvard College, all rights reserved.

- **Cost and Efficiency Improvements.** This quadrant represents a low amount of internal company, customer, and competitor connectivity and use of IT via the Internet and other networks. So one recommended strategy would be to focus on improving efficiency and lowering costs by using the Internet and the World Wide Web as a fast, low-cost way to communicate with customers, suppliers, and business partners. The use of E-mail and a company web site are typical examples.

- **Performance Improvement in Business Effectiveness.** Here a company has a high degree of internal connectivity and pressures to substantially improve its business processes, but external connectivity by customers and competitors is still low. A strategy of making major improvements in business effectiveness is recommended. For example, widespread internal use of Internet-based technologies like intranets can substantially improve information sharing and collaboration within the business.

- **Global Market Penetration.** A company that enters this quadrant of the matrix must capitalize on a high degree of customer and competitor connectivity and use of IT. Developing Internet-based applications to optimize interaction with customers and build market share is recommended. For example, outstanding web sites with value-added information services and online customer support would be one way to implement such a strategy.

- **Product and Service Transformation.** Here a company and its customers, suppliers, and competitors are extensively networked. Internet-based technologies, including web sites, intranets, and extranets, must now be implemented throughout the company's operations and business relationships. This enables a company to develop and deploy new Internet-based products and services that strategically reposition it in the marketplace. Using the Internet for online transaction processing of sales of products and services at company web sites, and electronic data interchange (EDI) with suppliers are typical examples of such strategic electronic commerce applications.

Internet Value Chains

In Section I, we explained how the value chain concept helps a company evaluate how to use information technology strategically. Value chains can also be used to strategically position a company's Internet-based applications to gain competitive advantage. Figure 9.22 is a value chain model that outlines several ways that a company's Internet connections with its customers could provide business benefits and opportunities for competitive advantage. For example, company-managed Internet newsgroups, chat rooms, and electronic commerce web sites are powerful tools for market research and product development, direct sales, and customer feedback and support [9].

Figure 9.23 illustrates how a company's Internet connections with its suppliers could be used for competitive advantage. Examples are electronic product catalogs at suppliers' web sites, and online shipping, scheduling, and status information that gives companies immediate access to up-to-date information from a variety of vendors. This can substantially lower costs, reduce lead times, and improve the quality of products and services.

McAffee Associates

Imagine a business plan where you develop a product that many businesses need, offer it free on the Internet on a trial basis to anyone, and provide high-quality customer and technical support, so the product is easy to use and maintain. Then after

---

Figure 9.22

An Internet value chain demonstrates the strategic business value of Internet-based applications that focus on a company's relationships with its customers.

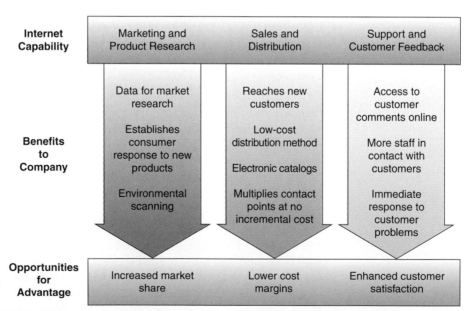

Source: Adapted from Mary Cronin, *Doing More Business on the Internet*, 2nd ed. (New York: Van Nostrand Reinhold, 1995), p. 61. Used by permission.

Figure 9.23

An Internet value chain for strategic applications with a company's suppliers.

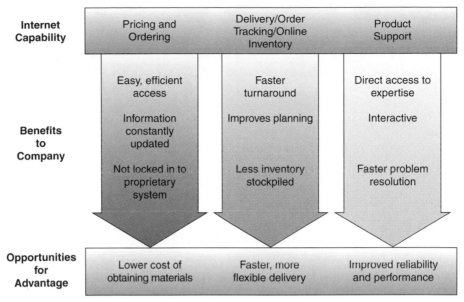

Internet Capability	Pricing and Ordering	Delivery/Order Tracking/Online Inventory	Product Support
Benefits to Company	Easy, efficient access Information constantly updated Not locked in to proprietary system	Faster turnaround Improves planning Less inventory stockpiled	Direct access to expertise Interactive Faster problem resolution
Opportunities for Advantage	Lower cost of obtaining materials	Faster, more flexible delivery	Improved reliability and performance

Source: Adapted from Mary Cronin, *Doing More Business on the Internet*, 2nd ed. (New York: Van Nostrand Reinhold, 1995), p. 58. Used by permission.

the fact, try to collect site license fees from corporations and institutions that are using your product. That is the business model of McAffee and Associates, the maker of McAffee VirusScan, one of the top antivirus programs for finding and eradicating computer viruses. The company and its products have been very successful. Their business gamble paid off and has been copied by many other companies [9]. See Figure 9.24.

Thus electronic distribution of software products over the Internet (and other online networks and bulletin board systems) is a vital component of many companies' Internet strategy. This minimizes the cost of manufacturing, packaging, shipping, distributing, and marketing products. Such cost savings enable McAffee to make large investments to maximize what they consider to be the key to competitive advantage: customer satisfaction.

If customers are very satisfied with a product, they will increase their use of it, renew their licenses, and recommend the product to others. So McAffee relies heavily on the Internet as the vehicle for distributing frequent, free product enhancements; encouraging customer participation in market research and product development; and providing top-quality customer service and technical support.

New software releases are made available for downloading to customers at the company's web site every six to eight weeks. The web site also provides access to product information and ordering systems, bulletin boards, discussion groups, and customer service and technical support. McAffee specialists participate in all discussion groups on the Internet and online services that relate to their product or its security and performance. This continual online interaction with their customers has made the entire company more customer-driven and responsive in product development and customer service, and given them a significant competitive advantage [9].

Figure 9.24

The home page of McAffee and Associates.

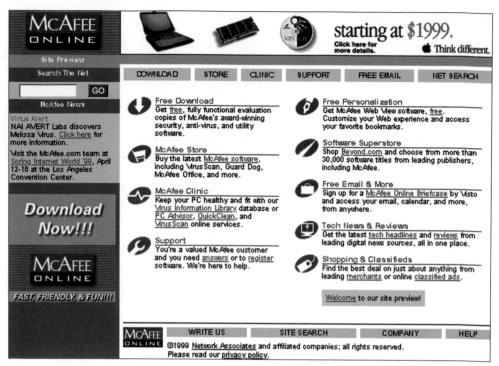

Courtesy of McAfee.com/Network Associates, Inc. McAfee and Network Associates are registered trademarks of Network Associates, Inc., and/or its affiliates in the United States and/or other countries.

The Challenges of Strategic IS

As we have seen in this chapter, the strategic use of information technology enables managers to look at information systems in a new light. No longer is the information systems function merely an operations necessity, that is, a set of technologies for processing business transactions, supporting business processes, and keeping the books of a firm. It is also more than a helpful supplier of information and tools for managerial decision making. Now the IS function can help managers develop competitive weapons that use information technology to implement a variety of competitive strategies to meet the challenges of the competitive forces that confront any organization. However, this is easier said than done.

> *We have learned over the past decade that it is not the technology that creates a competitive edge, but the management process that exploits technology; that there are not instant solutions, only difficult, lengthy, expensive implementations that involve organizational, technical, and market-related risk; and that competitive advantage comes from doing something others cannot match. If technology magically created competitive advantage for everyone, then there would effectively be no competitive edge for anyone. If innovation were easy, everyone would be an innovator. It is not easy, as evidenced by the many barriers to transforming IT from a problem to an opportunity. Among these barriers are the troubled history of IT in large organizations, particularly the limitations of the business management process; the culture gap between business and IS people; the rapid pace of technological change; and the immense and persistent difficulties associated with trying to integrate the many incompatible components of IT into a corporate platform* [21].

So successful strategic information systems are not easy to develop and implement, as Figure 9.25 illustrates. They may require major changes in the way a business operates, and in their relationships with customers, suppliers, competitors, and others. The

Figure 9.25 Examples of the success and failure of strategic information systems.

Initiative	Strategic Success: Automated Teller Machines	Strategic Failure: Home Banking
Stimulus	Cost structures of branches; pressure on margins	Successes of ATMs and corporate cash management systems; perceived large market of personal computer users
First Major Mover(s)	Citibank (1976)	Chemical Bank (Pronto system) (1980)
Customer Acceptance	Rapid and consistent; convenience the draw	Minimal; no player in United States or Europe ever established a critical mass of customers. Many entrants to the market dropped out, as did Chemical, in 1989
Catch-up Moves	"Shared access" networks (Cirrus, Monec); bank-specific networks; regional bank joint ventures	Mainly small-scale pilots and market tests; 19 American banks entered and abandoned the market, 1984–1989
First-Mover Actions	Expanded locations in New York and other states; kept other banks from adding their ATM cards to the Citibank electronic franchise	Pronto abandoned in 1989
Comments	Strategic necessity by 1982. Almost every bank in the United States began offering ATM services. Consumer pressures for shared access plus operating cost of own networks forced expensive retrofit of systems.	The classic instance of the unmet potential: no technology blockages, but no self-justifying benefits seen by target customers

Source: Adapted and reprinted by permission of The Harvard Business School Press from *Shaping the Future: Business Design through Information Technology* by Peter G. W. Keen (Boston: 1993), p. 248. Copyright © 1993 by Peter G. W. Keen.

competitive advantages that information technology produces can quickly fade away if competitors can easily duplicate them, and the failure of strategic systems can seriously damage a firm's performance. Many of the examples and cases in this chapter and text demonstrate the challenges and problems as well as the benefits of the strategic use of information technology. Thus, the effective use of strategic information systems presents managers with a major managerial challenge.

Sustaining Strategic Success

Figure 9.26 illustrates some of the factors that contribute to the success and sustainability of strategic information systems. Sustained success in using information technology strategically seems to depend on three sets of factors [22, 23].

- **The Environment.** A major environmental factor is the structure of an industry. For example, is it oligopolistic, that is, a closed structure with a few major players; or is it a wide open and level competitive playing field? Competitive restrictions and unique situations are environmental factors that involve political and regulatory restrictions to wide-open competition. For example, antitrust laws, patents, and government intervention can derail a company's plans for preemptive business use of IT.

- **Foundation Factors.** Unique industry position, organizational structure, alliances, assets, technological resources, and knowledge resources are foundation factors that can give a company a competitive edge in a market. If such a

Figure 9.26 Key factors for sustaining strategic success in the use of information technology.

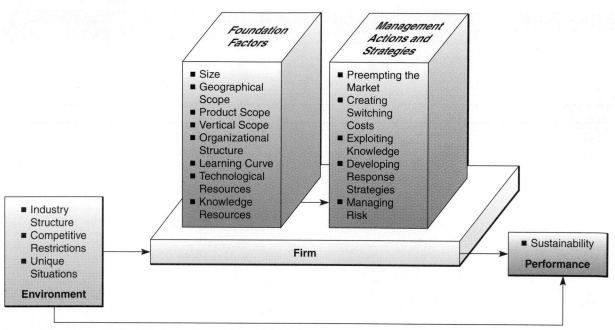

Source: Adapted from William Kettinger, Varun Grover, Subashish Guha, and Albert Segars, "Strategic Information Systems Revisited: A Study in Sustainability and Performance," *MIS Quarterly*, March 1994, p. 34. Reprinted with permission from the *MIS Quarterly*.

company develops a strategic business use of IT, they have a winning combination for strategic success.

- **Management Actions and Strategies.** None of the other factors mentioned will ensure success if a company's management does not develop and initiate successful actions and strategies that shape how information technology is actually applied in the marketplace. Examples include (1) preempting the market by being first and way ahead of competitors in strategic business uses of IT; (2) creating switching costs and barriers to entry; (3) implementing knowledge management and organizational learning; (4) developing strategies to quickly respond to the demands of customers and suppliers, and the catch-up moves of competitors; and (5) managing the business risks inherent in any strategic IT initiatives.

Figure 9.27 provides an overview of research findings on companies that are winners and losers in their strategic use of information technology [25]. Sustained winners include Air Products and Chemicals, American Airlines, Bergen Brunswig, DEC, Toys 'Я' Us, and Federal Express. These companies' investment in a specific strategic use of information technology continued to improve both their profitability and market share from 5 to 10 years after launching their strategic information systems. Sustained losers like Chase Manhattan, Mellon Bank, and United Airlines continued to suffer losses in profitability and market share for 5 to 10 years after making specific attempts to use IT strategically. As you can see, other companies had mixed success since they could not sustain profitability and market share for up to 5 years after introducing their strategic information systems.

So the lesson is clear. Sustained success in the strategic use of information technology is not a sure thing. Success depends on many environmental and foundation

Figure 9.27

Winners and losers in sustaining strategic advantage with IT. Sustained winners increased profits and market share for at least 5 to 10 years by strategic uses of information technology.

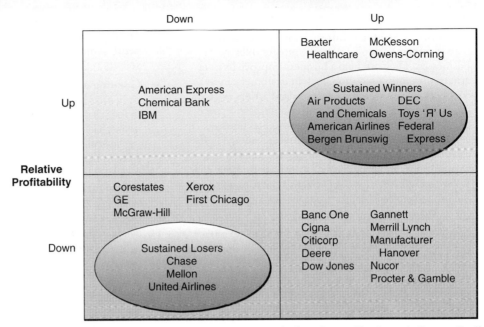

Relative Market Share

Down | Up

| Relative Profitability | |

Up

American Express
Chemical Bank
IBM

Baxter   McKesson
Healthcare   Owens-Corning

Sustained Winners
Air Products   DEC
  and Chemicals   Toys 'Я' Us
American Airlines   Federal
Bergen Brunswig   Express

Down

Corestates   Xerox
GE   First Chicago
McGraw-Hill

Sustained Losers
Chase
Mellon
United Airlines

Banc One   Gannett
Cigna   Merrill Lynch
Citicorp   Manufacturer
Deere   Hanover
Dow Jones   Nucor
                    Procter & Gamble

Source: Adapted from William Kettinger, Varun Grover, and Albert Segars, "Do Strategic Systems Really Pay Off? An Analysis of Classic Strategic IT Cases," *Information Systems Management* (New York: Auerbach Publications), Winter 1995, p. 39. © 1995 Research Institute of America. Used with permission.

factors, but also on the actions and strategies of a company's management team. As a future manager, developing strategic business use of information technology may be one of your biggest managerial challenges.

Summary

- **The Role of Strategic Information Systems.** Information systems can play several strategic roles in businesses. They can help a business improve its operations, promote innovation, lock in customers and suppliers, create switching costs, raise barriers to entry, build a strategic IT platform, and develop a strategic information base. Thus, information technology can help a business gain a competitive advantage in its relationships with customers, suppliers, competitors, new entrants, and producers of substitute products. Refer to Figure 9.3 for a summary of the uses of information technology for strategic advantage.

- **Reengineering Business Processes.** Information technology is a key ingredient in reengineering business operations by enabling radical changes to business processes that dramatically improve their efficiency and effectiveness. IT can play a major role in supporting innovative changes in the design of work flows, job requirements, and organizational structures in a company.

- **Improving Business Quality.** Information technology can be used to strategically improve the quality of business performance. In a total quality management approach, IT can support programs of continual improvement in meeting or exceeding customer requirements and expectations in quality, services, cost, responsiveness, and other features that have a significant impact on a firm's competitive position.

- **Becoming an Agile Competitor.** A business can use information technology to help it become an agile company. Then it can prosper in rapidly changing markets with broad product ranges and short model lifetimes in which it must process orders in arbitrary lot sizes, and can offer individualized products while maintaining high volumes of production. An agile company depends heavily on IT to help it: (1) enrich its customers with customized solutions to their needs; (2) cooperate with other businesses to bring products to market as rapidly and cost-effectively as possible; (3) coordinate the flexible, multiple organizational structures it uses; and (4) leverage the competitive impact of its people and information resources.

- **Creating a Virtual Company.** Forming virtual companies has become an important competitive strategy in today's dynamic global markets. Information technology plays an important role in providing computing and telecommunications resources to support the communications, coordination, and information flows needed. Managers of a virtual company depend on IT to help them manage a network of people, knowledge, financial, and physical resources provided by many business partners to quickly take advantage of rapidly changing market opportunities.

- **Building a Knowledge-Creating Company.** Lasting competitive advantage today can only come from the innovative use and management of organizational knowledge by knowledge-creating companies and learning organizations. Information technologies in knowledge management systems support the creation and dissemination of business knowledge, and its integration into new products, services, and business processes.

- **Using Internet Technologies.** The Internet, intranets, extranets, and other Internet-based technologies can be used strategically for competitive advantage. This may include major improvements in business efficiency and effectiveness, global market penetration, transforming products and services, and developing strategic applications and relationships with customers and business partners.

- **The Challenge of Strategic IS.** Successful strategic information systems are not easy to develop and implement. They may require major changes in how a business operates internally and with external stakeholders. Sustained success depends on many environmental and fundamental business factors, and especially on the actions and strategies of a company's management team. So developing strategic uses of information technology is a major managerial challenge.

Key Terms and Concepts

These are the key terms and concepts of this chapter. The page number of their first explanation is in parentheses.

1. Agile competitor (356)
2. Building a strategic IT platform (346)
3. Business process reengineering (351)
4. Competitive forces (340)
5. Competitive strategies (341)
6. Creating switching costs (345)
7. Developing a strategic information base (346)
8. Improving business processes (342)
9. Interorganizational information systems (358)
10. Knowledge-creating company (360)
11. Knowledge management system (360)
12. Leveraging investment in IT (346)
13. Locking in customers and suppliers (345)
14. Promoting business innovation (344)
15. Raising barriers to entry (346)
16. Strategic business use of Internet technologies (362)
17. Strategic information systems (340)
18. Strategic roles of information systems (341)
19. Sustaining competitive advantage (367)
20. Total quality management (353)
21. Value chain (347)
22. Virtual company (358)

Review Quiz

Match one of the key terms and concepts listed previously with one of the brief examples or definitions that follow. Try to find the best fit for answers that seem to fit more than one term or concept. Defend your choices.

_____ 1. A business must deal with customers, suppliers, competitors, new entrants, and substitutes.

_____ 2. Cost leadership, differentiation of products, and development of new products are examples.

_____ 3. Using investment in technology to keep firms out of an industry.

_____ 4. Making it unattractive for a firm's customers or suppliers to switch to its competitors.

_____ 5. Time, money, and effort needed for customers or suppliers to change to a firm's competitors.

_____ 6. Information systems that improve operational efficiency or promote business innovation are examples.

_____ 7. Information systems can help a business develop new products, services, and processes.

_____ 8. Information systems can help a business significantly reduce costs and improve productivity.

_____ 9. Information systems can help a business develop a strategic base of information.

_____ 10. A business can develop strategic capabilities in IT skills and resources.

_____ 11. Information systems can help a business develop electronic links to its customers and suppliers.

_____ 12. Highlights how strategic information systems can be applied to a firm's business processes and support activities for competitive advantage.

_____ 13. A business can find strategic uses for the computing and telecommunications capabilities it has acquired to run its operations.

_____ 14. A business can use information systems to build barriers to entry, promote innovation, create switching costs, and so on.

_____ 15. Information technology can help a business make radical improvements in business processes.

_____ 16. Programs of continual improvement in meeting or exceeding customer requirements or expectations.

_____ 17. A business can prosper in rapidly changing markets while offering its customers individualized solutions to their needs.

_____ 18. A network of business partners formed to take advantage of rapidly changing market opportunities.

_____ 19. Many companies use the Internet, intranets, and extranets to achieve strategic gains in their competitive position.

——— 20. Learning organizations that focus on creating, disseminating, and managing business knowledge.

——— 21. Information systems that manage the creation and dissemination of organizational knowledge.

——— 22. The competitive advantages of IT will disappear unless management implements strategies such as exploiting knowledge management.

Discussion Questions

1. Suppose you are a manager being pushed to use information technology to gain a competitive advantage in an important market for your company. What reservations might you have about doing so? Why?

2. How could a business use information technology to increase switching costs and lock in its customers and suppliers? Use business examples to support your answers.

3. How could a business leverage its investment in information technology to build a strategic IT platform that serves as a barrier to entry by new entrants into its markets?

4. Refer to the Real World Case on Ford Motor Company in the chapter. How else could Ford use IT to benefit from the expertise of its customers or suppliers instead of creating expertise within the company? Do you approve of this strategy? Why or why not?

5. What strategic role can information technology play in business process reengineering and total quality management?

6. How can information technology help a business form strategic alliances with its customers, suppliers, and others?

7. How could a business use the Internet, intranets, or extranets to form a virtual company or become an agile competitor?

8. Refer to the Real World Case on Office Depot and Staples in the chapter. How strategic is information technology to the success of a business today? Use Office Depot, Staples, or another company to illustrate your answer.

9. Information technology can't really give a company a strategic advantage, because most competitive advantages don't last more than a few years and soon become strategic necessities that just raise the stakes of the game. Discuss.

10. MIS author and consultant Peter Keen says: "We have learned over the past decade that it is not technology that creates a competitive edge, but the management process that exploits technology." What does he mean? Do you agree or disagree. Why?

Real World Problems

1. Barnes & Noble and Bertelsmann versus Amazon.com: Net Retail Strategies
Barnesandnoble.com: www.barnesandnoble.com. CEO: Stephen Riggio. 1998 revenues: $65 million (projected). Recent moves: Cash influx from Bertelsmann; parent company Barnes & Noble acquired Ingram Book Group. Key partners: Bertelsmann and AOL. Offerings: 600,000 titles. Prognosis: Now that its parent company owns the country's biggest book supplier (Ingram), barnesandnoble.com looms larger as an Amazon.com competitor. But it will be playing catch-up for the time being. For example, even with its land-based brand clout and aggressive marketing in 1998, its third-quarter sales ($17.2 million) were no match for Amazon's ($153.7 million).
Bertelsmann: www.bertelsmann.com. CEO: Thomas Middelhoff. 1998 revenues: $17 billion. Net retail offerings: Books, music. Plans to launch its own global online bookseller. Recent moves: Bought a 50 percent stake in barnesandnoble.com. Prognosis: The third-largest media company in the world now has a big foot in the Net retail door, with its $200 million investment in barnesandnoble.com.

As Amazon.com pushes outward from book selling, it won't be without competition from serious players aiming for a shot at Net retail dominance. The biggest salvo has come for Bertelsmann—the Germany-based publishing giant announced in October 1998 that it was paying $200 million for a 50 percent stake in Amazon's primary online competitor, barnesandnoble.com (now a joint venture between Bertelsmann and Barnes & Noble).

"This venture has one purpose," Bertelsmann CEO Thomas Middelhoff said shortly afterward in an interview with *Fortune:* "To compete with Amazon.com in the United States."

That Middelhoff had unsuccessfully proposed a Bertelsmann-Amazon partnership first—he reportedly even sent a corporate jet to fly Amazon.com CEO Jeff Bezos to Bertelsmann offices in Germany from a vacation spot in Turkey to try to close a deal—seems to have fueled a second blow. Barnes & Noble announced an agreement in November 1998 to buy the Ingram Book Group, the largest U.S. distributor (and supplier for 57 percent of Amazon's book purchases) for some $600 million in cash and stock.

Bertelsmann—the third-largest media company in the world, with divisions covering books, television, news media, and music—may be a relative newcomer to Internet retail, but it has international clout as a company that clearly "gets" the Net. The $17 billion company owns 45 percent of AOL Europe (as does America Online), and last year the two teamed up to buy CompuServe's European operations. The German giant also has a strategic partnership with Lycos, by which it helped launch the top portal in Europe.

Despite others' predictions of a commerce portal as its goal, the New York–based CEO of Bertelsmann's global online bookseller (BOL), Chip Austin, a former Prodigy executive, insists that as far as Net commerce goes, the company will stick to markets that it knows best—books and music, especially in Europe, where Amazon's recent launch will not go unchallenged.

"Amazon is going to try and expand globally into markets where they have never participated before, and they're going to try and extend their product areas where they don't have much experience. That's a lot of things that have to all go right."

Whether Bertelsmann/Barnesandnoble.com simply aims to dominate Net "media" retail in music, books, video, and software, here and abroad, or goes the "portal" route that many expect of Amazon, it promises to serve and volley the whole way, and with cash to spare.

a. Evaluate the strategic moves of Barnes & Noble and Bertelsmann against Amazon.com. Which move will prove most effective? Why?
b. What other strategic moves must Barnes & Noble and Bertelsmann make to compete more successfully against Amazon? Explain your reasoning.

Source: Adapted from Jeffrey Davis, "Mall Rats," *Business 2.0*, January 1999, pp. 41–50.

2. Shiva Corporation: Empowering Customers and Employees with Web Knowledge Management
Shiva Corporation is in the business of connecting employees, customers, and partners to business networks via remote access technology. However, in the past, customers had the option of calling the Shiva customer support desk for help. Shiva decided to take support matters one step further by providing a system that would make its customers self-reliant.

Using Verity's Information Server and CD Web Publisher software, Shiva built its Knowledge Management application. The solution provides customers with web-based answers to their technical support questions, access to online peer groups, CD-ROM-based product documentation, and a quarterly CD-ROM containing time-saving information.

The Knowledge Management solution took three months to develop. Within 45 days of use, it surpassed its financial break-even point. Shiva experienced a 22 percent drop in customer support calls in the first three months. Now, one out of four customers is getting answers on Shiva's web site or via the CD-ROM. Shiva's Knowledgebase area is now the second-most accessed section of the company's web site, with 110,000 people hitting the site every month, including Shiva's 500-plus employees worldwide.

The Knowledge Management application has helped foster a corporate culture in which technical information is shared fully and strategically rather than kept under lock and key. In-house staff can track common technical problems and determine what areas need improvement. Customers can obtain instant answers to their questions.

Shiva's Knowledge is updated primarily by the company's technical support and engineering departments, although anyone in the organization can enter a Knowledgebase article into the system. It then becomes accessible to everyone else via the company's intranet/extranet. Within the Knowledge Management application, the Lotus Notes Knowledgebase is converted to HTML and uploaded to a server. Then, the Verity software indexes all of the available documents regularly and ties all the information together, where it's available to users via the Web.

Shiva's Knowledge Management application has increased the company's ability to provide technical information to customers without requiring them to contact the company directly. The support centers now focus attention on more complex support issues. When these complex problems are solved, the information is then added to Shiva's Lotus Notes Knowledgebase and made available to customers via the Web and CD-ROM. Thus, with the help of information technology, Shiva has met its goal of making its customers and employees self-reliant.

a. How is knowledge management made easier by intranet and extranet technologies?

b. What is the business value and what are the risks of a strategy to make customers and employees more self-reliant?

Source: Adapted from "Helping Customers Help Themselves," *Intelligent Enterprise*, Advertising Section, January 5, 1999, p. R15.

3. Hewlett-Packard and furniture.com: The Business Value of Customer Service in E-Commerce

The big myth about E-commerce is that it's about as close to self-service as you can get. At last—or so the theory goes—companies no longer have to sweat customer hand-holding, staff huge call centers, and suffer the dings of customer gripes. But oh, how wrong that is. Four years into E-commerce, and the shrewdest web operators are finding that the velvet gloves treatment may be more crucial in cyberspace than it has ever been.

Gone are the days of the geographically captive customer, when merchants had the advantage of being the only store within driving distance. On the Web, the next shop is seconds away. What's more, it's open 24 hours. If cybershoppers can't get products or answers instantly—which happens all too often—they are off in a heartbeat. "Better service is no longer just a nice thing to do. It's mandatory," says Amir Aghdaei, Hewlett-Packard Co.'s call center manager.

That's the idea at furniture.com, of Worcester, Massachusetts, whose state-of-the-art digital aid provides a glimmer of the future. Visitors to its web site type in style preferences, and within seconds a live company rep is at their service, ready to talk via web chat or Netphone about the personalized showroom that has just been created and sent to their computer. From there, buyers can haggle over colors, fabrics, prices, and dimensions.

The service doesn't stop there. After the sale, customers are "adopted" by the reps, who E-mail or phone from time to time to handle complaints or offer a new fabric-coordinated accessory. The results: While shoppers who use the personalized showroom take 20 percent longer, the orders are, on average, 50 percent larger. CEO Andrew Brooks says furniture.com can afford to spend more on service because doing business over the Web is cheaper.

"The fundamental earth-shaking event that's being shaped by E-business is a radical shift in bargaining power from sellers to buyers," says Brooks. "What does that mean? Service is everything."

And E-service sells. Hewlett-Packard (HP) is using homegrown tracking software to create a database of corporate customers who call or E-mail for service. That way, HP can chart their concerns and, when they E-mail or call again, identify them by specialty before automatically routing them to agents with the right know-how. The payoff so far: an estimated $180 million in incremental sales. With those kinds of results, E-service can pay for itself.

a. Visit the www.furniture.com web site. How well is their customer service strategy being implemented? What is its business value?

b. How does Hewlett-Packard's "service sells" strategy differ from furniture.com's strategy? What is its business value?

Source: Reprinted from Marcia Stepanek, "You'll Wanna Hold Their Hands," *Business Week e.biz*, March 22, 1999, pp. EB 30–31, by special permission, copyright © 1999 by The McGraw-Hill Companies, Inc.

Application Exercises

1. Apex Products Inventory System

Apex Products is evaluating a proposal for the development of a new production and inventory management system that will allow it to use just-in-time techniques. It is estimated that the new system will allow Apex to operate with inventory levels equal to 10 days of production. In order to estimate the inventory cost savings from this system, you have been asked to gather information about current inventory levels at all of Apex's production facilities. You have received the following estimates of the value of current inventories and the value of resources used in a typical production day for each facility.

Facility	Inventory Value	Inventory Used per Production Day
Lakeside A	$12,572,000	$326,450
Lakeside B	18,473,500	402,500
Uptown	15,396,350	422,000
Industrial Park A	24,018,300	515,000
Industrial Park B	16,230,600	322,000

a. Create a spreadsheet based on the preceding estimates. Your spreadsheet should include a column showing the number of days of inventory currently held at each facility (inventory value divided by inventory used per production day). It should also include columns showing the inventory needed under the new system (inventory used per day times 10) and the reduction in inventory under the new system for each facility.

b. Assume that the annual cost of holding inventory is 9 percent times the level of inventory held. Add summary columns to your spreadsheet to show the savings at each site and the overall savings from the new system.

2. Electronic Commerce at ABC Company

ABC Company is considering developing a strategic system to sell products through its web site. None of ABC's direct competitors currently utilize electronic commerce, but the president of ABC thinks that electronic commerce is appropriate for ABC's industry and wants to be in a leadership position. You have been asked to assist in preparing a preliminary feasibility study for the system. Your analysis is to be restricted to the first five years of operation.

Staff from the information systems and marketing departments have developed the following estimates for your use. The IS department has estimated the cost of developing and maintaining this system across its first five years of operation. The marketing department estimates that sales will be $1,250,000 in year 2 (the system is expected to take one full year for initial development) and that sales will grow 40 percent per year thereafter. The departments also estimate that each dollar of electronic sales will contribute 30 cents to profit.

a. Based on these figures, construct a spreadsheet to analyze the costs and benefits of the proposed system. Projected sales for year 3 will be 1.4 times year 2 sales, year 4's sales will be 1.4 times year 3's sales, and so on. The benefits of the system are equal to new sales times the 30 percent contribution to profits. Your spreadsheet should include a column showing the net contribution (benefits minus system cost) for each year.

b. Assume that ABC Company requires a return of 25 percent on this type of investment. Add a net present value calculation to your spreadsheet and determine whether this project would be justified.

	Year 1	Year 2	Year 3	Year 4	Year 5
System cost:	$500,000	$250,000	$250,000	$300,000	$325,000
Projected sales:		$1,250,000	(40 percent growth per year)		
Sales contribution rate:	(30 percent contributions to profits in years 1–5)				

Review Quiz Answers

1. 4	5. 6	8. 8	11. 9	14. 18	17. 1	20. 10
2. 5	6. 17	9. 7	12. 21	15. 3	18. 22	21. 11
3. 15	7. 14	10. 2	13. 12	16. 20	19. 16	22. 19
4. 13						

Selected References

1. Applegate, Linda; F. Warren McFarlen; and James McKenney. *Corporate Information Systems Management: Text and Cases*. Burr Ridge, IL: Irwin/McGraw-Hill, 1996.

2. Bowles, Jerry. "Best Practices for Global Competitiveness." Special Advertising Section. *Fortune*, November 24, 1997.

3. Bowles, Jerry, and Josh Hammond. "Competing on Knowledge." Special Advertising Supplement, *Fortune*, September 19, 1996.

4. Callon, Jack. *Competitive Advantage through Information Technology*. New York: McGraw-Hill, 1996.

5. Caron, J. Raymond: Sirkka Jarvenpaa; and Donna Stoddard. "Business Reengineering at CIGNA Corporation: Experiences and Lessons from the First Five Years." *MIS Quarterly*, September 1994.

6. Cash, James I., Jr.; Robert G. Eccles; Nitin Nohria; and Richard L. Nolan, *Building the Information-Age Organization: Structure, Control, and Information Technologies*. Burr Ridge, IL: Richard D. Irwin, 1994.

7. Champy, James. "Now Batting Cleanup: Information Technology." *Computerworld*, October 28, 1996.

8. Clemons, Eric, and Michael Row. "Sustaining IT Advantage: The Role of Structural Differences." *MIS Quarterly*, September 1991.

9. Cronin, Mary. *Doing More Business on the Internet*. 2nd ed. New York: Van Nostrand Reinhold, 1995.

10. Cronin, Mary. *The Internet Strategy Handbook*. Boston: Harvard Business School Press, 1996.

11. Davenport, Thomas H. *Process Innovation: Reengineering Work through Information Technology*. Boston: Harvard Business School Press, 1993.

12. Davenport, Thomas H., and Donna Stoddard. "Reengineering: Business Change of Mythic Proportions." *MIS Quarterly*, June 1994.

13. El Sawy, Omar, and Gene Bowles. "Redesigning the Customer Support Process for the Electronic Economy: Insights from Strange Dimensions." *MIS Quarterly*, December 1997.

14. Evans, Phillip, and Thomas Wurster. "Strategy and the New Economics of Information." *Harvard Business Review*, September—October 1997.

15. Fayyad, Usama; Gregory Piatetsky-Shapiro; and Padhraic Smith. "The KDD Process for Extracting Useful Knowledge from Volumes of Data." *Communications of the ACM*, November 1996.

16. Frye, Colleen. "Imaging Proves Catalyst for Reengineering." *Client/Server Computing*, November 1994.

17. Garvin, David. "Building a Learning Organization." *Harvard Business Review*, July–August 1995.

18. Goldman, Steven; Roger Nagel; and Kenneth Preis. *Agile Competitors and Virtual Organizations: Strategies for Enriching the Customer*. New York: Van Nostrand Reinhold, 1995.

19. Hammer, Michael, and James Champy. *Reengineering the Corporation: A Manifesto for Business Revolution*. New York: HarperCollins, 1993.

20. Hibbard, Justin. "Spreading Knowledge." *Computerworld*, April 7, 1997.

21. Keen, Peter G. W. *Shaping the Future: Business Design through Information Technology*. Boston: Harvard Business School Press, 1991.

22. Kettinger, William; Varun Grover; Subashish Guha; and Albert Segars. "Strategic Information Systems Revisited: A Study in Sustainability and Performance." *MIS Quarterly*, March 1994.

23. Kettinger, William; Varun Grover; and Albert Segars. "Do Strategic Systems Really Pay Off? An Analysis of Classic Strategic IT Cases." *Information Systems Management*, Winter 1995.

24. Kettinger, William; James Teng; and Subashish Guha. "Business Process Change: A Study of Methodologies, Techniques, and Tools." *MIS Quarterly*, March 1997.

25. Maglitta, Joseph. "Know-How, Inc." *Computerworld*, January 15, 1996.

26. Mooney, John; Vijay Gurbaxani; and Kenneth Kramer. "A Process Oriented Framework for Assessing the Business Value of Information Technology." *The DATA BASE for Advances in Information Systems*, Spring 1996.

27. Neumann, Seev. *Strategic Information Systems: Competition through Information Technologies*. New York: Macmillan College Publishing Co., 1994.

28. Nonaka, Ikujiro. "The Knowledge Creating Company." *Harvard Business Review*, November–December 1991.

29. Pegels, C. Carl. *Total Quality Management: A Survey of Its Important Aspects*. Danvers, MA: boyd & fraser publishing co., 1995.

30. Porter, Michael, and Victor Millar. "How Information Gives You Competitive Advantage." *Harvard Business Review*, July–August 1985.

31. Prokesch, Steven. "Unleashing the Power of Learning: An Interview with British Petroleum's John Browne." *Harvard Business Review*, September–October 1997.

32. Resnick, Rosalind. "The Virtual Corporation." *PC Today*, February 1995.

33. Schonberger, Richard. "Is Strategy Strategic? Impact of Total Quality Management on Strategy." *Academy of Management Executive*, August 1992.

34. Siekman, Philip. "Why Infotech Loves Its Giant Job Shops." *Fortune*, May 12, 1997.

35. Zahedi, Fatemeh. *Quality Information Systems*. Danvers, MA: boyd & fraser publishing co., 1995.

Development and

Management

How can end users help develop information system solutions to solve business problems and pursue business opportunities? What managerial challenges do information systems pose for the end user managers of modern organizations? The three chapters of this module emphasize how managers and end users can develop and manage the use of information technology in a global information society.

Chapter 10, "Developing Business Solutions with Information Technology," introduces the traditional, prototyping, and end user approaches to the development of information systems, and discusses managerial issues in the implementation of information technology.

Chapter 11, "Enterprise and Global Management of Information Technology," emphasizes the impact of information technology on management and organizations, the importance of information resource management, and the managerial implications of global information technology.

Chapter 12, "Security and Ethical Challenges of Information Technology," discusses the controls needed for information system performance and security, as well as the ethical implications and societal impacts of information technology.

Developing Business Solutions

with Information Technology

Chapter Highlights

Section I
Developing Information System Solutions
Real World Case: SunAmerica Financial and A-DEC Inc.: Challenges in ERP Systems Development and Implementation
The Systems Approach
The Systems Development Cycle
Starting the Systems Development Process
A Case Study Example: Auto Shack Stores: Solving a Business Problem
Systems Analysis
Systems Design
Prototyping
Computer-Aided Systems Engineering
End User Development
Checklist for End User Development

Section II
Implementing Business Change with IT
Introduction
Real World Case: Computer Associates, Microsoft, and IBM: Business Users Rate Software Support
Managing Organizational Change
Implementing New Systems
Evaluating Hardware, Software, and Services
Other Implementation Activities

Learning Objectives

After reading and studying this chapter, you should be able to:

1. Describe and give examples to illustrate each of the steps of the information systems development cycle.

2. Explain how prototyping and computer-aided systems engineering have affected the process of information systems development for end users and information systems specialists.

3. Use the IS development process and the model of information system components from Chapter 1 and this chapter as problem-solving frameworks to help you propose information systems solutions to simple business problems.

4. Identify some of the major activities involved in the implementation process for managing technological change.

5. Discuss how end user resistance to changes in business processes or information technology can be minimized by end user involvement in systems development and implementation.

6. Identify the activities involved in the implementation of new information systems.

7. Describe several evaluation factors that should be considered in evaluating the acquisition of hardware, software, and IS services.

Section I

Developing Information System Solutions

Developing information system solutions to business problems is a responsibility of any business professional today. As a business end user you will be responsible for proposing or developing new or improved uses of information technology for your company. As a manager, you will also frequently manage the development efforts of information systems specialists and other end users. This section will show you how information system solutions that meet the business needs of end users and their organizations can be developed.

Analyzing SunAmerica and A-DEC

Read the Real World Case on SunAmerica Financial and A-DEC Inc. We can learn a lot about how difficult and complex it can be to install new software technology that requires major changes to business processes. See Figure 10.1

Roy Nakabara found himself doing project planning one month after SunAmerica had started an enterprise resource management (ERP) systems development project. Nakabara, who was called in to head the project, then had to deal with IT managers who had underestimated the complexity of modifying their present systems when installing a newly acquired ERP software suite. He also had to call in the executives of SunAmerica's business units to convince IT managers not to interfere with the work assignments of project team members so he could keep the project going properly.

Keith Bearden was brought in as CIO three months after A-DEC's new enterprise resource management system had been installed. He faced major resistance from users who had been inadequately trained and did not understand the new system. He also had to deal with an IT department that had underestimated the processing power needed to run the ERP system. It took A-DEC a year and doubled the cost of the

Figure 10.1

Roy Nakabara is vice president of cash services at SunAmerica Financial and project manager of their enterprise resource management system deployment.

Source: Alan Levenson.

SunAmerica Financial and A-DEC Inc.: Challenges in ERP Systems Development and Implementation

SunAmerica Financial

Roy Nakabara wasn't counting on being an ERP project manager. But that was before SunAmerica Inc.'s first choice to run its enterprise resource planning rollout quit a month into the project. Nakabara was next in line.

And so he suddenly found himself having to cope with all the pitfalls that can trip up business executives drafted to oversee application development project teams, from morale-busting work hours to disputes with information technology managers over resources.

Nakabara, vice president of cash services at SunAmerica Financial, had to declare a two-week time-out to take stock of the situation and put together a project plan. "We got off to a really rough start," Nakabara said in an interview at SunAmerica's accounting offices 36 floors above Los Angeles's Avenue of the Stars. "We were already 10 yards behind, which was hard to recover from."

SunAmerica's IT department also underestimated the complexity of building software interfaces to 18 mainframe applications that will still run other parts of the business, Nakabara said. And IT managers were pulling programmers from the ERP team to fix problems on the existing applications, a situation that led Nakabara to call in his bosses on the business side.

The business unit executives finally persuaded the IT managers to hire outside contractors to fix the mainframe applications. This freed up SunAmerica's programmers to focus on developing interfaces and tailoring the ERP package from Germany's SAP AG so it better fits SunAmerica's remaining systems.

A-DEC Inc.

Finally, A-DEC Inc. is starting to pull benefits out of its ERP system. But the dental equipment maker first had to endure more than a year of chaos and canceled orders. After turning on Baan Co.'s enterprise resource planning suite early in 1997, A-DEC fell behind on processing orders, building products, and then shipping the goods to dealers. Even some of its most loyal customers grew nervous about relying on the company.

"We lost a lot of business," said CIO Keith Bearden, who was brought in to manage A-DEC's information systems three months into the rollout. To get by, the Newberg, Oregon, company even had to fill some orders outside the Baan systems "because workers didn't understand it, and the performance was so bad," he said. At A-DEC, business changes initially were fought, Bearden said. End-user training also fell short at first, he said, and the information technology department underestimated the processing power that Baan's software required.

After Bearden was hired in mid-1997, he pulled together a stabilization team from all parts of the company. It took about six months of systems development work to fix the performance issues by changing databases and upgrading A-DEC's servers and network. Another six months were spent redesigning business processes and training users.

All that work basically doubled the cost of the project, Bearden said. "We spent a lot of money just cleaning up problems," he said. Even now, 50-plus key users spend 20 percent of their work time looking for ways to improve A-DEC's use of the software.

But the company now is getting some of the benefits it expected, Bearden said. For example, inventory levels have been cut by about 30 percent since the new system was put into use. And one of A-DEC's four product lines has been switched to a fast turnaround modular manufacturing approach that wasn't feasible before.

Case Study Questions

1. What stages of the systems development process (see Figure 10.4) do you recognize in this case? Explain how you recognize each one.

2. What mistakes in systems development, implementation, and project management do you recognize in this case?

3. How could each of these mistakes have been avoided?

Source: Adapted from Craig Steadman, "In Pinch, Exec Leads Crucial SAP Rollout," *Computerworld*, October 12, 1998, pp. 1, 84; and "ERP Pioneers," *Computerworld*, January 18, 1999, pp. 1, 24. Copyright 1998 and 1999 by Computerworld, Inc., Framingham, MA 01701. Reprinted from *Computerworld*.

project to change databases, upgrade servers, redesign business processes, and train users before the new system was operating properly and showing some of the business benefits for which it had been designed.

The Systems Approach

Suppose the chief executive of a firm where you are the sales manager asks you to find a better way to get information to the salespeople in your company. How would you start? What would you do? Would you just plunge ahead and hope you could come up with a reasonable solution? How would you know whether your solution was a good one for your company? Do you think there might be a systematic way to help you develop a good solution to the CEO's request? There is. It's a problem-solving process called **the systems approach.**

The systems approach to problem solving uses a systems orientation to define problems and opportunities and develop solutions. Studying a problem and formulating a solution involve the following interrelated activities:

1. Recognize and define a problem or opportunity using systems thinking.
2. Develop and evaluate alternative system solutions.
3. Select the system solution that best meets your requirements.
4. Design the selected system solution.
5. Implement and evaluate the success of the designed system.

Systems Thinking

Using **systems thinking** to understand a problem or opportunity is one of the most important aspects of the systems approach. Management consultant and author Peter Senge calls systems thinking *the fifth discipline.* Senge argues that mastering systems thinking (along with the disciplines of personal mastery, mental models, shared vision, and team learning) is vital to personal fulfillment and business success in a world of constant change. The essence of the discipline of systems thinking is "seeing the forest *and* the trees" in any situation by:

- Seeing *interrelationships* among *systems* rather than linear cause-and-effect chains whenever events occur.
- Seeing *processes* of change among *systems* rather than discrete "snapshots" of change, whenever changes occur [29].

One way of practicing systems thinking is to try to find systems, subsystems, and components of systems in any situation you are studying. This is also known as using a *systems context*, or having a *systemic view* of a situation. For example, the business organization or business process in which a problem or opportunity arises could be viewed as a system of input, processing, output, feedback, and control components. Then to understand a problem and solve it, you would determine if these basic systems functions are being properly performed.

Example   The sales function of a business can be viewed as a system. You could then ask: Is poor sales performance (output) caused by inadequate selling effort (input), out-of-date sales procedures (processing), incorrect sales information (feedback), or inadequate sales management (control)? Figure 10.2 illustrates this concept. ●

Figure 10.2

An example of systems thinking. You can better understand a sales problem or opportunity by identifying and evaluating the components of a sales system.

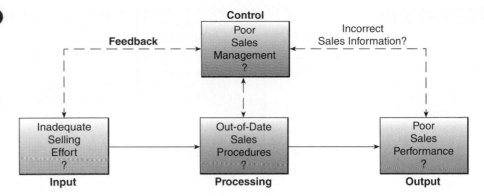

Figure 10.2

An example of systems thinking. You can better understand a sales problem or opportunity by identifying and evaluating the components of a sales system.

The Systems Development Cycle

When the systems approach to problem solving is applied to the development of information system solutions to business problems, it is called **information systems development** or *application development*. Most computer-based information systems are conceived, designed, and implemented using some form of systematic development process. In this process, end users and information specialists *design* information systems based on an *analysis* of the information requirements of an organization. Thus, a major part of this process is known as *systems analysis and design*. However, as Figure 10.3 shows, several other major activities are involved in a complete development cycle.

Using the systems approach to develop information system solutions involves a multistep process called the **information systems development cycle,** also known as the *systems development life cycle* (SDLC). Figure 10.4 illustrates what goes on in each stage of this process, which includes the steps of (1) investigation, (2) analysis, (3) design, (4) implementation, and (5) maintenance.

You should realize, however, that all of the activities involved are highly related and interdependent. Therefore, in actual practice, several developmental activities can occur at the same time, so different parts of a development project can be at different stages of the development cycle. In addition, analysts may recycle back at any time to repeat previous activities in order to modify and improve a system they are developing.

Finally, you should realize that developments such as prototyping, computer-aided systems engineering (CASE), and end user development are automating and changing

Figure 10.3

Developing information systems solutions to business problems is typically a multistep process or cycle.

Figure 10.4

The traditional information systems development cycle. Note how the five steps of the cycle are based on the stages of the systems approach. Also note the products that result from each step in the cycle, and that you can recycle back to any previous step if more work is needed.

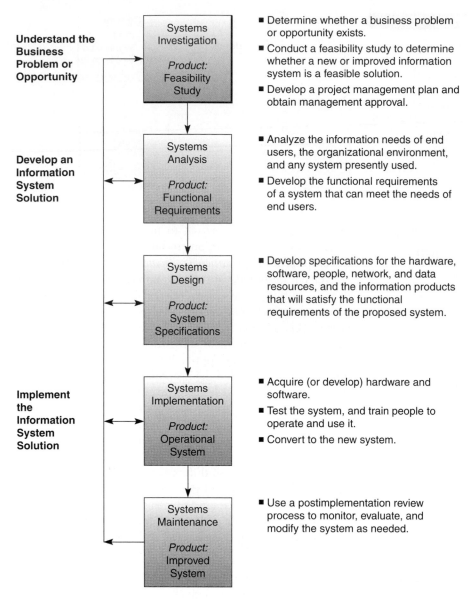

Understand the Business Problem or Opportunity

Systems Investigation

Product: Feasibility Study

- Determine whether a business problem or opportunity exists.
- Conduct a feasibility study to determine whether a new or improved information system is a feasible solution.
- Develop a project management plan and obtain management approval.

Develop an Information System Solution

Systems Analysis

Product: Functional Requirements

- Analyze the information needs of end users, the organizational environment, and any system presently used.
- Develop the functional requirements of a system that can meet the needs of end users.

Systems Design

Product: System Specifications

- Develop specifications for the hardware, software, people, network, and data resources, and the information products that will satisfy the functional requirements of the proposed system.

Implement the Information System Solution

Systems Implementation

Product: Operational System

- Acquire (or develop) hardware and software.
- Test the system, and train people to operate and use it.
- Convert to the new system.

Systems Maintenance

Product: Improved System

- Use a postimplementation review process to monitor, evaluate, and modify the system as needed.

some of the activities of information systems development. These developments are improving the quality of systems development and making it easier for IS professionals, while enabling more end users to develop their own systems. We will discuss them shortly. Now, let's take a look at each step of this development process.

Starting the Systems Development Process

Do we have a business problem (or opportunity)? What is causing the problem? Would a new or improved information system help solve the problem? What would be a feasible information system solution to our problem? These are the questions that have to be answered in the **systems investigation stage**—the first step in the systems development process. This stage may involve consideration of proposals generated by an information systems planning process, which we will discuss in Chapter 11. The investigation stage includes the preliminary study of proposed information system

Figure 10.5

Ways to gather information for systems development.

- Interviews with employees, customers, and managers.
- Questionnaires to appropriate end users in the organization.
- Personal observation, videotaping, or involvement in end user work activities.
- Examination of documents, reports, procedures manuals, and other documentation.
- Development, simulation, and observation of a model of the work activities.

solutions to end user business problems such as those facing Auto Shack Stores as described in the case study on the next page.

Feasibility Studies

Because the process of developing a major information system can be costly, the systems investigation stage frequently requires a preliminary study called a **feasibility study.** A feasibility study is a preliminary study that investigates the information needs of prospective users and determines the resource requirements, costs, benefits, and feasibility of a proposed project. You would use the methods of gathering information summarized in Figure 10.5 to collect data for a feasibility study. Then you might formalize the findings of this study in a written report that includes preliminary specifications and a developmental plan for the proposed system. If management approves the recommendations of the feasibility study, the development process can continue. See Figure 10.6

The goal of feasibility studies is to evaluate alternative systems and to propose the most feasible and desirable systems for development. The feasibility of a proposed system can be evaluated in terms of four major categories, as illustrated in Figure 10.7.

The focus of **organizational feasibility** is on how well a proposed information system supports the objectives of the organization and its strategic plan for information

Figure 10.6

If management approves the recommendations of the feasibility study team, the development process can continue.

Jon Riley/Tony Stone Images.

Auto Shack Stores: Solving a Business Problem

Auto Shack Stores is a chain of auto parts stores in Arizona, with headquarters in Phoenix. The firm has grown to 14 stores in just 10 years, and it offers a wide variety of automotive parts and accessories. Sales and profits have increased each year, but the rate of sales growth has failed to meet forecasts in the last three years. Early results for 1998 indicate that the rate of sales growth is continuing to drop, even with the addition of two new stores in 1997. Adding the new stores was the solution decided on by corporate management last year to reverse the trend in sales performance.

In recent meetings of corporate and store managers, the issue of computer use has been raised. Auto Shack uses computers for various information processing jobs, such as sales transactions processing, analysis of sales performance, employee payroll processing, and accounting applications. However, sales transactions by customers are still written up by salespeople. Also, corporate and store managers depend on computer-generated daily sales analysis reports that contain information that is always several days old.

Most store managers see the installation of a company-wide network of point-of-sale (POS) systems as a key component of any plan to reverse Auto Shack's sales trends. They believe using networks of POS terminals in each store would drastically shorten the time needed by a salesperson to write up a sale. This would not only improve customer service, it would free salespeople to sell to more customers. The managers call these the "selling floor" benefits of POS systems.

Another major point raised is that POS systems would allow immediate capture and processing of sales transaction data. Up-to-date sales performance information could then be made available to managers at personal computer workstations connected into the company's telecommunications network. This would provide the capability for information on sales performance to be tailored to each manager's information needs. Currently, managers have to depend on computer-produced daily sales analysis reports that use the same report format. Too much of a manager's time is being used to generate sales performance information not provided by the system. Managers complain they don't have enough time to plan and support sales efforts unless they make decisions without enough information.

The president of Auto Shack has resisted previous proposals to automate the selling process, based on his experience with the cost of computerizing other parts of the business. He knows automation would involve a large initial investment and resistance to the technology by some salespeople and managers. However, the continued disappointing sales performance has softened his position. Also, the president realized that POS systems have become commonplace in all types of retail stores. Auto Shack's major competitors have installed such systems, and their growth continues to outpace his own firm's. The company is failing to achieve its goal of increasing its share of the automotive parts market.

A team of store managers and systems analysts from the information services department conducted a feasibility study of the POS options facing Auto Shack. The study team made personal observations of the sales processing system in action and interviewed managers, salespeople, and other employees. Based on a preliminary analysis of user requirements, the team proposed a new sales processing system. This new system features new POS software and a telecommunications network of point-of-sale (POS) terminals and management workstations. After reviewing the feasibility study, the top management of Auto Shack faces a major business decision.

Figure 10.7

Organizational, economic, technical, and operational feasibility factors. Note that there is more to feasibility than cost savings or the availability of hardware and software.

Organizational Feasibility	Economic Feasibility
• How well the proposed system supports the strategic objectives of the organization	• Cost savings • Increased revenue • Decreased investment • Increased profits
Technical Feasibility	**Operational Feasibility**
• Hardware, software, and network capability, reliability and availability	• End user acceptance • Management support • Customer, supplier, and government requirements

Figure 10.7

Organizational, economic, technical, and operational feasibility factors. Note that there is more to feasibility than cost savings or the availability of hardware and software.

systems. For example, projects that do not directly contribute to meeting an organization's strategic objectives are typically not funded. **Economic feasibility** is concerned with whether expected cost savings, increased revenue, increased profits, reductions in required investment, and other types of benefits will exceed the costs of developing and operating a proposed system. For example, if a project can't cover its development costs, it won't be approved, unless mandated by government regulations or other considerations.

   Technical feasibility can be demonstrated if reliable hardware and software capable of meeting the needs of a proposed system can be acquired or developed by the business in the required time. Finally, **operational feasibility** is the willingness and ability of the management, employees, customers, suppliers, and others to operate, use, and support a proposed system. For example, if the software for a new system is too difficult to use, employees may make too many errors and avoid using it. Thus, it would fail to show operational feasibility. See Figure 10.8

Cost/Benefit Analysis. Feasibility studies typically involve **cost/benefit analysis.** If costs and benefits can be quantified, they are called tangible; if not, they are called intangible. Examples of tangible costs are the costs of hardware and software, employee salaries, and other quantifiable costs needed to develop and implement an IS solution. **Intangible costs** are difficult to quantify; they include the loss of customer goodwill or employee morale caused by errors and disruptions arising from the installation of a new system.

Figure 10.8

Examples of how a feasibility study measured the feasibility of the POS system proposed for Auto Shack Stores.

Organizational Feasibility	Economic Feasibility
• How well the proposed system fits the store's plans for integrating sales, marketing, and financial systems	• Savings in checkout costs • Increased sales revenue • Decreased investment in inventory • Increased profits
Technical Feasibility	**Operational Feasibility**
• Capability, reliability, and availability of POS hardware, software, and networks	• Acceptance of salespeople • Store management support • Customer acceptance

Figure 10.9

Possible benefits of computer-based information systems, with examples. Note that an opposite result for each of these benefits would be a cost or disadvantage of computer-based information systems.

Tangible Benefits	Example
● Increase in sales or profits	● Development of computer-based products
● Decrease in information processing costs	● Elimination of unnecessary documents
● Decrease in operating costs	● Reduction in inventory carrying costs
● Decrease in required investment	● Decrease in inventory investment required
● Increased operational efficiency	● Less spoilage, waste, and idle time

Intangible Benefits	Example
● Improved information availability	● More timely and accurate information
● Improved abilities in analysis	● Analytical modeling
● Improved customer service	● More timely service response
● Improved employee morale	● Elimination of burdensome job tasks
● Improved management decision making	● Better information and decision analysis
● Improved competitive position	● Systems that lock in customers
● Improved business image	● Progressive image as perceived by customers, suppliers, and investors

Tangible benefits are favorable results, such as the decrease in payroll costs caused by a reduction in personnel or a decrease in inventory carrying costs caused by reduction in inventory. **Intangible benefits** are harder to estimate. Such benefits as better customer service or faster and more accurate information for management fall into this category. Figure 10.9 lists typical tangible and intangible benefits with examples. Possible tangible and intangible costs would be the opposite of each benefit shown.

Systems Analysis

What is **systems analysis?** Whether you want to develop a new application quickly or are involved in a long-term project, you will need to perform several basic activities of systems analysis. Many of these activities are an extension of those used in conducting a feasibility study. Some of the same information-gathering methods are used, plus some new tools that we will discuss shortly. However, systems analysis is not a preliminary study. It is an in-depth study of end user information needs that produces *functional requirements* that are used as the basis for the design of a new information system. Systems analysis traditionally involves a detailed study of:

- The information needs of the organization and end users like yourself.
- The activities, resources, and products of any present information systems.
- The information system capabilities required to meet your information needs, and those of other end users.

Organizational Analysis

An **organizational analysis** is an important first step in systems analysis. How can anyone improve an information system if they know very little about the organizational environment in which that system is located? They can't. That's why the members of a development team have to know something about the organization, its management structure, its people, its business activities, the environmental systems it must deal with, and its current information systems. Someone on the team must know this information in more detail for the specific business units or end user workgroups that will be affected by the new or improved information system being proposed. For example, a new inventory control system for a chain of department stores cannot be designed unless someone on a development team knows a lot about the company and the types of business activities that affect its inventory. That's why business end users are frequently added to systems development teams.

Analysis of the Present System

Before you design a new system, it is important to study the system that will be improved or replaced (if there is one). You need to analyze how this system uses hardware, software, network, and people resources to convert data resources, such as transactions data, into information products, such as reports and displays. Then you should document how the information system activities of input, processing, output, storage, and control are accomplished.

For example, you might evaluate the format, timing, volume, and quality of input and output activities. Such *user interface* activities are vital to effective interaction between end users and computers. Then, in the systems design stage, you can specify what the resources, products, and activities should be to support the user interface in the system you are designing. Figure 10.10 illustrates an analysis-and-design approach that uses end user/IS teams and videos taken of employees at work to involve end users in a codevelopment effort.

Functional Requirements Analysis

This step of systems analysis is one of the most difficult. You may need to work as a team with systems analysts and other end users to determine your specific business information needs. For example, you need to determine what type of information your

Figure 10.10

An example of some of the activities that can be involved in analyzing a system and designing improvements. Note the use of end user/IS teams and codevelopment of design solutions.

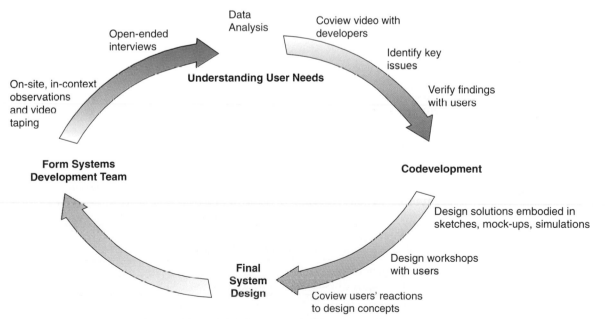

Source: Adapted from Françoise Brun-Cottan and Patricia Wall, "Using Video to Re-Present the User," *Communications of the ACM*, May 1995, p. 63. Copyright © 1995, Association of Computing Machinery. By permission.

Figure 10.11

Functional requirements specify information system capabilities required to meet the information needs of users.

- **User interface requirements.** The input/output needs of end users that must be supported by the information system, including sources, formats, content, volume, and frequency of each type of input and output.

- **Processing requirements.** Activities required to convert input into output. Includes calculations, decision rules, and other processing operations, and capacity, throughput, turnaround time, and response time needed for processing activities.

- **Storage requirements.** Organization, content, and size of databases, types and frequency of updating and inquiries, and the length and rationale for record retention.

- **Control requirements.** Accuracy, validity, safety, security, and adaptability requirements for system input, processing, output, and storage functions.

work requires; what its format, volume, and frequency should be; and what response times are necessary. Second, you must try to determine the information processing capabilities required for each system activity (input, processing, output, storage, control) to meet these information needs. *Your main goal is to identify what should be done, not how to do it.*

Finally, you should try to develop **functional requirements.** Functional requirements are end user information requirements that are not tied to the hardware, software, network, data, and people resources that end users presently use or might use in the new system. That is left to the design stage to determine. For example, Figure 10.11 outlines some of the key areas where functional requirements should be developed. Figure 10.12 shows examples of functional requirements for a sales transaction processing system at Auto Shack Stores.

Systems Design

Systems analysis describes *what* a system should do to meet the information needs of users. **Systems design** specifies *how* the system will accomplish this objective. Systems design consists of design activities that produce system specifications satisfying the functional requirements developed in the systems analysis stage.

User Interface, Data, and Process Design

A useful way to look at systems design is illustrated in Figure 10.13. This concept focuses on three major products, or *deliverables*, that should result from the design stage. In this framework, systems design consists of three activities: user interface, data, and process design. This results in specifications for user interface methods and products, database structures, and processing and control procedures.

Figure 10.12

Examples of functional requirements for a sales transaction processing system at Auto Shack Stores.

- **User Interface Requirements**
  Automatic entry of product data and easy-to-use data entry screens for salespeople.

- **Processing Requirements**
  Fast, automatic calculation of sales totals and sales taxes.

- **Storage Requirements**
  Fast retrieval and update of data from product, pricing, and customer databases.

- **Control Requirements**
  Signals for data entry errors and easy-to-read receipts for customers.

Figure 10.13   Systems design can be viewed as the design of user interfaces, data, and processes.

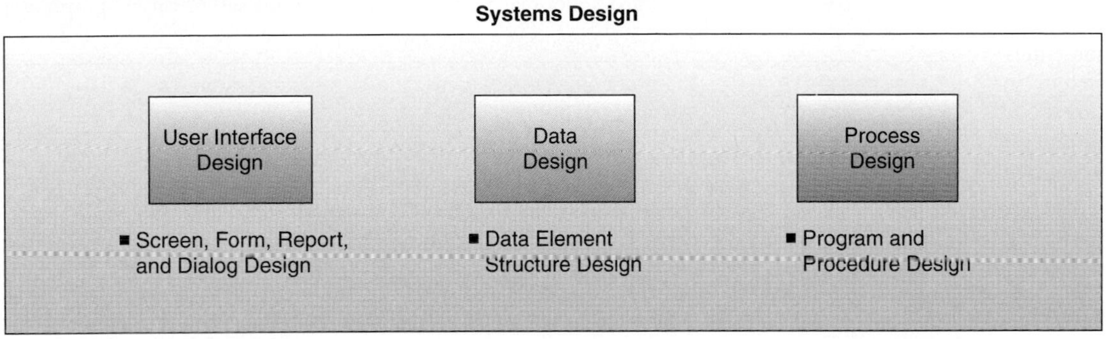

Systems Design

User Interface Design. The user interface design activity focuses on supporting the interactions between end users and their computer-based applications. Designers concentrate on the design of attractive and efficient forms of user input and output, such as easy-to-use Internet or intranet web pages. Or they may design methods of converting human-readable documents to machine-readable input, such as optical scanning of business forms.

As we will see shortly, user interface design is frequently a *prototyping* process, where working models or prototypes of user interface methods are designed and modified several times with feedback from end users. The user interface design process produces detailed design specifications for information products such as display screens, interactive user/computer dialogues (including the sequence or flow of dialogue), audio responses, forms, documents, and reports. Figure 10.14 gives examples of user interface design elements and guidelines suggested for the multimedia web pages of Internet and intranet web sites.

Data Design. The data design activity focuses on the design of the structure of databases and files to be used by a proposed information system. (Database design was discussed in Chapter 5.) The product of data design is detailed descriptions of:

- The *attributes* or characteristics of the *entities* (objects, people, places, events) about which the proposed information system needs to maintain information.
- The relationships these entities have to each other.
- The specific data elements (databases, files, records, etc.) that need to be maintained for each entity tracked by the information system.
- The *integrity rules* that govern how each data element is specified and used in the information system.

Process Design. The process design activity focuses on the design of *software resources*, that is, the programs and procedures needed by the proposed information system. Designers concentrate on developing detailed specifications for the software that will have to be purchased or developed by custom programming to meet user interface and data design specifications, and the functional requirements developed in the analysis stage.

Figure 10.14

Examples of user interface design elements and guidelines that could be used in designing multimedia web pages on Internet or intranet web sites.

Look	Web Page Design Elements
● Corporate	Background of marble or granite and embossed or carved graphics
	Conveys financial success and stability
● Hip/young	A lot of color, trendy icons, animation, and sound (the look of some of the popular e-zines)
● Innovative/creative	Independent graphics that form a cohesive whole even though they appear to float separately from one another; each graphic serves as a link to a different component of the intranet
● Aggressive	Action images—people moving, salespeople interacting with customers, contracts being signed
	Prominent place on the home page for bold announcements of the latest deal that was closed, the latest acquisition that was made, the latest milestone that was reached
● Family-oriented	Images of people

Web Page Design Guidelines

● **Keep it simple.** Avoid complex jargon, overwrought explanations, and confusing tangents. Always keep the customer's point-of-view in focus. Ask yourself, "What have they come here to do?" Then design a site that matches the answer.

● **Keep it clean.** Image isn't everything on the Net, but it certainly counts for a lot. A functional web site should avoid gratuitous displays of techno-tricks that clutter up the site.

● **Organize logically.** Go with the three-click rule: If users can't get to the core of the information they're looking for in three clicks, they'll abandon the search.

Sources: Adapted from Shel Holtz, *PC Week: The Intranet Advantage* (Emeryville, CA: Ziff-Davis Press, 1996), p. 104; and Chuck Martin, *The Digital Estate: Strategies for Competing, Surviving, and Thriving in an Internet-Worked World* (New York: McGraw-Hill, 1997), p. 134.

Because of the widespread use of client/server systems, software process design is frequently expressed as a "three-tier" architecture of processing services:

● **User services**—front-end client software that communicates with users through a graphical user interface.

● **Application services**—software modules that enforce business rules, process information, and manage transactions. Application services may reside on the client and server.

● **Data services**—data are made available to the application services software for processing. This is typically accomplished through database management system software [19].

System Specifications

System specifications formalize the design of an application's user interface methods and products, database structures, and processing and control procedures. Therefore, systems designers will frequently develop hardware, software, network, data, and personnel specifications for a proposed system. Systems analysts work with you so they can use your knowledge of your own work activities and their knowledge of computer-based systems to specify the design of a new or improved information system.

Figure 10.15

System specifications specify the details of a proposed information system.

- **User interface specifications:** The content, format, and sequence of user interface products and methods such as display screens, interactive dialogues, audio responses, forms, documents, and reports.
- **Database specifications:** Content, structure, distribution and access, response, maintenance, and retention of databases.
- **Software specifications:** The required software package or programming specifications of the proposed system, including performance and control specifications.
- **Hardware and network specifications:** The physical and performance characteristics of the equipment and networks required by the proposed system.
- **Personnel specifications.** Job descriptions of persons who will operate the system.

The final system design must specify what types of hardware resources (machines and media), software resources (programs and procedures), network resources (communications media and networks), and people resources (end users and information systems staff) will be needed. It must specify how such resources will convert data resources (stored in files and databases they design) into information products (displays, responses, reports, and documents). These specifications are the final product of the systems design stage. Figure 10.15 outlines some of the key characteristics that should be included in system specifications. Figure 10.16 shows examples of system specifications that could be developed for a point-of-sale system at Auto Shack Stores.

Prototyping

Prototyping is the rapid development and testing of working models, or **prototypes,** of new applications in an interactive, iterative process that can be used by both systems analysts and end users. Prototyping makes the development process faster and easier for systems analysts, especially for projects where end user requirements are hard to define. Thus, prototyping is sometimes called *rapid application design* (RAD).

Figure 10.16

Examples of system specifications for a new point-of-sale system at Auto Shack Stores.

- **User Interface Specifications**
  Use handheld optical scanning wands to automatically capture product data on bar-coded tags. Use data entry screens with key data highlighted for better readability.
- **Database Specifications**
  Develop databases that use a relational structure to organize access to all necessary customer and merchandise data.
- **Software Specifications**
  Develop or acquire a sales processing program that can accept entry of optically scanned bar codes, retrieve necessary product data, and compute sales amounts in less than one second. Acquire a relational database management package to manage stored databases.
- **Hardware and Network Specifications**
  Install POS terminals at each checkout station connected to a system of networked microcomputers in each store that are also connected to the corporate headquarters network.
- **Personnel Specifications**
  All hardware and software must be operable by regular store personnel. IS personnel should be available for hardware and software maintenance as needed.

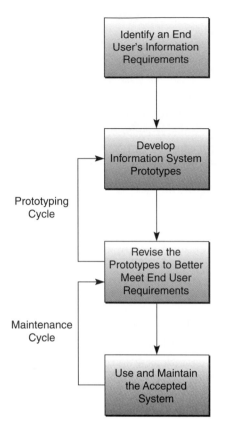

Figure 10.17

Application development using prototyping. Note how prototyping combines the steps of the systems development cycle and changes the traditional roles of information systems specialists and end users.

Identify an End User's Information Requirements

Develop Information System Prototypes

Prototyping Cycle

Revise the Prototypes to Better Meet End User Requirements

Maintenance Cycle

Use and Maintain the Accepted System

■ **Investigation/Analysis.** End users identify their information needs and assess the feasibility of several alternative information system solutions.

■ **Analysis/Design.** End users and/or systems analysts use application development packages to interactively design and test prototypes of information system components that meet end user information needs.

■ **Design/Implementation.** The information system prototypes are tested, evaluated, and modified repeatedly until end users find them acceptable.

■ **Implementation/Maintenance.** The accepted information system can be modified easily since most system documentation is stored on disk.

Prototyping has also opened up the application development process to end users because it simplifies and accelerates systems design. These developments are changing the roles of end users and information systems specialists in systems development. See Figure 10.17.

The Prototyping Process

Prototyping can be used for both large and small applications. Typically, large systems still require using the traditional systems development approach, but parts of such systems can frequently be prototyped. A prototype of a business application needed by an end user is developed quickly using a variety of application development packages. The prototype system is then repeatedly refined until it is acceptable.

As Figure 10.17 illustrates, prototyping is an iterative, interactive process that combines steps of the traditional systems development cycle. End users with sufficient experience with application development packages can do prototyping themselves. Alternatively, you could work with a systems analyst to develop a prototype system in a series of interactive sessions. For example, you could develop, test, and refine prototypes of management reports or data entry screens.

Usually, a prototype is modified several times before end users find it acceptable. Any program modules that are not generated by application development software can then be coded by programmers using conventional programming languages. The final version of the application system is then turned over to its end users for operational use. Figure 10.18 illustrates prototyping as a rapid application development process used by Netscape to develop its Navigator browser. Figure 10.19 outlines a typical prototyping-based systems development process for a business application.

Figure 10.18 Prototyping can be a rapid application development process, as demonstrated by these time-lines for the developmental stages of a new version of the Navigator browser.

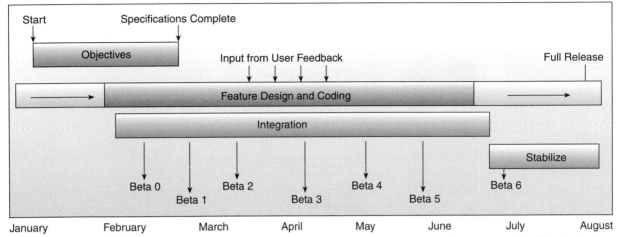

Computer-Aided Systems Engineering

Computer-aided systems engineering (CASE), which also stands for *computer-aided software engineering*, involves using software packages, called CASE tools, to perform many of the activities of the systems development life cycle. For example, software packages are available to help do business planning, project management, user interface prototyping, database design, and software development. Thus, CASE tools make a computer-aided systems development process possible. See Figures 10.20 and 10.21.

Using CASE Tools

Figure 10.20 emphasizes that CASE packages provide many computer-based tools for both the *front end* of the systems development life cycle (planning, analysis, and design) and the *back end* of systems development (implementation and maintenance). Note that server and workstation repositories help integrate the use of tools at both ends of

Figure 10.19

An example of a typical prototyping-based systems development process in business.

- **Team.** A few end users and IS developers form a team to develop a business application.
- **Schematic.** The initial prototype schematic design is developed.
- **Prototype.** The schematic is converted into a simple point-and-click prototype using prototyping tools.
- **Presentation.** A few screens and routine linkages are presented to users.
- **Feedback.** After the team gets feedback from users, the prototype is reiterated.
- **Reiteration.** Further presentations and reiterations are made.
- **Consultation.** Consultations are held with central IT developers/consultants to identify potential improvements and conformance to existing standards of the organization.
- **Completion.** The prototype is converted into a finished application.
- **Acceptance.** Users review and sign off on their acceptance of the new system.
- **Installation.** The new application software is installed on network servers.

Figure 10.20

The components of CASE. This is an example of the variety of software tools and repositories in an integrated CASE product.

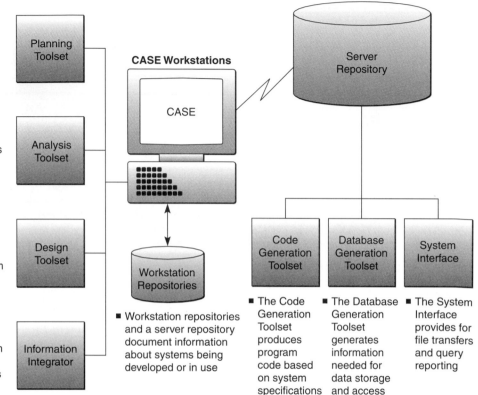

CASE Software Tools

- The Planning Toolset begins the development process with information strategy planning from a high-level, business vantage point

- The Analysis Toolset focuses on correctly capturing detailed business requirements early in the development process

- The Design Toolset provides detailed specifications of the system solution

- The Information Integrator integrates system specifications, checks them for consistency and completeness, and records them in the repositories

- Workstation repositories and a server repository document information about systems being developed or in use

- The Code Generation Toolset produces program code based on system specifications

- The Database Generation Toolset generates information needed for data storage and access

- The System Interface provides for file transfers and query reporting

the development cycle. The *system repository* is a computerized database for all of the details of a system generated with other systems development tools. The repository helps to ensure consistency and compatibility in the design of the data elements, processes, user interfaces, and other aspects of the system being developed.

Integrated CASE tools (called I-CASE) are now available that can assist all of the stages of systems development. Some of these CASE tools support *joint application design* (JAD), where a group of systems analysts, programmers, and end users can jointly and interactively design new applications. Finally, if the development of new systems can be called *forward engineering*, some CASE tools support *backward engineering*. That is, they allow systems analysts to inspect the logic of a program code for old applications, and convert it automatically into more efficient programs that significantly improve system effectiveness. For example, such CASE tools have played a major role in attempts to solve the year 2000 (Y2K) problem by automatically identifying and revising how yearly dates are handled by program code.

End User Development

In a traditional systems development cycle, your role as a business end user is similar to that of a customer or a client. Typically, you will make a request for a new improved system, answer questions about your specific information needs and information processing problems, and provide background information on your existing information

Figure 10.21

Sharper Image used the WebObjects application development package to create and test prototypes of dynamic web pages for the catalog of products at their web site.

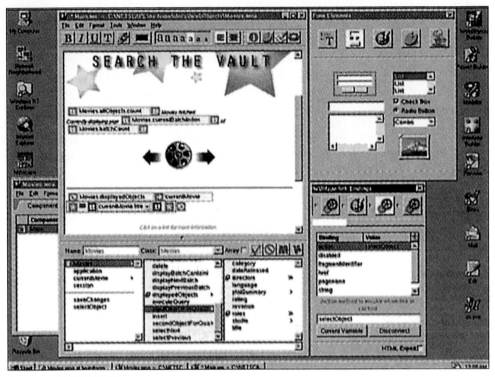

Courtesy of NeXT Software.

systems. Systems analysts and other IS professionals work with you to analyze your problem and suggest alternative solutions. When you approve the best alternative, it is designed and implemented. Here again, you may be involved in a prototyping design process or be on an implementation team with IS specialists.

However, in **end user development,** IS professionals play a consulting role while you do your own application development. Sometimes a staff of user consultants may be available to help you and other end users with your application development efforts. For instance, a *user services* group or *information center* may provide assistance for both mainframe and microcomputer applications development. This may include training in the use of application packages; selection of hardware and software; assistance in gaining access to organization databases; and, of course, assistance in analysis, design, and implementing your application.

Doing End User Development

In end user development, you and other end users can develop new or improved ways to perform your jobs without the direct involvement of IS professionals. The application development capabilities built into a variety of end user software packages have made it easier for many users to develop their own computer-based solutions. For example, you can use an electronic spreadsheet package as a tool to develop a way to easily analyze weekly sales results for the sales managers in a company. Or you could use a database management package to design data-entry displays to help sales clerks enter sales data, or to develop monthly sales analysis reports needed by district sales managers.

**Focus on IS
Activities**

End user development should focus on the fundamental activities of an information system: Input, processing, output, storage, and control. Figure 10.22 illustrates these system components and the questions they address.

In analyzing a potential application, you should focus first on the **output** to be produced by the application. What information is needed and in what form should it be presented? Next, look at the **input** data to be supplied to the application. What data are available? from what sources? and in what form? Then you should examine the **processing** requirements. What operations or transformation processes will be required to convert the available inputs into the desired output? Among software packages the developer is able to use, which package can best perform the operations required?

You may find that the desired output cannot be produced from the inputs that are available. If this is the case, you must either make adjustments to the output expected, or find additional sources of input data, including data stored in files and databases from external sources. The **storage** component will vary in importance in end user applications. For example, some applications require extensive use of stored data or the creation of data that must be stored for future use. These are better suited for database management development projects than for spreadsheet applications.

Necessary **control** measures for end user applications vary greatly depending upon the scope and duration of the application, the number and nature of the users of the application, and the nature of the data involved. For example, special procedures to restrict access to data are less needed if each application will be utilized either by only one individual serving as a developer/user or by a developer and a single additional user. Control measures are also needed to protect against accidental loss or damage to

Figure 10.22 End user development should focus on the basic information processing components of an information system.

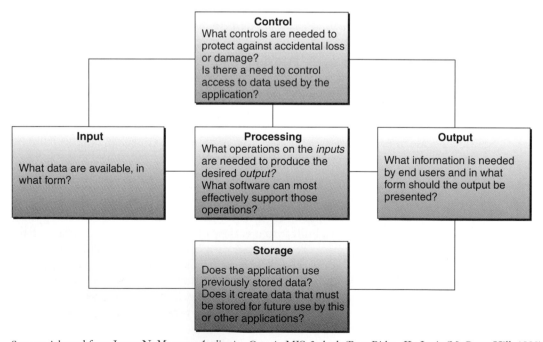

Source: Adapted from James N. Morgan, *Application Cases in MIS*, 3rd ed. (Burr Ridge, IL: Irwin/McGraw-Hill, 1999), p. 4.

an end user file. The most basic protection against this type of loss is simply to make backup copies of application files on a frequent and systematic basis. Another example of controls concerns spreadsheet applications that are used on a repeated basis or used by an individual other than their developer. The cell protection feature of spreadsheets that protects key cells from accidental erasure is a simple control measure to use when developing spreadsheet applications.

Checklist for End User Development

Figure 10.23 outlines key questions you can use as a checklist to begin the process of end user development illustrated in Figure 10.22. Also included are answers that identify generic system components that are typically found in most computer-based information systems in business. Use this detailed checklist as a tool to identify system components in any business application you are studying. Then use it again as a source of design features you may want to suggest for a new or improved system.

An **IS component matrix** can be used to document the results of using the checklist for end user development [25]. An IS component matrix views an information

Input of Data Resources
Question: How are data captured and prepared for processing? How should they be? What data resources are or should be captured?
Answers: Input data are frequently captured directly by transaction terminals (such as point-of-sale terminals) using devices such as optical scanners. Other input may be collected from *source documents* (such as payroll time cards) and converted to machine-sensible data by a *keyboarding* data entry process. Input into the system typically consists of:

- **Transaction data.** *Example:* Data describing sales transactions are captured by a point-of-sale terminal.
- **Database adjustments.** *Example:* A change in a customer's credit limit, using an online terminal in the credit department or processing a "credit increase request form" mailed in by a customer.
- **Inquiries.** *Example:* What is the balance owed on a customer's account?
- **Output of other systems.** *Example:* The output of a sales transaction processing system includes data needed as input by an inventory control system to reflect transactions that change the amount of inventory on hand.

Processing of Data Resources
Question: How are data manipulated and transformed into information? How should they be? What processing alternatives should be considered?
Answers: Data resources are subjected to sorting, summarizing, calculating, and other manipulation activities. Processing alternatives include batch processing and realtime processing. *Examples:*

- Calculating employee payroll.
- Sorting employee record by employee number.
- Summarizing employee payroll costs.
- Realtime processing of sales data from point-of-sale terminals.
- Nightly batch processing of deposited checks by banks.

Output of Information Products
Question: How is information communicated to users? How should it be? What information products are and should be produced?
Answers: Output typically takes the form of the following information products:

- **Reports.** *Example:* A sales analysis report outlining the sales made during a period by sales territory, product, and salesperson.

Figure 10.23

Concluded.

- **Documents.** *Example:* A paycheck or sales receipt.
- **Displays or responses.** *Example:* A video terminal displays the balance owed on a customer's account. The same information can be transmitted to a telephone by a computer audio-response unit.
- **Control listings.** *Example:* Each time an employee paycheck is printed, a line on a listing known as a payroll register is also printed and recorded on magnetic tape. This helps provide an audit trail for control purposes.
- **Input to other systems.** *Example:* Part of the output of a payroll system serves as input to a labor–cost accounting system and the general ledger system of the firm.

Storage of Data Resources
Question: How are data resources organized, stored, updated, and retrieved? How should they be?
Answers: Data resources are stored and organized into files and databases. This facilitates:

- Supplying data needed by the organization's information system applications. *Example:* The current credit balance of a customer is retrieved from a customer database by sales and accounting personnel.
- The updating of files and databases to reflect the occurrence of new business transactions. *Example:* A customer's credit balance is increased to reflect recent purchases on credit.

Control of System Performance
Question: How are input, processing, output, and storage activities monitored and controlled? How should they be? What control methods should be considered?
Answers: Input, processing, output, and storage activities must be controlled so that an information system produces proper information products and achieves its other objectives. Examples of typical control methods include:

- **Input controls.** *Example:* Formatted data entry screens warn users if input data exceed specified parameters.
- **Processing controls.** *Example:* Software may contain checkpoint routines that check the accuracy of intermediate results during processing.
- **Output controls.** *Example:* End users may check the accuracy of specified control totals in reports and control documents such as sales receipts.
- **Storage controls.** *Example:* Databases may be protected by security programs that require proper identification and authorization codes by end users.

system as a matrix of resources, products, and activities. It highlights how the activities of input, processing, output, storage, and control are accomplished, and how the use of people, hardware, network, and software resources supports the conversion of data resources into information products.

Figure 10.24 illustrates the use of an IS component matrix to document the basic components of a sales processing system for a retail store. Note how it spotlights the activities needed, resources used, and products produced by this information system. Some cells are left blank because information for each cell may not be available or applicable. However, duplicate entries are also possible, because the same resources and products can be used to support several information system activities. Thus, an IS component matrix serves its purpose by summarizing the information system components used in a real world information system.

Figure 10.24

An example of an IS component matrix for a sales processing system for a chain of retail stores. Note how it emphasizes some of the basic activities needed, resources used, and products produced by this information system.

Information System Activities	Hardware and Network Resources		Software Resources		People Resources		Data Resources	Information Products
	Machines	Media	Programs	Procedures	Specialists	Users		
Input	POS terminals Management workstations	Bar tags Mag stripe credit cards	Data entry program	Data entry procedures		Salesclerks Customers	Customer input data Product input data	Data entry displays
Processing	Mainframe computer Network servers Communications processors	Communications network media	Sales processing program Sales analysis program	Sales transaction procedures	Computer operators	Salesclerks Managers	Customer, inventory, and sales databases	Processing status displays
Output	POS terminals Management workstations	Paper reports and receipts	Report generator program Graphics programs	Output use and distribution procedures		Salesclerks Managers Customers		Sales analysis reports and displays Sales receipts
Storage	Magnetic disk drives	Magnetic disks	Database management program		Computer operators		Customer, inventory, and sales databases	
Control	Mainframe computer Network servers Communications processors POS terminals	Paper documents and control reports	Performance monitor program Security monitor program	Correction procedures	Computer operators	Salesclerks Managers Customers	Customer, inventory, and sales databases	Data entry displays Sales receipts Error displays and signals

Section II Implementing Business Change with IT

Introduction

The implementation process is the next major stage that follows the investigation, analysis, and design stages of the systems development process, as we discussed in Section I. Therefore, implementation is an important activity in the deployment of information technology to support the business changes planned by an organization and its end users.

Analyzing Computer Associates, Microsoft, and IBM

Read the Real World Case on Computer Associates, Microsoft, and IBM on the next page. We can learn a lot about the importance of vendor support of the software used by many businesses from this case. See Figure 10.25.

Computer Associates, Microsoft, and IBM are the three biggest software companies in the world. How they choose to provide support to business users of their software is a major criterion for any business that wants to acquire new software products.

Computer Associates' strategy of good support for a few major software products, and inadequate support for the rest, is not satisfactory for many of their users. Microsoft's strategy of providing in-depth service to the top 2,500 companies in the world, while providing great web site support for everyone else is not rated very highly by small business users, but seems more satisfactory to its customers. IBM has learned over the years how important software support is to its business users, except for its web site support, which needs to be improved to satisfy its customers.

Figure 10.25

Ron McCauley, IS director at Shari's Management Corporation, says he's moving away from Computer Associates' products because he isn't getting the software support he needs.

Source: Dan Lamont.

Computer Associates, Microsoft, and IBM: Business Users Rate Software Support

Computer Associates

"Dead last with a bullet," says Ron McCauley on learning of Computer Associates' (CA) low customer satisfaction rating. McCauley, who is the IS director at Shari's Management Corp. in Beaverton, Oregon, says he isn't getting the support he needs from CA.

McCauley was using MLink software for remote communication to his Unix environment before CA took control of the product when it acquired Legent. "In our experience, you have a package you like and then CA acquires the company, that's unfortunate," McCauley says. "We've seen a dramatic drop out in service for products now under CA's control."

This isn't new territory for the company. CA has consistently scored poorly on service issues in most *Computerworld* customer satisfaction surveys. That's because CA has acquired so many products that it's forced to choose which ones it will support while leaving the rest of its users to work out their own problems.

While our respondents disliked most web-site support offered by the vendors in the survey, CA's showing was especially poor. It alone failed to receive a single "very good" rating for its web site.

The good news: CA did receive a respectable grade for its mission-critical service, proving it can perform well when it wants to. "If you're on a mainline product such as the Unicenter TNG systems monitor, or Jasmine object database, you're probably happy with CA's support. It's the other 400-plus products that suffer," says McCauley.

Microsoft

The effectiveness of Microsoft's support depends on who you are, or whom you know. The company is highly selective in determining who receives its Premier Support plan, the very attentive service it's using to get deeper into the corridors of Fortune 500 corporations.

The very large—2,500 users or more—enterprise level companies fortunate enough to be included in Premier Support receive Microsoft's undivided and very effective attention. But the mediocre grades Microsoft received from *Computerworld*'s survey come largely from the rank-and-file companies that don't qualify for Premier class. These users, the vast majority of Microsoft business customers, are bounced to one of the company's many support partners.

Microsoft placed last among the five vendors in the survey (that also included Oracle and Novell) in the availability and helpfulness of its telephone staff, its preventative maintenance, and the quality of its basic as well as its mission-critical support.

One bright spot for Microsoft: Users really like its web-site support and gave it the highest grade of any in the survey. Respondents said that between its web site and its TechNet informational CD-ROM service, Microsoft is the best at letting its users help themselves. "Ninety percent of my IT questions are answered by the information on their site," says John Baldino, IT director at Wawa Food Markets Inc. in Philadelphia.

IBM

IBM's whatever-the-customer-wants approach to service has made it the benchmark by which other vendors are measured, according to several survey respondents. Big Blue scored highest in six of eight rating categories and achieved the highest customer-satisfaction grade in the entire survey for its emergency and mission-critical service.

IT managers gave the highest grades to the responsiveness and knowledge demonstrated by IBM's phone staff. IBM, they said, best follows the priorities users set when calling in problems. Priority 1 means a system is down. When that happens, IBM's goal is to connect the user to the person best qualified to fix the system within the hour. "They've hit it every time for us," says Janice Hardrath, information systems director at Aerostructures Corp. in Nashville. "When you set a higher priority to your problem, you always get a more experienced support person right away."

IBM lost ground in *Computerworld*'s survey over web-site support, however. Surveyed managers said IBM's site is OK for logging minor problems into a queue but not among the best when users need to quickly locate specific solutions. IBM wasn't alone in the area of weak web-based support, but it's certainly one place that IBM needs to work on.

Case Study Questions

1. How important is software support to a business? Explain.

2. What advice would you give Computer Associates, Microsoft, and IBM to help them improve their service?

3. What business strategies may explain the level and type of support provided by Computer Associates, Microsoft, and IBM?

Source: Adapted from Kevin Burden, "IBM Waxes, Others Wane," *Computerworld*, March 15, 1999, pp. 78–81. Copyright 1999 by Computerworld, Inc., Framingham, MA 01701. Reprinted from *Computerworld*.

Managing Organizational Change

IT increasingly changes jobs, skill needs, work, and relationships. Technical change has become synonymous with organizational change. Such change can be complex, painful, and disruptive. The people side of IT is often more difficult to anticipate and manage smoothly than is the technological side [20].

Typically, implementing changes in information technology is only part of a larger process of managing major changes in business processes, organizational structures, managerial roles, and employee work assignments. Organizations must implement a variety of management initiatives to help manage business change. For example, the involvement and commitment of top management is a basic requirement. A top management commitment is needed to support organizational changes generated by the reengineering of business processes or other work redesign activities [21].

End User Involvement

Any new ways of doing things generates some resistance by the people affected. Thus, the implementation of new computer-based work support technologies can generate fear and resistance to change by employees. For example, Figure 10.26 illustrates some of the major obstacles to knowledge management systems in business. Notice that **end user resistance** to sharing knowledge is the biggest obstacle to the implementation of knowledge management programs.

One of the keys to solving problems of end user resistance to new information technologies is proper education and training. Even more important is **end user involvement** in organizational changes, and in the development of new information systems.

Direct end user participation in systems development projects before a system is implemented is especially important in reducing the potential for end user resistance. That is why end users frequently are members of systems development teams and involved in the prototyping process. Such involvement helps ensure that end users assume ownership of a system, and that its design meets their needs. Systems that tend to inconvenience or frustrate users cannot be effective systems, no matter how technically elegant they are and how efficiently they process data.

Change Management

People and processes are a major focus of organizational **change management.** This includes activities such as developing innovative ways to measure, motivate, and reward performance. So is designing programs to recruit and train employees in the core competencies required in a changing workplace. Finally, change management involves

Figure 10.26

Obstacles to knowledge management systems. Note that end user resistance to knowledge sharing is the biggest obstacle.

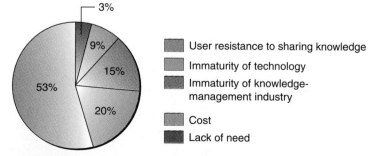

- User resistance to sharing knowledge
- Immaturity of technology
- Immaturity of knowledge-management industry
- Cost
- Lack of need

3%
9%
15%
53%
20%

Source: Adapted from Barb Cole-Gomolski, "Users Loathe to Share Their Know-How," *Computerworld*, November 17, 1997, p. 6. Copyright 1997 by Computerworld, Inc., Framingham, MA 01701. Reprinted from *Computerworld*.

analyzing and defining all changes facing the organization, and developing programs to reduce the risks and costs and to maximize the benefits of change. For example, implementing a reengineered business process might involve developing a *change action plan*, assigning selected managers as *change sponsors*, developing employee *change teams*, and encouraging open communications and feedback about organizational changes. To summarize, change experts recommend:

- Involve as many people as possible in reengineering and other change programs.
- Make constant change part of the culture.
- Tell everyone as much as possible about everything as often as possible, preferably in person.
- Make liberal use of financial incentives and recognition.
- Work within the company culture, not around it [22].

British Petroleum Exploration	British Petroleum Exploration (BPX), the $13 billion oil exploration division of British Petroleum Company, radically reengineered and downsized their IS function. Figure 10.27 outlines the dramatic statistics of this transformation. British Petroleum used a model of *purpose, people,* and *processes* as a change management tool to guide the complete and successful transformation of their IS function. The key was changing the purpose of the IS function from providing information systems for BPX to being responsible for planning the IT infrastructure needed to support the division's business. This was the foundation for subsequent changes in the *procedures* involved and the people required to implement these new IS *processes*. For example, IS people now act as business consultants and project managers on project teams that include business end users and representatives of IS processes that have been outsourced to other companies. See Figure 10.28.

Implementing New Systems

Once a new information system has been designed, it must be implemented. Figure 10.29 illustrates that the **systems implementation** stage involves hardware and software acquisition, software development, testing of programs and procedures, development of documentation, and a variety of conversion alternatives. It also involves the education and training of end users and specialists who will operate a new system.

Implementation can be a difficult and time-consuming process. However, it is vital in ensuring the success of any newly developed system, for even a well-designed system will fail if it is not properly implemented. Figure 10.30 outlines examples of

Figure 10.27

The dramatic statistics of the transformation of British Petroleum Exploration's IS function.

	1989	1992	1995
IS Budget	$360m	$170m	$132m
IS Personnel	1400	390	150
IS Applications	170	110	75
Percent Desktop MIPs to Mainframe MIPs	20%	85%	99%

Source: Adapted from John Cross, Michael Earl, and Jeffrey Sampler, "Transformation of the IT Function at British Petroleum," *MIS Quarterly*, December 1997, p. 402. Reprinted with permission from the *MIS Quarterly*.

Figure 10.28 British Petroleum Exploration used a change management model of purpose, processes, and people to guide the transformation of their IS function.

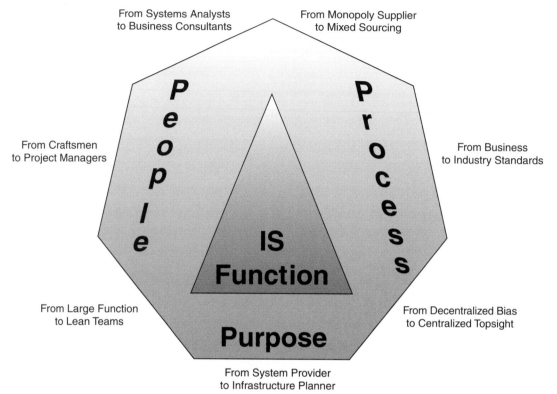

Source: Adapted from John Cross, Michael Earl, and Jeffrey Sampler, "Transformation of the IT Function at British Petroleum," *MIS Quarterly*, December 1997, p. 412. Reprinted with permission from the *MIS Quarterly*.

activities that Auto Shack Stores might use to implement its new point-of-sale systems. Figure 10.31 illustrates the activities and timelines that might be required to implement an intranet for a new employee benefits system in the human resources department of a company.

Figure 10.29 An overview of the implementation process. Implementation activities are needed to transform a newly developed information system into an operational system for end users.

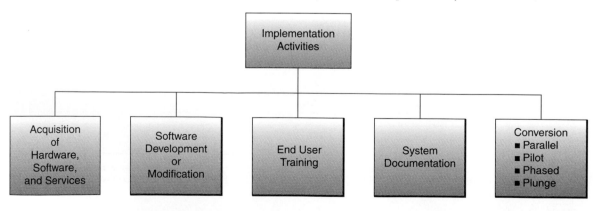

Figure 10.30 Examples of implementation activities for Auto Shack's new POS systems.

- Evaluate and acquire new hardware and software. Hardware includes computer systems, POS terminals, and telecommunications processors and network facilities. Software includes network management programs and POS transaction processing packages.
- Develop computer programs or make any necessary modifications to software packages that are acquired.
- Prepare training materials and documentation on how to operate the new POS system for managers and salespeople.
- Educate and train managers, salespeople, and information systems personnel to operate the new system.
- Test the system and make corrections until it operates properly.
- Convert to the new system on a phased store-by-store basis to minimize disruption. Use the first store converted as a pilot installation to help with testing and training.
- Perform a postimplementation audit within 30 days of each store's conversion to determine if the new POS systems are achieving their expected advantages.

Evaluating Hardware, Software, and Services

How do computer-using organizations evaluate and select hardware and software? Typically, they require suppliers to present bids and proposals based on system specifications developed during the design stage of systems development. Minimum acceptable physical and performance characteristics for all hardware and software requirements are established. Most large business firms and all government agencies formalize these requirements by listing them in a document called an RFP (request for proposal) or RFQ (request for quotation). Then they send the RFP or RFQ to appropriate vendors, who use it as the basis for preparing a proposed purchase agreement.

Computer users may use a *scoring* system of evaluation when there are several competing proposals for a hardware or software acquisition. They give each **evaluation factor** a certain number of maximum possible points. Then they assign each competing proposal points for each factor, depending on how well it meets the specifications

Figure 10.31

An example of the implementation process activities and timelines for a company installing an intranet-based employee benefits system in its human resource management department.

Implementation Activities	Month 1	Month 2	Month 3	Month 4
Acquire and install server hardware and software				
Train administrators				
Acquire and install browser software				
Acquire and install publishing software				
Train benefits employees on publishing software				
Convert benefits manuals and add revisions				
Create web-based tutorials for the intranet				
Hold rollout meetings				

Source: Adapted from Melanie Hills, *Intranet Business Strategy* (New York: John Wiley & Sons, 1997), p. 193. Reprinted with permission of John Wiley & Sons, Inc. Copyright © 1997 by John Wiley & Sons, Inc.

Figure 10.32 Evaluation scores for network hardware and software and their vendors.

Network operating systems

Overall satisfaction
Novell	3.80
Unix	3.76
Microsoft	3.73
IBM	3.71
Industry mean	3.77

Software quality
Unix	3.95
Novell	3.93
IBM	3.80
Microsoft	3.78
Industry mean	3.86

Electronic mail software

Overall satisfaction
Novell	3.79
Microsoft	3.64
Lotus	3.54
Industry mean	3.63

Software quality
Novell	3.88
Lotus	3.66
Microsoft	3.65
Industry mean	3.68

Wide area network hardware

Overall satisfaction
3Com	3.96
Cisco	3.91
Bay Networks	3.89
Cabletron	3.79
Industry mean	3.84

Cost of ownership
3Com	3.78
Bay Networks	3.64
Cisco	3.49
Cabletron	3.44
Industry mean	3.62

Source: Adapted from Kevin Burden, "Networking Survey: Edge Goes to Hardware Vendors," *Computerworld*, February 3, 1997, pp. 73–76. Copyright 1997 by Computerworld, Inc., Framingham, MA 01701. Reprinted from *Computerworld*.

of the computer user. Scoring each evaluation factor for several proposals helps organize and document the evaluation process. It also spotlights the strengths and weaknesses of each proposal. Figure 10.32 shows the results of a scoring process for network hardware and software based on scores assigned by more than 1,600 corporate network managers [4].

Whatever the claims of hardware manufacturers and software suppliers, the performance of hardware and software must be demonstrated and evaluated. Independent hardware and software information services (such as Datapro and Auerbach reporting services) may be used to gain detailed specification information and evaluations. Hardware and software should be demonstrated and evaluated. This can be done on the premises of the business or by visiting the operations of other computer users who have similar types of hardware or software.

Other users are frequently the best source of information needed to evaluate the claims of manufacturers and suppliers. That's why Internet newsgroups established to exchange information about specific software or hardware vendors and their products have become one of the best sources for obtaining up-to-date information about the experiences of users of the products.

Large computer users frequently evaluate proposed hardware and software by requiring the processing of special *benchmark* test programs and test data. Benchmarking simulates the processing of typical jobs on several computers and evaluates their performances. Users can then evaluate test results to determine which hardware device or software package displayed the best performance characteristics.

Hardware Evaluation Factors

When you evaluate computer hardware, you should investigate specific physical and performance characteristics for each hardware component to be acquired. This is true whether you are evaluating microcomputers, mainframes, or peripheral devices. Specific questions must be answered concerning many important factors. These **hardware evaluation factors** and questions are summarized in Figure 10.33.

Notice that there is much more to evaluating hardware than determining the fastest and cheapest computing device. For example, the question of possible

Figure 10.33

Figure 10.33

A summary of major hardware evaluation factors. Notice how you can use this to evaluate a computer system or a peripheral device.

Hardware Evaluation Factors	Rating
Performance What are its speed, capacity, and throughput?	
Cost What is its lease or purchase price? What will be its cost of operations and maintenance?	
Reliability What are the risk of malfunction and its maintenance requirements? What are its error control and diagnostic features?	
Availability When is the firm delivery date?	
Compatibility Is it compatible with existing hardware and software? Is it compatible with hardware and software provided by competing suppliers?	
Modularity Can it be expanded and upgraded by acquiring modular "add on" units?	
Technology In what year of its product life cycle is it? Does it use a new untested technology or does it run the risk of obsolescence?	
Ergonomics Has it been "human factors engineered" with the user in mind? Is it user-friendly, designed to be safe, comfortable, and easy to use?	
Connectivity Can it be easily connected to wide area and local area networks of different types of computers and peripherals?	
Scalability Can it handle the processing demands of a wide range of end users, transactions, queries, and other information processing requirements?	
Software Is system and application software available that can best use this hardware?	
Support Are the services required to support and maintain it available?	
Overall Rating	

obsolescence must be addressed by making a technology evaluation. The factor of ergonomics is also very important. Ergonomic factors ensure that computer hardware and software are user-friendly, that is, safe, comfortable, and easy to use. Connectivity is another important evaluation factor, since so many computer systems are now interconnected via Internet, intranet, and extranet networks.

Software Evaluation Factors

You should evaluate software according to many factors that are similar to those used for hardware evaluation. Thus, the factors of performance, cost, reliability, availability, compatibility, modularity, technology, ergonomics, and support should be used to evaluate proposed software acquisitions. In addition, however, the **software evaluation factors** summarized in Figure 10.34 must also be considered. You should answer the questions they generate in order to properly evaluate software purchases. For example, some software packages are notoriously slow, hard to use, or poorly documented. They are not a good choice, even if offered at attractive prices.

Figure 10.34

A summary of selected software evaluation factors. Note that most of the hardware evaluation factors in Figure 10.33 can also be used to evaluate software packages.

Software Evaluation Factors	Rating
Efficiency Is the software a well-developed system of computer instructions or objects that does not use much memory capacity or CPU time?	
Flexibility Can it handle its processing assignments easily without major modification?	
Security Does it provide control procedures for errors, malfunctions, and improper use?	
Connectivity Is it *network-enabled* so it can easily access the Internet, intranets, extranets, and other networks on its own, or by working with network browsers or other network software?	
Language Is it written in a programming language that is used by our own computer programmers?	
Documentation Is the software well documented? Does it include helpful user instructions?	
Hardware Does existing hardware have the features required to best use this software?	
Other Factors What are its performance, cost, reliability, availability, compatibility, modularity, technology, ergonomics, scalability, and support characteristics? (Use the hardware evaluation factor questions in Figure 10.33.)	
Overall Rating	

Evaluating IS Services

Most suppliers of hardware and software products and many other firms offer a variety of **IS services** to end users and organizations. Examples include assistance during installation or conversion of hardware and software, employee training, and hardware maintenance. Some of these services are provided without cost by hardware manufacturers and software suppliers.

Other types of IS services needed by a business can be outsourced to an outside company for a negotiated price. For example, *computer service centers* provide off-premises computer processing of customer jobs. *Systems integrators* take over complete responsibility for an organization's computer facilities when an organization outsources its computer operations. They may also assume responsibility for developing and implementing large systems development projects that involve many vendors and subcontractors. Value-added resellers (VARs) specialize in providing industry-specific hardware, software, and services from selected manufacturers. Many other services are available to end users, including systems design, contract programming, and consulting services. Evaluation factors and questions for IS services are summarized in Figure 10.35.

Other Implementation Activities

Testing

Testing, documentation, and training are keys to successful implementation of a new system. See Figure 10.36.

System testing involves testing hardware devices, testing and debugging computer programs, and testing information processing procedures. Programs are tested using test data that attempt to simulate all conditions that may arise during processing. In good programming practice, programs are subdivided into levels of modules to

Figure 10.35

Evaluation factors for IS services. These factors focus on the quality of support services computer users may need.

Evaluation Factors for IS Services	Rating
Performance What has been their past performance in view of their past promises?	
Systems Development Are systems analysis and programming consultants available? What are their quality and cost?	
Maintenance Is equipment maintenance provided? What are its quality and cost?	
Conversion What systems development, programming, and hardware installation services will they provide during the conversion period?	
Training Is the necessary training of personnel provided? What are its quality and cost?	
Backup Are several similar computer facilities available for emergency backup purposes?	
Accessibility Does the vendor have a local or regional office that offers sales, systems development, and hardware maintenance services? Is a customer hot line provided?	
Business Position Is the vendor financially strong, with good industry market prospects?	
Hardware Do they have a wide selection of compatible hardware devices and accessories?	
Software Do they offer a variety of useful system software and application packages?	
Overall Rating	

Figure 10.36

Successful IS implementation requires testing, training, and conversion activities.

Roger Tully/Tony Stone Images.

assist their development, testing, and maintenance. *Program testing* usually proceeds from higher to lower levels of program modules until the entire program is tested as a unit. The program is then tested along with other related programs in a final systems test. If computer-aided software engineering (CASE) methodologies are used, such program testing is minimized because automatically generated program code is more likely to be error-free.

An important part of testing is the review of prototypes of displays, reports, and other output. Prototypes should be reviewed by end users of the proposed systems for possible errors. Of course, testing should not occur only during the system's implementation stage, but throughout the system's development process. For example, you might examine and critique prototypes of input documents, screen displays, and processing procedures during the systems design stage. Immediate end user testing is one of the benefits of a prototyping process.

Documentation

Developing good user **documentation** is an important part of the implementation process. Examples include manuals of operating procedures and sample data entry display screens, forms, and reports. When computer-aided systems engineering methods are used, documentation can be created and changed easily since they are stored in a CASE system repository. Documentation serves as a method of communication among the people responsible for developing, implementing, and maintaining a computer-based system. Installing and operating a newly designed system or modifying an established application requires a detailed record of that system's design. Documentation is extremely important in diagnosing errors and making changes, especially if the end users or systems analysts who developed a system are no longer with the organization.

Training

Training is a vital implementation activity. IS personnel, such as user consultants, must be sure that end users are trained to operate a new system or its implementation will fail. Training may involve only activities like data entry, or it may also involve all aspects of the proper use of a new system. In addition, managers and end users must be educated in how the new technology impacts the company's business operations and management. This knowledge should be supplemented by training programs for any new hardware devices, software packages, and their use for specific work activities. Figure 10.37 illustrates how one business coordinated its training program with each stage of its implementation process for Internet access within the company.

Conversion Methods

The initial operation of a new computer-based system can be a difficult task. This typically requires a **conversion** process from the use of a present system to the operation of a new or improved application. Conversion methods can soften the impact of introducing new information technologies into an organization. Four major forms of system conversion are illustrated in Figure 10.38. They include:

- Parallel conversion.
- Phased conversion.
- Pilot conversion.
- Plunge or direct cutover.

Conversions can be done on a *parallel* basis, whereby both the old and the new system are operating until the project development team and end user management agree to switch completely over to the new system. It is during this time that the operations

Figure 10.37 How one company aligned its training programs with the implementation of Internet access for its employees.

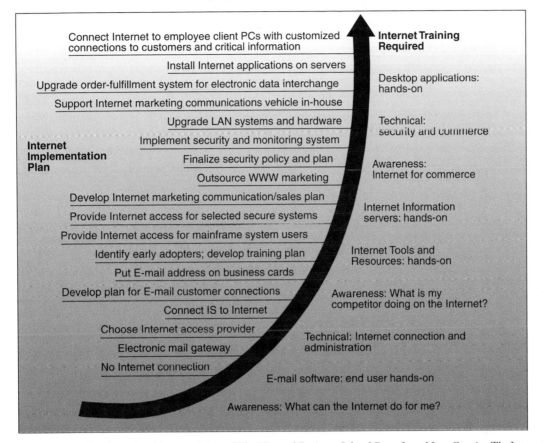

Source: Adapted and reprinted by permission of The Harvard Business School Press from Mary Cronin, *The Internet Strategy Handbook* (Boston: 1996), p. 198. Copyright © 1996 by the President and Fellows of Harvard College; all rights reserved.

and results of both systems are compared and evaluated. Errors can be identified and corrected, and the operating problems can be solved before the old system is abandoned. Installation can also be accomplished by a direct cutover or *plunge* to the newly developed system.

Conversion can also be done on a *phased basis*, where only parts of a new application or only a few departments, branch offices, or plant locations at a time are converted. A phased conversion allows a gradual implementation process to take place within an organization. Similar benefits accrue from using a *pilot conversion*, where one department or other work site serves as a test site. A new system can be tried out at this site until developers feel it can be implemented throughout the organization.

IS Maintenance

Once a system is fully implemented and is being used in business operations, the maintenance function begins. **Systems maintenance** is the monitoring, evaluating, and modifying of operational information systems to make desirable or necessary improvements. For example, the implementation of a new system usually results in the phenomenon known as the *learning curve*. Personnel who operate and use the system will make mistakes simply because they are not familiar with it. Though such errors

Figure 10.38

The four major forms of conversion to a new system.

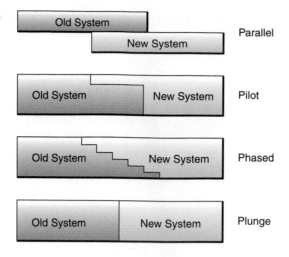

usually diminish as experience is gained with a new system, they do point out areas where a system may be improved.

Maintenance is also necessary for other failures and problems that arise during the operation of a system. End users and information systems personnel then perform a *troubleshooting* function to determine the causes of and solutions to such problems.

The maintenance activity includes a **postimplementation review** process to ensure that newly implemented systems meet the systems development objectives established for them. Errors in the development or use of a system must be corrected by the maintenance process. This includes a periodic review or audit of a system to ensure that it is operating properly and meeting its objectives. This audit is in addition to continually monitoring a new system for potential problems or necessary changes.

Maintenance also includes making modifications to a system due to changes in the business organization or the business environment. For example, new tax legislation, company reorganizations, and new business ventures usually require making a variety of changes to current business information systems.

Summary

- **The Systems Development Cycle.** End users and systems analysts should use a systems approach to help them develop information system solutions to business problems. This frequently involves an information systems development cycle where IS specialists and end users conceive, design, and implement computer-based information systems. The stages, activities, and products of the information systems development cycle are summarized in Figure 10.4.

- **Prototyping and CASE.** Major changes occurring in the traditional information systems development cycle include the use of prototyping tools and methodologies, which promote an iterative, interactive process that develops prototypes of user interfaces and other information system components. See Figures 10.17 and 10.19. Computer-aided systems engineering (CASE) software packages computerize and automate parts of the prototyping and systems development process.

- **End User Development.** The application development capabilities built into end user software packages have made it easier for end users to develop their own computer-based applications. End users should focus their development efforts on the system components of business processes that can benefit from the use of information technology, as summarized in Figures 10.22, 10.23 and 10.24.

- **Implementing Business/IT Change.** Implementation activities include managing the introduction and implementation of changes in business processes, organizational structures, job assignments, and work relationships resulting from reengineering projects, strategic business alliances, and the introduction of new technologies. Companies use change management programs to reduce the risks and costs and maximize the benefits of such major changes in business and information technology.

- **Implementing IS.** The implementation process for information system projects is summarized in Figure 10.39. Implementation involves acquisition, testing, documentation, training, installation, and conversion activities that transform a newly designed information system into an operational system for end users.

- **Evaluating Hardware, Software, and Services.** Business end users should know how to evaluate the acquisition of information system resources. IT vendors should present proposals based on specifications developed during the design stage of systems development. A formal evaluation process reduces the possibility of incorrect or unnecessary purchases of computer hardware or software. Several major evaluation factors, summarized in Figures 10.33, 10.34, and 10.35, can be used to evaluate hardware, software, and IS services.

Figure 10.39

An overview of the implementation process. Implementation activities are needed to transform a newly developed information system into an operational system for end users.

- **Acquisition**
  Evaluate and acquire necessary hardware and software resources and information system services. Screen vendor proposals.

- **Software Development**
  Develop any computer programs that will not be acquired externally as software packages. Make any necessary modifications to software packages that are acquired.

- **Training**
  Educate and train management, end users, and operating personnel. Use consultants or training programs to develop user competencies.

- **Testing**
  Test and make necessary corrections to the programs, procedures, and hardware used by a new system.

- **Documentation**
  Record and communicate detailed system specifications, including procedures for end users and IS personnel and examples of input/output displays and reports.

- **Conversion**
  Convert from the use of a present system to the operation of a new or improved system. This may involve operating both new and old systems in *parallel* for a trial period, operation of a *pilot* system on a trial basis at one location, *phasing* in the new system one location at a time, or an immediate *plunge* or *cutover* to the new system.

Key Terms and Concepts

These are the key terms and concepts of this chapter. The page number of their first explanation is given in parentheses.

1. Change management (404)
2. Computer-aided systems engineering (395)
3. Conversion methods (412)
4. Cost/benefit analysis (387)
5. Documentation (412)
6. Economic feasibility (387)
7. End user development (396)
8. End user involvement (404)
9. End user resistance (404)
10. Evaluation factors (407)
    a. Hardware (408)
    b. IS services (410)
    c. Software (409)
11. Feasibility study (385)
12. Functional requirements (389)
13. Implementation process (405)
14. Intangible (387)
    a. Benefits
    b. Costs
15. Operational feasibility (387)
16. Organizational analysis (388)
17. Organizational feasibility (385)
18. Postimplementation review (414)
19. Prototype (393)
20. Prototyping (393)
21. Systems analysis (388)
22. Systems approach (382)
23. Systems design (390)
24. Systems development life cycle (383)
25. Systems implementation (405)
26. Systems investigation (384)
27. Systems maintenance (413)
28. Systems specifications (392)
29. System testing (410)
30. Systems thinking (382)
31. Tangible (388)
    a. Benefits
    b. Costs
32. Technical feasibility (387)
33. User interface, data, and process design (390)

Review Quiz

Match one of the key terms and concepts listed previously with one of the brief examples or definitions that follow. Try to find the best fit for answers that seem to fit more than one term or concept. Defend your choices.

_____ 1. Using an organized sequence of activities to study a problem or opportunity using systems thinking.

_____ 2. Trying to recognize systems and the new interrelationships and components of systems in any situation.

_____ 3. Evaluating the success of a solution after it has been implemented.

_____ 4. Your evaluation shows that benefits outweigh costs for a proposed system.

_____ 5. The costs of acquiring computer hardware, software, and specialists.

_____ 6. Loss of customer goodwill caused by errors in a new system.

_____ 7. Increases in profits caused by a new system.

_____ 8. Improved employee morale caused by efficiency and effectiveness of a new system.

_____ 9. A multistep process to conceive, design, and implement an information system.

_____ 10. The first stage of the systems development cycle.

_____ 11. Determines the organizational, economic, technical, and operational feasibility of a proposed information system.

_____ 12. Cost savings and additional profits will exceed the investment required.

_____ 13. Reliable hardware and software are available to implement a proposed system.

_____ 14. Customers will not have trouble using a proposed system.

_____ 15. The proposed system supports the strategic plan of the business.

_____ 16. Studying in detail the information needs of users and any information systems presently used.

_____ 17. A detailed description of user information needs and the input, processing, output, storage, and control capabilities required to meet those needs.

_____ 18. The process that results in specifications for the hardware, software, people, network, and data resources and information products needed by a proposed system.

_____ 19. Systems design should focus on developing end user input/output methods, data structures, and programs and procedures.

_____ 20. A detailed description of the hardware, software, people, network, and data resources and information products required by a proposed system.

_____ 21. Acquiring hardware and software, testing and documenting a proposed system, and training people to use it.

_____ 22. Making improvements to an operational system.

_____ 23. Using software packages to computerize many of the activities in the systems development process.

_____ 24. A working model of an information system.

_____ 25. An interactive and iterative process of developing and refining information system prototypes.

_____ 26. Managers and business specialists can develop their own computer-based business applications.

_____ 27. End users should be part of organizational change and IS project teams.

_____ 28. Companies should try to minimize the risks and costs and maximize the benefits of major changes in business and technology.

_____ 29. Includes acquisition, testing, training, and conversion to a new system.

_____ 30. Performance, cost, reliability, technology, and ergonomics are examples.

_____ 31. Performance, cost, efficiency, language, and documentation are examples.

_____ 32. Maintenance, conversion, training, and business position are examples.

_____ 33. End users frequently resist the introduction of new technology.

_____ 34. Operate in parallel with the old system, use a test site, switch in stages, or cut over immediately to a new system.

_____ 35. Checking whether hardware and software work properly for end users.

_____ 36. A user manual communicates the design and operating procedures of a system.

_____ 37. Modifying an operational system by adding Internet web site access would be an example.

Discussion Questions

1. Why do you think prototyping has become a popular way to develop new computer-based business systems?

2. Refer to the Real World Case on SunAmerica Financial and A-DEC in the chapter. What are some of the costs to a business of a lack of proper project management for systems development projects?

3. How can a company use change management to minimize the risks and costs and maximize the benefits of changes in business and technology? Give several examples.

4. What are the three most important factors you would use in evaluating computer hardware? Explain why.

5. What are the three most important factors you would use in evaluating computer software? Explain why.

6. Assume that in your first week on a new job you are asked to use a type of software package that you have never used before. What kind of user training should your company provide to you before you start?

7. Refer to the Real World Case on Computer Associates, Microsoft, and IBM in the chapter. Should a vendor's web site become its primary source of software support? Why or why not?

8. What is the difference between the parallel, plunge, phased, and pilot forms of IS conversion? Which conversion strategy is best? Explain why.

9. What are several key factors in designing a successful Internet or intranet web site? Refer to Figure 10.14 as a starting point. Explain why the design factors you chose are important to web success.

10. Pick a task you would like to computerize. How could you use the steps of the information systems development cycle as illustrated in Figure 10.4 to help you? Use examples to illustrate your answer.

Real World Problems

1. Cyberian Outpost and Reel.com: Changing Web Site Design Requirements

Unlike longtime web surfers, newcomers to the Internet are less technically savvy than ever, causing a number of web retailers to revamp their web design and sales strategies accordingly. Newbies want to find items with a minimum of clicks, conduct business quickly, and be able to ask questions, experienced web merchants report. That means they're likely to frequent sites that are easy to navigate and have plenty of clear options for queries and feedback.

The change in Internet demographics is also creating opportunities to design sites for merchants whose target audience isn't primarily made up of affluent, highly educated men, which had been the major Internet demographic group. According to a study by the Pew Research Center for the People & the Press in Washington, 71 percent of adults who started using the Internet in the past year don't have a college degree; 52 percent were women; and 65 percent earn less than $50,000 a year. Only a quarter of new adult Internet users were younger than 30.

In contrast, longtime Internet enthusiasts "almost want it to be difficult" because they enjoy the challenge of making technology work, said Louise Cooper, vice president of worldwide marketing at online computer retailer Cyberian Outpost Inc. in Kent, Connecticut. Outpost recently revamped its web site (www.outpost.com) to make it "more intuitive, more obvious," Cooper said. There's an increase in information available on the home page, for example. And the company now promotes configured systems more than components for the do-it-yourselfer.

Outpost is also planning a new feature that will allow shoppers to calculate shipping costs before they place an order. "Shipping costs for web orders were a shock to a lot of people," Cooper said.

Dave Rochlin, vice president of marketing at Reel.com Inc. (www.reel.com) said the online video/digital videodisk store must rein in the temptation to be too cutting-edge in web site design because of novice users. That means not using new capabilities from the latest-release browsers or special software plug-ins unless a site specifically aims for a techno-sophisticate audience.

"We really have no discipline ourselves here," Rochlin said. "We have a lot of techno-savvy people, but we think a lot about web site usability. There's a huge portion of customers who only know how to get to the Web through America Online." Like many in Internet retailing, Rochlin said he believes there will be a major push to add web features that improve customer service this year, in part to cater to newcomers who want the same level of service on the Web that they get when shopping elsewhere.

a. What changes are occurring in the customers and design requirements of E-commerce web sites?

b. What other design changes would you recommend to improve retail web sites? Visit the web sites of several web retailers to get ideas.

Source: Adapted form Sharon Machris, "Web Retailers Retool for Mainstream Users," *Computerworld*, March 22, 1999, p. 40. Copyright 1999 by Computerworld, Inc., Framingham, MA 01701. Reprinted from *Computerworld*.

2. Clarke American Checks and Corning Inc.: Using the Web for ERP Software Training

If it's 10 A.M., workers at Clarke American Checks Inc. are firing up their web browsers for a collaborative training lesson on how to perform purchasing with their new SAP AG enterprise resource planning (ERP) software. During the daily sessions, end users in more than 20 locations either watch their colleagues perform simulated transactions with the software, or do it themselves.

Clarke American, a San Antonio–based check printer, is in a growing group of companies using web-based training to get workers up to speed on enterprise resource planning applications. Doing so can trim up to 75 percent off the cost of traditional training methods, such as instructor-led sessions, users said.

"Self-paced ERP training delivered via the Web is becoming a popular concept," said Ellen Julien, an analyst at International Data Corporation.

Users say training eats up 10 to 20 percent of an ERP project's budget and is one of the more vexing parts of an ERP development project. Many ERP systems have tricky user interfaces and are highly customized, making generic, computer-based training courses ineffective.

Some ERP software vendors offer training tools, but they may not cover all of the software's modules and often are expensive, users said. Classroom training is usually out of the question because of the high number of users who need to be trained.

At Corning Inc. in Corning, New York, the biggest ERP training challenge was "the large number of users we had to train in a short period of time," said training coordinator Maureen Smith. The company has been deploying various PeopleSoft modules for two years to about 5,000 users.

Corning considered delivering courses on CD-ROM, but "that was too hard to control and manage," said systems analyst Steve Ingram. And Corning's plan to train users via their private corporate network failed because access was too slow for remote users. Moving to the Web with the Web Pathlore Software training tool gave the trainers a central point to manage course content and make changes to update and improve the course, said Smith.

a. How important is user training for the successful implementation of a new system? Explain.

b. What are the advantages of web-based training for users of newly installed systems?

Source: Adapted from Barb Cole-Gomolski, "Companies Turn to Web for ERP Training," *Computerworld*, February 8, 1999, p. 4. Copyright 1999 by Computerworld, Inc., Framingham, MA 01701. Reprinted from *Computerworld.*

3. Automated Data Processing Inc.: Overcoming User Resistance to Customer Relationship Management

Forget notions of traditional field or sales force automation. Customer relationship management (CRM) systems incorporate features found in contact management, sales automation, call center management software, and more. Specifically, CRM provides a comprehensive view of the relationship between a business and its customers.

Naturally, senior managers at the accounting service firm Automated Data Processing Inc. (ADP) in Roseland, New Jersey, were thrilled at projections that a new CRM system would cut company costs by $450 million. But that wasn't the argument Howard Koenig used when he faced resistance from call center workers, sales representatives, and sales managers.

Call center workers were worried about the increased stress of having to enter much more detailed data whenever a customer called—and also about Big Brother–type monitoring of their every move. Sales-people were worried that automating the submission of new customer contacts would get in the way of closing deals.

So rather than point out how the new system would help the company, Koenig focused on allaying fears. "We had to demonstrate that the technology was going to make their jobs better," said Koenig, corporate vice president of operations and client services at ADP.

He showed call center workers how their managers would be able to better anticipate peak call times, thus improving staff scheduling. He showed them how having a history of each customer's interactions with the firm would lead to less-stressful encounters.

Sales representatives, on the other hand, were shown that they never would have to make a call without knowing about any outstanding issues on an account, Koenig says. And salespeople, who wouldn't get their commissions until a contract was officially processed, could track the progress of a deal through the system.

In addition to meeting company objectives, turnover among call center workers has been cut by more than 10 percent—"We believe the job is actually less stressful," Koenig says—and sales representatives have improved the retention of existing accounts by 5 percent.

a. How rational were the fears of call center workers, sales reps, and sales managers to the implementation of the new CRM system? Explain.

b. Do you agree with how Howard Koenig allayed the fears of each of the end user groups involved? Why or why not?

Source: Adapted from Alice LaPlante, "Eyes on the Customer," *Computerworld*, March 15, 1999, pp. 60–61. Copyright 1999 by Computerworld, Inc., Framingham, MA 01701. Reprinted from *Computerworld.*

Application Exercises

1. System Study Report

Study an information system described in a case study in this text or one used by an organization to which you have access. Write up the results in a system study report. Make a presentation to the class based on the results of your system study. Use the outline in Figure 10.40 as a table of contents for your report and the outline of your presentation. Use presentation software and/or overhead transparencies to display key points of your analysis.

2. Village Inn Restaurants: Doing End User Development

Village Inn Restaurants is a national chain of coffee shop restaurants. Typically, a server takes your order on a paper form, inserts it into a small terminal connected to an in-store network server, and enters appropriate data about your order. The computer produces a paper printout of your order in the kitchen for the cooks, calculates your bill, and prints the details of your order on the paper form. This form is

Figure 10.40   Outline of a system study report.

- **Introduction to the organization and information system.** Briefly describe the organization you selected and the type of information system you have studied.
- **Analysis of a current information system.** Identify the following system components of a business use of information technology in your report.
  - Input, processing, output, storage, and control methods currently used.
  - Hardware, software, networks, and people involved.
  - Data captured and information products produced.
  - Files and databases accessed and maintained.
- **Evaluation of the current information system.**
  - **Efficiency:** Does it do the job right? Is the information system well organized? Inexpensive? Fast? Does it require minimum resources? Process large volumes of data, produce a variety of information products?
  - **Effectiveness:** Does it do the right job? The way the end users want it done? Give them the information they need, the way they want it? Does it support the objectives of the organization? Provide significant business value?
- **Design and implementation of an information system proposal.**
  - Do end users need a new system or just improvements? Why?
  - What exactly are you recommending they do?
  - Is it feasible? What are its benefits and costs?
  - What will it take to implement your recommendations?

then returned to your table. When you are ready to leave, you give this form to the cashier, who keys data about your payment into a point-of-sale terminal.

Assume that some customers are complaining about slow service, which the cooks blame on incorrect orders by servers. Use the concepts of end user development as illustrated in Figures 10.4, 10.22, 10.23, and 10.39 to answer the following questions:

a. What specific steps would you take to study this problem and propose a solution?

b. What are three questions you would ask in a systems study interview?

c. What do you think the problem(s) is (are)? Why?

d. What are two possible solutions you can think of? What are their advantages and disadvantages?

e. If you had to choose one solution, what would it be? Why did you choose it?

f. How would you implement your solution?

3. Information Systems Maintenance at Premier Services

Users of information systems at Premier Services can request changes to systems by filling out a change request form and sending it to the group responsible for maintenance of the affected system. Premier has decided to assign a user, you, the authority and responsibility for coordinating the handling of change requests.

You have decided to maintain a database table listing the requester's name, the date the request was made, the name of the affected system, and the status of the request. The status field will be used to track the progress toward completing requested changes. As you receive a request, you will add a new record to the table marking its status as IP (in progress) and send the request on to the appropriate maintenance group. When changes are completed, you are notified by the maintenance team. At that point, you change the status to PA (pending approval). The user who submitted the request then evaluates the changes and either accepts or rejects the work. If they accept, the status is changed to Com (completed). If the changes are rejected, the status is returned to IP. A set of sample data for the system follows.

a. Create a database table to store this information and enter the sample data shown on page 421.

b. Create and print a report grouped by the name of the affected system that summarizes the status of all change requests.

c. Create and print a report on all requests whose status is not Com. The report should be sorted by request date from the oldest to the newest.

d. Create a query to retrieve a count of the number of change requests in each status category.

Request ID	Requester	Request Date	Affected System	Status
101	Jones, J.	12-Mar-99	Inventory	Com
102	Smith, R.	18-Apr-99	Purchasing	IP
103	Davis, I.	21-Apr-99	Sales	Com
104	Evans, R.	03-May-99	Purchasing	Com
105	Lewis, J.	15-May-99	Sales	PA
106	Tower, T.	14-Jun-99	Purchasing	IP
107	Jones, J.	01-Jul-99	Inventory	IP
108	Adams, J.	15-Jul-99	Purchasing	PA
109	Camber, D.	25-Jul-99	Inventory	IP

4. Creating a Personal Web Page

Create a personal web page for yourself using appropriate software recommended by your instructor. If you use Microsoft Word to create your web page, a brief description of special features of Word that are particularly useful in developing web pages is available on the web site for this textbook at www.mhhe.com/business/mis/obrien/obrien9e.

Your web page should actually include at least four separate HTML files that are linked together. Your web site should have a hierarchical structure beginning with a home page. The home page should contain links to the other, more detailed pages. You may also want to include bookmarks within a page linking to other sections of the same page and/or links to the web sites of others.

Review Quiz Answers

1. 22	7. 31*a*	13. 32	18. 23	23. 2	28. 1	33. 9
2. 30	8. 14*a*	14. 15	19. 33	24. 19	29. 13	34. 3
3. 18	9. 24	15. 17	20. 28	25. 20	30. 10*a*	35. 29
4. 4	10. 26	16. 21	21. 25	26. 7	31. 10*c*	36. 5
5. 31*b*	11. 11	17. 12	22. 27	27. 8	32. 10*b*	37. 27
6. 14*b*	12. 6					

Selected References

1. Belmonte, Richard, and Richard Murray. "Getting Ready for Strategic Change." *Information Systems Management*, Summer 1993.

2. Bowles, Jerry. "Best Practices for Global Effectiveness." Special Advertising Section, *Fortune*, November 24, 1997.

3. Brun-Cottan, Françoise, and Patricia Wall. "Using video to Re-Present the User." *Communications of the ACM*, May 1995.

4. Burden, Kevin. "Networking Survey: Edge Goes to Hardware Vendors." *Computerworld*, February 3, 1997.

5. Cafasso, Rosemary. "Few IS Projects Come in on Time, on Budget." *Computerworld*, December 12, 1994.

6. Clark, Charles; Nancy Cavanaugh; Carol Brown; and V. Sambamurthy. "Building Change-Readiness Capabilities in the IS Organization: Insights from the Bell Atlantic Experience." *MIS Quarterly*, December 1997.

7. Cole-Gomolski, Barb. "Users Loath to Share Their Know-How." *Computerworld*, November 17, 1997.

8. Cronin, Mary. *The Internet Strategy Handbook*. Boston: Harvard Business School Press, 1996.

9. Cross, John; Michael Earl; and Jeffrey Sampler. "Transformation of the IT Function at British Petroleum." *MIS Quarterly*, December 1997.

10. Davenport, Thomas H. *Process Innovation: Reengineering Work through Information Technology.* Boston: Harvard Business School Press, 1993.

11. El Sawy, Omar, and Gene Bowles. "Redesigning the Customer Support Process for the Electronic Economy: Insights from Storage Dimensions." *MIS Quarterly*, December 1997.

12. Forte, Gene, and Ronald Norman. "CASE: A Self-Assessment by the Software Engineering Community." *Communications of the ACM*, April 1992.

13. Grover, Varun; James Teng and Kirk Fiedler. "IS Investment Priorities in Contemporary Organizations." *Communications of the ACM*, February 1998.

14. Harkness, Warren; William Kettinger; and Albert Segars. "Sustaining Process Improvement and Innovation in the Information Services Function: Lessons Learned at the BOSE Corporation." *MIS Quarterly*, September 1996.

15. Hawson, James, and Jesse Beeler. "Effects of User Participation in Systems Development: A Longitudinal Field Experiment." *MIS Quarterly*, December 1997.

16. Hills, Melanie. *Intranet Business Strategies.* New York: John Wiley & Sons, 1997.

17. Holtz, Shel. *PCWeek: The Intranet Advantage.* Emeryville, CA: Ziff-Davis Press, 1996.

18. Iansiti, Marco, and Alan MacCormack. "Developing Products on Internet Time." *Harvard Business Review*, September–October 1997.

19. Kalakota, Ravi, and Andrew Whinston. *Electronic Commerce: A Manager's Guide.* Reading, MA: Addison-Wesley, 1997.

20. Keen, Peter G. W. *Shaping the Future: Business Design through Information Technology.* Boston: Harvard Business School, 1991.

21. Kettinger, William; James Teng; and Subashish Guha. "Business Process Change: A Study of Methodologies, Techniques, and Tools." *MIS Quarterly*, March 1997.

22. Maglitta, Joseph. "Rocks in the Gears: Reengineering the Workplace." *Computerworld*, October 3, 1994

23. Martin, Chuck. *The Digital Estate: Strategies for Competing, Surviving, and Thriving in an Internet-Worked World.* New York: McGraw-Hill, 1997.

24. Morgan, James N. *Application Cases in MIS.* 3rd ed. Burr Ridge, IL: Irwin/McGraw-Hill, 1999.

25. O'Brien, James A., and Craig A. VanLengen. "Evaluating Information Systems Documentation Techniques." *Journal of Information Systems Education*, Fall 1992.

26. Orlikowsky, Wanda. "CASE Tools as Organizational Change: Investigating Incremental and Radical Changes in Systems Development." *MIS Quarterly*, September 1993.

27. Pei, Daniel, and Carmine Cutone. "Object-Oriented Analysis and Design." *Information Systems Management*, Winter 1995.

28. Prokesch, Steven. "Unleashing the Power of Learning: An Interview with British Petroleum's John Browne." *Harvard Business Review*, September–October 1997.

29. Senge, Peter. *The Fifth Discipline: The Art and Practice of the Learning Organization.* New York: Currency Doubleday, 1994.

30. Whitten Jeffrey, and Lonnie Bentley. *Systems Analysis and Design Methods.* 4th ed. Burr Ridge, IL: Irwin/McGraw-Hill, 1998.

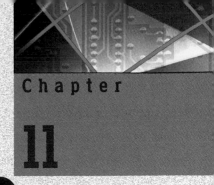

Chapter

11

Enterprise and Global

Management of Information

Technology

Chapter Highlights

Section I
Managing Information Resources and Technologies

Introduction

Real World Case: Chase Manhattan, Cigna, and PG&E: Business Managers of Information Technology

Managers and Information Technology

Organizations and Information Technology

Information Resource Management

Strategic Management

Operational Management

Resource Management

Technology Management

Distributed Management

Section II
Global Information Technology Management

Real World Case: Guy Carpenter & Co. and PRT Group: The Business Case for Global Software Development

The International Dimension

Global IT Management

Cultural, Political, and Geoeconomic Challenges

Global Business and IT Strategies

Global Business and IT Applications

Global IT Platforms

Global Data Issues

Global Systems Development

You and Global IT Management

Learning Objectives

After reading and studying this chapter, you should be able to:

1. Identify the major ways information technology has affected managers.

2. Explain how problems of information system performance can be solved by management involvement in IS planning and control.

3. Identify how information technology is affecting the structure and activities of organizations.

4. Identify the five major dimensions of the information resource management concept and explain how they affect the management of the information systems function.

5. Identify several cultural, political, and geoeconomic challenges that confront managers in the management of global information technology.

6. Explain the effect on global IT strategy of the trend toward a transnational business strategy by international business organizations.

7. Identify several considerations that affect the choice of IT applications, IT platforms, data definitions, and systems development methods by a global business.

Section I **Managing Information Resources and Technologies**

Introduction

The strategic and operational importance of information technology in business is no longer questioned.

> *In an increasingly competitive world, IT is critical to the development of more effective operational and management processes. To serve customers . . . companies need to be proficient in a half dozen key areas: reduced cycle times, reduced asset levels (for example, in inventories and people), faster development of new products, improved customer service, increasing empowerment of employees, and increased knowledge sharing and learning. Information technology is a critical resource for accomplishing all these goals [29].*

Thus, there is a real need for business end users to understand how to manage this vital organizational function. In this section, we will explore how IT affects managers and organizations, and stress the concept of *information resource management* as a key framework for managing information technology by both end user managers and IS managers. So whether you plan to be an entrepreneur and run your own business, a manager in a corporation, or a managerial-level professional, managing information system resources and technologies will be one of your major responsibilities.

Analyzing Chase Manhattan, Cigna, and PG&E

Read the Real World Case on Chase Manhattan, Cigna, and PG&E on the next page. We can learn a lot about the diverse IT management challenges and opportunities facing business managers today. See Figure 11.1.

Figure 11.1

June Yee Felix is a senior vice president at Chase Manhattan in charge of Chase's online bill payment service for corporate customers.

Source: Peter Gregoire.

Chase Manhattan, Cigna, and PG&E: Business Managers of Information Technology

June Yee Felix

It seems like many companies expect the growing ranks of new media/E-commerce executives, typically drawn from the sales and marketing ranks, to display the technology knowledge of Bill Gates, the sales and marketing acumen of Mary Kay, and the foresight of Gordon Moore. Says Jerry Colonna, managing partner of Flatiron Partners, a venture capital firm in New York City: "What we suddenly have is nontechnical executives responsible for strategy decisions that depend on understanding technology."

Take June Yee Felix, a senior vice president at Chase Manhattan. In February 1998 she was picked to start the bank's online bill-payment service for corporate customers. She knew little about E-commerce technology, so she began talking to experts at the bank and asking software suppliers for advice.

Within days she was deluged with calls from E-commerce consulting and research firms. After 20 one-on-one meetings with such experts, Felix chose three consulting firms to help her plan the new service. Of course, her division isn't the only unit of Chase trying to make the Web work. Other divisions have chosen other research firms, and now myriad studies circulate around the bank. Says a now wiser Felix: "My desk is covered with E-commerce reports."

Charles Baumann

Charles "Bud" Baumann wears both business and IT hats. He has let go of some of his day-to-day IT operations responsibility and moved further into growing Cigna Corporation's disability insurance business. "When you're on the business side, you have to let go of some of the reins," Baumann says. That means "trying to be more of a coach, counselor, negotiator, supporter" as opposed to directing how to implement an IT solution.

As vice president of IT at Cigna Integrated Care, Baumann is still in charge of integrating IS applications for Cigna's health care, disability, and workers' compensation units. But he spends half of his time as vice president of Cigna's Managed Disability unit, "developing a business plan for the technology, putting together the right business processes to make that technology work, and matching customer needs with our capabilities."

Meanwhile, the claims processing integration technology Baumann helps develop—now known as Cigna UniLynx—has been rolled out nationwide and is being fine-tuned. The ability to streamline the claims process by pulling together data from multiple applications is reducing disability costs by at least 15 percent, he says.

Geoff Jue

Geoff Jue is living proof of how a business/IT management partnership can work successfully. Jue moved into IT after 17 years in sales marketing and management at Pacific Gas and Electric Co., the regulated utility division of PG&E Corporation. Jue, who has an MBA and an undergraduate degree in engineering, says he felt it was time to try something new.

"I recognized IT as the agent of change, and I could only go so far in adding value on the business side," he says. So in 1997, Jue began working in the IT department on a customer information management system based on Aurum Software's SalesTrak. "I had no desire to go into IT until I started working in the Energy Services division," he recalls. "But working as a partner with IT here drew me in."

Today Jue is the director of customer relationship management systems at PG&E Energy Services in San Francisco and he says he's thrilled with his job. Jue manages a 16-person department of developers and programmers who are putting the finishing touches on one of the company's major customer management systems.

Case Study Questions

1. If you had June Yee Felix's job, what would be one of your next steps in accomplishing your E-commerce assignment? Why?

2. Do you approve of how Charles Baumann emphasizes IT in his activities as VP of Cigna's managed disability unit? Why or why not?

3. What does Geoff Jue's experience show you about what it takes to manage IT in business?

Source: Adapted from Daniel Roth, "My, What Big Internet Numbers You Have!" *Fortune*, March 15, 1999, pp. 114–20, © 1999 by Time Inc. All rights reserved; Robert Scheier, "Looking Back," *Computerworld*, January 14, 1999, pp. 99–100; and Bronwyn Fryer, "IT Hybrids, Your Next, Best Hire," *Computerworld*, February 8, 1999, p. 50. Copyright 1999 by Computerworld, Inc., Framingham, MA 01701. Reprinted from *Computerworld*.

June Yee Felix shows us how business executives today must quickly get up to speed in learning how to deploy information technology to support their companies' E-commerce initiatives. Charles Baumann demonstrates that whether he is acting as a VP of IT or a VP of a business unit, the business use of information technology stills plays a pervasive role in his management responsibilities. Geoff Jue demonstrates that you can move from a business management position to an IT management position if your previous business experience and your present IT position deal with the management of the business use of information technology.

Managers and Information Technology

Figure 11.2 illustrates that the competitive pressures of today's business and technology environment are forcing companies to rethink their use and management of information technology. Many business executives now see information technology as an enabling technology for managing the cross-functional and interorganizational processes that business units must have to successfully confront the competitive measures they face. For example, the Internet, intranets, extranets, and more cost-effective hardware and software are enabling individuals, teams, workgroups, business units, and organizations to be "wired together" in close business relationships that can provide the communication, coordination, and collaboration needed in today's competitive global marketplace [13].

Thus, information technology has become a major force for precipitating or enabling organizational and managerial change. Thanks to the Internet, intranets, extranets, and client/server networks, computing power and information resources are now more readily available to more managers than ever before. In fact, these and other information technologies are already promoting innovative changes in managerial decision making, organizational structures, and managerial work activities in companies around the world [12].

For example, the decision support capability provided by information systems technology is changing the focus of managerial decision making. Managers freed from number-crunching chores must now face tougher strategic policy questions in order to

Figure 11.2 Information technology must be managed to meet the challenges of today's business and technology environment.

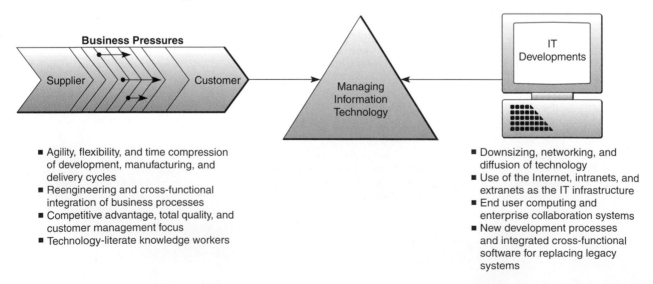

Business Pressures

Supplier ❯ Customer

Managing Information Technology

IT Developments

- Agility, flexibility, and time compression of development, manufacturing, and delivery cycles
- Reengineering and cross-functional integration of business processes
- Competitive advantage, total quality, and customer management focus
- Technology-literate knowledge workers

- Downsizing, networking, and diffusion of technology
- Use of the Internet, intranets, and extranets as the IT infrastructure
- End user computing and enterprise collaboration systems
- New development processes and integrated cross-functional software for replacing legacy systems

develop realistic alternatives for today's dynamic competitive environment. The use of the Internet, intranets, and enterprise collaboration systems to coordinate work activity is another example of the impact of information technology on management. Middle managers no longer need to serve as conduits for the transmission of operations feedback or control directives between operational managers and top management. Thus, many companies have experienced drastic reductions in the layers and numbers of middle management, and the dramatic growth of workgroups of task-focused teams of specialists [31].

Poor IS Performance

What is less clear [about IT], is how business executives can ensure that their firms benefit from new opportunities afforded by IT and avoid its well-known, oft-repeated pitfalls: botched development projects; escalating costs with no apparent economic benefits; organizational disruption; and technical glitches [20].

So, managing information technology is not an easy task. The information systems function has performance problems in many organizations. The promised benefits of information technology have not occurred in many documented cases. Studies by management consulting firms, computer user groups, and university researchers have shown that many businesses have not been successful in managing their computer resources and information services departments. Figure 11.3 dramatizes the results of research on what business users at over 500 companies feel are the major reasons why information technology fails to support business goals. Thus, it is evident that in many organizations information technology is not being used effectively, efficiently, or economically. For example:

- Information technology is not being used *effectively* by companies that use IT primarily to computerize traditional business processes instead of using it for

Figure 11.3

Performance problems in information systems. The major reasons why information technology does not support business goals according to a five-year survey of business users at over 500 companies.

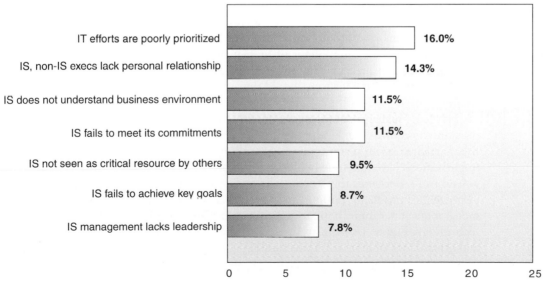

Source: Adapted from Jerry Luftman, "Align in the Sand," *Leadership Series*, *Computerworld*, February 17, 1997, p. 3. Copyright 1997 by Computerworld, Inc., Framingham, MA 01701. Reprinted from *Computerworld*.

decision support and innovative processes and products to gain competitive advantages.

- Information technology is not being used *efficiently* by information services groups that provide poor response times, frequent downtimes, incompatible systems, unintegrated data, and application development backlogs.
- Information technology is not being used *economically* in many cases. Information technology costs have risen faster than other costs in many businesses, even though the cost of processing each unit of data is decreasing due to dramatic price reductions and improvements in hardware and software technology.

Let's look at a real world example.

Empire Blue Cross/Blue Shield

Empire Blue Cross/Blue Shield is New York state's largest health care insurance company. In 1995, the company fired 20 percent of its IS staff and outsourced some of its IS services. Empire had employed over 1,000 IS workers and had annual expenditures for information services of $135 million.

The company had been migrating to a new claims processing system since 1992. About 50 percent of the 26 million claims the company handles annually are processed on the new system. Two mainframe-based legacy systems, both more than 25 years old, process the other half of the claims filed by the company's 5.4 million individual subscribers. The insurer also has completed two other systems under an estimated $160 million IS project that began in the late 1980s.

Performance of Empire's customer service systems was terrible. For example, the average time it took to process an institutional claim in the downstate region went up from 9.4 days to 14.7 days in 1995. Over 10 percent of customers trying to contact a customer service representative hung up before getting through, while 5 percent of customers received a busy signal. In addition, Empire's claims accounting systems proved unable to detect false claims, resulting in losses exceeding $40 million [21].

Management Involvement and Governance

What is the solution to problems of poor performance in the information systems function? There are no quick and easy answers. However, the experiences of successful organizations reveal that extensive and meaningful **managerial** and **end user involvement** is the key ingredient of high-quality information systems performance. Involving business managers in the governance of the IS function and end users in the development of IS applications should thus shape the response of management to the challenge of improving the business value of information technology [4, 42].

Involving managers in the management of IT (from CEO to the managers of business units) requires the development of *governance structures* that encourage their active participation in planning and controlling the business uses of IT. Thus, many organizations have developed policies and procedures that require managers to be involved in IT decisions that affect their business units. This helps managers avoid IS performance problems, outlined in Figure 11.3. Without this high degree of involvement, managers cannot hope to improve the strategic business value of information technology. Figure 11.4 illustrates several major levels of management involvement and governance of information technology.

- **Executive IT Committee.** Many organizations use an executive information technology committee of top executives to do strategic information system planning and to coordinate the development of major information systems projects.

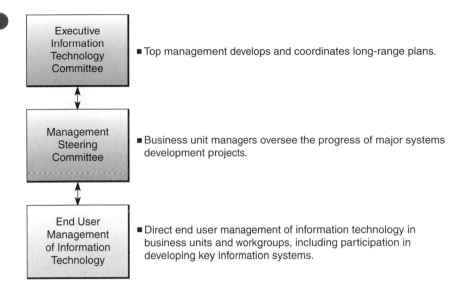

Figure 11.4

Levels of management involvement in IS governance. Successful information systems performance requires the involvement of business managers in IS governance.

■ Top management develops and coordinates long-range plans.

■ Business unit managers oversee the progress of major systems development projects.

■ Direct end user management of information technology in business units and workgroups, including participation in developing key information systems.

This committee includes senior management of the major divisions of the firm, as well as the *chief information officer* (CIO) of the organization, who is the senior executive responsible for governance of the IS function.

- **IT Steering Committee.** A steering committee of business unit managers, operating managers, and management personnel from the information services department may be created to oversee the progress of critical systems development projects. The committee meets on a regular basis to review progress made, to settle disputes, and to change priorities, if necessary.

- **End User Management.** End user managers must also accept their responsibility for managing the resources and quality of information systems and services within their business units and workgroups. This includes involvement in IS development projects that affect their business units, as well as managing the IS people, hardware, software, network, and data resources within their units.

Chemical Banking Corporation	Chemical Bank uses a business technology management council to set technology direction for the company. The council is chaired by Chemical's chief information officer. It includes the top IS executives from both central IS and Chemical's business units, senior non-IS executives from Chemical business units, and the controller's office. The council sets policies, standards, and guidelines that direct technology policies for both line managers and IS managers. The council has spun off subcommittees such as an information management committee. The committee is cochaired by the CIO, the CFO, and the head of credit policy. It establishes rules and principles for managing information across the company.

Organizations and Information Technology

One way to understand the organizational impact of information technology is to view an organization as a sociotechnical system. In this context, people, tasks, technology, culture, and structure are the basic components of an organization. Figure 11.5 illustrates this conceptual framework. This concept emphasizes that to improve an organization's performance, managers must (1) change one or more of these components and (2) take into account the relationships among these interdepartment components. This

Figure 11.5

Organizations as sociotechnical systems. Information systems must accommodate the people, tasks, technology, culture, and structure components and relationships of an organization.

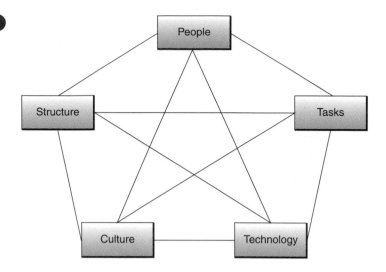

is especially important for the proper use of information technology. In the past, firms have used information systems technology to automate organizational tasks without giving sufficient consideration to its strategic impact on the organization. Thus, a major managerial challenge of information technology is to develop information systems that promote strategic improvements in how an organization supports its people, tasks, technology, culture, and structure.

People. Managers and knowledge workers are individuals with a variety of preferences for information and diverse capabilities for effectively using information provided to them. As we pointed out in Chapter 8, information systems can produce information products to meet the business requirements of end users and managers. Thus, management information, decision support, and executive information systems can provide prespecified or ad-hoc information tailored to a manager's decision-making requirements.

Tasks. The tasks of many organizations have become quite complex and inefficient over time. In many cases, information technology has been used to do the same old thing, only faster. However, as we discussed in Chapter 9, IT can play a major role in fighting organizational complexity by supporting the reengineering of business processes. For example, IT developments such as electronic data interchange dramatically reduce the need for several departments to be involved in preparing, authorizing, checking, and sending paper business documents. This can eliminate many manual tasks and required procedures and significantly improve communication and strategic cooperation between organizations.

Technology. The technology of computer-based information systems continues to grow more sophisticated and complex. However, this technology should not dictate the information needs of end users in the performance of their organizational tasks. It should accommodate the management culture and structure of each organization. For example, executive information systems overcame many of the objections of top executives to the lack of individual and task flexibility of previous types of management information systems. Internet and intranet-based business systems have also gained end user acceptance because of their easy-to-use browser-based graphical interfaces.

Culture. Organizations and their subunits have a culture that is shared by managers and other employees. That is, they have a unique set of organizational values and styles. For example, managers at some organizations share an informal, collegial, entrepreneurial spirit that stresses initiative, collaboration, and risk taking. Managers at other organizations may stress a more formal "do it by the book" or "go through the chain of command" approach. Naturally, the designs of information systems and information products must accommodate such differences. For example, managers in a corporate culture that encourages entrepreneurial risk taking and collaboration will probably favor executive information systems that give them quick access to forecasts about competitors and customers, and E-mail and other Internet and intranet systems that make it easy to communicate with colleagues anywhere.

Structure. Organizations structure their management, employees, and job tasks into a variety of organizational subunits. The IS function can no longer assume a hierarchical, centralized, organizational structure that it supports by centralizing processing power, databases, and systems development at the corporate headquarters level. This type of structure emphasizes gathering data into centralized databases and producing reports to meet the information needs of functional executives.

Instead, IT must be able to support a more decentralized, collaborative type of organizational structure, which needs more interconnected intranets or client/server networks, distributed databases, downsized computers, and systems development resources distributed to business unit and workgroup levels. Thus, information technology must emphasize quick and easy communication and collaboration among individuals, business units, and other organization workgroups, using electronics instead of paper. For example, information technologies such as the Internet, intranets, and extranets enable the development of interorganizational information systems and network organizational structures that are vital to the formation of the *virtual companies* discussed in Chapter 9.

Information Resource Management

IT has become the fourth major resource available to executives to shape and operate an organization. Companies have managed the other three major resources for years: people, money, and machines. But today IT accounts for more than 50% of the capital-goods dollars spent in the United States. It is time to see IT for what it is: a major resource that . . . can radically affect the structure of the organization, the way it serves customers, and the way it communicates both internally and externally [29].

Information resource management (IRM) is an IS management concept that organizes the management and mission of the information systems function into five major dimensions. Figure 11.6 illustrates this conceptual framework [33].

- **Strategic Management.** Information technology must be managed to contribute to a firm's strategic objectives and competitive advantages, not just for operational efficiency or decision support.
- **Operational Management.** Information technology and information systems can be managed by functional and process-based organizational structures and managerial techniques commonly used throughout other business units.
- **Resource Management.** Data and information, hardware and software, telecommunications networks, and IS personnel are vital organizational resources that must be managed like other business assets.

Figure 11.6

The information resource management (IRM) concept. Note that there are five major dimensions to the job of managing information system resources.

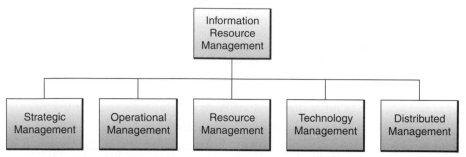

Source: Adapted from James A. O'Brien and James N. Morgan, "A Multidimensional Model of Information Resource Management," *Information Resources Management Journal*, Spring 1991, p. 4. Copyright © 1991, Information Resources Management Journal, Idea Group Publishing, Harrisburg, PA. Reprint by permission.

- **Technology Management.** All technologies that process, store, and communicate data and information throughout the enterprise should be managed as integrated systems of organizational resources.
- **Distributed Management.** Managing the use of information technology and information system resources in business units or workgroups is a key responsibility of their managers, no matter what their function or level in the organization.

Strategic Management

The IRM concept emphasizes a strategic management view that we emphasized in Chapter 9 and have stressed throughout this text. That is, the IS function must manage information technology so that it makes major contributions to the profitability and strategic objectives of the firm. Thus, the information systems function must change from an information services utility focused only on serving a firm's transaction processing or decision support needs. Instead, it must become a producer or packager of information products or an enabler of organizational structures and business processes that can give a firm a comparative advantage over its competitors. As we saw in Chapter 9, companies can develop strategic information systems to gain a competitive edge. Thus, information resource management focuses on developing and managing information systems that significantly improve operational efficiency, promote innovative products and services, and build strategic business alliances and information resources that can enhance the competitiveness of an organization.

The Chief Information Officer

Many companies have created a senior management position, the **chief information officer** (CIO), to oversee all use of information technology in their organizations and bring them into alignment with strategic business goals. Thus, all traditional computer services, telecommunications services, and other IS technology support services are the responsibility of this executive. Also, the CIO does not direct day-to-day information service activities. Instead, CIOs concentrate on long-term planning and strategy. They also work with other top executives to develop strategic uses of information technology that help make the firm more competitive in the marketplace. Many companies have also filled the CIO position with executives from the business functions or units outside the IS field. Such CIOs emphasize that the chief role of information technology is to help a company meet its strategic business objectives [24].

Strategic Information Systems Planning

Strategic IS management requires **strategic IS planning.** Figure 11.7 illustrates the activities and outputs of strategic IS planning. Companies do strategic IS planning with four main objectives in mind:

- **Business alignment.** Aligning investment in information technology with a company's business vision and strategic business goals.
- **Competitive advantage.** Exploiting information technology to create innovative and strategic business information systems for competitive advantage.
- **Resource management.** Developing plans for the efficient and effective management of a company's information system resources, including IS personnel, hardware, software, data, and network resources.
- **Technology architecture.** Developing technology policies and designing an information technology architecture for the organization [7].

The strategic IS planning process illustrated in Figure 11.7 is *business driven, not technology driven.* Notice that a business vision and business drivers, such as business process reengineering to achieve the best industry practices and the needs of customers and business partners, are what drive the planning process. Business/IT

Figure 11.7 Strategic planning uses a business vision and business drivers to create an IT architecture and tactical IS plans for the business use of information technology.

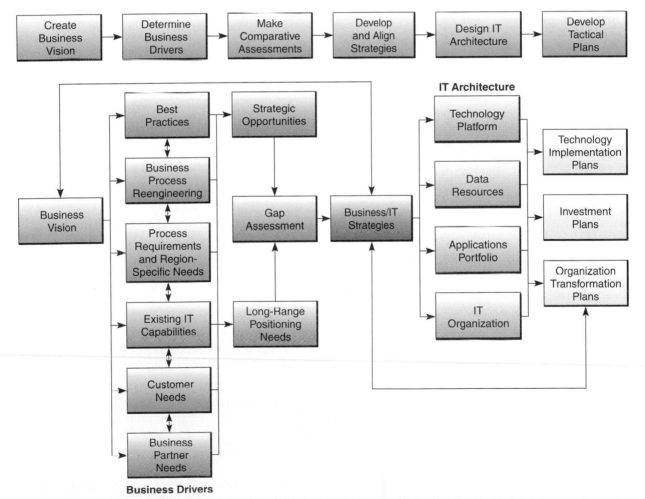

Source: Adapted and reprinted from Michael Mische, "Transnational Architecture: A Reengineering Approach," *Information Systems Management* (New York: Auerbach Publications), Winter 1995, p. 21. © 1995 Research Institute of America. Used with permission.

Figure 11.8 Strategic business/IT factors affect the priority of IS investment plans.

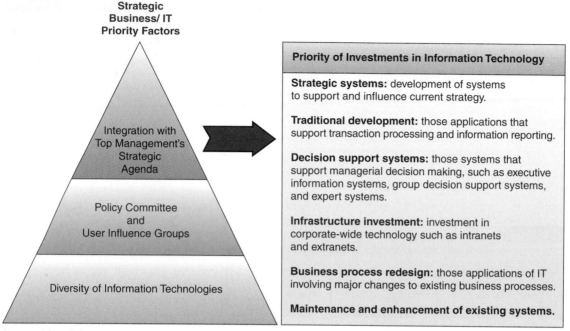

Source: Adapted from Varun Grover, James Teng, and Kirk Fiedler, "IS Investment Priorities in Contemporary Organizations," *Communications of the ACM*, February 1998, p. 42. Copyright © 1998, Association of Computing Machinery. By permission.

strategies can then be developed based on the strategic opportunities that are revealed. Only then can the IT architecture for the company be designed. For example, Figure 11.8 shows that investments in information technology must be aligned with top management's strategic agenda, earn a commitment from a company's IS policy committee and user groups, and support a diversity of information technologies.

Information Technology Architecture

Figure 11.7 also emphasizes that the **IT architecture** that is created by the strategic-planning process is a conceptual design, or blueprint, that includes the following major components:

● **Technology platform.** Computer systems, system and application software, and telecommunications networks provide a computing and communications infrastructure, or platform, that supports the use of information technology in the business.

● **Data resources.** Many types of operational and specialized databases, including data warehouses and Internet/intranet databases (as discussed in Chapter 5) store and provide data and information for business processes and managerial decision support.

● **Applications portfolio.** Business applications of information technology are designed as a diversified portfolio of information systems that support key business functions as well as cross-functional business processes. In addition, an applications portfolio should include support for interorganizational business linkages, managerial decision making, end user computing and collaboration, and strategic initiatives for competitive advantage.

● **IT organization.** The organizational structure of the IS function within a company and the distribution of IS specialists among corporate headquarters and business units can be designed or redesigned to meet the changing strategies of a business. The form of the IT organization depends on the managerial philosophy, business vision, and business/IT strategies formulated during the strategic planning process.

S. C. Johnson & Son, Inc.	S. C. Johnson & Son, more commonly known as Johnson Wax, emphasizes a portfolio management approach in its use of IS planning [15]. Johnson divides all IT applications into six portfolios according to the business function they support. These include sales, marketing, distribution, finance, manufacturing, and logistics. Each portfolio consists of a mix of computer-based applications that keep a particular business function operating successfully. An IS specialist serves as the manager of each application portfolio. Portfolio managers are given annual goals for the portfolio, which usually require them to lower the portfolio's fixed costs and come up with innovative IT solutions.
	The general managers of each Johnson business unit meet regularly with the IS staff to define major goals for improvements in business processes in their units. For example, they might want a 15 percent reduction in the cost of closing a sale, or a 5 percent reduction in inventory levels. Then an information technology team headed by a portfolio manager develops an IT strategy to meet these business goals. Finally, the IT team proposes systems development projects to create new systems or enhance present systems to meet the business unit's goals.

Operational Management

The IRM concept stresses that managerial functions and techniques and organizational structures common to most businesses can be used to manage information technology. Business and IS managers can use managerial techniques (such as planning models, financial budgets, and project management), and a mix of functional and process-based work groups and business units, just as they do in other major areas of the business.

> *A pure process oriented structure is not the optimal. Functional structures are necessary for technical and operational efficiencies while the process structures are key for end to end customer satisfaction* [39].

In many organizations, the information system's function is organized into a departmental or divisional unit. We will use the name *information services department* for this group, though other names (such as the MIS or IRM department) are also used. Information services departments perform several basic functions and activities. These can be grouped into three basic IS functions: (1) systems development, (2) operations, and (3) technical services. Figure 11.9 illustrates this grouping of information services functions and activities in a functional IS organizational structure.

However, operational management of IT can also be viewed from a process-based perspective. For example, Figure 11.10 illustrates the IS process architecture (ISPA-2) developed by the Society for Information Management (SIM), the international professional organization for IS executives. The eight major processes (or process classes) involved in an organization's IS function are outlined in this process-based view of IT management [38].

Centralization versus Decentralization

Experience has shown that information technology can support either the **centralization** or **decentralization** of information systems, operations, and decision making within computer-using organizations. For example, centralized computer facilities connected to all parts of an organization by telecommunications networks could allow

Figure 11.9

A functional organizational structure for an information services department. Note the activities that take place under each of the major functions of information services.

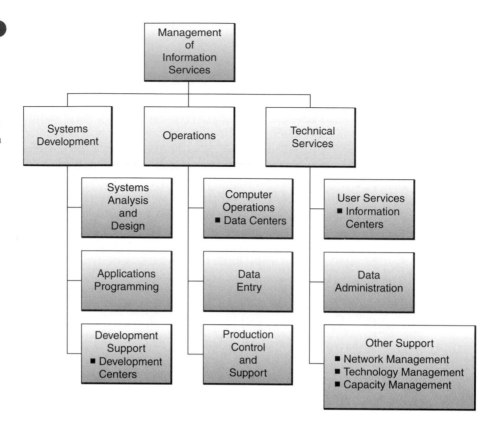

Figure 11.10

A process-based view of IT management developed by the Society for Information Management.

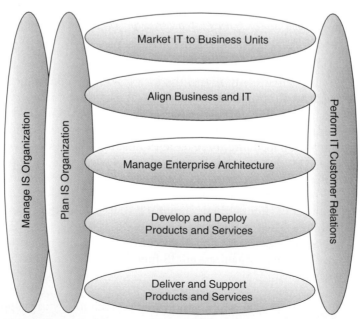

Source: Adapted from SIM International, *Information Systems Process Architecture*, Version 2.0 (Chicago: Society for Information Management, 1996), p. 9.

top management to centralize decision making formerly done by lower levels of management. It could also promote centralization of operations, which reduces the number of branch offices, manufacturing plants, warehouses, and other work sites needed by the firm.

On the other hand, intranets and distributed client/server networks of PCs and servers at multiple work sites allow top management to delegate more decision making to the managers of business units. Management could also decentralize operations by increasing the number of branch offices (or other company units) while still having access to the information and communications capabilities they need to control the overall direction of the organization.

Therefore, information technology can encourage either the centralization or decentralization of information systems, business operations, and management. The philosophy of top management, the culture of the organization, the need to reengineer its operations, and its use of aggressive or conservative competitive strategies all play major roles with information technology in shaping the firm's organizational structure and information systems architecture. For example, Figure 11.11 is a decentralized business-focused organizational structure for an IS function.

Figure 11.11

A business-focused organizational structure assigns delivery teams of IS specialists to business units and functions.

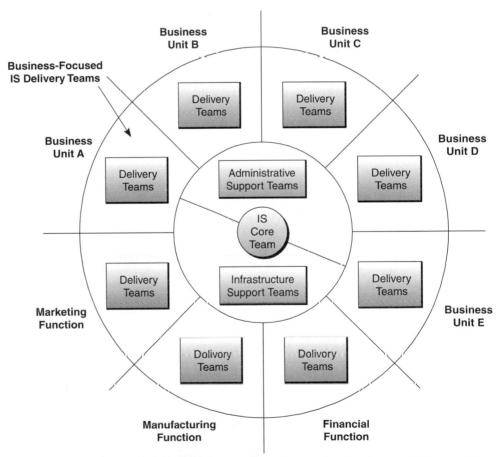

Source: Adapted from Robert Sloan and Hal Green, "Manufacturing Decision Support Architecture," *Information Systems Management* (New York: Auerbach Publications), Winter 1995, p. 14. © 1995 Research Institute of America. Used with permission.

Changing Trends

A radical shift is occurring in corporate computing—think of it as the recentralization of management. It's a step back toward the 1970s, when a data-processing manager could sit at a console and track all the technology assets of the corporation. Then came the 1980s and early 1990s. Departments got their own PCs and software; client/server networks sprang up all across companies.

Three things have happened in the past couple of years: The Internet boom inspired businesses to connect all those networks; companies put on to their intranets essential applications without which their businesses could not function; and it became apparent that maintaining PCs on a network is very, very expensive. Such changes create an urgent need for centralization [23].

In the early years of computing, the development of large mainframe computers and telecommunications networks and terminals caused a centralization of computer hardware and software, databases, and information specialists at the corporate level of organizations. Next, the development of minicomputers and microcomputers accelerated a **downsizing** trend, which prompted a move back toward decentralization by many business firms. Distributed client/server networks at the corporate, department, workgroup, and team levels came into being. This promoted a shift of databases and information specialists to some departments, and the creation of *information centers* to support end user and workgroup computing.

Lately, the trend is to establish tighter control over the management of the IS resources of an organization, while still serving the strategic needs of its business unit. This has resulted in a centralizing trend at some organizations and the development of hybrid structures with both centralized and decentralized components at others. Some companies have even spun off their information systems function into *IS subsidiaries* that offer information processing services to external organizations as well as to their parent company. Other corporations have **outsourced,** that is, turned over all or part of their information systems operations to outside contractors known as *systems integrators* or facilities management companies.

DuPont Corporation

DuPont, the giant global chemicals and energy company, reengineered its IS function, slashing annual spending on IS from $1.2 billion in 1980 to $770 million in 1994, a 40 percent cut. DuPont cut the number of people working in IS services by over 30 percent in the same period, from 7,000 to 4,800 employees. DuPont also cut back on the number of technologies it uses, and eliminated noneffective contractors. Nearly 200 data centers (computer centers) spread throughout the global company were merged into 40, according to Cinda Hallman, vice president of IS at DuPont. By 1996, DuPont had cut roughly 50 percent of its IT costs. DuPont is now operating IS as more of a business. For example, the IS group created customer services managers who work with business units to develop service level agreements. These agreements treat business units as internal customers and spell out their desired level of support and the costs. IS also established an application services control group to provide IS consulting support for those business units that need it [2, 28].

Managing Systems Development

Systems development management means managing activities such as systems analysis and design, prototyping, applications programming, project management, quality assurance, and system maintenance for all major business/IT development projects. Planning, organizing, and controlling the systems development function of an information services department is a major managerial responsibility. It requires managing the activities of teams of systems analysts, programmers, and end users working on a variety of information systems development projects. In addition, some systems development groups have established **development centers,** staffed with consultants to the professional programmers and systems analysts in their organizations. Their role is to evaluate new application development tools and to help information systems specialists use them to improve their application development efforts.

Managing IS Operations

IS operations management is concerned with the use of hardware, software, network, and personnel resources in the corporate or business unit **data centers** (computer centers) of an organization. Operational activities that must be managed include data entry, equipment operations, production control, and production support.

Most operations management activities are being automated by the use of software packages for computer system performance management. These **system performance monitors** monitor the processing of computer jobs, help develop a planned schedule of computer operations that can optimize computer system performance, and produce detailed statistics that are invaluable for effective planning and control of computing capacity. Such information evaluates computer system utilization, costs, and performance. This evaluation provides information for capacity planning, production planning and control, and hardware/software acquisition planning. It is also used in quality assurance programs, which stress quality control of services to end users. See Figure 11.12.

System performance monitors also supply information needed by **chargeback systems** that allocate costs to users based on the information services rendered. All costs incurred are recorded, reported, allocated, and charged back to specific end user

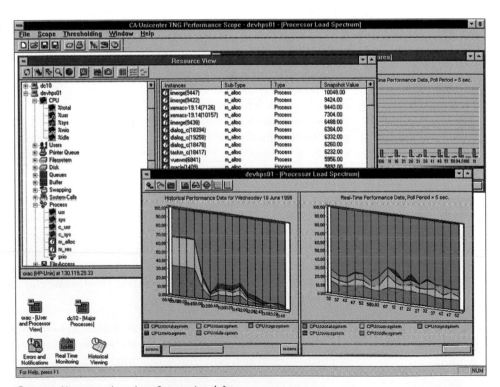

Figure 11.12

A computer system performance monitor in action. The CA-Unicenter TNG package can monitor and manage a variety of computer systems and operating systems.

Courtesy Computer Associates International, Inc.

departments, depending on their use of system resources. Under this arrangement, the information services department becomes a service center whose costs are charged directly to computer users, rather than being lumped with other administrative service costs and treated as an overhead cost.

Many performance monitors also feature **process control** capabilities. Such packages not only monitor but automatically control computer operations at large data centers. Some use built-in expert system modules based on knowledge gleaned from experts in the operations of specific computer systems and operating systems. These performance monitors provide more efficient computer operations than human-operated systems. They also are leading toward the goal of "lights out" data centers, where computer systems can be operated unattended, especially after normal business hours.

Resource Management

From an information resource management point of view, data and information, hardware and software, telecommunications networks, and IS personnel are valuable resources that should be managed for the benefit of the entire organization. If plant and equipment, money, and people are considered vital organizational resources, so should its data, information, and other information system resources. This is especially true if the organization is committed to building a strategic information resource base to be used for strategic IT applications, and if it wants to develop innovative products and services that incorporate information systems technology. We discussed managing data as an organizationwide resource through programs of data administration and data resource management in Chapter 5. In this chapter, let's now look at several human resource management issues.

Human Resource Management of IT

The success or failure of an information services organization rests primarily on the quality of its people. Many computer-using firms consider recruiting, training, and retaining qualified IS personnel as one of their greatest challenges. Managing information services functions involves the management of managerial, technical, and clerical personnel. One of the most important jobs of information services managers is to recruit qualified personnel and to develop, organize, and direct the capabilities of existing personnel. Employees must be continually trained to keep up with the latest developments in a fast-moving and highly technical field. Employee job performance must be continually evaluated and outstanding performances rewarded with salary increases or promotions. Salary and wage levels must be set, and career paths must be designed so individuals can move to new jobs through promotion and transfer as they gain in seniority and expertise.

For example, many firms provide information services personnel with individual career paths, opportunities for merit salary increases, project leadership opportunities, and attendance at professional meetings and educational seminars. These opportunities help provide the flexible job environment needed to retain competent personnel. Challenging technological and intellectual assignments and a congenial atmosphere of fellow professionals are other major factors frequently cited in helping to retain information services personnel.

Careers in Information Systems

Computers and their use in information systems have created interesting, highly paid, and challenging career opportunities for millions of men and women. Employment opportunities in the field of information technology are excellent, as organizations continue to expand their use of information technology. National employment surveys continually forecast shortages of qualified information systems personnel in many job

Figure 11.13

Providing end user
consulting services is a
major career opportunity
in information systems.

Index Stock.

categories. For these reasons, learning more about information technology may help
you decide if you want to pursue an IT-related career. Job opportunities in computers
and information systems are continually changing due to dynamic developments in information technology.

One major source of jobs is the computer industry itself. Thousands of companies
develop, manufacture, market, and service computer hardware and software, or provide related services such as end user training; Internet, intranet, and extranet applications and services; or business systems consulting. However, the biggest source of jobs
is in the hundreds of thousands of businesses, government agencies, and other organizations that use information technology. They need many types of IS managers and
specialists to help them support the work activities and supply the information needs
of their employees, managers, customers, suppliers, and other business partners. See
Figure 11.13.

Figure 11.14 gives valuable insight into the variety of job types and salaries com-
manded by many IS managers and specialists. Actual salaries range higher and lower
than the average for large companies shown, depending on such factors as the size and
geographic location of an organization.

Technology Management

An information resource management philosophy emphasizes that all technologies
that process, store, and deliver data and information must be managed as integrated
systems of organizational resources. Such technologies include the Internet, intranets,
and electronic commerce and collaboration systems, as well as traditional computer-
based information processing. These "islands of technology" are bridged by IRM and
become a primary responsibility of the CIO, since he or she is in charge of all information technology services. Thus, the information systems function can become "a
business within a business," whose chief executive is charged with strategic planning,
research and development, and coordination of all information technologies for the
strategic benefit of the organization.

Figure 11.14   Examples of important job categories and annual salaries in information services.

Top IS Management			
CIO/VP IS: $156,240	Director, IS/MIS: $104,075	Director, systems development $96,260	Director, IS operations: $90,425
Networks			
Director, networks: $86,970	Telecommunications manager: $75,305	Network administrator: $55,370	LAN manager: $60,585
Systems Development			
Systems project manager client/server: $74,345	Senior systems analyst: $63,145	Database manager: $75,850	Database analyst: $62,820
Electronic Commerce and Web Support			
Electronic commerce manager: $120,100	Internet strategy director: $114,700	Manager of Internet/intranet technology: $72,030	Webmaster/ Web designer: $56,750

Source: Adapted from "Enough is Enough: Computerworld's Twelfth Annual Salary Survey" by Leslie Goff, *Computerworld*, September 7, 1998, pp. 56–61, and "The New Web Walkers" by Natalie Engler, *Computerworld*, September 21, 1998, pp. 81–82. Copyright 1998 by Computerworld, Inc., Framingham, MA 01701. Reprinted from *Computerworld*.

Network Management

The rapid growth of the Internet, intranets, extranets, and client/server networks has made **network management** a major technology management function. This function is responsible for managing a company's Internet access, intranets and extranets, and the wide area networks and interconnected local area networks of client/server computing. These networks require a major commitment of hardware and software resources, as outlined in Chapter 4. They also require the creation of managerial and staff positions to manage their use. Thus, network management is responsible for overseeing the quality of all the telecommunications services that most businesses rely on today.

Network managers are usually responsible for evaluating and recommending the acquisition of Internet service providers, Internet and intranet servers and web browser suites, and communications hardware and software for workgroup and corporate client/server networks. They work with business unit managers to improve the design, operational quality, and security of the organization's telecommunications networks and services. They monitor and evaluate Internet, intranet, and other network usage, telecommunications processors (such as network servers and internetwork processors), network control software (such as network operating systems), and other network hardware and software resources to ensure a proper level of service to the users of a network. See Figure 11.15.

Telecommunications networks need a lot of managing to operate efficiently and effectively. That's why the quality of an organization's telecommunications managers and staff is a vital concern. Acquiring, training, and retaining good network managers, webmasters, and other network specialists is therefore a top priority. For example, a company's web site, intranets, and client/server networks need managers who are responsible for their management and maintenance. New servers and communications software must be installed; web pages, databases, and program files must be maintained; operations problems must be diagnosed and solved; and network security must be maintained. So manageability is a key managerial concern in any decision involving an organization's telecommunications network activities.

Figure 11.15

This web site management software monitors and evaluates web site usage and resources.

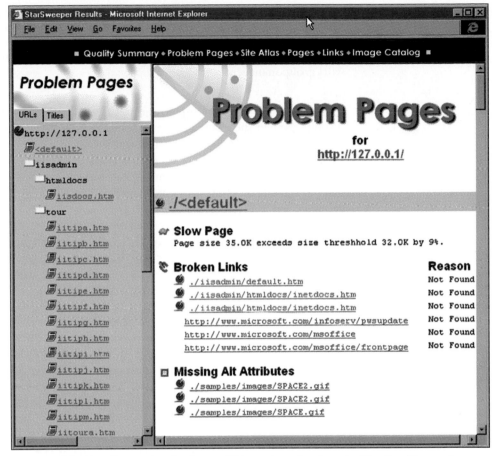

Courtesy of StarBase Corporation. StarSweeper™ is a registered trademark of StarBase Corporation.

Advanced Technology Management

The management of rapidly changing technology is important to any organization. Changes in information technology, like the rise of the PC, client/server networks, and the Internet and intranets, have come swiftly and dramatically and are expected to continue into the future. Developments in information systems technology have had, and will continue to have, a major impact on the operations, costs, management work environment, and competitive position of many organizations. Therefore, many firms have established separate groups to identify, introduce, and monitor the assimilation of new information systems technologies into their organizations, especially those with a high payoff potential [8]. These organizational units are called technology management, emerging technologies, or advanced technology groups.

Such **advanced technology groups** (ATGs) typically report to the chief information officer and are staffed with former senior systems analysts and other specialists in information systems technology. Their job is to monitor emerging technological developments and identify innovative developments that have high potential payoffs to the firm. Then they work with end user managers and information services management to introduce new technologies into the firm. They also audit a firm's current applications of technology so they can recommend improvements.

Distributed Management

Responsibility for managing information technology is increasingly being distributed to the managers of an organization at all levels and in all functions. Information resource management is not just the responsibility of an organization's chief information officer. If you're a manager, IRM is one of your responsibilities, whether you are a manager of a company, a department, a workgroup, or a functional area. This is especially true as the Internet, intranets, and client/server networks drive the responsibility for managing information systems out to all of an organization's functional and workgroup managers.

Managing End User Computing

The number of people in organizations who use computers to help them do their jobs has outstripped the capacity of many information services departments. As a result, teams and workgroups of end users must use PC workstations, software packages, and the Internet, intranets, and other networks to develop and apply information technology to their work activities. Organizations have responded by creating **user services,** or *client services,* functions to support and manage this explosion in end user and workgroup computing.

End user computing provides both opportunities and problems for end user management. For example, some firms create an **information center** group staffed with user liaison specialists, or help desks with end user "hot-lines." IS specialists with titles such as user consultant, account executive, or business analyst may be assigned to end user workgroups. These specialists perform a vital role by troubleshooting problems, gathering and communicating information, coordinating educational efforts, and helping end users with application development. Their activities improve communication and coordination between end user workgroups and the corporate information services department and avoid the runaround that can frustrate end users.

In addition to these measures, most organizations still establish and enforce policies for the acquisition of hardware and software by end users and business units. This ensures their compatibility with company standards for hardware, software, and network connectivity. See Figure 11.16. Also important is the development of applications with proper controls to promote correct performance and safeguard the integrity of corporate and departmental networks and databases [14]. We will discuss such IS controls in Chapter 12.

Figure 11.16 The benefits derived from company IT standards.

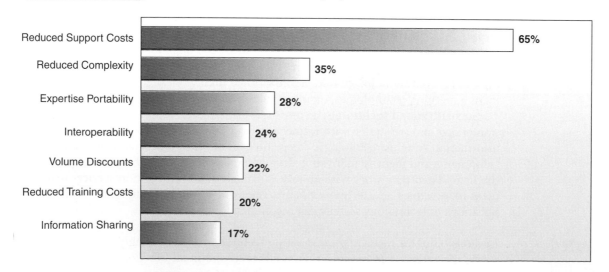

Managing Internet Access

The Net is still a limited, risky, and ill-understood resource that cries out for thoughtful management. Governing employee use is new territory. Network capacity remains an issue. And viruses, security, and legal issues are real concerns [45].

Managing Internet access within organizations is a major new management responsibility. Providing Internet access to employees raises several challenging managerial issues. One example is network capacity, which is a prime concern at many companies. Heavy Internet use by employees can overrun the capacity of client/server networks. Many were not designed to handle the large network loads generated by World Wide Web multimedia traffic and other Internet uses. For example, when its corporate networks began to slow down a few years ago, Allied Signal Aerospace shut off all "noncritical" Internet applications by its employees in order to regain network capacity [45].

Other management issues besides network capacity include questions concerning legitimate worktime use of the Internet by employees and liability for the contents of employee E-mail on the Net. Developing company standards for such issues is another managerial responsibility. We will discuss such issues in Chapter 12. Figure 11.17 spotlights these and other managerial concerns, and outlines suggestions for managing Internet access at the enterprise and business unit level.

Figure 11.17 Suggestions for managing Internet access in business.

Internet Access Checklist

Management
- Define who has responsibility for granting Internet access, managing its use, and enforcing the rules.
- Write conduct standards and policies on Internet use and educate employees. It's the best way to head off harassment suits, libel issues, and other legal problems.

Network Capacity
- Do a baseline assessment of your network capacity. Assess your network's current performance level. You should also evaluate the network demands and performance expectations of your current applications.
- Put into place a method for measuring the impact of Internet access once it's rolled out. The impact on the network and the additional usage will change from what was initially estimated.
- Provide proper training to your IS staff. Be sure they are capable of providing Internet support.

Politics
- Get key executives to buy into your Internet plan. You will need them to champion your plan as costs go up and as you invest in upgrades or infrastructure improvements.
- Before you plan, reach a consensus with line management on how much Internet access should be allowed.
- Make sure non-IS department heads know of your plan. Their budgets likely will have to support the network expansion needed to handle the increased load.

Source: Adapted from Randy Weston, "The Internet: Managing the Connection," *Computerworld*, September 16, 1996, p. 6. Copyright 1996 by Computerworld, Inc., Framingham, MA 01701. Reprinted from *Computerworld*.

Global Information Technology Management

It's no secret that international dimensions are becoming more and more important in managing a business in the internetworked global economies and markets of today. Whether you become a manager in a large corporation or the owner of a small business, you will be affected by international business developments, and deal in some way with people, products, or services whose origin is not from your home country.

Analyzing Guy Carpenter & Co. and PRT Group

Read the Real World Case on Guy Carpenter & Co. and PRT Group on the next page. We can learn a lot about the challenges and opportunities for companies involved in global software development. See Figure 11.18.

Companies like Guy Carpenter & Co. are hiring offshore IT development groups like the PRT Group in Barbados to help them develop software for vital business processes. In this case, PRT Barbados is staffing one-half of the team that is developing a new web-based insurance brokerage system. Guy Carpenter's goal is to lower development costs and to avoid having to find and hire qualified software developers in the United States.

Companies are choosing PRT Barbados because it employs a skilled international workforce of English-speaking developers who are working on several projects for a variety of U.S. corporations, including a new contract with Netscape for Internet application development and training.

The International Dimension

Even a quick tour of commercial sites on the World Wide Web demonstrates the variety and vitality of the Internet's [international] business community. A bakery in Jerusalem and a Caribbean art gallery share web space with multinational giants like AT&T, IBM, Hitachi, and Siemens. On a home page based in Singapore, managers of small

Figure 11.18

John Gropper, CIO of Guy Carpenter & Co. hired the PRT Group in Barbados to develop their web-based brokerage system.

Source: Giorgio Palmisano.

Guy Carpenter & Co. and PRT Group: The Business Case for Global Software Development

India, Ireland, Israel, Barbados, Bulgaria . . . more U.S. companies are shipping more software projects to these and other offshore sites in the ongoing scramble to beat information technology skill shortages, visa caps, and ever-rising labor costs.

In the past year, U.S. IT projects shipped to India alone ballooned by almost 60 percent, according to India's National Association of Software Service Companies. That represents nearly 200,000 jobs and will account for a software export market of about $4 billion by year's end.

And it's not just COBOL coding work. Mission-critical projects ranging from real-time stock trading applications to electronic-commerce systems are moving offshore to third-party service providers and new software development facilities established abroad by U.S. companies.

One big reason is it's a lot cheaper. For example, software teams with a ratio of 25 on-site workers to 75 workers offshore in India can expect to pay a blended hourly rate of about $37, compared with an average rate of $75 to $100 for an all-U.S. team, according to Chris Kizzier, an offshore outsourcing consultant in Portland, Oregon.

Other big factors contributing to the offshore boom include the ever-increasing speed and reliability of communications technology and better project-management discipline. "With advancements in communications and the Internet, the world has shrunk down to the size of a pea, and the fact that you might be 9,000 miles away is irrelevant once you put the right project management disciplines in place," Kizzier said.

In the past 15 months, five U.S. companies—including Boston-based Liberty Mutual Insurance Co.—have opened IT research and development centers in and around Belfast, Ireland. So far, Liberty Mutual has hired 60 Irish software developers—all of whom get at least six months of training at Liberty's offices in the United States—to work on C++ and Java-based applications among others. "There's definitely a labor cost savings, plus there are tax incentives for locating in Ireland," said Chris Gravel, U.S. operations manager at Liberty's Belfast based software center.

Meanwhile, Guy Carpenter & Co., a $450 million New York reinsurance company, has outsourced development of a web-based insurance brokerage system to PRT Group Ltd., which operates out of Bridgetown, Barbados. "We have half the team on site in New York, and half the people in Barbados," said John Gropper, CIO at Guy Carpenter. The two groups are connected via a high-speed communications link, and Barbados is a four-hour flight from New York.

With this kind of project management and communication in place, "there's very little difference in executing a project on the other side of the world versus executing it on the other side of the street," Kizzier said.

PRT Group is just a short stroll from a sun-drenched, white-sand Caribbean beach, housed in a 55,000-square-foot software development center, staffed by about 200 English-speaking IT workers from India, Jamaica, Malaysia, the United Kingdom, and elsewhere around the globe. They work on software development and maintenance projects for U.S. clients, including J.P. Morgan & Co. and Prudential Insurance Company of America, which have both invested in the company, and Travelers Corp. and Pfizer Inc.

"Our strategy has always been to import brainpower from other parts of the world to help Barbados develop that talent internally," said PRT Barbados President Srinivasan Viswanatha, who is known to everyone simply as "Vishy." Vishy left a highly successful post as head of Citicorp's offshore development center in India to join PRT Barbados in 1995. Eventually, several of his former co-workers from India joined him as did programmers and software developers like Pamela Alleyne from Malaysia; Stephen Vitoria, a programmer/analyst from England; and Gail Campbell, a team leader from Jamaica.

In 1999, PRT Barbados was looking to get into the training and Internet application development business, having just signed a partnership agreement with Netscape Communications Corp. Within six months, PRT expects to hire 100 Netscape developers and trainers.

Case Study Questions

1. What are the benefits and limitations of the offshore development of software for a business?

2. Do you think it is a good idea for Guy Carpenter & Co. to have half of its development team in New York and half in Barbados? Why or why not?

3. What are the advantages of software development in a country like Barbados for U.S. companies? For a company like the PRT Group? For international IT workers?

Source: Adapted from Julia King, "Exporting Jobs Saves IT Money," *Computerworld*, March 15, 1999, p. 24; and "Sun and Pay Lures Coders to Barbados Outsourcer," *Computerworld*, March 15, 1999, p. 24. Copyright 1999 by Computerworld, Inc., Framingham, MA 01701. Reprinted from *Computerworld*.

Canadian companies make trade contracts and discuss export arrangements. Real estate brokers in South Africa link with investment firms in London. India Web documents the fine points of doing business in Calcutta, while Dow Jones Information Services provides up-to-date news and business analysis. The list of products and services available on the Web now reads like a global Yellow Pages; it is difficult to think of any type of business not represented somewhere in the online world. [11].

So international issues in business management are vitally important today. This means that international issues in accounting, marketing, finance, productions/operations, human resource management, and, of course, information systems and information technology are also very important to business success. Properly designed and managed information systems using appropriate information technologies are a key ingredient in international business. They provide vital information resources needed to support business activity in global markets.

Global IT Management

Figure 11.19 illustrates the major dimensions of the job of managing **global information technology** that we will cover in this section. Notice that all global IT activities must be adjusted to take into account the cultural, political, and geoeconomic challenges that exist in the international business community. Developing appropriate business and IT strategies for the global marketplace should be the first step in **global IT management.** Once that is done, end user and IS managers can move on to developing the portfolio of applications needed to support business/IT strategies; the hardware, software, and network technology platforms to support those applications; the data management methods to provide necessary databases; and finally the systems development projects that will produce the global information systems required.

Cultural, Political, and Geoeconomic Challenges

"Business as usual" is not good enough in global business operations. The same holds true for global IT management. There are too many cultural, political, and geoeconomic (geographic and economic) realities that must be confronted in order for a business to succeed in global markets. As we have just said, global IT management must focus on developing global business IT strategies and managing global application portfolios, technologies, platforms, databases, and systems development projects. But managers must also accomplish that from a perspective and through methods that take into account the cultural, political, and geoeconomic differences that exist when doing business internationally.

Figure 11.19

The major dimensions of global IT management.

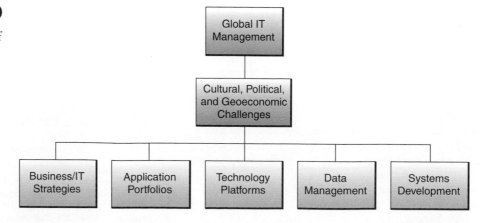

For example, a major **political challenge** is that many countries have rules regulating or prohibiting transfer of data across their national boundaries (transborder data flows), especially personal information such as personnel records. Others severely restrict, tax, or prohibit imports of hardware and software. Still others have local content laws that specify the portion of the value of a product that must be added in that country if it is to be sold there. Other countries have reciprocal trade agreements that require a business to spend part of the revenue they earn in a country in that nation's economy [37].

Geoeconomic challenges in global business and IT refer to the effects of geography on the economic realities of international business activities. The sheer physical distances involved are still a major problem, even in this day of Internet telecommunications and jet travel. For example, it may still take too long to fly in specialists when IT problems occur in a remote site. It is still difficult to communicate in realtime across the world's 24 time zones. It is still difficult to get good-quality telephone and telecommunications service in many countries. There are still problems finding the job skills required in some countries, or enticing specialists from other countries to live and work there. Finally, there are still problems (and opportunities) in the great differences in the cost of living and labor costs in various countries [31]. All of these geoeconomic challenges must be addressed when developing a company's global business and IT strategies.

Cultural challenges facing global business and IT managers include differences in languages, cultural interests, religions, customs, social attitudes, and political philosophies. Obviously, global IT managers must be trained and sensitized to such cultural differences before they are sent abroad or brought into a corporation's home country. Other cultural challenges include differences in work styles and business relationships. For example, should one take one's time to avoid mistakes, or hurry to get something done early? Should one go it alone or work cooperatively? Should the most experienced person lead, or should leadership be shared? The answers to such questions depend on the culture you are in and highlight the cultural differences that might exist in the global workplace. Let's take a look at several recent examples involving the Internet and electronic commerce.

Challenges in Europe and China

The English term *home page* is translated as "pagina inicial," or first page, in Spanish and "page d'accueil," or welcome page, in French. Icons that a novice American web surfer would easily recognize, such as an American-style mailbox, do not speak as clearly to many overseas users. Its color and shape do not immediately convey for Europeans the notion of sending mail. Thus, a more universal icon would be an envelope [19].

In Germany, a vendor by law cannot accept payment via credit card until two weeks after the order has been sent. And you can't display a swastika on a computer screen. "Yet if Amazon.com has books that use swastikas as artwork or within the text, who is legally responsible for breaking German law?" asks Mark Stevensen, an analyst for Ovum Ltd. of London. Most Internet systems are not sophisticated enough to block orders from specific regions or countries to avoid breaking the law by shipping forbidden products to a particular country [24].

At U.S.-based Prodigy, Inc., the first online service recognized by the Chinese government, cultural differences include the fact that the Chinese are accustomed to paying cash in advance for business services. So Prodigy needed to adjust its billing and payment policies to reflect this comfort level. "That was our single biggest impediment: the payment policy," said Paul DeLacey, president and CEO of Prodigy. He said cultural differences make it essential to establish local companies staffed with locals [24].

Global Business and IT Strategies

How much of a business need is there for global information technology? That is, do we need to use IT to support our company's international business operations? Figure 11.20 helps answer these questions by showing that many firms are moving toward **transnational strategies** in which they integrate their global business activities through close cooperation and interdependence among their international subsidiaries and their corporate headquarters. Businesses are moving away from (1) multinational strategies where foreign subsidiaries operate autonomously; (2) international strategies in which foreign subsidiaries are autonomous but are dependent on headquarters for new processes, products, and ideas; or (3) global strategies, where a company's world-wide operations are closely managed by corporate headquarters [22, 32].

In the transnational approach, a business depends heavily on its information systems and appropriate information technologies to help it integrate its global business activities. Instead of having independent IS units at its subsidiaries, or even a central-ized IS operation directed from its headquarters, a transnational business tries to develop an integrated and cooperative worldwide hardware, software, and telecom-munications architecture for its IT platform. Figure 11.21 illustrates how transnational business and IT strategies were implemented by global companies [45].

Figure 11.20 Companies operating internationally are moving toward a transnational business strategy. Note some of the chief differences between international, global, and transnational business and IT strategies.

International	Global	Transnational
• Autonomous operations.	• Global sourcing.	• Virtual operations via global alliances.
• Region specific.	• Multiregional.	• World markets and mass customization.
• Vertical integration.	• Horizontal integration.	
• Specific customers.	• Some transparency of customers and production.	• Global order fulfillment and customer service.
• Captive manufacturing.	• Some cross regionalization.	• Transparent manufacturing.
• Customer segmentation and dedication by region and plant.		• Global sourcing and logistics.
		• Dynamic resource management.

Information Technology Characteristics

International	Global	Transnational
• Standalone systems.	• Regional decentralization.	• Logically consolidated, physically distributed, network connected.
• Decentralized/no standards.	• Interface dependent.	• Common global data resources.
• Heavy reliance on interfaces.	• Some consolidation of applica-tions and use of common systems.	• Integrated systems.
• Multiple systems, high redundancy and duplication of services and operations.	• Reduced duplication of operations.	• Internet, intranet, extranet applications.
• Lack of common systems and data.	• Some worldwide IT standards.	• Transnational IT policies and standards.

Source: Adapted and reprinted from Michael Mische, "Transnational Architecture: A Reengineering Approach," *Information Systems Man-agement* (New York: Auerbach Publications), Winter 1995, p. 18. © 1995 Research Institute of America. Used with permission; and Nicholas Vitalari and James Wetherbe, "Emerging Best Practices in Global Systems Development," in *Global Information Technology and Systems Management*, Prashant Palvia et al., editors (Marietta, GA: Ivy League Publishing, 1996), p. 336.

Figure 11.21   Examples of how transnational business and IT strategies were implemented by global companies.

Tactic	Global Alliances	Global Sourcing and Logistics	Global Customer Service
Examples	British Airways / US Air KLM / Northwest Qantas / American	Benetton	American Express
IT Environment	Global network (online reservation system)	Global network, EPOS terminals in 4000 stores, CAD/CAM in central manufacturing, robots and laser scanner in their automated warehouse	Global network linked from local branches and local merchants to the customer database and medical or legal referrals database
Results	• Coordination of schedules • Code sharing • Coordination of flights • Co-ownership	• Produce 2000 sweaters per hour using CAD/CAM • Quick response (in stores in 10 days) • Reduced inventories (just-in-time)	• Worldwide access to funds • "Global Assist" Hotline • Emergency credit card replacement • 24-hour customer service

Source: Adapted from Nicholas Vitalari and James Wetherbe, "Emerging Best Practices in Global System Development," in *Global Information Technology and Systems Management*, Prashant Palvia et al., editors (Marietta, GA: Ivy League Publishing, 1996), pp. 338–42.

Global Business and IT Applications

The applications of information technology developed by global companies depend on their business and IT strategies and their expertise and experience in IT. However, their IT applications also depend on a variety of **global business drivers,** that is, business requirements caused by the nature of the industry and its competitive or environmental forces. One example would be companies like airlines or hotel chains that have global customers, that is, customers who travel widely or have global operations. Such companies will need global IT capabilities for online transaction processing so they can provide fast, convenient service to their customers or face losing them to their competitors. The economies of scale provided by global business operations are another business driver that requires the support of global IT applications [18].

Companies whose products are available worldwide would be another example of how business needs can shape global IT. For example, Coca-Cola or Pepsi might use teleconferencing to make worldwide product announcements, and use computer-based marketing systems to coordinate global marketing campaigns. Other companies with global operations have used IT to move parts of their operations to lower-cost sites. For example, Citibank moved its credit card processing operations to South Dakota; American Airlines moved much of its data entry work to Barbados; and other firms have looked to Ireland and India as sources of low-cost software development [31]. Figure 11.22 summarizes some of the business requirements that make global IT a competitive necessity [18].

Of course, many global IT applications, particularly finance, accounting, and office applications, have been in operation for many years. For example, most multinational companies had global financial budgeting and cash management systems, and more recently office automation applications such as fax and E-mail systems. However, as global operations expand and global competition heats up, there is increasing pressure for companies to install global transaction processing applications for their customers and suppliers. Examples include global point-of-sale (POS) and customer service

Figure 11.22

Business drivers for global IT. These are some of the business reasons behind global IT applications.

● **Global customers.** Customers are people who may travel anywhere or companies with global operations. Global IT can help provide fast, convenient service.
● **Global products.** Products are the same throughout the world or are assembled by subsidiaries throughout the world. Global IT can help manage worldwide marketing and quality control.
● **Global operations.** Parts of a production or assembly process are assigned to subsidiaries based on changing economic or other conditions. Only global IT can support such geographic flexibility.
● **Global resources.** The use and cost of common equipment, facilities, and people are shared by subsidiaries of a global company. Global IT can keep track of such shared resources.
● **Global collaboration.** The knowledge and expertise of colleagues in a global company can be quickly accessed, shared, and organized to support individual or group efforts. Only global IT can support such enterprise collaboration.

systems for customers and global electronic data interchange (EDI) systems for suppliers. In the past, such systems relied almost exclusively on privately constructed or government-owned telecommunications networks. But the fast-growing business use of the Internet, intranets, and extranets for electronic commerce has made such applications much more feasible for global companies.

Chase Manhattan Bank

Chase Manhattan Bank is an example of a global company with global information systems for customer service. At Chase's Global Securities Services (GSS), more than 200 managers around the world use the Account Service Planning and Analysis (ASPA) system. ASPA, along with two related systems, helps GSS develop service and production plans, as well as monitor success against these plans according to customer service expectations and revenue targets. By quickly analyzing specific customer service data by various dimensions, Chase is able to identify key service problems in its global transaction processing systems and drill down through countries and customer accounts anywhere in the world, zero in on the problem, and take corrective action to prevent recurrence.

A customer service manager in any of Chase's service centers around the world can check for problems in performance with a few mouse clicks on a PC. A typical problem could be something like dividend or settlement payments taking longer than normal. Once a service problem is identified, the GSS customer service manager can use the system to analyze the situation and, working with the customer—who may be unaware of the problem—put together a program that will correct the problem within a specific time limit [3].

Global IT Platforms

The choice of technology platforms (also called the technology infrastructure) is another major dimension of global IT management. That is, what hardware, software, telecommunications networks, and computing facilities will be needed to support our global business operations? Answering this question is a major challenge of global IT management. The choice of a global IT platform is not only technically complex but also has major political and cultural implications.

For example, hardware choices are difficult in some countries because of high prices, high tariffs, import restrictions, long lead times for government approvals, lack of local service or spare parts, and lack of documentation tailored to local conditions. Software choices can also present unique problems. Software packages developed in Europe may be incompatible with American or Asian versions, even when purchased from the same hardware vendor. Well-known U.S. software packages may be unavailable because there is no local distributor, or because the software publisher refuses to supply markets that disregard software licensing and copyright agreements [18].

Establishing computing facilities internationally is another global challenge. Companies with global business operations usually establish or contract with systems integrators for additional data centers in their subsidiaries in other countries. These data centers meet local and regional computing needs, and even help balance global computing workloads through communications satellite links. However, offshore data centers can pose major problems in headquarter's support, hardware and software acquisition, maintenance, and security.

That's why many global companies turn to systems integrators like EDS or IBM to manage their overseas operations. For example, more than 80,000 companies use the IBM Global Network, which reaches 850 cities in more than 100 countries [10]. See Figure 11.23.

The Internet as a Global IT Platform

What makes the Internet and the World Wide Web so important for international business? This interconnected matrix of computers, information, and networks that reaches tens of millions of users in over one hundred countries is a business environment free of traditional boundaries and limits. Linking to an online global infrastructure offers companies unprecedented potential for expanding markets, reducing costs, and improving profit margins at a price that is typically a small percentage of the corporate communications budget. The Internet provides an interactive channel for direct communication and data exchange with customers, suppliers, distributors, manufacturers, product developers,

Figure 11.23

The global telecommunications command center of Electronic Data Systems.

Bill Gallery/Stock Boston.

- Will you have to develop a new navigational logic to accommodate cultural preferences?
- What content will you translate, and what content will you create from scratch to address regional competitors or products that differ from those in the United States?
- Should your multilingual effort be an adjunct to your main site, or will you make it a separate site, perhaps with a country-specific domain name?
- What kinds of traditional and new media advertising will you have to do in each country to draw traffic to your site?
- Will your site get so many hits that you'll need to set up a server in a local country?
- What are the legal ramifications of having your web site targeted at a particular country, such as laws on competitive behavior, treatment of children, or privacy?

Source: Adapted from Alice LaPlante, "Global Boundaries.com," Global Innovators Series, *Computerworld*, October 6, 1997, p. 17. Copyright 1997 by Computerworld, Inc., Framingham, MA 01701. Reprinted from *Computerworld*.

financial backers, information providers—in fact, with all parties involved in a given business venture [11].

Decisions about telecommunications networks are vital to establishing a technology platform for any company and present major challenges in global IT management. In previous chapters and sections, we discussed some of the managerial opportunities and challenges posed by the Internet, intranets, extranets, and other telecommunications network technologies. Obviously, global networks like the Internet that cross many international boundaries can make such issues even more challenging and strategic. See Figure 11.24.

So the Internet and the World Wide Web have now become vital components in international business and commerce. Within a few years, the Internet, with its interconnected network of thousands of networks of computers and databases, has established itself as a technology platform free of many traditional international boundaries and limits. By connecting their businesses to this online global infrastructure, companies can expand their markets, reduce communications and distribution costs, and improve their profit margins without massive cost outlays for new telecommunications facilities.

That's because the Internet, along with its related intranet and extranet technologies, such as client/server and virtual private networks, provides a low-cost interactive channel for communications and data exchange with employees, customers, suppliers, distributors, manufacturers, product developers, financial backers, information providers, and so on. In fact, all parties involved can use the Internet and other related networks to communicate and collaborate to bring a business venture to its successful completion [11]. However, as Figure 11.25 illustrates, much work needs to be done to bring Internet access and electronic commerce to more people in more countries. But the trend is clearly on continued expansion of the Internet as it becomes a pervasive IT platform for global business.

Global Data Issues

Global data issues have been a subject of political controversy and technology barriers in global business operations for many years. A major example is the issue of **transborder data flows** (TDF), in which business data flow across international borders over the telecommunications networks of global information systems. Many countries

Figure 11.25	How Forrester Research evaluated the electronic commerce status of 45 countries. Rankings are based on market size, technology penetration, and cultural/political climate.

Categories	Countries	Comments
Superpowers	● United States	To maintain its position, the United States must drop crypto restrictions.
Contenders	● Germany, United Kingdom, Japan, Canada	Government initiatives position Japan to overtake Germany and the UK.
Gateways	● Singapore, the Netherlands, Belgium, the former Hong Kong	Singapore's bid to become an "intelligent island" will falter unless it abandons online censorship.
Sprinters	● Finland, Sweden, Denmark, Norway, New Zealand	Simple, innovative public policy is a strength across the board.
Stragglers	● France, Australia, Italy, South Korea, Spain	These potentially lucrative markets are in danger of being left behind.
Wild Cards	● Switzerland, Austria, Ireland, Israel, South Africa	Look to the wild-card countries for the gateways and sprinters of the future.
Low Techs	● Mexico, Malaysia, Greece, Brazil, Chile, Indonesia, Czech Republic, Portugal, Turkey, Argentina, Venezuela, Colombia, Poland, Thailand	The next few years will determine which of these markets will move up and which will stay behind.
Resisters	● China, Saudi Arabia, India, Philippines, Russia, Pakistan, Iran	These countries are either too technologically underdeveloped or too politically isolated to become electronic commerce players in the foreseeable future.

Source: Adapted from Alice LaPlante, "Global Boundaries.com," Global Innovators Series, *Computerworld*, October 6, 1997, p. 9. Copyright 1997 by Computerworld, Inc., Framingham, MA 01701. Reprinted from *Computerworld*.

view TDF as violating their national sovereignty because transborder data flows avoid customs duties and regulations for the import or export of goods and services. Other countries may view transborder data flows as a violation of their privacy legislation since, in many cases, data about individuals are being moved out of the country without stringent privacy safeguards. Still others view transborder data flows as violating their laws to protect the local IT industry from competition, or their labor regulations for protecting local jobs [7].

Figure 11.26 outlines some of the fears and responses of several countries to global data issues. Notice that this includes not only transborder data flows but also regulation of files and databases, content of Internet web sites, and software that can provide service encryption of data. Recent research seems to indicate that data issues have not been as much of a problem for global business as had been feared. This is due primarily to difficulties in enforcing such laws, especially given the wide-open nature of the Internet and to efforts by host countries to encourage foreign investment and electronic commerce. However, the data business issues that still seem politically sensitive are those that affect the movement of personal data in payroll and personnel applications [7, 18, 36].

Other important global data issues are concerned with global data management and standardization of data. Common data definitions are necessary for sharing data among the parts of an international business. Differences in language, culture, and technology platforms can make global data standardization quite difficult. For example, a sale may be called "an 'order booked' in the United Kingdom, an 'order

Figure 11.26

Global data issues. Note the fears and responses by some countries to the issues of transborder data flows, control of global databases, content of Internet web sites, and export of encryption software.

Country	Presumed Fear	Actual Response
Brazil	Information colonialism and a lack of development of a domestic information industry.	All companies must maintain copies of all databases physically within the country; offshore processing is prohibited.
Canada	Exportation of corporate information to headquarters in other countries (especially the United States). Abuses of the personal privacy of its citizens. Loss of cultural and national sovereignty.	Banking Act prohibits processing data transactions outside of the country unless approved by the government. Limitations on the number of direct access links for international data transmission and limitations on satellite usage.
France	Basically the same as Canada.	Imposition of taxes and duties on information and information transfers. Requires every database maintained in France to be registered with the government.
Germany	A lack of development of a domestic information industry. Abuses of personal privacy.	Regulations that favor the domestic IT and telecommunications industry. Data records on German nationals must be kept in Germany. Prohibitions against pornographic or racist web sites.
Sweden	Abuses of privacy. Domestic economic data may not be accessible if stored abroad.	Has a data protection law and a commission to license and approve all data systems. Prohibits offshore processing and storage of data.
Taiwan	National and economic security.	Government monitoring of data transmissions.
United States	National and domestic security.	Prohibitions against export of software that can provide secure encryption of data.

Source: Adapted from William Carper, "Societal Impacts and Consequences of Transborder Data Flows," in Shailendra Palvia et al., *The Global Issues of Information Technology Management*, p. 443. Copyright © 1992, Idea Group Publishing, Harrisburg, PA. Reprinted by permission; and Sari Kalin, "The Importance of Being Multiculturally Correct," Global Innovators Series, *Computerworld*, October 6, 1997, p. 8. Copyright 1997 by Computerworld, Inc., Framingham, MA 01701. Reprinted from *Computerworld*.

scheduled' in Germany, and an 'order produced' in France" [37]. However, businesses are moving ahead to standardize data definitions and structures. By moving their subsidiaries in data modeling and database design, they hope to develop a global data architecture that supports their global business objectives [18].

Global Systems Development

Just imagine the challenges of developing efficient, effective, and responsive applications for business end users domestically. Then multiply that by the number of countries and cultures that may use a global IT system. That's the challenge of managing global systems development. Naturally, there are conflicts over local versus global system requirements, and difficulties in agreeing on common system features such as multilingual user interfaces and flexible design standards. And all of this effort must take place in an environment that promotes involvement and "ownership" of a system by local end users. Thus, one IT manager estimates that

> *it takes 5 to 10 times more time to reach an understanding and agreement on system requirements and deliverables when the users and developers are in different countries. This is partially explained by travel requirements and language and cultural differences, but technical limitations also contribute to the problem* [18].

Figure 11.27

The global use of information technology depends on international systems development efforts.

John Moore/The Image Works.

Other systems development issues arise from disturbances caused by systems implementation and maintenance activities. For example: "An interruption during a third shift in New York City will present midday service interruptions in Tokyo." Another major development issue relates to the trade-offs between developing one system that can run on multiple computer and operating system platforms, or letting each local site customize the software for its own platform [18]. See Figure 11.27.

Systems Development Strategies

Several strategies can be used to solve some of the systems development problems that arise in global IT. First is transforming an application used by the home office into a global application. However, often the system used by a subsidiary that has the best version of an application will be chosen for global use. Another approach is setting up a *multinational development team* with key people from several subsidiaries to ensure that the system design meets the needs of local sites as well as corporate headquarters.

A third approach is called *parallel development*. That's because parts of the system are assigned to different subsidiaries and the home office to develop at the same time, based on the expertise and experience at each site. Another approach is the concept of *centers of excellence*. In this approach, an entire system may be assigned for development to a particular subsidiary based on their expertise in the business or technical dimensions needed for successful development. Obviously, all of these approaches require development team collaboration and managerial oversight to meet the global needs of a business. So global systems development teams are making heavy use of the Internet, intranets, groupware, and other electronic collaboration technologies [18, 44].

You and Global IT Management

Most companies fail to have in place a coherent information technology strategy. Their IT infrastructure does not match or facilitate their emerging global business strategy. Few multinationals have discovered the potential of computer and communications technology to transform their operations on a global basis. A company may have a single product sold globally, but no globally rationalized product database. It may be fighting a battle for centralized control when the business strategy needs to be different for each national market. It most likely has many different national data centers when it could better serve strategy with regionalized data processing of selected applications and resources [37].

Now that we have covered the basic dimensions of global IT management, it is time to acknowledge that much work remains to be done to implement global IT strategies. As a future business user of IT, the global business success of your company or business unit will be in your hands. But now at least you know the dimensions of the problems and opportunities that arise from the use of information technology to support global business operations.

First, you must discover if your company has a global business strategy and a strategy for how information technology can support global business operations. If not, you can begin to play a role, however small, in developing such strategies. Then you must discover or help develop the IT applications to support your global business activities. This includes providing your ideas for the hardware, software, and telecommunications platform and databases you need to do business globally. This process can be a gradual one. For example, as a managerial end user, you can follow the lead of a global corporation that laid out the five basic actions it had to accomplish to become a truly successful global company, as shown in Figure 11.28.

As a manager, entrepreneur, or managerial professional, global IT management will be one of your many managerial responsibilities. Like other areas of global business management, it requires an added dimension of sensitivity to the cultural, political, and geoeconomic realities of doing business with people in other countries. But it also offers an exciting challenge of competing successfully in a dynamic global arena to bring your products or services to customers throughout the world.

Figure 11.28 Basic steps toward becoming a global company.

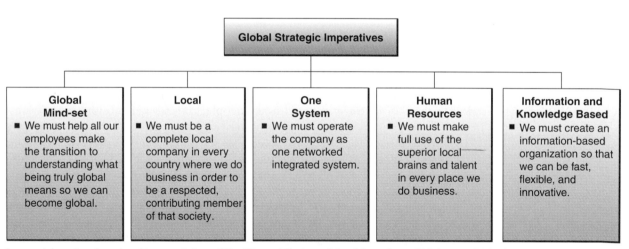

Source: Adapted and reprinted by permission of The Harvard Business School Press from *Globalization, Technology, and Competition: The Fusion of Computers and Telecommunications in the 1990s* by Stephen P. Bradley, Jerry A. Hausman, and Richard L. Nolan. Boston: 1993, p. 248. Copyright © 1993 by the President and Fellows of Harvard College, all rights reserved.

Summary

- **Managers and IT.** Information technology is changing the distribution, relationships, resources, and responsibilities of managers. That is, IT is eliminating layers of management, enabling more collaborative forms of management, providing managers with significant information and computing resources, and confronting managers with a major information resource management challenge.

- **IS Performance.** Information systems are not being used effectively, efficiently, or economically by many organizations. The experiences of successful organizations reveal that the basic ingredient of high-quality information system performance is extensive and meaningful management and user involvement in the governance of information technology. Thus, managers may serve on executive steering committees and create an IS management function within their business units.

- **Organizations and IT.** The people, tasks, technology, culture, and structure of an organization affect how it will organize and use information technology. Thus, many variations exist, which reflect the attempts of organizations to tailor their organizational structures and applications to their particular business activities and management philosophy, as well as to the capabilities of centralized or distributed information systems. Lately, the trend has been to a combination of centralized and distributed arrangements for the management of information technology.

- **Information Resource Management.** Managing the use of information technology in an organization has become a major managerial responsibility. End user managers should use an information resource management approach to manage the data and information, hardware and software, telecommunications networks, and people resources of their business units and workgroups for the overall benefit of their organizations. The information systems function in an organization may be headed by a chief information officer who oversees the organization's strategic planning and use of information technology (strategic management). IRM also involves managing data and IS personnel (resource management), telecommunications, and advances in information technologies (technology management). The activities of information services can be grouped into basic functions and processes such as systems development, operations, and technical services (operational management).

- **Managing Global IT.** The international dimensions of managing global information technology include dealing with cultural, political, and geoeconomic challenges posed by various countries; developing appropriate business and IT strategies for the global marketplace; and developing a portfolio of global IT applications and a technology platform to support them. In addition, database management methods have to be developed and systems development projects managed to produce the global information systems that are required to compete successfully in the global marketplace.

- **Global Business and IT Strategies and Issues.** Many businesses are becoming global companies and moving toward transnational business strategies in which they integrate the global business activities of their subsidiaries and headquarters. This requires that they develop a global IT platform, that is, an integrated worldwide hardware, software, and telecommunications network architecture. Global companies are increasingly using the Internet and related technologies as a major component of this IT platform to develop and deliver global IT applications that meet their unique global business requirements. Global IT and end user managers must deal with restrictions on the availability of hardware and software, restrictions on transborder data flows and movement of personal data, and difficulties with developing common data definitions and system requirements.

Key Terms and Concepts

These are the key terms and concepts of this chapter. The page number of their first explanation is in parentheses.

1. Centralization or decentralization (435)
   a. Information systems (437)
   b. Operations and management (437)
2. Chargeback systems (439)
3. Chief information officer (432)
4. Cultural, political, and geoeconomic challenges (448)

5. Data center (439)

6. Development center (439)

7. Downsizing (438)

8. End user services (444)

9. Global business drivers (451)

10. Global information technology (448)

11. Global IT management (448)

   a. Applications (451)

   b. Business/IT strategies (450)

   c. Data issues (454)

   d. IT platforms (452)

   e. Systems development (456)

12. Human resource management of IT (440)

13. Impact of information technology

   a. On management (426)

   b. On organizations (429)

14. Information center (444)

15. Information resource management (431)

   a. Five dimensions of IRM (431)

16. Information services functions (435)

17. Information systems performance (427)

18. Information technology architecture (434)

19. Management involvement (428)

20. Operations management (439)

21. Organizations as sociotechnical systems (429)

22. Outsourcing IS operations (438)

23. Strategic IS planning (432)

24. System performance monitor (439)

25. Systems development management (438)

26. Technology management (441)

27. Telecommunications network management (442)

28. Transborder data flows (454)

29. Transnational strategy (450)

Review Quiz

Match one of the key terms and concepts listed previously with one of the brief examples or definitions that follow. Try to find the best fit for the answers that seem to fit more than one term or concept. Defend your choices.

____ 1. Managers now have a lot of information processing power, and responsibility for information systems.

____ 2. Information technology affects the people, tasks, technology, culture, and structure of organizations.

____ 3. Information system resources can be distributed throughout an organization or consolidated in corporate data centers.

____ 4. Information systems can help management increase the number of regional and branch offices or consolidate operations.

____ 5. The management of data, information, hardware, software, and IS personnel as organizational resources.

____ 6. Managing information technology is a distributed responsibility focusing on the strategic management of IS resources and technology.

____ 7. Information systems have not been used efficiently, effectively, and economically.

____ 8. A management steering committee is an example.

____ 9. End users need an end user services group, or other forms of liaison, consulting, and training support.

____ 10. Includes the basic functions of systems development, operations, and technical services.

____ 11. An executive that oversees all information systems technology for an organization.

____ 12. Managing systems analysis and design, computer programming, and systems maintenance activities.

____ 13. Planning and controlling data center operations.

____ 14. Corporate locations for computer system operations.

____ 15. A support group for an organization's professional programmers and systems analysts.

____ 16. A support group for an organization's end users.

____ 17. Rapidly changing technological developments must be anticipated, identified, and implemented.

____ 18. Using outside contractors to provide and manage IS operations.

_____ 19. A company's use of the Internet, intranets, and extranets must be developed, administered, and maintained.

_____ 20. Software that helps monitor and control computer systems in a data center.

_____ 21. The cost of IS services may be allocated back to end users.

_____ 22. Recruiting and developing information services employees.

_____ 23. Many business firms are replacing their mainframe systems with networked PCs and servers.

_____ 24. Develops business/IT strategies and an IT architecture for the IS function.

_____ 25. Using IT to support a company's international business operations.

_____ 26. Integrating global business activities through cooperation among international subsidiaries and corporate headquarters.

_____ 27. Differences in customs, governmental regulations, and the cost of living are examples.

_____ 28. Global customers, products, operations, resources, and collaboration.

_____ 29. Applying IT to global transaction processing systems is an example.

_____ 30. The goal of some organizations is to develop integrated worldwide networks for global electronic commerce.

_____ 31. Transborder data flows and security of personal databases are top concerns.

_____ 32. Standardizing computer systems, software packages, telecommunications networks, and computing facilities.

_____ 33. Agreement is needed on common user interfaces and other design features in global IT.

_____ 34. Global telecommunications networks like the Internet move data across national boundaries.

Discussion Questions

1. What has been the impact of information technology on the work relationships, activities, and resources of managers?

2. What can end user managers do about performance problems in the use of information technology and the development and operation of information systems in a business?

3. Refer to the Real World Case on Chase Manhattan, Cigna, and PG&E in the chapter. Which of the three business/IT jobs in the case would you prefer (a) now, and (b) 10 years from now? Why?

4. How is information technology affecting the structure and work roles of modern organizations? For example, will middle management wither away? Will companies consist primarily of self-directed project teams of knowledge workers? Explain your answers.

5. Should the IS function in a business be centralized or decentralized? What recent developments support your answer?

6. Refer to the Real World Case on Guy Carpenter & Co. and PRT Group in the chapter. Would you hire an offshore IT group to develop new software for one of your company's vital business processes? Why or why not?

7. How will the Internet, intranets, and extranets affect each of the components of global IT management, as illustrated in Figure 11.19? Give several examples.

8. How might cultural, political, or geoeconomic challenges affect a global company's use of the Internet? Give several examples.

9. Will the increasing use of the Internet by firms with global business operations change their move toward a transnational business strategy? Explain.

10. How might the Internet, intranets, and extranets affect the business drivers or requirements responsible for a company's use of global IT, as shown in Figure 11.22? Give several examples to illustrate your answer.

Real World Problems

1. SAP AG, Sara Lee, AeroGroup, and Others: Failures in Business and IT Management

The year was 1998, a year filled with great promises for the apparel and shoe industry. The economy was strong, skirt lengths were rising to new heights, and the stock market was humming. Furthermore, much of the apparel and footwear industry buzzed with anticipation. Software giant SAP AG of Waldorf, Germany, was about to launch what seemed to be the solution to the industry's manufacturing and distribution problems. In January, industry participants rang in the year celebrating SAP's Apparel/Footwear Solution (AFS) software, which several companies had been co-developing with SAP for two years. A tailored version of SAP's R/3 enterprise resource planning (ERP) software, Juggernaut, AFS promised to untangle the knot of variables—style, size, color, and so on—that had stymied earlier attempts at production and distribution integration.

But the mood was decidedly grim in a small office complex in the tiny German village of Hallbergmoos. There, in one of the buildings that housed SAP's AFS development effort, five IT staffers from Sara Lee Hosiery were making a startling discovery. After eight months of poring over code in intense collaboration with AFS programmers, the Sara Lee team was shocked to find that SAP had decided six months earlier to ax a key function on which their business implementation depended.

In 1999 the gloom in Hallbergmoos spread. The buoyant anticipation that greeted AFS's debut has evaporated, at least at some companies. In its place is stoicism, mingled with muted panic and dead silence. Several AFS projects have been delayed, and at one—AeroGroup International, the Edison, New Jersey–based maker of the Aerosoles line of casual shoes—it was cancelled.

At AeroGroup International, CIO Jeffrey Zonenshine, CEO Jules Schneider, and executive vice president Richard Morris cancelled AFS and pulled back from installing what other industry officials now consider an incomplete and overly expensive solution to the company's problems.

All of the AeroGroup participants share the blame for the fiasco. AeroGroup's executive team may have been overly confident in their ability to deal with the technological challenges inherent in implementing a major new ERP system. Furthermore, they based their selection of AFS, in part, on the fact that the other contender, the Style package from JBA International, was viewed as an IBM AS/400 package that re-

quired JBA's implementation support, and AeroGroup officials didn't want to be locked into a proprietary system. But many other footwear companies in the industry use JBA, such as Kenneth Cole, Candie's, and Rocky's Shoes and Boots. Evidently, AeroGroup has realized its error and has since purchased the JBA software product.

The consulting firms involved in the project also bear some responsibility, especially the lead implementation partner. The Eisner Consulting unit of Richard Eisner & Co. of New York is an experienced SAP implementation partner that was familiar with the apparel and footwear industry. Why did it proceed with the project when anyone with even a passing familiarity with ERP, SAP's R/3, and AeroGroup could see that this project reeked of risk? And what about SAP? Of course it's naïve in the extreme to expect a vendor to decline to sell a product to an inappropriate buyer. The capitalist system might mean caveat emptor (buyer beware) to some, but what is SAP's responsibility to its customers?

a. What are some of the causes of the failures in the installation of SAP's AFS software product at the companies in this case?

b. How could such problems have been avoided?

Source: Adapted from Deborah Asbrand, "Peering across the Abyss: Clothing and Shoe Companies Cross the ERP Chasm," *Datamation*, January 1999; and Larry Marion, "Autopsy of a Debacle," *Datamation*, February 1999, at www.datamation.com. © 1999 by EarthWeb Inc.

2. Cisco Systems, Tech Data, and the Chicago Stock Exchange: The New Business CIO

Cisco Systems' chief information officer, Peter Solvik, is the antithesis of the glass-house MIS director who oversees technology decisions. He is responsible not only for Cisco's Internet-based customer service tools, wide and local area networks, business applications, and telecommunications, but also for overseeing Cisco's Internet business organization. Under his leadership, the Cisco Connection Online site recently surpassed a $4 billion annual run rate. Solvik also reports on Cisco's technology strategy to its board of directors, taking the company's technology decisions to the highest level.

Like Solvik, a handful of new CIOs in U.S. corporations are increasingly taking on business decisions in addition to the technology decisions that have traditionally defined their role. Driven by Internet advances, globalization, and corporate downsizing, progressive companies are hiring CIOs who can connect the products and processes of their various business units to IT know-how. These executives are transforming IT from a cost center into a profit center. And some of them are on their way to becoming the next generation of technology business leaders.

A good example is John Lochow, CIO of Tech Data, a $12 billion distributor of personal computer products that serves about 70,000 resellers and has a 400-person IT department. Lochow was hired in January 1998 to help Tech Data add new technology-based customer services to its back-office operation. Prior to joining TechData, Lochow was Bell Canada's first-ever CIO. "It was my responsibility to help Bell Canada become competitive. I came in to maximize the investment the company was making in IT," he says. "And I've done the same at TechData." For example, Lochow implemented a financial model to ensure that IT is managed like a business, and he oversaw the rollout of a new suite of electronic commerce products, which generated $200 million in revenues within a few months.

The Chicago Stock Exchange, like Tech Data, is counting on the new generation of CIOs to help it stay competitive in the online era. CIO Steve Randich, who came to the Chicago exchange two years ago with a background in management consulting, recently took on the future of the company's main product, its automatic trading system. "I'm responsible for helping us meet business goals in each of our target markets because 60 to 70 percent of the business initiatives we identify have a significant IT component," he says.

a. Why are many CIOs taking on business as well as technology responsibilities today?

b. How do Peter Solvik, John Lochow, and Steve Randich support your answer to the previous question?

Source: Adapted from Nikki Goth Itoi, "The New CIO," *Red Herring*, February 1999, pp. 68–70.

3. EDS, Oracle, and GM-Opel: Call Centers for IT Support in Europe

Near the airport of Antwerp in Belgium, a drab 13-story building rises above weedy lots stacked with cargo containers. Dingy shipping offices occupy most of the sprawling structure. But take the elevator to the eighth floor, and you see a different scene. Here, about 125 workers for Electronic Data Systems Corporation sit in front of computers at brightly lit workstations, chattering into headsets.

French, Dutch, German, and English fill the air. On one side, an operator is helping a caller from France's aluminum giant Pechiney straighten out a software bug. Across the room another agent is telling a salesman at Eural, a Belgian financial-services firm, how to enter a new customer's account into his com-

puter. On an average day, these operators will deal with some 600 problems phoned in from as many as 18 different European countries.

Welcome to one of Europe's fastest-growing and most important new businesses. From Belfast to Naples, workers are donning headsets and staffing service centers set up to deal with sales and problems for clients ranging from banks to carmakers to software houses. These new service outfits go by a variety of names; the most common are customer contact centers or, simply, call centers.

Software maker Oracle Corporation uses a sophisticated call center to handle sales. The Dublin facility employs 350, most with business-school or engineering degrees. They cover companies in Europe, the Middle East, and Africa, selling software costing $40,000 or less to a total of 30 countries. That frees up Oracle's field sales force to concentrate on more complex deals of higher value, says managing director Eric Duffaut.

At General Motors Opel unit, call centers help the company keep in touch with dealers and customers alike. The company has contracted with EDS to provide information technology services in Europe. EDS runs a network of centers to deal with problems car owners encounter with their vehicles. Other centers help dealers with the software that links them to GM distribution centers.

The EDS center is one of the most ambitious in Europe. It is part of a network of nine such operations that handle software problems for EDS clients. The company built a service center near Antwerp because this area is known as one where people speak many languages. Nearly everyone in the city speaks both Dutch and French, while college graduates who have acquired English, German, and Spanish are also common. Many workers at the EDS center are graduates of colleges in the Antwerp area renowned for churning out language whizzes.

EDS required fluency in four languages, and the Antwerp facility works in nine: French, German, English, Dutch, Spanish, Italian, Swedish, Portuguese, and Norwegian. There are also operators who can deal with Russian, Icelandic, and Danish.

EDS pays beginning operators $1,800 a month—$27,720 per year. That compares with a minimum wage of $19,000 in Belgium—not bad for a twentysomething college graduate in a country with 8.6 percent unemployment. EDS teaches its workers the ins and outs of troubleshooting computer software and promises them a promotion to a corporate job after two years. "I am very satisfied," says Isabelle Arntz, a 25-year-old operator who works in English, Dutch, French, and Spanish.

a. What is the business value of establishing call centers in Europe?

b. Should the companies in this case also establish European web sites to provide software support? Why or why not?

Source: Reprinted from Stanley Reed, "Wired Collar Workers," *Business Week*, February 1, 1999, pp. 122E2–122E4 by special permission, copyright © 1999 by The McGraw-Hill Companies, Inc.

Application Exercises

1. Updating Apex Products Human Resources System

The human resources information system at Apex Products is seriously outdated. Limitations of the current system require human resources employees to make numerous manual calculations with the attendant risk of error. Two alternatives have been proposed: (1) Development of an entirely new system by Apex's IS department, and (2) purchase of a third-party human resources software package and modification as needed to meet Apex's needs. A spreadsheet will be used to estimate the costs and benefits of these alternatives over the next 10 years. Costs and benefits will be measured in terms of changes relative to the current system, so that if neither alternative shows a positive return, the existing system will be retained.

Benefits of the new system would come in the form of reduced processing time by human resources staff. Because an internally developed system can be better tailored to Apex's needs, it is expected to create greater time savings than the purchased system alternative. The cost of an hour's work by the average human resources employee is $18 including benefits. Assume the following:

Development: Will require two years to complete with costs of $300,000 the first year and $250,000 the second year. Will save 17,000 hours of labor per year, beginning in year 3.

Purchase: Will cost $275,000 plus an additional $100,000 to adapt it; would be operational within a year. Will save 11,000 hours of labor per year, beginning in year 2.

a. Based on these figures, develop a spreadsheet showing the costs and benefits of each alternative over the next 10 years.

b. Modify your spreadsheet so that it includes calculations of the net present value of each investment assuming a required return on investment of 15 percent.

c. Describe which alternative you would choose and why you would choose it.

2. Worldwide Technical Support at Acme Services

Your organization, Acme Services, has extensive worldwide operations including information systems department staff at locations throughout the world. In order to provide 24-hour technical support, users can call any support facility worldwide to obtain help with their technical problems. Three categories of technical support are available from separate support groups: hardware support, networking support, and database/applications support.

You have been asked to put together a database application that will record the location, hours of operation (based on U.S. Eastern Standard time), type of support provided, and phone number of each support facility. A sample set of data follows.

City	Country	Start Hour	End Hour	Support Type	Phone Number
Berlin	Germany	1:00	12:00	Database/Apps	3183
Bombay	India	21:00	13:00	Network	3093
Boston	United States	8:00	18:00	Hardware	3826
Boston	United States	8:00	20:00	Network	3814
Chicago	United States	9:00	21:00	Database/Apps	2819
Denver	United States	10:00	21:00	Hardware	1809
Honolulu	United States	13:00	1:00	Network	1817
Manchester	England	2:00	14:00	Hardware	1004
Manchester	England	2:00	15:00	Network	2761
Melbourne	Australia	19:00	8:00	Database/Apps	1920
Melbourne	Australia	19:00	10:00	Hardware	1933

a. Create an appropriate database table for these data and populate it with the data shown.
b. Create a report listing all of the data grouped by type of support so that a user could identify all possible sources for a given type of support.

c. Create a query that will allow users to enter the type of support they need and be shown a list of centers offering that type of support.

Review Quiz Answers

1. 13*a*	6. 15*a*	11. 3	16. 14	21. 2	26. 29	31. 11*c*
2. 13*b*	7. 17	12. 25	17. 26	22. 12	27. 4	32. 11*d*
3. 1*a*	8. 19	13. 20	18. 22	23. 7	28. 9	33. 11*e*
4. 1*b*	9. 8	14. 5	19. 27	24. 23	29. 11*a*	34. 28
5. 15	10. 16	15. 6	20. 24	25. 10	30. 11*b*	

Selected References

1. Alter, Allan. "Harmonic Convergence." In "The Premier 100." *Computerworld*, November 16, 1998.

2. Bowles, Jerry. "Making the Most of Your Technology Investment." *Fortune*, Special Advertising Section, December 9, 1996.

3. Bowles, Jerry. "Quality 2000: The Next Decade of Progress." *Fortune*, Special Advertising Supplement, October 3, 1994.

4. Boynton, Andrew; Robert Zmud; and Gerry Jacobs. "The Influence of IT Management Practice on IT Use in Large Organizations." *MIS Quarterly*, September 1994.

5. Bradley, Stephen P.; Jerry A. Hausman; and Richard L. Nolan. *Globalization, Technology, and Competition: The Fusion of Computers and Telecommunications in the 1990s.* Boston: Harvard Business School Press, 1993.

6. Brandel, Mary. "Think Global, Act Local." *Computerworld Global Innovators*, Special Section, March 10, 1997.

7. Carper, William. "Societal Impacts and Consequences of Transborder Data Flows." In *The Global Issues of Information Technology Management*, ed. Shailendra Palvia et al. Harrisburg, PA: Idea Group Publishing, 1992.

8. Cash, James I., Jr.; Robert G. Eccles; Nitin Nohria; and Richard L. Nolan. *Building the Information-Age Organization.* Burr Ridge, IL: Richard D. Irwin, 1994.

9. *Collaborative Solutions.* New York: IBM Corporation, 1997.

10. Corbett, Michael. "Outsourcing: Creating Competitive Advantage through Specialization, Alliances, and Innovation." *Fortune*, Special Advertising Section, October 14, 1996.

11. Cronin, Mary. *Global Advantage on the Internet.* New York: Van Nostrand Reinhold, 1996.

12. Davenport, Thomas H. *Process Innovation: Reengineering Work through Information Technology.* Boston: Harvard Business School Press, 1993.

13. Davenport, Thomas. "Saving Its Soul: Human-Centered Information Management." *Harvard Business Review*, March–April 1994.

14. Doolittle, Sean. "Standardizing Systems." *PC Today.* October 1997.

15. El Sawy, Omar, and Gene Bowles. "Redesigning the Customer Support Process for the Electronic Economy: Insights from Storage Dimensions." *MIS Quarterly*, December 1997.

16. Grover, Varun; James Teng; and Kirk Fiedler. "IS Investment Opportunities in Contemporary Organizations." *Communications of the ACM*, February 1998.

17. Haeckel, Stephan, and Richard Nolan. "Managing by Wire." *Harvard Business Review*, September–October 1993.

18. Ives, Blake, and Sirkka Jarvenpaa. "Applications of Global Information Technology: Key Issues for Management." *MIS Quarterly*, March 1991.

19. Kalin, Sari. "The Importance of Being Multiculturally Correct." Global Innovators Series, *Computerworld*, October 6, 1997.

20. Keen, Peter G. W. *Shaping the Future: Business Design through Information Technology*. Boston: Harvard Business School, 1991.

21. King, Julia, and Thomas Hoffman. "Troubled Insurer to Get IS." *Computerworld*, May 29, 1995.

22. King, William, and Vikram Sethi. "A Framework for Transnational Systems." In *The Global Issues of Information Technology Management*, ed. Shailendra Palvia et al. Harrisburg, PA: Idea Group Publishing, 1992.

23. Kirkpatrick, David. "Back to the Future with Centralized Computing." *Fortune*, November 10, 1997.

24. LaPlante, Alice. "Global Boundaries.com." Global Innovators Series, *Computerworld*, October 6, 1997.

25. LaPlante, Alice. "No Doubt about IT." *Computerworld*, August 15, 1994.

26. Levis, John, and Peter Von Schilling. "Lessons from Three Implementations: Knocking Down Barriers to Client/Server." *Information Systems Management*, Summer 1994.

27. Luftman, Jerry. "Align in the Sand." Leadership Series. *Computerworld*, February 17, 1997.

28. Maglitta, Joseph. "CIOs Warned to Get Their Shops in Shape." *Computerworld*, November 7, 1994.

29. Martin, Bob; Gene Batchelder; Jonathan Newcomb; John Rockart; Wayne Yetter; and Jerome Grossman. "The End of Delegation? Information Technology and the CEO." *Harvard Business Review*, September–October 1995.

30. Martin, Michael. "When Info Worlds Collide." *Fortune*, October 28, 1996.

31. McFarlan, F. Warren. "The Expert's Opinion." *Information Resources Management Journal*, Fall 1991.

32. Mische, Michael. "Transnational Architecture: A Reengineering Approach." *Information Systems Management*, Winter 1995.

33. O'Brien, James A., and James N. Morgan. "A Multidimensional Model of Information Resource Management." *Information Resources Management Journal*, Spring 1991.

34. Palvia, Prashant; Shailendra Palvia; and Edward Roche, eds. *Global Information Technology and Systems Management*. Marietta, GA: Ivy League Publishing, 1996.

35. Palvia, Shailendra; Prashant Palvia; and Ronald Zigli, eds. The *Global Issues of Information Technology Management*. Harrisburg, PA: Idea Group Publishing, 1992.

36. Petty, Terrence. "European Officials Agree with U.S. on Internet Guideline." *PC Today*, September 1997.

37. Roche, Edward M. *Managing Information Technology in Multinational Corporations*. New York: Macmillan, 1992.

38. Rowell, Jan. "Getting Control of TCO." Special Advertising Supplement. *Computerworld*, November 17, 1997.

39. SIM International. *Information Systems Process Architecture*. Version 2.0. Chicago: Society for Information Management, 1996.

40. SIM International. "Leading Companies Find Success Using SIM's IS Process Architecture." SIM Working Group Publications, July 1996.

41. Simpson, David. "Will NCs Save You a Bundle?" *Datamation*, May 1997.

42. Sloan, Robert, and Hal Green. "Manufacturing Decision Support Architecture." *Information Systems Management*, Winter 1995.

43. Strassman, Paul. *The Squandered Computer*. New Canaan, CT: The Information Economics Press, 1997.

44. Verity, John. "Gaining an Edge: It's All about IT." In "The Premier 100." *Computerworld*, November 16, 1998.

45. Vitalari, Nicholas, and James Wetherbe. "Emerging Best Practices in Global Systems Development." In *Global Information Technology and Systems Management*, ed. Prashant Palvia et al. Marietta, GA: Ivy League Publishing, 1996.

46. Weston, Randy. "The Internet: Managing the Connection." Leadership Series. *Computerworld*, September 16, 1996.

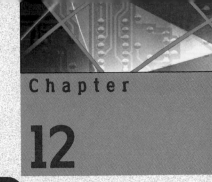

Security and Ethical

Challenges of Information

Technology

Chapter Highlights

Section I
Security and Control Issues in Information Systems
Why Controls Are Needed
Real World Case: BuyDirect and Others: Credit Card Fraud in E-Commerce
Information System Controls
Facility Controls
Procedural Controls
Auditing Information Systems

Section II
Ethical and Societal Challenges of Information Technology
Real World Case: Warroom Research and Sun-Trust Banks: Defending Networks from Cyberattacks
The Ethical Dimension
Ethical and Societal Dimensions of IT
Privacy Issues
Computer Crime
Health Issues
Societal Solutions
You and Ethical Responsibility

Learning Objectives

After reading and studying this chapter, you should be able to:

1. Identify several types of information system controls, procedural controls, and facility controls and explain how they can be used to ensure the quality and security of information systems.

2. Discuss ways to control the performance and security of the use of the Internet by businesses and their end users and trading partners.

3. Identify several ethical issues in how information technology affects employment, individuality, working conditions, privacy, crime, health, and solutions to societal problems.

4. Propose several ways that managerial end users can help to lessen the harmful effects and increase the beneficial effects of information technology.

Security and Control Issues in Information Systems

Why Controls Are Needed

As a manager, you will be responsible for the control of the quality and performance of information systems in your business unit. Like any other vital business assets, the resources of information systems hardware, software, networks, and data need to be protected by built-in controls to ensure their quality and security. That's why controls are needed.

Analyzing BuyDirect and Others

Read the Real World Case on BuyDirect and Others on the next page. We can learn a lot from this case about the threat of credit card fraud and the defensive measures a company can take in E-commerce transactions. See Figure 12.1.

Businesses engaged in electronic commerce on the Web are finding that credit card fraud is a major threat to both their profitability and survival. Companies like BuyDirect experienced fraud rates in excess of 20 percent, especially from international sales, when they first started E-commerce on the Web. Such losses also made them vulnerable to losing their financing from banks, which would put them out of business. By installing antifraud software, tough screening procedures, and other measures, BuyDirect and other companies have been able to reduce their credit card fraud rates to less than 1 percent.

What Controls Are Needed

Effective controls provide **information system security,** that is, the accuracy, integrity, and safety of information system activities and resources. Controls can minimize errors, fraud, and destruction in the internetworked information systems that interconnect today's end users and organizations. Effective controls also provide **quality assurance** for information systems. That is, they can make a computer-based

Figure 12.1

William Headapohl, president of BuyDirect Inc., says credit card fraud almost overwhelmed their web site business until they installed elaborate security software and procedures.

Source: Gary Laufman Photography.

BuyDirect and Others: Credit Card Fraud in E-Commerce

Electronic-commerce merchants focus on making customers feel safe inside their virtual stores. But achieving that same level of protection for merchants themselves is a much tougher proposition that IT managers say isn't happening fast enough. "It's like we've triple-locked the bank vault only to get mugged on the sidewalk outside," say Danny Sullivan, a webmaster who recently uncovered a major online credit-card scam in the United Kingdom.

In some cases, fraudulent transactions accounted for 20 percent or more of Web merchants' sales until managers got wise and installed antifraud software. "There were days when we had more fraud than legitimate sales," one chief technology officer said. Another online merchant who asked not to be named said one bank had dropped him for having unacceptably high fraud rates, forcing him to turn to a far more "high-risk" bank to continue accepting customer cards. "We got our fraud down now, but we've been warned that if it ever exceeds 1 percent of our total, we're out. That, of course, means instant bankruptcy," he said.

Fraud nearly vanquished San Francisco–based BuyDirect Inc. when it opened for business in 1996, said William Headapohl, president of the online software store. "Our fraud rate was unacceptably high and banks wanted to drop us. If we hadn't had strong financial backing and worked hard to reduce our fraud rates, we would have been put out of business pretty quickly."

Using antifraud software and elaborate screening systems, the company reduced its fraud rate to under 1 percent. "The more it costs, the more someone will try to steal it," said Headapohl. "One of our first defenses was not to sell the really expensive products online."

Selling internationally is one of the key reasons for starting an electronic-commerce site, yet foreign sales are the riskiest of all. "Our international fraud rates were so bad in the beginning, we thought we were going to have to exclude overseas sales altogether," Headapohl said. "Companies like ours were routinely seeing fraud rates in excess of 20 percent.

The greatest concentrations of credit-card thieves come from Romania, Egypt, Russia, Belarus, Israel, Thailand, Pakistan, and Mexico, merchants and law enforcement officials said. The problem is so bad, in fact, that many merchants refuse to do business with buyers in these countries.

Usually, the amounts lost in online transactions are too small to warrant attention by law enforcement officials.

"Everyone we've talked with had absolutely no success getting police interested, even for amounts as high as $50,000," said Audri Lanford of Scambusters (www.scambusters.org), a fraud-alert web site for online retailers.

One reason for the problem is that it's too easy to purchase stolen cards: A valid credit-card number and expiration date can be had for as little as $25 online, said Ramzi Saffouri, a consultant at fraud-detection software maker Advanced Software Applications in Pittsburgh. And according to the U.S. Federal Bureau of Investigation, you can buy the magnetic stripes and holograms to create a counterfeit card online for about $40.

Most successful web merchants avoid fraud by outsourcing credit-card verification to third parties with sophisticated (and expensive) neural-net antifraud software. Or they develop their own antifraud systems. Another approach is to take verification procedures off-line and check cards manually.

The best defense involves screening practices based on online retailers' most typical sales. Web site personnel and E-commerce software can check for addresses that don't match and other suspicious details. For example, many merchants, including airlines, refuse transactions in which the shipping address doesn't match the billing address on the card. "We triangulate," Headapohl says. "It's just common sense, if they say they're from the U.K., their card is Japanese, and the shipping address is in Beverly Hills, call and check."

A combination of two defense strategies, analysts said, provides the best of both worlds: expert authorization handling and expert knowledge of your company's customer base.

Cast Study Questions

1. How does credit card fraud happen on the Internet?
2. What steps should a business take to protect itself from credit card fraud in electronic commerce?
3. Visit the E-commerce web site of a company. What steps are being taken to minimize credit card fraud in E-commerce transactions?

Source: Adapted from Cynthia Morgan, "Web Merchants Stung by Fraud," Computerworld, March 8, 1999, p. 24; and "Protecting Your Web Site against Credit Card Fraud, Computerworld, March 8, 1999, p. 71. Copyright 1999 by Computerworld, Inc., Framingham, MA 01701. Reprinted from Computerworld.

Figure 12.2

Security requirements for electronic commerce.

● **Privacy**	The ability to control who sees (or cannot see) information and under what terms
● **Authenticity**	The ability to know the identities of communicating parties
● **Integrity**	The assurance that stored or transmitted information is unaltered
● **Reliability**	The assurance that systems will be available when needed and will perform consistently at an acceptable level of quality
● **Blocking**	The ability to block unwanted information or intrusions

Source: Adapted from Ravi Kalakota and Andrew Whinston, *Electronic Commerce: A Manager's Guide* (Reading, MA: Addison-Wesley, 1977), p. 135. © 1997 by Addison-Wesley Publishing Company Inc. Reprinted by permission of Addison-Wesley Longman, Inc.

information system more free of errors and fraud and able to provide information products of higher quality than manual types of information processing. This can help reduce the potential negative impact (and increase the positive impact) that information technology can have on business survival and success and the quality of life in society. However, much work needs to be done before adequate controls are implemented in many companies. Figure 12.2 outlines the security requirements that companies must establish to provide secure electronic commerce using the Internet, intranets, and extranets for electronic commerce.

Three major types of controls must be developed to ensure the quality and security of information systems. These control categories, illustrated in Figure 12.3 are:

● Information system controls.

● Procedural controls.

● Facility controls.

Figure 12.3

The controls needed for information system security. Specific types of controls can be grouped into three major categories: information systems, procedural, and facility controls.

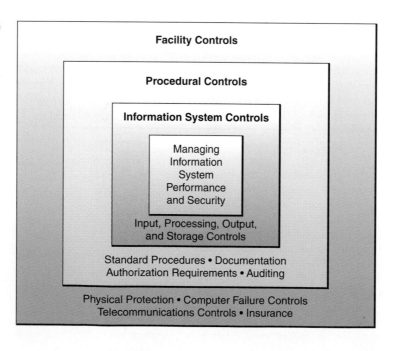

Information System Controls

Information system controls are methods and devices that attempt to ensure the accuracy, validity, and propriety of information system activities. Controls must be developed to ensure proper data entry, processing techniques, storage methods, and information output. Thus, information system controls are designed to monitor and maintain the quality and security of the input, processing, output, and storage activities of any information system. See Figure 12.4.

Input Controls

Have you heard the phrase *garbage in, garbage out,* (GIGO)? Figure 12.5 shows why controls are needed for the proper entry of data into an information system. Examples include passwords and other security codes, formatted data entry screens, audible error signals, templates over the keys of key-driven input devices, and prerecorded and prenumbered forms. Some realtime systems record all entries into the system on magnetic tape *control logs* that preserve evidence of all system inputs. Computer software can include instructions to identify incorrect, invalid, or improper input data as it enters the computer system. For example, a data entry program can check for invalid codes, data fields, and transactions. Also, the computer can be programmed to conduct "reasonableness checks" to determine if input data exceed certain specified limits or are out of sequence. This includes the calculation and monitoring of selected **control totals.**

Data entry and other systems activities are frequently monitored by the use of control totals. For example, a *record count* is a control total that consists of counting the total number of source documents or other input records and comparing this total to the number of records counted at other stages of input preparation. If the totals do not match, a mistake has been made. Batch totals and hash totals are other forms of control totals. A *batch total* is the sum of a specific item of data within a batch of

Figure 12.4

Examples of information system controls. Note that they are designed to monitor and maintain the quality and security of the input, processing, output, and storage activities of an information system.

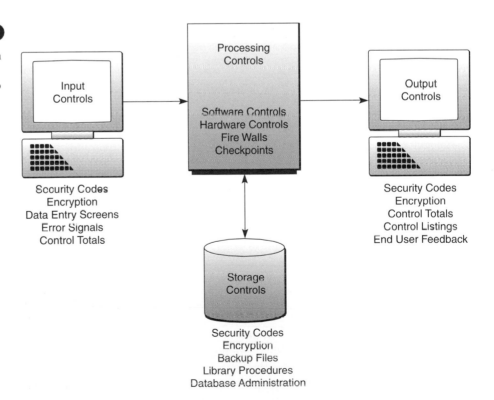

Input Controls

Security Codes
Encryption
Data Entry Screens
Error Signals
Control Totals

Processing Controls

Software Controls
Hardware Controls
Fire Walls
Checkpoints

Output Controls

Security Codes
Encryption
Control Totals
Control Listings
End User Feedback

Storage Controls

Security Codes
Encryption
Backup Files
Library Procedures
Database Administration

Figure 12.5

Garbage in, garbage out. Input controls are needed for the proper entry of data into a computer system.

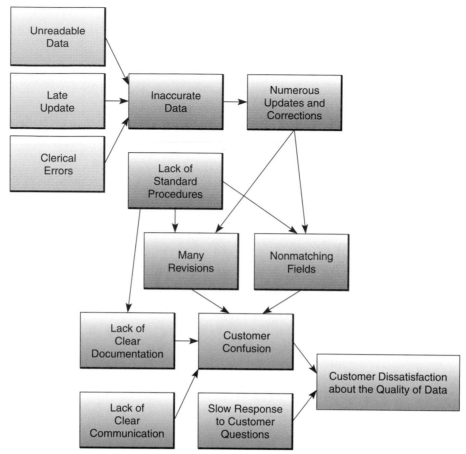

transactions, such as the sales amounts in a batch of sales transactions. *Hash totals* are the sum of data fields that are added together for control comparisons only. For example, employee Social Security numbers could be added to produce a control total in the input preparation of payroll documents.

Processing Controls

Once business data are entered correctly into a computer system, they must be processed properly. Processing controls are developed to identify errors in arithmetic calculations and logical operations. They are also used to ensure that data are not lost or do not go unprocessed. Processing controls can include hardware controls and software controls.

Hardware Controls. Hardware controls are special checks built into the hardware to verify the accuracy of computer processing. Examples of hardware checks include:

- **Malfunction detection circuitry** with a computer or telecommunications processor that can monitor their operations. For example, *parity checks* are made to check for the loss of the correct number of bits in every byte of data processed or transmitted on a network. Another example is *echo checks* that require a device or circuit to return a signal to verify that it was properly activated.

- **Redundant components.** For example, multiple read-write heads on magnetic disk drives check and promote the accuracy of reading and recording activities.
- **Special-purpose microprocessors and associated circuitry** that may be used to support remote diagnostics and maintenance. These allow off-site technicians to diagnose and correct some problems via network links to the computer.

Software Controls. Some software controls ensure that the right data are being processed. For example, the operating system or other software checks the internal file labels at the beginning and end of magnetic disk and tape files. These labels contain information identifying the file as well as provide control totals for the data in the file. These internal file labels allow the computer to ensure that the proper storage file is being used and that the proper data in the file have been processed.

Another major software control is the establishment of checkpoints during the processing of a program. *Checkpoints* are intermediate points within a program being processed where intermediate totals, listings, or "dumps" of data are written on magnetic tape or disk or listed on a printer. Checkpoints minimize the effect of processing errors or failures, since processing can be restarted from the last checkpoint (called a rollback), rather than from the beginning of the program. They also help build an *audit trail*, which allows transactions being processed to be traced through all of the steps of their processing.

Output Controls

How can we control the quality of the information products produced by an information system? Output controls are developed to ensure that information products are correct and complete and are available to authorized users in a timely manner. Several types of output controls are similar to input control methods. For example, control totals on output are usually compared with control totals generated during the input and processing stages. Control listings can be produced that provide hard copy evidence of all output produced.

Access to the online output of computer networks is typically controlled by security codes that identify which users can receive output and the type of output they are authorized to receive. Prenumbered output forms can be used to control the loss of important output documents such as stock certificates or payroll check forms. Finally, end users should be encouraged to provide feedback on the quality of the output. This is an important function of systems maintenance and quality assurance activities.

Storage Controls

How can we protect our data resources? First, control responsibilities for files of computer programs and organizational databases may be assigned to data center specialists and database administrators. These employees are responsible for maintaining and controlling access to the program libraries and databases of the organization. Second, many databases and files are protected from unauthorized or accidental use by security programs that require proper identification before they can be used. Typically, operating systems or security monitors protect the databases of realtime processing systems from unauthorized use or processing accidents. Account codes, passwords, and other **security codes** are frequently used to allow access to authorized users only. A catalog of authorized users enables computer systems to identify eligible users and determine which types of information they are authorized to receive.

Typically, a multilevel **password** system is used. First, an end user logs on to the computer system by entering his or her unique identification code, or user ID. The end user is then asked to enter a password in order to gain access into the system. (Passwords should be changed frequently and consist of unusual combinations of upper- and lowercase letters and numbers.) Next, to access an individual file, a unique file name must be entered. In some systems, the password to read the contents of a file is different from that required to write to a file (change its contents). This feature adds another level of protection to stored data resources. However, for even stricter security, passwords can be scrambled, or *encrypted*, to avoid their theft or improper use, as we will discuss shortly. In addition, *smart cards*, which contain microprocessors that generate random numbers to add to an end user's password, are used in some secure systems.

Many firms also use **backup files,** which are duplicate files of data or programs. Such files may be stored off-premises, that is, in a location away from the computer center, sometimes in special storage vaults in remote locations. Many realtime processing systems use duplicate files that are updated by network links. Files are also protected by *file retention* measures that involve storing copies of master files and transaction files from previous periods. If current files are destroyed, the files from previous periods are used to reconstruct new current files. Usually, several generations of files are kept for control purposes. Thus, master files from several recent periods of processing (known as *child, parent, grandparent* files, etc.) may be kept for backup purposes.

Facility Controls

Facility controls are methods that protect an organization's computing and network facilities and their contents from loss or destruction. Computer networks and computer centers are subject to such hazards as accidents, natural disasters, sabotage, vandalism, unauthorized use, industrial espionage, destruction, and theft of resources. Therefore, various safeguards and control procedures are necessary to protect the hardware, software, network, and vital data resources of a company. This is especially vital as more and more companies engage in electronic commerce on the Internet.

Network Security

Security of a network may be provided by specialized system software packages known as **system security monitors.** See Figure 12.6. System security monitors are programs that monitor the use of computer systems and networks and protect them from unauthorized use, fraud, and destruction. Such programs provide the security measures needed to allow only authorized users to access the networks. For example, identification codes and passwords are frequently used for this purpose. Security monitors also control the use of the hardware, software, and data resources of a computer system. For example, even authorized users may be restricted to the use of certain devices, programs, and data files. Additionally, security programs monitor the use of computer networks and collect statistics on any attempts at improper use. They then produce reports to assist in maintaining the security of the network.

Encryption. Encryption of data has become an important way to protect data and other computer network resources especially on the Internet, intranets, and extranets. Passwords, messages, files, and other data can be transmitted in scrambled form and unscrambled by computer systems for authorized users only. Encryption involves using special mathematical algorithms, or keys, to transform digital data into a scrambled code before they are transmitted, and to decode the data when they are received. The most widely used encryption method uses a pair of public and private keys unique to each individual. For example, E-mail could be scrambled and encoded using a unique *public key* for the recipient that is known to the sender. After the E-mail is transmitted, only the recipient's secret *private key* could unscramble the message. See Figure 12.7.

Using CA-Unicenter
TNG. The security
monitor module of
CA-Unicenter TNG
performance monitor
system has identified an
attempt at unauthorized
access. Note the virtual
reality interface.

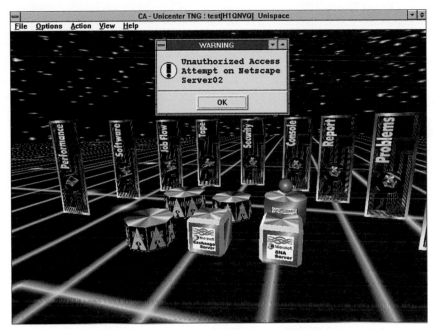

Courtesy of Computer Associates International, Inc.

Encryption programs are sold as separate products or built into other software
used for the encryption process. There are several competing software encryption
standards, but the top two are RSA (by RSA Data Security) and PGP (pretty good privacy), a popular encryption program available on the Internet. Software products including Microsoft Windows NT, Novell Netware, Lotus Notes, and Netscape
Communicator offer encryption features using RSA software.

Fire Walls. Another important method for control and security on the Internet and
other networks is the use of **fire wall** computers and software. A network fire wall is a
"gatekeeper" computer system that protects a company's intranets and other computer
networks from intrusion by serving as a filter and safe transfer point for access to and
from the Internet and other networks. It screens all network traffic for proper passwords or other security codes, and only allows authorized transmissions in and out of
the network. Fire walls have become an essential component of organizations connecting to the Internet, because of its vulnerability and lack of security. Figure 12.8 illustrates an Internet/intranet fire wall system for a company.

Fire walls can deter, but not completely prevent, unauthorized access (hacking)
into computer networks. In some cases, a fire wall may allow access only from trusted
locations on the Internet to particular computers inside the fire wall. Or it may allow
only "safe" information to pass. For example, a fire wall may permit users to read
E-mail from remote locations but not to run certain programs. In other cases, it is impossible to distinguish safe use of a particular network service from unsafe use and so
all requests must be blocked. The fire wall may then provide substitutes for some network services (such as E-mail or file transfer) that perform most of the same functions
but are not as vulnerable to penetration.

**Physical
Protection
Controls**

Providing maximum security and protection for an organization's computer and network resources requires many types of controls. For example, computer centers and
end user work areas are protected through such techniques as identification badges,

Figure 12.7 How public key/private key encryption works.

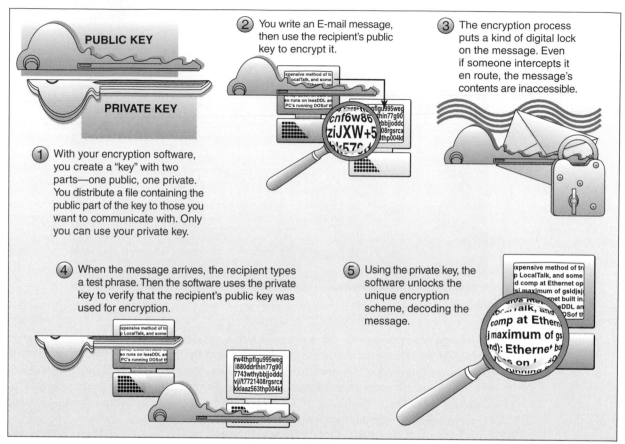

PUBLIC KEY

PRIVATE KEY

① With your encryption software, you create a "key" with two parts—one public, one private. You distribute a file containing the public part of the key to those you want to communicate with. Only you can use your private key.

② You write an E-mail message, then use the recipient's public key to encrypt it.

③ The encryption process puts a kind of digital lock on the message. Even if someone intercepts it en route, the message's contents are inaccessible.

④ When the message arrives, the recipient types a test phrase. Then the software uses the private key to verify that the recipient's public key was used for encryption.

⑤ Using the private key, the software unlocks the unique encryption scheme, decoding the message.

Source: Adapted from Jeffrey Rothfeder, "No Privacy on the Net," *PC World*, February 1997, pp. 224–25. Reprinted with the permission of *PC World* Communications Inc.

electronic door locks, burglar alarms, security police, closed-circuit TV, and other detection systems. Computer centers may be protected from disaster by such safeguards as fire detection and extinguishing systems; fireproof storage vaults for the protection of files; emergency power systems; electromagnetic shielding; and temperature, humidity, and dust controls. Protecting computer systems and networks is a major challenge now that so many companies are internetworked via intranets, extranets, and the Internet. See Figure 12.9.

Biometric Controls

Biometric controls are a fast-growing area of computer security. These are security measures provided by computer devices that measure physical traits that make each individual unique. This includes voice verification, fingerprints, hand geometry, signature dynamics, keystroke analysis, retina scanning, face recognition, and genetic pattern analysis. Biometric control devices use special-purpose sensors to measure and digitize a *biometric profile* of an individual's fingerprints, voice, or other physical trait. The digitized signal is processed and compared to a previously processed profile of the individual stored on magnetic disk. If the profiles match, the individual is allowed entry into a computer facility or given access to information system resources.

Figure 12.8   An example of the Internet and intranet fire walls in a company's networks.

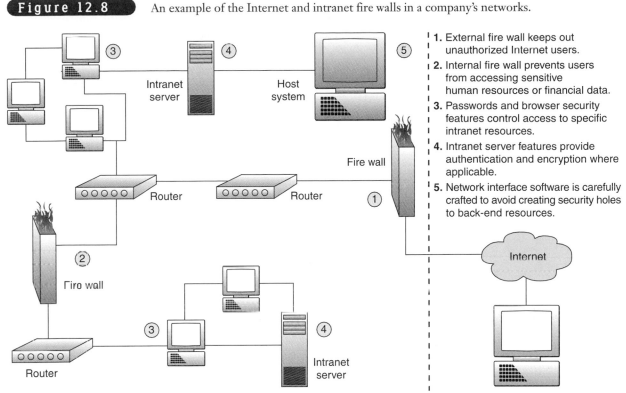

1. External fire wall keeps out unauthorized Internet users.
2. Internal fire wall prevents users from accessing sensitive human resources or financial data.
3. Passwords and browser security features control access to specific intranet resources.
4. Intranet server features provide authentication and encryption where applicable.
5. Network interface software is carefully crafted to avoid creating security holes to back-end resources.

Source: Adapted from Lenny Liebman, "Are Intranets Safe?" *Communications Week*, August 5, 1996, p. 77.

Computer Failure Controls

Sorry, the computer is down is a well-known phrase to many end users. A variety of controls can prevent such computer failure or minimize its effects. Computer systems fail for several reasons—power failure, electronic circuitry malfunctions, telecommunications network problems, hidden programming errors, computer viruses, computer operator errors, and electronic vandalism. The information services department typically takes steps to prevent equipment failure and to minimize its detrimental effects. For example, computers are available with automatic and remote maintenance capabilities. Programs of preventive maintenance of hardware and management of software updates are commonplace. Adequate electrical supply, air-conditioning, humidity control, and fire prevention standards are a prerequisite. A backup computer system capability can

Figure 12.9

Network security is a major challenge for many companies.

- More than 50% of all respondents reported unauthorized use of their computer systems within the last year.
- 47% of users reported a security invasion via the Web, up 10% over the previous year.
- 50% have no emergency response team.
- 60% have no network intrusion policy.
- 50% of the companies that have an intrusion policy still have no policy for preserving evidence.

Source: Adapted from Laura Didio, "Detecting Intrusions Is Only a Start," *Computerworld*, November 17, 1997, p. 68. Copyright 1997 by Computerworld, Inc., Framingham, MA 01701. Reprinted from *Computerworld*.

Figure 12.10

Methods of fault tolerance in computer-based information systems.

Layer	Threats	Fault Tolerant Methods
Applications	Environment, hardware and software faults	Application-specific redundancy and rollback to previous checkpoint
Systems	Outages	System isolation, data security, system integrity
Databases	Data errors	Separation of transactions and safe updates, complete transaction histories, backup files
Networks	Transmission errors	Reliable controllers; safe asynchrony and handshaking; alternative routing; error-detecting and error-correcting codes
Processes	Hardware and software faults	Alternative computations, rollback to checkpoints
Files	Media errors	Replication of critical data on different media and sites; archiving, backup, retrieval
Processors	Hardware faults	Instruction retry; error-correcting codes in memory and processing; replication; multiple processors and memories

Source: Adapted from Peter Neumann, *Computer-Related Risks* (New York: ACM Press, 1995), p. 231. Copyright © 1995, Association for Computing Machinery, Inc. By permission.

be arranged with *disaster recovery* organizations. Major hardware or software changes are usually carefully scheduled and implemented to avoid problems. Finally, highly trained data center personnel and the use of performance and security management software help keep a company's computer system and networks working properly.

Many firms also use **fault tolerant** computer systems that have redundant processors, peripherals, and software that provide a *fail-over* capability to back up components in the event of system failure. This may provide a *fail-safe* capability where the computer system continues to operate at the same level even if there is a major hardware or software failure. However, many fault tolerant computer systems offer a *fail-soft* capability where the computer system can continue to operate at a reduced but acceptable level in the event of a major system failure. Figure 12.10 outlines some of the fault tolerant capabilities used in many computer systems and networks.

Procedural Controls

Procedural controls are methods that specify how an organization's computer and network resources should be operated for maximum security. They help to ensure the accuracy and integrity of computer and network operations and systems development activities.

Standard Procedures and Documentation

Typically, an IS organization develops and follows standard procedures for the operation of information systems. Using standard procedures promotes quality and minimizes the chances of errors and fraud. It helps both end users and IS specialists know what is expected of them in operating procedures and system quality. In addition, documentation of the systems and software design and the operation of the system must be developed and kept up-to-date. Documentation is invaluable in the maintenance of a system as needed improvements are made.

Authorization Requirements

Requests for systems development and program changes are frequently subjected to a review process before authorization is given. For example, program changes requested by end users or generated by maintenance programmers must typically be approved by a systems development manager after consultation with the affected business unit. Conversion to new hardware, software, and network components and installation of newly developed information systems are also typically subjected to a formal notification and scheduling procedure. This minimizes their detrimental effects on the accuracy and integrity of ongoing system and network operations.

Disaster Recovery

Natural and man-made disasters do happen. Hurricanes, earthquakes, fires, floods, criminal and terrorist acts, and human error can all severely damage an organization's computing resources, and thus the health of the organization itself. Many organizations, like airlines, banks, and online services, for example, are crippled by losing even a few hours of computing power. Many firms could survive only a few days without computing facilities. That's why organizations develop **disaster recovery** procedures and formalize them in a *disaster recovery plan*. It specifies which employees will participate in disaster recovery and what their duties will be; what hardware, software, and facilities will be used; and the priority of applications that will be processed. Arrangements with other companies for use of alternative facilities as a disaster recovery site and offsite storage of an organization's databases are also part of an effective disaster recovery effort.

Controls for End User Computing

Many end user–developed applications are performing extremely important business functions. Instead of merely being systems for personal productivity or decision support, these applications are supporting the accomplishment of important business activities that are critical to the success and survival of the firm. Thus, they can be called *company-critical* end user applications.

Figure 12.11 outlines controls that can be observed or built into all company-critical end user applications. Many companies are insisting on such end user controls to protect themselves from the havoc that errors, fraud, destruction, and other hazards could cause to these critical applications and thus to the company itself. The controls involved are those that are standard practice in applications developed by professional IS departments. However, such controls are more easily ignored in the rush to develop end user systems.

Figure 12.11 emphasizes a major point for managerial end users. Who is ultimately responsible for ensuring that proper controls are built into company-critical applications? Business unit managers are! This emphasizes once again that all managers must accept the responsibility for managing the computer network and information system resources of their teams, workgroups, departments, and other business units.

Figure 12.11

Criteria and controls for company-critical end user applications.

• Methods for testing user-developed systems for compliance with company policies and work procedures.
• Methods for notifying other users when changes in mission-critical user-developed systems are planned.
• Thorough documentation of user-developed systems.
• Training several people in the operation and maintenance of a system.
• A formal process for evaluating and acquiring new hardware and software.
• Formal backup and recovery procedures for all user systems.
• Security controls for access to user and company computer systems, networks, and databases.

Auditing Information Systems

An information services department should be periodically examined, or audited, by internal auditing personnel from the business firm. In addition, periodic audits by external auditors from professional accounting firms are a good business practice. Such audits should review and evaluate whether proper and adequate information system controls, procedural controls, facility controls, and other managerial controls have been developed and implemented. There are two basic approaches for **auditing information systems**—that is, auditing the information processing activities of computer-based information systems. They are known as (1) auditing around the computer system and (2) auditing through the computer system.

Auditing around the computer system involves verifying the accuracy and propriety of the input of data and output produced without evaluating the software that processed the data. This is a simpler and easier method, but does not trace a transaction through all of its stages of processing and does not test the accuracy and integrity of the software used. Therefore, it is recommended only as a supplement to other auditing methods.

Auditing through the computer system involves verifying the accuracy and integrity of the software that processes the data, as well as the input of data and output produced by the computer systems and networks. Auditing through the computer requires a knowledge of computer system and network operations and software development. Some firms employ special *EDP auditors* for this assignment. They may use special test data to test processing accuracy and the control procedures built into the software. The auditors may develop special test programs or use audit software packages. See Figure 12.12.

EDP auditors use such programs to process their test data. Then they compare the results produced by their audit programs with the results generated by the computer user's own programs. One of the objectives of such testing is to detect the presence of unauthorized changes or patches to computer programs. Unauthorized program patches may be the cause of unexplainable errors or may be used for fraudulent

Figure 12.12

An example of the capabilities of an audit software package. This package analyzes database rules and identifies any data records that deviate from those rules.

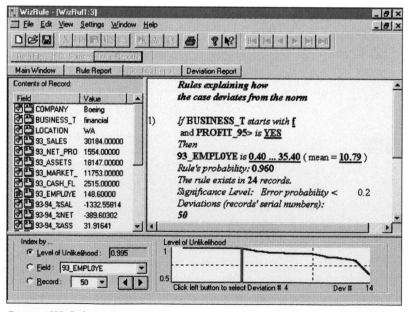

Courtesy WizSoft.

purposes. Another important objective of such auditing procedures is to test the integrity of an application's *audit trail.*

An **audit trail** can be defined as the presence of documentation that allows a transaction to be traced through all stages of its information processing. This journey may begin with a transaction's appearance on a source document and may end with its transformation into information on a final output document or report. The audit trail of manual information systems was quite visible and easy to trace. However, computer-based information systems have changed the form of the audit trail. Now auditors must know how to search electronically through magnetic disk and tape files of past activity to follow the audit trail of most business systems.

Many times, this *electronic audit trail* takes the form of *control logs* that automatically record all computer network activity on magnetic disk or tape devices. This audit feature can be found on many online transaction processing systems, performance and security monitors, operating systems, and network control programs. Software that records all network activity is also widely used on the Internet, especially the World Wide Web, as well as corporate intranets and extranets. Such an audit trail helps auditors check for errors or fraud, but also helps IS security specialists trace and evaluate the trail of hacker attacks on computer networks.

Section II ▸ Ethical and Societal Challenges of Information Technology

Ethical questions are involved in many strategic decisions, such as investment in human resources, modernization, product development and service, marketing, environmental decisions, and executive salaries. Often strategic issues may significantly affect the firm's performance and are characterized by their novelty, complexity, and speed. Obviously, such threats or opportunities may involve a large ethical component [18].

We are in the midst of an **information revolution,** in which information technology has dramatically magnified our ability to acquire, manipulate, store, and communicate information. Thanks to information technology, especially Internet technologies, we have electronic tools that let us retrieve and communicate information in seconds to practically any person, in any place, at any time of the day. Thanks to IT, we can now communicate easily, work cooperatively, share resources, and make decisions, all electronically. But also thanks to IT, it has now become possible to engage in ethical or unethical business practices electronically anywhere in the world.

Analyzing Warroom Research and Sun-Trust Banks

Read the Real World Case on Warroom Research and Sun-Trust Banks on the next page. We can learn a lot from this case about the network security issues and challenges that surround the business use of information technology. See Figure 12.13.

Mark Gembicki's company helps companies test their networks for system vulnerabilities that could be discovered and exploited by network attackers. Network penetration testing helps companies like Sun-Trust Banks improve their computer

Figure 12.13

Mark Gembicki heads Warroom Research Inc., an IT security consulting firm that performs penetration tests on network fire walls.

Source: Katherine Lambert.

Warroom Research and Sun-Trust Banks: Defending Networks from Cyberattacks

On his 17th birthday, Mark Gembicki started work at the U.S. National Security Agency's (NSA) Research and Development unit—plucked out of high school after testing off the charts in electronics and computer science. In 1987, Gembicki helped form InfoTek Systems, which produced technology now used in cable boxes. His current venture, Warroom Research Inc. in Annapolis, Maryland, is a consulting firm that performs penetration tests on fire walls. "While CEOs and CIOs appear on TV telling reporters their networks have never been hit," say Gembicki, now 33, "we're getting the real truth from their security administrators."

One way to get management to take information security more seriously is to perform penetration testing, in which a company uses automated software tools to probe its own systems for security holes. That shows management the vulnerabilities that are found and their implications, Gembicki says. "There's shock value in attack and penetration work," he notes.

John Wylder, a senior vice president at Sun-Trust Banks, Inc., in Atlanta, agrees that showing management the results of penetration tests can be effective, provided security vulnerabilities are clearly related to business concepts. "You can say that hackers could have downloaded the customer list for your Jacksonville office—that will get their attention," he says.

Network penetration testing took on a new urgency after TV networks aired dramatic stories of international attacks on U.S. Defense Department computer networks.

But security analysts said that those attacks are more likely the work of a new generation of automated scanning and attack software that simulate coordinated, multinational probes. A bulletin released by the CIO Institute (www.cio.org), a private organization of U.S. government CIOs, said that in late 1998, security experts began noticing widespread use of sophisticated scanning tools that mask their activities in a barrage of what appear to be multinational attacks.

The new scanners are more malignant than their predecessors because they can spread out attacks to hide below the monitoring thresholds of audit trails and intrusion-detection software. They enable crackers to automate the entire process of identifying computer systems, locating known vulnerabilities, and exploiting those holes to gain network access.

For example, scanner software called NMap performs decoy scans using any number of Internet addresses. NMap allows a relatively unsophisticated cracker, located in the same city as the target network, to quickly scan a system for network vulnerabilities, and then to launch an attack that mimics a coordinated group of international cyberattackers.

To defend against this new generation of scanning tools, companies should establish automated monitoring and auditing procedures along with rapid system administration response, security experts said. Smart organizations are running automated vulnerability scans several times per year.

The CIO Institute said companies should encourage competition among their vulnerability testing teams. They should include an inside team, an outside team from a systems integrator or accounting firm, and another from a smaller specialized security organization. Once holes are located, companies must then allocate trained staff to make sure the holes are closed before they are exploited by cybercriminals.

"The bottom line is, we should not worry about building bigger, faster, and better information systems. We should address the real challenge: building more effective systems that are designed to be secure," adds Gembicki.

Case Study Questions

1. What is the business value of network penetration testing?

2. What do hackers hope to gain from attacks on business networks?

3. How should organizations protect themselves from network attacks by the new generation of attack scanners?

Source: Adapted from Laura Didio, "Future Tense," *Computerworld*, January 4, 1999, p. 42; Gary Anthes, "Lotsa Talk, Little Walk," *Computerworld*, September 21, 1998, pp. 70–71; Ann Harrison, "New Generation of Scanning Tools Masks Source of Attack," *Computerworld*, March 15, 1999, p. 8; and "When Good Scanners Go Bad," *Computerworld*, March 22, 1999, p. 66. Copyright 1999 by Computerworld, Inc., Framingham, MA 01701. Reprinted from *Computerworld*.

networks to protect vital business databases and systems from theft or destruction. By highlighting any system weaknesses, network penetration testing also provides a major incentive to company executives to spend the funds to defend their networks from attacks by hackers using a new generation of attack scanner software.

The Ethical Dimension

Why is it important for you to understand the ethical dimensions of working in business and using information technology? As a future managerial end user, it will be your responsibility to make decisions about business activities and the use of IT, which may have an ethical dimension that must be considered.

For example, should you electronically monitor your employees' work activities and electronic mail? Should you let employees use their work computers for private business or take home copies of software for their personal use? Should you electronically access your employees' personnel records or workstation files? Should you sell customer information extracted from transaction processing systems to other companies? These are a few examples of the types of decisions you will have to make that have a controversial ethical dimension. So let's take a closer look at ethical considerations in business and information technology.

Ethical Foundations

People may use **ethical philosophies** or hold *ethical values* that guide them in ethical decision making. For example, four basic ethical philosophies are: egoism, natural law, utilitarianism, and respect for persons [10]. Briefly, these alternative ethical philosophies are:

Egoism. What is best for a given individual is right.

Natural law. Humans should promote their own health and life, propagate, pursue knowledge of the world and God, pursue close relationships with other people, and submit to legitimate authority.

Utilitarianism. Those actions are right that produce the greatest good for the greatest number of people.

Respect for persons. People should be treated as an end and not as a means to an end; and actions are right if everyone adopts the moral rule presupposed by the action.

Ethical values are more specific ethical concepts that people hold, and are heavily influenced by one's cultural background. For example, Figure 12.14 lists several Western and non-Western values. Notice that these values converge to support three basic ethical values that are common across many cultures today [10].

There are many **ethical models** of how humans apply their chosen ethical philosophies to the decisions and choices they have to make daily in work and other areas of their lives. For example, one theory focuses on people's decision-making processes and stresses how various factors or our perceptions of them affect our ethical decision-making process. Figure 12.15 illustrates this model. Notice how individual attributes; personal, professional, and work environments; and governmental/legal and social environments may affect our decision processes and lead to ethical or unethical behavior.

Another example is a *behavioral stage theory*, which says that people go through several stages of moral evolution before they settle on one level of ethical reasoning. In this model, if you reach the final stage of moral evolution, your actions are guided by self-chosen ethical principles, not by fear, guilt, social pressure, and so on.

Business Ethics

Business ethics is concerned with the numerous ethical questions that managers must confront as part of their daily business decision making. For example, Figure 12.16

Figure 12.14	Non-Western	Western	Common Values
Western and non-Western values and how they converge to support three common ethical values.	• Kyosei (Japanese): Living and working together for the common good. • Dharma (Hindu): The fulfillment of inherited duty. • Santutthi (Buddhist): The importance of limited desires. • Zakat (Muslim): The duty to give alms to the Muslim poor.	• Individual liberty • Egalitarianism • Political participation • Human rights	• Respect for human dignity • Respect for basic rights • Good citizenship

Source: Adapted and reprinted by permission of *Harvard Business Review* from Thomas Donaldson, "Values in Tension: Ethics Away from Home," September–October 1996, p. 7. Copyright © 1996 by the President and Fellows of Harvard College; all rights reserved.

outlines some of the basic categories of ethical issues and specific business practices that have serious ethical consequences. Notice that the issues of employee privacy, security of company records, and workplace safety are highlighted because they have been major areas of ethical controversy in information technology.

How can managers make ethical decisions when confronted with business issues such as those listed in Figure 12.16? Several important alternatives based on theories of corporate social responsibility can be used [33, 34].

- **The stockholder theory** holds that managers are agents of the stockholders, and their only ethical responsibility is to increase the profits of the business without violating the law or engaging in fraudulent practices.

- **The social contract theory** states that companies have ethical responsibilities to all members of society, which allow corporations to exist based on a social contract. The first condition of the contract requires companies to enhance the economic satisfaction of consumers and employees. They must do that without polluting the environment or depleting natural resources, misusing political power, or subjecting their employees to dehumanizing working conditions. The second condition requires companies to avoid fraudulent practices, show respect for their employees as human beings, and avoid practices that systematically worsen the position of any group in society.

- **The stakeholder theory** maintains that managers have an ethical responsibility to manage a firm for the benefit of all its stakeholders, which are all individuals and groups that have a stake in or claim on a company. This usually includes the corporation's stockholders, employees, customers, suppliers, and the local community. Sometimes the term is broadened to include all groups who can affect or be affected by the corporation, such as competitors, government agencies, special interest groups, and the media. Balancing the claims of conflicting stakeholders is obviously not an easy task for managers.

Ethical and Societal Dimensions of IT

Figure 12.17 illustrates several important aspects of the ethical and societal dimensions of information technology. It emphasizes that the use of information technology in business has major impacts on society, and thus raises serious ethical considerations in areas such as privacy, crime, health, working conditions, individuality, employment,

Figure 12.15 . A model of ethical decision making. Note the factors that may affect our ethical decision-making process.

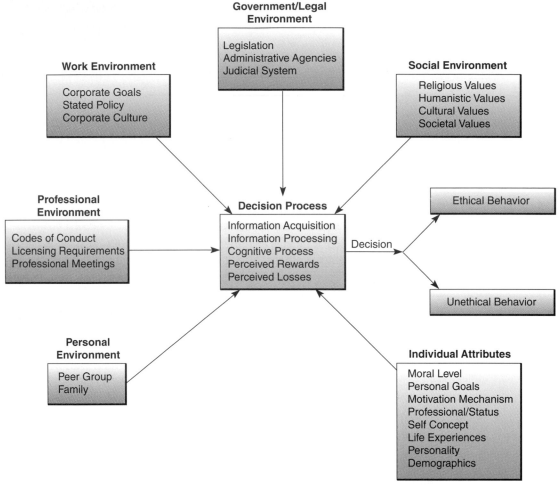

Source: Adapted from "A Behavioral Model of Ethical and Unethical Decision Making" by Michael Bonner, Clarence Grotto, Jerry Gravander, and Mark Tuttle, *Journal of Business Ethics*, June 1987, pp. 265–280. Reprinted by permission of Kluwer Academic Publishers.

and the search for societal solutions through IT. However, you should realize that information technology can have a beneficial effect as well as a negative effect in each of these areas. For example, computerizing a production process may have the adverse effect of eliminating jobs, and the beneficial effect of improving the working conditions and job satisfaction of employees that remain, while producing products of higher quality at less cost. So your job as a managerial end user should involve managing your work activities and those of others to try to minimize the negative effects of IT and maximize its beneficial effects. That would represent an ethically responsible use of information technology. Figure 12.18 lists four *ethical principles* that can serve as guidelines in the implementation of any form of technology [27].

IT and Employment

The impact of information technology on **employment** is a major ethical concern and is directly related to the use of computers to achieve automation. There can be no doubt that the use of information technology has created new jobs and increased

Figure 12.16

Basic categories of ethical business issues. Information technology has caused ethical controversy in the areas of employee privacy, security of company records, and workplace safety.

Equity	Rights	Honesty	Exercise of Corporate Power
Executive Salaries	Corporate Due Process	Employee Conflicts	Political Action Committees
Comparable Worth	Employee Health	of Interest	*Workplace Safety*
Product Pricing	Screening	*Security of Company*	Product Safety
	Employee Privacy	*Records*	Environmental Issues
	Sexual Harassment	Inappropriate Gifts	Disinvestment
	Affirmative Action	Advertising Content	Corporate Contributions
	Equal Employment	Government Contract	Social Issues Raised by
	Opportunity	Issues	Religious Organizations
	Shareholder Interests	Financial and Cash	Plant/Facility Closures and
	Employment at Will	Management Procedures	Downsizing
	Whistle-blowing	Questionable Business	
		Practices in Foreign	
		Countries	

Source: Adapted from The Conference Board, "Defending Corporate Ethics," in Peter Madsen and Jay Shafritz, *Essentials of Business Ethics* (New York: Meridian, 1990), p. 18.

productivity, while also causing a significant reduction in some types of job opportunities. Computers used for office information processing or for the numerical control of machine tools are accomplishing tasks formerly performed by many clerks and machinists. Also, jobs created by information technology within a computer-using organization require different types of skills and education than do the jobs eliminated by computers. Therefore, individuals may become unemployed unless they can be retained for new positions or new responsibilities.

Figure 12.17

Major aspects of the ethical and societal dimensions of information technology. Remember that IT can have both a positive and a negative effect on society in each of the areas shown.

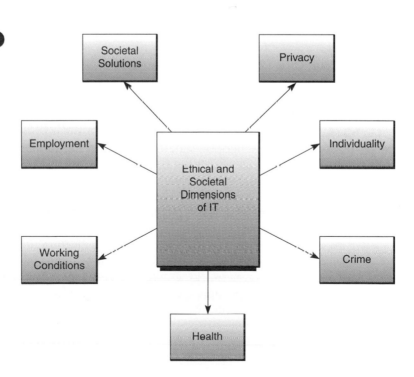

Figure 12.18

Ethical principles to help evaluate the potential harms or risks of the business use of IT.

- **Proportionality.** The good achieved by the technology must outweigh the harm or risk. Moreover, there must be no alternative that achieves the same or comparable benefits with less harm or risk.
- **Informed Consent.** Those affected by the technology should understand and accept the risks.
- **Justice.** The benefits and burdens of the technology should be distributed fairly. Those who benefit should bear their fair share of the risks, and those who do not benefit should not suffer a significant increase in risk.
- **Minimized Risk.** Even if judged acceptable by the other three guidelines, the technology must be implemented so as to avoid all unnecessary risk.

However, there can be no doubt that information technology has created a host of new job opportunities for the manufacture, sale, and maintenance of computer hardware and software, and for other information system services. Many new jobs, including Internet webmasters, systems analysts, computer programmers, and user consultants, have been created in computer-using organizations. New jobs have also been created in service industries that provide services to the computer industry and to computer-using firms. Additional jobs have been created because information technology makes possible the production of complex industrial and technical goods and services that would otherwise be impossible to produce. Thus, jobs have been created by activities that are heavily dependent on information technology, in such areas as space exploration, microelectronic technology, and scientific research.

IT and Individuality

A frequent criticism of information technology concerns its negative effect on the **individuality** of people. Computer-based systems are criticized as impersonal systems that dehumanize and depersonalize activities that have been computerized, since they eliminate the human relationships present in noncomputer systems. Although it is more efficient for an information system to deal with an individual as a number than as a name, many people feel a loss of identity when they seem to be "just another number."

Another aspect of the loss of individuality is the regimentation of the individual that seems to be required by some computer-based systems. These systems do not seem to possess any flexibility. They demand strict adherence to detailed procedures if the system is to work. The negative impact of IT on individuality is reinforced by horror stories that describe how inflexible and uncaring computer-based systems are when it comes to rectifying their own mistakes. Many of us are familiar with stories of how computerized customer billing and accounting systems continued to demand payment and send warning notices to a customer whose account has already been paid, despite repeated attempts by the customer to have the error corrected.

However, computer-based systems can be ergonomically engineered to accommodate **human factors** that minimize depersonalization and regimentation. People-oriented and user-friendly information systems can thus be developed. The computer hardware, software, networks, graphical user interface, and other IT capabilities that make such systems possible are increasing rather than decreasing. For example, the widespread use of personal computers and the Internet has dramatically improved the development of people-oriented end user and workgroup information systems. Even everyday products and services have been improved through microprocessor-powered "smart" products.

IT and Working Conditions

Information technology has eliminated monotonous or obnoxious tasks in the office and the factory that formerly had to be performed by people. For example, word processing and desktop publishing make producing office documents a lot easier to do, while robots have taken over repetitive welding and spray painting jobs in the automotive industry. In many instances, this allows people to concentrate on more challenging and interesting assignments, upgrades the skill level of the work to be performed, and creates challenging jobs requiring highly developed skills in the computer industry and within computer-using organizations. Thus, information technology can be said to upgrade the quality of work because it can upgrade the *quality of working* conditions and the content of work activities.

Of course, it must be remembered that some jobs created by information technology—data entry, for example—are quite repetitive and routine. Also, to the extent that computers are utilized in some types of automation, IT must take some responsibility for the criticism of assembly-line operations that require the continual repetition of elementary tasks, thus forcing a worker to work like a machine instead of like a skilled craftsperson. Many automated operations are also criticized for relegating people to a "do-nothing" standby role, where workers spend most of their time waiting for infrequent opportunities to push some buttons. Such effects do have a detrimental effect on the quality of work, but they must be compared to the less burdensome and more creative jobs created by information technology.

Computer Monitoring. One of the most explosive ethical issues concerning the quality of work is **computer monitoring.** That is, computers are being used to monitor the productivity and behavior of millions of employees while they work. Supposedly, computer monitoring is done so employers can collect productivity data about their employees to increase the efficiency and quality of service. However, computer monitoring has been criticized as unethical because it monitors individuals, not just work, and is done continually, thus violating workers' privacy and personal freedom. For example, when you call to make a reservation, an airline reservation agent may be timed on the exact number of seconds he or she took per caller, the time between calls, and the number and length of breaks taken. In addition, your conversation may also be monitored. See Figure 12.19.

Computer monitoring has been criticized as an invasion of the privacy of employees because, in many cases, they do not know that they are being monitored or don't know how the information is being used. Critics also say that an employee's right of due process may be harmed by the improper use of collected data to make personnel decisions. Since computer monitoring increases the stress on employees who must work under constant electronic surveillance, it has also been blamed for causing health problems among monitored workers. Finally, computer monitoring has been blamed for robbing workers of the dignity of their work. In effect, computer monitoring creates an "electronic sweatshop," where workers are forced to work at a hectic pace under poor working conditions.

Political pressure is building to outlaw or regulate computer monitoring in the workplace. For example, public advocacy groups, labor unions, and many legislators are pushing for action at the state and federal level in the United States. The proposed laws would regulate computer monitoring and protect the worker's right to know and right to privacy. In the meantime, lawsuits by monitored workers against employers are increasing. Jury awards to workers have been in the hundreds of thousands of dollars [11]. So computer monitoring of workers is one ethical issue that won't go away.

Figure 12.19

Computer monitoring can be used to record the productivity and behavior of people while they work.

Dennis Brack/Black Star.

Privacy Issues

Information technology makes it technically and economically feasible to collect, store, integrate, interchange, and retrieve data and information quickly and easily. This characteristic has an important beneficial effect on the efficiency and effectiveness of computer-based information systems. However, the power of information technology to store and retrieve information can have a negative effect on the **right to privacy** of every individual. For example, confidential E-mail messages by employees are monitored by many companies. Personal information is being collected about individuals every time they visit a site on the World Wide Web. Confidential information on individuals contained in centralized computer databases by credit bureaus, government agencies, and private business firms has been stolen or misused, resulting in the invasion of privacy, fraud, and other injustices. The unauthorized use of such information has seriously damaged the privacy of individuals. Errors in such databases could seriously hurt the credit standing or reputation of an individual.

Some of the important privacy issues being debated in business and government include the following [39]:

- Accessing individuals' private E-mail conversations and computer records, and collecting and sharing information about individuals gained from their visits to Internet web sites and newsgroups (violation of privacy).

- Always knowing where a person is, especially as mobile and paging services become more closely associated with people rather than places (computer monitoring).

- Using customer information to market additional business services (computer matching).

- Collecting telephone numbers and other personal information to build individual customer profiles (unauthorized personal files).

- Using automated equipment either to originate calls or to collect caller information (caller identification).

Privacy on the Internet

If you don't take the proper precautions, anytime you send an E-mail, access a web site, post a message to a newsgroup, or use the Internet for banking and shopping . . . whether you're online for business or pleasure, you're vulnerable to anyone bent on collecting data about you without your knowledge. Fortunately, by using tools like encryption and anonymous remailers—and by being selective about the sites you visit and the information you provide—you can minimize, if not completely eliminate, the risk of your privacy being violated [29].

The Internet is notorious for giving its users a feeling of anonymity, when in actuality, they are highly visible and open to violations of their privacy. Most of the Internet and its World Wide Web and newsgroups are still a wide open, unsecured electronic frontier, with no tough rules on what information is personal and private. Information about Internet users is captured legitimately and automatically each time you visit a web site or newsgroup and recorded as a "cookie file" on your hard disk. Then the web site owners, or online auditing services like WebTrack and Doubleclick, may sell the information from cookie files and other records of your Internet use to third parties. To make matters worse, much of the net and Web are easy targets for the interception or theft by hackers of private information furnished to web sites by Internet users [29].

Figure 12.20 outlines some key sources you can use to find out more on how your privacy can be violated, as well as protected, on the Internet and the Web. For example, sensitive E-mail can be protected by encryption, if both E-mail parties use compatible encryption software like PGP or RSA. Newsgroup postings can be made privately by sending them through *anonymous remailers* that protect your identity when you add your comments to a discussion. You can ask your Internet service provider not to sell your name and personal information to mailing list providers and other

---

Figure 12.20

Some of the sources for information about privacy on the Internet.

Internet Privacy Sources	
● **Center for Democracy and Technology** http://www.cdt.org	Internet censorship, privacy, cryptography, and federal legislation regarding the Internet are issues of CDT concern. Demo shows you info collected on you when you browse.
● **The Stalker's Home Page** http://pages.ripco.com:8080/~glr/stalk.html	Lots of Internet privacy resources, plus searchable databases.
● **Discreet Data** http://www.discreetdata.com	Check out just how much of your vital personal data is available to online sleuths.
● **The Replay Remailer** http://www.replay.com/remailer	Anonymous remailers like The Replay, which lets you shield your identity online, can protect you from newsgroup snoops and demographics-hungry marketing firms.

Source: Adapted from Jeffrey Rothfeder, "No Privacy on the Net," *PC World*, February 1997, pp. 228–29. Reprinted with permission of *PC World* Communications Inc.

marketers. Finally, you can decline to reveal personal data and interests on online service and web site user profiles to limit your exposure to electronic snooping [29].

Corporate E-Mail Privacy

Companies differ on their privacy policies, especially as they apply to their corporate electronic mail systems. For example, First Bancorporation of Ohio vows that it will never monitor the E-mail system used by its more than 1,000 employees. It views E-mail correspondence as private. However, Eastman Kodak's policy states that it retains the right to monitor employee E-mail on its networks. But the company says that it will exercise that right only if there is reason to suspect that an employee is involved in illegal or unauthorized activity. The Bank of Boston, on the other hand, has a written policy banning all use of computers for personal business, and warns employees that it will actively monitor E-mail on its computer networks to enforce that policy. To underscore its reasons, the bank revealed that it had discovered an employee running a gambling operation and handicapping dog races over its E-mail system [23, 30].

Computer Matching

Computer profiling and mistakes in the **computer matching** of personal data are other controversial threats to privacy. Individuals have been mistakenly arrested and jailed, and people have been denied credit because their physical profiles or personal data have been used by profiling software to match them incorrectly or improperly with the wrong individuals. Another threat is the unauthorized matching of computerized information about you extracted from the databases of sales transaction processing systems, and sold to information brokers or other companies. A more recent threat is the unauthorized matching and sale of information about you collected from Internet web sites and newsgroups you visit, as we discussed earlier. You are then subjected to a barrage of unsolicited promotional material and sales contacts as well as having your privacy violated [8, 30].

Privacy Laws

In the United States, the Federal Privacy Act strictly regulates the collection and use of personal data by governmental agencies (except for law enforcement investigative files, classified files, and civil service files). The law specifies that individuals have the right to inspect their personal records, make copies, and correct or remove erroneous or misleading information. It also specifies that federal agencies (1) must annually disclose the types of personal data files they maintain, (2) cannot disclose personal information on an individual to any other individual or agency except under certain strict conditions, (3) must inform individuals of the reasons for requesting personal information from them, (4) must retain personal data records only if it is "relevant and necessary to accomplish" an agency's legal purpose, and (5) must "establish appropriate administrative, technical, and physical safeguards to ensure the security and confidentiality of records" [32].

Other government **privacy laws** also attempt to enforce the privacy of computer-based files and communications. For example, in the United States, the Electronic Communications Privacy Act and the Computer Fraud and Abuse Act prohibit intercepting data communications messages, stealing or destroying data or trespassing in federal-related computer systems. Since the Internet includes federal-related computer systems, privacy attorneys argue that the laws also require notifying employees if a company intends to monitor Internet usage. Another example is the Computer Matching and Privacy Act, which regulates the matching of data held in federal agency files to verify eligibility for federal programs.

Computer Libel and Censorship

The opposite side of the privacy debate is the right of people to know about matters others may want to keep private (freedom of information), the right of people to express their opinions about such matters (freedom of speech), and the right of people

Figure 12.21

How to protect yourself from spam.

How to Fight Spam
1. Use E-mail filters to automatically dump messages with headers that contain hints of spam, such as "xxx," "make money," or "!!!"
2. Sort incoming E-mail into folders to make deleting spam easier.
3. Don't respond to spam, even if the author promises to remove you from the mailing list.
4. Use dual E-mail accounts—one for public surfing, one for key correspondence with colleagues and family.
5. Use spam blockers provided on America Online and CompuServe.
6. Don't fill in the "member's profile" on AOL. Spammers troll those for leads.
7. Don't fill in registration forms at web sites unless the purveyor promises not to sell or exchange your name and information.
8. Don't complain about spam in Usenet newsgroups or on mailing lists. Doing so wastes more resources.
9. Complain to legislators.
10. Don't counterspam the offender's mailbox. The reply address usually doesn't work.

Source: Adapted from Barb Cole-Gomolski, "Quick Fixes Are of Limited Use in Deterring Forced Diet of Spam," *Computerworld*, October 20, 1997, p. 6. Copyright 1997 by Computerworld, Inc., Framingham, MA 01701. Reprinted from *Computerworld*.

to publish those opinions (freedom of the press). Some of the biggest battlegrounds in the debate are the bulletin boards, E-mail boxes, and online files of the Internet and public information networks such as America Online and the Microsoft Network. The weapons being used in this battle include *spamming*, *flame mail*, libel laws, and censorship.

Spamming is the indiscriminate sending of unsolicited E-mail to many Internet users. Spamming is the favorite tactic of mass-mailers of unsolicited advertisements, or *junk E-mail*. Figure 12.21 outlines several ways that Internet users can protect themselves from spam, which is slowly being curbed by anti-spam legislation.

Flaming is the practice of sending extremely critical, derogatory, and often vulgar E-mail messages (*flame mail*), or electronic bulletin board postings to other users on the Internet or online services. Flaming is especially prevalent on some of the Internet's special-interest newsgroups. There have been several incidents of racist or defamatory messages that have led to calls for censorship and lawsuits for libel. In addition, the presence of sexually explicit photographs and text at many World Wide Web locations has triggered lawsuits and censorship actions by the institutions involved [28]. More recently, the Communications Decency Act of the U.S. Telecommunications Deregulation and Reform Bill of 1996 tried to ban the sending of "indecent" material over the Internet and online services, but was declared unconstitutional by the U.S. Supreme Court [37].

Computer Crime

Computer crime is the threat caused by the criminal or irresponsible actions of computer users who are taking advantage of the widespread use of computer networks in our society. It thus presents a major challenge to the ethical use of IT. Computer crime poses serious threats to the integrity, safety, and quality of most business information systems, and thus makes the development of effective security methods a top priority. See Figure 12.22

Figure 12.22

Types of computer crime. Note the many ways that computer systems and networks have been misused for criminal purposes.

Mode	Misuse Type
External	
1. Visual spying	Observing of keystrokes or screens
2. Misrepresentation	Deceiving operators and users
3. Physical scavenging	Dumpster-diving for printout
Hardware misuse	
4. Logical scavenging	Examining discarded/stolen media
5. Eavesdropping	Intercepting electronic or other data
6. Interference	Jamming, electronic or otherwise
7. Physical attack	Damaging or modifying equipment, power
8. Physical removal	Removing equipment and storage media
Masquerading	
9. Impersonation	Using false identities external to computer systems
10. Piggybacking attacks	Usurping communications lines, workstations
11. Spoofing attacks	Using playback, creating bogus nodes and systems
12. Network weaving	Masking physical whereabouts or routing
Pest programs	Setting up opportunities for further misuse
13. Trojan horse attacks	Implanting malicious code, sending letter bombs
14. Logic bombs	Setting time or event bombs (a form of Trojan horse)
15. Malevolent worms	Acquiring distributed resources
16. Virus attacks	Attaching to programs and replicating
Bypasses	Avoiding authentication and authority
17. Trapdoor attacks	Utilizing existing flaws
18. Authorization attacks	Password cracking, hacking tokens
Active misuse	Writing, using, with apparent authorization
19. Basic active misuse	Creating, modifying, using, denying service, entering false or misleading data
20. Incremental attacks	Using salami attacks
21. Denials of service	Perpetrating saturation attacks
Passive misuse	Reading, with apparent authorization
22. Browsing	Making random or selective searches
23. Inference, aggregation	Exploiting database inferences and traffic analysis
24. Covert channels	Exploiting covert channels or other data leakage
Inactive misuse	Willfully failing to perform expected duties, or committing errors of omission
Indirect misuse	Preparing for subsequent misuses, as in offline preencryptive matching, factoring large numbers to obtain private keys, autodialer scanning

Source: Adapted from Peter Neumann, *Computer-Related Risks* (New York: ACM Press), p. 231. Copyright © 1995, Association for Computing Machinery, Inc. By permission.

Computer Crime Laws

One way to understand computer crime is to see how current laws view such criminal offenses. A good example of this is the U.S. Computer Fraud and Abuse Act of 1986. In a nutshell, this law says that computer crime involves access of "federal interest" computers (used by the federal government), or operating in interstate or foreign commerce (1) with intent to defraud, (2) resulting in more than a $1,000 loss, or (3) to gain access to certain medical computer systems. Trafficking in computer access passwords is also prohibited. Penalties for violations of this law are severe. They include 1 to 5 years in prison for a first offense, 10 years for a second offense, and 20 years for three or more offenses. Fines could range up to $250,000 or twice the value of the stolen data [9].

The Association of Information Technology Professionals (AITP) has worked with federal and state agencies to develop computer crime laws. In its Model Computer Crime Act, the AITP defines computer crime as including (1) the unauthorized use, access, modification, and destruction of hardware, software, data, or network resources; (2) the unauthorized release of information; (3) the unauthorized copying of software; (4) denying an end user access to his or her own hardware, software, data, or network resources; and (5) using or conspiring to use computer resources to illegally obtain information or tangible property.

Examples of Computer Crime

Another way to understand computer crime is to examine examples of major types of criminal activity involving computers. Typically, this involves the theft of money, services, software, and data; destruction of data and software, especially by computer viruses; malicious access, or hacking on the Internet or other computer networks; and violations of privacy.

Crime on the Internet.

Widely publicized attacks by hackers on the Internet have splashed the open electronic playground with a dose of cold reality and sent newcomers scrambling to beef up network security plans. In recent years, as the Internet has changed from the casual chat line of the academic and research communities to the playground of the computationally hip, attacks have increased. The influx has created a new breed of intruder who uses sophisticated software programs designed to automatically probe the Internet looking for system weaknesses [3].

Someone breaks into computer systems at Rice University and steals files of thousands of passwords, changes passwords, and destroys several files. Someone takes over a student's account on a computer at Northern Arizona University and sends a racist E-mail message to over 15,000 Internet users worldwide. Someone breaks into computers at IBM, Sprint, and an Internet service provider and sends an electronic bomb of thousands of angry E-mail messages to *Wired* magazine and a pair of *Newsday* reporters, jamming their Internet mailbox and knocking them off the Net. Someone breaks into the heavily protected computer networks of General Electric, causing them to disconnect from the Internet for three days. Network security specialists at the Boeing Corporation notice that someone has hacked their way into the defense contractor's computer networks intent on stealing a vital list of Boeing passwords [1, 12, 29]. How can such incidents happen?

Hackers can monitor E-mail, web server access, or file transfers to extract passwords or steal network files, or to plant data that will cause a system to welcome intruders. A hacker may also use remote services that allow one computer on a network to execute programs on another computer to gain privileged access within a network. Telnet, a tool for interactive use of remote computers, can help a hacker discover information to plan other attacks. Hackers have used Telnet to access a computer's E-mail port, for example, to monitor E-mail messages for passwords and other information about privileged user accounts and network resources. These are just some of the typical types of computer crimes that hackers commit on the Internet on a regular basis. That's why Internet security measures like encryption and fire walls, as discussed in this chapter, are so vital to the success of electronic commerce and other business uses of the Internet.

Money Theft. Many computer crimes involve the theft of money. In many cases, they are "inside jobs" that involve fraudulent alternation of computer databases to cover the tracks of the employees involved. For example, in the famous Volkswagen AG case of 1987, a group of company executives altered computerized foreign exchange accounting files to hide their theft of almost $253 million. A lot of unsuccessful frauds have been reported, but many have been foiled more by accident than by vigilance. For example, in 1988, the Union Bank of Switzerland was automatically processing a money transfer of $54.1 million, when a computer failure caused a manual check of the transaction that revealed it was fraudulent [28].

More recent examples involve the use of the Internet: widely publicized was the theft of $11 million from Citibank in late 1994. Russian hacker Vladimir Levin and his accomplices in St. Petersburg used the Internet to electronically break into Citibank's mainframe systems in New York. They then succeeded in transferring the funds from several Citibank accounts to their own accounts at banks in Finland, Israel, and California [28].

Of course, the scope of such financial losses is much larger than the incidents reported. Most companies don't reveal that they have been targets or victims of computer crime. They fear scaring off customers and provoking complaints by shareholders. In fact, several British banks, including the Bank of London, paid hackers more than a half million dollars not to reveal information about electronic break-ins. The American Society for Industrial Security estimates that computer crime may be costing U.S. corporations as much as $63 billion a year [28].

Service Theft. The unauthorized use of computer systems and networks is called *service theft*. A common example is unauthorized use of company-owned computer networks by employees. This may range from doing private consulting or personal finances, or playing video games, to unauthorized use of the Internet on company networks. Network monitoring software, called *sniffers*, is frequently used to monitor network traffic to evaluate network capacity, as well as reveal evidence of improper use. See Figure 12.23.

For example, 98 employees at Pacific Northwest National Laboratory in Richland, Washington, were disciplined when audits of system usage revealed that they used lab computers on their own time to access pornographic sites on the Web. Pacific Northwest National Laboratory became suspicious that employees were abusing the Internet when the staff set up sniffers to measure Net traffic and found lots of hits going out

Figure 12.23

Using Internet monitoring software. This package shows you the top web sites accessed during an hour of monitoring.

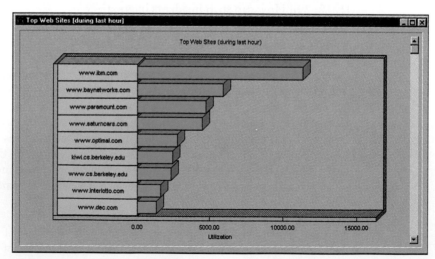

Courtesy of Optimal Network Corporation.

Figure 12.24

The hits made in one day to non-work-related web sites at an anonymous manufacturing company with 381 end users.

Use of Non-Work-Related Web Sites			
Uncategorized personal page	16,939	Personal pages	1,062
Sex	16,473	Fluff sites	466
Online sales	10,333	Gambling	322
Sports	6,657	Nonmainstream publications	315
Entertainment	4,182	Drugs	222
Dotted decimal domains (e.g., 198.68.36.46/adultsrus)	2,245	Lifestyle	113
		Games	104
Job search	1,583	Humor	48
Gross or indecent	1,291	Criminal skills	1

Source: Adapted from Patrick Dryden, "Users Go on Bandwidth Patrol," *Computerworld*, March 18, 1996, p. 61. Copyright 1996 by Computerworld, Inc., Framingham, MA 01701. Reprinted from *Computerworld*.

to *Playboy*, *Penthouse*, and other sites from the lab's network. Another similar incident occurred at Sandia National Labs in Albuquerque, New Mexico. Sixty-four employees, contractors, and college interns were disciplined for viewing Internet pornography on company time and their own time, using Sandia's computer networks [37]. See Figure 12.24.

Software Theft. Computer programs are valuable property and thus are the subject of theft from computer systems. However, unauthorized copying of software, or **software piracy,** is also a major form of software theft. Several major cases involving the unauthorized copying of software have been widely reported. These include lawsuits by the Software Publishers Association, an industry association of software developers, against major corporations that allowed unauthorized copying of their programs. Lotus Development Corporation and other software companies have also won lawsuits against competitors who marketed copies or clones that had the look and feel of their popular software packages.

Unauthorized copying is illegal because software is intellectual property that is protected by copyright law and user licensing agreements. For example, in the United States, commercial software packages are protected by the Computer Software Piracy and Counterfeiting Amendment to the Federal Copyright Act. In most cases, the purchase of a commercial software package is really a payment to license its fair use by an individual end user. Therefore, many companies sign *site licenses* that allow them to legally make a certain number of copies for use by their employees at a particular location. Other alternatives are *shareware*, which allows you to make copies of software for others, and *public domain software*, which is not copyrighted.

Data Alteration or Theft. Making illegal changes or stealing data is another form of computer crime. For example, an employee of the University of Southern California was convicted of taking payments from students and using the university's computer system to change their grades in return. Other reported schemes involved using computer networks to make changes in credit information, and changes in Department of Motor Vehicles' records that facilitated the theft of the cars to which the records referred. More recently, employees of the U.S. Social Security Administration were indicted for using the SAA's computer networks to obtain and sell confidential personal information to *information brokers.* Also indicted were Virginia state police and other officers who sold criminal histories from the National Crime Information Center network. Internet hacker Kevin Mitnick was convicted in 1996 of stealing thousands of credit card numbers and other business data from companies on the Internet [37].

Malicious Access. Hacking, in computerese, is the obsessive use of computers, or the unauthorized access and use of networked computer systems. Illegal hackers (also called *crackers*) may steal or damage data and programs. One of the issues in hacking is what to do about a hacker who commits only *electronic breaking and entering;* that is, gets access to a computer system, reads some files, but neither steals nor damages anything. This situation is common in computer crime cases that are prosecuted. In several states, courts have found that the typical computer crime statute language prohibiting malicious access to a computer system did apply to anyone gaining unauthorized access to another's computer networks [29].

Computer Viruses: Destruction of Data and Software. One of the most destructive examples of computer crime involves the creation of **computer viruses** or *worms.* Virus is the more popular term but, technically, a virus is a program code that cannot work without being inserted into another program. A worm is a distinct program that can run unaided. In either case, these programs copy annoying or destructive routines into the networked computer systems of anyone who accesses computers infected with the virus or who uses copies of magnetic disks taken from infected computers. Thus, a computer virus or worm can spread destruction among many users. Though they sometimes display only humorous messages, they more often destroy the contents of memory, hard disks, and other storage devices. Copy routines in the virus or worm spread the virus and destroy the data and software of many computer users. See Figure 12.25.

Computer viruses enter a computer system typically through illegal or borrowed copies of software, or through network links to other computer systems. Copies of software downloaded from electronic bulletin boards can be another source of viruses. A virus usually copies itself into the files of a computer's operating system. Then the virus spreads to main memory and copies itself onto the computer's hard disk and any inserted floppy disks. The virus spreads to other computers through telecommunications links or floppy disks from infected computers. Thus, as a good end user computing practice, you should avoid using software from questionable sources without checking for viruses. You should also regularly *use antivirus programs* that can help diagnose and remove computer viruses from infected files on your hard disk or in a network. See Figure 12.26.

Health Issues

The use of information technology in the workplace raises a variety of **health issues.** Heavy use of computers is reportedly causing health problems like job stress, damaged arm and neck muscles, eye strain, radiation exposure, and even death by computer-caused accidents. For example, computer monitoring is blamed as a major cause of computer-related job stress. Workers, unions, and government officials criticize computer monitoring as putting so much stress on employees that it leads to health problems [9, 11].

People who sit at PC workstations or visual display terminals (VDTs) in fast-paced, repetitive keystroke jobs can suffer a variety of health problems known collectively as

Figure 12.25

Facts about computer viruses.

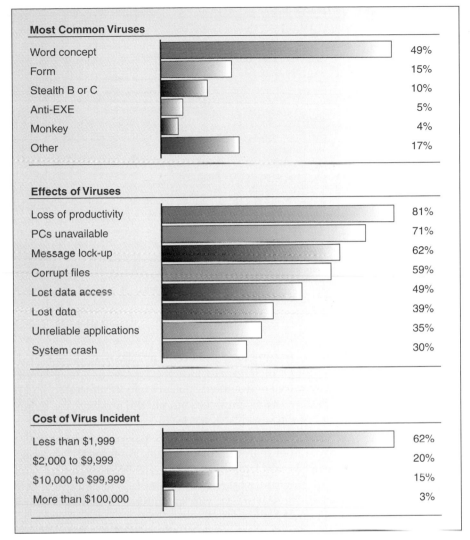

Most Common Viruses

Word concept	49%
Form	15%
Stealth B or C	10%
Anti-EXE	5%
Monkey	4%
Other	17%

Effects of Viruses

Loss of productivity	81%
PCs unavailable	71%
Message lock-up	62%
Corrupt files	59%
Lost data access	49%
Lost data	39%
Unreliable applications	35%
System crash	30%

Cost of Virus Incident

Less than $1,999	62%
$2,000 to $9,999	20%
$10,000 to $99,999	15%
More than $100,000	3%

Source: National Computer Security Association, Carlisle, PA, 1997.

cumulative trauma disorders (CTDs). Their fingers, wrists, arms, necks, and backs may become so weak and painful that they cannot work. Many times strained muscles, back pain, and nerve damage may result. In particular, some computer workers may suffer from *carpal tunnel syndrome*, a painful, crippling ailment of the hand and wrist that typically requires surgery to cure [21].

Prolonged viewing of video displays causes eyestrain and other health problems in employees who must do this all day. Radiation caused by the cathode ray tubes (CRTs) that produce most video displays is another health concern. CRTs produce an electromagnetic field that may cause harmful radiation of employees who work too close for too long in front of video monitors. Some pregnant workers have reported miscarriages and fetal deformities due to prolonged exposure to CRTs at work. However, several studies have failed to find conclusive evidence concerning this problem. Still, several organizations recommend that female workers minimize their use of CRTs during pregnancy [9, 11].

Figure 12.26

An example of the display from an antivirus program to eliminate computer viruses.

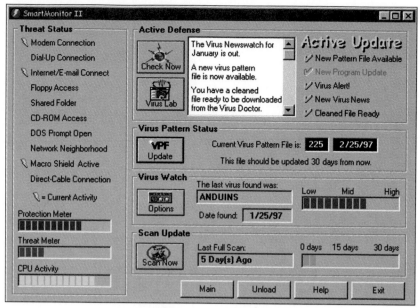

Courtesy of Touchstone Software.

Ergonomics

Solutions to some of these health problems are based on the science of **ergonomics,** sometimes called *human factors engineering*. The goal of ergonomics is to design healthy work environments that are safe, comfortable, and pleasant for people to work in, thus increasing employee morale and productivity. Ergonomics stresses the healthy design of the workplace, workstations, computers and other machines, and even software packages. Other health issues may require ergonomic solutions emphasizing job design, rather than workplace design. For example, this may require policies providing for work breaks from heavy VDT use every few hours, while limiting the CRT exposure of pregnant workers. Ergonomic job design can also provide more variety in job tasks for those workers who spend most of their workday at computer workstations. See Figure 12.27.

Societal Solutions

Before we conclude this section, it would be good to emphasize that information technology can have many beneficial effects on society. We can use information technology to solve human and social problems through **societal solutions** such as medical diagnosis, computer-assisted instruction, governmental program planning, environmental quality control, and law enforcement. For example, computers can help diagnose an illness, prescribe necessary treatment, and monitor the progress of hospital patients. Computer-assisted instruction (CAI) allows a computer to serve as tutor, since it uses conversational computing to tailor instructions to the needs of a particular student. This is a tremendous benefit to students, especially those with learning disabilities.

Information technology can be used for crime control through various law enforcement applications. For example, computerized alarm systems allow police to identify and respond quickly to evidences of criminal activity. Computers have been used to monitor the level of pollution in the air and in bodies of water, to detect the sources of pollution, and to issue early warnings when dangerous levels are reached. Computers are also used for the program planning of many government agencies in

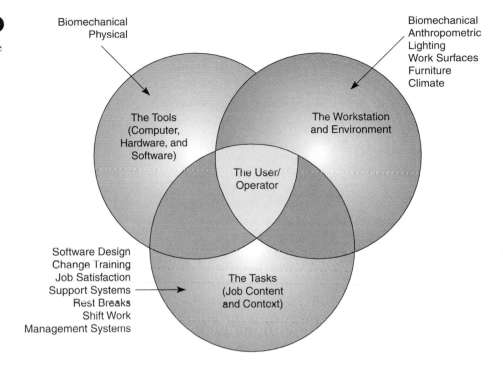

Figure 12.27

Ergonomic factors in the workplace. Note that good ergonomic design considers tools, tasks, the workstation, and environment.

Biomechanical
Physical

Biomechanical
Anthropometric
Lighting
Work Surfaces
Furniture
Climate

The Tools
(Computer,
Hardware, and
Software)

The Workstation
and Environment

The User/
Operator

Software Design
Change Training
Job Satisfaction
Support Systems
Rest Breaks
Shift Work
Management Systems

The Tasks
(Job Content
and Context)

such areas as urban planning, population density and land use studies, highway planning, and urban transit studies. Computers are being used in job placement systems to help match unemployed persons with available jobs. These and other applications illustrate that information technology can be used to help solve the problems of society.

You and Ethical Responsibility

As a business end user, you have a responsibility to promote ethical uses of information technology in the workplace. Whether you are a manager, end user, or IS professional, you should accept the ethical responsibilities that come with your work activities. That includes properly performing your role as a vital human resource in the computer-based information systems you help develop and use in your organization. In this section, we have outlined several ethical principles that can serve as the basis for ethical conduct by managers, end users, and IS professionals. But what more specific guidelines might help your ethical use of information technology?

One way to answer this question is to examine statements of responsibilities contained in codes of professional conduct for IS professionals. A good example is the code of professional conduct of the Association of Information Technology Professionals (AITP), an organization of professionals in the computing field. Its code of conduct outlines the ethical considerations inherent in the major responsibilities of an IS professional. Figure 12.28 is a portion of the AITP code of conduct.

End users and IS professionals would live up to their ethical responsibilities by voluntarily following such guidelines. For example, you can be a **responsible end user** by (1) acting with integrity, (2) increasing your professional competence, (3) setting high standards of personal performance, (4) accepting responsibility for your work, and (5) advancing the health, privacy, and general welfare of the public. Then you would be demonstrating ethical conduct, avoiding computer crime, and increasing the security of any information system you develop or use.

AITP Standards of Professional Conduct

In recognition of my obligation to my employer I shall:

- Avoid conflicts of interest and ensure that my employer is aware of any potential conflicts.
- Protect the privacy and confidentiality of all information entrusted to me.
- Not misrepresent or withhold information that is germane to the situation.
- Not attempt to use the resources of my employer for personal gain or for any purpose without proper approval.
- Not exploit the weakness of a computer system for personal gain or personal satisfaction.

In recognition of my obligation to society I shall:

- Use my skill and knowledge to inform the public in all areas of my expertise.
- To the best of my ability, ensure that the products of my work are used in a socially responsible way.
- Support, respect, and abide by the appropriate local, state, provincial, and federal laws.
- Never misrepresent or withhold information that is germane to a problem or a situation of public concern, nor will I allow any such known information to remain unchallenged.
- Not use knowledge of a confidential or personal nature in any unauthorized manner to achieve personal gain.

As a business end user, you should insist that the ethical and societal dimensions of information technology be considered when computer-based information systems are being developed and used. For example, a major design objective should be to develop systems that can be easily and effectively used by people. The objectives of the system must also include protection of the privacy of the individuals and the defense of the system against computer crime. The potential for misuse and malfunction of a proposed system must be analyzed and controlled to minimize such effects on its users. Thus, control hardware, software, and procedures must be included in the systems design.

It should be obvious to you that many of the detrimental effects of information technology are caused by individuals or organizations that are not accepting the ethical responsibility for their actions. Like other powerful technologies, information technology possesses the potential for great harm or great good for all humankind. If managers, end users, and IS professionals accept their ethical responsibilities, then information technology can help make this world a better place for all of us.

Summary

- **IS Security and Control.** One of the most important responsibilities of the management of computer-using business firms is to assure the security and quality of its information services activities. Controls are needed that ensure the accuracy, integrity, and safety of the information system activities and resources of the organization and its end users. Such controls attempt to minimize errors, fraud, and destruction, and can be grouped into three major categories: (1) information system controls, (2) procedural controls, and (3) facility controls, as summarized in Figures 12.3 and 12.4.

- **The Ethical Foundations of IT.** Business and IT activities involve many ethical considerations. Various ethical philosophies and models of ethical behavior may be used by people in forming ethical judgments.

These serve as a foundation for ethical principles and codes that can serve as guidelines for dealing with ethical business issues that may arise in the use of information technology.

- **Ethical and Societal Dimensions of IT.** The vital role of information technology in business and society raises serious ethical and societal issues in terms of the impact of IT on employment, individuality, working conditions, computer monitoring, privacy, computer matching, health, and computer crime. Managerial end users and IS professionals can help solve the problems of improper use of IT by assuming their ethical responsibilities for the ergonomic design, beneficial use, and enlightened management of information technology in our society.

Key Terms and Concepts

These are the key terms and concepts of this chapter. The page number of their first explanation is in parentheses.

1. Audit trail (481)
2. Auditing information systems (480)
3. Backup files (474)
4. Biometric controls (476)
5. Business ethics (484)
6. Computer crime (493)
   a. Examples (495)
   b. Laws (494)
7. Computer matching (492)
8. Computer monitoring (489)
9. Computer virus (498)
10. Control totals (471)
11. Controls for end user computing (479)
12. Disaster recovery (479)
13. Encryption (474)
14. Ergonomics (500)
15. Ethical and societal impacts of IT (485)
    a. Employment (486)
    b. Health (498)
    c. Individuality (488)
    d. Privacy (490)
    e. Societal solutions (500)
    f. Working conditions (489)
16. Ethical models (484)
17. Ethical philosophies (484)
18. Facility controls (474)
19. Fault tolerant (478)
20. Fire wall (475)
21. Flaming (493)
22. Hacking (498)
23. Human factors (488)
24. Information system controls (471)
25. Information system security (468)
26. Network security (474)
27. Passwords (473)
28. Privacy laws (492)
29. Procedural controls (478)
30. Responsible end user (501)
31. Security codes (473)
32. Software piracy (497)
33. Spamming (493)
34. System security monitor (474)

Review Quiz

Match one of the key terms and concepts listed previously with one of the brief examples or definitions that follow. Try to find the best fit for the answers that seem to fit more than one term or concept. Defend your choices.

_____ 1. Ensuring the accuracy, integrity, and safety of information system activities and resources.

_____ 2. Control totals, error signals, backup files, and security codes are examples.

_____ 3. Documentation and authorization requirements are examples.

_____ 4. Fire and access detection systems are examples.

_____ 5. Software that can control access and use of a computer system.

_____ 6. A computer system can continue to operate even after a major system failure if it has this capability.

_____ 7. A computer system that serves as a filter for access to and from other networks by a company's networked computers.

_____ 8. Periodically examine the accuracy and integrity of computer processing.

_____ 9. The presence of documentation that allows a transaction to be traced through all stages of information processing.

_____ 10. Managerial end users are responsible for information system controls in their business units.

_____ 11. Using your voice or fingerprints to identify you electronically.

_____ 12. A plan to continue IS operations during an emergency.

_____ 13. The sum of subtotals must equal a grand total.

_____ 14. Scrambling data during its transmission.

_____ 15. Passwords, user IDs, and account codes are examples.

_____ 16. Network fire walls and security monitors protect network resources.

_____ 17. Examples include egoism, natural law, utilitarianism, and respect for persons.

_____ 18. Ethical choices may result from decision-making processes, cultural values, or behavioral stages.

_____ 19. Managers must confront numerous ethical questions in their businesses.

_____ 20. Sending unsolicited E-mail indiscriminately.

_____ 21. Employees may have to retrain or transfer.

_____ 22. Computer-based systems may depersonalize human activities.

_____ 23. Constant long-term use of computers at work may cause health problems.

_____ 24. Personal information is in computer-accessible files.

_____ 25. Computer-based monitoring of environmental quality is an example.

_____ 26. Tedious jobs are decreased and jobs are made more challenging.

_____ 27. Using computers to identify individuals that fit a certain profile.

_____ 28. Regulate the collection, access, and use of personal data.

_____ 29. Using computers to monitor the activities of workers.

_____ 30. People need a variety of capabilities when operating computers.

_____ 31. Using computers to steal money, services, software, or data.

_____ 32. Legislation makes it illegal to access a computer with intent to defraud.

_____ 33. Unauthorized copying of software.

_____ 34. Electronic breaking and entering into a computer system.

_____ 35. A program makes copies of itself and destroys data and programs.

_____ 36. Sending extremely critical, derogatory, and vulgar E-mail messages.

_____ 37. Designing computer hardware, software, and workstations that are safe, comfortable, and easy to use.

_____ 38. End users should act with integrity and competence in their use of information technology.

Discussion Questions

1. What can be done to improve security on the Internet? Give examples of hardware, software, network, and other controls and security measures.

2. What potential security problems do you see in the increasing use of intranets and extranets in business? What might be done to solve such problems? Give several examples.

3. What artificial intelligence techniques can a business use to improve computer security and fight computer crime?

4. What controls are needed for improved security in end user computing? Give an example of three controls that could be used at your school or work.

5. What is disaster recovery? How could it be implemented at your school or work?

6. Refer to the Real World Case on BuyDirect and Others in the chapter. How could law enforcement officials help business fight credit card fraud in E-commerce?

7. Is there an ethical crisis in business today? What role does information technology play in unethical business practices?

8. What business decisions will you have to make as a manager that have both an ethical and IT dimension? Give several examples to illustrate your answer.

9. Refer to the Real World Case on Warroom Research and Sun-Trust Banks in the chapter. Do you feel that the PCs and networks you use are properly protected? Why or why not?

10. What would be examples of one positive and one negative effect of the use of information technology for each of the ethical and societal dimensions illustrated in Figure 12.17? Explain several of your choices.

Real World Problems

1. **Wal-Mart versus Amazon.com: Ethical Issues in E-Commerce Competition**

Wal-Mart is the 800-pound gorilla in the $1.7 trillion U.S. retail universe, breaking $130 billion in sales in 1998, and opening hundreds of new outlets around the world in 1999. "We want to dominate North America first," proclaims CEO David Glass, "then South America and then Asia and then Europe."

Strange as it might seem, you won't find much cheering in the executive offices in Bentonville, Arkansas, these days, even amid talk of global domination. For months, a quiet but portentous battle over theft of trade secrets—with potentially huge ramifications for the future of online commerce—was brewing between the offline megastore and its would-be Internet counterpart: the swift and wiry 80-pound gorilla of online retail, Amazon.com.

In October 1998, the cannon finally fired on the flea: Wal-Mart filed a long-awaited lawsuit against Amazon accusing it of conspiring to hire away key Wal-Mart information systems personnel and to replicate its logistics and data warehousing systems—all key ingredients in the company's long-term success. Between August 1997 and July 1998, more than a dozen of Wal-Mart's key information systems personnel—beginning with CIO Richard Dalzell (who left to become Amazon's CIO) and ending with logistics exec Jimmy Wright (who became Amazon's first chief logistics officer in July 1998)—flew the corporate coop in Bentonville. They took new jobs at either Seattle-based Amazon or Redmond, Washington–based DrugStore.com, the budding Net retailer that hopes to sell over-the-counter and prescription drugs online. It's backed by Amazon's venture-capital big brother, Kleiner Perkins Caufield & Byers.

"Why else is a Seattle company coming to Arkansas to recruit?" asked Wal-Mart spokesperson Mike Maher. "They hired away 15 of our employees who have very specific knowledge of what we have. If they haven't already started doing it, it's inevitable they will re-create our proprietary system."

So what might Amazon have wanted so badly from the Wal-Mart brains to help launch it into the next generation of online retail? Consider that the world's biggest store is also the ringleader of information technology in the retail industry. Wal-Mart's 25-terabyte database is second only to the U.S. government's. The company has pioneered virtually every modern high-tech retailing technique—including bar code scanners, point-of-sale systems, data warehousing, and just-in-time delivery. At Wal-Mart, Dalzell presided over an IT group that helped it slash $1.4

billion from inventory costs during 1997. More recently, the company continues to mine its massive database, analyzing sales from all of its stores down to the contents of each shopping cart. Managing these logistical challenges, especially for such a large conventional retailer, is expensive; Wal-Mart spends $500 million annually on IT alone—the equivalent of Amazon's total projected revenues for 1998.

And logistics is exactly where Amazon needs help. "The E-commerce market is now very much about mastering the distribution and fulfillment process," says Kate Delhagen, Forrester Research's director of online retail analysis. "It's also about acquiring a customer database, beefing that up, and extracting maximum revenue from it. . . . But as Amazon has grown, CEO Jeff Bezos has realized that this is just as much about mastering the logistics and the distribution challenges."

Such as? The clunky tasks inextricably tied to the physical world: shipping, handling, returns, payment processing, avoiding credit card fraud, and inventory management. Enter Wal-Mart, its renowned back-end expertise—and, eventually, a lawsuit.

a. Do you think that Amazon's hiring of Wal-Mart IS employees is an ethical business/IT practice? Why or why not?

b. How should the dispute between Wal-Mart and Amazon.com be settled? Explain your reasoning.

Source: Adapted from Jeffrey Davis, "Mall Rats," *Business 2.0*, January 1999, pp. 40–50.

2. Happy99, Melissa, and Kelly Services: E-Mail Viruses and Antivirus Software

Computer viruses continue to be a major threat to business computers and networks, and their presence in E-mail traffic is a growing menace, say security experts. Let's look at a few examples and see how one company protects itself from the threat of E-mail viruses.

Happy99.exe

The Happy99.exe virus or worm started making its way around the Internet early in 1999, sending hundreds of copies of itself via E-mail attachments and newsgroup postings. According to Helsinki, Finland, data security firm Data Fellows Inc., the worm does not attempt to destroy files on infected machines, but it sends E-mails and newsgroup postings without the victim's knowledge and can cause network slowdowns or even crash corporate E-mail servers.

The worm, so designated because it can replicate on its own, arrives as an E-mail or newsgroup attachment and infects only users who run the attachment. Once they do, all victims see is a window with a fireworks display. But behind the scenes, the worm alters the host computer's windsock32.dll file, the computer's doorway to the Internet. Then, each time a user initiates E-mail or newsgroup activity, by either receiving or sending E-mail or posting to a newsgroup, Happy99 spams the newsgroup or E-mail recipient with copies of itself.

Melissa

If you receive an E-mail with the subject line "Important message from . . . ," be suspicious. If that message comes with a Word document attached called "List.Doc," you've likely been sent the Word/Melissa macro virus or worm. And if you open the document, it will send copies of itself to 50 E-mail addresses it gleans from your personal E-mail file. That gives it the ability to propagate very quickly—much quicker than the Happy99.exe worm, according to virus experts.

The document itself contains a list of 73 pornographic web sites, along with user names and passwords for those sites. The virus can allow documents to be E-mailed to other people without warning, a potential security breach that should worry businesses and governments. About 60,000 users were infected at the company that made the first complaint, said Srivhes Sampath, general manager of McAfee Online. "It pretty much brings mail systems to a halt. . . . We've never seen anything spread like this."

Kelly Services, Inc.

Employment agency Kelly Services, Inc., is using server-based virus filtering technology to crush E-mail bugs—and has found some early success. Kelly has about 5,000 employees. About 60 percent of the company uses Lotus Notes for E-mail and about 40 percent use browser-based E-mail.

When Kelly adopted Lotus Notes, many users gained their first access to external E-mail. As the system was rolled out, the number of E-mail messages grew exponentially, "which gave us greater exposure to newer strains of viruses," said Mike Littleton, a network systems engineer and leader of Kelly Services' antivirus project—a team dedicated to tracking E-mail bugs. In 1999 Kelly transmitted 500,000 to 1 million messages per month globally, he said.

Late in 1997, the company noticed it had contracted "Imposter E," a Word macro virus, and tried to fight it off desktop-by-desktop. But by July of 1998, the number of virus alerts had increased significantly.

So Kelly adopted Trend Micro's server-based ScanMail antivirus software. With ScanMail, PCs can be monitored from a central location and software/virus pattern updates can be done automatically. The server-based antivirus software lets software administrators track alerts back to an individual user so they can isolate virus hot spots. And because Kelly can configure every workstation in one shot, that guarantees antivirus consistency. Since Kelly deployed Scan-Mail, the company has had fewer virus alerts than ever before, Littleton said.

a. What damage is caused to business users and networks by E-mail viruses like Happy99.exe and Melissa?

b. How should a business and its users protect their PCs and networks from computer viruses?

Source: Adapted from Roberta Fusaro, "Kelly Fights E-Mail Bugs at Server," Computerworld, February 15, 1999, p. 66, Copyright 1999 by Computerworld, Inc., Framingham, MA 01701. Reprinted from Computerworld.; and Bob Sullivan, "Happy99.exe Worm Spreads Quickly," and "Melissa Macro Worms around Web," at www.msnbc.com/news, March 27, 1999.

3. Rima Berzin and Excite: Privacy Trade-offs in E-Commerce

Rima Berzin recently inherited a laptop computer from her husband and began an intense two-day honeymoon with the Internet. She went all the way; buying jeans at Gap, browsing for books at Barnesandnoble.com, and registering for Martha Stewart's online journal. While Berzin was shopping, something un-Martha happened: Her spree left muddy digital footprints all over the Net.

Berzin, a Manhattan mother of two, is like a lot of other people just stepping onto the Web. When a friend told her how much personal information she had swapped for the convenience of home shopping, she was angry at first, then confused. On Berzin's first visit to Gap, hidden files called "cookies" were deposited on her computer. Other software whirred into action to track and analyze her online behavior. Marketers didn't know her name at first, but the anonymity evaporated when Berzin made her first purchase. "You can say no to being tracked," says the former strategic planning executive, "but it takes a great deal of work, and sometimes it pays to say yes."

No one hacked Berzin's credit card or stole her identity. The apprehensions that engulfed Berzin are more far-reaching than fear of theft and resonate across society. Personal details are acquiring enormous financial value. They are the new currency of the digital economy. Indeed, a $50 billion freight train called electronic commerce is bearing down on Berzin and millions of consumers now venturing forth on the Net. That train is powered by an insatiable need for personal information—details about what individuals do online that help businesses zero in on customers.

E-commerce, more than conventional business, needs this personal connection for several reasons.

Despite their lofty stock valuations, web-based businesses with little or no earnings can't afford to constantly solicit new customers. They need repeat business.

At Excite Inc., for example, customers who exchange tidbits about themselves in return for a personalized experience—in the form of selected news, movie listings, or local weather—return to the site roughly 20 times more often than those who don't, says Joe Kraus, Excite's co-founder and senior vice president. Armed with loyal customers, Excite can then pile on additional services and boost its income. It can offer advertisers banner ads and "pop-ups" aimed only at the customers deemed most likely to respond.

However, many E-consumers are starting to understand that what companies discover can hurt them. First comes the nuisance: a blizzard of junk mail. Then come the real dangers: Companies on the Web that know consumers' shopping habits and history can engage in sophisticated kinds of discrimination. If a business finds out that you, for example, are not a big spender, it may leave you dangling on help lines, refuse to notify you of juicy deals and discounts, or cut you off as a customer. And you won't even known you've been a victim.

Then there's the danger that the discrimination could be based on information that is false or out of date. "There hasn't been a data system built yet that is not fraught with inaccuracy," warns privacy activist Robert Ellis Smith. Even when information is correct, it may be damaging—and none of anyone's business.

As companies race to collect personal data and exploit them, consumers are being confronted with urgent trade-offs and choices about how to cover their tracks in cyberspace—or whether they should. If they decide not to hide, how should they be compensated for the information they reveal? Businesses also face arduous trade-offs. Rightly, they fear a backlash over breaches of privacy. Cries for regulation have already begun. If consumers like Berzin opt to conceal themselves or bolt from the Net or bind it in new laws, E-commerce could choke in its infancy.

a. Is it an ethical business/IT practice for companies on the Web to collect information about you and your web activities? Why or why not?

b. What should companies and individuals do to settle this privacy issue?

Source: Reprinted from Edward Baig, Marcia Stepanek, and Neil Gross, "Privacy," Business Week, April 5, 1999, pp. 84–90, by special permission, copyright © 1999 by The McGraw Hill Companies, Inc.

Application Exercises

1. Computer Ethics:
Abusing Internet Access in the Workplace
Employers who give Internet access to their staffs are sending out a message: Look at porn, lose a paycheck.

Faced with international controversies over pornography and hate speech on the Internet, employers are setting policies to limit Internet usage to business purposes. They also are penalizing employees who send out abusive electronic mail, "flame" people on Usenet, or visit inappropriate sites on the World Wide Web. And they are cautioning employees to remember that out on the Net, they represent their companies, not just themselves.

For most companies, an Internet usage policy is straightforward. It generally informs employees that their Internet access is a company resource that should be used only for their jobs.

"3M's policy is simply put: that the Web must be used for business purposes. If people get on and abuse it, then you've got a problem with that individual and need to handle it," said Luke Crofoot, a marketing services supervisor at 3M in St. Paul, Minnesota. Crofoot said he opposes draconian measures to control Internet use. "What really gets under my skin is the people who want to censor the world and place on me the burden of creating the infrastructure of what should and should not be censored," he said. Trying to control employee use of the Internet is nonproductive, he added. It is better to educate people about how to use the Internet and accept that at first they will spend a lot of time online looking up non-business-related content, Crofoot said.

That approach may work for companies that give employees a lot of independence, said Barry Weiss, a partner at Gordon & Glickson, a Chicago law firm that specializes in information technology legal issues. But for firms that want more control over their employees, the best solution is to develop detailed Internet usage policies, he added. Companies that have detailed Internet usage policies in place or are developing them include the Chase Manhattan Bank NA; Johnson Controls, Inc.; Pioneer Hi-Bred International Inc.; and Monsanto Co.

But some attorneys take a tougher stance. "Employees are under the misapprehension that the First Amendment applies in the workplace—it doesn't," said Neal J. Friedman, a Washington attorney who specializes in online law. "Employees need to know they have no right of privacy and no right of free speech using company resources."

a. How are some employees abusing the online access provided by their companies?
b. What should companies do to curb such abuses of their computing resources?
c. Do you agree with Neal Friedman that "employees . . . have no right of privacy and no right of free speech using company resources"? Why or why not?

Source: Adapted from Mitch Wagner, "Firms Spell Out Appropriate Use of Internet for Employees," *Computerworld*, February 5, 1996, pp. 56–58. Copyright 1996 by Computerworld, Inc., Framingham, MA 01701. Reprinted from *Computerworld*.

2. Your Internet Job Rights: Three Ethical Scenarios
Whether you're an employer or an employee, you should know what your rights are when it comes to Internet use in the workplace. Mark Grossman, a Florida attorney who specializes in computer and Internet law, gives answers to some basic questions.

Scenario 1
Nobody told you that your Internet use in the office was being monitored. Now you've been warned you'll be fired if you use the Internet for recreational surfing again. What are your rights?

Bottom line. When you're using your office computer, you have virtually no rights. You'd have a tough time convincing a court that the boss invaded your privacy by monitoring your use of the company PC on company time. You should probably be grateful you got a warning.

Scenario 2
Your employees are abusing their Internet privileges, but you don't have an Internet usage policy. What do you do?

Bottom line. Although the law isn't fully developed in this area, courts are taking a straightforward approach: If it's a company computer, the company can control the way it's used. You don't need an Internet usage policy to prevent inappropriate use of your company computers. To protect yourself in the future, distribute an Internet policy to your employees as soon as possible.

Scenario 3
Employee John Doe downloads adult material to his PC at work, and employee Jane Smith sees it. Smith then proceeds to sue the company for sexual harassment. As the employer, are you liable?

Bottom line. Whether it comes from the Internet or from a magazine, adult material simply has no place in the office. So Smith could certainly sue the company for making her work in a sexually hostile environment. The best defense is for the company to have an Internet usage policy that prohibits visits to adult sites. (Of course, you have to follow through. If someone is looking at adult material in the office, you must at least send the offending employee a written reprimand.) If the company lacks a strict Internet policy, though, Smith could prevail in court.

Ethical Questions

a. Do you agree with the advice of attorney Mark Grossman in each of the scenarios? Why or why not?

b. What would your advice be? Explain your positions.

c. Identify any ethical philosophies, values, or models you may be using in explaining your position in each of the scenarios.

Source: Adapted from James Martin. "You Are Being Watched," *PC World*, November 1997, p. 258. Reprinted with the permission of *PC World* Communications Inc.

Review Quiz Answers

1. 25	7. 20	13. 10	19. 5	24. 15d	29. 8	34. 22
2. 24	8. 2	14. 13	20. 33	25. 15e	30. 23	35. 9
3. 29	9. 1	15. 31	21. 15a	26. 15f	31. 6	36. 21
4. 18	10. 11	16. 26	22. 15c	27. 7	32. 6b	37. 14
5. 34	11. 4	17. 17	23. 15b	28. 28	33. 32	38. 30
6. 19	12. 12	18. 16				

Selected References

1. Anthes, Gary. "Internet Hackers Hit GE, Others." *Computerworld*, December 5, 1994.

2. Anthes, Gary. "Lotsa Talk, Little Walk." In "Managing." *Computerworld*, September 21, 1998.

3. Anthes, Gary, and James Daly. "Internet Users Batten Down Hatches." *Computerworld*, February 7, 1994.

4. Bahar, Richard. "Who's Reading Your E-Mail?" *Fortune*, February 3, 1997.

5. Bloom, Paul; Robert Adler; and George Milne. "Identifying the Legal and Ethical Risks and Costs of Using New Information Technologies to Support Marketing Programs." In *The Marketing Information Revolution*, ed. Robert C. Blattberg, Rashi Glazer, and John D. C. Little. Boston: Harvard Business School Press, 1994.

6. Cheswick, William, and Steven Bellovin. "In Depth: Repelling the Wily Hacker." *Computerworld*, May 16, 1994.

7. Cole-Gomolski. "Quick Fixes Are of Limited Use in Deterring Force Diet of Spam." *Computerworld*, October 20, 1997.

8. Culnane, Mary. "How Did They Get My Name? An Exploratory Investigation of Consumer Attitudes toward Secondary Information Use." *MIS Quarterly*, September 1993.

9. Dejoie, Roy; George Fowler; and David Paradice, eds. *Ethical Issues in Information Systems*. Boston: boyd & fraser, 1991.

10. Donaldson, Thomas. "Values in Tension: Ethics Away from Home." *Harvard Business Review*, September–October 1996.

11. Dunlop, Charles, and Rob Kling, eds. *Computerization and Controversy: Value Conflicts and Social Choices*. San Diego: Academic Press, 1991.

12. Elmer-DeWitt, Phillip. "Terror on the Internet." *Time*, December 12, 1994.

13. Freeman, Edward. "When Technology and Privacy Collide: Encoded Encryption and the Clipper Chip." *Information Systems Management*, Spring 1995.

14. Fried, Louis. "Information Security and New Technology." *Information Systems Management*, Summer 1994.

15. Galbraith, Craig, and Gregory Merrill. "The Politics of Forecasting: Managing the Truth," *California Management Review*, Winter 1996.

16. Ganesan, Ravi, and Ravi Sandhu, guest editors. "Security in Cyberspace." Special Section, *Communications of the ACM*, November 1994.

17. Harrington, Susan. "What Corporate America Is Teaching about Ethics." *Academy of Management Executive* 5, no. 1 (1991).

18. Johnson, Deborah. "Ethics Online." *Communications of the ACM*, January 1997.

19. Kalakota, Ravi, and Andrew Whinston. *Electronic Commerce: A Manager's Guide.* Reading, MA: Addison-Wesley, 1997.

20. Kallman, Earnest, and John Grillo. *Ethical Decision Making and Information Technology: An Introduction with Cases.* New York: Mitchel McGraw-Hill, 1993.

21. Keppler, Kay. "A New Kind of Cutting Edge." *AI Expert*, February 1995.

22. Knouse, Stephen, and Robert Giacalone. "Ethical Decision Making in Business," *Journal of Business Ethics*, May 1992.

23. LaPlante, Alice. "Net Cops." *Computerworld*, March 11, 1996.

24. Liebman, Lenny. "Are Intranets Safe?" *Communications Week*, August 5, 1996.

25. Madsen, Peter, and Jay Shafritz, eds. *Essentials of Business Ethics.* New York: Meridian, 1990.

26. Martin, James. "You Are Being Watched." *PC World*, November 1997.

27. McFarland, Michael. "Ethics and the Safety of Computer Systems." *Computer*, February 1991.

28. Neumann, Peter. *Computer-Related Risks.* New York: ACM Press, 1995.

29. Rothfeder, Jeffrey. "Hacked! Are Your Company Files Safe?" *PC World*, November 1996.

30. Rothfeder, Jeffrey. "No Privacy on the Net." *PC World*, February 1997.

31. Schuler, Doug, guest editor. "Social Computing." Special Section, *Communications of the ACM*, January 1994.

32. Slater, Derek. "Cyberspace and the Law." *Computerworld*, December 5, 1994.

33. Smith, H. Jefferson, and John Hasnas. "Debating the Stakeholder Theory." *Beyond Computing*, March–April 1994.

34. Smith, H. Jefferson, and John Hasnas. "Establishing an Ethical Framework," *Beyond Computing*, January–February 1994.

35. Stark, Andrew. "What's the Matter with Business Ethics?" *Harvard Business Review*, May–June 1993.

36. Tate, Priscilla. "Internet Security: Can Best Practices Overcome Worst Perils?" White Paper. *Computerworld*, May 4, 1998.

37. Wagner, Mitch. "Firms Spell Out Appropriate Use of Internet for Employees." *Computerworld*, February 5, 1996.

38. Willard, Nancy. *The Cyberethics Reader.* Burr Ridge, IL: Irwin/McGraw-Hill, 1997.

39. Wolinsky, Carol, and James Sylvester. "From Washington: Privacy in the Telecom Age." *Communications of the ACM*, February 1992.

40. Zahedi, Fatemeh. *Quality of Information Systems.* Danvers, MA: boyd & fraser, 1995.

Accounting Information Systems
Information systems that record and report business transactions, the flow of funds through an organization, and produce financial statements. This provides information for the planning and control of business operations, as well as for legal and historical record-keeping.

Active Data Dictionary
A data dictionary that automatically enforces standard data element definitions whenever end users and application programs use a DBMS to access an organization's databases.

Ad Hoc Inquiries
Unique, unscheduled, situation-specific information requests.

Ada
A programming language named after Augusta Ada Byron, considered the world's first computer programmer. Developed for the U.S. Department of Defense as a standard high-order language.

Agile Competition
The ability of a company to profitably operate in a competitive environment of continual and unpredictable changes in customer preferences, market conditions, and business opportunities.

Algorithm
A set of well-defined rules or processes for the solution of a problem in a finite number of steps.

Analog Computer
A computer that operates on data by measuring changes in continuous physical variables such as voltage, resistance, and rotation. Contrast with Digital Computer.

Analytical Database
A database of data extracted from operational and external databases to provide data tailored to online analytical processing, decision support, and executive information systems.

Analytical Modeling
Interactive use of computer-based mathematical models to explore decision alternatives using what-if analysis, sensitivity analysis, goal-seeking analysis, and optimization analysis.

Applet
A small limited-purpose application program, or small independent module of a larger application program.

Application Development
See Systems Development.

Application Generator
A software package that supports the development of an application through an interactive terminal dialogue, where the programmer/analyst defines screens, reports, computations, and data structures.

Application Portfolio
A planning tool used to evaluate present and proposed information systems applications in terms of the amount of revenue or assets invested in information systems that support major business functions.

Application Software
Programs that specify the information processing activities required for the completion of specific tasks of computer users. Examples are electronic spreadsheet and word processing programs or inventory or payroll programs.

Application-Specific Programs
Application software packages that support specific applications of end users in business, science and engineering, and other areas.

Arithmetic-Logic Unit (ALU)
The unit of a computing system containing the circuits that perform arithmetic and logical operations.

Artificial Intelligence (AI)
A science and technology whose goal is to develop computers that can think, as well as see, hear, walk, talk, and feel. A major thrust is the development of computer functions normally associated with human intelligence, for example, reasoning, inference, learning, and problem solving.

ASCII: American Standard Code for Information Interchange
A standard code used for information interchange among data processing systems, communication systems, and associated equipment.

Assembler
A computer program that translates an assembler language into machine language.

Assembler Language
A programming language that utilizes symbols to represent operation codes and storage locations.

Asynchronous
Involving a sequence of operations without a regular or predictable time relationship. Thus operations do not happen at regular timed intervals, but an operation will begin only after a

previous operation is completed. In data transmission, involves the use of start and stop bits with each character to indicate the beginning and end of the character being transmitted. Contrast with Synchronous.

Audit Trail
The presence of media and procedures that allow a transaction to be traced through all stages of information processing, beginning with its appearance on a source document and ending with its transformation into information on a final output document.

Automated Teller Machine (ATM)
A special-purpose transaction terminal used to provide remote banking services.

Automation
The automatic transfer and positioning of work by machines or the automatic operation and control of a work process by machines, that is, without significant human intervention or operation.

Back-End Processor
Typically, a smaller general-purpose computer that is dedicated to database processing using a database management system (DBMS). Also called a database machine.

Background Processing
The automatic execution of lower-priority computer programs when higher-priority programs are not using the resources of the computer system. Contrast with Foreground Processing.

Backward-Chaining
An inference process that justifies a proposed conclusion by determining if it will result when rules are applied to the facts in a given situation.

Bandwidth
The frequency range of a telecommunications channel, which determines its maximum transmission rate. The speed and capacity of transmission rates are typically measured in bits per second (BPS). Bandwidth is a function of the telecommunications hardware, software, and media used by the telecommunications channel.

Bar Codes
Vertical marks or bars placed on merchandise tags or packaging that can be sensed and read by optical character-reading devices. The width

and combination of vertical lines are used to represent data.

Barriers to Entry
Technological, financial, or legal requirements that deter firms from entering an industry.

BASIC: Beginner's All-Purpose Symbolic Instruction Code
A programming language developed at Dartmouth College that is popular for microcomputer and time-sharing systems.

Batch Processing
A category of data processing in which data are accumulated into batches and processed periodically. Contrast with Realtime Processing.

Baud
A unit of measurement used to specify data transmission speeds. It is a unit of signaling speed equal to the number of discrete conditions or signal events per second. In many data communications applications it represents one bit per second.

Binary
Pertaining to a characteristic or property involving a selection, choice, or condition in which there are two possibilities, or pertaining to the number system that utilizes a base of 2.

Biometric Controls
Computer-based security methods that measure physical traits and characteristics such as fingerprints, voice prints, retina scans, and so on.

Bit
A contraction of "binary digit." It can have the value of either 0 or 1.

Block
A grouping of contiguous data records or other data elements that are handled as a unit.

Branch
A transfer of control from one instruction to another in a computer program that is not part of the normal sequential execution of the instructions of the program.

Browser
See Web Browser.

Buffer
Temporary storage used to compensate for a difference in rate of flow of data or time of occurrence of events, when transmitting data from one device to another.

Bug
A mistake or malfunction.

Bulletin Board System (BBS)
A service of online computer networks in which electronic messages, data files, or programs can be stored for other subscribers to read or copy.

Bundling
The inclusion of software, maintenance, training, and other products or services in the price of a computer system.

Bus
A set of conducting paths for movement of data and instructions that interconnects the various components of the CPU.

Business Ethics
An area of philosophy concerned with developing ethical principles and promoting ethical behavior and practices in the accomplishment of business tasks and decision making.

Business Information System
Information systems within a business organization that support one of the traditional functions of business such as marketing, finance, or production. Business information systems can be either operations or management information systems.

Business Process Reengineering (BPR)
Restructuring and transforming a business process by a fundamental rethinking and redesign to achieve dramatic improvements in cost, quality, speed, and so on.

Byte
A sequence of adjacent binary digits operated on as a unit and usually shorter than a computer word. In many computer systems, a byte is a grouping of eight bits that can represent one alphabetic or special character or can be packed with two decimal digits.

C
A low-level structured programming language that resembles a machine-independent assembler language.

C++
An object-oriented version of C that is widely used for software package development.

Cache Memory
A high-speed temporary storage area in the CPU for storing parts of a program or data during processing.

Calendaring and Scheduling
Using electronic calendars and other groupware features to automatically schedule, notify, and remind the computer networked members of teams and workgroups of meetings, appointments, and other events.

Capacity Management
The use of planning and control methods to forecast and control information processing job loads, hardware and software usage, and other computer system resource requirements.

Case-Based Reasoning
Representing knowledge in an expert system's knowledge base in the form of cases, that is, examples of past performance, occurrences, and experiences.

Cathode Ray Tube (CRT)
An electronic vacuum tube (television picture tube) that displays the output of a computer system.

CD-ROM
An optical disk technology for microcomputers featuring compact disks with a storage capacity of over 500 megabytes.

Cellular Phone Systems
A radio communications technology that divides a metropolitan area into a honeycomb of cells to greatly increase the number of frequencies and thus the users that can take advantage of mobile phone service.

Central Processing Unit (CPU)
The unit of a computer system that includes the circuits that control the interpretation and execution of instructions. In many computer systems, the CPU includes the arithmetic-logic unit, the control unit, and the primary storage unit.

Change Management
Managing the process of implementing major changes in information technology, business processes, organizational structures, and job assignments to reduce the risks and costs of change, and optimize its benefits.

Channel
(1) A path along which signals can be sent. (2) A small special-purpose processor that controls the movement of data between the CPU and input/output devices.

Chargeback Systems
Methods of allocating costs to end user departments based on the information services rendered and information system resources utilized.

Chat Systems
Software that enables two or more users at networked PCs to carry on online, realtime text conversations.

Check Bit
A binary check digit; for example, a parity bit.

Check Digit
A digit in a data field that is utilized to check for errors or loss of characters in the data field as a result of data transfer operations.

Checkpoint
A place in a program where a check or a recording of data for restart purposes is performed.

Chief Information Officer
A senior management position that oversees all information technology for a firm concentrating on long-range information system planning and strategy.

Client
(1) An end user. (2) The end user's networked microcomputer in client/server networks. (3) The version of a software package designed to run on an end user's networked microcomputer, such as a web browser client, a groupware client, and so on.

Client/Server Network
A computing environment where end user workstations (clients) are connected to network servers and possibly to mainframe superservers.

Clock
A device that generates periodic signals utilized to control the timing of a computer. Also, a register whose contents change at regular intervals in such a way as to measure time.

Coaxial Cable
A sturdy copper or aluminum wire wrapped with spacers to insulate and protect it. Groups of coaxial cables may also be bundled together in a bigger cable for ease of installation.

COBOL: COmmon Business Oriented Language
A widely used business data processing programming language.

Code
Computer instructions.

Cognitive Science
An area of artificial intelligence that focuses on researching how the human brain works and how humans think and learn, in order to apply such findings to the design of computer based systems.

Cognitive Styles
Basic patterns in how people handle information and confront problems.

Cognitive Theory
Theories about how the human brain works and how humans think and learn.

Collaborative Work Management Tools
Software that helps people accomplish or manage joint work activities.

Common Carrier
An organization that supplies communications services to other organizations and to the public as authorized by government agencies.

Communications Satellite
Earth satellites placed in stationary orbits above the equator that serve as relay stations for communications signals transmitted from earth stations.

Competitive Advantage
Developing products, services, processes, or capabilities that give a company a superior business position relative to its competitors and other competitive forces.

Competitive Forces
A firm must confront (1) rivalry of competitors within its industry, (2) threats of new entrants, (3) threats of substitutes, (4) the bargaining power of customers, and (5) the bargaining power of suppliers.

Competitive Strategies
A firm can develop cost leadership, product differentiation, and business innovation strategies to confront its competitive forces.

Compiler
A program that translates a high-level programming language into a machine-language program.

Computer

A device that has the ability to accept data; internally store and execute a program of instructions; perform mathematical, logical, and manipulative operations on data; and report the results.

Computer-Aided Design (CAD)

The use of computers and advanced graphics hardware and software to provide interactive design assistance for engineering and architectural design.

Computer-Aided Engineering (CAE)

The use of computers to simulate, analyze, and evaluate models of product designs and production processes developed using computer-aided design methods.

Computer-Aided Manufacturing (CAM)

The use of computers to automate the production process and operations of a manufacturing plant. Also called factory automation.

Computer-Aided Planning (CAP)

The use of software packages as tools to support the planning process.

Computer-Aided Software Engineering (CASE)

Same as Computer-Aided Systems Engineering, but emphasizing the importance of software development.

Computer-Aided Systems Engineering (CASE)

Using software packages to accomplish and automate many of the activities of information systems development, including software development or programming.

Computer Application

The use of a computer to solve a specific problem or to accomplish a particular job for an end user. For example, common business computer applications include sales order processing, inventory control, and payroll.

Computer-Assisted Instruction (CAI)

The use of computers to provide drills, practice exercises, and tutorial sequences to students.

Computer-Based Information System

An information system that uses computer hardware and software to perform its information processing activities.

Computer Crime

Criminal actions accomplished through the use of computer systems, especially with intent to defraud, destroy, or make unauthorized use of computer system resources.

Computer Ethics

A system of principles governing the legal, professional, social, and moral responsibilities of computer specialists and end users.

Computer Generations

Major stages in the historical development of computing.

Computer Graphics

Using computer-generated images to analyze and interpret data, present information, and do computer-aided design and art.

Computer Industry

The industry composed of firms that supply computer hardware, software, and services.

Computer-Integrated Manufacturing (CIM)

An overall concept that stresses that the goals of computer use in factory automation should be to simplify, automate, and integrate production processes and other aspects of manufacturing.

Computer Matching

Using computers to screen and match data about individual characteristics provided by a variety of computer-based information systems and databases in order to identify individuals for business, government, or other purposes.

Computer Monitoring

Using computers to monitor the behavior and productivity of workers on the job and in the workplace.

Computer Program

A series of instructions or statements, in a form acceptable to a computer, prepared in order to achieve a certain result.

Computer System

Computer hardware as a system of input, processing, output, storage, and control components. Thus a computer system consists of input and output devices, primary and secondary storage devices, the central processing unit, the control unit within the CPU, and other peripheral devices.

Computer Terminal

Any input/output device connected by telecommunications links to a computer.

Computer Virus or Worm

Program code that copies its destructive program routines into the computer systems of anyone who accesses computer systems that have used the program, or anyone who uses copies of data or programs taken from such computers. This spreads the destruction of data and programs among many computer users. Technically, a virus will not run unaided, but must be inserted into another program, while a worm is a distinct program that can run unaided.

Concurrent Processing

The generic term for the capability of computers to work on several tasks at the same time, that is, concurrently. This may involve specific capabilities such as overlapped processing, multiprocessing, multiprogramming, multitasking, parallel processing, and so on.

Connectivity

The degree to which hardware, software, and databases can be easily linked together in a telecommunications network.

Context Diagram

The highest level data flow diagram. It defines the boundaries of a system by showing a single major process and the data inputs and outputs and external entities involved.

Control

(1) The systems component that evaluates feedback to determine whether the system is moving toward the achievement of its goal and then makes any necessary adjustments to the input and processing components of the system to ensure that proper output is produced. (2) A management function that involves observing and measuring organizational performance and environmental activities and modifying the plans and activities of the organization when necessary.

Control Listing

A detailed report that describes each transaction occurring during a period.

Control Totals
Accumulating totals of data at multiple points in an information system to ensure correct information processing.

Control Unit
A subunit of the central processing unit that controls and directs the operations of the computer system. The control unit retrieves computer instructions in proper sequence, interprets each instruction, and then directs the other parts of the computer system in their implementation.

Conversion
The process in which the hardware, software, people, network, and data resources of an old information system must be converted to the requirements of a new information system. This usually involves a parallel, phased, pilot, or plunge conversion process from the old to the new system.

Cooperative Processing
Information processing that allows the computers in a distributed processing network to share the processing of parts of an end user's application.

Cost/Benefit Analysis
Identifying the advantages or benefits and the disadvantages or costs of a proposed solution.

Critical Success Factors
A small number of key factors that executives consider critical to the success of the enterprise. These are key areas where successful performance will assure the success of the organization and attainment of its goals.

Cross-Functional Information Systems
Information systems that are integrated combinations of business information systems, thus sharing information resources across the functional units of an organization.

Cursor
A movable point of light displayed on most video display screens to assist the user in the input of data.

Cybernetic System
A system that uses feedback and control components to achieve a self-regulating capability.

Cylinder
An imaginary vertical cylinder consisting of the vertical alignment of tracks on each surface of magnetic disks that are accessed simultaneously by the read/write heads of a disk drive.

Data
Facts or observations about physical phenomena or business transactions. More specifically, data are objective measurements of the attributes (characteristics) of entities such as people, places, things, and events.

Data Administration
A data resource management function that involves the establishment and enforcement of policies and procedures for managing data as a strategic corporate resource.

Database
A collection of logically related records or files. A database consolidates many records previously stored in separate files so that a common pool of data serves many applications.

Database Administration
A data resource management function that includes responsibility for developing and maintaining the organization's data dictionary, designing and monitoring the performance of databases, and enforcing standards for database use and security.

Database Administrator
A specialist responsible for maintaining standards for the development, maintenance, and security of an organization's databases.

Database Maintenance
The activity of keeping a database up-to-date by adding, changing, or deleting data.

Database Management Approach
An approach to the storage and processing of data in which independent files are consolidated into a common pool, or database, of records available to different application programs and end users for processing and data retrieval.

Database Management System (DBMS)
A set of computer programs that controls the creation, maintenance, and utilization of the databases of an organization.

Database Processing
Utilizing a database for data processing activities such as maintenance,

information retrieval, or report generation.

Data Center
An organizational unit that uses centralized computing resources to perform information processing activities for an organization. Also known as a computer center.

Data Conferencing
Users at networked PCs can view, mark up, revise, and save changes to a shared whiteboard of drawings, documents, and other material.

Data Design
The design of the logical structure of databases and files to be used by a proposed information system. This produces detailed descriptions of the entities, relationships, data elements, and integrity rules for system files and databases.

Data Dictionary
A software module and database containing descriptions and definitions concerning the structure, data elements, interrelationships, and other characteristics of a database.

Data Entry
The process of converting data into a form suitable for entry into a computer system. Also called data capture or input preparation.

Data Flow Diagram
A graphic diagramming tool that uses a few simple symbols to illustrate the flow of data among external entities, processing activities, and data storage elements.

Data Management
Control program functions that provide access to data sets, enforce data storage conventions, and regulate the use of input/output devices.

Data Mining
Using special-purpose software to analyze data from a data warehouse to find hidden patterns and trends.

Data Model
A conceptual framework that defines the logical relationships among the data elements needed to support a basic business or other process.

Data Modeling
A process where the relationships between data elements are identified and defined to develop data models.

Data Planning
A corporate planning and analysis function that focuses on data resource management. It includes the responsibility for developing an overall information policy and data architecture for the firm's data resources.

Data Processing
The execution of a systematic sequence of operations performed upon data to transform it into information.

Data Resource Management
A managerial activity that applies information systems technology and management tools to the task of managing an organization's data resources. Its three major components are database administration, data administration, and data planning.

Data Warehouse
An integrated collection of data extracted from operational, historical, and external databases, and screened, edited, and standardized for retrieval and analysis (*data mining*), to provide business intelligence for managerial decision making.

Debug
To detect, locate, and remove errors from a program or malfunctions from a computer.

Decision-Making Process
A process of intelligence, design, and choice activities that result in the selection of a particular course of action.

Decision Support System (DSS)
An information system that utilizes decision models, a database, and a decision maker's own insights in an ad hoc, interactive analytical modeling process to reach a specific decision by a specific decision maker.

Demand Reports and Responses
Information provided whenever a manager or end user demands it.

Desktop Publishing
The use of microcomputers, laser printers, and page-makeup software to produce a variety of printed materials, formerly done only by professional printers.

Desktop Videoconferencing
The use of end user computer workstations to conduct two-way interactive video conferences.

Development Centers
Systems development consultant groups formed to serve as consultants to the professional programmers and systems analysts of an organization to improve their application development efforts.

Digital Computer
A computer that operates on digital data by performing arithmetic and logical operations on the data. Contrast with Analog Computer.

Digitizer
A device that is used to convert drawings and other graphic images on paper or other materials into digital data that are entered into a computer system.

Direct Access
A method of storage where each storage position has a unique address and can be individually accessed in approximately the same period of time without having to search through other storage positions. Same as Random Access. Contrast with Sequential Access.

Direct Access Storage Device (DASD)
A storage device that can directly access data to be stored or retrieved, for example, a magnetic disk unit.

Direct Data Organization
A method of data organization in which logical data elements are distributed randomly on or within the physical data medium. For example, logical data records distributed randomly on the surfaces of a magnetic disk file. Also called direct organization.

Direct Input/Output
Methods such as keyboard entry, voice input/output, and video displays that allow data to be input into or output from a computer system without the use of machine-readable media.

Disaster Recovery
Methods for ensuring that an organization recovers from natural and human-caused disasters that affect its computer-based operations.

Discussion Forum
An online network discussion platform to encourage and manage online text discussions over a period of time among members of special interest groups or project teams.

Distributed Databases
The concept of distributing databases or portions of a database at remote sites where the data are most frequently referenced. Sharing of data is made possible through a network that interconnects the distributed databases.

Distributed Processing
A form of decentralization of information processing made possible by a network of computers dispersed throughout an organization. Processing of user applications is accomplished by several computers interconnected by a telecommunications network, rather than relying on one large centralized computer facility or on the decentralized operation of several independent computers.

Document
(1) A medium on which data have been recorded for human use, such as a report or invoice. (2) In word processing, a generic term for text material such as letters, memos, reports, and so on.

Documentation
A collection of documents or information that describes a computer program, information system, or required data processing operations.

Downsizing
Moving to smaller computing platforms, such as from mainframe systems to networks of personal computers and servers.

Downtime
The time interval during which a device is malfunctioning or inoperative.

DSS Generator
A software package for a decision support system that contains modules for database, model, and dialogue management.

Duplex
In communications, pertaining to a simultaneous two-way independent transmission in both directions.

EBCDIC: Extended Binary Coded Decimal Interchange Code
An eight-bit code that is widely used by mainframe computers.

Echo Check
A method of checking the accuracy of transmission of data in which the received data are returned to the sending device for comparison with the original data.

Economic Feasibility
Whether expected cost savings, increased revenue, increased profits, and reductions in required investment exceed the costs of developing and operating a proposed system.

EDI: Electronic Data Interchange
The electronic transmission of source documents between the computers of different organizations.

Edit
To modify the form or format of data. For example: to insert or delete characters such as page numbers or decimal points.

Edit Report
A report that describes errors detected during processing.

EFT: Electronic Funds Transfer
The development of banking and payment systems that transfer funds electronically instead of using cash or paper documents such as checks.

Electronic Commerce
The buying and selling, marketing and servicing, and delivery and payment of products, services, and information over the Internet, intranets, extranets, and other networks, between an internetworked enterprise and its prospects, customers, suppliers, and other business partners.

Electronic Communications Tools
Software that helps you communicate and collaborate with others by electronically sending messages, documents, and files in data, text, voice, or multimedia over the Internet, intranets, extranets, and other computer networks.

Electronic Conferencing Tools
Software that helps networked computer users share information and collaborate while working together on joint assignments, no matter where they are located.

Electronic Data Processing (EDP)
The use of electronic computers to process data automatically.

Electronic Document Management
An image processing technology in which an electronic document may consist of digitized voice notes and electronic graphics images, as well as digitized images of traditional documents.

Electronic Mail
Sending and receiving text messages between networked PCs over telecommunications networks. E-mail can also include data files, software, and multimedia messages and documents as attachments.

Electronic Meeting Systems (EMS)
Using a meeting room with networked PCs, a large screen projector, and EMS software to facilitate communication, collaboration, and group decision making in business meetings.

Electronic Payment Systems
Alternative cash or credit payment methods using various electronic technologies to pay for products and services in electronic commerce.

Electronic Spreadsheet Package
An application program used as a computerized tool for analysis, planning, and modeling that allows users to enter and manipulate data into an electronic worksheet of rows and columns.

Emulation
To imitate one system with another so that the imitating system accepts the same data, executes the same programs, and achieves the same results as the imitated system.

Encryption
To scramble data or convert it, prior to transmission, to a secret code that masks the meaning of the data to unauthorized recipients. Similar to enciphering.

End User
Anyone who uses an information system or the information it produces.

End User Computing Systems
Computer-based information systems that directly support both the operational and managerial applications of end users.

Enterprise Collaboration Systems
The use of groupware tools and the Internet, intranets, extranets, and other computer networks to support and enhance communication, coordination, collaboration, and resource sharing among teams and workgroups in an internetworked enterprise.

Enterprise Model
A conceptual framework that defines the structures and relationships of business processes and data elements,

as well as other planning structures, such as critical success factors, and organizational units.

Enterprise Resource Planning (ERP)
Using integrated cross-functional software to reengineer, integrate, and automate the basic business processes of a company to improve its efficiency, agility, and profitability.

Entity Relationship Diagram (ERD)
A data planning and systems development diagramming tool that models the relationships among the entities in a business process.

Entropy
The tendency of a system to lose a relatively stable state of equilibrium.

Ergonomics
The science and technology emphasizing the safety, comfort, and ease of use of human-operated machines such as computers. The goal of ergonomics is to produce systems that are user-friendly: safe, comfortable, and easy to use. Ergonomics is also called human factors engineering.

Exception Reports
Reports produced only when exceptional conditions occur, or reports produced periodically that contain information only about exceptional conditions.

Executive Information Systems (EIS)
An information system that provides strategic information tailored to the needs of top management.

Executive Support System (ESS)
An executive information system with additional capabilities, including data analysis, decision support, electronic mail, and personal productivity tools.

Expert System (ES)
A computer-based information system that uses its knowledge about a specific complex application area to act as an expert consultant to users. The system consists of a knowledge base and software modules that perform inferences on the knowledge and communicate answers to a user's questions.

Extranet
A network that links selected resources of the intranet of a company with its customers, suppliers, and other business partners, using the Internet or

private networks to link the organizations' intranets.

Facilities Management
The use of an external service organization to operate and manage the information processing facilities of an organization.

Fault Tolerant Systems
Computers that have multiple central processors, peripherals, and system software and that are able to continue operations even if there is a major hardware or software failure.

Faxing (Facsimile)
Transmitting and receiving images of documents over the telephone or computer networks using PCs or fax machines.

Feasibility Study
A preliminary study that investigates the information needs of end users and the objectives, constraints, basic resource requirements, cost/benefits, and feasibility of proposed projects.

Feedback
(1) Data or information concerning the components and operations of a system. (2) The use of part of the output of a system as input to the system.

Fiber Optics
The technology that uses cables consisting of very thin filaments of glass fibers that can conduct the light generated by lasers at frequencies that approach the speed of light.

Field
A data element that consists of a grouping of characters that describe a particular attribute of an entity. For example: the name field or salary field of an employee.

Fifth Generation
The next generation of computing, which will provide computers that will be able to see, hear, talk, and think. This would depend on major advances in parallel processing, user input/output methods, and artificial intelligence.

File
A collection of related data records treated as a unit. Sometimes called a data set.

File Management
Controlling the creation, deletion, access, and use of files of data and programs.

Financial Information Systems
Information systems that support financial managers in the financing of a business and the allocation and control of financial resources. Include cash and securities management, capital budgeting, financial forecasting, and financial planning.

Fire Wall Computer
Computers, communications processors, and software that protect computer networks from intrusion by screening all network traffic and serving as a safe transfer point for access to and from other networks.

Firmware
The use of microprogrammed read-only memory circuits in place of hardwired logic circuitry. See also Microprogramming.

Floating Point
Pertaining to a number representation system in which each number is represented by two sets of digits. One set represents the significant digits or fixed-point "base" of the number, while the other set of digits represents the "exponent," which indicates the precision of the number.

Floppy Disk
A small plastic disk coated with iron oxide that resembles a small phonograph record enclosed in a protective envelope. It is a widely used form of magnetic disk media that provides a direct access storage capability for microcomputer systems.

Flowchart
A graphical representation in which symbols are used to represent operations, data, flow, logic, equipment, and so on. A program flowchart illustrates the structure and sequence of operations of a program, while a system flowchart illustrates the components and flows of information systems.

Foreground Processing
The automatic execution of the computer programs that have been designed to preempt the use of computing facilities. Contrast with Background Processing.

Format
The arrangement of data on a medium.

FORTRAN: FORmula TRANslation
A high-level programming language widely utilized to develop computer programs that perform mathematical computations for scientific, engineering, and selected business applications.

Forward Chaining
An inference strategy that reaches a conclusion by applying rules to facts to determine if any facts satisfy a rule's conditions in a particular situation.

Fourth-Generation Languages (4GL)
Programming languages that are easier to use than high-level languages like BASIC, COBOL, or FORTRAN. They are also known as nonprocedural, natural, or very-high-level languages.

Frame
A collection of knowledge about an entity or other concept consisting of a complex package of slots, that is, data values describing the characteristics or attributes of an entity.

Frame-Based Knowledge
Knowledge represented in the form of a hierarchy or network of frames.

Front-End Processor
Typically a smaller, general-purpose computer that is dedicated to handling data communications control functions in a communications network, thus relieving the host computer of these functions.

Functional Requirements
The information system capabilities required to meet the information needs of end users. Also called system requirements.

Fuzzy Logic Systems
Computer-based systems that can process data that are incomplete or only partially correct, that is, fuzzy data. Such systems can solve unstructured problems with incomplete knowledge, as humans do.

General-Purpose Application Programs
Programs that can perform information processing jobs for users from all application areas. For example, word processing programs, electronic spreadsheet programs, and graphics programs can be used by individuals

for home, education, business, scientific, and many other purposes.

General-Purpose Computer
A computer that is designed to handle a wide variety of problems. Contrast with Special-Purpose Computer.

Generate
To produce a machine-language program for performing a specific data processing task based on parameters supplied by a programmer or user.

Genetic Algorithm
An application of artificial intelligence software that uses Darwinian (survival of the fittest) randomizing and other functions to simulate an evolutionary process that can yield increasingly better solutions to a problem.

Gigabyte
One billion bytes. More accurately, 2 to the 30th power, or 1,073,741,824 in decimal notation.

GIGO
A contraction of "Garbage In, Garbage Out," which emphasizes that information systems will produce erroneous and invalid output when provided with erroneous and invalid input data or instructions.

Global Company
A business that is driven by a global strategy so that all of its activities are planned and implemented in the context of a whole-world system.

Global Information Technology
The use of computer-based information systems and telecommunications networks using a variety of information technologies to support global business operations and management.

Globalization
Becoming a global enterprise by expanding into global markets, using global production facilities, forming alliances with global partners, and so on.

Goal-Seeking Analysis
Making repeated changes to selected variables until a chosen variable reaches a target value.

Graphical User Interface
A software interface that relies on icons, bars, buttons, boxes, and other images to initiate computer-based tasks for users.

Graphics
Pertaining to symbolic input or output from a computer system, such as lines, curves, and geometric shapes, using video display units or graphics plotters and printers.

Graphics Pen and Tablet
A device that allows an end user to draw or write on a pressure-sensitive tablet and have the handwriting or graphics digitized by the computer and accepted as input.

Graphics Software
A program that helps users generate graphics displays.

Group Decision Making
Decisions made by groups of people coming to an agreement on a particular issue.

Group Decision Support System (GDSS)
A decision support system that provides support for decision making by groups of people.

Group Support Systems (GSS)
An information system that enhances communication, coordination, collaboration, decision making, and group work activities of teams and workgroups.

Groupware
Software to support and enhance the communication, coordination, and collaboration among networked teams and workgroups, including software tools for electronic communications, electronic conferencing, and cooperative work management.

Hacking
(1) Obsessive use of a computer.
(2) The unauthorized access and use of computer systems.

Handshaking
Exchange of predetermined signals when a connection is established between two communications terminals.

Hard Copy
A data medium or data record that has a degree of permanence and that can be read by people or machines.

Hardware
(1) Machines and media. (2) Physical equipment, as opposed to computer programs or methods of use. (3) Mechanical, magnetic, electrical, elec-

tronic, or optical devices. Contrast with Software.

Hash Total
The sum of numbers in a data field that are not normally added, such as account numbers or other identification numbers. It is utilized as a control total, especially during input/output operations of batch processing systems.

Header Label
A machine-readable record at the beginning of a file containing data for file identification and control.

Heuristic
Pertaining to exploratory methods of problem solving in which solutions are discovered by evaluation of the progress made toward the final result. It is an exploratory trial-and-error approach guided by rules of thumb. Opposite of algorithmic.

Hierarchical Data Structure
A logical data structure in which the relationships between records form a hierarchy or tree structure. The relationships among records are one to many, since each data element is related only to one element above it.

High-Level Language
A programming language that utilizes macro instructions and statements that closely resemble human language or mathematical notation to describe the problem to be solved or the procedure to be used. Also called a compiler language.

Homeostasis
A relatively stable state of equilibrium of a system.

Host Computer
Typically a larger central computer that performs the major data processing tasks in a computer network.

Human Factors
Hardware and software capabilities that can affect the comfort, safety, ease of use, and user customization of computer-based information systems.

Human Information Processing
A conceptual framework about the human cognitive process that uses an information processing context to explain how humans capture, process, and use information.

Human Resource Information Systems (HRIS)
Information systems that support human resource management activities such as recruitment, selection and hiring, job placement and performance appraisals, and training and development.

Hybrid AI Systems
Systems that integrate several AI technologies, such as expert systems and neural networks.

Hypermedia
Documents containing multiple forms of media, including text, graphics, video, and sound, that can be interactively searched, like Hypertext.

Hypertext
Text in electronic form that has been indexed and linked (hyperlinks) by software in a variety of ways so that it can be randomly and interactively searched by a user.

Hypertext Markup Language (HTML)
A popular page description language for creating hypertext and hypermedia documents for World Wide Web and intranet web sites.

Icon
A small figure on a video display that looks like a familiar office or other device such as a file folder (for storing a file) or a wastebasket (for deleting a file).

Image Processing
A computer-based technology that allows end users to electronically capture, store, process, and retrieve images that may include numeric data, text, handwriting, graphics, documents, and photographs. Image processing makes heavy use of optical scanning and optical disk technologies.

Impact Printers
Printers that form images on paper through the pressing of a printing element and an inked ribbon or roller against the face of a sheet of paper.

Index
An ordered reference list of the contents of a file or document together with keys or reference notations for identification or location of those contents.

Index Sequential
A method of data organization in which records are organized in sequential order and also referenced by an index. When utilized with direct access file devices, it is known as index sequential access method, or ISAM.

Inference Engine
The software component of an expert system, which processes the rules and facts related to a specific problem and makes associations and inferences resulting in recommended courses of action.

Information
Information is data placed in a meaningful and useful context for an end user.

Information Architecture
A conceptual framework that defines the basic structure, content, and relationships of the organizational databases that provide the data needed to support the basic business processes of an organization.

Information Center
A support facility for the end users of an organization. It allows users to learn to develop their own application programs and to accomplish their own information processing tasks. End users are provided with hardware support, software support, and people support (trained user consultants).

Information Float
The time when a document is in transit between the sender and receiver, and thus unavailable for any action or response.

Information Processing
A concept that covers both the traditional concept of processing numeric and alphabetic data, and the processing of text, images, and voices. It emphasizes that the production of information products for users should be the focus of processing activities.

Information Quality
The degree to which information has content, form, and time characteristics that give it value to specific end users.

Information Resource Management (IRM)
A management concept that views data, information, and computer resources (computer hardware, software, networks, and personnel) as valuable organizational resources that should be efficiently, economically, and effectively managed for the benefit of the entire organization.

Information Retrieval
The methods and procedures for recovering specific information from stored data.

Information Superhighway
An advanced high-speed Internet-like network that connects individuals, households, businesses, government agencies, libraries, schools, universities, and other institutions with interactive voice, video, data, and multimedia communications.

Information System
(1) A set of people, procedures, and resources that collects, transforms, and disseminates information in an organization. (2) A system that accepts data resources as input and processes them into information products as output.

Information System Model
A conceptual framework that views an information system as a system that uses the resources of hardware (machines and media), software (programs and procedures), people (users and specialists), and networks (communications media and network support) to perform input, processing, output, storage, and control activities that transform data resources (databases and knowledge bases) into information products.

Information System Specialist
A person whose occupation is related to the providing of information system services. For example: a systems analyst, programmer, or computer operator.

Information Systems Development
See Systems Development.

Information Systems Planning
A formal planning process that develops plans for developing and managing information systems that will support the goals of the organization. This includes strategic, tactical, and operational planning activities.

Information Technology (IT)
Hardware, software, telecommunications, database management, and other information processing technologies used in computer-based information systems.

Information Theory
The branch of learning concerned with the likelihood of accurate transmission or communication of messages subject to transmission failure, distortion, and noise.

Input
Pertaining to a device, process, or channel involved in the insertion of data into a data processing system. Opposite of Output.

Input/Output (I/O)
Pertaining to either input or output, or both.

Input/Output Interface Hardware
Devices such as I/O ports, I/O busses, buffers, channels, and input/output control units, which assist the CPU in its input/output assignments. These devices make it possible for modern computer systems to perform input, output, and processing functions simultaneously.

Inquiry Processing
Computer processing that supports the realtime interrogation of online files and databases by end users.

Instruction
A grouping of characters that specifies the computer operation to be performed.

Intangible Benefits and Costs
The nonquantifiable benefits and costs of a proposed solution or system.

Integrated Circuit
A complex microelectronic circuit consisting of interconnected circuit elements that cannot be disassembled because they are placed on or within a "continuous substrate" such as a silicon chip.

Integrated Packages
Software that combines the ability to do several general-purpose applications (such as word processing, electronic spreadsheet, and graphics) into one program.

Intelligent Agent
A special-purpose knowledge-based system that serves as a software surrogate to accomplish specific tasks for end users.

Intelligent Terminal
A terminal with the capabilities of a microcomputer that can thus perform many data processing and other functions without accessing a larger computer.

Interactive Marketing
A dynamic collaborative process of creating, purchasing, and improving products and services that builds close relationships between a business and its customers, using a variety of services on the Internet, intranets, and extranets.

Interactive Processing
A type of realtime processing in which users can interact with a computer on a realtime basis.

Interactive Video
Computer-based systems that integrate image processing with text, audio, and video processing technologies, which makes interactive multimedia presentations possible.

Interface
A shared boundary, such as the boundary between two systems. For example, the boundary between a computer and its peripheral devices.

Internet
The Internet is a rapidly growing network of thousands of business, educational, and research networks connecting millions of computers and their users in over 100 countries.

Internetwork Processor
Communications processors used by local area networks to interconnect them with other local area and wide area networks. Examples include switches, routers, hubs, and gateways.

Internetworked Enterprise
A business that uses the Internet, intranets, extranets, and other computer networks to support electronic commerce and other business processes, managerial decision making, and team and workgroup collaboration within the enterprise and among its customers, suppliers, and other business partners.

Internetworks
Interconnected local area and wide area networks.

Interoperability
Being able to accomplish end user applications using different types of computer systems, operating systems, and application software, interconnected by different types of local and wide area networks.

Interorganizational Information Systems
Information systems that interconnect an organization with other organizations, such as a business and its customers and suppliers.

Interpreter
A computer program that translates and executes each source language statement before translating and executing the next one.

Interrupt
A condition that causes an interruption in a processing operation during which another task is performed. At the conclusion of this new assignment, control may be transferred back to the point where the original processing operation was interrupted or to other tasks with a higher priority.

Intranet
An Internet-like network within an organization. Web browser software provides easy access to internal web sites established by business units, teams, and individuals, and other network resources and applications.

Inverted File
A file that references entities by their attributes.

IS Component Matrix
A matrix that documents how hardware, software, people, network, and data resources support an information system's input, processing, output, storage, and control activities to produce information products for end users.

IT Architecture
A conceptual design for the implementation of information technology in an organization, including its hardware, software, and network technology platforms, data resources, application portfolio, and IS organization.

Iterative
Pertaining to the repeated execution of a series of steps.

Java
An object-oriented programming language designed for programming realtime, interactive web-based applications in the form of applets for use on clients and servers on the Internet, intranets, and extranets.

Job
A specified group of tasks prescribed as a unit of work for a computer.

Job Control Language (JCL)
A language for communicating with the operating system of a computer to identify a job and describe its requirements.

Joystick
A small lever set in a box used to move the cursor on the computer's display screen.

K
An abbreviation for the prefix kilo-, which is 1,000 in decimal notation. When referring to storage capacity it is equivalent to 2 to the 10th power, or 1,024 in decimal notation.

Key
One or more fields within a data record that are used to identify it or control its use.

Keyboarding
Using the keyboard of a microcomputer or computer terminal.

Knowledge Base
A computer-accessible collection of knowledge about a subject in a variety of forms, such as facts and rules of inference, frames, and objects.

Knowledge-Based Information System
An information system that adds a knowledge base to the database and other components found in other types of computer-based information systems.

Knowledge Engineer
A specialist who works with experts to capture the knowledge they possess in order to develop a knowledge base for expert systems and other knowledge-based systems.

Knowledge Management
Organizing and sharing the diverse forms of business information created within an organization. Includes managing project and enterprise document libraries, discussion databases, hypermedia web site databases, and other types of knowledge bases.

Knowledge Workers
People whose primary work activities include creating, using, and distributing information.

Language Translator Program
A program that converts the programming language instructions in a computer program into machine language code. Major types include assemblers, compilers, and interpreters.

Large-Scale Integration (LSI)
A method of constructing electronic circuits in which thousands of circuits can be placed on a single semiconductor chip.

Layout Forms and Screens
Tools used to construct the formats and generic content of input/output media and methods for the user interface, such as display screens and reports.

Legacy Systems
The older, traditional mainframe-based business information systems of an organization.

Light Pen
A photoelectronic device that allows data to be entered or altered on the face of a video display terminal.

Line Printer
A device that prints all characters of a line as a unit.

Liquid Crystal Displays (LCDs)
Electronic visual displays that form characters by applying an electrical charge to selected silicon crystals.

List Organization
A method of data organization that uses indexes and pointers to allow for nonsequential retrieval.

List Processing
A method of processing data in the form of lists.

Local Area Network (LAN)
A communications network that typically connects computers, terminals, and other computerized devices within a limited physical area such as an office, building, manufacturing plant, or other worksite.

Locking in Customers and Suppliers
Building valuable relationships with customers and suppliers that deter them from abandoning a firm for its competitors or intimidating it into accepting less-profitable relationships.

Logical Data Elements
Data elements that are independent of the physical data media on which they are recorded.

Logical System Design
Developing general specifications for how basic information systems activities can meet end user requirements.

Loop
A sequence of instructions in a computer program that is executed repeatedly until a terminal condition prevails.

Machine Cycle
The timing of a basic CPU operation as determined by a fixed number of electrical pulses emitted by the CPU's timing circuitry or internal clock.

Machine Language
A programming language where instructions are expressed in the binary code of the computer.

Macro Instruction
An instruction in a source language that is equivalent to a specified sequence of machine instructions.

Mag Stripe Card
A plastic wallet-size card with a strip of magnetic tape on one surface; widely used for credit/debit cards.

Magnetic Disk
A flat circular plate with a magnetic surface on which data can be stored by selective magnetization of portions of the curved surface.

Magnetic Ink
An ink that contains particles of iron oxide that can be magnetized and detected by magnetic sensors.

Magnetic Ink Character Recognition (MICR)
The machine recognition of characters printed with magnetic ink. Primarily used for check processing by the banking industry.

Magnetic Tape
A plastic tape with a magnetic surface on which data can be stored by selective magnetization of portions of the surface.

Mainframe
A larger-size computer system, typically with a separate central processing unit, as distinguished from microcomputer and minicomputer systems.

Management Functions
Management as a process of planning, organizing, directing, and controlling activities.

Management Information System (MIS)
A management support system that produces prespecified reports, displays, and responses on a periodic, exception, or demand basis.

Management Levels
Management as the performance of planning and control activities at the strategic, tactical, and operational decision-making levels of an organization.

Management Support System (MSS)
An information system that provides information to support managerial decision making. More specifically, an information-reporting system, executive information system, or decision support system.

Managerial End User
A manager, entrepreneur, or managerial-level professional who personally uses information systems. Also, the manager of the department or other organizational unit that relies on information systems.

Managerial Roles
Management as the performance of a variety of interpersonal, information, and decision roles.

Manual Data Processing
Data processing that requires continual human operation and intervention and that utilizes simple data processing tools such as paper forms, pencils, and filing cabinets.

Manufacturing Information Systems
Information systems that support the planning, control, and accomplishment of manufacturing processes. This includes concepts such as computer-integrated manufacturing (CIM) and technologies such as computer-aided manufacturing (CAM) or computer-aided design (CAD).

Marketing Information Systems
Information systems that support the planning, control, and transaction processing required for the accomplishment of marketing activities, such as sales management, advertising, and promotion.

Mass Storage
Secondary storage devices with extra-large storage capacities such as magnetic or optical disks.

Master File
A data file containing relatively permanent information that is utilized as an authoritative reference and is usually updated periodically. Contrast with Transaction File.

Mathematical Model
A mathematical representation of a process, device, or concept.

Media
All tangible objects on which data are recorded.

Megabyte
One million bytes. More accurately, 2 to the 20th power, or 1,048,576 in decimal notation.

Memory
Same as Storage.

Menu
A displayed list of items (usually the names of alternative applications, files, or activities) from which an end user makes a selection.

Menu Driven
A characteristic of interactive computing systems that provides menu displays and operator prompting to assist an end user in performing a particular job.

Meta Data
Data about data; data describing the structure, data elements, interrelationships, and other characteristics of a database.

Microcomputer
A very small computer, ranging in size from a "computer on a chip" to a small typewriter-size unit.

Micrographics
The use of microfilm, microfiche, and other microforms to record data in greatly reduced form.

Microprocessor
A microcomputer central processing unit (CPU) on a chip. Without input/output or primary storage capabilities in most types.

Microprogram
A small set of elementary control instructions called microinstructions or microcode.

Microprogramming
The use of special software (microprograms) to perform the functions of special hardware (electronic control circuitry). Microprograms stored in a read-only storage module of the control unit interpret the machine language instructions of a computer program and decode them into elementary microinstructions, which are then executed.

Microsecond
A millionth of a second.

Middleware
Software that helps diverse networked computer systems work together, thus promoting their interoperability.

Midrange Computer
A computer category between microcomputers and mainframes. Examples include minicomputers, network servers, and technical workstations.

Millisecond
A thousandth of a second.

Minicomputer
A small (e.g., the size of a desk) electronic, digital, stored-program, general-purpose computer.

Model Base
An organized collection of conceptual, mathematical, and logical models that express business relationships, computational routines, or analytical techniques. Such models are stored in the form of programs and program subroutines, command files, and spreadsheets.

Modem
(MOdulator-DEModulator) A device that converts the digital signals from input/output devices into appropriate frequencies at a transmission terminal and converts them back into digital signals at a receiving terminal.

Monitor
Software or hardware that observes, supervises, controls, or verifies the operations of a system.

Mouse
A small device that is electronically connected to a computer and is moved by hand on a flat surface in order to move the cursor on a video screen in the same direction. Buttons on the mouse allow users to issue commands and make responses or selections.

Multidimensional Structure
A database model that uses multidimensional structures (such as cubes or cubes within cubes) to store data and relationships between data.

Multimedia Presentations
Providing information using a variety of media, including text and graphics

displays, voice and other audio, photographs, and video segments.

Multiplex
To interleave or simultaneously transmit two or more messages on a single channel.

Multiplexer
An electronic device that allows a single communications channel to carry simultaneous data transmission from many terminals.

Multiprocessing
Pertaining to the simultaneous execution of two or more instructions by a computer or computer network.

Multiprocessor Computer Systems
Computer systems that use a multiprocessor architecture in the design of their central processing units. This includes the use of support microprocessors and multiple instruction processors, including parallel processor designs.

Multiprogramming
Pertaining to the concurrent execution of two or more programs by a computer by interleaving their execution.

Multitasking
The concurrent use of the same computer to accomplish several different information processing tasks. Each task may require the use of a different program, or the concurrent use of the same copy of a program by several users.

Nanosecond
One billionth of a second.

Natural Language
A programming language that is very close to human language. Also called very-high-level language.

Network
An interconnected system of computers, terminals, and communications channels and devices.

Network Architecture
A master plan designed to promote an open, simple, flexible, and efficient telecommunications environment through the use of standard protocols, standard communications hardware and software interfaces, and the design of a standard multilevel telecommunications interface between end users and computer systems.

Network Computer
A low-cost networked microcomputer with no or minimal disk storage, that depends on Internet or intranet servers for its operating system and web browser, Java-enabled application software, and data access and storage.

Network Computing
A network-centric view of computing in which "the network is the computer," that is, the view that computer networks are the central computing resource of any computing environment.

Network Data Structure
A logical data structure that allows many-to-many relationships among data records. It allows entry into a database at multiple points, because any data element or record can be related to many other data elements.

Neural Networks
Computer processors or software whose architecture is based on the human brain's meshlike neuron structure. Neural networks can process many pieces of information simultaneously and can learn to recognize patterns and programs themselves to solve related problems on their own.

Node
A terminal point in a communications network.

Nonimpact Printers
Printers that use specially treated paper and that form characters by laser, thermal (heat), electrostatic, or electrochemical processes.

Nonprocedural Languages
Programming languages that allow users and professional programmers to specify the results they want without specifying how to solve the problem.

Numerical Control
Automatic control of a machine process by a computer that makes use of numerical data, generally introduced as the operation is in process. Also called machine control.

Object
A data element that includes both data and the methods or processes that act on those data.

Object-Based Knowledge
Knowledge represented as a network of objects.

Object-Oriented Language
An object-oriented programming (OOP) language used to develop programs that create and use objects to perform information processing tasks.

Object Program
A compiled or assembled program composed of executable machine instructions. Contrast with Source Program.

OEM: Original Equipment Manufacturer
A firm that manufactures and sells computers by assembling components produced by other hardware manufacturers.

Office Automation (OA)
The use of computer-based information systems that collect, process, store, and transmit electronic messages, documents, and other forms of office communications among individuals, work groups, and organizations.

Offline
Pertaining to equipment or devices not under control of the central processing unit.

Online
Pertaining to equipment or devices under control of the central processing unit.

Online Analytical Processing (OLAP)
A capability of some management, decision support, and executive information systems that supports interactive examination and manipulation of large amounts of data from many perspectives.

Online Transaction Processing (OLTP)
A realtime transaction processing system.

Open Systems
Information systems that use common standards for hardware, software, applications, and networking to create a computing environment that allows easy access by end users and their networked computer systems.

Operand
That which is operated upon. That part of a computer instruction that is identified by the address part of the instruction.

Operating Environment
Software packages or modules that add a graphics-based interface between end users, the operating system, and their application programs, and that may also provide a multitasking capability.

Operating System
The main control program of a computer system. It is a system of programs that controls the execution of computer programs and may provide scheduling, debugging, input/output control, system accounting, compilation, storage assignment, data management, and related services.

Operation Code
A code that represents specific operations to be performed upon the operands in a computer instruction.

Operational Feasibility
The willingness and ability of management, employees, customers, and suppliers to operate, use, and support a proposed system.

Operations Support System (OSS)
An information system that collects, processes, and stores data generated by the operations systems of an organization and produces data and information for input into a management information system or for the control of an operations system.

Operations System
A basic subsystem of the business firm that constitutes its input, processing, and output components. Also called a physical system.

Opportunity
A basic condition that presents the potential for desirable results in an organization or other system.

Optical Character Recognition (OCR)
The machine identification of printed characters through the use of light-sensitive devices.

Optical Disks
A secondary storage medium using laser technology to read tiny spots on a plastic disk. The disks are currently capable of storing billions of characters of information.

Optical Scanner
A device that optically scans characters or images and generates their digital representations.

Optimization Analysis
Finding an optimum value for selected variables in a mathematical model, given certain constraints.

Organizational Feasibility
How well a proposed information system supports the objectives of an organization's strategic plan for information systems.

Output
Pertaining to a device, process, or channel involved with the transfer of data or information out of an information processing system. Opposite of Input.

Outsourcing
Turning over all or part of an organization's information systems operation to outside contractors, known as systems integrators or facilities management companies.

Packet
A group of data and control information in a specified format that is transmitted as an entity.

Packet Switching
A data transmission process that transmits addressed packets such that a channel is occupied only for the duration of transmission of the packet.

Page
A segment of a program or data, usually of fixed length.

Paging
A process that automatically and continually transfers pages of programs and data between primary storage and direct access storage devices. It provides computers with multiprogramming and virtual memory capabilities.

Parallel Processing
Executing many instructions at the same time, that is, in parallel. Performed by advanced computers using many instruction processors organized in clusters or networks.

Parity Bit
A check bit appended to an array of binary digits to make the sum of all the binary digits, including the check bit, always odd or always even.

Pascal
A high-level, general-purpose, structured programming language named after Blaise Pascal. It was developed by Niklaus Wirth of Zurich in 1968.

Pattern Recognition
The identification of shapes, forms, or configurations by automatic means.

PCM: Plug Compatible Manufacturer
A firm that manufactures computer equipment that can be plugged into existing computer systems without requiring additional hardware or software interfaces.

Pen-Based Computers
Tablet-style microcomputers that recognize handwriting and hand drawing done by a pen-shaped device on their pressure-sensitive display screens.

Performance Monitor
A software package that monitors the processing of computer system jobs, helps develop a planned schedule of computer operations that can optimize computer system performance, and produces detailed statistics that are used for computer system capacity planning and control.

Periodic Reports
Providing information to managers using a prespecified format designed to provide information on a regularly scheduled basis.

Peripheral Devices
In a computer system, any unit of equipment, distinct from the central processing unit, that provides the system with input, output, or storage capabilities.

Personal Information Manager (PIM)
A software package that helps end users store, organize, and retrieve text and numerical data in the form of notes, lists, memos, and a variety of other forms.

Physical System Design
Design of the user interface methods and products, database structures, and processing and control procedures for a proposed information system, including hardware, software, and personnel specifications.

Picosecond
One trillionth of a second.

Plasma Display
Output devices that generate a visual display with electrically charged particles of gas trapped between glass plates.

Plotter
A hard-copy output device that produces drawings and graphical displays on paper or other materials.

Pointer
A data element associated with an index, a record, or other set of data that contains the address of a related record.

Pointing Devices
Devices that allow end users to issue commands or make choices by moving a cursor on the display screen.

Pointing Stick
A small buttonlike device on a keyboard that moves the cursor on the screen in the direction of the pressure placed upon it.

Point-of-Sale (POS) Terminal
A computer terminal used in retail stores that serves the function of a cash register as well as collecting sales data and performing other data processing functions.

Port
(1) Electronic circuitry that provides a connection point between the CPU and input/output devices. (2) A connection point for a communications line on a CPU or other front-end device.

Postimplementation Review
Monitoring and evaluating the results of an implemented solution or system.

Presentation Graphics
Using computer-generated graphics to enhance the information presented in reports and other types of presentations.

Prespecified Reports
Reports whose format is specified in advance to provide managers with information periodically, on an exception basis, or on demand.

Private Branch Exchange (PBX)
A switching device that serves as an interface between the many telephone lines within a work area and the local telephone company's main telephone lines or trunks. Computerized PBXs can handle the switching of both voice and data.

Problem
A basic condition that is causing undesirable results in an organization or other system.

Procedure-Oriented Language
A programming language designed for the convenient expression of procedures used in the solution of a wide class of problems.

Procedures
Sets of instructions used by people to complete a task.

Process Control
The use of a computer to control an ongoing physical process, such as petrochemical production.

Process Design
The design of the programs and procedures needed by a proposed information system, including detailed program specifications and procedures.

Processor
A hardware device or software system capable of performing operations upon data.

Program
A set of instructions that cause a computer to perform a particular task.

Programmed Decision
A decision that can be automated by basing it on a decision rule that outlines the steps to take when confronted with the need for a specific decision.

Programmer
A person mainly involved in designing, writing, and testing computer programs.

Programming
The design, writing, and testing of a program.

Programming Language
A language used to develop the instructions in computer programs.

Programming Tools
Software packages or modules that provide editing and diagnostic capabilities and other support facilities to assist the programming process.

Project Management
Managing the accomplishment of an information system development project according to a specific project plan, in order that a project is completed on time, and within its budget, and meets its design objectives.

Prompt
Messages that assist a user in performing a particular job. This would include error messages, correction suggestions, questions, and other messages that guide an end user.

Protocol
A set of rules and procedures for the control of communications in a communications network.

Prototype
A working model. In particular, a working model of an information system that includes tentative versions of user input and output, databases and files, control methods, and processing routines.

Prototyping
The rapid development and testing of working models, or prototypes, of new information system applications in an interactive, iterative process involving both systems analysts and end users.

Pseudocode
An informal design language of structured programming that expresses the processing logic of a program module in ordinary human language phrases.

Pull Marketing
Marketing methods that rely on the use of web browsers by end users to access marketing materials and resources at Internet, intranet, and extranet web sites.

Push Marketing
Marketing methods that rely on web broadcasting software to push marketing information and other marketing materials to end users' computers.

Quality Assurance
Methods for ensuring that information systems are free from errors and fraud and provide information products of high quality.

Query Language
A high-level, humanlike language provided by a database management system that enables users to easily extract data and information from a database.

Queue
(1) A waiting line formed by items in a system waiting for service. (2) To arrange in or form a queue.

RAID
Redundant array of independent disks. Magnetic disk units that house many interconnected microcomputer hard

disk drives, thus providing large, fault tolerant storage capacities.

Random Access
Same as Direct Access. Contrast with Sequential Access.

Random Access Memory (RAM)
One of the basic types of semiconductor memory used for temporary storage of data or programs during processing. Each memory position can be directly sensed (read) or changed (write) in the same length of time, irrespective of its location on the storage medium.

Reach and Range Analysis
A planning framework that contrasts a firm's ability to use its IT platform to reach its stakeholders, with the range of information products and services that can be provided or shared through IT.

Read Only Memory (ROM)
A basic type of semiconductor memory used for permanent storage. Can only be read, not "written," that is, changed. Variations are Programmable Read Only Memory (PROM) and Erasable Programmable Read Only Memory (EPROM).

Realtime
Pertaining to the performance of data processing during the actual time a business or physical process transpires, in order that results of the data processing can be used to support the completion of the process.

Realtime Processing
Data processing in which data are processed immediately rather than periodically. Also called online processing. Contrast with Batch Processing.

Record
A collection of related data fields treated as a unit.

Reduced Instruction Set Computer (RISC)
A CPU architecture that optimizes processing speed by the use of a smaller number of basic machine instructions than traditional CPU designs.

Redundancy
In information processing, the repetition of part or all of a message to increase the chance that the correct information will be understood by the recipient.

Register
A device capable of storing a specified amount of data such as one word.

Relational Data Structure
A logical data structure in which all data elements within the database are viewed as being stored in the form of simple tables. DBMS packages based on the relational model can link data elements from various tables as long as the tables share common data elements.

Remote Access
Pertaining to communication with the data processing facility by one or more stations that are distant from that facility.

Remote Job Entry (RJE)
Entering jobs into a batch processing system from a remote facility.

Report Generator
A feature of database management system packages that allows an end user to quickly specify a report format for the display of information retrieved from a database.

Reprographics
Copying and duplicating technology and methods.

Resource Management
An operating system function that controls the use of computer system resources such as primary storage, secondary storage, CPU processing time, and input/output devices by other system software and application software packages.

Robotics
The technology of building machines (robots) with computer intelligence and humanlike physical capabilities.

Routine
An ordered set of instructions that may have some general or frequent use.

RPG: Report Program Generator
A problem-oriented language that utilizes a generator to construct programs that produce reports and perform other data processing tasks.

Rule
Statements that typically take the form of a premise and a conclusion such as If-Then rules: If (condition), Then (conclusion).

Rule-Based Knowledge
Knowledge represented in the form of rules and statements of fact.

Scalability
The ability of hardware or software to handle the processing demands of a wide range of end users, transactions, queries, and other information processing requirements.

Scenario Approach
A planning approach where managers, employees, and planners create scenarios of what an organization will be like three to five years or more into the future, and identify the role IT can play in those scenarios.

Schema
An overall conceptual or logical view of the relationships between the data in a database.

Scientific Method
An analytical methodology that involves (1) recognizing phenomena, (2) formulating a hypothesis about the causes or effects of the phenomena, (3) testing the hypothesis through experimentation, (4) evaluating the results of such experiments, and (5) drawing conclusions about the hypothesis.

Secondary Storage
Storage that supplements the primary storage of a computer. Synonymous with Auxiliary Storage.

Sector
A subdivision of a track on a magnetic disk surface.

Security Codes
Passwords, identification codes, account codes, and other codes that limit the access and use of computer-based system resources to authorized users.

Security Monitor
A software package that monitors the use of a computer system and protects its resources from unauthorized use, fraud, and vandalism.

Semiconductor Memory
Microelectronic storage circuitry etched on tiny chips of silicon or other semiconducting material. The primary storage of most modern computers consists of microelectronic semiconductor storage chips for random access memory (RAM) and read only memory (ROM).

Semistructured Decisions
Decisions involving procedures that can be partially prespecified, but not enough to lead to a definite recommended decision.

Sensitivity Analysis
Observing how repeated changes to a single variable affect other variables in a mathematical model.

Sequential Access
A sequential method of storing and retrieving data from a file. Contrast with Random Access and Direct Access.

Sequential Data Organization
Organizing logical data elements according to a prescribed sequence.

Serial
Pertaining to the sequential or consecutive occurrence of two or more related activities in a single device or channel.

Server
(1) A computer that supports telecommunications in a local area network, as well as the sharing of peripheral devices, software, and databases among the workstations in the network.
(2) Versions of software for installation on network servers designed to control and support applications on client microcomputers in client/server networks. Examples include multiuser network operating systems and specialized software for running Internet, intranet, and extranet web applications, such as electronic commerce and enterprise collaboration.

Service Bureau
A firm offering computer and data processing services. Also called a computer service center.

Smart Products
Industrial and consumer products, with "intelligence" provided by built-in microcomputers or microprocessors that significantly improve the performance and capabilities of such products.

Software
Computer programs and procedures concerned with the operation of an information system. Contrast with Hardware.

Software Package
A computer program supplied by computer manufacturers, independent software companies, or other computer users. Also known as canned programs, proprietary software, or packaged programs.

Software Piracy
Unauthorized copying of software.

Software Suites
A combination of individual software packages that share a common graphical user interface and are designed for easy transfer of data between applications.

Solid State
Pertaining to devices such as transistors and diodes whose operation depends on the control of electric or magnetic phenomena in solid materials.

Source Data Automation
The use of automated methods of data entry that attempt to reduce or eliminate many of the activities, people, and data media required by traditional data entry methods.

Source Document
A document that is the original formal record of a transaction, such as a purchase order or sales invoice.

Source Program
A computer program written in a language that is subject to a translation process. Contrast with Object Program.

Special-Purpose Computer
A computer designed to handle a restricted class of problems. Contrast with General-Purpose Computer.

Spooling
Simultaneous peripheral operation online. Storing input data from low-speed devices temporarily on high-speed secondary storage units, which can be quickly accessed by the CPU. Also, writing output data at high speeds onto magnetic tape or disk units from which it can be transferred to slow-speed devices such as a printer.

Stage Analysis
A planning process in which the information system needs of an organization are based on an analysis of its current stage in the growth cycle of the organization and its use of information systems technology.

Standards
Measures of performance developed to evaluate the progress of a system toward its objectives.

Storage
Pertaining to a device into which data can be entered, in which they can be held, and from which they can be retrieved at a later time. Same as Memory.

Strategic Information Systems
Information systems that provide a firm with competitive products and services that give it a strategic advantage over its competitors in the marketplace. Also, information systems that promote business innovation, improve operational efficiency, and build strategic information resources for a firm.

Strategic Opportunities Matrix
A planning framework that uses a matrix to help identify opportunities with strategic business potential, as well as a firm's ability to exploit such opportunities with IT.

Structure Chart
A design and documentation technique to show the purpose and relationships of the various modules in a program.

Structured Decisions
Decisions that are structured by the decision procedures or decision rules developed for them. They involve situations where the procedures to follow when a decision is needed can be specified in advance.

Structured Programming
A programming methodology that uses a top-down program design and a limited number of control structures in a program to create highly structured modules of program code.

Structured Query Language (SQL)
A query language that is becoming a standard for advanced database management system packages. A query's basic form is SELECT . . . FROM . . . WHERE.

Subroutine
A routine that can be part of another program routine.

Subschema
A subset or transformation of the logical view of the database schema that is required by a particular user application program.

Subsystem
A system that is a component of a larger system.

Supercomputer
A special category of large computer systems that are the most powerful available. They are designed to solve massive computational problems.

Superconductor
Materials that can conduct electricity with almost no resistance. This allows the development of extremely fast and small electronic circuits. Formerly only possible at super cold temperatures near absolute zero. Recent developments promise superconducting materials near room temperature.

Supply Chain
The network of business processes and interrelationships among businesses that are needed to build, sell, and deliver a product to its final customer.

Supply Chain Management
Integrating management practices and information technology to optimize information and product flows among the processes and business partners within a supply chain.

Switch
(1) A device or programming technique for making a selection. (2) A computer that controls message switching among the computers and terminals in a telecommunications network.

Switching Costs
The costs in time, money, effort, and inconvenience that it would take a customer or supplier to switch its business to a firm's competitors.

Synchronous
A characteristic in which each event, or the performance of any basic operation, is constrained to start on, and usually to keep in step with, signals from a timing clock. Contrast with Asynchronous.

System
(1) A group of interrelated or interacting elements forming a unified whole. (2) A group of interrelated components working together toward a common goal by accepting inputs and producing outputs in an organized transformation process. (3) An assembly of methods, procedures, or techniques unified by regulated interaction to form an organized whole. (4) An organized collection of people, machines, and methods required to accomplish a set of specific functions.

System Flowchart
A graphic diagramming tool used to show the flow of information processing activities as data are processed by people and devices.

System Software
Programs that control and support operations of a computer system. System software includes a variety of programs, such as operating systems, database management systems, communications control programs, service and utility programs, and programming language translators.

System Specifications
The product of the systems design stage. It consists of specifications for the hardware, software, facilities, personnel, databases, and the user interface of a proposed information system.

System Support Programs
Programs that support the operations, management, and users of a computer system by providing a variety of support services. Examples are system utilities and performance monitors.

Systems Analysis
(1) Analyzing in detail the components and requirements of a system. (2) Analyzing in detail the information needs of an organization, the characteristics and components of presently utilized information systems, and the functional requirements of proposed information systems.

Systems Approach
A systematic process of problem solving that defines problems and opportunities in a systems context. Data are gathered describing the problem or opportunity, and alternative solutions are identified and evaluated. Then the best solution is selected and implemented, and its success evaluated.

Systems Design
Deciding how a proposed information system will meet the information needs of end users. Includes logical and physical design activities, and user interface, data, and process design activities that produce system specifications that satisfy the system requirements developed in the systems analysis stage.

Systems Development
(1) Conceiving, designing, and implementing a system. (2) Developing information systems by a process of investigation, analysis, design, implementation, and maintenance. Also called the systems development life cycle (SDLC), information systems development, or application development.

Systems Development Tools
Graphical, textual, and computer-aided tools and techniques used to help analyze, design, and document the development of an information system. Typically used to represent (1) the components and flows of a system, (2) the user interface, (3) data attributes and relationships, and (4) detailed system processes.

Systems Implementation
The stage of systems development in which hardware and software are acquired, developed, and installed; the system is tested and documented; people are trained to operate and use the system; and an organization converts to the use of a newly developed system.

Systems Investigation
The screening, selection, and preliminary study of a proposed information system solution to a business problem.

Systems Maintenance
The monitoring, evaluating, and modifying of a system to make desirable or necessary improvements.

Systems Thinking
Recognizing systems, subsystems, components of systems, and system interrelationships in a situation. Also known as a systems context or a systemic view of a situation.

Tangible Benefits and Costs
The quantifiable benefits and costs of a proposed solution or system.

Task and Project Management
Managing team and workgroup projects by scheduling, tracking, and charting the completion status of tasks within a project.

Task Management
A basic operating system function that manages the accomplishment of the computing tasks of users by a computer system.

TCP/IP
Transmission control protocol/Internet protocol. A suite of telecommunications network protocols used by the

Internet, intranets, and extranets that has become a de facto network architecture standard for many companies.

Technical Feasibility
Whether reliable hardware and software capable of meeting the needs of a proposed system can be acquired or developed by an organization in the required time.

Technological Implementation
Formal programs of implementation-support activities to encourage user acceptance and productive use of reengineered business processes and new information technologies.

Technology Management
The establishment of organizational groups to identify, introduce, and monitor the assimilation of new information system technologies into organizations.

Telecommunications
Pertaining to the transmission of signals over long distances, including not only data communications but also the transmission of images and voices using radio, television, and other communications technologies.

Telecommunications Channel
The part of a telecommunications network that connects the message source with the message receiver. It includes the hardware, software, and media used to connect one network location to another for the purpose of transmitting and receiving information.

Telecommunications Control Program
A computer program that controls and supports the communications between the computers and terminals in a telecommunications network.

Telecommunications Controller
A data communications interface device (frequently a special-purpose mini- or microcomputer) that can control a telecommunications network containing many terminals.

Telecommunications Monitors
Computer programs that control and support the communications between the computers and terminals in a telecommunications network.

Telecommunications Processors
Internetwork processors such as switches and routers, and other devices such as multiplexers and communications controllers that allow a communications channel to carry simultaneous data transmissions from many terminals. They may also perform error monitoring, diagnostics and correction, modulation-demodulation, data compression, data coding and decoding, message switching, port contention, and buffer storage.

Telecommuting
The use of telecommunications to replace commuting to work from one's home.

Teleconferencing
The use of video communications to allow business conferences to be held with participants who are scattered across a country, continent, or the world.

Telephone Tag
The process that occurs when two people who wish to contact each other by telephone repeatedly miss each other's phone calls.

Teleprocessing
Using telecommunications for computer-based information processing.

Terabyte
One trillion bytes. More accurately, 2 to the 40th power, or 1,009,511,627,776 in decimal notation.

Text Data
Words, phrases, sentences, and paragraphs used in documents and other forms of communication.

Throughput
The total amount of useful work performed by a data processing system during a given period of time.

Time Sharing
Providing computer services to many users simultaneously while providing rapid responses to each.

Total Quality Management
Planning and implementing programs of continuous quality improvement, where quality is defined as meeting or exceeding the requirements and expectations of customers for a product or service.

Touch-Sensitive Screen
An input device that accepts data input by the placement of a finger on or close to the CRT screen.

Track
The portion of a moving storage medium, such as a drum, tape, or disk, that is accessible to a given reading head position.

Trackball
A rollerball device set in a case used to move the cursor on a computer's display screen.

Transaction
An event that occurs as part of doing business, such as a sale, purchase, deposit, withdrawal, refund, transfer, payment, and so on.

Transaction Document
A document produced as part of a business transaction. For instance: a purchase order, paycheck, sales receipt, or customer invoice.

Transaction File
A data file containing relatively transient data to be processed in combination with a master file. Contrast with Master File.

Transaction Processing Cycle
A cycle of basic transaction processing activities including data entry, transaction processing, database maintenance, document and report generation, and inquiry processing.

Transaction Processing System (TPS)
An information system that processes data arising from the occurrence of business transactions.

Transaction Terminals
Terminals used in banks, retail stores, factories, and other work sites that are used to capture transaction data at their point of origin. Examples are point-of-sale (POS) terminals and automated teller machines (ATMs).

Transborder Data Flows (TDF)
The flow of business data over telecommunications networks across international borders.

Transform Algorithm
Performing an arithmetic computation on a record key and using the result of the calculation as an address for that record. Also known as key transformation or hashing.

Transnational Strategy
A management approach in which an organization integrates its global business activities through close cooperation and interdependence among its

headquarters, operations, and international subsidiaries, and its use of appropriate global information technologies.

Turnaround Document
Output of a computer system (such as customer invoices and statements) that is designed to be returned to the organization as machine-readable input.

Turnaround Time
The elapsed time between submission of a job to a computing center and the return of the results.

Turnkey Systems
Computer systems where all of the hardware, software, and systems development needed by a user are provided.

Unbundling
The separate pricing of hardware, software, and other related services.

Uniform Resource Locator (URL)
An access code (such as http://www.sun.com) for identifying and locating hypermedia document files, databases, and other resources at web sites and other locations on the Internet, intranets, and extranets.

Universal Product Code (UPC)
A standard identification code using bar coding, printed on products that can be read by the optical supermarket scanners of the grocery industry.

Unstructured Decisions
Decisions that must be made in situations where it is not possible to specify in advance most of the decision procedures to follow.

User-Friendly
A characteristic of human-operated equipment and systems that makes them safe, comfortable, and easy to use.

User Interface
That part of an operating system or other program that allows users to communicate with it to load programs, access files, and accomplish other computing tasks.

User Interface Design
Designing the interactions between end users and computer systems, including input/output methods and the conversion of data between human-readable and machine-readable forms.

Utility Program
A standard set of routines that assists in the operation of a computer system by performing some frequently required process such as copying, sorting, or merging.

Value-Added Carriers
Third-party vendors who lease telecommunications lines from common carriers and offer a variety of telecommunications services to customers.

Value-Added Resellers (VARs)
Companies that provide industry-specific software for use with the computer systems of selected manufacturers.

Value Chain
Viewing a firm as a series or chain of basic activities that add value to its products and services and thus add a margin of value to the firm.

Videoconferencing
Realtime video and audio conferencing (1) among users at networked PCs (desktop videoconferencing), or (2) among participants in conference rooms or auditoriums in different locations (teleconferencing). Videoconferencing can also include whiteboarding and document sharing.

Videotex
An interactive information service provided over phone lines or cable TV channels.

Virtual Communities
Groups of people with similar interests who meet and share ideas on the Internet and online services and develop a feeling of belonging to a community.

Virtual Company
A form of organization that uses telecommunications networks and other information technologies to link the people, assets, and ideas of a variety of business partners, no matter where they may be located, in order to exploit a business opportunity.

Virtual Machine
Pertaining to the simulation of one type of computer system by another computer system.

Virtual Mall
An online multimedia simulation of a shopping mall with many different interlinked retail web sites.

Virtual Memory
The use of secondary storage devices as an extension of the primary storage of the computer, thus giving the appearance of a larger main memory than actually exists.

Virtual Private Network
A secure network that uses the Internet as its main backbone network to connect the intranets of a company's different locations, or to establish extranet links between a company and its customers, suppliers, or other business partners.

Virtual Reality
The use of multisensory human/computer interfaces that enable human users to experience computer-simulated objects, entities, spaces, and "worlds" as if they actually existed.

Virtual Storefront
An online multimedia simulation of a retail store shopping experience on the Web.

Virtual Team
A team whose members use the Internet, intranets, extranets, and other networks to communicate, coordinate, and collaborate with each other on tasks and projects, even though they may work in different geographic locations and for different organizations.

VLSI: Very-Large-Scale Integration
Semiconductor chips containing hundreds of thousands of circuits.

Voice Conferencing
Telephone conversations shared among several participants via speaker phones or networked PCs with Internet telephone software.

Voice Mail
Unanswered telephone messages are digitized, stored, and played back to the recipient by a voice messaging computer.

Voice Recognition
Direct conversion of spoken data into electronic form suitable for entry into a computer system. Also called voice data entry.

Volatile Memory
Memory (such as electronic semiconductor memory) that loses its contents when electrical power is interrupted.

Wand
A handheld optical character recognition device used for data entry by many transaction terminals.

Web Browser
A software package that provides the user interface for accessing Internet, intranet, and extranet web sites. Browsers are becoming multifunction universal clients for sending and receiving E-mail, downloading files, accessing Java applets, participating in discussion groups, developing web pages, and other Internet, intranet, and extranet applications.

Web Publishing
Creating, converting, and storing hyperlinked documents and other material on Internet or intranet web servers so they can easily be shared via web browsers with teams, workgroups, or the enterprise.

What-If Analysis
Observing how changes to selected variables affect other variables in a mathematical model.

Whiteboarding
See Data Conferencing.

Wide Area Network (WAN)
A data communications network covering a large geographic area.

Window
One section of a computer's multiple-section display screen, each of which can have a different display.

Wireless LANs
Using radio or infrared transmissions to link devices in a local area network.

Word
(1) A string of characters considered as a unit. (2) An ordered set of bits (usually larger than a byte) handled as a unit by the central processing unit.

Word Processing
The automation of the transformation of ideas and information into a readable form of communication. It involves the use of computers to manipulate text data in order to produce office communications in the form of documents.

Workgroup Computing
Members of a networked workgroup may use groupware tools to communicate, coordinate, and collaborate, and to share hardware, software, and databases to accomplish group assignments.

Workstation
(1) A computer system designed to support the work of one person. (2) A high-powered computer to support the work of professionals in engineering, science, and other areas that require extensive computing power and graphics capabilities.

World Wide Web (WWW)
A global network of multimedia Internet information sources.

Name Index

Abramson, Michael L., 338
Adelman, Ken, 148
Adler, Robert, 509
Aghdaei, Amir, 374
Ahrens, Judith, 199
Aldinger, Norman, 40
Allbaugh, Gaylin, 311
Alleyne, Pamela, 447
Alter, Allan, 465
Anderson, Heidi, 247, 291
Andreessen, Marc, 247, 263, 291
Andrews, Tim, 310, 311
Anthes, Gary, 483, 509
Applegate, Linda, 376
Arntz, Isabelle, 463
Asbrand, Deborah, 247, 462
Ashline, Peter, 335
Atwood, Thomas, 199
Austin, Chip, 373

Babcock, Charles, 199
Baer, Tony, 183, 291
Bahar, Richard, 509
Baig, Edward, 507
Balance, Craigg, 166, 248
Baldino, John, 403
Barksdale, Jim, 291
Barr, Keith, 163, 164
Batchelder, Gene, 44, 466
Batterson, David, 89
Baumann, Charles, 425, 426
Bearden, Keith, 380, 381
Beath, Cynthia Mathis, 9, 44
Beaudoin, Scott, 149
Beeler, Jesse, 422
Begley, Sharon, 335
Belcher, Lloyd, 335
Bellomy, Donald, 125
Bellovin, Steven, 509

Belmonte, Richard, 421
Ben-Israel, Ron, 163
Bentley, Lonnie, 422
Bernard, Ryan, 252, 291
Berzin, Rima, 507
Bezos, Jeff, 202, 203, 224, 373, 506
Bikson, Tora, 269, 292
Blackburn, David, 335
Blattberg, Robert C., 9, 247, 335, 509
Bloom, Paul, 509
Blum, Scott, 223–224
Bly, Bob, 291
Boardman, Tom, 197
Bock, Ed, 53
Bonner, Michael, 486
Borders, Jeff, 100, 174
Botchner, Ed, 335
Bowles, Gene, 361, 362, 377, 422, 465
Bowles, Jerry, 273, 291, 376, 421, 465
Boylan, Jo Ann, 332
Boynton, Andrew, 465
Brack, Dennis, 59, 61, 490
Bradley, Allen, 335
Bradley, Stephen P., 16, 44, 458, 465
Brandel, Mary, 465
Bray, Hiawatha, 89
Brooks, Andrew, 374
Brown, Carol, 421
Brown, Derek, 131
Brown, Eric, 288
Brown, Kathryn, 251
Bruegger, Dave, 199
Brun-Cottain, Françoise, 389, 421
Burden, Kevin, 267, 335, 403,
      408, 421
Burns, Christine, 95
Burrows, Peter, 89, 95
Buta, Paul, 335
Bylinsky, Gene, 335

Cafasso, Rosemary, 10, 199, 421
Callon, Jack, 376
Calloway, D. Wayne, 299
Campbell, Gail, 447
Campbell, Ian, 261, 291
Caron, J. Raymond, 354, 376
Carpenter, Guy, 446
Carper, William, 456, 465
Carr, Houston, 166
Carrol, Michael, 248
Case, Stephen M., 130–132
Cash, James I., Jr., 44, 376, 465
Cavanaugh, Nancy, 421
Cerullo, Michael J., 219, 248
Champy, James, 44, 338, 376
Chan, Hock Chuan, 199
Charles, Cindy, 4
Chatterjee, Samir, 135
Chell, Cam, 125
Chen, H., 278, 291
Cheswick, William, 509
Child, Robert, 243
Clark, Charles, 421
Clemons, Eric, 376
Cohen, Susan, 269, 292
Cole, Kenneth, 462
Cole-Gomolski, Barb, 291, 404, 419, 421,
    493, 509
Collins, Tom, 95
Colonna, Jerry, 425
Conchatre, Michael, 49
Connors, Bob, 332
Cook, Jim, 4, 5
Cooper, Louise, 243, 418
Cope, Jim, 65
Corbett, Michael, 465
Cox, Earl, 335
Cox, Nancy, 259, 291
Cressman, George, 41
Cronin, Mary, 44, 166, 248, 335, 363, 364,
    365, 376, 413, 421, 465
Cross, John, 405, 406, 422
Cruz, Kathy, 94, 95
Culnane, Mary, 509
Cutone, Carmine, 199, 422

Dahl, Tom, 183
Daly, James, 509
Dalzell, Richard, 505–506
Darling, Charles, 303, 335
Davenport, Thomas, 17, 44, 205, 248, 344,
    352, 376, 422, 465
Davis, Elaine, 250, 251
Davis, Jeffrey, 131, 203, 224, 373, 506

Deck, Stewart, 248, 295, 332
Dejoie, Roy, 509
DeLacey, Paul, 450
Delhagen, Kate, 506
Devoney, Chris, 91
DiDio, Laura, 335, 477, 483
Dillon, Nancy, 197
DiStefano, Bob, 41
Donaldson, Thomas, 485, 509
Doolittle, Sean, 166, 291, 442, 444, 465
Dryden, Patrick, 497
Duffaut, Eric, 463
Dukker, Stephen, 88, 89
Dunlop, Charles, 509
Dunsky, Pam, 294, 295

Earl, Michael, 405, 406, 422
Ebert, Charles, 126
Eccles, Robert G., 44, 376, 465
Edison, Thomas, 163
Egan, Richard, 335
Elmer-DeWitt, Phillip, 509
El Sawy, Omar, 361, 362, 377, 422, 465
Engler, Natalie, 442
Enwall, Jim, 88
Ericsson, Maria, 128, 187, 199
Eskow, Dennis, 248
Evans, Phillip, 376
Ewusi-Mensah, Kewku, 44

Fayyad, Usama, 179, 376
Feigenbaum, Edward, 312
Felix, June Yee, 424, 426
Fernandez, Tony, 166, 291
Fiedler, Kirk, 422, 434, 465
Finkelstein, Richard, 186, 335
Finnie, Charles, 243
Fitzgerald, Michael, 257, 291
Forte, Gene, 422
Foster, Jason, 66–68
Fowler, George, 509
Freeman, Edward, 509
Freeman, Eva, 88, 335
Freeman, Mark, 89
Frerichs, Kenny, 148, 149
Fried, Louis, 510
Frye, Colleen, 352, 376
Fryer, Bronwyn, 425
Furlong, John, 95
Fusaro, Roberta, 5, 507

Gagne, Cathleen, 291
Galbraith, Craig, 510
Gallery, Bill, 453

Ganesan, Ravi, 510
Gantz, John, 295
Garner, Rochelle, 350
Garvin, David, 376
Gates, Bill, 295, 425
Gembicki, Mark, 482, 483
Giacalone, Robert, 510
Glass, David, 505
Glazer, Rashi, 9, 247, 335, 509
Goff, Leslie, 246, 442
Gold, Elliot, 291
Goldberg, David, 335
Goldman, Steven, 376
Goldstein, Robert, 191, 199
Goodhue, Chris, 67
Gorry, G. Anthony, 335
Gove, Alex, 224
Gow, Kathleen, 140, 248, 291
Gravander, Jerry, 486
Gravel, Chris, 447
Grecco, Michael, 202
Green, Hal, 437, 466
Green, Heather, 89
Greenlar, 214
Gregoire, Peter, 424
Grey, Howard, 208
Grillo, John, 510
Gropper, John, 446, 447
Gross, Neil, 507
Grossman, Jerome, 44, 466
Grotto, Clarence, 486
Grover, Varun, 199, 368, 376, 422, 434, 465
Guha, Subashish, 368, 376, 422
Gurbaxani, Vijay, 377
Gurley, J. William, 224
Guyon, Janet, 91

Haeckel, Stephan, 465
Hallman, Cinda, 438
Halper, Mark, 248
Halpern, Marcia, 40–41
Hamblin, Matt, 164
Hamel, Gary, 248
Hamm, Steve, 95, 339
Hammer, Michael, 16, 44, 376
Hammond, Josh, 376
Hardrath, Janice, 403
Harkness, Warren, 422
Harrington, Susan, 510
Harrison, Ann, 483
Haskin, David, 291
Hasnas, John, 510
Hausman, Jerry A., 16, 44, 458, 465
Hawk, Keith, 295

Hawson, James, 422
Headapohl, William, 468, 469
Hellweg, Eric, 311
Henderson, Rik, 335
Herringshaw, Chris, 248
Hershey, Al, 66–68
Hesney, Douglas T., 73
Hibbard, Justin, 376
Higgins, Kelly, 335
Hills, Melanie, 44, 263, 264, 291, 407, 422
Hodges, Judy, 248
Hoffman, Thomas, 197, 251, 466
Holtz, Shel, 291, 392, 422
Hoopes, L., 278, 291
Horwitt, Elisabeth, 49
Houston, Carr, 247
Hsu, P., 278, 291
Huff, Sid, 336

Iansiti, Marco, 395, 422
Ingram, Steve, 419
Inmon, W.H., 178
Itoi, Nikki Goth, 463
Ives, Blake, 466

Jablonowski, Mark, 335
Jacobs, April, 87, 91
Jacobs, Gerry, 465
Jacobsen, Ageneta, 128, 187, 199
Jacobsen, Ivar, 128, 187, 199
Janal, Daniel, 248
Jarvenpaa, Sirkka, 354, 376, 466
Jenkings, Avery, 199
Jiang, James, 248
Johnson, Deborah, 510
Johnson, Stella, 349
Jones, Wynn, 266, 267
Jordan, Graeber, 287
Joseph, Suresh, 149
Judge, Paul C., 169
Jue, Geoff, 425, 426
Julien, Ellen, 418

Kalakota, Ravi, 15, 166, 207, 208, 230, 232, 238, 248, 291, 303, 335, 422, 470, 510
Kalin, Sari, 456, 466
Kalish, David, 91
Kallman, Earnest, 510
Kasparov, Garry, 60, 61
Kastner, Peter, 248
Kay, Mary, 425
Keen, Peter G.W., 44, 166, 248, 367, 376, 422, 466
Kelley, Mary, 311

Kennedy, Ken, 91
Keppler, Kay, 510
Kerin, John, 182, 183
Kettinger, William, 368, 376, 422
King, James, 335
King, Julia, 41, 126, 335, 447, 466
King, Nelson, 291
King, William, 466
Kirkpatrick, David, 91, 466
Kizzier, Chris, 447
Klein, Kristina, 216
Kling, Rob, 509
Knouse, Stephen, 510
Koenig, Howard, 419
Kramer, Kenneth, 377
Kraus, Joe, 507
Kroenke, David, 199
Kupfer, Andrew, 166
Kurszweil, Raymond, 335
Kwock, Kee Wei, 199

Lai, Vincent, 335
Lambe, Dave, 259, 265
Lambert, Katherine, 482
Lamont, Dan, 402
Lanford, Audry, 469
LaPlante, Alice, 248, 291, 335, 419, 454, 455, 466, 510
Lasker, Harry, 336
Laube, David, 287, 291
Laufman, Gary, 468
Lawrence, Bill, 109, 110
Lee, Sooun, 199
Levenson, Alan, 380
Levin, Vladimir, 496
Levis, John, 466
Levitan, Jeff, 349, 350
Levitt, Lee, 292
Levy, Henry, 40
Liebman, Lenny, 477, 510
Liss, Samantha, 243
Little, John D.C., 9, 247, 335, 509
Littleton, Mike, 506
Lochow, John, 463
Loeb, Larry, 248
Lorents, Alden, 199
Loshin, Peter, 246, 248
Luechtefeld, Monica, 350
Luftman, Jerry, 466
Lundquist, Christopher, 311
Lynn, Renee, 53

MacCormack, Alan, 395, 422
Machlis, Sharon, 20, 243, 244, 311, 418

Madsen, Peter, 487, 510
Maglitta, Joseph, 292, 377, 422, 466
Mahan, Suruchi, 248
Maher, Mike, 505
Mailoux, Jacquiline, 336
Mankin, Don, 269, 292
Margolin, George, 163
Marion, Larry, 40, 462
Markus, M. Lynn, 9, 44
Martin, Bob, 44, 466
Martin, Chuck, 166, 209, 248, 392, 422
Martin, James, 216, 509, 510
Martin, Michael, 466
Martinez, Gina, 88
Mathaisel, Bernard, 338, 339
May, Thomas, 248
McBratney, Melissa, 197
McCarthy, John, 312
McCauley, Ron, 402, 403
McCracken, Harry, 163
McCulloch, Warren, 312
McFarlan, F. Warren, 376, 466
McFarland, Michael, 510
McKeen, James D., 199
McKenney, James, 376
McNealy, Scott, 255
McNeill, F. Martin, 336
Medich, Cathy J., 223
Merrill, Gregory, 510
Middelhoff, Thomas, 373
Millar, Victor, 377
Millette, Eric, 94
Milne, George, 509
Minsky, Marvin, 312
Mische, Michael, 433, 450, 466
Mitnick, Kevin, 498
Miyaki, Sandi, 125
Mooney, John, 377
Moore, Gordon, 425
Moore, John, 457
Morgan, Cynthia, 469
Morgan, James N., 199, 398, 422, 432, 466
Morris, Richard, 462
Morton, Michael Scott, 335
Moschella, David, 44
Moskowitz, D., 99
Moxiey, Dave, 41
Mullison, Suzanne, 264
Murray, Richard, 351, 421

Nagel, Roger, 376
Nakabara, R., 380, 381
Nash, Kim, 292
Neumann, Peter, 44, 292, 478, 494, 510

Neumann, Seev, 44, 377
Newcomb, Jonathan, 6, 44, 466
Newell, Allen, 312
Newmann, Peter, 44
Niedorf, Steve, 17
Nohria, Nitin, 44, 376, 465
Nolan, Richard L., 16, 44, 376, 458, 465
Nonaka, Ikujiro, 377
Norman, Ronald, 422
Norton, David, 336
Nunamaker, J.F., 278, 291

O'Brien, Atiye, 292
O'Brien, James A., 422, 432, 466
O'Reilly, Tim, 248
Orenstein, David, 110, 125, 126, 333
Orlikowsky, Wanda, 422
Orwig, R., 278, 291
Ouellett, Tim, 59, 60, 91
Overbeek, Will Van, 66

Palmisano, Giorgio, 446
Palvia, Prashant, 466
Palvia, Shailendra, 466
Panatera, Lawrence, 292
Papows, Jeff, 292
Paradice, David, 509
Pegels, C. Carl, 355, 377
Pei, Daniel, 199, 422
Pelaez, Jose Luis, 70
Perin, Constance, 292
Perlman, Steve, 131
Perry, Chip, 243
Perry, David, 244
Peterson, Mike, 333
Petty, Terrence, 466
Phillips, Ronald, 292
Piatetsky-Shapiro, Gregory, 179, 376
Picatrill, Lisa, 91
Pimentel, Ken, 336
Pittman, Robert W., 130–132
Pitts, Walter, 312
Pizi, Anthony, 95
Porter, Michael, 377
Preis, Kenneth, 376
Price, Mike, 349
Prince, Michael, 110, 196–197
Prokesch, Steven, 377, 422
Pussurach, Patiwat, 248
Pyle, Raymond, 248

Radcliff, Deborah, 67
Randich, Steve, 463
Reed, Stanley, 464

Rees, Dennis, 87
Reichard, Kevin, 292
Reinhardt, Andy, 89, 95
Renard, D., 248
Resnick, Rosalind, 377
Resnick, Seth, 168
Rice, Ted, 294
Riggio, Stephen, 373
Riley, Jon, 385
Roche, Edward M., 466
Rochlin, Dave, 5, 418
Rockart, John, 44, 466
Rosenblatt, Frank, 312
Roth, Daniel, 425
Rothfeder, Jeffrey, 476, 491, 510
Row, Michael, 376
Rowell, Jan, 466
Rubin, Elaine, 243
Ruettgers, Michael C., 168, 169
Rystedt, Rex, 109

Saffouri, Ramzi, 469
Sager, Ira, 87
Sambamurthy, V., 421
Sampath, Srivhes, 506
Sampler, Jeffrey, 405, 406, 422
Sams, Ruth, 89
Sandhu, Ravi, 510
Sandler, Jeff, 248
Sankar, Chetan, 199
Satzinger, John, 336
Schaffer, Richard, 311
Scheier, Robert, 248, 292, 299, 425
Schneider, Jules, 462
Schonberger, Richard, 377
Schuler, Barry, 131
Schuler, Doug, 510
Segars, Albert, 368, 376, 422
Seltzer, Bill, 349, 350
Senge, Peter, 382, 422
Senn, James A., 234
Sethi, Vikram, 466
Seybold, Patricia, 248
Shaffer, Alan, 19, 20
Shafritz, Jay, 487, 510
Shank, Roger, 312
Shaw, Stephen, 291
Siau, Keng Leng, 199
Sibbald, Peter, 48
Siekman, David, 126
Siekman, Philip, 377
Silver, Mark, 9, 44
Simon, Herbert, 312
Simpson, David, 91, 466

Skeet, Rob, 125
Slater, Derek, 510
Slitz, John, 199
Sliwa, Carol, 287, 288
Sloan, Robert, 437, 466
Smith, H. Jefferson, 510
Smith, Heather A., 199
Smith, Jim, 125
Smith, Maureen, 418
Smith, Padhraic, 179, 376
Smith, Robert Ellis, 507
Smith, Victoria Hall, 41
Snedecor, Dan, 339
Snelling, Angela, 20, 36
Snow, Andy, 19
Snyder, Charles, 166, 247
Solanki, Vimal, 149
Solvik, Peter, 462
Spanbauer, Scott, 110
Spiegler, Israel, 199
Stark, Andrew, 510
Stauffer, Brian, 110
Steadman, Craig, 199, 381
Steiner, Laurie, 223
Stepanek, Marcia, 95, 339, 374, 507
Stevens, Christopher, 248
Stevensen, Mark, 449
Stewart, Jim, 49
Stoddard, Donna, 354, 376
Storey, Veda, 191, 199
Strassman, Paul, 466
Strom, David, 292
Sullivan, Bob, 507
Sullivan, Danny, 469
Sully, Sandy, 288
Sumners, Paul, 213
Sylvester, James, 510

Taptich, Brian, 89, 224
Tate, Priscilla, 510
Teixeira, Kevin, 336
Teng, James, 199, 376, 422, 434, 465
Tetzeli, Rick, 289
Thomson, Andrew, 164
Thro, Ellen, 336
Torvalds, Linus, 109, 110
Truong, Lam H., 292
Tucker, Jay, 236, 248
Tucker, Michael, 248
Tully, Roger, 411
Tumey, Peggy, 264
Turing, Alan, 312

Turner, Danny, 266
Tuttle, Mark, 486

VandeHel, Jim, 20, 36
Vandenbosch, Betty, 336
Van DeZande, Doug, 250
VanLengen, Craig A., 422
Van Overbeek, Will, 66
Vanzura, Rick, 196
Verity, John, 466
Viswanatha, Srinivasan, 447
Vitalari, Nicholas, 450, 451, 466
Vitoria, Stephen, 447
Voltz, Tom, 287
Von Schilling, Peter, 466

Wadman, Tim, 48, 49
Wagner, Mitch, 336, 508, 510
Wainwright, Julie, 224
Wall, Patricia, 389, 421
Wallace, Bob, 166, 339
Walther, Eckart, 227, 257
Waltner, Charles, 292
Watson, Hugh, 335, 336
Watterson, Karen, 336
Weinstein, Lauren, 292
Welz, Gary, 335
Weston, Randy, 206, 445, 466
Wetherbe, James, 450, 451, 466
Whinston, Andrew, 15, 166, 207, 208, 230, 232, 238, 248, 291, 303, 335, 422, 470, 510
Whitten, Jeffrey, 422
Wiener, Norbert, 312
Wilard, Nancy, 510
Wilkinson, Joseph W., 219, 248
Wilson, Linda, 199
Winston, Patrick, 314, 336
Wolinsky, Carol, 510
Woodrum, Jeff, 251
Wright, Jimmy, 505
Wurster, Thomas, 376
Wylder, John, 483

Yetter, Wayne, 44, 466

Zahedi, Fatemeh, 377, 472, 510
Zander, Ed, 91
Zerega, Blaise, 149
Zigli, Ronald, 466
Zmud, Robert, 465
Zonenshine, Jeffrey, 462

Organizational Index

Aberdeen Group, 125
Acquired Intelligence, 327
A-DEC Inc., 380–381
Adobe Systems, Inc., 102, 103
Advanced Manufacturing Council, 232
Advanced Micro Devices (AMD), 67, 88, 89
Advanced Software Applications, 469
AeroGroup International, 462
Aerostructures Corp., 403
AgriMail.com, 243
Airborne Express, 343
Air Products and Chemicals, 368, 369
Alaska Airlines, 13
Allied Signal Aerospace, 445
Amazon.com, 13, 20, 131, 202–204, 224,
    228–229, 311, 373, 449, 505–506
American Airlines, 12–13, 14, 140, 368, 369,
    451; see also AMR Corp.
American Express, 238, 347, 369
American General Finance Inc., 87
American Mobile Satellite, 151
American Society for Industrial Security, 496
America Online (AOL), 130–132, 138, 203,
    228, 277, 373, 418, 493
America's Job Bank, 216
AmeriServe Inc., 87
Amp, Inc., 141
AMR Corp., 14, 345; see also American
    Airlines
A&M Records, 13
Analog Devices, Inc., 40
Andrea Electronics, 71
AOL Europe, 373
Apache International, 110
Apple Computer, 64, 88, 89, 114
Aptex Software, 311, 312, 316
Arby's, 303
Arthur D. Little, Inc., 141
ASD Catalogs, 66–68

Aspect Telecommunications, 94, 95
Association of Information Technology
    Professionals (AITP), 495, 501, 502
@Home, 131, 163
ATI Technologies, 89
AT&T, 114, 138, 159, 259, 446
AT&T WorldNet, 138
Auerbach, 408
Aurum Software, 425
Austin-Hayne, 217
AutoConnect, 243
Automated Data Processing Inc. (ADP), 419
Automotive Network Exchange (ANX), 149
Automotive Systems Group, 212
Auto Shack Stores, 386, 390, 393, 406, 407
Autoweb Interactive, 228

Baan Co., 40, 205, 381
BancOne, 346, 369
Bank of America, 178–179
Bank of Boston, 492
Bank of Montreal, 41
Barnes & Noble, 131, 203, 228, 373, 507
Barnesandnoble.com, 507
BARTNAGEL.COM, 148
Battelle Pacific Northwest Laboratories, 258
Baxter Healthcare, 369
Bay Networks, 408
BC Telecom (BC TEL), 250–252
BCT.TELUS Communications, Inc., 251
Bechtel Corp., 258
Bell Canada, 463
Bergen Brunswig, 368, 369
Bertelsmann, 203, 373
Best Buy, 88
Bestware, Inc., 220
Beyond Software, 49
Black Star, 59, 61, 490
Black & Veatch, 141

Blockbuster Entertainment Group, 5
Blue Cross/Blue Shield (Empire), 428
Boeing Corp., 40, 287, 495
BookServe.com, 224
Borders Books and Music, 196
Brightware, 311
British Petroleum Exploration (BPX), 405, 406
Broadvision Inc., 243
Burger King, 87
Burlington Coat Factory, 109, 110, 196–197
Buy.com, 223–224
BuyDirect Inc., 468, 469

Cabletron, 408
Cadence Design Systems, 260–262
Candie's, 462
CareerMosaic, 216
CareerPath.com, 216
Caterpillar, 319
CDNow Inc., 203, 228, 243
Center for Democracy and Technology, 491
Charles Schwab, 13, 169, 287, 310–312
Chase Manhattan Bank, 311, 368, 369, 424, 425, 452
Chemdex Corp., 243, 244
Chemical Bank, 367, 369, 429
Chicago Stock Exchange, 182–184, 462–463
CH2M Hill Inc., 258
Chrysler Corp., 212, 343–344
CIGNA Corp., 353, 354, 369, 424, 425
CIO Institute, 483
Cisco Systems, 143, 169, 359–360, 408, 462–463
Citibank, 344, 367, 451, 496
Citicorp, 343, 369, 447
Citrix Systems, 125
Clarke American Checks Inc., 418
Coca-Cola Co., 131, 451
Collabra, 164
Comcast, 163
CommerceNet, 223
Compaq, 67, 169, 224
CompareNet, 203
CompuServe, 131, 493
Computer Associates International, Inc. (CA), 67, 116, 402–403, 439, 475
COMSAT Personal Communication, 151, 152
Comshare, Inc., 34, 308
Conoco, Inc., 307
Consolidated Freightways, 18, 343
Consolidated Rail, 303

Corel, 98, 101, 102, 105, 110, 115, 270
Corestates, 369
Corning Inc., 418–419
Costco, 88
Countrywide Home Loans, 262
COVIA, 345
CUC International, 131, 141
CyberCash, 237, 239
CyberCoin, 238, 239
Cyberian Outpost Inc., 243, 418
Cyrix, 67, 88

DaimlerChrysler, 212, 343–344
Dassault Systems, 343
DataBeam Corp., 274
Data Fellows Inc., 506
DataMasters, 216
Datapro, 408
Dayton Hudson Corp., 333
DB2, 196
Deere & Co., 18, 343, 369
Dell Computers, 67, 169
Delta Air Lines, 169
Designs Inc., 343
DigiCash, 238
Digital Equipment Corp. (DEC), 183, 282, 368, 369
Diner's Club International, 69, 76, 238
Discreet Data, 491
Diversified Investment Advisors, Inc., 48, 49
Dow Chemical, 87
Dow Jones, 310–311, 369, 448
Dow Jones Information Services, 448
Dragon Systems, 71
The Dreyfus Corp., 13
DrugStore.com, 505
Ducks Unlimited Canada, 48, 49
DuPont, 438

Earthlink Network, 138
Eastman Kodak Co., 492
EchoStar, 131
EFTC Corp., 243
Egghead.com, 94, 95
Electronic Data Systems (EDS), 453, 463–464
emachines Inc., 88–89
EMC Corp., 20, 36, 168–170
Empire Blue Cross/Blue Shield, 428
Enron Energy Services, 182–184
Enterprise Products, 310–312
Environmental Protection Agency (EPA), 218

Equal Employment Opportunity
 Commission (EEOC), 218
Ernst & Young LLP, 66–68
E*Trade, 222, 224
Excite Inc., 131, 137, 311, 507

Farmers Insurance Group, 197
Federal Bureau of Investigation (F.B.I.), 469
Federal Express, 13, 18, 260, 303, 343,
 368, 369
First Bancorporation of Ohio, 492
First Chicago, 369
First Union Corp., 13, 197
First Virtual, 238
Flatiron Partners, 425
Florida State University, 89
Ford Motor Co., 212, 319, 338–340
Forrester Research, 149, 250, 251, 288,
 455, 506
Frost & Sullivan, 149
furniture.com, 374
FutureLink, 125

GameServe.com, 224
Gannett, 369
Gap, 507
Gartner Group, 49, 67, 250
GE Information Services, 234
Genentech Inc., 244
General Electric (GE), 147, 183, 234, 318,
 369, 495
General Motors (GM), 463–464
GE Trading Process Network, 147
Glaxo Wellcome, 250–252
GlobalLink New Media, 20, 36
GM-Opel, 463–464
Gould Paper Corp., 258
Great Plains Software, 125
GroupSystems, 278
Gulf States Paper, 213
Guy Carpenter & Co., 446, 447

Halco Business Products, 40–41
Hamilton Corp., 359–360
Hastings Entertainment, 258
Helsinki University, 110
Hewlett-Packard, 54, 59, 62, 67, 73, 110,
 114, 115, 374
Hitachi, 49, 88, 317, 446
Hitachi Data Systems, 88
Holiday Inns, 13
Hotlinks, Inc., 164

HRLive, 214–216
Hudson's, 333

IBM, 49, 53, 55, 58, 59, 60, 61, 64, 67, 71,
 87, 88, 89, 95, 110, 114, 115, 126, 155,
 169, 188, 196, 197, 234, 238, 295, 304,
 311, 319, 332, 369, 402–403, 408, 446,
 453, 462, 495
IBM Advantis, 234
IceGroup, 203
ichat, Inc., 277
The Image Bank, 17
The Image Works, 214, 457
Index Stock Photography Inc., 69, 441
Industrial Matematic International, 206
INFORM, 304
Information Advantage, 303, 333
Information Resources Inc. (IRI), 206,
 208–209
Informix, 188
Infoseek, 131, 137, 316
Info Tech, 5
InfoTek Systems, 483
Ingram Book Group, 373
Ingram Entertainment, 224
Intel, 55, 64, 65, 67, 89, 113, 114, 274
Intellichoice, Inc., 141
Intellsat, 151
International Data Corp. (IDC), 40, 87, 250,
 256, 260, 418

J.P. Morgan & Co., 447
Jabil Circuit, 359–360
Jay Jacobs, 109, 110
JBA International, 462
JCPenney, 238, 263
JFax, 272
JobSmart, 216
Johnson Controls, 212
Johnson & Higgins, 141
Johnson Wax, 435
Junglee, 203

Kelly Services, Inc., 506–507
Kendall-Jackson Wines, 277
KeyCorp, 258, 309, 332
Key Technology Service, 332
KFC, 87
Kinko's, 275
Kleiner Perkins Caufield & Byers, 505
KPMG, 258
K-Swiss, 277

Lands' End, 13, 228
Levi Strauss, 303, 343
Levitz Furniture, 18, 343
Lexis-Nexis Inc., 294–295
Liberty Mutual Insurance Co., 447
Linux, 109, 110
Liquid Audio, 107
Lockheed Martin, 258–259, 266–268, 319
Lotus Development Corp., 11, 98, 101, 103, 104, 105, 106, 107, 108, 115, 120, 173, 175, 190, 270, 276, 277, 279, 280, 282, 306, 374, 408, 475, 497
Lucent Technologies, 267
Lycos, 373

MacMillan Bloedel Corp., 327
Macromedia, 107
Manufacturers Hanover, 369
Manugistics, Inc., 206
Mapics, Inc., 211
MapInfo, Inc., 304
Marshall Field's, 333
Marshall Industries, 233, 262
MasterCard International, 148, 149, 238, 301
Matsushita Electric, 319
McAfee Online, 506
McAffee Associates, 364–366
McDonald's, 131
McGraw-Hill, 369
MCI WorldCom, 148, 149, 169
McKesson Corp., 18, 343, 369
Media Metrix, 243
MediaOne, 131
MediaOne Express, 163
Mellon Bank, 41, 368, 369
Merrill Lynch, 18, 95, 277, 343, 346, 369
Mervyn's, 333
Metacrawler, 138
Meta Group, 49
Metaphase, 40
Metropolitan Life, 18, 343
Micro Focus Group, 126
Microsoft Corp., 55, 56, 88, 94, 95, 98, 99, 101, 102, 103, 105, 106, 108, 110, 113, 114, 115, 116, 120, 121, 126, 131, 137, 155, 173, 174, 238, 267, 270, 271, 272, 273, 277, 279, 280, 282, 295, 321–322, 402–403, 408, 475, 493
MicroStrategy Inc., 295, 332
Midstate Realty, 40
Milacron Inc., 19, 20–21, 36
The Monsterboard, 216
Morgan Stanley & Co., 320
Motorola, 64, 114

MovieFone, Inc., 141
The Mutual Group, 48, 49
Mutual Life of Canada, 49
MySimon, 311

NASA, 319
National Association of Software Service Companies, 447
National Computer Security Association, 499
National Crime Information Center, 498
National Security Agency (NSA), 483
National Semiconductor, 89
Nations Bank, 277
Navistar, 18, 343
NCD, 55, 57
NCR, 295, 303
NDC Health Information Services, 332
NetBuy, 243
NetChannel, 56
NetDynamic, 251
NetFlix.com, 4, 5, 6
Net Perceptions, 243
Netscape Communications Corp., 99–100, 101, 108, 110, 131, 137, 155, 156, 164, 227, 237, 238, 244, 251, 257, 265, 270, 271, 272, 276, 277, 279, 288, 394, 447, 475
NetWare, 155
Network Alchemy, 148, 149
Network Wizards, 137
New Light Industries, 317
Newsday, 495
NeXT Software, 397
Nortel Networks, 230–231
Norton Utilities, 65, 116
Novell, 94, 108, 115, 270, 279, 280, 282, 408, 475
NSA, 483
N2K, 131, 203
Nucor, 369

Object Design, 183
Occupational Safety and Health Administration (OSHA), 218
Office Depot, 88, 349–350
1-800-flowers, 131
Onyx Corp., 125
OpenConnect, 49
Open Market Inc., 20, 36
Open Text, 280, 282
Oracle Corp., 56, 88, 110, 183, 184, 188, 189, 205, 206, 228, 463
Ovum Ltd, 449
Owens-Corning, 369

Pacific Bell Internet Services, 311
Pacific Northwest National Laboratory,
    496–497
Paine Webber, 95
Parker Hannifin Corp., 258
Peapod, 141
Pechiney, 463
Penthouse, 497
Peoples Bank & Trust Co., 332
PeopleSoft, 205, 251, 418
Pepsi, 451
PepsiCo, 299, 304
Pew Research Center for the People and
    the Press, 418
Pfizer Inc., 447
PG&E Corp., 424, 425
Philips Magnavox, 56
Photo Researchers, 53
PlanetAll, 203
Platinum Technology, 303
Playboy, 497
Port of Los Angeles, 260
Preview Travel, 131
PriceWaterhouseCoopers, 149
Procter & Gamble, 343, 345, 369
Prodigy, Inc., 449–450
PRT Group Ltd., 446, 447
Prudential Insurance Co. of America, 447

Quark, 102

RCA, 56, 131
RealAudio, 228
RealNetworks, 107
Recreational Equipment Inc. (REI), 125
Red Hat Software, 110
Reel.com, 5, 224, 418
Rentrak Corp., 343
The Replay Remailer, 491
Result Communications Ltd., 125–126
Rice University, 495
Richard Eisner & Co., 462
RJR Nabisco, 234
Rockwell International, 258
Rocky's Shoes and Boots, 462
Ross Operating Valves, 357
RSA Data Security, 475

S.C. Johnson & Son, 435
SABRE Decision Technologies, 303
Samsung Electronics, 89
Sandia National Labs, 497
SAP AG, 381, 418, 462
SAP America, 205, 251

Sara Lee Hosiery, 462
Scambusters, 469
Schnuck Markets, 141
Seagage Technology, 89
Sears, 238
Sedgwick James Inc., 304
Seibel Systems, 125
Sempra Energy, 258
Sento Corp., 163–164
Setco Industries, 18, 343
Shari's Management Corp., 402, 403
Sharper Image, 141, 397
Shiva Corp., 373–374
Shop.org, 243
Siemens, 446
Silicon Graphics, 59
Simon & Schuster, 6
Snap-on Inc., 263
Softbank, 223, 224
Software Publishers Association, 497
Sony, 56
SpeedServe, 224
Sprint, 495
The Stalkers Home Page, 491
Staples, 349–350
Sterling Software, 234
Stock Boston, 453
The Stock Market, 53, 70, 73
Storage Dimensions, 361–362
Strategic Pricing Group, 41
Structural Dynamics Research Corp., 339
SunAmerica Financial, 380–381
Sun Microsystems Inc., 55, 57, 95, 114, 120,
    131, 169, 223, 225, 226, 254–256, 320,
    355–356
Sun-Trust Banks, Inc., 482–483
SYGMA, 202
Symantec, 121
Syntellect Interactive Services, 235, 236
Sysco Corp., 87

Taco Bell, 87
Target Stores, 333
TCI, 163
Tech Data, 462–463
Telefónica, 244
Tel-Save, 131
Thinking Machines, 315
3Com, 408
Time Warner, 277
Tinwald Corp., 115
Tokyo Stock Exchange, 317
Tony Stone Images, 208, 385, 411
Toshiba, 75, 83, 317

Toshiba Image Bank, 75, 83
Touchstone Software, 500
Toys 'R' Us, 343, 368, 369
Travelers Corp., 447
Trend Micro, 506–507
Trilogy, 40
TSAI (Telefónica Services Avanzados de
    Información), 244
Tyson Foods, 258

Union Bank of Switzerland, 496
Unisys Corp., 126, 303
United Airlines, 368, 369
U.S. Defense Department, 483
U.S. Department of Defense, 319
U.S. Federal Bureau of Investigation
    (F.B.I.), 469
U.S. National Security Agency (NSA), 483
U.S. Social Security Administration, 497–498
University of Southern California, 497
Unix, 408
US West Inc., 125–126, 163–164, 259,
    264–265, 287

Vanguard Group, 41
Van Waters & Rogers (VW&R), 87–88
Ventana Corp., 279
Verity Inc., 311, 321, 373–374
Versant, 183

VideoServe.com, 224
VIP Systems Inc., 126
Virtual Emporium, 228
VISA International, 169, 238
Visible Decisions, 320
VocalTech, 271
Volkswagen AG, 496
Volpe Brown Whelan & Co., 243

Wall Data, 49
Wal-Mart, 197, 343, 345, 505–506
Warm Boot, 99
Warroom Research Inc., 482–484
Wawa Food Markets Inc., 403
Web Pathlore Software, 419
Whirlpool Corp., 13
White Pine, 274
Winamp, 107
Wired, 495
Worldcom/MCI, 244

Xerox, 369
Xilinx Inc., 288

Yahoo!, 131, 137, 138, 203, 224, 277
Young & Rubicam, 324

Zona Research, 250

Subject Index

Acceptance phase, prototyping, 395
Accessibility, IS services, 411
Accessing databases; see Databases
Accounting information systems, 218–221
  accounts payable, 219, 220
  accounts receivable, 219, 220
  general ledger, 219, 221
  inventory control, 219, 220
  online, 218
  order processing, 218–219
  payroll, 219, 220–221
Accounts payable systems, 219, 220
Accounts receivable systems, 219, 220
Accuracy, 29
Active data dictionaries, 174
Active matrix LCDs, 75
Active misuse computer crime, 494
Ada, 118
Adaptability, 358
Adaptive learning systems, 313, 361
Adaptive system, 23
Additions, 28
Advanced technology groups (ATGs), 443
Advanced technology management, 443
Advertising and promotion, 208–209
Agents, intelligent; see Artificial
    intelligence (AI)
Agile competitors, 356–357
Agile manufacturing, 211
Agility, 356
AITP Standards of Professional
    Conduct, 502
Alliance strategies, 341, 342, 343
Analysis
  business change implementation, 402–403
  and design, prototyping, 394
  of information requirements, 383
Analytical capability, IT, 344

Analytical modeling, 304–307
Anonymous remailers, 491
Antivirus programs, 498, 506–507
Applets, 120–121, 146, 254
Application development, 104, 383
  DBMS, 176
  using prototyping, 394
Applications
  fault tolerance and, 478
  global IT management, 451–452
Application services, 392
Applications of extranets, 262–265
Applications of intranets, 253–256
Application software, 26, 94–108
  desktop publishing (DTP), 101–102
  electronic mail (e-mail), 100–101, 138, 271,
      283, 492
  electronic spreadsheets, 102–103
  for end users, 97–98
  groupware, 106–108
  integrated packages, 98–99
  multimedia presentations, 104–106
  personal information managers (PIM), 106
  presentation graphics, 104–105
  software suites, 98–99
  trends, 96–97
  web browsers, 99–100
  word processing, 101–102
Application-specific software, 97
Applications portfolio, IRM and, 434
Application trends, business
    telecommunications, 136
Architecture
  communications, 150, 156–158
  technology, electronic commerce, 225–226
Archival storage, 82
Arithmetic-logic unit, 63
ARPANET, 136

Artificial intelligence (AI), 31–32, 310–328
 adaptive-learning systems, 313
 application areas, 313
 cognitive science, 313
 decision support, 314
 domains of, 312–314
 expert systems; *see* Expert systems (ES)
 fuzzy logic systems, 313, 316–317
 genetic algorithms, 313, 317–318
 information retrieval, 314
 intelligent agents, 313, 320–322
  information agents, 320
  information brokers, 320
  information filters, 320
  information management agents, 320
  interface tutors, 320
  network navigation agents, 320
  presentation agents, 320
  role-playing agents, 320
  search agents, 320
  user interface agents, 320
 knowledge-based systems, 313
 natural interfaces, 314
 neural networks, 313, 314–316
 objectives, 310
 robotics, 313, 314
 virtual reality (VR), 314, 318–320
ASCII, 78
Assembler, 121
Assembler languages, 117
ATM (asynchronous transfer mode), 159–160
Attributes, 170–171, 391
Auditing
 around the computer system, 480
 through the computer system, 480
 information systems, 480–481
Audit trail, 473, 481
Authenticity, e-commerce and, 470
Automation, 210–211, 344
Automational capability, IT, 344
Availability, 328, 409

Backbone network, 144
Back end, of systems development, 395
Background mode, 113
Backup, IS services, 411
Backup files, 474
Backup systems, 68
Backward engineering, 396
Bandwidth alternatives, telecommunications, 158–159
Bar coding, 72
Barriers to entry, 346
BASIC, 118

Basic machine instructions, 64
Batch processing, 33
 online, 235
Batch total, 471
Baud rate, 158
Behavioral stage theory, 484
Benchmark, 408
Best business practices, 347
Bill of materials, 214
Binary representation, 77
Biometric controls, 476
Biometric profile, 476
Bit, 78
Bloatware, 98
Blocking, e-commerce and, 470
Borderless, 358
Broadband, 159
Browsers, 99–100, 142
Building a strategic IT platform, 342, 346
Bulletin board systems (BBS), 275
Business alignment, 433
Business applications, IS, 7
Business change implementation; *see*
  Implementing business change;
  Implementing new systems
Business-driven IS, 433
Business effectiveness, the Internet and, 363
Business end users, IS and, 6–7
Business ethics, 484–485; *see also* Ethical and
  societal challenges of IT
Business functions, 205
Business information systems, 35, 201–222
 accounting IS; *see* Accounting information
  systems
 cross-functional information systems,
  204–205
 financial management systems, 221–222
  capital budgeting, 222
  cash management, 221
  financial forecasting and planning, 222
  online investment management, 221–222
 human resources IS; *see* Human resources
  information systems
 IS in business, 202–204
 manufacturing IS; *see* Manufacturing
  information systems
 marketing IS; *see* Marketing information
  systems
Business innovation, promoting, 341, 342,
 343, 344
Business operations
 intranets and, 254
 support of, 10–12
Business position, IS services, 411

Business processes, 205
  improvement of, 342–344
Business process reengineering (BPR), 16,
  351–353
Business quality improvement, 353–356
Business telecommunications; *see*
  Telecommunications
Business-to-business commerce, 225,
  231–234
  electronic data interchange (EDI); *see*
    Electronic data interchange (EDI)
  supply-chain management (SCM), 232
  wholesaling on the Web, 232–233
Business-to-consumer commerce, 225,
  226–229
  retailing on the Web, 227–229, 373
    incentives, 228
    look and feel, 228
    performance and service, 227
    personalization, 227
    security and reliability, 228
    socialization, 227
Business use of the Internet, 138–139
Business value, 133
  of extranets, 262
  of the Internet, 140–141
  of intranets, 256–262
Bus network, 155
Busses, 65
Bypasses, 494
Byte, 78

Cable modems, 163
Cache memory, 62–63
Calendaring and scheduling, 279, 283
Capital budgeting, 222
Careers in IS, 440–441
Carpal tunnel syndrome, 499
Case-based information system, 322, 323
CASE (computer-aided software/systems
  engineering), 111, 122, 395 396
Case managers, 352
Cash management systems, 221
Catalog server, 257
Cathode ray tube (CRT), 75
CAVEs (cave automatic virtual
  environments), 319
CD-R, 82
CD-ROM, 68, 82
CD-ROM drives, 68
CD-RW, 82
Cells, 152
Cell switching technology, 159
Cellular phone systems, 152

Censorship, computer, 492–493
Centers of excellence, 457
Centralized IRM, decentralized vs., 431,
  435–437
Central processing unit (CPU), 61, 62–63
Certificate server, 257
Change action plan, 405
Change management, 404–405
Change sponsors, 405
Change teams, 405
Channel management, 232
Channels, 63, 141
  telecommunications, 142, 150
Character, 170
Chargeback systems, 439–440
Chat rooms, 138, 277, 283
Checkpoints, 473
Chief information officer (CIO), 429, 432,
  462–463
Child files, 474
CICS (Customer Identification Control
  System), 155
Circuit switching, 159
Clarity, 29
Classification, 28
  ES and, 325
Clients, 145
Client/server computing, 31
Client/server networks, 50, 52, 58, 145
Client services, 444
Clip art, 102
Clock speed, 65
Coaxial cable, 150–151
COBOL, 118, 126
Cognitive science, 313
Collaboration; *see also* Enterprise
  collaboration systems
  global, 452
  manufacturing networks, 212
  software, 108, 270
  workgroups, 268
Collaborative work management tools,
  279–283
  calendaring and scheduling, 279, 283
  knowledge management, 282, 283
  task and project management, 279–280,
    283
  workflow systems, 280–281, 283
Command-driven interfaces, 112
Communication, enterprise collaboration
  and, 254, 266
Communications Decency Act, 493
Communications media, 27
Communications satellites, 151

Communities of interest, 209, 276
Community, targeted marketing and, 209
Company-critical applications, 479
Comparisons, 28
Compatibility, 409
Compensation analysis, 217
Competitive forces, 340
Competitive strategy concepts, 16–18,
        340–341, 433
    cost strategies, 16–17, 18
    differentiation strategies, 17, 18,
        341–343
    innovation strategies, 17–18, 341–344
Compilers, 117, 121
Completeness, 29
Completion phase, prototyping, 395
Complex data type, 188
Complexity criteria, ES, 328
Computer-aided design (CAD), 57, 213
Computer-aided engineering (CAE),
        213–214
Computer-aided manufacturing (CAM),
        57, 211
Computer-aided software engineering
        (CASE), 111, 122
Computer-aided systems engineering
        (CASE), 395–396
Computer-assisted instruction (CAI), 500
Computer-based IS, 30
Computer crime, 493–500
    computer viruses, 498, 506–507
    data alteration or theft, 497–498
    on the Internet, 495
    laws, 494–495
    malicious access, 498
    money theft, 495–496
    service theft, 496–497
    software theft, 497
Computer Fraud and Abuse Act, 492
Computer hardware; *see* Hardware
Computer-integrated manufacturing (CIM),
        210–212
Computer libel and censorship, 492–493
Computer matching, 492
Computer Matching and Privacy Act, 492
Computer monitoring, 489
Computer peripherals, 26, 66–83
    backup systems, 68
    CD-ROM drives, 68
    digital cameras, 74
    hard disk drives, 68
    input technology trends, 68–69
    magnetic ink character recognition
        (MICR), 74

Computer peripherals—*Cont.*
    magnetic stripe technology, 73
    monitors, 68
    optical scanning, 72–73
    output technology and trends, 74–76
    pen-based computing, 70–71
    pointing devices, 69–70
    printers, 68
    scanners, 68
    smart cards, 73–74
    storage trends and trade-offs, 76–83
        direct and sequential access, 79
        magnetic disk storage, 80–81
        magnetic tape storage, 81–82
        optical disk storage, 82–83
        semiconductor memory, 79–80
    voice recognition and response, 71–72
Computer service centers, 410
Computer Software Piracy and
    Counterfeiting Amendment, 497
Computer systems
    central processing unit (CPU), 61, 62–63
    fault tolerant, 478
    generations of, 50–52
        first, 51
        second, 51–52
        third, 52
        fourth, 52
        fifth, 52
    mainframe, 49, 50, 57–59, 88
    microcomputers; *see* Microcomputers
    midrange, 50, 57
    multiple processors and, 63–64
    primary storage unit, 63
    processing, 61
        speeds, 64–65
    RISC processors, 64
    secondary storage, 63
Computer telephony integration, 163–164
Computer terminals, 56
Computer viruses, 498, 506–507
Computers, telecommunications, 142
Conciseness, 29
Configurations, ES and, 325
Connectivity, 135
    hardware evaluation factor, 409
    software evaluation factor, 410
Consolidation, OLAP and, 300
Consultation phase, prototyping, 395
Contact lists, 106
Content, targeted marketing and, 209
Content dimension, information quality, 29
Context, targeted marketing and, 209
Continuous speech recognition (CSR), 71

Control, 22, 61; *see also* Security and control
IS component matrix, 401
of system performance, 28, 30
Control listings, 399
Control logs, 471, 481
Control of system performance, 399
Control requirements, 390
Control requirements analysis, 390
Control software, telecommunications, 142
Control totals, 471
Control unit, 63
Conversion, IS services, 411
Conversion methods, 412–413
Cookie file, 491
Coordination, enterprise collaboration
and, 266
Corporate e-mail privacy, 492
Corporate intranets, HRM and, 216
Cost, 409
Cost barriers, 133
Cost/benefit analysis, systems
development, 387
Cost efficiency improvement, the Internet
and, 363
Cost leadership strategy, 341–343
Cost strategies, 16–17, 18, 341–343
Coupled processor, 63
C programming language, 118
Crackers, 498
Creating switching costs, 345
Credit card fraud, 469
Crisp data, 316
Critical success factors (CSFs), 307
Cross-functional IS, 35, 204–205
Crossware, 254
Cultural challenges, to global IT
management, 449
Culture, organizations and IT, 431
Cumulative trauma disorders (CTDs), 499
Currency, 29
Customer database, 172
Customers, global, 452
Customer value and the Internet, 229–231
Cybernetic system, 21
Cybersickness, 319

Data, information vs., 27
Data administration, 181
Data alteration or theft, 497–498
Database adjustments, 399
Database administration, 180
data administration, 181
data planning, 180
Database administrators (DBAs), 173

Database design, 191–193
Database development, 104, 173–174,
191–193
database design, 191–193
data planning, 192
Database interrogation, 104, 174–175
Database maintenance, 104, 175
online transaction processing, 235
Database management, 103–104,
168–199, 196
approach, 172–173
benefits of, 181
data resource management, 168, 180–181
foundation data concepts, 170–171
character, 170
field, 170–171
file, 171
record, 171
limitations of, 181
object technology on the Web, 188
systems (DBMS); *see* Database
management systems (DBMS)
technical foundations of, 182–193
Database management systems (DBMS),
115–116, 172
data dictionary, 173–174
major uses
application development, 104
database development, 104
database interrogation, 104
database maintenance, 104
database management, 103–104
object-oriented (OODBMS), 187–188
software, 173–176
application development, 176
database development, 173–174
database interrogation, 174–175
database maintenance, 175
graphical queries, 174–175
natural queries, 174–175
SQL queries, 174
Databases, 30, 171–172
accessing, 188–190
direct access, 190–191
key fields, 188
sequential access, 189–190
data mining, 177, 178–179, 197
data warehouses, 176–177, 197, 295
distributed, 177
external, 177–178
fault tolerance and, 478
hypermedia, 177, 179–180
object vs. relational, 183
operational, 176

Databases—*Cont.*
  production, 176
  statistical data banks, 177
  subject area (SADB), 176
  transaction, 176
  types of, 176–179
Database specifications, 393
Database structures, 184–188
  evaluation of, 187–188
  hierarchical, 184
  multidimensional, 184–186
  network, 184
  object-oriented, 186–187
  relational, 184
Data centers, 439
Data conferencing, 272–273, 283
Data definition language (DDL), 173
Data design, 390–392
Data dictionary, 173–174
Data entry, 28
  online, 235
Data glove, 318
Data issues, global IT management and,
    454–456
Data manipulation language (DML), 176
Data marts, 177
Data mining, 177, 178–179, 197
Data modeling, 192
Data planning, 180, 192
Data processing, 27, 28
Data resource management, 168, 180–181
Data resources, 7, 25, 26–27
  IRM and, 434
Data services, 392
Data warehouses, 176–177, 197, 295
Datum, 27
Debuggers, 122
Decentralized IRM, centralized vs., 431,
    435–437
Decision making, support of, 10–12
Decision management, ES and, 325
Decision room, 272, 278
Decision structure, 297
Decision support systems (DSS), 31, 32, 34,
    35, 301–307, 332–333
  AI and, 314
  analytical modeling, 304–307
  geographic information systems (GIS),
      303–304
  goal seeking analysis, 305, 306
  management reporting vs., 302
  models and software, 302–303
  optimization analysis, 305, 306–307
  sensitivity analysis, 305–306

Decision support systems (DSS)—*Cont.*
  software, 302–303
  what-if analysis, 305
Deliverables, 390
Demand reports and responses, 298–299
Demodulation, 153
Demographics, targeted marketing and, 209
Design, 383
  ES and, 325
  prototyping, 394
Desktop accessory packages, 279
Desktop publishing (DTP), 101–102
Desktops, 52
Desktop videoconferencing, 267, 273
Detail, 29
Developing a strategic information base,
    346–347
Development centers, 439
Development processes, IS, 7
Dharma, 485
Diagnostics, ES and, 325
Differentiation strategy, 17, 18, 341, 342, 343
Digital cameras, 74
Digital cash, 238
Digital currency, 238
Digital modems, 153
Digital network technologies, 135
Digital signal processors (DSPs), 55
Digital wallet, 237–238
Digitizer pen, 71
Direct access, 79, 190–191
Direct access storage devices (DASDs), 79
Direct organization methods, 190
Directory server, 257
Disaster recovery, 478, 479
Discrete speech recognition, 71
Discussion databases, 276
Discussion forums, 138, 275–277, 283
Discussion tracking, 276
Disintermediation capability, IT, 344
Displays or responses, 399
Distributed databases, 177
Distributed management, 431, 443–445
  end user computing, 444
  Internet access, managing, 445
Distribution management, 232
Document and report generation, online,
    235–236
Documentation
  business change implementation, 412
  software evaluation factor, 410
  standard procedures and, 478
Document file, 171
Document image management, 280

Document management library, 72
Documents, 101
  end-user development, 399
Domain criteria, ES, 328
DOS, 114
Downloads, 138
Downsizing, 52, 145, 296, 438
Drill down, 300, 307
Dual scan LCDs, 75
Dumb terminals, 56
DVD, 82
Dynamic system, 21

Echo checks, 472
Economical use of IT, 428
Economic feasibility, 387
EDP auditors, 480
E-engineering, 339
Efficiency, 9
  improvement, 342
  IT use and, 428
  software evaluation factor, 410
Egoism, 484
Electronic audit trail, 481
Electronic breaking and entering, 498
Electronic cash, 238
Electronic commerce, 13–14, 133, 139–140,
    223–239
  business model, 24
  business-to-business commerce; *see*
      Business-to-business commerce
  business-to-consumer commerce; *see*
      Business-to-consumer commerce
  customer relationship management, 243,
    374, 419
  customer value and the Internet, 229–231
  data resource management, 169, 196
  electronic payments and security, 236–239
    electronic funds transfer (EFT), 237
  ethical issues, 505–506
  foundations of, 225
  in-store, 125
  intermediaries, 243–244
  internal business processes, 225
  knowledge management, 373–374
  online transaction processing, 235–236
    batch processing, 235
    data entry, 235
    database maintenance, 235
    document and report generation,
      235–236
    inquiry processing, 236
    realtime processing, 235
    transaction processing, 235

Electronic commerce—*Cont.*
  privacy trade-offs, 507
  retail strategies, 373
  security and control for, 236–239, 469, 470
  small business served by, 5
  start-up challenges, 5
  strategic applications, 350
  successful, 203
  technologies, 225–226
Electronic Communications Privacy Act, 492
Electronic communication tools, 271–272,
    283
  electronic mail (e-mail), 100–101, 138, 271,
    283, 492
  faxing, 283
  Internet phone and fax, 271
  voice mail, 283
  Web publishing, 271–272, 283
Electronic conferencing tools, 272–279, 283
  chat systems, 138, 277, 283
  data conferencing, 272–273, 283
  discussion forums, 275–277, 283
  electronic meeting systems (EMS), 272,
    277–279, 283
  teleconferencing, 273, 274–275
  videoconferencing, 273–275, 283
  voice conferencing, 272–273, 283
Electronic data interchange (EDI), 140, 147,
    233–234, 452
  Internet-based, 244
Electronic data processing (EDP), 30
Electronic funds transfer (EFT), 140, 237
Electronic mail (e-mail), 100–101, 138, 271,
    283, 492
  viruses, 506–507
Electronic meeting systems (EMS), 272,
    277–279, 283
Electronic mouse, 69
Electronic payment systems, 236–239
  electronic funds transfer (EFT), 237
Electronic social fields, 268
Electronic spreadsheets, 102–103
Employee self-service (ESS), 216
Employment, ethics and; *see* Ethical and
    societal challenges of IT
Encapsulation, 186
Encryption, 474–475
End-user development, 396–401
  checklist for, 399–400
  control listings, 399
  control of system performance, 399
  database adjustments, 399
  displays or responses, 399
  documents, 399

End-user development—*Cont.*
  input controls, 399
  input of data resources, 399
  input to other systems, 399
  inquiries, 399
  output controls, 399
  output of information products, 399
  output to other systems, 399
  processing controls, 399
  processing of data resources, 399
  storage controls, 399
  storage of data resources, 399
  transaction data, 399
End user(s), 24
  application software for, 97–98
  computing, 31, 479
  development; *see* End-user development
  involvement, 404, 428
  management, 429
  perspective, IS, 8
  resistance, 404
  responsible, 501–502
Enterprise collaboration, 14, 32, 33, 35,
    132–133, 139, 249–292; *see also*
    Enterprise collaboration systems
  desktop videoconferencing, 267
  extranets and, 262–263, 288
    future of, 263–265
  intranets and; *see* Intranets
Enterprise collaboration systems, 32, 33, 35,
    266–283
  collaborative work management tools; *see*
      Collaborative work management tools
  communication and, 266
  components of, 268–269
  coordination and, 266
  electronic communication tools,
      271–272, 283
  electronic conferencing tools; *see*
      Electronic conferencing tools
  electronic mail, 100–101, 138, 271
  groupware for, 270
  Internet phone and fax, 271
  teams, 268
  Web publishing, 271–272, 283
  workgroups, 268
Enterprise internetworking, 32
Enterprise management perspective, IS, 8–10
Enterprise model, 192
Enterprise resource planning (ERP), 40, 205,
    206, 380, 381, 418–419, 462
Enterprise server, 257
Entities, 171, 192, 391
Entity relationship diagrams (ERDs), 192

Environment, 23
  programming, 122
  strategic success and, 367
EPROM (erasable programmable read only
    memory), 80
Ergonomics, 500, 501
  hardware evaluation factor, 409
Ethical and societal challenges of IT,
    482–502
  AITP Standards of Professional
      Conduct, 502
  business ethics, 484–485
  computer crime; *see* Computer crime
  electronic commerce, 505–506
  employment and, 486–490
    computer monitoring, 489
    individuality, 488
    working conditions, 489
  ethical foundations, 484
  health issues, 498–500
  privacy issues; *see* Privacy issues
  responsible end users, 501–502
  societal solutions, 500–501
Ethical models, 484
Ethical philosophies, 484
Ethical principles, 486, 488
Ethical responsibilities, 8
Ethical values, 484
Evaluation factors
  hardware, 407, 408–409
  IS services, 411
  software, 407, 409–410
Excellence, 358
Exception reports, 298
Executive information systems (EIS), 31, 32,
    34, 35, 307–310
Executive IT committee, 428–429
Expertise criteria, ES, 328
Expert systems (ES), 21, 31–32, 34, 35, 313,
    322–328
  applications, 322–325
    classification, 325
    configurations, 325
    decision management, 325
    design, 325
    diagnostics, 325
    maintenance, 325
    process monitoring/control, 325
    scheduling, 325
    selection, 325
    troubleshooting, 325
  benefits of, 327–328
  case-based reasoning, 322, 323
  components of, 322

Expert systems (ES)—*Cobt.*
  developing, 325–327
    frame-based knowledge, 322, 323
    inference engine, 322
    knowledge base, 322
    knowledge engineering, 326–327
    limitations of, 329
    object-based knowledge, 322, 323
    rule-based knowledge, 322, 323
    shell, 322, 325
    software resources, 322
    systems development, 325–327
    value of, 327–328
Explicit knowledge, 360
External computer crime, 494
External databases, 177–178
Extranets, 9, 32, 144–145
    for enterprise collaboration, 288
    future of, 263–264
    role of, 262–263

Facility controls, 474–478
    biometric controls, 476
    computer failure controls, 477
    fault tolerance methods, 478
    network security, 474–475, 477
    physical protection controls, 475–476
Fail-over capability, 478
Fail-safe capability, 478
Fail-soft capability, 478
Fault tolerance, 63, 81, 235, 478
Faxing, 271, 283
Feasibility studies, systems development
    process, 385–388
Federal Copyright Act, 497
Federal Privacy Act, 492
Feedback, 21–22
Feedback phase, prototyping, 395
Fiber optics, 151
Field, 30, 170–171
Fifth discipline, 382
Fifth-generation computing, 52
File(s), 30, 171
    fault tolerant, 478
    management of, 112
    retention of, 474
File server, 143–144
Financial forecasting and planning, 222
Financial management, 232
Financial management systems, 221–222
Fire walls, 475
First-generation computing, 51
First-generation languages, 116–117
Fixed-length records, 171

Flame mail, 493
Flatbed scanners, 72
Flattened organizational structures, 296
Flexibility, software evaluation factor, 410
Flexible manufacturing systems, 211
Floppy disks, 80–81
Form dimension, information quality, 29
FORTRAN, 118
Forward engineering, 396
Foundation concepts, IS, 7
Foundation data concepts, 170–171
Foundation factors, strategic success and,
    367–368
Foundations, of electronic commerce, 225
Fourth-generation computing, 52
Fourth-generation languages (4GLs), 97,
    116, 118–119
Frame-based information system, 322
Frame-based knowledge, 322, 323
Frame relay, 159
Freeware, 109–110
Frequency, 29
Frequency division multiplexing (FDM), 154
Front end, of systems development, 395
Front-end computers, 57
Front-end processor, 142
Functional requirements, 388–390
Fuzzy data, 313
Fuzzy logic systems, 313, 316–317

Garbage in, garbage out (GIGO), 471
Gateway, 155
General ledger systems, 219, 221
General-purpose application programs,
    97–98
Generations of computing, 50–52
Genetic algorithms, 313, 317–318
Geoeconomic challenges, to global IT
    management, 449
Geographical capability, IT, 344
Geographic information systems (GIS),
    303–304
Geographics barriers, 133
Gigabytes, 78
Global business drivers, 451
Global internetworking, 32
Global IT management, 446–458
    applications, 451–452
    cultural challenges, 449
    data issues, 454–456
    geoeconomic challenges, 449
    the Internet as global IT platform,
        453–454
    platforms, 452–454

Global IT management—*Cont.*
political challenge, 449
software development, 447
strategies, 450–451
systems development and, 456–457
transnational strategies, 450–451
Globalization, IT and, 14–16
Global market penetration, the Internet
and, 363
Global software development, 447
Goal seeking analysis, 305, 306
Governance structures, 428
Governmental reporting, human resources
and, 218
Grandparent files, 474
Graphical image file, 171
Graphical programming interface, 122
Graphical queries, 174–175
Graphical user interface (GUI), 69, 98,
112, 175
Graphics tablet, 71
Group decision support systems (GDSS), 278
Group memory, 278
Group support systems (GSS), 278
Groupware, 98, 106–108
for enterprise collaboration systems, 270
Growth strategies, 341–343

Hacking, 498
Handshaking, 157
Hard disk drives, 68, 81
Hardware, 7, 47–91
computer peripherals; *see* Computer
peripherals
computer systems; *see* Computer systems
as IS services evaluation factor, 411
as software evaluation factor, 410
Hardware controls, 472–473
Hardware evaluation factors, 407, 408–409
Hardware misuse computer crime, 494
Hardware resources, 25, 26
Hardware specifications, 393
Hash totals, 472
Health issues
ergonomics, 500, 501
of IT, 498–500
Hierarchical database structures, 184
High-level languages, 117–118
Host computer, 142
HTML (Hypertext Markup Language), 101,
102, 105, 120–121, 180
Hub, 155
Human factors, 488
Human factors engineering, 500

Human information processing, 313
Human resource management (HRM),
214–216, 440–441
Human resources information systems,
214–218
compensation analysis, 217
governmental reporting, 218
human resource management (HRM), 214
and corporate intranets, 216
and the Internet, 214–216
staffing the organization, 216–217
training and development, 217
Hyperarchy, 358
Hyperlinks, 120
Hypermedia, 105
Hypermedia databases, 177, 179–180
Hypertext, 105

Image processing, 82
Impact of IT
on management, 426–427
on organizations, 429–430
Implementation/maintenance,
prototyping, 394
Implementing business change, 402–422
analyzing, 402–403
change management, 404–405
conversion methods, 412–413
documentation, 412
end user involvement, 404
Implementing new systems, 405–407
hardware evaluation, 407, 408–409
implementing new systems, 405–407
IS services evaluation, 407, 410, 411
IS services maintenance, 413–414
managing organizational change, 404
software evaluation, 407, 409–410
testing, 410–412
training, 412
Improving business processes, 342–344
Inactive misuse computer crime, 494
Incentives, retailing on the Web, 227–228
Index, 190
Indexed sequential access method
(ISAM), 190
Indirect misuse computer crime, 494
Individuality, employment and, 488
Industry trends, business
telecommunications, 134–135
Inference engine, 322
Information, data vs., 27
Information agents, 320
Information appliance, 56
Information brokers, 320, 498

Information center, 444
Information filters, 320
Information management agents, 320
Information overload, 271
Information processing, 27, 28; *see also*
    Processing
Information products, 25, 28, 36
Information quality, 29
Information resource management (IRM),
    424–445
  distributed management, 431, 443–445
    end user computing, 444
    Internet access, managing, 445
  five dimensions of, 431–432
  managers and IT; *see* Managers and IT
  operational management; *see* Operational
    management
  organizations and IT, 429–431
    culture, 431
    people, 430
    structure, 431
    tasks, 430
    technology, 430
  resource management, 112, 431, 433,
    440–441
  strategic management; *see* Strategic
    management
  technology management, 431, 441–443
    advanced technology management, 443
    network management, 442
Information retrieval, AI and, 314
Information services, department, 435
Information superhighway, 136
Information systems (IS), 21, 26, 48–65, 268;
    see also Information technology (IT)
  activities, 28–30, 36
    control of system performance, 28, 30
    input, 28
    output, 28–29
    processing, 28
    storage, 28, 30
  analysis; *see* Systems analysis
  approach, 382–383
  boundary, 23
  business applications, 7, 202–204; *see also*
    Business information systems
  business end users and, 6–7
  business process reengineering (BPR), 16
  competitive advantage with IT; *see*
    Information technology (IT)
  components, 23–24
    matrix, 399–400, 401
  context, 382
  control; *see* IS Controls

Information systems (IS)—*Cont.*
  cross-functional IS, 35
  decision support systems, 32, 34, 35
  defined, 7
  design; *see* Systems design
  development; *see* Systems development
  end-user perspective, 8
  foundation concepts, 7
  fundamentals of, 19–36
  implementation, 405–407
  importance of, 4–5
  input, 61
  integrators, 410, 438
  the Internet, 12–13
  internetworked enterprises, 13–14
  investigation stage, 384, 386
  maintenance, 413–414
  management challenges, 7
  management programs, 111
  model, 23
  operations management, 439–440
  output, 61
  overview, 30–36
  performance, 439
  real world of, 6
  recognizing, 36
  repository, 396
  resources; *see* IS resources
  roles of, 10–12
  security, 468, 474
  services, 410
    evaluation, 407, 410, 411
    maintenance, 413–414
  specialists, 8, 24
  specifications, 392–393
  storage; *see* Storage
  strategic; *see* Strategic information systems
  testing, 410–412
  thinking, 382–383
  transaction processing systems, 32, 33, 35
  trends in, 30–32
  types of; *see* Types of IS
Information technology (IT), 7, 8; *see also*
    Information systems (IS)
  applications of, 9
  architecture, 433, 434–435
    applications portfolio, 434
    data resources, 434
    electronic commerce, 225–226
    IT organization, 434–435
    strategic management and, 434–435
    technology platform, 342, 346, 434,
      452–454
  business failure/success with, 40

Information technology (IT)—*Cont.*
　competitive advantage with; *see*
　　Competitive strategy concepts
　ethical and societal challenges of; *see*
　　Ethical and societal challenges of IT
　failures, 462
　globalization and, 14–16
　organization, 434–435
　platforms, 342, 346, 434, 452–454
　software support, European, 463–464
　steering committee, 429
　success and failure of, 10
　targeting customers with, 41
Informational capability, IT, 344
Informed consent, 488
Inheritance, 186
Inkjet printers, 76
Innovation strategies, 17–18, 341–344
Input, 21, 28, 61
　controls, 399, 471–472
　of data resources, 399
　IS component matrix, 401
　to other systems, 399
　technology trends, 68–69
Inquiries, 236, 399
Inquiry processing, online, 236
Installation phase, prototyping, 395
Instruction set, 64
Insurance industry, DSS and, 303
Intangible benefits, systems
　development, 388
Intangible costs, systems development, 387
Integrated circuits, 52
Integrated packages, 98–99
Integration, 211
Integrity
　e-commerce and, 470
　rules, 391
Intelligent agents, 97, 313, 320–322
Intelligent terminals, 56
Interactive marketing, 205–207
Interface, 23
Interface tutors, 320
Internal business applications,
　telecommunications, 133
Internal business processes, electronic
　commerce, 225
The Internet, 12–13, 27, 32; *see also*
　Telecommunications; World Wide Web
　(WWW)
　computer crime on, 495
　electronic commerce; *see* Electronic
　　commerce
　as global IT platform, 453–454

The Internet—*Cont.*
　human resource management (HRM) and,
　　214–216
　interactive marketing process on,
　　206–207
　Internet phone and fax, 271
　intranets and, 252
　networking technologies, 135
　privacy on, 491–492
　strategic advantage with; *see* Strategic
　　information systems
　TCP/IP protocol, 158
　technologies, 135–136
　value chains, 364–366
Internetwork processors, 155
Internetworked enterprises, 13–14, 130
Internetworking of computing, 14, 27–28
Interoperability, 135
Interorganizational information systems, 341,
　342, 343
Interorganizational networks, 146–147
Interpreters, 117, 121
Interrelationships, among systems, 382
Intranets, 9, 32, 144–145, 250–262
　applications of, 253–256
　　business operations and
　　　management, 254
　　communications and collaboration, 254
　　Web publishing, 254
　business value of, 256–262
　　measuring, 259–260
　　publication cost savings, 258–259
　　training and development cost
　　　savings, 259
　for enterprise collaboration, 288
　future of, 263–265
　the Internet and, 252
　managing, 287–288
　portals, 287–288
　self-service, 251
　technology resources, 256
Inventory control systems, 219, 220
Inventory file, 171
Inventory management, 232
Investigation/analysis, prototyping, 394
Investment management, online, 221–222
IS; *see* Information systems (IS)
IS controls, 61, 471–474
　hardware controls, 472–473
　input controls, 471–472
　output controls, 473
　processing controls, 472–473
　software controls, 473
　storage controls, 473–474

IS resources, 7–8, 24–28, 36
  data, 25, 26–27
  data vs. information, 27
  hardware, 25, 26
  information products, 25
  network, 25, 27–28
  people, 24–25
    end users, 24
    IS specialists, 24
  software, 25, 26
IT; *see* Information technology (IT)

Java, 120–121
Joint application development (JAD), 396
Jukeboxes, 82
Junk e-mail, 271, 493
Justice, 488

Key fields, 188
Key transformation, 190
Kilobytes, 78
Knowledge, needed about IS, 6–10
Knowledge base, 322, 361
Knowledge-based information systems
    (KBIS), 32, 313, 322
Knowledge capability, IT, 344
Knowledge capture, 361
Knowledge-creating companies, 360–362
Knowledge engineering, 326–327
Knowledge engineers, 326, 361
Knowledge management, 34–35, 282, 283,
    360, 373–374
Knowledge management systems (KMS),
    34–35, 360–361
Knowledge retrieval, 361
Knowledge workers, 8
Kyosei, 485

Language, software evaluation factor, 410
Language processors, 121
Language translator programs, 121–122
Laser printers, 76
Learning curve, 413
Learning loops, 361
Learning organizations, 360
Legacy systems, 145
Level of management decision making, 296
Leveraging investment in IT, 346
Leveraging strategic IT platform, 342, 346
Libel, computer, 492–493
Linux, 109, 110, 114
Liquid crystal displays (LCDs), 70, 75
Local area networks (LANs), 143–144, 153
Lock in customers and suppliers, 345

Logical views, 170, 192
Look and feel, retailing on the Web, 227
Low-earth orbit (LEO) satellites, 151
LSI (large-scale integration), 52

Machine control, 212
Machine languages, 116–117
Machines, 26
The Macintosh System, 114
Macroinstructions, 117
Magnetic cores, 52
Magnetic disk storage, 80–81
Magnetic ink character recognition
    (MICR), 74
Magnetic stripe technology, 73
Magnetic tape storage, 81–82
Mail server, 257
Mainframe computer systems, 49, 50,
    57–59, 88
Main memory, 63
Main microprocessor, 62
Maintenance
  ES and, 325
  IS services evaluation factors, 411
Malfunction detection circuitry, 472
Malicious access, 498
Management actions, strategic success
    and, 368
Management challenges, IS, 7
Management information systems (MIS),
    30–31, 32, 34, 35, 297–301
  management reporting alternatives,
    298–299
    demand reports and responses, 298–299
    exception reports, 298
    periodic scheduled reports, 298
    push reporting, 299
  online analytical processing (OLAP),
    299–301
    consolidation, 300
    drill-down, 300
    slicing and dicing, 300
Management reporting alternatives, 298–299
Management support systems, 32, 33–34,
    35, 297
Managerial decision support, 293–336
  artificial intelligence (AI); *see* Artificial
    intelligence (AI)
  decision support systems (DSS); *see*
    Decision support systems (DSS)
  executive information systems (EIS),
    307–310
  information, decisions, and management,
    296–297

Managerial decision support—*Cont.*
  information, decisions, and
    management—*Cont.*
     operational management, 296
     strategic management, 296
     tactical management, 296
    management IS; *see* Management
     information systems (MIS)
Managerial pyramid, 296
Managers and IT, 426–430
  end user management, 429
  executive IT committee, 428–429
  IT steering committee, 429
  poor IS performance, 427–428
Managing organizational change, 404
Manufacturing execution systems (MES),
  211–212
Manufacturing information systems, 210–214
  collaborative manufacturing networks, 212
  computer-aided engineering (CAE),
    213–214
  computer-aided manufacturing (CAM),
    57, 211
  computer-integrated manufacturing
    (CIM), 210–212
  machine control, 212
  manufacturing execution systems (MES),
    211–212
  process control, 212
  robotics, 212–213
Manufacturing resource planning, 211
Many-to-many relationships, 184
Marketing information systems, 205–210
  advertising and promotion, 208–209
  interactive marketing, 205–207
  market research and forecasting, 209–210
  promotion, 208–209
  sales and product management, 208
  sales force automation, 207–208
  targeted marketing, 207, 209
Market research and forecasting, 209–210
Masquerading, 494
Massively parallel processing (MPP), 63–64
Mass storage, 82
Master file, 171
Material requirements planning (MRP), 211
Media, 29, 142
  telecommunications; *see*
    Telecommunications
Medium, 141
Medium-band, 159
Megabytes, 78
Megahertz, 65
Memory, 61, 79–80

Memory caches, 65
Memory chips, 52
Menu-driven interfaces, 112
Mesh network, 155
Metadata, 173
Metropolitan area networks, 143
Microcomputers, 50, 52–56
  computer terminals, 56
  multimedia systems, 55
  network computers, 55–56
Micropayment systems, 238
Microprocessors, 52
Microseconds, 64
Middleware, 115, 135, 155
Midrange computer systems, 50, 57
Millisecond, 64
Minicomputers, 57
Minimized risk, 488
Minisupercomputers, 60
MIPS, 64–65
Mnemonics, 117
Model bases, 302
Model Computer Crime Act, 495
Models, DSS, 302–303
Modems, 153, 163
Modularity, 409
Modulation, 153
Money theft, 495–496
Monitors, 68
MS-DOS, 114
Multidimensional database structures,
  184–186
Multimedia authoring systems, 55
Multimedia presentations, 104–106
Multimedia systems, 55
Multinational development team, 457
Multiple processors, 63–64
Multiplexers, 153–155
Multiprocessor, 63
Multiprogramming, 113
Multitasking, 113

Nanoseconds, 64
Natural interfaces, AI and, 314
Natural language query, 175
Natural languages, 96–97, 118, 175, 314
Natural law, 484
Natural queries, 174–175
Natural user interface, 68
Network architectures, 150, 156–158
  Internet TCP/IP, 158
  OSI model, 158
Network-centric computing, 145–146
Network computers, 55–56, 87, 146

Network computing, 145–146
Network database structures, 184
Network fault tolerance, 478
Network interface card, 143
Network management, 115, 155, 442
Network navigation agents, 320
Network operating systems, 115, 142, 144
Network resources, 25, 27–28
Networks; *see* Telecommunications
Network security, 474–475, 477, 483
Network servers, 53, 57, 142, 144
Network specifications, 393
Network structure, 358
Network support, 27–28
Network topologies, 150, 155–156
Neural networks, 64, 313, 314–316
Neurons, 314
Newsgroups, 137, 276
News server, 257
Nonprocedural languages, 118
Notebooks, 52
Numerical control, 212

Object, 186
Object-based information system, 322
Object-oriented database management
    systems (OODBMS), 187–188
Object-oriented database structures, 186–187
Object-oriented programming (OOP),
    119–120
Object technology, on the Web, 188
Objects, 119, 171
OFF state, 78
Office automation systems, 279
Offline devices, 68
One-to-many relationships, 184
Online accounting systems, 218
Online analytical processing (OLAP), 186,
    299–301
    consolidation, 300
    drill-down, 300
    slicing and dicing, 300
Online behavior, targeted marketing
    and, 209
Online devices, 68
Online HRM systems, 214–216
Online investment management, 221–222
Online service providers, 131, 164
Online transaction processing systems, 21,
    235–236
ON state, 78
On-the-fly execution, 121
Open-source software, 109–110
Open systems, 23, 135, 158

Open Systems Interconnection (OSI)
    model, 158
Operating systems, 52, 95, 111–114
    functions, 112–113
        file management, 112
        resource management, 112
        task management, 112–113
        user interface, 112
    popular, 112
Operational databases, 176
Operational feasibility, 387
Operational management, 296, 431, 435–440
    centralized vs. decentralized, 435–437
    changing trends, 438
    IS operations, 439–440
    systems development management,
        438–439
Operations, global, 452
Operations support systems, 32–33, 35
Opportunism, 358
Optical character recognition (OCR), 72
Optical disk storage, 82–83
Optical scanning, 72–73
Optimization analysis, 305, 306–307
Order, 29
Order processing, 218–219
Organizational analysis, 388–389
Organizational feasibility, 385
Organizations
    and IT; *see* Information resource
        management (IRM)
    as sociotechnical systems, 429–431
OS/2, 114
Output, 21, 28–29, 61
    controls, 399, 473
    of information products, 399
    IS component matrix, 401
    of other systems, 399
    printed, 76
    technology and trends, 74–76
    video, 75
Outsourcing, 438

Packet radio, 152
Packet switching, 159
Page composition, 102
Page makeup, 102
Parallel conversion, 412–413
Parallel development, 457
Parallel processing, 60
Parallel processor, 63
Parent files, 474
Parent objects, 186
Parity checks, 472

Pascal, 118
Passive data dictionaries, 174
Passive misuse computer crime, 494
Passwords, 473–474
Payment management, 232
Payroll file, 171
Payroll systems, 219, 220–221
Pen-based computing, 70–71
People, organizations and IT, 430
People resources, 24–25
Performance, 29
  hardware evaluation factor, 409
  IS services evaluation factors, 411
  and service, retailing on the Web, 227
  monitors, 116
Periodic scheduled reports, MIS and, 298
Peripherals; *see* Computer peripherals
Personal Communications Services
    (PCS), 152
Personal computers, 52; *see also*
    Microcomputers
  business vs. consumer, 67
  inexpensive, 88–89
Personal digital assistants (PDAs), 50, 53
Personal information managers (PIM), 106
Personalization, retailing on the Web, 227
Personnel management, 214
Personnel specifications, 393
Pest programs, 494
Phased conversion, 413
Physical design of databases, 192
Physical protection controls, 475–476
Physical views, 192
Picoseconds, 64
Pilot conversion, 413
Platforms, global IT, 452–454
Plunge conversion, 413
Pointer fields, 188
Pointing devices, 69–70
Pointing stick, 70
Political challenge, to global IT
    management, 449
Poor IS performance, managers and IT,
    427–428
Postimplementation review, 414
Present systems, analysis of, 389
Presentation, 29
Presentation agents, 320
Presentation graphics, 104–105
Presentation phase, prototyping, 395
Primary key field, 188
Primary storage unit, 63
Printed output, 76
Printers, 68

Privacy issues, 490–493
  computer libel and censorship, 492–493
  computer matching, 492
  corporate e-mail, 492
  e-commerce and, 470, 507
  on the Internet, 491–492
  laws regarding, 492
Privacy laws, 492
Private key, 474, 476
Procedural controls, 478–479
Procedural languages, 96
Procedures, 26
Process control, 32, 33, 35, 212, 325, 440
Process design, 390–392
Processes, fault tolerant, 478
Processes of change, among systems, 382
Processing, 21, 28, 61
  controls, 399, 472–473
  of data resources, 399
  IS component matrix, 401
  requirements, 390
  speeds, 64–65
Processors
  fault tolerance and, 478
  telecommunications; *see*
      Telecommunications
Process teams, 268, 352
Production databases, 176
Production operations, 210
Productivity packages, 97
Products, global, 452
Product transformation, the Internet and,
    363–364
Professional workstations, 52
Programmable logic controllers (PLCs), 212
Programming editor, 122
Programming environment, 122
Programming languages, 116–121
  assembler languages, 117
  fourth-generation languages, 118–119
  high-level languages, 117–118
  HTML; *see* HTML (Hypertext Markup
    Language)
  Java, 120–121
  language translator programs, 121–122
  machine languages, 116–117
  object-oriented, 119–120
  packages, 121–122
Programming packages, 121–122
Programming tools, 122
Programs, 26
Program testing, 412
Project management, enterprise
    collaboration systems, 279–280, 283

Project teams, 268
PROM (programmable read only memory), 80
Promoting business innovation, 17–18, 341–344
Promotion, 208–209
Proportionality, 488
Protocols, 155, 156–158
Prototyping, 391, 393–395
    analysis/design, 394
    database specifications, 393
    design/implementation, 394
    hardware specifications, 393
    implementation/maintenance, 394
    investigation/analysis, 394
    network specifications, 393
    personnel specifications, 393
    software specifications, 393
    user interface specifications, 393
Proxy server, 257
Psychographics, targeted marketing and, 209
Publication cost savings, intranets and, 258–259
Public domain software, 497
Public key, 474, 476
Push reporting, 299

Quality assurance, 468–469
Quality control, 353–354
Quality improvement, 342, 353–356
Quality of working conditions, 489
Query language, 116, 174

RAID, 81
Raising barriers to entry, 346
Random access, 79
Random access memory (RAM), 63, 77, 79, 80
Rapid application development (RAD), 393
Reader-sorters, 74
Read only memory (ROM), 63, 80
Real-time (online) processing, 33, 235
Receiver, 141
Record, 30, 171
Record count, 471
Redundant components, 473
Reengineering, 16, 351–353
Registers, 62–63, 65
Reiteration phase, prototyping, 395
Relational database structures, 184
Relations, 184
Relevance, 29
Reliability
    e-commerce and, 470
    hardware evaluation factor, 409

Report generator, 174
Reporting alternatives, 298–299
Resource management, 112, 431, 433, 440–441
Resources
    global, 452
    IS; *see* Information systems (IS)
Respect for persons, 484
Responsible end users, 8, 501–502
Retail industry, DSS and, 303
Retailing on the Web, 227–229, 373
    incentives, 228
    look and feel, 228
    performance and service, 227
    personalization, 227
    security and reliability, 228
    socialization, 227
RFP (request for proposal), 407
RFQ (request for quotation), 407
Right to privacy, 490
Ring network, 155
RISC processors, 64
Robotics, 212–213, 313, 314
Role-playing agents, 320
Roles, of IS, 10–12; *see also* Strategic information systems
Rollback, 473
Root record, 184
Router, 155
Rule-based information system, 322

Sales and product management, 208
Sales force
    automation, 206, 207–208
    management, 232
Santutthi, 485
Scalability, 409
Scanners, 68
Scheduling
    enterprise collaboration systems, 279, 283
    ES and, 325
Schemas, 192
Schematics phase, prototyping, 395
Scope, 29
Scoring system, 407
Search agents, 320
Secondary storage, 63
Second-generation computing, 51–52
Second-generation languages, 117
Secure Electronic Transaction (SET), 238
Secure Socket Layer (SSL), 237
Security and control, 468–481
    auditing information systems, 480–481
    authorization requirements, 478–479

Security and control—*Cont.*
  controls, need for, 468–470
  disaster recovery, 478, 479
  of electronic commerce, 236–239, 470
  for end user computing, 479
  facility controls; *see* Facility controls
  information system controls; *see*
    Information systems (IS)
  monitors, 116
  procedural controls, 478–479
  security codes, 473
  software evaluation factor, 410
  standard procedures and
    documentation, 478
Selection, ES and, 325
Semantics, 118
Semiconductor memory, 79–80
Semistructured decisions, 297
Sender, 141
Sensitivity analysis, 305–306
Sequential access, 79, 189–190
Sequential capability, IT, 344
Sequential organization, 189
Servers, 145; *see also* Client/server networks
  catalog, 257
  certificate, 257
  directory, 257
  enterprise, 257
  file, 143–144
  mail, 257
  network, 53, 57, 142, 144
  news, 257
  proxy, 257
  superservers, 58
Services; *see* Information systems (IS)
Service theft, 496–497
Service transformation, the Internet and,
    363–364
Set-top boxes, 56
Shareware, 114, 497
Simplification, 210
Site licenses, 497
Slicing and dicing, OLAP and, 300
Slide shows, 105
Small business, on World Wide Web, 5,
    40–41
Smart cards, 73–74, 474
Sniffers, 496
Social contract theory, 485
Social fields, 268
Socialization, retailing on the Web, 227
Societal solutions, 500–501
Sociotechnical systems, organizations as,
    429–431

Software, 7, 26, 93–128, 96, 109–122
  antivirus, 498, 506–507
  applications; *see* Application software
  controls, 473
  database management systems (DBMS),
    115–116
  DSS, 302–303
  evaluation factors, 407, 409–410
  hardware evaluation factor, 409
  interface, 109
  as IS services evaluation factor, 411
  network management programs, 115
  open-source (freeware), 109–110
  operating systems; *see* Operating systems
  overview, 109–111
  piracy, 497
  programming languages; *see* Programming
    languages
  public domain, 497
  rental of, 125–126
  resources, 25, 26, 322, 391
  specifications, 393
  suites, 96, 98–99
  surrogate, 320
  system development programs, 111
  system management programs, 111
  telecommunications, 150, 155
  theft, 497
  training, on World Wide Web, 418–419
  vendor support, 403
Sorting, 28
Source documents, 28, 68–69
Spamming, 271, 493
Speaker-independent voice recognition, 72
Special-purpose microprocessors, 473
Spread spectrum, 153
Staffing, 216–217
Stakeholder theory, 485
Standard procedures and documentation, 478
Standards of Professional Conduct, 502
Star network, 155
Statements, 117
Statistical data banks, 177
Statistical time division multiplexer, 154
Stockholder theory, 485
Storage, 28, 30, 61; *see also* Computer
    peripherals
  controls, 399, 473–474
  of data resources, 399
  IS component matrix, 401
  requirements, 390
Storage area networks (SANs), 196–197
Strategic advantage; *see* Strategic information
    systems

Strategic business alliances, 140, 341, 342, 343
Strategic business use of Internet technologies; *see* Strategic information systems
Strategic information base, developing, 346–347
Strategic information systems, 10–12, 16, 32, 35, 337–377
  agile competitor, becoming, 356–357
  alliance strategies, 341, 342, 343
  business process reengineering (BPR), 351–353
  business quality improvement, 353–356
  challenges for using, 366–367
  competitive strategy concepts, 340–341
  cost leadership strategy, 341, 342, 343
  differentiation strategy, 17, 18, 341, 342, 343
  efficiency improvement and, 342
  growth strategies, 341, 342, 343
  innovation strategy, 17–18, 341, 342, 343, 344
  the Internet, using, 362–366
    business effectiveness improvement, 363
    cost efficiency improvement, 363
    global market penetration, 363
    Internet value chains, 364–366
    product transformation, 363–364
    service transformation, 363–364
  IT platforms and, 342, 346
  knowledge-creating companies, 360–362
  planning, 432
  quality improvement and, 342
  roles for, 341–347
    barriers to entry, raising, 346
    business innovation, promoting, 17–18, 341–344
    business process improvement, 342–344
    leveraging strategic IT platform, 342, 346
    lock in customers and suppliers, 345
    strategic information base, developing, 346–347
    switching costs, creating, 345
  sustaining strategic success, 367–369
    environment and, 367
    foundation factors, 367–368
    management actions and strategies, 368
  value chains, 347–348
  virtual companies, creating, 358–360
Strategic knowledge base, 347
Strategic management, 296, 431, 432–435
  business alignment, 433

Strategic management—*Cont.*
  chief information officer (CIO), 432
  competitive advantage, 433
  IT architecture, 434–435
    applications portfolio, 434
    data resources, 434
    IT organization, 434–435
    technology platform, 342, 346, 434, 452–454
  resource management, 433
  strategic IS planning, 432
  technology architecture, 433
Strategies, global IT management, 450–451
Structural barriers, 133
Structure, organizations and IT, 431
Structure criteria, ES, 328
Structured decisions, 297
Subject area databases (SADB), 176
Subschemas, 192
Subsidiaries, IS, 438
Subsystem, 23
Summarization, 28
Supercomputer, 59
Superservers, 58
Supplier management, 232
Supply chain management (SCM), 205, 232
Support, 409
Support processor, 63
Surfing, Internet, 138
Sustaining competitive advantage, 367–369
Switch, 155, 156, 159–160
Switching costs, creating, 345
Syntax, 118
Systemic view, 382
Systems analysis, 383, 388–390, 390
  functional requirements analysis, 389–390
    control requirements, 390
    processing requirements, 390
    storage requirements, 390
    user interface requirements, 390
  organizational analysis, 388–389
  present systems, analyzing, 389
Systems concepts, 21–23, 60–62
  control, 22
  feedback, 21–22
  input, 21
  output, 21
  processing, 21
Systems design, 390–393
  application services, 392
  control requirements, 390
  database specifications, 393
  data design, 390–392
  data services, 392

Systems design—*Cont.*
  hardware specifications, 393
  network specifications, 393
  personnel specifications, 393
  process design, 390–392
  processing requirements, 390
  software specifications, 393
  storage requirements, 390
  systems specifications, 392–393
  user interface, data, and process design,
    390–391
  user interface specifications, 393
  user services, 392
Systems development, 7, 379–422
  computer-aided systems engineering
    (CASE), 395–396
  cycle, 383–384
  end-user development, 396–401
  global IT management and, 456–457
  as IS services evaluation factor, 411
  life cycle (SDLC), 383
  management, 438–439
  process for, 384–388
    feasibility studies, 385–388
    prototyping; *see* Prototyping
  programs, 111
  prototyping; *see* Prototyping
  systems analysis; *see* Systems analysis
  systems approach, 382–383
  systems design; *see* Systems design
  systems development; *see* Systems
    development
  systems development cycle, 383–384
  systems thinking, 382–383

Tables, 171, 184
Tactical management, 296
Tangible benefits, systems development, 388
Tangible costs, systems development,
  387–388
Targeted marketing, 207, 209
Task management, 112–113, 279–280,
  283, 430
Teams
  enterprise collaboration, 268
  prototyping phase, 395
Technical feasibility, 387
Technical foundations of database
  management; *see* Database management
Technology, 358
  architecture; *see* Information
    technology (IT)
  electronic commerce, 225–226
  hardware evaluation factor, 409

Technology—*Cont.*
  infrastructure, global, 452–454
  organizations and IT, 430
  platforms, 342, 346, 434, 452–454
  resources, intranets, 256
  trends, business telecommunications,
    135–136
Technology management, 431, 441–443
  advanced technology management, 443
  network management, 442
Telecommunications, 7, 129–166
  applications, 132–133
  bandwidth alternatives, 158–159
  channels, 142, 150
  computer telephony integration, 163–164
  DSS and, 303
  the Internet and, 129–132, 134, 136–141
    applications of, 137–138
    business use of the Internet, 138–139
    business value of, 140–141
    electronic commerce, 139–140
    enterprise communications and
      collaboration, 139
    strategic business alliances, 140
  media, 150–153
    cellular phone systems, 152
    coaxial cable, 150–151
    communications satellites, 151
    fiber optics, 151
    terrestrial microwave, 151
    twisted-pair wire, 150
    wireless LANs, 153
  monitors, 115, 142, 155
  networks, 27–28, 141–142
    architectures, 150, 156–158
      Internet TCP/IP, 158
      OSI model, 158
    channels, 142, 150
    computers, 142
    control software, 142
    management of, 442
    processors, 142, 150, 153–155
    protocols, 155, 156–158
    terminals, 142
    topologies, 150, 155–156
    types of, 142–147
      client/server networks, 145
      extranets, 144–145
      interorganizational networks, 146–147
      intranets, 144–145
      local area networks (LANs), 143–144
      metropolitan area networks, 143
      network computing, 145–146
      wide area networks (WANs), 143

Telecommunications—*Cont.*
  processors, 142, 150, 153–155
    internetwork, 155
    modems, 153
    multiplexers, 153–155
  software, 155
  switching alternatives, 155, 156, 159–160
  technical alternatives, 148–160
  trends in, 134–136
    application trends, 136
    industry trends, 134–135
    technology trends, 135–136
  value of, 133–134
Teleconferencing, 273, 274–275
Telepresence, 318
Teleprocessing (TP), 155
Templates, 105
Terabytes, 78
Terminals, 142
Terrestrial microwave, 151
Testing, systems, 410–412
Text data, 101
Third-generation computing, 52
Third-generation languages, 117
Threaded discussions, 276
Time barriers, 133
Time dimension, information quality, 29
Time division multiplexing (TDM), 154
Time elements, 64–65
Timeliness, 29
Time management, 279
Time period, 29
Timesharing, 113
Topology, communications, 150, 155–156
Total quality management (TQM), 211,
    353–356
Touchpad, 70
Touch screens, 70
Trackball, 70
Tracking capability, IT, 344
Trackpoint, 70
Training and development, 217
  business change implementation and, 412
  cost savings, intranets and, 259
  IS services evaluation factors, 411
Transactional capability, IT, 344
Transaction data, 399
Transaction databases, 176
Transaction file, 171
Transaction processing, 32, 33, 35
  cycle, 235–236
  online, 235
Transaction terminals, 56
Transborder data flows (TDF), 454–456

Transistors, 51
Transnational strategies, global IT
    management, 450–451
Tree network, 156
Trends
  in application software, 96–97
  in computer systems, 50–52
  IRM, 438
  in IS, 30–32
  in telecommunications, 134–136
    application trends, 136
    industry trends, 134–135
    technology trends, 135–136
Troubleshooting, 414
  ES and, 325
Trust-based, 358
Twisted-pair wire, 150
Types of IS, 32–35
  enterprise collaboration systems; *see*
      Enterprise collaboration systems
  enterprise management perspective, 8–10
  executive information systems, 32, 34, 35
  expert systems; *see* Expert systems (ES)
  knowledge management systems, 34–35,
      360–361
  management information systems; *see*
      Management information
      systems (MIS)
  management support systems; *see*
      Management support systems
  operations support systems, 32–33, 35
  process control systems, 32, 33, 35,
      212, 440

U.S. Computer Fraud and Abuse Act of
    1986, 494
U.S. Telecommunications Deregulation and
    Reform Bill of 1996, 493
Universal client, 99
Universal Product Code (UPC), 72
UNIX, 114
Unstructured decisions, 297
Updates, 28
User interfaces, 28, 112, 389
  agents, 320
  design, 390–391
  requirements analysis, 390
  specifications, 393
User services, 392, 444
Utilitarianism, 484
Utilities, 116

Vacuum tubes, 51
Value-added carriers, 159

Value-added resellers (VARs), 410
Value chains, 347–348
    Internet, 364–366
Variable-length records, 171
Video monitors, 75
Video output, 75
Videoconferencing, 273–275, 283
Virtual communities, 209, 276
Virtual companies, 140, 431
    characteristics of, 358
    creating, 358–360
Virtual corporation, 358
Virtual discussion groups, 276
Virtual machines, 113
Virtual memory, 112
Virtual organization, 358
Virtual private networks (VPNs), 144–145,
    149, 262
Virtual reality (VR), 314, 318–320
Virtual teams, 14, 108, 139, 268
Visual programming, 119–120
VLSI (very-large-scale integration), 52, 76
Voiceband, 159
Voice conferencing, 272–273, 283
Voice mail, 283
Voice-messaging computers, 72
Voice recognition and response, 71–72, 74
Volatility, 80
Von Neuman design, 64
VRML (virtual reality modeling
    language), 319

Walker, 318
Wands, 72

Web browsers, 99–100, 142
Web page design, 392, 418
Web publishing, 120, 271–272, 283
    intranets and, 254
Websheet, 103
What-if analysis, 103, 305
Whiteboarding, 272–273
Wholesaling on the Web, 232–233
Wide area networks (WANs), 143
Windows operating system, 114
Windows terminal, 55
Wireless LANs, 153
Wizards, 97
Word processing, 101–102
Workbench, 122
Workflow systems, 280–281, 283
Workgroups, 268
Working conditions, 489
Workstation computers, 53
World Wide Web (WWW), 136; *see also*
    The Internet
    browsers, 99–100
    page design elements, 392
    retailing on, 227–229
    small businesses on, 5, 40–41
    software training on, 418–419
    wholesaling on, 232–233
WORM (write once, read many), 82
Worms (computer viruses), 498, 506–507
WYSIWYG, 102

Year 2000 problem (Y2K), 396

Zakat, 485

Chapter 7

Information Systems for Enterprise Collaboration

Real World Cases

1. Glaxo Wellcome and BC Telecom: The Business Value of Self-Service Intranets, p. 251
2. Lockheed Martin Corporation: Improving Team Collaboration via Desktop Videoconferencing, p. 267

Real World Problems

1. The Boeing Company: Managing the Intranet Explosion, p. 287
2. US West and Charles Schwab & Co.: The Business Case for Intranet Portals, p. 287
3. Xilinx, Inc.: Using Intranets and Extranets for Enterprise Collaboration, p. 288

Chapter 8

Information Systems for Managerial Decision Support

Real World Cases

1. Lexis-Nexis Inc.: Using a Data Warehouse and Web-Based Tools for Decision Support, p. 295
2. Dow Jones and Charles Schwab & Co.: Web Applications of Intelligent Agents and Neural Nets, p. 311

Real World Problems

1. Key Corp. and Peoples Bank: Using Decision Support Systems in Banking, p. 332
2. NDC Health Information Services: Web-Based Decision Analysis and Reporting, p. 332
3. Dayton Hudson Corporation: Using Decision Support Systems in Retailing, p. 333

Chapter 9

Information Systems for Strategic Advantage

Real World Cases

1. Ford Motor Company: E-Engineering Global Business Processes, p. 339
2. Office Depot versus Staples: Competing with Internet Technologies, p. 350

Real World Problems

1. Barnes & Noble and Bertelsmann versus Amazon.com: Net Retail Strategies, p. 373
2. Shiva Corporation: Empowering Customers and Employees with Web Knowledge Management, p. 373
3. Hewlett-Packard and furniture.com: The Business Value of Customer Service in E-Commerce, p. 374